Jas. E. Mitchell

A STUDENT'S MANUAL

OF

ENGLISH CONSTITUTIONAL HISTORY

A

STUDENT'S MANUAL

OF

ENGLISH CONSTITUTIONAL

HISTORY

BY

DUDLEY JULIUS MEDLEY, M.A.

PROFESSOR OF HISTORY IN THE UNIVERSITY OF GLASGOW

SOMETIME EXAMINER IN THE HONOUR SCHOOL OF MODERN HISTORY, OXFORD

AND IN THE HISTORICAL TRIPOS, CAMBRIDGE

FOURTH EDITION

Oxford

B. H. BLACKWELL, 50 AND 51 BROAD STREET

London

SIMPKIN, MARSHALL, HAMILTON, KENT & CO.

1907

PREFACE

SUBSTANTIAL changes were made in the Second Edition of this book published in 1898. The Third Edition (1902) was practically a reprint of the Second. But in the light of recent conclusions it is necessary to modify some of the views then held. Professor Maitland's work marks an important epoch in the study of our early institutions, and his death is an irreparable loss to historical scholarship. But in certain subjects — the individualism of the early English vill, the typical importance of the county borough — his brilliant exposition raised a suggestive interpretation to the level of an universal principle. The constructive work of Professor Vinogradoff, and the destructive criticism of Professor Tait, have recalled us to a more balanced position. Mr Chadwick's learned treatise is not for young students; but I have not hesitated to refer to some of the many interesting points which it illustrates. The work of these authors, however, touches but a small portion of the whole subject. The main part of the book stands as it has stood since 1898, and I have been careful throughout to keep the original plan both in the general headings of the chapters, and in the particular subjects of each section. A text-book should not be so transformed out of recognition in its outward shape that teachers are put to the necessity of learning to find their way about a new edition as if it were an entirely new book.

TABLE OF CONTENTS

---◇---

INTRODUCTION

CHAPTER I

The Land and its Inhabitants

CHAPTER II

THE EXECUTIVE

CHAPTER III

The Legislature

CHAPTER IV

The House of Commons—Its Form

CHAPTER V

The House of Commons in Action

CHAPTER VI

THE EXECUTIVE AND LEGISLATURE IN CONFLICT

CHAPTER VII

ADMINISTRATION OF JUSTICE

CHAPTER VIII

POLICE AND LOCAL ADMINISTRATION

CHAPTER IX

LIBERTY OF THE SUBJECT

CHAPTER X

REVENUE AND TAXATION

CHAPTER XI

The Church

APPENDIX

Some Important Cases in Constitutional Law

ABBREVIATED REFERENCES TO AUTHORS AND BOOKS USED THROUGHOUT THIS VOLUME.

	Referred to as
ANSON, Sir W., *Law and Custom of the Constitution* (vol. i. 3rd edition; vol. ii. 2nd edition)	Anson.
BROOM, H., *Constitutional Law* (2nd edition by Denman, 1885)	Broom.
CHADWICK, H. M., *Studies on Anglo-Saxon Institutions*	Chadwick.
Dialogus de Scaccario, edited by A. Hughes, C. G. Crump, and C. Johnson	*Dialog. de Scac.*
DICEY, Prof. A. V., *Law of the Constitution* (5th edition)	Dicey.
DOWELL, S., *History of Taxation and Taxes in England*	Dowell.
English Historical Review	*E. H. R.*
GARDINER, S. R., *History of England from the Accession of James I* (10 vols.)	Gardiner.
———*Constitutional Documents of the Puritan Revolution*	*Const. Docts.*
GEE, Rev H., and HARDY, W. J., *Documents Illustrative of English Church History*	Gee & Hardy.
GROSS, CHARLES, *The Gild Merchant*	Gross.
HALLAM, H., *Constitutional History of England* (3 vols. cr. 8vo. 1876)	Hallam.
HOLDSWORTH, W. S., *History of English Law*	Holdsworth.
LECKY, W. H., *History of England in the Eighteenth Century* (8 vols., 8vo., 1878-1887)	Lecky.
M'KECHNIE, W. S., *Magna Carta*	M'Kechnie.
MAITLAND, Prof. F. W., *Domesday Book and Beyond*	*Domesday.*
MAKOWER, FELIX, *Constitutional History of the Church of England* (trans.)	Makower.

Referred to as

MAY, Sir T. ERSKINE, *Constitutional History of England* (5th edition, 3 vols., cr. 8vo., 1875) .   Erskine May.

PIKE, L. O., *Constitutional History of the House of Lords* . . . .   Pike.

POLLOCK, Sir F. and MAITLAND, Prof. F. W., *History of English Law* (1st edition) . .   *P. and M.*

PORRITT, E., and A. G., *The Unreformed House of Commons* . . . .   Porritt.

PROTHERO, G. W., *Statutes and Constitutional Documents*, 1559-1625 . . . .   Prothero.

REDLICH, JOSEF, and HURST, F. W., *Local Government in England* . . . . .   Redlich and Hurst.

Report of the Ecclesiastical Courts Commission .   *E. C. C.*

ROBERTSON, C. G., *Select Statutes, Cases, and Documents*, 1660-1832 . . . .   Robertson.

STUBBS, Bishop W., *Constitutional History of England* . . . . . .   *S. C. H.*

——*Lectures on Early English History* . .   *E. E. H.*

——*Select Charters* . . . . .   *S. C.*

THAYER, J. B., *Development of Trial by Jury* (Boston)   Thayer.

THOMAS, E. C., *Leading Cases in Constitutional Law* (2nd edition) . . . . .   Thomas.

VINOGRADOFF, Prof. P., *Growth of the Manor* .   Vinogradoff.

ENGLISH CONSTITUTIONAL HISTORY

INTRODUCTION

§ 1. AMONG systems of government the English Consti- Character-
tution holds a pre-eminent place; for it is the result of a istics of the English
practically unbroken development of thirteen hundred years. Constitu-
Perhaps for this reason among others, during the last century tion.
and a half it has been freely copied. Nearly every progressive nation of the world now possesses a system of government
by an executive of ministers and a deliberative body of two
chambers. It may be said, without fear of contradiction, that
this form originated in England; and its prevalence throughout
Europe and America is the result of conscious imitation. But
there is this one great difference between the original and all
the imitations—that, whereas all foreign constitutional governments sprang Minerva-like from the brain of the legislator, the
English Constitution is the result of forces and influences which
have been at work for thirteen successive centuries; and while
we can, by reference to a written document, gain a sufficiently
accurate acquaintance with the governmental method of most
foreign parliamentary constitutions, our knowledge of our own
constitutional arrangements has to be sought as much in
customs as in definite law. The results are so important as
to excuse, and indeed to necessitate, a further examination.

A Constitution has been defined as the product of 'all rules, Flexible
which directly or indirectly affect the distribution, or the and rigid Constitu-
exercise of the sovereign power in the State.'[1] It might justly tions.
be thought that such rules in each particular country would be [1] Dicey, 22.

as infinitely various as is the history of each country from that of any other; but, as a matter of fact, the sum total of such rules may be distinguished into two classes. The dividing line is to be found in the method by which any fundamental change may be carried out in the structure of the Constitution. Thus in our own English system, any change, whether great or small, whether fundamental or merely corrective, is carried out by the process of ordinary legislation. To such a Constitution, of which as yet England is the sole example, the epithet *Flexible* has been applied; and in such a Constitution the Parliament or legislative body is of necessity the sovereign power, for there is nothing to hinder it from changing or annulling at will all the laws of the commonwealth. All other parliamentary constitutions have been conveniently labelled as *Rigid*, inasmuch as the whole or some part of them can be changed only by some extraordinary method of legislation. For they spring from a written document, in which the sovereign power may be said thenceforth to repose.[1] Thus there is a difference between a legislative and a constituent assembly, such as has only twice been realized in England, at the epochs of the Restoration and the Revolution; and there is a marked distinction between fundamental laws which can only be touched by a constituent assembly, and ordinary laws which fall within the competence of the ordinary legislature.

From the division between these two kinds of Constitution there follow three noteworthy results. In the first place, *the rights of individuals are guaranteed*, in a rigid Constitution, by a fundamental article in the Constitution; whereas in the flexible Constitution of England they depend on the indirect, but no less sure, safeguards of judicial decisions and specified legal remedies. Again—and perhaps as a necessary consequence of this difference—beyond the fundamental laws strictly so called, the founders of all rigid Constitutions have been irresistibly tempted to fill them with a number of articles which merely state advantageous maxims of policy unsecured by any guarantee; whilst the piecemeal growth of the flexible Constitution of England has inseparably connected the means of enforcing a right with the right itself.[2] Finally, the term *unconstitutional* undergoes a change according as it is applied to an act or law under a flexible, or under a rigid Constitution;

[1] Anson, i. 34.

Results of the difference.

[2] Dicey, 190.

for, whereas in England it implies something that is opposed to the *spirit* of the Constitution, but brings no immediate penalty with itself; in a country under a rigid documentary Constitution, the unconstitutional act of an individual or of an assembly is one either beyond the competence of those who commit it, and so ipso facto void, or which incurs a punishment affixed to it in the written articles of the Constitution. In such a case the terms 'unconstitutional' and 'illegal' are identical. This distinction will explain the meaning of the boast that England is governed by an *unwritten* Constitution.

But it does not follow that the English Constitution has no bases. Indeed, although it will be found that in one sense of the term the taunt of a foreign writer is true, that we have no Constitution;[1] yet we may look in two directions for the guarantees of the ordinary action of our machinery of government. In the first place, an important part of the ordinary law of the land is formed by what is called Public or *Constitutional Law*, which, consisting (like the rest of the Common law) of parliamentary statutes and of judicial decisions based upon precedents, is merely for convenience distinguished from Private Law which governs the relations of individuals to each other: for, both alike are enforced by the ordinary courts of law. The more impalpable part of the English Constitution, and that which marks it off more clearly from rigid Constitutions, is contained in the *Conventions of the Constitution.* These are practices or rules, with which the law courts immediately have no concern, but whose object it is to ensure the harmonious working of the various members of the sovereign body, the Crown-in-Parliament. It is these informal understandings alone which for two hundred years have prevented the exercise of the royal veto on bills passed by Parliament; which have caused the House of Lords to yield to the clearly expressed wishes of the nation, and which ensure the resignation of a ministry when it has been defeated on an important vote in the House of Commons.

Nor is this all; for, while it would seem at first sight as if the only guarantee for the maintenance of these understandings could be found in a powerfully expressed public opinion, a little reflection will show that they are merely as it were a first line of defence, and that in the end their violation involves a conflict

Marginal notes:

Bases of the English Constitution.

[1] De Tocqueville; quoted in Dicey, 21.

Connection between the Law and the Customs of the Constitution.

with the law.[1]   Thus the repudiation of the convention in any one of the three cases stated above, would result in the refusal of supplies by the House of Commons, which could only be obtained by the king and the ministry through other than legal means.   So true is this within certain limitations, that the difference between rigid and flexible Constitutions seems to resolve itself merely into a difference between an immediate and an ultimate appeal to the law.   In the two cases, however, the functions of the law courts are to be carefully distinguished. In a rigid Constitution it is within the power of the judges to treat as unconstitutional, and therefore illegal, any act of the executive or legislature which is at variance with the written articles of the Constitution ; whereas in England the judicial bench can only decide whether the deeds of individuals are illegal or a violation of the letter of the law, although sub-sequent legislation can destroy the value of such decision as a precedent.

The Roman or Teutonic origin of the English Constitution.

§ 2. The English Constitution then, or the system and institutions under which we are governed, is a growth and not a manufacture ; and, consequently, more than in the case of any other nation, its history is expressive of the character and development of the people who possess it.   But it is possible to exaggerate the divergence between the course of English history and that of the kindred nations of the continent.   However great the later differences may be, the English tongue, if not the people, was originally of that same so-called Aryan type which is common to most of the European nations, as well as to large portions of the Asiatic world.   To it belonged alike the Celtic peoples of the Gaels and Britons, and the Teutonic tribes, which in succession occupied this island.   Again, no less than the rest of Western Europe, Britain passed under the Roman yoke, and for three and a half centuries formed a province of the Roman Empire ; while in the train of the legions ultimately came that Christian faith which formed so strong a leavening and binding influence among the progressive nations of the world.   But for some years it has been an accepted truth among English historical students, that the only cataclysm of which our history has to tell, began with the arrival on the shores of Britain of those Teutonic tribes whose descendants undoubtedly form the staple portion of the population in modern England. This theory has not gone without challenge either in the past or at the present day. Its acceptance or rejection makes the history of the previous inhabitants of this island either a piece of pure antiquarianism or an important element in the formation of our present life.

The two preliminary incursions by Caesar (B.C. 55 and 54) into Britain, with which its history begins, were followed after an interval of nearly a century by renewed invasions, ending in the conquest of the southern portion of the island and its occupation for 360 years. The ordinary Roman organization with a staff of the customary officials was introduced, and the different parts of the country were connected by great roads. But Britain lay too far away to feel the effect of Roman colonization. The imperial rule was little more than a military occupation; and, so far as evidence remains, it affected a handful of towns, whether municipia, of which there is only one known example, or coloniæ, which numbered at least four. Outside these two sets of organized bodies, which differed in little save in name, lay the districts which probably continued in the possession of native tribes ruled by their chiefs, retaining their own language and, at any rate at first, their own customary law. The compulsory withdrawal of the Roman legions at the beginning of the fifth century left the country a prey to internal factions. The antagonism between the Romanized dwellers in the towns and the native population of the country districts has probably been overstated; and the theory that when the latter welcomed the incursions of their more than dubious kinsmen, the Picts, the former summoned the Saxon pirates who were already familiar with the coast, seems to be based on no reliable evidence. Both invaders, however, did come; and the plundering raids of the Saxons gave way to systematic invasion, and, finally, to a conquest which did not cease until, a century and a half later, it had placed the conquerors in possession of all Eastern Britain south of the Forth.

The Conquest of Britain.

Here the different interpretations of the effect of this conquest part company. Of late years it has been *assumed that the English conquest of Britain was to be distinguished sharply from the conquest of Gaul by the kindred tribes of the Franks;* for, whereas in the latter case the Romanized inhabitants of Gaul

The theory of absolute Teutonic predominance.

gave to their new conquerors far more than they received from them, it is held that in Britain alone the imperfect extent of the Roman civilization on the one side, and, on the other, the irreconcilable attitude of the Britons towards the new comers, resulted in *a war of practical extermination* by the Saxons, which in the end left behind none of the Romano-Celtic civilization to affect the settlers. 'Everywhere but in Britain,' Mr Freeman tells us, 'the invaders gradually adopted Christianity . . . gradually learned to speak some form, however corrupt, of the language of Rome . . . respected the laws and the arts of Rome . . . and the local divisions, and the local nomenclature survived the conquest.'[1] In Britain, on the contrary, 'the English wiped away everything Celtic as well as everything Roman as thoroughly as everything Roman was wiped out of Africa by the Saracen conquerors of Carthage.'[2]   As a result, the English retained their heathen worship, and owed their subsequent conversion to Christianity to other sources than the surviving and attenuated British Church: they retained their language almost free from any intermixture of Roman or Celtic words, until the conversion brought in a certain number of words of ecclesiastical Latin: 'the vestiges of Romano-British law,' says Dr. Stubbs, 'which have filtered through local custom into the common law of England . . . are infinitesimal':[3] 'no dream of ingenious men,' says Mr. Freeman again, 'is more groundless than that which seeks to trace the franchises of English cities to a Roman source'; and finally, the 'local nomenclature is everywhere essentially Teutonic.'[4]   As a reason for this clean sweep it is pointed out that least of all the Teutonic tribes had the invaders of Britain previously come into contact with the Roman Empire.   Thus no terms were kept between them and the inhabitants of the island.   For one hundred and fifty years the English waged a war of practical if not literal extermination.   The Britons fled before their conquerors to the western side of the island, and so complete was the separation between the two peoples, that when, a century after the first settlement, Augustine came with his gift of Christianity to the English, the British Church remained aloof and refused to help him in his work.   On this land, so cleared of its former inhabitants and their civilization,

[1] *Norm. Conq.* i. 16.

[2] *Ibid.* 1. 20.

[3] *S. C. H.* § 28.

[4] *Norm. Conq.* i. 17.

450-600.

597.

the English tribes settled down and reproduced in all essential details of their society as they had lived it in their previous homes. For, 'conquest under the circumstances,' says Dr. Stubbs, 'compelled colonization and migration . . . the invaders came in families and kindred, and in the full organization of their tribes . . . even the slaves were not left behind. The cattle of their native land were, it would appear, imported too.'[1] Thus Mr. Green contends that 'the settle- ment of the conquerors was nothing less than a transfer of English society in its fullest form to the shores of Britain. It was England that settled down on British soil';[2] and although, with Dr. Stubbs again, 'it is unnecessary to suppose that a migrating family exactly reproduced its old conditions,' yet it is substantially true to say that 'the new life started at the point at which the old had been broken off.'[3]

[1] *S. C. H.* § 31.

[2] *Making of England,* 154.

[3] *S. C. H.* § 31.

To this reading of early English history the advocates of the continued existence of Romano-Celtic influences give a flat denial. According to their contention, it was through the Romanized Celts that the civilization of the previous inhabitants chiefly, though not entirely, reached the new conquerors. The whole evidence produced by the upholders of this opinion, goes to *rebut the theory of the exceptional character of the English invasion of Britain*. They deny not only the possibility but the fact of the extermination of the Britons, and assert in the most uncompromising manner the unavoidable intermixture of the Britons and their conquerors, and the consequent far-reaching effect of the Romanized institutions of the former, on whatever Teutonic organization 'was brought in the keels of the invaders.' The *evidence* for this is drawn from many sources. Of these, the most direct is afforded by the language of the invaders. Instead of the 'few Celtic, and the still fewer Latin words' which 'found their way into English from the first days of the conquest,'[4] and which form two very small exceptions to the purely Low Dutch character of the English language, it has been maintained that 'hundreds of common words' relating not merely to domestic employments (such as would be transmitted by the female slaves, who alone are generally allowed to have been saved from extermination), but even to government, 'may still be traced in the limited Anglo-Saxon and Welsh voca-

The theory of Roman and Celtic survivals.

[4] *Norm. Conq.* i. 17

bularies'; while rather more than a hundred Latin words, often to be found also in Welsh, prove the abiding influence of the Roman tongue. The retention of Celtic words also in relation to 'the arts of weaving, boat-building, carpentry, and smith's work,'[1] would seem to show that the invaders accepted the teaching of their captives in some of the more skilful occupations. But besides this practically direct evidence, it has been conjectured[2] that a resistance which was sufficiently stubborn to protract the conquest for 150 years, would tell in favour of a compromise rather than of wholesale extermination. Christianity did not come to mitigate the fury of the invaders until the conquest was nearly accomplished; but the method of its introduction into Kent and its immediate success seem to argue that the ground had been prepared by a continued exercise of the rites of worship in the old church of St. Martin which was set aside for the use of Æthelberht's Christian queen. It has even been asserted that Celtic missionaries lent their aid to Augustine and his followers in their labour of conversion. And if continuity can be traced in the language, the religion and the arts of the days of the Roman occupation, it may well be believed that the Roman organization, both social and political, would not perish. Thus it has been asserted[3] that Roman *territoria*, which hypothetically followed the boundaries of the British tribal lands, were presided over by an official called the *comes civitatis*, and that in these is to be found the origin of the small kingdoms of the Heptarchic period, and, therefore, ultimately of the English *shire*, together with that of the Anglo-Saxon *ealdorman*. But while all this remains no more than mere assertion, some evidence has been adduced in favour of the continued life of lesser organizations, whether the *villa* or private estate, cultivated by a bailiff and servile tenants, or (less conclusively) the *municipium* with its *collegia*, which became the English *burh* with its *gilds*. Under these circumstances it would almost naturally follow that 'Roman law has formed the basis of the Saxon family system, and of the laws of property'; while the only possible conclusion would be with Mr. Pearson that 'the Saxon Conquest . . . did not break up society; it only added a new element to what it found. The Saxon state was built up on the ruins of the past.'[4]

[1] Pearson, *Hist. of Eng.* i. 102.

[2] Brewer, *English Studies,* 64-74.

[3] Scarth, *Roman Britain,* 225.

[4] *Hist. of Eng.* i. 103.

Such are the two diametrically opposite interpretations of the evidence as to the early history of the country. Is it possible to arrive at a definite conclusion? Perhaps, for the present, the question must be left to the antiquarians, whose material, when collected, it will fall to the lot of the historian to interpret. It is, however, necessary for our immediate purpose to note the precise points of contention between the two rival theories, and thus to indicate the direction in which future evidence may be expected to point. At the outset it may be noticed that the difference between the two schools, which for the sake of the contrast has been presented stripped of all qualifications, is, by their introduction, considerably and appreciably modified. It is, of course, the extreme theory of the advocates of a purely Teutonic origin which suffers by their introduction. Thus Mr. Freeman acknowledges that 'the literal extirpation of a nation is an impossibility';[1] and all advocates of Teutonic influences allow of the survival among the English of women and slaves of British blood. The cities too, though the destruction was such that in many cases their very sites have passed away, may sometimes have remained in possession of their former inhabitants, but in dependence on their conquerors. It is even not improbable that the greater men made terms for themselves with the invaders; while it is most likely that on the western borderland, where the two races joined, large numbers of the Britons remained mingled with the new comers. There are instances of the existence of patches of country, such as the small kingdom of Elmet or Leeds, which seem to have remained for a while under their old rulers and only gradually to have been assimilated by the surrounding English population; and it has even been conjectured that in places where local industries survived, such as the smelting in the Forest of Dean and the lead mines of the Peak, the old population of skilled workmen remained and kept up their special organization.[2] Again, despite the general prevalence of Teutonic nomenclature, it is not to be denied that the designations of local features of the country often retained such Celtic forms as pen, dun, ock, combe, and exe.[3] None of these admissions would of themselves settle the question against the school of the writers who make them. But they are willing to go even

Qualifications of the pure Teutonic theory.

[1] *Norm. Conq.* i. 18.

[2] Cunningham, *Eng. Ind. and Com.* i. 65.

[3] Green, *Making of England*, 138.

further. It is, perhaps, not wonderful that Roman Britain should have set the bounds of the settlement of the English, and that thus 'the political structure of its provinces had an influence on the settlement of the invaders, and even the social life as far as it was controlled by roads, boundary marks of estates, and fields'; but the same writer seems almost to surrender his whole position when he acknowledges that 'it was thus that the Roman Vill often became the English township: that the boundaries of its older masters remained the bound marks of the new: that serf and læt took the place of colonus and slave: while the system of cultivation was probably in the case of both peoples sufficiently identical to need little change in field or homestead.'[1] The modifications of the theory of pure Teutonic descent are, then, both numerous and important, though it is difficult to meet the summary judgement of a high authority 'that all these probabilities only bring out more strongly the improbability of any commixture or amalgamation of the races.'[2]

In passing to the precise points of contention between the rival theories of English origins, it will not be necessary to dwell on what may be described as the older class of arguments, which constitute the bulk of those just given on the side of the Romano-Celtic school of writers; for, these are avowedly conjectures unsubstantiated by continuous historical proof and resting in the main on such striking analogies between the Roman and the English system as might be accounted for by similarity of circumstances. Under this head come the identification of the territoria and the shires, the municipium and the burh, the collegia and the gilds, and the descent of the 'trinoda necessitas'—the threefold obligation on every English landowner of repairing the bridges and walls and serving in the local militia—from similar duties which lay upon the manorial lords of the Roman occupation. The arguments drawn from anthropological considerations,[3] such as the study of human skulls found in ancient tombs, are so highly technical, even if the results are not in themselves conflicting, that no apology need be made for omitting them. It is over *the system of land ownership* that the strife at present rages. Did the English settle in that system of free village communities which one interpretation of the accounts given by

---

[1] *Making of England*, 148.

[2] *S. C. H.* § 28.

The early land system as interpreted by (1) the Teutonic School.

[3] Greenwell, *British Barrows*.

Caesar and Tacitus represents as the basis of their social organization in the German lands whence they came? or did they accept from the inhabitants of the island that system of individual and absolute ownership which was established by the Romans in all their provinces? Both schools agree that the cultivation of the land was carried on by a common and co-operative method. The question, therefore, may be defined as a dispute *whether it was their freedom or their serfdom that these cultivators possessed in common.* Now, German writers have fashioned for us a social organization to which they have given the questionable title of the Mark.[1] This was a village community which had grown from the expansion of one family into several households. These had kept together for successive generations and had settled down side by side on the same clearing in the primaeval forests. Their settlement was characterized by a supposed common *kinship* among the inhabitants; a common, or rather equal, *ownership* of the land belonging to the community; and the *cultivation* of that land according to a common method. To the head of each family was allotted, besides a separate and permanent dwelling, a definite share with his neighbours in the arable land which for fairness' sake was annually redivided, and a proportionate share in the woods and pastures which were not temporarily divided but continued to be held in common. Much has been made of the difference in method of cultivation between a two-field and a three-field system. In the former, all the lands outside the woods and waste would be divided annually into two; in the latter, into three great portions. Of these, in the rudimentary agriculture of the time, each portion in rotation would be suffered to lie fallow: the one or the two remaining portions would be annually redistributed among the cultivators who would be bound, each on his own share, to grow a certain kind of crops. The three-field may denote a more advanced stage of agriculture than the two-field system, in that it gives scope for a more extensive rotation of crops; but much may be accounted for by the difference of circumstances and of soil.

Out of this somewhat hypothetical social system a few enthusiasts have endeavoured to develop the whole of the early English Constitution. More moderate writers who

The 'Mark system.'

[1] Kemble, *Saxons in England,* i. 35.

(2) The Romano-Celtic School.

equally believe in it as a social basis common to the whole of the so-called Aryan race, whether in Europe or in Asia, point out that, inasmuch as the development of many nations of Aryan race has evidently been arrested and they themselves have been reduced to insignificance, the social life of the English could not have been based on the mark system alone.[1] Indeed, on the most favourable hypothesis it was merely an agricultural system, and the equality which underlay it would naturally disappear with the frequency of inter-tribal war and the resulting opportunities of acquisition and the satisfaction of ambitious desires. But the advocates of the continued existence of Romano-Celtic influences *deny the existence of the mark system altogether.* One critic,[2] with reference to its elaboration by German writers, has called it 'a figment of the Teutonic imagination,' and has pointed out that there is not a single real instance of the use of the word 'marca' in the sense of landownership by a community. Caesar and Tacitus furnish the earliest accounts of the Teutonic invaders of Britain, but their evidence may be interpreted in support of a theory of individual ownership with at least as much plausibility as it has been cited to prove the existence of a system of common ownership as well as common cultivation. The analogies with the village community of India have been denied: the parallels from Russia and elsewhere are otherwise explained. As a last refuge, some of the Teutonic school have asserted that the system itself existed, though the application of the term 'mark' may have been unwarranted. But even for this final position no room is left, for it is contended by the opponents that early German law is based on the assumption of private land-ownership; that the only alternative is the possession of rights by the family, and that the term *common* merely denotes the enjoyment by two or more individual owners.[3] It should be pointed out that, however important may be the place of this question in the discussion of origins, it does not enter very practically into the course of English history; for, 'although traces still remain of common land tenure at the opening of Anglo-Saxon history, absolute ownership of land in severalty was established and becoming the rule.'[4]

The existence of individual ownership at the very outset of

[1] *S. C. H.* § 19.

[2] M. F. de Coulanges, *Recherches sur quelques problèmes d'histoire,* 322-340.

[3] Ashley, Introduction to F. de Coulanges' *Origin of Property in Land,* xvi.-xx.

[4] *S. C. H.* § 36.

English history, is argued upon two further postulates. That, so far as evidence carries us, the *system of cultivation during the Roman occupation of Britain was manorial* is, with reservations, admitted on all hands. In other words, the Roman *villa* was an estate belonging to an individual owner, who probably cultivated it by a villicus or steward, through the medium of coloni, semi-servile cultivators of small plots of their own, and of servi who were absolutely at the lord's disposal. It must further be premised that the English accepted the system of ownership and cultivation which they found established in the island. Such a supposition is possible only on the theory of a large Romano-Celtic survival. Now, in addition to the arguments already given in disproof of the theory of extermination, it should be noticed that the Welsh poets who chronicle the invasion, complain that 'a race of Romanized Britons, whom they call Loegrians, took part with the invaders against their Keltic kinsmen.'[1] But the real connecting link between the old inhabitants and their new conquerors is supposed to have been made by a pre-existing Teutonic population whom the Romans, in pursuance of their common policy, deported into Britain and settled in the south-eastern portion of the island.[2] These would be likely to welcome the invaders and to impart to them the civilization which they themselves had learnt. If together with these Teutons is reckoned the Celtic population which survived in the cities and even in a servile condition in the country, there would be ample means through which the social organization of the old inhabitants could be impressed upon their conquerors; while, if the accounts of Caesar and Tacitus are pressed into the service as witnesses to the existence of individual property among the Saxon tribes, in principle the organization of the old and the new elements of the population would not be appreciably different.

In the present state of our knowledge it is inadvisable, even if it were possible, to attempt a definite decision in favour of one or other of these rival theories. Probably we should press neither to its extreme conclusions. And anyhow our business is not with the earliest forms of social organization even among the Aryan race. The construction of 'a normal programme' of social progression for mankind at large has justly been

Means of transmitting Roman and Celtic influences.

[1] Pearson, *Hist. of Eng.* i. 100.

[2] Dr. Stubbs denies this. *S. C. H.* § 29.

Conclusions.

[1] *Domesday*, 345. Jenks, *Law and Politics in the Middle Ages*, 149.

stigmatized as 'idle and unscientific.'[1] We must take our evidence as we find it, and in its interpretation we must carefully avoid reading into it the ideas of a more scientific and a better ordered age. Thus it has been well said that 'one of the most unfortunate consequences of the mark theory has been to create a vague impression that any condition lower than absolute freedom was altogether exceptional in early English

[2] Ashley, *op. cit.* xxxviii.

society.'[2] But freedom is an altogether relative term ; for in early society unfreedom does not by any means denote rightlessness, and infinite may be the stages between the class immediately above the absolute serf and the few individuals who possess privileges of an exceptional kind.

Within the limit of a few pages it is impossible to deal with the innumerable variations of the two opposite theories of the origin of English society. In the following chapter an attempt will be made merely to summarize the conclusions of the greatest weight. But our earliest direct evidence is so scanty and so scattered that at every step we are treading on disputed ground, and although we may be nearer than our predecessors to an attainment of the truth, many of our conclusions must to the end remain matters of pure conjecture.

CHAPTER I

THE LAND AND ITS INHABITANTS

§ 3. THE idea of a landowning corporation is a legal idea The original which is said to arise late in the evolution of legal ideas and settlements to be one which 'primitive man . . . could not for the life of of the Anglo-Saxons. him have grasped.[1] But on the other hand 'there seems to [1] Maitland, be hardly anything more certain in the domain of archaic law *Survival of* than the theory that the soil was originally owned by groups *Archaic* and not by individuals.'[2] We are, however, not yet in the *Communities.* domain of legal ideas ; while we are dealing with a time when Rev. ix. 226. the early pastoral pursuits were only gradually giving way to [2] Vinogra- agriculture and when the management of the pasture remained doff, *Growth* of equal importance with the cultivation of the arable land.[3] *of the Manor,* This is to be remembered whether we are speaking of the [3] *Ibid.* 16-19 ; conquered Celts or the victorious English. It may be true 179-182. that the typical Celtic settlement was a family group occupy- ing either one common dwelling-house or a hamlet of several houses,[4] whereas the typical Teutonic group was the tun or [4] *Ibid.* village. But the larger village groups were not unknown to 146-148. Celtic society in Britain, especially in connection with markets and places of common meeting ; and it is generally agreed that the Roman occupation did little if anything to disturb the arrangements of daily life among the native population. Thus, apart from the thin veneer of Christianity there must have been little to separate the conquered from the conquerors in their method of supplying their ordinary needs. Differences of race and language are surely sufficient to account for the bitter nature of the struggle between Celt and Saxon. But no writer of credit now holds the theory of complete extermination of the conquered people. It was Celtic civilization practically unmodified by Roman accretions, with which the Saxons

15

came in contact. The invaders ignored the typically Roman organizations of the town settlements and the villas of great landowners—both of which were suffered to fall into decay ; on the other hand, they appropriated without any difficulty the settlements of the Celtic population with or without the ultimate acquiescence of the original owners.

Thus, whatever our view of the relations of invader and invaded, in all Teutonic villages as in all Celtic settlements outside the few Roman villas, cultivation was carried on by co-operation of the inhabitants upon a common system. Such co-operative agriculture was necessary because the allotments made for the use of each household consisted of separate strips of land of a roughly uniform size in each of the fields set apart for purposes of tillage. Thus the share of each individual head of a household would be scattered over a considerable area, and on a similar principle his share in the unstinted waste land and the valuable meadows was carefully regulated in accordance with the size of his holding. The whole system bears witness to the original equality of the householders.[1] Individual enterprise and convenience of communication were less important than the maintenance of this primitive principle. It was essentially a system in which rights of pasture remained of primary importance.[2] Whether under a two-field or a three-field system of agriculture there was always one great division of the cultivable area lying fallow and available for the necessary pasture close at hand. The rest of the land— the arable, on which the attention of modern writers is usually concentrated—would be ploughed by teams of oxen supplied in equal proportion by the holders of the land which they traversed. It has been held that this system of common cultivation merely conceals the fact that the several strips of the arable were the individual possessions of the holders. Proof either way seems impossible, but the evidence of a later age when common cultivation was still the rule, would seem to show the householder so restricted in the disposal and the management of his tenement by the rules recognised and enforced within the community, that we may well decline to consider the question of private ownership as worth discussion under the circumstances.

A further point of interest arises as to the character and size

[1] *Domesday*, 337.

[2] Vinogradoff, 180-181.

of these village groups. Here it is necessary to distinguish. So far as we can argue from the evidence of Domesday as to the course of previous social history there is a significant difference between the eastern and western sides of the country. In the west and south-west we are in a land of hamlets — the typical settlement of Celtic social life,— and each unit of social organization is dependent on some thegn. This points to the acceptance by the English conquerors of boundaries and agrarian arrangements which originated in Celtic times. In the east, 'the home of liberty'—to which may be added the north—by the time of the Norman Conquest the inhabitants of the English village communities are also dependent, but severally dependent in very varying degrees of dependence on many different lords. It was upon the north and east that the Danish invasions fell; but even that cannot account for the difference. The thegn who imposed himself upon the Celts of the west is supposed by some writers to have carried on a manorial system that originated with the Romans.[1] He was rather the individual adventurer whose superior prowess gained his acceptance as their lord by the natives while, in return for the payment of tribute, he left them in possession of their holdings. Such arrangements came late in the period of the conquest when the first feelings of hostility between the two races had worn away. The small size of the Celtic settlements lent itself to the establishment of such individual authority. But it would probably be a mistake to suppose that the English village community was by contrast a populous body. The normal holding of the ordinary house-holder seems to have been a hide : and though we may regard this rather as a share than as an uniform measurement,[2] all evidence points to it as denoting a considerable extent of land. Thus, it may be true that the original village communities of the Anglo-Saxons were few in number of inhabitants and aristocratic in tone.[3] In many parts it may have been quite possible to supply the necessary work for the cultivation of the scattered strips by the labour of Celtic slaves. Under these circumstances, even in the eastern parts of the country the development of 'the manorializing process' would not have been difficult, and the influence of the Danes, a nation of freeholders, would be limited to checking, in the

[1] Seebohm, *English Village Community*.

[2] Vinogradoff, 151-152.

[3] *Domesday*, 336.

c

districts where they settled, this growth of individual authority at the expense of the ordinary freeman.

The cause of this development is to be found in the fact that 'war begat the king,' and that, when once he was begotten, continuous war between the various tribes and races in the island tended to a constant increase of his authority. Thus, with the needs and power of the state there would be a corresponding increase of the royal rights and claims. Of such rights the most important in a primitive community would be those arising out of the land. In no sense would the king be regarded as supreme landowner. No doubt as a great thegn he would be the owner of extensive lands; but so long as the title to the crown remained strictly elective, it would be impossible to distinguish between those which were attached to his official rank and others which he might hold as a private individual. Whatever he held would in all probability equally descend according to the custom of the folk. So, at any rate at first, would all land descend. The original allotments of the invading English host need not be described as alod,[1] ethel,[2] heirland, or even as family land.[3] These are all terms invented by modern writers to express a contrast, of whose existence the extant documents give no suggestion. Every head of a family held his hide or share in the land of the village community by right or custom of the folk to which he belonged. In this sense all land throughout England, even the King's own estates, may be described as *folkland*.[4] But what the king had as king was a claim to certain dues from all the folklands, and these had so completely become his own property that he could dispose of them to others. It may not be denied that he granted away actual estates, either out of his own private property or out of the waste lands. But such grants would not be extensive; for the rights of his own folk would limit his sphere of generosity; while, so far as extant evidence goes, he always seems to be granting land already occupied. Thus it seems likely that his alienations, as they came to be called, took the form of grants, not of estates in land, but of rights, of a *superiority*, as it has been styled, over the land and the freemen living upon it.[5] These grants were made by charters or landbooks, of which there remain about

Species of Tenures.

[1] Lodge, *Essays in A. S. Law*, 68.

[2] Kemble, *Saxons in Eng.* I. 118.

[3] Lodge, *op. cit.*

(1) Folkland.

[4] *E. H. R.* VIII. 1-17.

The growth of a manorial system from above.

(2) Bookland.

[5] *Domesday*, 232.

twelve hundred of varying degrees of genuineness. By far
the greater number of them are made in favour of some
church or monastery; the motive of the gift is stated as
the desire of the giver to save his soul or to win pardon for
his misdeeds: threats of such awful spiritual penalties as
excommunication and eternal damnation are denounced
against any one interfering with the gift, and the deed is
confirmed with the cross and signature of the king, followed
by those of the witnessing and assenting members of the
Witenagemot, and by words of attestation or confirmation
of such of them as are bishops. Even when the grant is
made to a layman the whole charter bears an ecclesiastical
character. Seldom in the case of either ecclesiastic or
layman is there any stipulation of services in return for the
grant. The common form of charter is an absolute gift
of a certain extent of land with its appurtenances in the
shape of fields, woods, waters, and such like. Alongside of
this there appears from an early period a clause of immunity
which becomes common in the later grants, exempting the
land from all burdens except the three military obligations
which came to be known as the 'trinoda necessitas.' Now
such exemption could not mean that the inhabitants of those
lands should in future be released from payments of all kinds.
The gift was for the benefit of the donee, not of the inhabitants; so that it does not seem unreasonable to suppose
that the gift consisted of a transfer of those dues which had
hitherto been paid to the Crown. *Bookland*, then, implied
a different kind of title to that over folkland. In fact, *the
same piece of land could be both bookland and folkland*;[1] for the
right to the land itself would be regulated by the custom of
the particular folk, while the right to the royal dues of various
kinds from the inhabitants would be under the terms of the
book which bestowed them. Two other important characteristics of bookland may be noted. In the first place, it is
probable that folklaw did not contemplate the alienation of
land by the holder. The Church, however, encouraged it,
and introduced landbooks to facilitate it in the holder's lifetime, and wills which should take effect at his death. In
either case the holders of bookland who wished to alienate,
either lay or ecclesiastical, fortified themselves against the

[1] *Domes-
day*, 257.

claims of the folk by obtaining the consent of the king to such alienation. But even so the power of alienation, with at least the implied assent of the donor, may be regarded as a distinctive mark of bookland.[1] To this, in the second place, may be added the liability of such land to revert to the king if its holder neglected such services as still lay upon it or died leaving no heirs. Here bookland is to be contrasted, not with folkland, but with another form of landholding, far more common than bookland and likely to be confused with it. Bookland, properly so called, was a very rare subject of grant; it only appears in connection with ecclesiastical bodies or great thegns;[2] it could only be bestowed by the king with the advice or under the attestation of his ʿcouncillors; its creation was a royal *privilegium*. On the other hand it was only at a comparatively late period in Anglo-Saxon history that private individuals conveyed rights in land by written charter. But meanwhile, as in the case of the ʿprecariumʾ abroad, in England ecclesiastical bodies from whatever cause granted extensive *loans of land* to great men. Such loans would be either the temporary alienation of a superiority in the case of wide tracts of land[3] or occupation of the land itself. In either case there would be stipulations for rent or services, while the loan of a superiority would probably involve a stipulation for that patronage or protection of the grantor which played such an important part in other countries. The ecclesiastical grantors tried to prevent these loans from becoming permanent by limiting them to a grant for three successive lives. But the difference between a gift and a loan was not kept entirely clear.[4] Prelates with the power of pronouncing the anathema of the Church, sometimes made loans by a written form, a book, which was a real protection to the holder; and such grants might loosely be called grants of bookland. But there was this important difference, that even when made by book these loans reverted, on forfeiture for crime or neglect, not to the king, but to the grantor of the loan. At the same time so great was the hold which a loan for three lives established upon the land that the difference between bookland and loan-land was rapidly disappearing, and at the time of the Norman Conquest the formula of dependent tenure (*A* holds land of *B*), the mark of feudalism, which seemed applicable to

[1] Vinogradoff, 244-248.

(3) Læn-land.

[2] *Domesday*, 257.

[3] *Ibid.* 300-302.

[4] *Ibid.* 296.

bookland, might also be regarded as not inapplicable to the
infinitely larger class of holders of a læn.[1]

Thus from an early period we may trace a tendency towards
the building up of a landholding hierarchy. By means of a
book the king for ever alienated to a Church the superiority
over a certain district of the country; by means of what also
purported to be a book the Church for a time alienated part of
that superiority to a thegn, who exercised it immediately over
the cultivator of the soil. Now such a process would account
for the dependent vills which Domesday records in the south
and south-west. It does not offer an explanation of the more
sporadic dependence of individual villagers which is the
characteristic of the eastern shires. In fact an adequate explanation of the condition of the English people at the time
of the Norman Conquest is only to be found in an attempt to
understand the part played by the practice of *Commendation*.[2]
In the process of conquest the old kindred groups of the
English tribes seem to have lost their corporate sense, and
during the anarchic period of the Heptarchy the central power
was too weak to take their place as the protector of the ordinary
householder. The small man who could not stand alone fled
to the patronage of the greater, and 'commended' himself to
some wealthy ecclesiastical corporation or to the protection
of a neighbouring thegn. This process of subjection then
dates from an early period. And when the land was beset by
constant Danish attacks the custom became almost universal.
A 'social transformation' took place, by which the whole
land became reorganized on the basis of a military and
landowning aristocracy. Now, the protection thus accorded,
emphasized as it was by a personal oath of fealty,[3] did
not in the first instance give the lord any rights over the
land of the commended man. It would be enough for the
lord that he had a retainer to follow him to battle; while, if
any injury was done to his vassal, in addition to the wergild
paid to the family or the injured man, the lord could claim
for himself the further payment of a manbot.[4] But, inasmuch
as one of the chief desires of the commended man was to
obtain the lord's warranty of the title by which he held his
land, it became a not uncommon practice for the man to
include his land in the act of commendation.[5] Even when

[1] *Domesday*, 317.

The growth of a manorial system from below.

[2] Vinogradoff, 126-128; 213-220.

[3] Cf. *S. C.* 67, Edmund I.

[4] *Domesday*, 70.

[5] *Ibid.* 71.

the commendation was merely personal, 'in one way or another' the lord seems to have got rights over the land which constitute, as it were, 'an alienable and hereditary seignory.'[1] As a result the purchaser of the land buys it subject to the lord's rights over it; these rights can be alienated piecemeal or even can descend to co-heirs. Domesday shows us men who were commended half to one lord and half to another for the same holding. At a later date the lawyers inseparably connected commendation with rights of private jurisdiction: the commended man was of necessity in his lord's 'soke.' It is important, therefore, to notice that, in the Domesday record of the eastern counties at any rate, it was 'extremely common for a man to be bound to one lord by commendation and to another lord by soke.'[2] We may carry still further the possibilities of Anglo-Saxon cross-relationships: for we note that there were some men who could withdraw from a lord, and could transfer to another not merely their personal fealty nor even the commendation of their land, but actually the soke or rights of jurisdiction over it.[3] In fact this power of provisional commendation seems to strike across deeper social divisions, and to divide the English freeholders into two broad classes—those who could and those who could not go with their land where they would. The difference may be due to the fact that while some holders merely formed part of a seignory which had been booked to some church or thegn, but still lay under the national obligation of the 'trinoda necessitas'; others had been endowed with loans of land for the discharge of a specific service, and therefore held their land on condition of discharging such service in person.

Despite the scanty evidence before the Conquest and the confusing terminology of Domesday, three social grades may be broadly distinguished among the English. Tacitus notes this number among the German tribes — nobiles, ingenui, servi: and it seems probable that on their arrival in Britain the invading tribes were composed of an hereditary noble caste called *Eorls*, a mass of non-noble freemen described as *Ceorls*, and a small following of *theows* or slaves whose numbers would be swollen by the captive Britons. But even before the conquest of Britain noble birth as such was ceasing

[1] *Domesday*, 75.

[2] *Ibid*. 103. Cf. also Pollock, *Oxford Lectures*, 123.

[3] *Domesday*, 100.

Social ranks.

to hold its unique privileges. Tacitus tells us of the Comitatus, a band of free companions surrounding the chief.[1] When the conquest had exalted the successful chief into the king, his comites or *gesiths*, to use the English equivalent, would be the first to obtain tracts of the newly-conquered land. But all the king's gesiths did not become landowners,[2] and the distinction was perhaps marked by the introduction of the term *Thegn*. This is said to denote a servant in the royal household as contrasted with the free companion, the gesith.[3] But the members of the royal household would be more than personal attendants of the king. The minister or miles—for by such terms was the word thegn rendered—soon became a member of a territorial nobility, while the gesiths henceforth denote personal attendants on the king. The term eorl also drops out of use.[4] The name, however, survived, sometimes as part of a comprehensive phrase to denote the whole of the English people (eorl and ceorl),[5] sometimes as a convenient and familiar description of the great officials of the court and nation, the class from whom would be taken the ealdormen or provincial governors. Meanwhile the thegns pursue a chequered career. It is true that after the time of Alfred they all have the same legal status as expressed by a similar wergild of 1200 shillings. But this is the only point of similarity between all the members of the class. The term is applied equally to the great ealdorman, to the king's thegn, the thegn of any other lord, the ordinary 'scirthegn' who as the holder of five hides is responsible for the defence of the shire, and, finally, to the ceorl who by the acquisition of certain possessions has thriven to thegn-right. In theory perhaps every thegn is a member of an hereditary caste, a gesithcund-man, who stands in certain personal relations to the king or to some superior thegn, and who, as the owner of five hides, is bound to military service with his followers.[6] As a matter of fact, the practice of equal division of land under the folklaw would soon produce a class of poor, if not actually landless thegns ; while the exigency of military service opened the social rank to any ceorl who had accumulated the requisite quantity of land, and had placed himself or had been placed in the necessary relation to a lord.

Below the Nobilis in Tacitus' description came the Ingenuus,

[1] *S. C.* 57. § 13.

[2] *Ibid.* 62. § 51.

[3] *E. H. R.* IV. 723-729.

[4] Cf. Jenks, *op. cit.* 76.

[5] *S. C.* 65. § 1, and 67 : cap. VIII. 2, and 75, Cnut's Charter.

[6] *Domesday*, 164.

the ordinary freeman, the *Ceorl* of Anglo-Saxon history, who, in everything except a certain social precedence, is described as the equal of the nobilis. The name evidently covers classes of very different social status. In laws dealing with grades of rank the twelfhynde man is contrasted with the twihynde man. Obviously the reference is to the amount of wergild. And while the former, whose life was valued at 1200 shillings, is treated as synonymous with the thegn, he is contrasted now with the twihynde man, now with the ceorl.[1] The ceorl, then, was a man whose wergild amounted to 200 shillings. But in the laws of Alfred and earlier, mention is found of an intermediate class—the sixhynde man. A law of Ine draws a contrast between a gesithcund landowner and one who does not own land, and if we may identify the former with the twelfhynde thegn, perhaps the sixhynde man may denote at any rate one class of the landless men of gesithcund rank.[2] Under the same head may be ranged such British landowners as continued under English rule. After the time of Alfred this intermediate class disappears by name. But in one of Alfred's laws the sixhynde man is synonymous with the radcniht, and the record of some of the Western shires of the Midlands in Domesday mentions a class of radchenistres and radmanni [3] who can scarcely be other than the representatives of the earlier sixhynde men. The most comprehensive English term for this and parallel classes, such as the Danish drengs in Lancashire,[4] was perhaps the word 'geneat.'[5] This denoted the holder of a small free tenement in return for which he paid 'gafol' or rent, and whose characteristic service was the duty of carrying and riding on errands of all kinds. He was, in fact, a kind of lesser military tenant, the representative of the sergeant-at-arms of the feudal period. Domesday records many other local names for this class of non-noble freemen : these were due to the local jurors through whom the information was collected. The most characteristic terms have been supposed to be the English sokemen, and the Latin liberi homines. These are sometimes spoken of as denoting the only classes of non-noble freemen mentioned in Domesday. They are found chiefly in the east of the country, but are not unknown in the Midlands, and even in the south-eastern shires, and are commonly supposed to be the product of Danish influence.

[1] Chadwick, 78, 88.

[2] *Ibid.* 95.

[3] Victoria, *County Hist. of Worcestershire*, 250.

[4] *Domesday*, 66.

[5] Vinogradoff, 220, 232.

But we should in all likelihood treat them merely as local representatives of the better kind of ceorl. They were men who had kept at least their economic freedom, and discharged their obligations to their lord, chiefly by the payment of some kind of rent. Perhaps the liberi homines owned no lord, for, until the advent of the Norman feudal lawyers, there still remained a certain number of small owners who held their land by witness of the shire: the sokemen evidently denoted that class who, holding their land in accordance with ancient custom, yet had come to owe suit at the court of some neighbouring thegn.[1] But the rise in importance of the thegn class was steadily degrading the position of the ordinary freeman. The ceorl, or tunesman, inhabitant of a tun or village, was originally the head of a household in an agrarian community. In some cases he would increase his original share of a single hide to five hides, and acquire the status of a thegn: in other cases he might find himself the owner of an infinitesimal portion of his forefathers' original share. On such a small holder, the king's 'feorm' or the lord's 'gafol' would fall with oppressive weight, and it may be that the levy of Danegeld put the finishing touch to his degradation.[2] This class came to be especially denoted by the term 'gebur.' A peasant holder of a few acres, so poor that he was dependent on his lord for the means of cultivation, he has not yet sunk to the servile position accorded to the Norman villan; for he has once been a member of a free village community.[3] The typical ceorl who has retained his place in the common cultivation of the village community, is represented in Domesday by the term 'villanus.' An almost equally numerous class are the bordarii. We scarcely hear of them except in Domesday, while the cottarii, who are few in number in that inquest, figure largely in subsequent records. Both these names probably denote the class of crofters or cottagers who, personally free, yet cultivated plots of ground too small to be included in the system of common ploughing.[4] From them were drawn the labourers on the lord's own land, and among them was found room for the younger members of a numerous family and for those who, from whatever cause, had sunk in social status.

Below them in the social scale, Domesday records the existence of some 25,000 servi, or slaves.[5] In the seventh

[1] Vinogradoff, 341.

[2] Domesday, 8, 25, 324.

[3] Vinogradoff, 234-235.

[4] Ibid. 338.

[5] Domesday, 27-34. Vinogradoff, 332-336.

century the laws of Æthelberht of Kent distinguish between the theow and the læt, but of the latter nothing further is heard on English soil. The Anglo-Saxon theow was not a mere chattel. In some parts of the country so many slaves are registered that they cannot have been entirely menials. They were no doubt annexed to a particular holding; but the Church tried to secure to them the benefit of their savings, and the criminal law accorded a pecuniary compensation in the shape of a small wergild to the family of a murdered slave. The effect of the police system of the country, to make the lord answerable for the production of his freemen no less than of his slaves, must have helped to raise the status of the inferior class. Manumissions in Anglo-Saxon times were frequent, but the freedman had no special social status. Except in the small class of coliberti, whose name bears witness to the practice of freeing slaves in groups, the freed slaves merely swelled the ranks of the men personally free, who held land burdened with servile duties.

§ 4. It was a society of this amorphous type that was developed into the Feudal system whose general features are so familiar. The word FEUDALISM is used to describe the social system of western Europe for about seven centuries. During so long a period this system naturally suffered many changes; tenancy at will grew into tenancy for life, which in its turn was extended into a heritable holding. But the characteristic of the whole period was what has been described as the union of the two relationships of lord with man and lord with vassal.[1] Thus feudalism, or feudo-vassalism, as it has been more correctly called, contained both a social element based upon land-tenure, and a political element expressed by homage and fealty. It is the first of these elements which chiefly concerns us here. We have noticed the cross-relationships of Anglo-Saxon days, due to the absence of any necessary connection between landholding and service. Grants from the Crown were made on the basis of the king's general sovereignty over land and people. Thus, with the sanction of the Witan, the king gave away the ownership of large tracts of land and of extensive rights over land; yet the one did not necessarily imply the other. But with the advent of the Norman lawyers, landholding and service

The introduction of Feudalism.

[1] *P. and M.* 44.

became inseparably connected. In the feudal theory, the king became the supreme landowner, and all land was held immediately or mediately of him.[1] Those holding immediately of the king were his tenants-in-chief, a name applied at first to the immediate tenants of all lands irrespective of the particular tenure, then appropriated to the immediate tenants of the Crown, and finally reserved for such of them as held of the Crown on condition of military service. But just as the Crown had enfeoffed them or granted them feuda or fiefs, with right of inheritance for their heirs, so by a similar process known as subinfeudation or the creation of sub-fiefs, would they carve out portions of their estates and make them over to tenants to hold on condition of rendering in return services of various kinds. This process might be continued through a succession of holders, all of whom below the king are described as mesne lords or mesnes, and are regarded as holding the land in service (in servitio), the immediate lord of any tenant being his capitalis dominus, and the immediate tenant of any lord, in early days at least, his tenant-in-chief. Finally, the tenant actually in occupation by himself or his servants, was said to hold the land in demesne (in dominio suo). Cases are known of no less than nine lords above the tenant in demesne, all of whom were regarded as holding one and the same estate of land, and not by any means necessarily on the same tenure.[2] Moreover, an individual tenant could hold his lands of many different lords and by a great variety of *tenures*, that is, of services to be discharged in return for the land; so that it becomes apparent that the important point of feudalism, as a system of land tenure, was not so much the status of the individual holder as the due performance of the stipulated services.[3] These services, so far as they were exacted from freeholders, were of four kinds, which may be described as military, spiritual, serviential, or merely free, but not falling under any of these three heads.

(1) *Military.* The duty of the tenant to attend his lord's summons to the field of battle is popularly regarded as the essential feature of the feudal system. It was, however, only one, though by far the most common, subject of bargain between lord and tenant. In England a large majority of the king's tenants-in-chief held their land by tenure of knight

[1] Vinogradoff, 293-295.

[2] *P. and M.* i. 211-212. Feudal Tenures.

[3] *Ibid.* i. 215.

service (per servitium militare) as it was called. In its simplest form this involved the obligation of supplying on summons one fully armed warrior to the lord's military array. No legal stipulations were ever made as to length or place of service, but custom early tended to fix the former at forty days in the year, while the question of place of service was practically never raised until after the loss of Normandy. The effect of the existence of this tenure on the military arrangements of the country will be dealt with more fittingly in speaking of the army. Here our concern is with its social aspects. The original obligation of every freeman to military service seems in the course of Anglo-Saxon history to have been replaced by an obligation on all communities, whether shire or burh, to supply a fixed contingent. The unit of service was perhaps a rateable area of five hides ; but as there was little necessary connection between the rateable and the actual area, the number of the contingent was not governed, except very roughly, by the size of the community which supplied it.[1] Under the Normans the unit of military service was one knight's fee ; but as an expression of land measurement its meaning was as vague as the five hides of pre-Norman times. For, in contrast to the various conjectures of former writers, it is now generally allowed, that in return for his grants of land William the Conqueror laid upon a large number of his followers the obligation of supplying a fixed number of knights.[2] There is evidence which would lead us to believe that the arrangement was based upon a unit of five knights, and that it was made without any reference to the size of the tenant's estate. At any rate, in William's agreements with the ecclesiastical nobles and corporations who held the greater part of their land by ordinary lay tenure, the number of knights stipulated for was probably governed by the custom of pre-Norman times, and the difficulty of obtaining even this small contingent not unfrequently resulted in a successful attempt to reduce the obligation. For, the service due from the estate of a tenant-in-chief of the Crown was due equally from the whole of that estate, and was a liability which overrode any arrangement between the tenant and his sub-tenants. A tenant might provide for the discharge of the military service which he owed, by enfeoffing a number of persons who would agree to

Tenure by Knight service.

[1] Vinogradoff, 219, 281.

[2] Round, Feudal Studies, 261.

be responsible for it. That number might consist of part, or all, or even more than all of the amount of service due. In any case it was entirely a matter of the personal convenience of the individual tenant-in-chief who made the arrangement.[1] Thus it is of little profit to inquire the exact meaning of a knight's fee. It may have been an extent of land corresponding to the Anglo-Saxon standard division of five hides: it may have denoted the pecuniary worth of land to the extent of an annual value of £20.[2] Practically it must have been the extent or the value for which a mesne lord could induce a tenant to discharge the obligation. The difficulty of arriving at any conclusion on the matter is further complicated by the power which the lord not unfrequently exercised of imposing on a new tenant other obligations in addition to the discharge of military service. This was especially the case when the introduction of the payment of scutage in lieu of military service changed a personal into a merely pecuniary burden which could be divided up among a number of small holders.[3] Besides their portion of the scutage due from the whole of the divided knight's fee, the lord would exact from such small tenants rent in the shape of payment of various kinds; and although the payer of the smallest possible sum under the name of scutage ranked as a tenant by military service, yet in his social position he would differ in no way from the simple freeman holding by socage tenure;[4] so that the introduction of scutage, and the consequent subdivision of the knight's fee, played an important part in the destruction of the exclusive nature of the military side of feudalism.

With a knight's fee is often coupled a *Barony*. This was the name given to the lands of a great tenant-in-chief of the Crown, and though it would no doubt generally contain a number of knight's fees, there is no reason to suppose with some writers that it was a fixed number of thirteen and a third which alone fell under this description.[5] A barony once formed was regarded as an indivisible whole: if it escheated, that is, reverted to the Crown, it was not merged with the king's estates, but was almost immediately granted out to a fresh tenant; nor, if it came into the hands of the holder of another barony, were the two united; the payments due from the holder

[1] *P. and M.* i. 232-245.

[2] *S. C. H.* § 96. Round, *op. cit.* 295.

[3] *P. and M.* i. 252-255.

[4] *Ibid.* i. 256.

Tenure by barony.

[5] Cf. Hallam, *Middle Ages*, iii. 6. M'Kechnie, 236.

[1] *P. and M.*
i. 259-261.
had to be made separately upon each.[1]   But the chief importance of the idea of a barony lies in the division which it
gradually produced in the military tenants-in-chief of the
Crown.   Soon after the Conquest the holders of an earl's or
baron's barony began to form a class by themselves, apart
from the simple tenants by knight service of the Crown; and
in course of time the division was recognized and emphasized
by the practice of the administration.   Thus the greater
barons—*majores barones*, the holders of baronies—were those
who were entitled to a special summons to council or camp,
and whose money transactions were all carried on directly
with the Exchequer.   The lesser tenants—*barones secundae
dignitatis* or, more simply, *minores*—found the sheriff interposed between themselves and the Crown.   To him they paid
their feudal dues, which were fixed in amount long before
those of the greater barons; through him they received their
summons to assembly or array, and under him they mustered
so long as the feudal levy was employed.   The full importance
of the distinction between these two classes will be clear when
we are dealing with the early history of Parliament.

Tenure by
serjeanty.
[2] *P. and M.*
i. 262-271.
(2) *Serviential.*[2]   The essence of feudalism was the render of
service in return for the grant of land.   But while all tenants
owed service, the name *servientes* or serjeants came to denote
a particular class of tenants.   The majority of those holding
by this tenure would have to render service in person; for
under this head come, as tenants of the Crown, the officers of
the royal household, of whom the greater soon cease to serve
in person; the various officials, high and low, connected with
the forests; royal messengers and artizans whose duty it was
to maintain the royal palaces.   The serjeants of mesne lords
would be officials fulfilling corresponding positions in a lower
circle.   But there were some enumerated among the serjeants,
both of the Crown and of mesne lords, whose duty consisted
in finding a man, or several men, to serve with arms of a prescribed kind in the royal army.   In this way the king obtained,
both directly and through the medium of his tenants, a small
but useful force of light armed troops and commissariat officers
on whom he could permanently rely.   Probably the only way
of defining the tenure of serjeanty is by noting what it was
held to involve.   Thus a tenant by serjeanty was held to be

unable to alienate his land, or even without his lord's leave
to create a tenancy of any kind; while the close personal
relation to which the name bore witness, was marked by the
arbitrary character of the feudal dues exacted from serjeants
long after those of all other classes had been definitely settled
in amount.   In course of time the serjeanties held of the
Crown, like the military tenants-in-chief of the Crown, fell into
two classes, and, whatever the reason, the result was that
a tenant by grand serjeanty was expected to do service in
person, while over him or rather his heir, if a minor, and all his
possessions, the king established a claim of prerogative wardship which utterly overrode even the superior claims of other
lords : at the same time tenure by petty serjeanty came to be [1] Bateson,
little more than the annual delivery to the lord of some merely *Mediæval*
nominal acknowledgment of his lordship.[1]   But the serjeanty *England*
of the Crown might be only one among several tenures by 249-250.
which such tenants held various portions of their lands.   In [2] *S. C.* 301.
such cases a clause of Magna Carta saved the rights of mesne § 37.
lords, and denied to the Crown the application of the claims of *P. and M.*
prerogative wardship.[2] i. 302.
M'Kechnie,
429.

(3) *Spiritual.*   The tenure known as *Frankalmoin, Free* Tenure by
Alms, Libera Elemosyna at first included all land given from frankal-
religious motives.   But the name came to be specially reserved moin.
for such as was given, whether by the king or by mesne lords,
to religious persons or corporations without stipulation for
service of any kind.   The effect of such grant was twofold.[3] [3] *P. and M.*
In the first place, the donor's lord would have agreed with him i. 223-225.
for certain services.   These had still to be performed, and
would most likely be a matter of arrangement between donor
and donee.   All that the former could do was to free the land,
which was the subject of his gift, from all secular services
towards himself.   But it might be a real injury to his lord that
he should substitute for himself, as the person responsible for
the discharge of the services due, the rector of a church or
the corporation of a cathedral or monastery, who could perhaps
with difficulty be called to account.   In the second place,
land held in frankalmoin was that land which was subject to
the jurisdiction of the ecclesiastical courts alone.   This is
allowed by the Constitutions of Clarendon[4] which only claim [4] *S. C.* 139.
that the king's justiciar should decide the preliminary question § 9.

whether the land in dispute is or is not held on tenure of
frankalmoin ; that decided in the affirmative, there is no
question that the remaining stages of the dispute must be
heard before the ecclesiastical tribunal. But by a series of
measures, too complicated for enumeration here, [1] the lawyers
succeeded in minimizing the action of the ecclesiastical courts
in relation to land, so that the contrast drawn in the article of
the Constitutions of Clarendon just mentioned between *laicum
feodum* and *elemosyna* ceased to have any significance, and
in the thirteenth century even land held 'in free pure and
perpetual alms' might be regarded as in lay fee. [2]

[1] See *P. and M.* i. 226-228.

[2] See *P. and M.* i. 229.

(4) *All other free tenures.* The most widespread description
of the ordinary freeholders in Domesday is either as *liberi
homines* and *qui libere tenuerunt* which is found, though with
very varying frequency, from east to west of mid-England ; or
—simplest method of all and one of the most common—by
a mere mention of the holder under his proper name. In the
course of the next two centuries all other designations of such
tenants were swallowed up in the one description of tenure in
socage. The original sokeman was a peasant landowner of
the twihynde class who did suit at the court of a thegn. The
term was not itself extended, and the word socager did not
arise until the fourteenth century. Meanwhile all the free
non-military tenures came to be classed as tenures in socage.
But this was only by degrees. Thus for some time after the
Norman Conquest the tenure of a baron or prelate other than
tenure by knight service was known as tenure 'in fee farm,'
that is, one in which the fee or inheritance has been let at a
perpetual rent. [3] Magna Carta speaks of this tenure in the
same connection with socage, [4] but a century later it had
entirely disappeared. Again, although by the end of the
thirteenth century tenure by knight service had practically
become tenure by payment of scutage, yet mention is found
of military service in connection with socage tenants as a
liability which was formerly imposed upon them. [5] But it will
be clear from the various origin of tenure in socage that the
name covered very unequal classes of persons. It is not
surprising, therefore, that in the course of time there should
be found a division between Free and Bond Socage. Concerning the origin of the former class of tenants there has been

[1] *P. and M.* i. 273.

[4] *S. C.* 301. § 37.

[5] *P. and M.* i. 275.

much dispute, but it seems sufficient to think of them as
the descendants of the more substantial kinds of free non-
military tenants mentioned in Domesday. The sochemanni
of Domesday may have been 'normally holders of land lying
in common fields,'[1] but the free socmen of the fourteenth
century were large landowners whose holdings might even
be detached economically from the manor of their lord
and cultivated by their own tenants, and these might even
include others holding of them on a socage tenure. The
holders in bond or villan socage differed from the unfree
tenants whose name they shared, only in the extra security of
possession which might arise from the protection of the royal
as opposed to the manorial courts.[2] So far we have seen the
negative character of socage—it was, at least in its fully
developed form, essentially non-military. As a positive form
of land tenure it involved services and payments of widely
varying kinds ; so that the old legal definition which attributed
to it as the only incident the payment of rent, must be entirely
abandoned. The services would range from some purely
nominal duty of a personal kind, through agricultural work of
a more or less onerous character, which, however, might or
might not be performed in person. The payments consisted
of rent in kind or money, at one end of the scale being the
duty of rendering to the lord 'some small article of luxury'
such as a pair of gloves, at the other end a sum of money
representing something like the full agricultural value of the
land. Lastly, in many cases the liabilities of socage tenants
comprised a mixture of personal services and payments in
money or in kind.[3]

In further illustration of these various classes of free tenures
three points especially may be selected for development—(1)
the gradual establishment of the exclusive claims of the eldest
male heir in the succession ; (2) the divorce of any necessary
connection between the tenure of land and the personal status
of the tenant, status tending rather to attach itself to land
than to persons ; (3) the definition, both as to occasion and
amount, of the specially feudal rights which the lords could
exercise over their tenants.

(1) *The growth of primogeniture.* Under the Anglo-Saxons
the land of almost all those who ultimately held as tenants

[1] Pollock, *E. H. R.* xi. 229.

[2] Vinogradoff, *Villainage in England,* chap. iii. *P. and M.* i. 374-379.

[3] *P. and M.* i. 271-272.

Primogeniture.

D

in socage was divided, according to the dictates of natural justice, equally among all the sons.[1] But in the case of the thegns, or at any rate the holders of great estates in bookland, their military obligations would make it important that the landed possessions for which they were due should remain intact. That the inheritance of one was an exception even in the highest class, seems probable from the numerous entries found in Domesday of thegns who are described as holding their land *pariter* or *in paragio*.[2] This has been interpreted as describing a group of co-heirs holding an undivided inheritance, of whom one, sometimes distinguished as the senior, was held responsible to the king for the services due from the land. But it seems very doubtful whether, even in Normandy at the time of the Norman Conquest, the hereditary character of even the great feudal fiefs had been firmly established. At any rate, hereditary rights in them had only very recently been admitted by the overlord.[3] Thus it was not the example of the Norman nobles which brought about the application of a rule of exclusive succession to all the military fiefs in England. The cause is rather to be found in the enormous strength of the administrative power built up by the Norman and early Plantagenet kings. It seems probable that William and his sons insisted rather on 'impartible succession' than on a strict enforcement of the rule of primogeniture. It was with the military fiefs alone that the king would concern himself; for, a diminution of the holding might mean an inability not only to discharge the requisite duty (and all military service in England was service to the Crown), but also to pay necessary feudal dues. Thus the recognition of the responsibility of one out of a number of co-heirs and co-owners for those purposes which were most important in the eyes of the administration, would ultimately result in the recognition of his responsibility for all purposes, a recognition enforcible in the royal courts. And the most obvious rule, and the one most free from all chance of dispute, would be one which placed the responsibility upon the eldest son irrespective of all other claims whatsoever. The stronger the administration, the more complete was the form of primogeniture which ruled the succession to military holdings. The powerful king must have no manner of doubt where rests the duty of military service. Thus English

[2] *E. H. R.*
xi. 228.
P. and M.
ii. 261.
Domesday,
145.

[3] *P. and M.*
i. 48-49.

law far out-stripped Norman law in the rigidity of the rules of succession which it recognized.   There seems little doubt that primogenitary succession was in the first instance enforced from above; its denial of the dictates of natural justice made it unpopular with the landholding classes; its simplicity as a working rule commended it strongly to the royal officials.[1]   Natural justice and political expediency struggled against each other, until the formulation of the machinery of government under Henry II placed a weapon in the hands of the Crown which no sentiment, however strong, could gainsay or resist. The principle of primogeniture, established in one class, spread by degrees to all classes, especially as the judgements of the king's courts superseded or appropriated local or customary law.   Tenants by military service occupied by far the largest portion of English soil.   As the introduction of payment in lieu of military service encouraged the subdivision of military holdings, the number of military tenants increased until, by the end of the twelfth century, they formed by far the larger portion of all the free tenants of the country.   Then, as the power of the king's courts grew at the expense of the manorial courts, it became necessary even for tenants in socage to establish a prescriptive right to a partible inheritance, and those who could do so became constantly fewer in number;[2] while in the smaller holdings the necessity of keeping together the cattle used for tillage, would operate as a very real check upon too minute a subdivision.[3]   So rapidly did the rule spread that even the holdings of many among the unfree villan tenants had ceased to be partible, the descent being regulated by some custom of inheritance enforced by the manorial court. But this custom was not always in favour of the succession of the eldest son.   The town of Nottingham contained an English and a French borough lying side by side, and in 1327 lawyers found that while in the latter the holdings of the burgesses descended by primogeniture, many of those in the English borough descended by custom to the youngest son.   Hence the *Borough English* which writers have popularized as the name for a tenure which should at least be distinguished as Ultimogeniture, but whose limited prevalence scarcely justifies the importance attached to it, at any rate in English history.[4]

[1] *P. and M.* ii. 258-262.

[2] *Ibid.* ii. 264-267.

[3] Vinogradoff, *Vill. in Eng.* 251.

[4] *P. and M.* i. 631; ii. 277-281. Vinogradoff, 314.

(2) *Divorce of tenure and personal status.* It has been said
that mediaeval, no less than modern, law recognized the interest
of several tenants in the same plot of ground. Moreover, each
tenant might hold by a different tenure—that is, the agreement
as between any one of those tenants and the tenant who held
immediately of him might be of quite a different nature to the
agreement made between the latter and his tenant. Thus the
lord of a tenant in villenage might himself hold his land in
free socage from the abbot of a monastery who held it in
frankalmoin of a tenant by knight service of the Crown. In
such an hypothetical case four different sets of services were
due from the land, and the claims to them had arisen from
four separate bargains.[1] All who had an interest in the land
were regarded as having, in legal phraseology, seisin or possession of it; but while the actual cultivating occupier, provided
he were a freeman, was seised of the land in demesne, all
others who had any interest in it were said to be seised of it in
service. But the constant creation of new tenures in connection
with the same piece of land caused a gradual separation to be
made in the mind between the obligations due from the
holding itself and those due from any particular tenant of that
holding. This was expressed in the law, which by degrees
came to regard any given mesne lord as seised not of the land
itself, but of certain kinds of services due from it. So much,
indeed, did such services come to be regarded as a single
whole that, in course of time, precisely the same remedies were
available to a lord whose tenant failed to perform the stipulated
services, as had been originally devised for an occupying tenant
who had been disseised or turned out of his holding.[2] But,
further, the services themselves admitted of distinction. Those
which arose from a bargain between any individual subtenant
and his lord were described as *Intrinsec*, in contrast to services
which were already incumbent on the land as the result of an
agreement between the lord and his superior lord, and which
were known as *Forinsec* services. The intrinsec service of the
subtenant might, or might not, include the whole or part of the
forinsec service, which lay upon the land before his bargain
was made with the person who enfeoffed him. In either case
these terms were relative, and the intrinsec service of a mesne
lord to his superior lord would be forinsec as regards the

[1] *P. and M.*
i. 276-277.

[2] *Ibid.* ii.
39, 127,
146.

bargain between the mesne lord and his subtenant.[1] The
important point is that the service due from each particular
piece of land came to be everything, and the actual status
of the holder of the land a matter of comparative indifference.
It is scarcely possible to overrate the effect of this manner of
regarding the tenure of land in breaking up the social system
of the middle ages. Great nobles thought it no degradation
to hold land on socage tenure of mesne lords far below them
in the social scale, or even to undertake the more precarious
liabilities of the unfree villan holders ; and in the first half of
the thirteenth century the king's judges were on the point
of giving to freemen holding villan land a recognition which
would have seriously altered the whole position of the unfree
class, and would have anticipated by nearly three centuries the
actual course of events.[2]

(3) *The Feudal Incidents.* Among the various services and
payments with which free tenures were burdened, there were
a certain number which are known as the Feudal Incidents,
i.e. as inseparably incident to that tenure in chivalry or by
knight service which is generally regarded as the essential, or
at least the typical, element of the feudal system. But many
of them were known in England long before the Norman
Conquest, and in the feudal system itself they were by no
means to be found only in connection with tenure by knight
service. But the Norman Conquest affected them as it affected
every department of English life[3]—it simplified such obligations
by interpreting them according to a few uniform rules, and by
tending to translate them into terms of payments in money.
Thus, broadly speaking, the rights of the lord over his free tenant
under the feudal system may be divided into (i) actual payments, whether on a fixed occasion as the Relief, or casual as
the Aids ; (ii) the privilege of such protection of the heir or
heiress during minority as is expressed in the terms Wardship
and Marriage ; (iii) the ever present chance that his seisin of
the land in service might by forfeiture or escheat become his
seisin of it in demesne.

(i) (*a*) *Relevium or Relief.*[4] It may be conjectured that
in prehistoric times the lord fitted out his dependant with
whatever was necessary for the exercise of the latter's calling.
Thus to the soldier he would give arms, to the husbandman

[1] *P. and M.* i. 216.

[2] Maitland, *Law Quart. Rev.* vii. 174-175.

The incidents of Feudal Tenure.

[3] Vinogradoff, 295-298.

[4] *P. and M.* i. 239-299.

the needful stock for his farm; and on the death of the follower this equipment would return to the lord who gave it. To the military equipment was applied the term Heriot (heregeatu, i.e. military apparel), but it is possible that at an early period in Anglo-Saxon times a gift of land took the place of the original horse and arms, although the render to the lord by the heir of equipments of a certain kind still bore witness to the practice of an earlier date. Thus the laws of Cnut provide for such payment in the case of three grades of landowners in the event of their dying without having made provision for it in their wills.[1] Whether or not, as is generally supposed, the heriot implied an original personal connection between the lord and the late tenant, while the relief represented a life-relationship between the two based on land, the Normans at once translated the existing heriot into a relief, and in Domesday the two terms seem to be used interchangeably. But they were not merged. The rule of primogeniture or even of inheritance was not established even in the military holdings until some time after the Norman Conquest, so that for a long time the relief represented an actual bargain between the lord and the incoming tenant, and thus bore witness to the former's possession of the land in question. In England, at any rate, it was paid by every one who succeeded a free tenant irrespective of relationship. The heriot, on the other hand, bore a far more personal flavour, and the evidence of manorial 'extents' or surveys shows that it was paid by the villan classes, who continued for some generations undoubtedly to hold their tenements at the will of the lord.[2] It is possible that the earlier interpretation of the meaning of the heriot may be merely a reading back into Anglo-Saxon times, and an extension to the higher classes of the community, of that personal connection which the later law-books feigned between the lord and his unfree tenants. But as the relief became gradually fixed,[3] all connection between it and the heriot ceased. With a probable reference to the extortionate conduct of his brother, Henry I in his Coronation Charter promised that reliefs should be 'just and lawful' on the part both of the king and of other overlords.[4] This was interpreted by the legal writers of his time with reference to Cnut's law, which, however, Henry himself did

[1] S. C. 74. § 72.

[2] Vinogradoff, Growth of Manor, 347. Villainage in Eng. 159.

[3] M'Kechnie, 230-232.

[4] S. C. 100. § 2.

not maintain.   The amounts paid as relevium, both to the king
by his tenants-in-chief and to the mesne lords by theirs, were
still matters of bargain in each individual case between lord
and tenant.   But the great legal authorities of Henry II's
reign note that, while the old method obtained for baronies,
the relief for a knight's fee had become fixed at 100 shillings,
and the liability of the holder of socage land was a whole
year's rent.[1]   The Articles of the Barons demanded the ancient
relief,[2] and in consequence Magna Carta further defined the
relief to be paid by the barony of an earl or baron as a fixed
sum of £100.[3]   But there seems to have been some doubt
about the amount to be paid by a baron's barony, which
before the end of Edward I's reign was reduced to 100
marks.[4]   It was not, however, until the reign of Edward I
that in the case of serjeanties the exchequer in practice
limited its exaction to a whole year's rent.[5]   But while
every lord was entitled to a relief from the heir to a free
tenement, he was not entitled to enforce his claim by occupation of the land if the heir had already obtained seisin.
On the other hand, 'primer seisin' was a prerogative right
of the Crown ; the heir of the royal tenant-in-chief could not
lawfully obtain possession until inquest had ascertained his
right, homage had been done, and he had at least given
security for the payment of his relief.[6]

   (b) *Auxilium or Aid.*[7]   The close relationship which was
supposed to exist between the lord and his men gave the
former an excuse for demanding from his tenants pecuniary
aid on all kinds of occasions.   It was to the interest of the
tenants to limit the number of such occasions.   Thus under
Henry II a great legal authority defines them as the knighting
of the lord's eldest son, the marriage of his eldest daughter,
and a contribution towards payment of the relief which his
lord owes to an overlord.[8]   Magna Carta finally sanctioned
the two former together with a third for ransoming the
lord from captivity.[9]   These were omitted from subsequent
editions of the charter, but nevertheless they came to be
known as the three regular feudal aids.   Presumably the
amount payable for ransoming a lord from captivity must
have depended upon circumstances ; in the case of Richard I
the Crown vassals were called upon for an aid at the rate

[1] *S. C.* 163. c. 4.
[2] *Ibid.* 290. § 1.
[3] *Ibid.* 297. § 2.
[4] Bémont, *Chartes des Libertés Anglaises*, 47, note 6.
[5] M'Kechnie, 230-233.
[6] *P. and M.* i. 292. M'Kechnie, 78-79.
[7] *P. and M.* i. 330-332. M'Kechnie, 80-82, 302-306.
[8] *S. C.* 163. c. 8.
[9] *Ibid.* 297. § 12.

[1] *S. C.* 252.
Rog.
Hoved. iii.
210.
[2] *Ibid.* 450.
c. 36.
[3] 25 Edw. III
stat. 5.
c. 11.

of 20 shillings on the knight's fee.[1]   Under Edward I this same amount was fixed by statute for the two other occasions in the case of owners of a knight's fee or of £20 worth of land in socage tenure held from a mesne lord,[2] and in 1351 was extended to the tenants-in-chief of the Crown.[3]

But the lords did not consider that the settlement of these aids precluded them from exacting others for such purposes as payment of a debt or of a fine to the king or even for the stocking of their land, and the theories of the lawyers helped them to regard the extent of their claims upon their vassals as dependent upon circumstances.   Thus Magna Carta provides that no aid, except the three specified aids, should be imposed without the leave of the Commune Concilium Regni; that even such aid should be reasonable, and that mesne lords should

[4] *S. C.* 289-
299. §§ 12, 15.
[5] *Ibid.* 459.
§ 6.

exact no aid at all except on the three specified occasions;[4] while the Confirmatio Cartarum again forbids illegal aids.[5] But probably the greatest safeguard was the growth of that strong administrative machine which made it practically impossible for a lord to collect an aid without the authority of the king and the help of the royal officers.   The Acts of 1275 and 1351, however, must have destroyed the legal theory of the optional character of such aids.   With the decay of the feudal system the payment of the three aids by the tenants of mesne lords must have practically ceased.   The Crown never had a second occasion to raise a ransom; but the two remaining aids were exacted from time to time, though at such long intervals as to give them the appearance of extortions.

[6] *P. and M.*
i. 299-310.
M'Kechnie,
75-76, 242-
248, 428.

(ii) (a) *Custodia or Wardship.*[6]   Since every feudal grant was conditional on the performance of services, if the tender years of the heir in succession prevented him from fulfilling his obligations, the lord, whether king or mesne lord, in theory resumed possession by asserting a right of wardship during the minority.   Henry I in his Coronation Charter

[7] *S. C.* 100-
101. §§ 3, 4.

promised that the right should not be abused,[7] but there is evidence that he used it as a means of raising money.   This was possible, because the rights of a guardian were regarded as property and, as such, were saleable and even disposable by will.   In the fully formulated law of the thirteenth century the lord of a tenant by knight service or by military serjeanty not only was possessed of the person of the heir, but could

take for his own use the rents and profits of the land so long
as he committed no waste. If the tenant held of several lords,
the guardianship of his person was the right of the lord from
whom his family derived their most ancient title to the land;
while the different tenements of which the estate was composed
would fall under the guardianship of their respective lords.
If, however, the king was among these lords, his claim overrode that of all the other lords, and the wardship both of
the heir's person and of all his lands, no matter from whom
they were held, went to the king by the right of 'prerogative
wardship.' The abuse of these rights did not pass without
an occasional attempt at a remedy. Henry I extended the
custom in the guardianship of socage lands to lands held by
military service, by transferring the guardianship of the heir of
such land to the widow of the next of kin.[1] The Assize of
Northampton, however, restores it to the lord,[2] though Magna
Carta provides that guardians should only take 'reasonable'
profits and should not abuse their trust.[3]

In the case of *socage* tenants the rules of guardianship were
in theory far more equitable. The guardian was the next of
kin among those who could not inherit, and this would most
commonly be the mother : the compulsory supervision lasted
only to the fifteenth year, when the heir could choose his own
guardian for the remainder of his minority. Moreover, the
Provisions of Westminster[4] (§ 12, confirmed in Stat. Marlb. § 17)
made an important difference between the guardian in chivalry
and in socage, by holding the latter accountable to the heir
for his administration of the estate. On the abolition of
military tenures under Charles II these rules were extended
to all holdings, and a statute placed the choice of guardians
in the father's hands.

(*b*) *Maritagium or Marriage.*[5] One of the most important
results of guardianship was the right of regulating the marriage
of the ward. The earliest shape taken by this right is the
power of rejecting the chosen suitor of an heiress. The
foundation of such a right was the supreme interest of the lord
in providing for the fit and faithful administration of the
military service and other duties which lay upon the estate.
This would not be possible if the heiress married a cripple
or an enemy of the lord. But the right was soon extended.

[1] *S. C.* 101.
§ 4.
[2] *Ibid.* 151.
§ 4.
[3] *Ibid.* 297.
§§ 4, 5.

[4] *Ibid.* 403.

[5] *P. and M.*
i. 299-310.
M'Kechnie,
77.

Henry I's charter promises no abuse in the marriage of daughters,[1] and even the great law-book of Henry II's day mentions only the marriage of women : but there is evidence that even in the reign of Henry I heirs could not marry without their lord's consent, and instances of the sale by the king of the rights involved in this last development of guardianship are so numerous under Henry II's sons as to prove that it was a growing custom under Henry II himself. In the fully developed law of the thirteenth century no tenant holding by knight service could lawfully give his daughter in marriage without his lord's consent. The law (Magna Carta § 6,[2] Stat. Marlb. § 17) contented itself with forbidding the lord to force his tenant into a disparaging union. Such temperate provisions may show that these rights of wardship and marriage were not so oppressive as some writers have supposed.[3] The ward could always marry his or her choice on payment of a substantial fine to the king or other lord, and the cases were probably few in which large sums were raised by the suggestion on the lord's part of a series of unacceptable suitors. Anyhow, the lords found them profitable rights ; and while the liability to military service was easily compounded for or exchanged for a tenure of a different kind, the other liabilities involved in the original tenure by knight service were carefully preserved and on every occasion extended.

(iii) The recovery of the land by the lord through *Forfeiture* or *Escheat*.[4]

It has been pointed out that the basis of the feudal system was a contract wherein the tenants undertook to perform certain services in return for a grant of land. The estate reverted to the lord on failure of the heir to perform his portion of the contract. But the lord early lost the power of evicting a tenant for mere non-performance of his services. He possessed, of course, several methods of calling the tenant to account, but a description of them belongs too strictly to the province of legal procedure to concern us here. There remained, however, two occasions on which the land escheated to the lord. 'Only God,' quotes the great lawyer of Henry II's day, 'can make an heir, not man.' Thus, if the tenant died without legal heirs, his estate reverted to the lord. Moreover, if a tenant were outlawed—a very common occurrence in the

middle ages—or if he were convicted of one of the graver
offences which come under the head of felony, the king claimed
an ancient right of wasting his land for a year and a day; but
after that, it escheated to the lord.[1] If, however, the tenant
were convicted of treason, his blood was considered corrupted,
his heirs could not inherit, and, no matter from whom the land
was held, it was claimed as forfeit by the king.

Perhaps enough has been said to show that although the
growth of the king's court may have helped to simplify and
unify the relations of classes and the variety of tenures, yet
society in England remained after the Norman Conquest an
exceedingly complicated structure. A whole series of lords
might claim rights of many different kinds based upon their
interest in the same piece of land; an individual tenant might
hold his land of a number of different lords on a great variety
of tenures. Each individual and each tenement under the
feudal system has to be viewed in many relations, and the
most accurate definition of feudal tenure is that which finds
it to be 'a complex of personal rights and real rights,' i.e. in
connection with both individual tenants and the tenements
which they hold.[2] Nor is this complexity much removed
when we go on to examine what is generally regarded as the
social unit of feudal society—the lord's manor. Yet such
examination is not without its use; for, although the relations
of any single tenant or of any single acre of land are exceedingly complex, the tenements and tenants, viewed in any
one of their relations, do conform to one or other of a
few general types, and may be best depicted by gathering
them into an unit which, though its importance is overrated,
was sufficiently widespread to form the basis of instructive
generalizations.

§ 5. The word MANOR was not a technical term of
mediaeval law. Writers of post-feudal times give it certain
definite characteristics which centre round the right to hold
a court. It has been thought that in Domesday the word was
used to denote 'a house against which geld is charged.'[3] But
this is to narrow the object of the compilation of Domesday
to a knowledge of the taxable capacity of the county in terms
of the Danegeld. Seeing, however, that estates with manorial
organization already existed before the Conquest, interspersed

[1] M'Kechnie,
395-396.

[2] P. and M.
i. 214.

The
Manor

[3] Domesday,
120.
Vinogra-
doff, 3co.

with free village communities and the territorial organization of the hundred, and that all kinds of social groups were described by the commissioners as Manors, it seems more feasible to suppose that the object of the survey was the more general one of organizing the country on the basis familiar to the conquerors of the ideas of tenure and service. Anyhow, in the language of the thirteenth century the word Manor comes to correspond to the ordinary modern use of the word Estate. No doubt it implies an area and a more or less continuous area of a certain size, but the name is found in connection with tenements of such various extent that perhaps the only definition of a manor is that it was 'a complex of rights over lands and tenements.'[1]

In idea it may be said that the manor tended to become approximated to a jurisdictional, a geographical, and an economic unit. Of these marks that which is most inseparably, because almost invariably, in later times at least, connected with a manor is its use as an unit for the exercise of *jurisdiction*. Much will be said of the manorial courts in dealing with the organization of justice. Here it is only necessary to remark that there are cases in which the lord exercised rights over so small a number of cottagers or even over free tenants in respect of so small a part of their holdings, that it was practically impossible for him to hold a court for them. Nevertheless, in the thirteenth century, if there was one necessary characteristic of a manor rather than another, it was the recognition of the lord's right to hold a court. But it does not seem to have been at all necessary that a manor should form a *geographical* unit. Perhaps originally it was identical with the vill of public law. But as early as Domesday this had ceased to be the case,[2] and in succeeding centuries the constant creation of new estates not only broke up the vills into several manors, but even caused the boundaries of vill and manor to cut across each other ; so that it is no uncommon thing to find the lands of one manor intermixed with those of another manor.[3] Thus, it has been said, the fact that any particular piece of land formed part of one manor rather than of another seemed a mere matter of convenience.[4] Or perhaps, again, the manor may have originated as an *economic* unit. It did not, however, necessarily remain so, nor did manors of later formation ever of necessity

[1] *P. and M.* i. 592. Cf. also *Domesday*, 107 et seq.

As an unit for various purposes.

[2] *Domesday*, 129.

[3] *Ibid.* 136.

[4] *P. and M.* i. 593.

bear this character. It would be difficult, perhaps impossible, to make scattered holdings conform to a common system of cultivation. Any given holding would tend to conform for convenience' sake to the system in vogue on the neighbouring land, irrespective of the actual manor to which it might happen to belong ; while the practice which often prevailed, of letting all the lands of the manor out of the lord's own hand and simply retaining the rents and the jurisdiction of the court, would at once do away with an economic unity which was founded on the necessity of helping in the cultivation of the lord's demense.

For, in an agricultural community, all the arrangements of the manor aimed at procuring a supply of labour for this purpose. The principle of common cultivation, whether it be a relic of freedom or of slavery, still existed—that is, cultivation by co-operation and in accordance with a common system. *Common cultivation in the Manor.* Thus all who took part in it, including the lord and the priest, held their share of land scattered up and down in strips of varying but roughly uniform size over the whole arable portion of the estate ; while they turned out their cattle into the pasture and their pigs into the woods in number regulated in strict proportion to the size of their tenements. There is some reason to believe that in general even the lord considered himself to be morally bound by these restrictions. The object, of course, was to maintain an equality between similar classes of tenants and to ensure a correspondence between the size of the tenements and the services due from them ; but, in view of the apparent actual dissimilarity in the amount, it has been suggested that the principle of this equality was agrarian, the statutable size of the unit of measurement varying with the nature of the ground, and quality not quantity being thus the measure of division.[1] Or it may be that, for purposes of distribution of rents and services, the tenements were reduced to an artificial uniformity ; for, where comparison is possible, a considerable difference is found between the rateable and the actual size. Finally, it has been conjectured that for purposes of taxation the local assessors, ' by means of rules of thumb, which they do not explain to us,' brought into some relation with each other in their assessment the size, the annual value, and the necessary agricultural labour of the individual tenements,

[1] Vinogradoff, *Vill. in Eng.* 240.

and thus by a reckoning couched in terms of the money's worth of each portion—librate, marcate, solidate—produced the theoretical uniformity between the various classes of tenants, which apparently existed.[1] But this delusive system of equality of holdings is subordinate to a twofold or rather threefold division of the whole of the lands in any given manor. The first of these divisions consisted of the *demesne lands* of the manor, which were themselves divided into the (*a*) demesne, strictly so called, or what would now be known as the home-farm, and (*b*) the villenagium or holdings of the villan tenants, of which in the eyes of the lawyers the lord had the seisin or possession no less than he had of the lands which he reserved for his own immediate use. The remaining portion of the lands of the manor were composed of the tenements of those who held of the lord by some *freehold* tenure.

[1] *P. and M.* i. 347.

Although separate portions are found, the lord's demesne in its narrowest sense consisted for the most part of strips intermixed with those of his tenants, following the same course of husbandry and, after harvest, similarly thrown into the open fields for pasture. The affairs of the demesne and of the manor generally were regulated by a series of officers with fixed duties.[2] (1) Over all the manors of a lord would be set a *Seneschal* or steward, generally a lawyer, who combined the functions of a land-agent and a judge or president of the courts. (2) To each manor there would be a *Bailiff* or beadle, an outsider appointed by the lord, who would watch his interests, collect the numerous and petty labour rents, and attend the neighbouring market to sell produce and buy stock. These functions were often undertaken at a fixed rent, and gained for their performer the name of *firmarius*. (3) In each manor also there would be a *Reeve*, or *praepositus*, nominated from among the peasants, mostly at their own choice, and in any case the representative of their interests. His responsibility for the due performance of the villans' services made it an undesirable office; and the duty of serving in this capacity became obligatory on every holder of a certain small quantity of land, and thus came to be regarded as a mark of servile tenure. Below these three individuals were ranged three classes of officials. These were (*a*) economic, such as the head reaper and shepherd; (*b*) judicial, like summoners

Manorial officials.

[2] *Vill. in Eng.* 317-320. Ashley, *Econ. Hist.* i. 11-12.

and servers of writs ; and (c) domestic, who would be drawn from the growing surplus population. Such of these three classes as were foremen and responsible servants, would be paid by a remission of the liabilities, whether in work or money, which were due from their holdings. The influence of such responsible positions often enabled their holders, in course of time, to gain a footing among the free tenants of the manor.

Such of the demesne lands as the lord did not keep in his own hands he distributed among his villani. One of the most complicated of historical problems is the actual position of the unfree tenant under the feudal system—that successor of the Saxon ceorl who, as we are often told, was degraded by the Norman lawyers into the unfree Norman villanus, and whose whole position has been thoroughly obscured by the utter discrepancy between the facts as we find them in the manorial records, and the theories of all lawyers from Glanvill to Blackstone. In the first place, according to these lawyers, a distinction was to be made between villans *regardant* (i.e. attached to land), and villans in *gross* (i.e. attached to the person of the lord) ; but this has been conclusively proved[1] to be baseless. The same person might come under both heads according to the connection in which he was mentioned. Thus a villan regardant was a villan in relation to a particular manor, and was so called by a lord in proving his claim to that villan's services ; while a villan in gross needed no further qualification—he was all that his title implied, and was viewed in no particular aspect. For, the villan was attached to the manor as a whole, and not, like the Roman colonus, to a particular plot within it ; he was thus a personal dependant, though the dependence was enforced through the medium of a territorial lordship. *The lawyers, however, set themselves to assimilate his position to that of the colonus.* Save in one special case, to be noted presently, there was no difference in their eyes between one unfree tenant and another. Servus, nativus, and villanus are equivalent terms. The individuals of the class which they describe were all rooted to the soil (*ascriptitii glebae*), whence they could not move without the lord's permission. Such a tenant had no protection against his lord ; for the king's court would not interfere so long as the punishments inflicted

The holdings of the villan tenants.

Legal theory of villenage.

[1] *Vill. in Eng.* 48-55. Cf. also *P. and M.* i. 396-397.

by the lord did not extend to injury to life or limb. Nor was it possible for him by any effort of his own to shake himself free from such bondage. Since not only his possessions, but even his very person, belonged to his lord, he could not gain his freedom by purchase.[1] He was dependent on the compassionate generosity of strangers, or on the liberality of his lord. But even here we are warned that, while the lord could release his villan from obligations towards himself and his heirs, this did not preclude the claims of another, even if the villan so freed had attained to knightly rank.[2]

And yet even the lawyers acknowledged the existence of certain indirect ways by which the villan could gain his freedom. Residence for a year and a day in a chartered town or on the king's demesne, was perhaps the most common of these. The same effect was produced by the reception of Holy Orders, which the Constitutions of Clarendon[3] forbid without the leave of the lord. And if the lord can free his villan, says Bracton,[4] much more can he let him a piece of land by agreement; and a breach of this agreement comes under the cognizance of the king's courts, and can be remedied by the assize. Nor was this all: in numberless ways the law gradually recognized the existence of the villans as members of the commonwealth. Although legally, as we have seen, they could own no property, for them as well as for freemen Magna Carta[5] allows certain exemptions from the liabilities to heavy fines; while under Henry III, in 1237,[6] the members of the Commune Concilium are said to grant to the king an income-tax of 8d. in the pound on behalf of themselves *and their villans*, an unnecessary addition unless the latter had possessions of their own. Again, the property, not being their own but their lord's, could legally be sold in payment of their lord's debts; but it is a lawyer who records[7] that in the order of such sale the villan's chattels should be taken last. Under Henry II the Assize of Arms (§§ 3 and 12)[8] limits its operation to freemen; but under Henry III we find it extended[9] so as to include the villan population; for the villans are sworn to arms (1225 and 1252), and their arms are included among that portion of their goods which is exempted from taxation. Finally, they are legally disqualified for attendance at the local courts;[10] but numerous are the proofs of their

[1] *S. C.* 162.

[2] For explanations see *Vill. in Eng.* 87. *P. and M.* i. 411 note.

Limitations to the legal theory.

[3] *S. C.* 140. § 16.

[4] Lib. iv. cap. 28, fol. 208.

[5] *S. C.* 299. § 20.

[6] *Ibid.* 366.

[7] *Ibid.* 237.

[8] *Ibid.* 154, 156

[9] *Ibid.* 356, 371.

[10] *Ibid.* 106, xxix.

employment on royal business, from the collection of evidence for Domesday to the presentment of criminal and fiscal matters before the king's commissioners.[1]

[1] S. C. 86, 257.

But the lawyers have not been alone to blame for hasty generalizations on this point. Economic writers have divided the villan class into *villans proper*, the unfree tenants of the common fields of the manor, who were responsible for supplying the plough teams by co-operation; and the *bordars* and *cottars* already mentioned (p. 25). This division is convenient, but does not appear to correspond with facts. The bordars, who in Domesday form more than thirty per cent. of the enumerated population (between 70,000 and 80,000), disappear almost entirely from subsequent records; while the cottars, who reached only 5,000 at the same period, never rose to the dignity of a separate class.

Classes of villans.

The villan class may be dealt with as a whole. The names to denote it are as numerous as the points from which the villan is viewed. They sometimes allude to *status*, such as servus and nativus; sometimes to *tenure*, as in villanus and rusticus: more rarely the *nature of the services* gives rise to such descriptions as operarius and custumarius; or the *size of the holding* supplies the form virgatarius or yerdling. As the commutation of services which had begun before the Conquest gives the clue to rare names found in Domesday,[2] such as censuarii and gablatores, so the normal holding of the villan, a virgate of thirty acres, explains such expressions as a full and a half villan (plenarius aut dimidius villanus : half yerdling). The unit of the manorial system was the hide of 120 acres of arable, the amount of land which might be cultivated by one normal plough drawn by eight oxen.[3] The number of oxen requisite, as well as the respective size of the individual holdings, would naturally vary with the quality of the soil. But a fourth part of a hide, or a rough measurement of thirty acres, was now regarded as the normal holding of the villan tenant. It was on these two units, the hide and the virgate, that all calculations of services were made; and, although the acquisition of villan land by freeholders must have slightly altered the position of the lord towards the individual holders, the duties remained as a fixed quantity entered in the manorial rolls, and were practically subject neither to increase on the part of the lord

Villan tenure.

[2] Ashley, *Econ. Hist.* vol. i. pt. i. 22.

[3] Vinogradoff, 161. Round, *Feudal England*, 63. *Domesday*, 501.

nor to substantial diminution by the tenant.   But this must not be overstated.   It was at the lord's initiative that many of the villan tenants were allowed to commute their personal services for payments in money or kind.   And it was not to the lord's interest to get rid of a tenant.   It has been noted that only for two purposes would he wish to do so—to lay out a forest or to found a monastery.   But evidence does seem to show [1] that, at any rate as time went on, the class of landlords—the monasteries — which, while most tenacious of their rights, would also be more likely to maintain a high ideal of justice, did not hesitate to increase the burdens of their villan tenants. The only place where a villan could get redress was in the manorial court, and it cannot have been easy to obtain a judgment against the lord in his own court.

[1] *P. and M.* i. 360.

Obligations of manorial tenants.

The ordinary agricultural obligations of the tenants were of three kinds—(1) *Week-work*, or labour on the lord's demesne for two or three days a week during the greater part of the year, and for four or five days in the summer time.   This labour ranged from the ploughing incumbent on the holders of virgates down to the manual duties of the cottars and other humble tenants.   Perhaps at first all obligations to service came under the head of week-work ; but at an early period the socage tenants and, in imitation of them, the more successful villans must have obtained an exchange of such onerous duties for (2) *Precariae, Precationes* or Boon-days, work during the harvest when the tenant's whole time was at the lord's disposal.   It was no inconsiderable check upon the lord that manorial custom carefully defined the amount of a day's work, and exacted from the lord food of a certain kind and quantity. We should note that many tenants owed both week-work and precariae.   The third kind of obligations may be distinguished as (3) *Gafol* or tribute, fixed payments in money or kind which, though often most minute, reached in the aggregate to a considerable sum.   The greater number of such payments have been concisely divided into [2] (*a*) such as were based on the lord's right of jurisdiction, e.g. tithing-penny or wite-penny, and (*b*) such as might represent some return for a share in the lord's rights over wastes and waters, e.g. fishsilver or woodsilver.   To these obligations must be added others of an occasional nature, such as tallage or merchet, which can perhaps

[2] *P. and M.* i. 348.

best be dealt with as the outcome rather of the villan's personal status than of his tenure ; 'fold-soke' which forced the tenant's sheep to lie upon the lord's land for the sake of the manure ; and the aggravating and profitable 'suit of mill' which bound the tenant to take his corn to the lord's mill for grinding.

For the most part these obligations were imposed upon free and unfree tenants alike. Doubtless from the first there were tenants of both classes who paid rent in money or produce ; but the majority gradually commuted their personal services for such payments, in stages which may be traced through the manorial records. An occasional commutation of a single kind of task in any given year would be followed in time by the permanent commutation of that task, and so by degrees of all the various personal labours of that particular tenant. Such commutation was a mere matter of calculation on the part of the lord. The unwilling service of the holder of a considerable tenement, especially at harvest time when he required all his labour on his own fields, would exchange to the benefit of the lord for an equivalent rent, and the work of the lord's demesne would be done by the smaller tenants and especially by free labourers, who could be hired to work at such times as they could spare from the cultivation of their own lands. This increase in the number of free labourers was brought about chiefly in three ways—all at the initiative of the lord. Thus the lord would (i) carve out portions from his own demesne lands, or (ii) enclose parts of the waste and let them at money rents, often to servants occupied in the administration of the manor. But perhaps the chief creation of free tenancies came from (iii) the commutation of personal services. It was on the holdings of the socage tenants that the process was begun, and its extension to the villans would, at first at any rate, tend to approximate their position to that of the free tenants in whose path they so closely followed. Thus the payment of money rent as contrasted with personal service would soon cease to be, if it ever had been, a test of free tenure. The only reliable test would seem to have been whether the king's court would or would not take any notice of a particular tenant. The enumeration of services afforded no clue ; the fact of commutation was common to free and unfree alike. But action or refusal to

Commutation of obligations.

Test of free and unfree tenure.

act on the part of the king's court was the effect and not the origin of the particular tenure. The judges would be guided by the fact of the certainty or uncertainty, not of the amount of the services to be rendered by the tenant, but of the particular kind to be rendered on a particular day.   It was not so much that his obligations were without measure (for they were all strictly fixed), but that, in Bracton's words, 'he knows not to-day what he should do on the morrow.'   Thus it was only by constant reference to the lord's will that his daily duties could be settled, while even if the lord did choose to go behind manorial custom and to increase the obligations, the villan was practically without remedy.[1]

[1] *P. and M.* i. 351-354.

Origin of copyhold tenure.

The manorial custom which secured the villan in such rights as he possessed must have become greatly strengthened by the reduction of those claims to writing. The use of written rolls spread from the king's courts to the manorial courts, and on the records of the latter were gradually entered the lord's dealings with his villan tenants. To these records the villan could appeal in the manorial court even against his lord, and although for many generations to come the king's judges would put no limit to the lord's arbitrary rights, yet it must have been peculiarly difficult for a lord to violate his own written and witnessed agreement with his tenant. Thus the tenant who hitherto had held by custom of the manor, and was in consequence sometimes described as *custumarius*, was now thought of as holding by roll of court, and even before long, when he was given a duplicate of the entry which bore on his holding, by copy of court roll. This process seems to have begun about the middle of the thirteenth century, and two centuries later the customary tenant has become the copyholder known to modern law. The existence of this tenure is rapidly becoming a matter of merely antiquarian interest, for the power of enfranchisement conferred within the last century by statute on both lords and tenants is extinguishing the remaining copyholds.

Villan Status.

So much for villan tenure: it remains to say something of the *personal status of a villan holder*. The nominal extent of the lord's powers over him have been already touched on. He was absolutely at the disposal of the lord; for, although the villan could not leave his land without the lord's permission, the lord could sell the villan with his tenement. Unlike a chattel, he belonged to the manor and formed part of the freehold.[1] The villan was also liable to sundry heavy payments such as tallage and special aids; and he laboured under many disabilities such as *merchet* or the fine for marrying his daughter, a fine for selling a horse or an ox, the liability to be tallaged high and low (de haut en bas), and the necessity of serving in his turn as reeve.[2] But the limitations to the lord's power far outweighed these disadvantages. Although towards the lord alone the villan was in a position of serfdom, yet even as against his lord he was protected from the forfeiture of his 'wainage' or instruments of labour[3] and from injury to life or limb; while the power of the lord in the exaction of his services applied in general not to the quantity, which was settled and recorded, but to the kind of work which the villan should perform. Moreover, beyond the bounds of the manor and away from the power of the lord the influences which made for freedom were irresistibly strong. Not only was there considerable migration, despite regulations to limit it and the exaction of a poll-tax (chevagium) by the lord in maintenance of his claim, but away from the manor a villan was treated as a freeman, so long as his servile status had not been proved. And the procedure in such trials was also favourable to liberty; for, the only proof accepted was the acknowledged servile status of the ancestors of the person claimed. Thus the position of the villan as regards his lord has been described as a condition of unprotectedness rather than of rightlessness.[4] And yet this was only true of the villan in a civil capacity. From the reign of Henry II at least, the criminal law made practically no distinction beween free and unfree classes. The extant pleas of the royal courts scarcely reveal a consciousness or afford a proof of a distinction between the two. There seems to have been some difference in the payment of the Murdrum and in the method of Ordeal; but early in the thirteenth century both these disappeared. On the other hand, villans, as well as freemen, could use the royal courts to gain redress for injuries; the frankpledge —an essentially free institution in idea and origin—came to be composed chiefly of villans, who through its agency became connected with the Sheriff's Turn; while the ordinary courts of the hundred and shire were attended by a representative

[1] But see Vinogradoff, 346.

[2] *P. and M.* i. 350; 355-356.

[3] But see M'Kechnie, 343.

[4] *P. and M.* i. 400.

body composed of the reeve and four villan tenants from each
vill.

We are now in a position to understand the full significance
of the central fact in the economic history of mediaeval England
—namely the Black Death, with its necessary accompaniment,
the Peasant Revolt.   Towards the middle of the fourteenth
century the success of the villans in commuting their services
seems to have encouraged those who had not been so successful, to refuse the performance of their services.   Even with
the customary tenants there was much dissatisfaction at the
lord's retention of liabilities like the merchet and of small
payments of various kinds to mark their servitude.   At such

a moment the visitation of the Black Death swept away an
almost incredible proportion of the population, and, in consequence of the resulting scarcity and costliness of labour, the
lords would no doubt use the manorial courts to enforce the
performance of such services as had not been commuted and
the strict payment of all commutation fees, while by the
Statute of Labourers the governing classes tried to stereotype

the old rate of wages.   There is no need to suppose[1] that the
lords attempted to demand the performance of the services
which had been commuted.   The Peasant Revolt (1381) which
followed was to no small extent fanned by the doctrine,
founded on Wycliffe's teaching, that, as it was lawful to
withdraw tithes from priests who lived in sin, so 'servants
and tenants may withdraw their services and rents from their

lords that live openly a cursed life.'[2]   The demands of the villans
varied from place to place, and the most common of them
was, in words, that land should be no more than fourpence an
acre; but their real desire was for a free tenure of their land
by the abolition of the remaining servile payments exacted by
the lord.   This, rather than the desire to obliterate the records

of the services already commuted,[3] explains their attack upon
the manorial rolls.   The revolt failed immediately, and perhaps
even its ultimate success in destroying mediaeval serfdom was
not so great as is generally assumed.   The Land and Stock
lease, by which the lord stocked the land for his tenant in
anticipation of the day when he could resume the old methods
of cultivation, gave way, after an experiment of some seventy
years, to an extension of the system of tenant-farming on leases

which had been already in use. But remnants of villenage were to be found perhaps as long as feudal tenure lasted,[1] and methods of common cultivation, whatever their origin, existed in different parts of England down to the beginning of the nineteenth century.

[1] M. Kova-levsky, *Archae-ological Review*, i. 444.

§ 6. The causes which brought about the commutation of services for rents tended also to reduce the profits of landlord cultivation. It has been reckoned[2] that, as a result of the Black Death and the rise in the price of labour, such profits had sunk from twenty to about four per cent. The landlords sought refuge in the creation of leaseholds. They ceased to be cultivators and became mere rent receivers. But in the fifteenth century along-side of the leaseholders and copyholders there appears a third important class, namely the *yeomen*, who on the whole repre-sent the small freeholders of the feudal manor. The limit of the class may be said to lie between those who were eligible for the magistracy and those who possessed the franchise and were called to serve on juries. A statute of 1430 limited the parliamentary franchise to freeholders of the annual value of forty shillings. But the yeomen must have found their way into Parliament; for a statute of 1445 forbids the con-stituencies to return valetti or esquires as their members. Yet notwithstanding this apparent check, they were popularly regarded as the mainstay of the country. Fortescue, the Lancastrian judge, in a laudatory passage of comparison between England and the Continent, draws attention to their flourishing state, and is followed by the social writers of Elizabeth's time. But in the fifteenth and early sixteenth centuries, the market commanded by English wool on the Continent encouraged the formation of large sheep farms. This led to a diminution of the arable land and the enclosure of common lands for the lord's benefit, proceedings which bore hardly on the villan and the free labourer alike; for they led to the eviction of the former and lessened the demand for agricultural labour. The freeholders too could not fail to be affected by so great a change, though the rise in prices which followed the diffusion of specie from the American mines affected them less than almost any class; for, while they obtained a greater price for their produce, their labour, supplied as it was by themselves and their families, did not

Yeomen freeholders.

[2] Thorold Rogers, *Six Cents. of W. and W.* 230.

8 Hen. VI. c. 7.

23 Hen. VI. c. 14.

increase in cost. At the same time, the legislature, representing the Crown and the landed gentry, did everything in
its power to protect them. Small holdings were encouraged,
and a maximum limit was set to the size of a flock of sheep,
and, by whatever means, the class of yeomen was saved to
form the backbone of the parliamentary party in the Civil
War. But their day was gone by. Contemporaries reckoned
them as forming one-sixth of the population of England in
the seventeenth century, and at its close their actual numbers
were estimated at between 160,000 and 180,000. But as a
class they were ignorant and conservative in agricultural habits,
and after the Civil War they took no political initiative. Thus
they lent no aid to the Revolution of 1688, which paved the
way for their extinction. For, the Revolution was the victory
of the great Whig landowners, who in their jealousy of the
rising mercantile class—their political allies—spared no efforts
to keep ahead of them in the race for wealth. To this end
they did everything for the encouragement of agriculture.
They offered a bounty on the export of corn ; they passed
bills through Parliament for the enclosure of common fields,
and, as individuals, they introduced on their estates improved
methods of cultivation from Holland. The result was most
disastrous to the yeomen.[1] The introduction of the factory
system destroyed those domestic industries on which they
had fallen back in bad times ; and the decay of the small
country towns, which followed on the consolidation both of
industry and of farms, deprived them of their markets. At
the same time, they were too poor, if not too ignorant, to
take advantage of the improved methods of agriculture,
and in their poverty they were bought out from their small
freeholds by great landowners or wealthy founders of new
families.

The mention of enclosures brings us to the important subject of common lands from which the enclosures were made.
Rights of common were of various kinds ; but here we need
concern ourselves only with the most important—common of
pasture, or the right enjoyed both by freeholders and by villans
of turning out a certain number of cattle to feed either on the
waste of the manor, as was most usual, or on the fields after
the hay harvest was gathered.[2] These latter were often called

Margin notes:
1515.
1534.

1689.

[1] Toynbee,
*Indust.
Rev.* 65.

Common
Lands.

[2] Vinogradoff,
171-174.

'Lammas lands,' because it was on old Lammas day (August 12) that the enclosures were removed; and the right exercised over them came to be known in law as 'common of shack.' The right of common enjoyed by the freeholders was chiefly of two kinds—(1) common *appendant* or annexed by custom to the freehold as forming part of the manor, and (2) common *appurtenant* belonging by definite grant to a freehold, which did not necessarily form part of the manorial system of cultivation.   Of these the former would be exercised over both the Lammas lands and the waste, the latter as a general rule over the waste alone.   But the villan tenants, and after them the copyholders, enjoyed similar rights of common extending over both classes of land, though their rights rested merely on the custom of the manor.   The legal theory of the manor *gave the whole estate into the lord's hand*[1] subject only to the diminution of such rights as he might have granted away.   Thus whether it was freeholders asserting their claim to the Lammas lands, or copyholders turning out cattle upon the waste, it was only by permission of the lord that these could be done.   Such permission however, once given, became binding as the common law of the land, and although legally it was only the freeholders who could enforce such rights, they carried with them the interests of the villans, in conjunction with whom the prevailing customs had been defined and enforced in the manorial court.   Thus any freeholder with a right of common could prevent his lord from appropriating any portion of the common land, and could enforce his right in the king's court by a special process known as assize of common.[2]   The Statute of Merton in 1236 first allowed the lord to approve, i.e. to enclose with a view to profit, the common lands of the manor, provided he left sufficient for the tenants' wants, a point which may have been settled by a jury according to local custom. But this only applied to commons appendant, and the lord was not able to touch commons appurtenant until a clause in the Statute of Westminster II (1285) allowed him to deal similarly with such of them as were held by prescriptive right, although he could not revoke any definite grant made by himself or his predecessors.

But this legal theory of the right of common was perhaps untrue to history, and certainly unjust in practice.   Apart

Marginal notes:
Legal theory of rights of common.

[1] Vinogradoff, 311.

[2] *P. and M.* i. 162.

20 Hen. III. c. 4.

13 Ed. I. c. 46.

Historical origin.

from the unfortunately recurring question of the Roman origin of the manor in England, it has been held on the one side, that although some manors may have sprung from the voluntary dependence on a lord of freemen and freedmen who would accept all privileges at his hands; yet a great many of the manors now or formerly existing represent ancient communities in which, little by little, the authority of the community was engrossed by the most considerable man in it, until he became the lord and the other landholders sank into his dependants;[1] and that the privileges of the former would naturally be modelled on the customs which kept their ground among the latter. Thus whether it is the common system of cultivation, or the rights of common enjoyed by the inhabitants of all manors, they equally represent the *imposition of the lord on a free village community*, and his successful encroachment on their primitive rights.

A doubt, however, has been expressed whether the community as such ever had any primitive rights. A system of common cultivation, we are told, may well be the outcome, not of the abstract idea of common ownership or kinship, but of primitive agricultural needs, and it can be maintained not by any legal recognition of the communal custom, but merely by the common law of trespass.[2] It is because of this necessary economic interdependence that we find the lord treating his villan tenants as members of a community having duties towards himself; he imposes amercements on them, he lets them his demene lands on lease. But the money to be collected, whether for the amercement or the rent, is collected from individuals with separate holdings and a responsibility for payment proportionate to the size or character of their holdings; it is a 'joint and several' liability for the whole amount of the necessary payment. It is asserted that the same principle applied to the apparently communal rights of the villan tenants. They were not rights which attached to the community as such, but the tenants in villenage enjoyed them, e.g. rights of pasture, because those rights were treated as part of the tenements which they held. In fact the inhabitants of the original manors, if they began as a body of freemen, regarded themselves not as a community of common owners but as a group of co-owners: and rights of pasture

[1] Compare Pollock, *Land Laws* (1st edit.), with (3rd edit.) 41-42.

[2] Maitland, *Survival of Archaic Communities*, Law Quart. Rev. ix. 224-225.

were, therefore, rights attached to certain individuals, which were exercised in common because more valuable thereby to each, but nevertheless as 'several,' separate rights.[1]

[1] P. and M. i. 619-620.

Enclosures.

Whichever of these views may be the right one, the practical injustice of the legal theory of the origin of common rights is clear from the refusal of the law to consider the claims of any other inhabitants than freeholders or copyholders of the manor, even though the privilege may have been enjoyed unquestioned for an unknown length of time; while it was not until 1836 that the legislature betrayed the least consciousness that the exercise of such rights, as affected by the question of enclosures, concerned any except the lord and, in a less degree, the manorial tenants. But by that time the mischief had gone too far for remedy. A combination of circumstances led to the accumulation of those large estates of the fifteenth century which threatened, through the practices of *livery* and *maintenance*, to reproduce the worst evils of unmitigated feudalism. Self-interest caused the landowners to throw together large tracts of land. Nothing hindered this policy so much as the system of common cultivation; and the abolition of the system necessitated the eviction of the tenants who practised it. These would now be chiefly the remains of the old tenants in villenage or, as they were coming to be called, the customary or copyhold tenants. Under Edward IV the law courts seem to have begun to take cognizance of the rights of the heir of a customary tenant who held a grant of inheritance; but—though this is a point of much dispute,[2]— it is doubtful whether there was any legal protection until a much later period for the ordinary villan. It has been maintained that, without incurring legal penalties, the lords could, throughout the fifteenth century, evict all copyholders, and in the early years of the sixteenth century such of them as held no grants. Even into the reign of Henry VIII there is evidence of wholesale evictions; nor does the Tudor legislation, which tried to stem the current in the direction of great estates, betray the least consciousness that the practices against which it is aimed were in any sense unlawful. 'They (the Acts of Parliament) lay down that "houses of husbandry" ought to be maintained, on the ground that it is desirable that men should find employment; but they never provide

[2] Cf. I. S. Leadam, in *Trans. R. Hist. Soc.* 1892, and *E. H. R.* vol. viii.

means by which the copyholders could enforce their *legal* rights, if they had any.'[1]

[1] Ashley, *Econ. Hist.* vol. i. pt. 2, 280.

But although the result of these forcible enclosures was a displacement of large portions of the agricultural population, and was therefore serious as far as it went, yet no great permanent harm was done.   The population was not increasing so as to outstrip the means of subsistence : the extraordinary maritime development of Elizabeth's age gave occupation to the hardier spirits ; while the spread of textile industries among the cottage population in the seventeenth century helped to strengthen the position of small holders of all kinds.   But the desire of the landed aristocracy to keep pace with the growing wealth of the merchants and the consequent encouragement of the proffered bounty to agriculture, caused the landowners to do all in their power to foster the growth of great estates.

Their effect on (1) the landlord and farmer.

For this purpose, as in the matter of the bounty, recourse was had to Parliament ; and, since commonable rights had now become recognized by the law courts, it needed Acts of the legislature to legalize enclosures.   In this way three million acres of common land were dealt with by the land-lords in the eighteenth century, and six million more in the early years of the nineteenth century.   But the growing feeling, possibly of complex origin, that such enclosures were an infringement of the rights of the public and not of the commoners alone, has led to the resistance offered in courts of law and to the statutory curtailment of the landlords' powers.   Of the details of these nothing can here be said. We need only notice some of the more serious results. Despite the greed of the landowners, and despite even the agricultural improvements which they introduced, the popula-tion grew so fast that, after the middle of the eighteenth century, the importation of corn began to exceed the amount exported ; in 1773 the liberty to export was curtailed, and in 1814 the bounty on export was abolished.

(The Corn Laws.)

But the growth of population had an even more serious result for the landed interest.   Together with the bounty of five shillings per quarter so long as the home price was not above 48 shillings, in the interests of the home growers the legislature maintained the prohibitive import duties which had been imposed first in 1670.   But the feeling of the country was in favour of using the import duties for the purpose of maintaining a level price. By an Act of 1773, associated with the name of Burke, this was fixed at 48 shillings, which in 1791 was increased by the pressure of the farmers to 54 shillings, and after the great war in 1815 to 80 shillings, above which the import duties became merely nominal or altogether ceased. But these attempts completely failed; for, while the price of corn during the Continental wars of 1792-1815 rose so high that, in order to feed the starving people, Parliament had to offer bounties on importation, for the succeeding decade it fell much below the limit selected by the legislature. In 1828 the idea of a sliding scale, attributed to Canning, fixed a varying tariff of import duties until the price rose to 73 shillings, when the duty became nominal. But this had no better effect than the previous simpler system; and in 1846 Sir Robert Peel, after one attempt at readjustment of the sliding scale, became a convert to the principles of Cobden, and almost with a single Act removed the import duties altogether. Whatever the real cause may be, the schemes of the landed interest to manipulate first the export and then the import duties to its advantage have redounded to its own confusion. The interest was perhaps a little too much confined to that of the landlords and farmers; for, meanwhile, a second result of the enclosure of the commons had been the rapid impoverishment of the agricultural labourers and their severance from the land. We have already noticed the decay of the yeomen. But if the enclosures bore hardly, as undoubtedly they did, upon them, much more were they the cause of suffering to the tenant of a mere cottage and garden.

It has been said that since the break up of the manorial system the most prosperous time for the agricultural labourer was the fifteenth century, and in a less degree the first half of the eighteenth century; while the periods of his greatest degradation were the first half of the seventeenth and the first quarter of the nineteenth century.[1] But the policy of the landlords in the formation of large sheep farms, the known continuance of villenage, and the record of wholesale evictions may well make us pause before we assent to the prosperity of the labourer under the Lancastrians;[2] while it has been

(2) the labourers.

[1] Thorold Rogers, *op. cit.* 522.

[2] Cf. *Social England,* ii. 381-386.

pointed out that, had there been any severe and widespread distress at the beginning of the seventeenth century, it would have coloured such democratic risings as those of the Levellers and others during the Commonwealth.[1]   As a matter of fact, the continued existence of commonable rights and the spread of cottage industries must have placed the labourer in a fairly comfortable position ; and although the policy of the great landowners of the eighteenth century deprived him of the former, and the growth of the factory system extinguished the latter, the rise in wages which followed the introduction of improved agricultural methods, prevented the real change in the labourer's condition from becoming apparent till towards the close of the century.   Then the enormously increased rent and prices went to the benefit of the landlord ; and the labourer, debarred from an increase of wages through the vicious action of the old Poor Law, found himself reduced to starvation point, with no means of keeping the cow or the geese which had made up to him for the deficiencies in a weekly wage, and no chance of supplementing his agricultural work by the produce of his loom.   At the same time, until 1824 combination was treated as conspiracy, and until 1834 the old Poor Law continued to supplement the wages out of the parochial rates.

§ 7. So far we have investigated the various kinds of tenure and modes of agricultural life, which emanated from the manorial system of the middle ages.   It remains to enquire how far the LAW modified the conditions of the only species of feudal tenure which at first it recognized, namely, that of the freeholders, and in particular of those who held on condition of military service.

It has been shown already that in the feudal theory a life grant of an estate was alone possible ; and although circumstances and convenience caused the establishment of primogeniture both in custom and in law, and ultimately for both military and non-military estates alike, yet the theory was so far observed that inheritance by descent only existed when it was expressly specified in the original grant.

Thus interest in land was of two kinds—for life or in fee ; for, with the establishment of primogeniture the word *feudum* came to denote rights of inheritance.   But the difference

[1] Ashley, *Pol. Sci. Quart.* iv. 404.

The Land Laws.

between the two kinds of interests was not thought of as
a difference in quality of ownership.   Behind the claims of
every tenant for life there must of necessity stand the claims
of a tenant in fee ; but none the less the only difference
between the two is that the interest of the tenant for life is one
of definite duration, whereas that of the tenant in fee runs on
for time which no man can define.[1]   Now, the most practical
test of ownership lies in the power of disposing at will of the
thing owned.   The feudal theory of life ownership was so far
retained as to render it impossible to leave land by will
(alienation 'post mortem') ; but the circumstances attending
the Norman Conquest caused the recognition of the right of
alienation 'inter vivos'—the grant or sale of land during the
owner's lifetime.   For it would be only by such means that
the tenants-in-chief of the Crown would be able to secure the
proper discharge of the military service which they owed
to the king, or that the Church would be induced to lend its
powerful aid to the Crown ; while the growth of a class of professional lawyers would raise a great influence in favour of the
free alienation of landed property.   Such alienation would
take chiefly one of two forms [2]—it might be alienation by
(1) *substitution* of one tenant for another, in which case there
would be no alteration or readjustment of services, but the lord
might get an incapable and uncongenial tenant in the place of
one with whom he stood on friendly terms.   The commoner
form of alienation would be by (2) *subinfeudation*, or grant of
a portion of the estate to be held of the grantor.   In such
a case the lord's rights would not be destroyed ; but since
their efficient discharge might well depend on the behaviour of
the sub-tenant whom he could not control, their exaction might
become precarious, and since the terms on which the new tenant
held might be quite different from those by which the grantor
held of his lord, that lord's rights might be seriously diminished
in value.   For when the time came for the exercise of such
profitable rights as were implied in the words wardship or
escheat, instead of having absolute control over the tenement,
the lord might find the land already occupied by tenants from
whom he was bound to accept the perhaps utterly insignificant
rents in return for which they had been enfeoffed or invested
with their land.

[1] *P. and M.*
ii. 6-13.

[2] *Ibid.* i.
310.

The power of alienation being once granted, the alienor
had it in his power to regulate the future devolution of the
land by the form of his gift (forma doni).   His liberty in this
respect seems to have been regulated by the law merely in
a negative way—that is, everything was permissible in the
form of an alienation except such as the law expressly forbade.
But the interpretation of the terms of any particular alienation
was in the hands of the lawyers, and, as will be seen, they did
not lose their opportunity.   The forms in common use which
call for remark were of two kinds—(1) a gift of the *Fee Simple
Absolute* by a grant to a man and *his heirs*.[1]   At first such a gift
was taken to mean what it said, and a tenant holding by such
a grant could not alienate without the consent of his heir-at-
law.   But in the early years of the thirteenth century such
consent seems no longer to have been necessary, a man's heirs
were interpreted to mean those whom he chose to appoint as
such, and the form itself was commonly changed to 'his heirs
and assignees.'   But this very free interpretation of the lawyers
was not at all in accordance with popular opinion, and in the
second reissue of the charter under Henry III in 1217, a small
attempt was made to restrain the absolute freedom which
was allowed, by a clause which prohibited a freeman from
disposing of so much of his land as would prevent him from
doing, with the remainder, the service due to the lord.[2]   In the
same document the special prohibition of such alienation in
favour of ecclesiastical corporations began the Mortmain laws,
which will be dealt with under a separate head.   The king
made use of the feeling against alienation to establish as
a prerogative right the necessity of his licence to his tenants-in-
chief for such alienation of their lands.   But the efforts of
those tenants-in-chief in the charter of 1217 completely failed.
Usually, however, it has been supposed that Edward I allowed
his barons to triumph in the Statute of Westminster III,
commonly called *Quia Emptores*.   This enacted that every
creation of a new manor should place the new tenant
in the same relation to his lord's lord as was occupied by
the lord who had enfeoffed him.   The effect of this, of
course, was to put an end to the creation of new manors
by subinfeudation.   But recently it has been pointed out
that the statute also compelled the great barons to grant to

1217.

1290.

their tenants complete freedom of alienation by substitution, and that since this extended even to the substitution of several tenants for one, the resulting difficulties were precisely the same as had arisen out of subinfeudation, and consequently the benefit of the statute to the great lords was not so complete as is commonly assumed.[1] At any rate, however much [1] *P. and M.* or little other lords gained, the king's prerogative rights were i. 318. untouched, and it was only by special legislation that in years to come the uncontrolled exercise of the king's claims could be brought by degrees within reasonable limits.

It was just at the very time when this disingenuous interpretation of the meaning of the word 'heirs' was gaining acceptance that a second form of gift became common, which attempted to limit the devolution of land to a special class of heirs by (2) a grant made to *the heirs of the body* of the original donee,[2] i.e. his direct descendants.   But the lawyers were not [2] *Ibid.* ii. to be beaten.   At the beginning of the thirteenth century it 15-19. was not uncommon for a grant to be made to a man and his heirs 'if he shall have an heir of his body,' and such a grant was interpreted by the lawyers to imply, and consequently to depend for the validity of its limitation upon, the condition of the birth of such an heir.   If he was born, and whether he remained alive or not, the condition was fulfilled, and what had hitherto been a conditional gift became an estate in fee simple absolute of which the grantee could dispose as he wished.   The opinion of the great lords on this reading of the law is to be found in a clause of the Petitions of the Barons in 1258,[3] but no answer seems to have been given [3] *S. C.* 386. to their complaints until 1285, when the Statute of West- § 27. minster II provided in its first section, known as *De Donis* 1285. *Conditionalibus*, that, if a conditional fief had been alienated, the heir could, on the death of the grantee, recover the fief from the person to whom it had been alienated; while, if there was no heir alive, the original grantor or his heir could recover it from the holder as if issue had never been born.

The effect of this statute was to create not only a limited Restraint but also an inalienable estate; and since it did not pretend to on alienabe a fee simple either absolute or conditional, it was regarded tion. as a new species of estate and called a *Fee Tail*, i.e. a fee or estate, taillé or cut off from the fee simple and the freedom of

F

disposition which accompanied it.   Thus, whatever happened during the lifetime of the holder of the estate, his heirs were bound to inherit ; no disposal of it could bar their claim, for the estate was entailed on them and they were the tenants in tail.   'Such is the legal and only correct meaning of the term entail which nowadays is constantly used to express the far more complicated scheme of modern settlements.' [1]

[1] Pollock, *Land Laws*, 68.

New methods of alienation.

But from the very first this effective check on the power of alienation met with considerable resistance.   The inviolability of an entail rendered titles insecure, since an old entail might be proved and no time could bar it.   Moreover, not only was the king unable to punish treason by forfeiture of an estate in tail, but the smaller landowners, as they became impoverished in the Wars of the Roses, increasingly felt the drawback on the power of free disposition.   Thus all classes, except the great landowners in whose behalf the statute had been passed, were interested in obtaining a relaxation of the practice.   The nobles, however, were strong enough to keep what they had won ; and only indirectly could the wishes of their tenants or the ingenuity of lawyers break through the hated barrier.

(1) Application of Warranty.

The first method employed for this purpose was the application, within necessary limits, to estates in fee tail of doctrines originally devised for the use of tenants in fee simple.   By the doctrine of *Warranty*, which in the case of personal property or chattels dated back to early Teutonic law, a purchaser whose possession was disputed would 'vouch to warranty' the vendor of the article, so that the vendor would be obliged either to defend his title or, if the claimant established his right, to make recompense to the purchaser of the article from him. 'In the development of the English law of land the doctrine of warranty was applied mainly to the obligation on the part of the donor of land and his heirs to defend the obligation of the donee and his heirs' [2] to the extent of giving, if necessary, to the representative of the donee lands of equal value to those of which he had been deprived.   Now, the holder of an estate tail was regarded as the owner of the freehold within the limit of his lifetime ; if he went further and alienated the fee simple, which was legally beyond his power, yet the burden lay with his heirs of establishing their claim by process of law ; while, if the alienation had been accompanied by a warranty,

[2] Digby, *Hist. Law Real Prop.*, 4th ed., 80, note.

those very persons who on the alienor's death would make a claim, would find themselves bound by their ancestor's action to defend the title of the present holder or to compensate him, if evicted, with lands of equal value. Thus 'it was often possible for the actual possessor of land to give to a purchaser a better title than he had himself.'[1]

1 Pollock, *Land Laws*, 82.

This same doctrine of Warranty was again brought into use in a more effectual method of 'barring an entail' which was established in the fifteenth century. A friend of the tenant in tail would claim to be the holder of the fee simple, and would bring an action against him for its recovery. The tenant in tail would then vouch to warranty another friend who impersonated the donor or heir of the donor of the estate in tail. After some further forms, which need not be specified, the second friend, representing the original donor, would disappear; judgement would go against him by default, and the lands would be awarded in fee simple to the first friend, who would convey them to the former tenant in tail as an estate in fee simple. This elaborate process was called a *Common Recovery*, and its applicability to estates in fee tail is generally, though not without question,[2] agreed to have been established by the case of *Taltarum* in 1472, whence it lasted as a mere matter of form until an alteration of the law in 1833. Two important points remain. The only claim to compensation which the dispossessed heirs of the tenant in tail might have, would be against the second friend who had been vouched to warranty, and who in the eyes of the law would have to provide for the heirs lands of equal value with those of which they had been dispossessed. This was a serious liability; but it was practically nullified by the customary selection of a humble official of the court to play the part required. Meanwhile, there was no legal guarantee that the first friend, who by decision of the court was the holder of the fee simple, would fulfil his part in the understanding and dispose of those lands at the will of the original tenant in tail. But by the end of the fifteenth century the dictates of honour had given way to the jurisdiction of the Chancellor; and the elaborate ingenuity of attorneys gradually secured the safe working of the whole procedure.

(2) Recoveries.

2 Pollock, *Land Laws*, 87, note.

A third method of 'barring an entail' was the use of a process known as a *Fine of Lands*. This was also a collusive

(3) Fines.

suit, differing from a Recovery both in being an action not pursued to judgement, but compromised by the defendant abandoning his claim, and in its less complete and effective barring of all possible claims.   The effect of the process was to bar the claim of all who did not urge it within a year and a day.   It was abolished under Edward III, but restored under Henry VII, in the Statute of Fines, with an extension of time to five years.   Its application, however, to the case of tenants in tail was not definitely allowed until 1541.   The process was finally abolished, together with that of Recoveries, by the Act of 1833, which allows a tenant in tail, by the simple, if costly, enrolment of a deed in Chancery, to make himself or any one else a tenant in fee simple.

4 Hen. VII. c. 24.

32 Hen. VIII. c. 36.

3 & 4 Will. IV. c. 74.

Uses.

The attempt to make an estate inviolable had thus broken down before the ingenuity of the lawyers, and it was necessary for the great landowners, whether sole or corporate, to defend their property from legal liabilities by discovering some more subtle means of evading the Common law.   From the time of the Norman Conquest onwards cases are found in which lands were conveyed to be held in trust for some particular person or purpose.   The method was not unknown among private owners, but it was employed chiefly to secure endowment for some particular person, whether private or official, or some especial portion of the work—such as library or infirmary—in a monastery.[1]   It was popularized by the Franciscans whose special vow of poverty precluded them from accepting endowments.   But there was nothing to prevent a pious donor from leaving land to the corporation of a borough who should hold it 'to the use of' the friars.   This system of double ownership was now freely adopted by the great landowners, and by the practice of *Uses*, as it was called, an estate was left to a man and his heirs for the use of some one else and his heirs.   Such a disposition could of course be made to take effect either in a man's lifetime or after his death ; and by this means the power of regulating an interest in land by will, which had died out at the Conquest, was practically recovered.   The legal owner, who alone was recognized by the Common law, was technically called the *feoffee to uses* ; and the beneficial owner, who had no legal standing, was distinguished as *cestui que use*.   Thus the right of the beneficial owner rested at first merely on moral or

[1] *P. and M.* ii. 226-230.

religious obligation, so that it was often possible for the feoffee
to uses to suffer forfeiture, to alienate or to create charges
upon the lands, and thus to defeat the intention of the original
donor without any remedy on the part of the unfortunate cestui
que use.   But with the growth of the equitable jurisdiction of
the Chancellor came the enforcement of the right of cestui que
use by legal means ; for, as an ecclesiastic, the Chancellor
would especially concern himself with anything which bound
the conscience, and, as a churchman, would be interested in
all evasions of the Act of Mortmain ; while as 'depositary of
the undefined prerogative of the Crown' he would be petitioned
to intervene against any individual too powerful to be touched
by the Common law or in cases for which the Common law
provided no remedy.   Moreover, the Chancellor acted by writ
of *Subpoena* commanding the person complained of to appear
before him 'under penalty'; and his decrees were from the
first enforced by 'attachment,' i.e. arrest and imprisonment
for contempt of court.   This gave the Chancellor a power, not
possessed by the common law courts, of enforcing contracts ;
and, in the exercise of that power, he would not only restrain
the feoffee to uses from dealing with the land as he liked
to the detriment of cestui que use, but even bind him over to
carry out the lawful wishes of cestui que use with regard to
the disposition, by sale or otherwise, of that beneficial interest,
whether during lifetime or in accordance with the will of cestui
que use.

    But this legal enforcement of Uses only served to stereotype Results of
many unfortunate evils ; and legislation was necessary to check their enforcement.
the application of the system in many possible directions.   For,
until the restraint imposed by an Act of 1391, lands could be 15 Ric. II.
held by an individual to the use of a religious corporation, and c. 5.
the Act of Mortmain could be thus evaded.   Again, a debtor,
by making over the legal ownership of his land to another who
should hold it to the debtor's use, very effectually contrived
to evade his creditors, until an Act of 1376 restrained such 50 Edw. III.
collusive conveyance with intent to defraud.   The practice c. 6.
was equally convenient for the protection of a disseisor, i.e.
a wrongful possessor of land ; for he would secure his tenure by
making over the land to some great lord whom it would be
difficult to oust and who would consent to hold it to the use of

1 Ric. II.
c. 9.
the disseisor.   This too was met by an Act of 1377.   Finally, it was an indispensable weapon whether against the king to avoid forfeiture for treason, or against the overlord who would claim escheat on the failure of heirs, so long as the legal ownership remained in the treasonous or the heirless person.

Remedies.
1 Ric. III.
c. 1.

4 Hen. VII.
c. 17.

27 Hen.
VIII. c. 10.
The only remedy was to *assimilate the position of the beneficial to that of the legal owner.*   This was partly done by two Acts, of which one (1483) made valid the dispositions of cestui que use without the consent of the feoffee to uses, while the other (1488) gave to the lord the wardship of the heir of cestui que use ; but it was the great *Statute of Uses* of 1535 which definitely converted the beneficial into the legal owner, and made the former accountable to his lord for all feudal services and dues.   This had the further effect of destroying the power —which had become both possible and common with the growth of Uses—of disposing of interests in land by will.   But the result of the Act was directly the reverse of its purpose. The interpreters of the Common law held that the Act had provided for only one transfer from the legal to the beneficial owner, so that no account could be taken of any further interest.   ' An use,' said the judges without any apparent reason, ' cannot be engendered of an use.'   Thus, if land was left to *A* to the use of *B* to the use of *C*, the Statute was held to be satisfied in the securing of *B*'s interest ; *C*'s claims were left as before to the jurisdiction of the Chancellor, and the distinction was restored between the equitable and legal estate which it had been a main object of the Statute to extinguish. These second Uses became the *Trusts* of modern law.   Again, the restriction placed by the practical extinction of Uses on the power of Wills, was so unpopular among the landowners that as early as 1540 its restoration within limits was found

32 Hen.
VIII. c. 1.
necessary.   The Statute of Wills allowed a tenant in fee simple to dispose by will of all lands held in socage, and of two-thirds of any lands held by military tenure.

Abolition of
feudal tenure.
But the military tenure was doomed.   The services due from it, long obsolete, were regarded as an unnecessary burden, though the system of uses for some time alleviated their pressure.   Under Henry VIII not only were Uses abolished, but a special Court of Wards and Liveries was

created for the express purpose of asserting more effectually the feudal rights of the Crown. The result was a strenuous endeavour to get rid of the feudal tenures. The first attempt under James I, known as the Great Contract, failed because the king refused to surrender *all* his rights. But the Long Parliament abolished Distraint of Knighthood;[1] and in 1645 the Commons and Lords at Westminster voted the abolition of the Court of Wards and Liveries, and of military tenures by the substitution of tenure in socage.[2] This was confirmed by the Parliament of 1656, and finally by the Long Parliament of the Restoration in 1661. Henceforth, under the Statute of Wills, it became possible to dispose by will of all lands held in fee simple, which could now be held only on the one tenure of socage.

[1] Gardiner, *Documents of Puritan Rev.* 121.

[2] *Ibid.* 207.

12 Car. II. c. 24.

Two subjects remain for consideration—the Mortmain Laws and the Modern Strict Settlement.

Mortmain Laws.

Land granted to a religious house was held either in frank-almoin or, more commonly, in fee simple by military tenure. But in this case the fact that the holder was a corporation and therefore never died, caused loss to the lords of all those dues which came from the lucrative items of Relief, Wardship, Marriage, Forfeiture or Escheat. Such land was said to have fallen in mortuâ manu, 'since from the majority of legal claims it was practically void or dead.' Thus it was the interest of the superior lords to restrain such grants on the part of their pious or dying tenants. In answer to the Petitions of the Barons[3] the Provisions of Westminster[4] in 1259 forbade ecclesiastics to enter on the land of any one without the leave of the superior lord; but this clause was omitted in the sanctioning Statute of Marlborough in 1267. But the vague and ineffective forty-third Article of the Charter of 1217,[5] which had been construed as prohibiting all grants of land to religious houses, was defined and extended by the third great Act in Edward I's land legislation known as *De Viris Religiosis*, which forbade such grants to all corporations, lay as well as ecclesiastical. But the class which was interested in the evasion of the Statute was too large and powerful to acquiesce in the prohibition. The terms of the Statute were held to apply only to acquisition of land by gift or sale, and not to land gained by process of law. Thus recourse was had to

[3] *S. C.* 383.

[4] § 10.

[5] *Ibid.* 404. § 14.

[5] *Ibid.* 347.

7 Edw. I. 1279.

the medium of a Recovery by which the ecclesiastics collusively sued the occupying tenant, who thereupon made default, and the land was adjudged in fee simple to the designing monks. But the Crown and the overlords would not tamely submit to so large a loss of their rights. The Statute of Westminster II placed in the hands of a jury the determination of the right of the claimants to the land, and, in case of its disallowance, gave the land in forfeiture to the overlord. The ecclesiastics returned to the charge armed with the method of Uses, until they were effectually and finally restrained by the Act of 1391. Henceforth there were only two methods of getting over the restriction—by licence from the Crown or the mesne lords, if any, until an Act of 1695-6 removed the necessity for the consent of the latter; or through exemptions made by statute in favour of particular corporations or classes of corporations, such as the Universities and Colleges of Oxford and Cambridge, Eton and Winchester, or limited Companies.[1] But Mortmain has long ceased to be a danger to the Constitution and the effects of the more recent Acts (51 and 52 Vict. c. 42, s. 2 as amended by 54 and 55 Vict. c. 73, s. 5) must be sought in the domain of technical law.

13 Edw. I. c. 32.

7 & 8 Will. III. c. 37.

[1] Digby, 217.

Strict Settlements.

It is only possible to indicate the chief points connected with the growth of the complicated and technical process known as a *Strict* or *Family Settlement*. We have noticed the desperate effort made by the smaller landowners after the passing of De Donis to break through the entail which was then engrafted on the law, and how from the fifteenth century they were able to do so by the use of a Recovery, and from the sixteenth century by a Fine, until both methods were extinguished in 1833. But although it was quite impossible to prevent a tenant in tail from exchanging his holding for an estate in fee simple, something could be done on the part of the great landowners to keep their estates from alienation; and here they found the lawyers able and willing to help them. The perfection of the form of Strict Settlement is generally attributed to the legal ingenuity of Sir Orlando Bridgman, Lord Keeper in succession to Clarendon; but for some time previously it had been in preparation.

After the Statute De Donis the grant of an estate for life to *A* might be followed by the grant of an estate tail to his son *B*.

B's son *C* would be the 'tenant in tail in remainder' who on coming of age could, with the consent of *B*, but only on that condition, break the entail and obtain a fee simple of which he could dispose as he pleased. But in process of time there arose a gradually recognized distinction between a *vested* and a *contingent* remainder. By the former, 'an estate of future enjoyment' was conferred in a pre-determined order on certain persons already in existence; whereas the latter provided for the descent of the land to a life as yet unborn. In accordance with this distinction it was settled that the final tenancy in tail could be conferred on the unborn child of an as yet unmarried though living tenant for life, and in order to prevent the indefinite inalienability of the estate, about the middle of the eighteenth century it came to be ultimately recognized by the application of the 'rule against perpetuities,' that the furthest limit of time for which an estate can at any one moment be tied up and rendered inalienable, is the attainment of the legal majority by the first tenant in tail mentioned in the settlement, at which period the tenant in tail can exercise his discretion of keeping or breaking the entail.[1] But in order that the estate may be handed down through generations, as far as possible inviolate, it became customary for the son (the unborn tenant in tail) on his coming of age, in consideration perhaps of a substantial allowance from his father, to break the entail and, in conjunction with the father, who after 1833 was known as the Protector of the settlement, to make a re-settlement of the estate upon his as yet unborn son or sons in succession. Thus the son in his turn becomes a mere tenant for life of his estate, and no alienation of the property can be made until his own as yet unborn son comes of age.

[1] Pollock, *Land Laws*, 122-128.

CHAPTER II

THE EXECUTIVE

The Crown and the Council

Divisions
of govern-
ment.

*Pruet
King.
Lawgiver*

§ 8. IN the art of government, as in any other practical work, progress may be traced in an increasing subdivision of functions, and it is as a provision for better administration, and not as a security to civil liberty, that in process of time the work of government becomes more specialized. These functions fall roughly but naturally into three. (1) In a highly advanced state the duty of making the law belongs to the whole body politic, and in any case the law-maker, the holder of the *legislative* power, is the real sovereign of the country. (2) All modern constitutions recognize that the interpreters of the law, the *judicial* bench, should be separate from those who make it; otherwise there is no security against arbitrary stretches of authority under a legal guise. (3) Even more necessary is the division between the *executive*, or administrating body, and the judges; otherwise the same persons would be the doers of possibly illegal acts and the judges of the legality of them when done. The student of constitutional history has to learn the late recognition of even these broad and obvious distinctions. For convenience' sake, however, the question will be treated from the modern standpoint, and this threefold division will be taken for granted. But inasmuch as the most prominent power in an early stage of organization is the executive, which both issues isolated ordinances and then applies them, historical accuracy demands that it should be noticed first. The formation of a definite legislature which draws up scientific and permanent laws, is a much later process. With its growth the executive loses much of its early initiatory authority, and

Chap. ii.

Chap. iii.-v.

74

tends more and more to become a mere agent of the sovereign power. Laws cannot be interpreted until they have been made; so that logical necessity, as well as historical accuracy, dictates the treatment of the judiciary last in order of the three. But Chap. vii. the executive does not surrender its exclusive power of initiation without a severe struggle; and the longest and most interesting chapter in the history of the English Constitution tells of the rivalry between a small and highly centralized Chap. vi. executive on the one side, and on the other a large and invertebrate but representative legislature.

The executive in England is formed of an hereditary monarch, holding the crown under certain religious restrictions, and a council which, though always nominally composed of ministers of the Crown, has actually undergone considerable change. Each of these must be separately considered.

§ 9. The historical position of the CROWN in the English Constitution will be realized best from a description, first, of the *title* by which at various periods it has been held, and next, of that theoretical basis of the kingly power known as the *royal prerogative*.

Before the migration of the English folk to Britain, the general system of government as described by Tacitus was that of a national assembly of all fully qualified freemen, for whose final decision the items of business had been prepared by a small committee composed of the elected magistrates.[1] A few of the tribes had adopted royalty; but in such cases the kings were elected from among the nobles and occupied an honorary position as impersonating the unity of the tribe; though even at this early stage a strong ruler could make his position much more real, especially by the advancement of his favourites to high office.[2] The particular circumstances of the conquest of Britain, especially the continuous warfare, forced all the tribes under kingly rule. 'War begat the king'; the successful chief assured for himself a permanent position. But this position was not as yet fortified by theories of sovereignty. The English king was a powerful chief asserting ever-increasing claims over his subjects and adorned with the insignia of royalty—the throne, the crown, the sceptre, standard and lance.[3] But both in idea and in practice was the monarchy *elective*, and although by gentile rule the choice of the Witan

Title to the Crown.

[1] *Germania,* c. 11. (1) Election.

[2] *Ibid.* c. 25.

[3] *S. C. H.* §§ 59-62.

was restricted to the members of one family, the most competent individual of that family would be chosen; while the elective idea was further kept alive by the occasional use of the power of deposition. Nor, despite the very changed position of the Norman conquerors, did the elective idea disappear at once. William, claiming to succeed Eadward the Confessor as his lawful heir, submitted himself to the election of the Witan, and the continued existence of the idea was ensured alike by the personal character of kingship which made all the early rulers kings of the English people and not of the land ; by the ceremony of coronation, involving as it did a recommendation to and election by the people and an oath of good government by the king himself, and by the circumstances under which each of the three later Norman kings succeeded to the throne : for both William II and Henry I had to make good their title against their elder brother Robert, and Stephen was opposed by the dynastically superior claim of Matilda. Moreover, from William II to Henry II each monarch issued a sealed charter in confirmation of the promises which he had made.[1]

[1] M'Kechnie, 116.

But this theory of election, modified as it was by the hereditary claims of one family, was gradually superseded by the growth of the idea of *pure hereditary right*. So long as it lay with the Witan or Great Council to make the actual choice, the ceremony of election and the resulting coronation were essential to the exercise of royal authority, and between the death of the previous monarch and the election of his successor there was an actual interregnum during which it was no one's business to maintain peace and order in the country. But the feudal theories which were worked out after the Norman Conquest did much to mitigate the evils of this elective system. For the election by the Witan was substituted the homage of the vassals ; while 'the feudal land law assimilated the descent of the Crown to the descent of an estate in fee simple.'[2] Thus for a personal basis was substituted a territorial basis, and the king and representative of the people became the king and owner of the land. Another influence was at work in the same direction. Hereditary right soon tended to include an *indefeasible claim*. The lawful successor could in no case be deprived of his right, for such right was of divine origin. The

[2] Anson, ii. 58.

(2) Hereditary right.

old divinity of descent claimed by the heathen Saxons for
their kings, had now given way to divinity of office: for the
Church desired to enforce on the holder of the Crown the
sense of responsibility; while the lawyers of the twelfth century,
incited by the increased influence of the Roman law, sought
to strengthen the authority of the law by exalting that of the [1] *S. C. H.* § 158.
theoretical lawgiver.[1]

It was in accordance with this hereditary view of kingship Its estab-
that Richard I and John omitted the issue of coronation lishment.
charters. John, moreover, was the first to describe himself
on the Great Seal as Rex Angliae.[2] Henry III, though a [2] M'Kechnie, 217-220.
mere child ascending the throne at a critical moment, was
accepted without demur;[3] while Edward I was proclaimed in [3] *S. C. H.* § 170.
his absence and reigned for nearly two years before his coronation. This was the first constitutional recognition of the
altered character of kingship.[4] After his reign the proofs are [4] *Ibid.* § 179.
abundant. Thus, Edward II dated his reign from the day
after his father's death, and a new coronation oath was framed
to express the changed position of the Crown;[5] Edward III [5] *Ibid.* § 249.
proclaimed the peace before his coronation. Richard II's
reign supplies two most remarkable proofs. He was accepted,
although a minor and despite the existence of several uncles
who had taken a prominent part in public affairs. This cir-
cumstance seems to have duly impressed itself upon him, for
on his deposition he refused to renounce the spiritual honour
of the royal character imposed on him by his coronation and
his unction:

> ' Not all the water in the rough rude sea
>   Can wash the balm off from an anointed King.'[6]   [6] Shake-
speare,
From the succeeding century come two striking cases of the *Rich. II.*
influence of arguments based on hereditary claims. Henry IV, Act iii.
beyond and above his election and the homage of the royal Sc. 2.
vassals, went out of his way to revive an old tradition in favour
of the superior claim of Edmund Crouchback, the brother of
Edward I and the ancestor of the Lancastrian line. But,
although his claim deceived no one, the tendency to which it
bore witness was more completely exemplified when Richard,
Duke of York, and his son Edward IV triumphed over the
Lancastrians. In theory their claim was based merely on
hereditary right, and such a claim was held to be superior to

[1] *S. C. H.*
§ 458.

(3) Act of
Parliament.

[2] Stubbs,
*Lectures
on Mediaeval
and Modern
History*,
345.

[3] Anson,
ii. 61.

25 Hen.
VIII. c. 22.

28 Hen.
VIII. c. 7.

35 Hen.
VIII. c. 1.

13 Eliz. c. 1.

[4] Prothero,
58-59.

election, to oaths of fealty and to the ceremony of coronation.[1]

But this apparently complete triumph of the hereditary principle was almost immediately followed by the *revival in a slightly changed form of the old principle of election.* Henry VII claimed the Crown by hereditary right,[2] but his legal title was derived from an Act of Parliament which settled the Crown on himself and the heirs of his body. Indeed, it has been justly said that 'from this time forth our history illustrates the conflict between two views of kingship . . . title by descent and title by choice of Parliament,' which 'came to express two different views of kingship.'[3] Under the Tudors the latter title was frequently asserted. Thus, the Act of Royal Succession settled the Crown on the issue of Anne Boleyn; a later Act not only settled the succession on the children of Jane Seymour, to the exclusion of those of Katherine of Aragon or of Anne Boleyn, but even, in the event of the king surviving his own issue, conferred on him the power, either by letters patent or by will, of naming whomsoever he wished as his successor; and another Act reinstated the children of Katherine and Anne, while still leaving to the king, in the last resort, the power of nominating his successor. Under Elizabeth, again, the power of Parliament as against the claims of Mary Queen of Scots was most strenuously affirmed. An Act of 1571 declared it treasonable to maintain that the law and statutes did not limit the succession to the throne, or that any particular person except the issue of the queen was lawful heir, before the same should be so established and affirmed by Act of Parliament.[4] Thus Parliament did not now claim to assert its elective power on the death of each sovereign, but only in the event of a break in the royal line. But under the Stuarts circumstances forced forward the alternative view of hereditary right. The complete severance of the feudal bond required something which should fill its place. The studies of the Renaissance caused a revival of the patriarchal theories of monarchy; while, in the decadence of the Empire, the powers once attributed to the temporal head of Christendom were now claimed for the kings of the respective nations. Thus the mediaeval theory of divine right, with its twofold assertion that kings derived their authority from God and that such authority was absolute, once more came to the front; and the special circumstances under which the Stuarts obtained the throne, added a new and more dangerous tenet in the insistence on the hereditary character of monarchy. For, Henry VIII had used the power conferred on him by Parliament to exclude the Scotch line from the throne. Yet despite this it was the representative of that line who was now in possession, and there could be no more positive proof of the futility of attempting by human endeavour to defeat the will of God. The Church was willing to go even further and, in opposition to the Jesuit doctrine of the papal right of deposition, to maintain the absolute sinfulness of resistance to the monarchy. But James condemned the canons of 1606 in which this was asserted, pointing out that, in that case, if a foreign ruler seized the throne the people would have no right to overthrow him.[1] [1] Gardiner, i. 289-291.

The two rival theories finally joined issue in the case of James II ; and on his flight from the kingdom it was asserted, in the Declaration of Right, that he had abdicated and that thereby the throne became vacant. The convention then proceeded to offer the throne jointly to William and Mary. By the Bill of Rights the succession was limited to the heirs of Mary, then to Anne her sister and her heirs, and then to those of William by another wife.[2] In 1700 the Act of Settlement added, after the lines enumerated in 1689, the person and descendants of Sophia, Electress of Hanover;[3] and it is under this final settlement that the Crown is at present held. But it is important to notice with Hallam[4] that the great work of the Revolution of 1688 was that it broke the line of succession. 'The changes which then took place were either declarations of principle or changes of practice, and of actual legal limitation there was but little. Parliament had settled the succession to the Crown before, and it settled the succession again,' and yet it will be found that 'the conception of a royal prerogative superior to all the rules of law had survived the catastrophe of the Rebellion.'[5] We are thus led naturally to our second illustration of the historical position of the Crown—the history of the development of the royal prerogative.

The modern title to the Crown.

[2] S. C. 525.

[3] Ibid. 529.

[4] Hallam, iii. 92.

[5] Anson, ii. 64.

§ 10. It has been shown that the monarchy was in its origin the representative of the people. So long as this aspect was *The Royal Prerogative.*

predominant, there could be no question of special rights or
powers on the part of the monarch. As the head of a feudal
society his position was limited and defined in theory by the
action of a feudal council of his tenants-in-chief. Thus it was
not until all trace of the old representative character of the
Crown had been wiped out by the feudal theory of the king's
proprietary right, that any definition of the royal prerogative
became possible. The royal power now came to be regarded
as inherent, and this view grew side by side with the hereditary,
as opposed to the elective, right to the title. Already, since
the days of Henry II, the clergy and the lawyers had been at
work. The former made use of the Scriptures to enforce on
the king the sense of responsibility; and on the people the
religious duty of obedience, of which they were the first to
feel the embarrassing effects. Meanwhile the lawyers, with the
aid of the revived Civil Law of Rome, built up the systems of
allegiance, fealty and homage. Thus Glanvill applied to Henry
II the maxim of Justinian that the pleasure of the king has
the force of law; while the author of the Dialogus de Scaccario [1]
asserts that the king's deeds are not to be judged by men. [2]
This was nothing else than the assertion of absolute power.
No wonder, then, that when, with the growth of Parliament,
national demands are formulated and rights made good, it
seems as if 'royalty becomes in theory more absolute as in
practice it is limited more and more by the national will.' [3]
The result was that the theory of the prerogative, as it emerged,
expressed not only that the king might do anything except
what he had especially promised not to do, but even that he
might repudiate any obligation which he thought to stand in
the way of or to tell against his sovereign right. Thus the
prerogative was a kind of inexhaustible reservoir on which the
king could draw at need, and of which, at the best, portions
alone could be cut off by separate and oft-repeated acts of the
people. All power was inherent in the king; everything
emanated from him; he was the supreme landowner, the
source of justice; in himself individually was summed up the
State. The painfully-won rights of the people seemed scarcely
to touch the exercise of the royal power; for, beyond these
definite claims made from time to time by Parliament, there
extended the region of undefined prerogative.

[1] *S. C.* 169.

[2] *S. C. H.*
§ 158.

[3] *Ibid.*
§ 273.

It was in accordance with this theory that the judges of the Stuart kings defined the prerogative as twofold. It contained the king's ordinary power, which he exercised in accordance with the will of Parliament; and his extraordinary power, which was for the good of the State and could not be diminished.[1] In this view the ordinary power was that which the king had practically surrendered, and the exercise of which, so far as the king was concerned, was subject to custom and to statute. As far as it was regulated by statute, the king could not lawfully act without the concurrence of Parliament, and such powers really ceased to form part of the royal prerogative. Moreover, custom had rendered the consent of his Council necessary to the king's action in certain cases. This might or might not be a real limiting power: it was so under the early Lancastrians, while the Tudors and Stuarts exercised their prerogative through the Council. Again, the Law Courts might have formed a limit to the royal authority; but the use of royal writs, the royal power of pardon and the entire dependence of the judges on the Crown minimized the force of such a check.[2] There were, besides, other attributes and rights of the Crown which it shared with no body in the kingdom. Such were those rights drawn from the position of the king as feudal lord, and carrying with them not only powers incidental to the ownership of an estate, but also the conception of treason and allegiance as matters personal to the sovereign.[3] Such also were certain attributes, the result of legal theory, which for convenience' sake established the important maxims that the king never dies, and that the king can do no wrong.[4]

With certain additions, then, the royal prerogative may be defined as the *discretionary power of the Crown*.[5] So long as this was exercised on the whole in the interests of the people, even when as against individuals it was subject to no legal check, there was little complaint. But in the hands of the Stuarts the definition of the prerogative went alongside of the claim of hereditary and indefeasible right. Thus the Revolution of 1688 materially affected the position of the Crown in both these points. The struggle between Crown and Parliament for the right to say the final word, ended in the complete victory of Parliament. But we have seen that the legal changes which

Its definition under the Stuarts.

[1] Cf. Prothero, 341.

[2] Anson, ii. 19.

[3] S. C. H. § 462.

[4] Anson, ii. 4.

[5] Anson, ii. 2-3.
Cf. Hearn, *Govt. of England*, 18.
Hearn, 113-123.

Effect of the Revolution upon it.

resulted were very slight. In theory, the Crown kept all the prerogatives which had descended to it from times past. It was still the fountain of justice and of honour : the ministers were still its servants : it still called and dissolved Parliament. But none of these powers could now be used except with the popular approval ; and indeed it was only too likely that many of them would have to be employed in direct opposition to the personal wishes of the Crown. The Bill of Rights prohibited the maintenance of that standing army which the later Stuarts had inherited from Cromwell, and the observance of this pro-hibition was secured by the custom of limiting the parliamentary grant for the army to a single year ; so that, at any rate for the maintenance of an army, annual sessions became necessary. The last of the king's dangerous prerogatives went when the Act of Settlement took from the Crown the power of dismissing

[1] *S. C.* 531.

the judges at pleasure,[1] and when the gradual growth of party government had identified the servants of the Crown with the nominees of the people.

Its present position.

While, then, in theory the prerogatives of the Crown remain almost intact, the checks upon them have become real. The Council is now the Cabinet or representative of the majority in Parliament : the Law Courts are not amenable to arbitrary interference ; the Judges need no longer fear dismissal for decisions adverse to the personal wishes of the Crown. And yet the personal influence of the Crown need not be under-rated. The monarch is permanent while the ministers change. He is consulted and supplied with full information on every topic. In the course of a lengthy reign his experience is bound to be of considerable value and weight. Thus, although the royal prerogatives have to be exercised in accordance with law or an equally binding custom, a clever sovereign must, and an evil-disposed sovereign might, wield an influence the extent of which it is difficult to calculate.[2]

[2] Cf. Bage-hot, *Eng. Const.* 75 et seq.

Regencies.

§ 11. Ever since the firm establishment of the principle of hereditary monarchy it has been the accepted legal maxim that 'the king never dies'; in other words, that there can be no abeyance of the royal functions. But, if the heir succeeds to the throne at the moment of his predecessor's death, there are occasions during the lifetime of a reigning monarch when, from one cause or another, he is incapable of discharging the

duties of his office.   Such incapacity is of two kinds.   It may
be *temporary*, caused either by absence from the kingdom, by
a vacancy created by deposition, or by that infancy of the
wearer of the crown which is inseparable from hereditary
monarchy.   The incapacity may also be *permanent*, such as
would be caused by severe illness or insanity on the part of
the monarch.   Of all these our history affords numerous
instances; but the point of constitutional importance in each
case is the particular provision which was made for the discharge of the royal functions.

   Absence from the kingdom [1] was fairly frequent when, as under For tem-
the Norman and early Angevin sovereigns, the English king porary ab-
was also the ruler of a great continental empire.   Accordingly, 1 Anson,
the Norman kings created an official, analogous to the Norman ii. 76-78.
seneschal or steward, to whom pre-eminently after a time was
applied the common judicial title of (1) *justiciar*.   Under
William I merely temporary, under William II the justiciar
became the permanent lieutenant of the kingdom and the head
of the whole judicial and financial machinery of government.
So great an office was at first given to ecclesiastics who could
not make it hereditary; but Henry II felt himself sufficiently
free from any chance of dictation by a baronial holder of
the office, and accordingly appointed laymen.   His sons, however, returned to the previous practice.   With the fall of
Hubert de Burgh the office lost its unique position.   The 1232.
justiciar may or may not be traceable in the Chief Justice of
the Court of King's Bench, but his great political position was
ultimately taken by the Chancellor.   Consequently, on the king's
absence other provision had to be made, and, during Henry III's 1254.
expedition into Gascony, the queen and the Earl of Cornwall
were made (2) *Custodes regni*.   This practice was followed on
subsequent occasions, the last instance being the appointment of Queen Caroline, wife of George II.   Meanwhile, resort 1732.
was had occasionally to a third method.   The exceptional
absence of Edward I at the beginning of his reign had been
met by the appointment of a committee of the Concilium,
nominated beforehand and confirmed by the magnates.   Queen
Mary, the wife of William III, was empowered by statute to
exercise the royal prerogative in her husband's absence.   But
after her death it became customary to appoint (3) *Lords* 1695.

Justices under the Great Seal, whose powers were specified in the letters patent which gave them their commission. Henceforth this was the usual method of providing for the absence of the monarch, and was used so late as 1837, when a provisional appointment was made to take effect in the event of the queen's death while the heir (the King of Hanover) was abroad. The improved methods of communication in recent years have rendered it practically unnecessary to make any provision for the occasional absence of the sovereign.

In vacancy of the throne.

[1] Anson, ii. 80-81.

A temporary vacancy of the royal office has more than once been created by the *deposition of the reigning monarch*.[1] In all three cases which call for notice, much attention has been paid to forms. Both Edward II and Richard II were themselves practically forced to be consenting parties to their own dethronement. For Edward II alone was there an heir ready, in whose name was summoned the Parliament which pronounced the deposition. It was only after the throne had actually been declared vacant that Henry IV, on the one occasion, and William III and Mary on the other, were accepted by the assemblies which they themselves had been instrumental in calling together. Finally, James II did not wait for a formal deposition, but left the throne vacant by a timely flight which, to salve over the consciences of the believers in divine and indefeasible right, was construed into a voluntary abdication.

During a minority.

The *minority* of a newly ascended monarch has given frequent occasion for the appointment of guardians and Councils of Regency. The methods of appointment have been almost as numerous as the cases. Thus, for Henry III the (1) *Barons* appointed William Marshall, Earl of Pembroke, as *Rector Regis et Regni*, together with a small assistant council. For Richard II a Council of Regency was provided by the joint action of the young king himself and the magnates. On the accession of Edward V, his father's Privy Council assumed the power and appointed Richard, Duke of Gloucester, as Protector. On two occasions the (2) *reigning king* has made provision for his successor, and in each case have his arrangements been modified. Thus, Henry V appointed the Duke of Bedford Regent in France and the Duke of Gloucester to the parallel office in England. But immediately on his death the Lords made Bedford First Counsellor in England also, only giving the power to Gloucester

in his absence.   Parliament subsequently added sixteen coun-
sellors.   In accordance with an Act of Parliament, 'the first
Regency Act and the only one of the kind that ever took
effect,'[1] Henry VIII nominated a Council of Regency, which
on his death promptly altered the intention of the late king
by making Somerset Protector, in which act it was upheld by
the lords and the young king himself.   All modern provisions
for a regency are of course made by (3) *Act of Parliament.*
Already in the case of Edward III Parliament had appointed a
Council of Regency ; while for Henry VI they had considerably
modified the dispositions of his father.   In 1751, on the death
of Frederick Prince of Wales, an Act of Parliament provided
a Regent if necessary in the person of the Princess Dowager
of Wales, and nominated a Council to whom the reigning king
could make four additions.   In 1765 a severe illness, from
which George III had just recovered, seemed to make it
prudent to provide for the event of his death.   The king, with
his high notions of the royal prerogative, claimed the right of
nominating as Regent any person whom he chose.   He was,
however, obliged to give way, and a Regency Act empowered
him to nominate either the Queen, the Princess Dowager of
Wales or any descendant of George II.   Subsequent Regency
Acts were those of 1830 appointing the Duchess of Kent,
and of 1840 appointing the Prince Consort to a like office
in the event of the then heir succeeding as a minor to the
throne.

A more permanent kind of incapacity which has beset the
occupants of the throne has come from *severe illness ending in
actual insanity.*   Of this our history affords two important
instances.   In the case of Henry VI, on the occasion of his
first illness, in 1454, the Lords chose the Duke of York as
Protector, and their choice was embodied in an Act of Parliament.[2]   On the second occasion, in 1455, the Lords at the
request of the Commons again nominated the Duke of York,
whose appointment was ratified in letters patent by the king
himself.[3]   The proceedings in the case of George III were
complicated by political considerations.   The simplest method
would have been to imitate the Convention Parliament of 1688
and, by an Address, to request the obvious person to assume
the functions of royalty.   But this 'obvious person,' the Prince

[1] Anson, ii. 78.
28 Hen. VIII. c. 7, s. 23.

1751.

1765.

In mental incapacity of the monarch.

[2] *S. C. H.* § 349.

[3] *Ibid.* § 351.

1788-9.

of Wales, was deeply committed to the cause of the parliamentary Opposition, and Pitt, the Prime Minister, knew that his appointment would be followed by the instalment of the Opposition in office, with a majority purchased by all the means of influence at the disposal of the Crown. Pitt, therefore, determined to impose restrictions on the exercise of the prerogative in the hands of the Prince, and an Act of Parliament rather than an Address became the necessary procedure. Political animosity caused the two parliamentary parties to reverse the principles which for a century they had respectively upheld. Fox, the leader of the Opposition, although acknowledging that it was the duty of Parliament to declare at what period the Regent should assume power, yet maintained that when Parliament had so decided, the Prince of Wales had as clear a right to the attributes of sovereignty as if the king were already dead. Pitt, on the other hand, was driven to declare that, except by decision of Parliament, the Prince had no more right to the Regency than any other subject of the Crown.[1] This argument, as Fox asserted, introduced the principle of election into the first branch of the legislature, which was as unconstitutional as the introduction of heredity into the House of Commons. But a more practical difficulty still remained. Procedure by statute necessitated the royal assent which, under the circumstances, was impossible. The solution of this difficulty to which Pitt resorted has incurred the condemnation of constitutional lawyers. The two Houses were to authorize the Chancellor to put the Great Seal to letters patent appointing one commission for opening Parliament, and another commission which should give its assent to the Regency Bill. Before the bill passed the king recovered; but on his relapse in 1810 the same method was employed, and a bill containing restrictions on the Regent's power in the matter of the creation of peers and the grant of offices and pensions,[2] received the royal assent by a commission appointed by Parliament.[3] Many eminent lawyers united in condemnation of this 'phantom king,' whose will was a mere echo of that of 'the other two estates,' and thereby robbed of all meaning the exercise of the power which still lay in the royal prerogative. 'The precedent established,' says an historian,[4] 'was a revolutionary one,' and he adds his belief that 'if England should ever again pass through a period

[1] Robertson, 177-178. Lecky, v. 103-111; vi. 416-429. Erskine May, *Const. Hist.* i. 175-183.

[2] Robertson, 171.

[3] *Ibid.* 181.

[4] Lecky, v. 124.

of revolution, and if it should be thought desirable to throw over that revolution a colour of precedent and legality, this page of history will not be forgotten.'

§ 12. The bond between sovereign and subject is to be found in the Oath of Allegiance. Together with Fealty and Homage, it dates from the time of a fully developed feudal sovereignty. All three words express various sides of the relations between a feudal monarch and his people.[1] Thus *Fealty* (foi) was the promise of the military follower to be personally faithful : *Homage* was definitely connected with the bestowal of land ; while *Allegiance* was due from every member of the community, whether he were a landholder or not.[2] But with the decay of the feudal status the two former sank into mere ceremonies ; and although the establishment of an efficient system of police had rendered superfluous the exaction of an oath, allegiance is still due not only from citizens, in which case it is called *natural*, but also from resident aliens under the name of *local* allegiance. Originally the territorial nature of feudal sovereignty not only extended the duty of allegiance over all who were born in the country irrespective of their parentage, but even made such allegiance perpetual. The Naturalization Act of 1870, however, enables a British born subject to become, by renunciation of allegiance, a naturalized subject of a foreign power.

Relations between sovereign and subject.

[1] *S. C. H.* § 463.

Allegiance.

[2] Anson, ii. 69-71.

33 & 34 Vict. c. 14. s. 7.

The betrayal of allegiance constituted *Treason*. The LAW OF TREASON formed perhaps the strongest bulwark of the royal power. It grew with the growth of kingship. Thus in the earlier Anglo-Saxon laws the difference between the life of the king and that of an ordinary freeman is one merely of degree : both were estimated in money, though of course at widely different sums. As the king's position increased, his life became of increasing value, until it reached a point at which harm done to his person could not be atoned for save with the life of the wrong-doer. It is this *difference in kind between injury to the king and injury to an individual*, which constitutes the law of treason. The first hint of the change is found in Alfred's law that any man plotting against the king's life should be 'liable in his life and in all that he has.'[3] But for the present the king shared this position, as he shared the benefit of Eadmund's oath of fealty,[4] with other lords.

The Law of Treason.

[3] *S. C.* 62. c. 4.

[4] *Ibid.* 67.

1086.

William the Conqueror's Oath of Allegiance at Salisbury, together with the whole policy which he inaugurated, must have made it impossible for the lords to compete any longer with the Crown. The great legal writers of Angevin times have nothing to say in respect of the lord. They draw their definitions largely, though not exclusively, from the Roman law of 'Majestas.'[1] But the application of the law by the judges was very vague and apparently arbitrary. The only discoverable principle seems to have been the desire to extend the interpretation of a breach of allegiance as far as possible, so that the condemned person should lose his 'benefit of clergy' or right to trial by an ecclesiastical court, and the king should obtain the forfeiture of the criminal's land and goods, which, in the case of a conviction for felony, would have escheated to the superior lord. The commonest form of accusation—laid against the Despencers in 1321 and again in 1326, and against Mortimer in 1331—was that of 'accroaching royal power.' At last, in 1348, on the adjudication as treason of a mere case of highway robbery, the Commons asked for a definition of this offence of accroachment. Although the king returned, as his immediate answer, that cases should be decided by the judges as they arose, four years later came the first attempt to embody the principle in statute law. In 1351 the *Statute of Treasons*, following closely on the lines laid down by the great jurist Bracton,[2] defined and limited treason to seven heads. These were (a) compassing or imagining the death of the king, the queen or their eldest son and heir; (b) violating the king's companion, eldest unmarried daughter or eldest son's wife; (c) levying war against the king in his realm; (d) adhering to and aiding the king's enemies in his realm and elsewhere; (e) counterfeiting the king's Great or Privy Seal; (f) issuing false money; and (g) slaying the Chancellor, Treasurer or Justices whilst discharging their offices. To these was added a proviso to the effect that Parliament might adjudge as treason, although not specified in the Act, any political misdeed of which a future offender might be convicted. The terms of this Act are most general. 'It enumerates,' it has been said,[3] 'the only crimes likely to be committed against a popular king who has an undisputed title, and as to the limits of whose legal power there is no serious dispute.' In short, 'it protects

Its early history.

[1] *S. C. H.*
§ 463.
Cf. *P. and M.* ii. 502.

25 Edw. III.
st. 5.

[2] *Lib.* iii.
cap. 3, fol.
118 *b*.

Edward III.'s Statute of Treasons.

[3] Stephen,
*Hist.
Crim. Law*,
ii. 250.

Its great defect.

nothing but the personal security of the king.' It seems probable that the mild and incomplete wording of the Act was due to the power and popularity of the reigning king.[1] On some such supposition alone can we account for all *omission from the Act of political conspiracy for the king's deposition, as apart from plots for his assassination, and until such conspiracy has become open war.*

[1] But see P. and M. ii. 507, note.

This serious defect was remedied in three different ways. In the first place, the proviso at the end of the Statute practically allowed *Parliament to create an ex post facto treason.* Legal writers have disputed whether this proviso referred to parliamentary action in a judicial or a legislative capacity. In the former case it would concern the House of Lords alone ; and it was in such a capacity that in 1387-8, at the instigation of the Lords Appellant, Parliament proceeded against Richard II's favourites. But for some reason this method of operation seems to have ceased, and Parliament proceeded by a bill of attainder which involved no definition, rather than by impeachment on formulated charges. A second method of overcoming the defects of Edward III's Act was by *additional legislation.* This, however, was only intended to be temporary. The only permanent addition made for two centuries to the statute law on the subject of treason was the Act of Henry VII of obedience to the king *de facto* as opposed to any king *de jure,*[2] which was intended to quiet tender consciences by justifying to future generations, and possibly under altered circumstances, their present obedience. Of temporary Acts there were many from Richard II onwards. Thus an Act of 1397 was repealed in 1401, and another of 1414 in 1442. But it is to the Tudor times that we must look for the most numerous instances of this method of fortifying the Crown. During the seventy years of struggle for sovereignty in England between the Crown and the Pope, this was one of the weapons to which the Crown most naturally resorted in order to ensure from its subjects the recognition of the position which, for the first time, it found necessary so carefully to define. Thus Henry VIII forced through Parliament no less than nine Acts creating new treasons. Of these, four upheld the king against the papal power, the chief being the Act of Supremacy which made it treason to deny the king's title as head of the Church.

Remedies. (1) Action of Parliament.

(2) Temporary Legislation.

11 Hen. VII. c. 1.

[2] Hallam, i. 9.

1533-1603.

26 Hen. VIII. c. 1.

The severity of their provisions has been overrated, for many of them were already included in Edward III's law, while others can be paralleled from the legislation of William III and Anne, to which no such character has been applied.   The remaining five Acts, which 'are beyond all question of terrible severity,'[1] dealt with the question of the succession, and made it treason to alter the settlement or to cast any doubt on the validity or the nullity respectively of the king's various marriages. Under Edward VI, while all the specially created treasons of his father were abolished, three others were placed on the statute book, namely, a denial of the king's supremacy (1547); riots of a certain specified kind (1549); and the denunciation of the king as an heretic or usurper (1551).   These were all in their turn repealed by Mary, but the Spanish marriage was defended by making it treason to deny Philip's title of king consort.   The same Act made it treason to pray for the queen's death.   One of the first measures of Elizabeth's reign was to re-enact this statute with an application to the new sovereign.[2] Circumstances demanded further definitions.   In 1571 the Pope's bull of deposition was met by Acts making it treason to deny the power of the queen and Parliament to limit the succession, or to call the queen heretic, schismatic or usurper, or to bring papal bulls into England.[3]   A statute of 1581 was aimed against the Pope's power of absolving subjects from their allegiance,[4] and this was re-enacted by James I in 1606; while in 1585 another Act was called forth by the machinations of the Jesuits.[5]   Similar circumstances in later reigns produced resort to similar expedients.   In 1661 it was made treason to imagine any bodily injury to the king;[6] in 1702, to hinder or attempt to hinder the next in succession to the throne according to the Act of Settlement;[7] and in 1707, to assert by writing or printing the right to the crown of any other person than the next in succession according to the Act of Settlement, or to deny the power of the sovereign and Parliament to limit the succession.[8]

Meanwhile, the third, and by far the most important, method of filling the gaps left by the Treason Statute had become firmly established.   The place which, some legal writers think, was meant to be filled by Parliament in its judicial capacity, was taken by the bench of judges.   A consensus of *judicial decisions*

[1] Stephen, *Hist. Crim. Law*, ii. 258.

[1] & 2 Phil. and Mary, c. 10.

[2] I Eliz. cap. 5. Prothero, 23.

[3] 13 Eliz. caps. 1 & 2. Prothero, 57-63.

[4] 23 Eliz. c. i. Prothero, 74-76. *Ibid.* 257.

[5] 27 Eliz. c. 2. Prothero, 83-86.

[6] 13 Car. II. s. 1. c. 1.

[7] I Anne, c. 16.

[8] 6 Anne, c. 66.

(3) Interpretation of Judges.

established the principle that the words of Edward III's Act were intended to bear a much wider than their literal interpretation. In accordance with this principle, a *conspiracy to levy war* was construed as an overt act of imagining the king's death. This interpretation seems to have been finally established at the end of Elizabeth's reign when, in the case of the Earl of Essex, the judges advised the Lords that 1600. 'in every rebellion the law intendeth as a consequent the compassing the death and deprivation of the king.' Possibly the late repeal of the severe treason laws of Henry VIII's reign exposed the defects of Edward III's law and so encouraged lawyers to make good the deficiencies 'by strained artificial constructions.' The same principle was applied to expressions of opinion. Thus *spoken words* could not be construed as an overt act, but they were held to expound an overt act. On the other hand, *words committed to writing* were held to be overt acts, while under the Stuarts, in the cases of *Peacham* (1615)[1] and *Algernon Sidney* (1683),[2] the [1] Hallam, judges actually interpreted *unpublished writings* in the same i. 343. way. In short, the imagining of the king's death has been [2] *Ibid.* ii. held to include an intention of 'anything whatever which 459. under any circumstances may possibly have a tendency, however remote, to expose the king to personal danger or to the forcible deprivation of any part of the authority incidental to his office.'[3] The *levying of war against the king in his* [3] Stephen, *realm* was construed in a similar fashion. According to the *Hist.* wording of the clause, the extent of the violence employed did ii. 268. not signify. Provided it was aimed against the king, it was treason. The original object was perhaps to distinguish between insurrections and private wars; but when these latter ceased, all disturbances must of necessity be against the king's government. From this sweeping interpretation great lawyers, like Chief Justices Coke and Hale, tried to escape by making a distinction between mere riots and actual rebellion, founded on the object of the disturbance. Thus a special and local tumult, aiming, for example, at the throwing down of enclosures, would be included under the former head; while a general political movement to compel the action of the government in some particular direction, would fall under the more serious charge of treason. But the judges as a body were not so lenient, and as late as 1668, in the case of *Messenger*, they pronounced a riot of apprentices for the purpose of pulling down houses of bad repute, to be treason; and in 1710, in the case of *Dammaree*,[1] they similarly treated a charge of destroying dissenting meeting houses in the riots connected with the trial of Dr. Sacheverell. In 1715, however, this power of judicial interpretation was considerably checked, and the Riot Act removed local riots from the action of the treason law, by making it a felony for rioters to refuse to disperse at the command of a magistrate.[2]

[1] Robertson, 296-298.

1 Geo. I. c. 5.

[2] *Ibid.* 114.

(4) Statute Law.

These far-fetched interpretations, which have been described 'by way of odium' as the Law of Constructive Treason, were brought to a test towards the end of the eighteenth century in the cases of *Lord George Gordon* (1780), of *Hardy* and of *Horne Tooke* (1794).[3] In all these instances the reading of the law—which was accepted by the council for the prisoners and was expounded by the judge to the jury—was this constructive law; but there seems little doubt that the acquittal of the prisoners in all these cases did 'in a popular sense' discredit this extreme latitude of interpretation. At any rate, in 1795 came the first modern supplementary law of treason, and the Act 36 Geo. III c. 7, which was made perpetual in 1817, both embodied the constructive interpretations put by lawyers on the 'compassing of the king's death,' and enumerated all the steps towards the death or deposition of the monarch or the coercion of him and of Parliament. This was followed by the Treason Felony Act of 1848, which converted into felonies all those acts which had now been brought under the head of 'compassing the king's death,' except such as were aimed at the person of the sovereign. Thus the terrible charge of treason, with all its attendant severities, has been defined and narrowed. Statute law has supplanted the Common law. As in so many other ways, instead of the State being identified with the king, the king is now merged in the State.

[3] Erskine May ii. 308-309.

57 Geo. III. c. 6.

11 & 12 Vict. c. 12.

Procedure in trials of treason.

The change in the *procedure* in trials for treason had been more rapid than the change in the law. Originally the trials were grossly unfair. The greatest latitude of procedure was allowed; the prisoner himself was cross-examined, and all kinds of evidence, written as well as oral, were accepted against him. A law of Edward VI attempted some remedy

1552.

by making two witnesses necessary to prove an act of treason. [1] [1] Hallam,
But this was of slight effect. Under the Tudors the two i. 40.
witnesses bore testimony to different facts, and even, as
in the trial of Babington on the plea that he was indicted 1586.
under the Act of Edward III, the necessity of two witnesses
was waived. But in 1696 an Act required that both witnesses 7 & 8 Will.
should testify to the same overt act or to two overt acts III. c. 3.
under the same head of treason. It moreover provided that
the prisoner should receive a copy of the indictment and
a panel of the jury some days before the trial, and gave him
the assistance of counsel and the power to compel the attendance of witnesses, all of which had hitherto been denied. [2] [2] Robertson,
Finally, while with the definition of treason the death penalty 84-87.
had been correspondingly reduced, the terrible surroundings
of the penalty itself were removed. Originally the condemned
man was liable to be hanged, drawn and quartered, and his
lands and goods were forfeit. But the bodily liabilities were
mitigated by two Acts of George III, which permitted of
beheadal, and in 1870 forfeitures for treason were abolished
and the punishment itself was reduced to hanging.

§ 13. The Crown was assisted in the work of administration The Curia
by a COUNCIL. In early English times no difference is to be Regis.
found between the administrative and the legislative body in
the kingdom. Both powers were centred in the Witan. But
of central administration there was little. The Ealdormen
ruled their provinces and the sheriffs their shires ; but it was
just in the absence of connection between central and local
governments that the fatal weakness of the early English
government lay.

An attempt has been made to discover the germs of an
administrative body in England before the Conquest,[3] but, [3] Green,
whatever its value, it is to the initiative of the Normans that *Conquest*
we must attribute the first definite and successful discrimination *of Eng-*
between the different departments and functions of government. *land,*
The chief result of the Norman Conquest was the establish- 542-548.
ment of a strong kingship in England. It was round and out Early Nor-
of this personal authority of the king that the whole adminis- man central
trative arrangements of the English Constitution may be said tion.
to have developed. William seems to have had a Curia or
Concilium, terms which for a century at least were apparently

interchangeable. It is scarcely likely to have been a definitely organized body; but a nucleus would be formed by the holders of the chief administrative offices, who would in the first instance be supplied from the members of the royal household, and would each be in charge of a separate department which he would administer through a special staff of servants. This seems to have been, as nearly as we can discover, the form of government under William I and his immediate successor. But such a system depended too entirely on the personal influence of the king. In the absence of trained officials and recognized methods of administration these offices were placed in the hands of the nobles and clergy. But many of the nobles were also entrusted with the chief posts of local government—the sheriffdoms, which in some few cases they contrived to make hereditary. The singularly united action of William and Archbishop Lanfranc alone prevented the inevitable oppression of the people by the royal servants, or rather postponed it until the next reign. The earliest organization of some governmental system has sometimes been attributed to that powerful favourite of William II who, as the chronicler reports, 'drove and commanded all his gemots all over England,'[1] but a recent writer will not allow that any good thing could come out of the evil genius of Ranulf Flambard.[2] It may, however, be allowable to conjecture that he showed how much could be raised from the people by the strenuous and logical application of the system of land tenure which William I had worked out. For it was possibly the success of Flambard's methods which incited Henry I to break the promise made in his coronation charter that he would return to old custom in the matter of amercements.[3] But had Henry stopped here, there would have been nothing new to record. To him or to his minister, Bishop Roger of Salisbury, must belong the credit of a statesmanship which perceived that regular exactions, however heavy, are borne more cheerfully than those which are spasmodic and irregular. Already there must have been some kind of financial organization for the receipt of the payments made by the sheriffs on account of the ferms of the shire and the danegeld: but of this organization we have only indirect evidence.[4] Now, however, during the Justiciarship of Bishop

[1] *S. C. H.* § 120.

[2] Round, *Feudal England*, 226-229.

[3] *S. C.* 101. § 8.

[4] Round, *Commune of London*, 65-66. 1107-1137.

Roger, there comes into existence a permanent body, to which perhaps gradually the name Scaccarium or Exchequer became technically attached, and which, probably for the first time, brought together into one administrative body all the official heads of the departments, to whom for this special purpose were added a certain number of trained financiers. Two circumstances may be said to have aided its formation. In the first place, Henry began to train a race of official nobility, the Clintons and Bassets, to take the place of the too powerful feudal nobility on whom the kings had hitherto been obliged to rely : secondly, the great official posts seem to have begun to fall apart into two classes, the more ceremonial becoming hereditary among the feudal nobles, whilst those of a more purely administrative character remained to be filled, at the disposal of the king, by clerks or laymen of his new nobility. But we must be careful not to overestimate the existing amount of organization. The development of a formulated system of government is in any case a slow process, and in mediaeval England it was so slow that even at the beginning of Henry II's reign his ministers were little more than officers of his household.[1] Thus it is not surprising that 'even under Henry I the word scaccarium is by no means of common occurrence.'[2] The full body met only twice a year to receive the sheriffs' accounts, and the ordinary financial business would no doubt be done, as perhaps it had hitherto been done, by the Treasurer and his staff.[3] Still, it was a permanent body consisting of definite persons, and organized for a definite piece of work ; and in the intervals of its sessions its members, with the title ' barones scaccarii,' were sent round the country, often in conjunction with the sheriffs, primarily for financial business, but incidentally also for judicial business. Thus they seem to have been called equally barones scaccarii and justiciarii ; but it has been pointed out that, although they were probably experienced financiers and administrators, they were not necessarily trained lawyers.[4] In fact as yet there were no trained lawyers ; for there was no law, except the Roman and Canon law, in which they could be trained. It was the organization of Henry II's reign which first gave the means for the reduction and systematization of local customs into one uniform Common law. For, although Henry II raised

[1] Stubbs, *Introd. to Bened. Abbas.* ii. p. xxi.

[2] *S. C. H.* § 126.

[3] *Dialogus de Scaccario,* Introduction, 13 et seq.

[4] *P. and M.* i. 87.

the Exchequer from the ruin into which all government had fallen in Stephen's time, and made great efforts to secure for it the service of specialists, even foreigners, it was to the judicial organization of the country that he turned his particular attention. The greatest obstacles to good government were the power which had been allowed to fall into the hands of the sheriffs, and the class privileges claimed by the barons and the clergy. Direct legislation might do something, but administrative organization would do more; and, great as was the importance of the Assizes of Clarendon and Northampton, it was the regulation of the visits of the itinerant justices, the establishment of a permanent judicial body and the evolution of the whole system of writs which brought about the supremacy of the Common law of the land over the feudal law of the manorial courts or the ecclesiastical law of the Catholic Church. The history of each of these will be told in another place. Here it is important to notice that for some time to come all the committees gradually formed to administer separate branches of government, were in theory mere delegations from the central and quite indefinite body of the Curia Regis. Thus the Exchequer was the *Curia Regis ad Scaccarium*; the judicial court of five judges formed in 1178 to remain with the king and hear the plaints of the people, was the *Curia Regis de Banco*; even the itinerant justices, though consisting only of a few professional judges mingled with a number of local delegates, were said to hold a Curia Regis as they went round the country.[1] In course of time these delegated bodies obtained a form of their own; and, in any case, whatever was the authority which had been delegated to them, a reserve of power was always deemed to lie in the king and the whole Curia of which they were supposed to form a part. Thus in 1178 it was expressly said that the questions which could not be settled by the five judges who should remain at the Curia Regis, were to be referred for hearing and settling to the king and his sapientes.[2] By this vague term the chronicler intended, no doubt, to describe the body that would perhaps a century later be known as the King in Council —the mainspring of the administration of the country. To this strictly executive Council under the Normans and early Angevins, by way of distinction, has sometimes been applied

[1] *P. and M.* i. 135, 180.

[2] *S. C.* 131. *Ben. Abb.* i. 207.

the term Aula Regis. But it has been pointed out recently[1]
that the Aula dealt merely with affairs of the royal household,
and it may well be questioned whether, until the end of the
thirteenth century, there was anything to distinguish. For, the
general conduct of the administration would naturally be the
last point in which the king would allow himself to be 'fettered
by a routine which would stiffen into law.'[2] Thus it seems
probable that throughout the reign of Henry II the government
of the country continued to be administered in departments
whose only point of contact was the person and will of the
king.

§ 14. It is to the minority of Henry III that Dr. Stubbs
has taught us to look for the first rudiments of a central
administrative council—that is, to a time when there existed
a Council of Regency which owed its appointment and
summons, not to the personal will of the king, but to the
nomination of the Commune Concilium.[3] But there is reason
to think that the Council of Regency was a mere temporary
arrangement, and that we have no warrant for believing that
until well into the reign of Edward I, there was any organized
Council except the Commune Concilium. This had been
recognized for grants of taxation by Magna Carta.[4] On all
other matters—legislation, the administration of equity, general
political discussion—the king took counsel with such persons
as he chose to summon, and these for the time being formed
his council. Thus the Council even under Edward I can
only be described as perhaps mainly a body of officers, that is,
'of men who in one capacity or another are doing the king's
work, and receiving the king's pay.'[5] The only permanent
organization in close contact with the king was the Chancery
—the office of the Chancellor, whom Dr. Stubbs characterizes
as the king's secretary of state for all departments.[6] He
would be surrounded by a number of clerks who have, not
inappropriately, been described as under-secretaries of state,
and many of whom were ecclesiastics holding high preferment
and trained students of Roman and Canon Law. It was as
yet a long time before the Chancery was to become a judicial
tribunal. It was at present a great secretarial bureau, a kind
of permanent civil service. Nearly everything emanating from
the Crown ultimately took the form of a document drawn

[1] Pike, 27, note.

[2] Maitland, Select Pleas of Crown, Introd. xvi.

[3] S. C. H. § 171, 230.

[4] S. C. 299. § 14.

[5] Maitland, Memoranda de Parliamento.

[6] S. C. H. § 121.

H

up in Chancery and sealed with the Great Seal. Hence the quantity of rolls of all kinds—close, patent, fine, charter and others—which form some of the most valuable material for tracing the early development of the administrative arrangements of the country. Under Henry II it was established that no action could be begun in the king's courts without an originating writ issued from Chancery, which became the warrant of the royal judges for entertaining the action. Many of these writs were issued in answer to petitions addressed to the Crown, and as the number of these petitions increased, it was perhaps for the reception and answer of them that a central administrative council first began to be formed. For, many of these petitions could only be answered when the king was surrounded by his councillors or, in other words, when he was holding a 'parliamentum' or colloquy, and arrangements were made in 1280 and again in 1293 for the sorting of the numerous written requests which were now preferred to the Crown on all kinds of matters, and for the reference of the more important of them to the king in his Council.[1] But not even yet can the Council as such be said to have formed a separate, well-defined body; for, the answers of the king in his Council are enrolled sometimes on the rolls of the more strictly professional court held *coram rege*, which was coming to be known as the King's Bench, sometimes on the Chancery rolls, and sometimes on the newly formed Parliament rolls, which also contained the records of a body described by a contemporary lawyer as 'the king in his Council in his Parliament,' —apparently the judicial side of the Commune Concilium.[2]

It is to the last half of the fourteenth century that we must look for the clear setting apart of the Council into a body which was to exercise special functions of its own. About the middle of the century Chancery was separated off into a court for the hearing of certain classes of cases by the direction to suitors to appear 'before our Council in our Chancery,' and 'to do and accept as our court shall adjudge.'[3] Far more important was the separation of Council from Parliament.[4] One of the most useful powers exercised by the king in his Council in his Parliament was that of interposing at intermediate stages in any suit for the purpose of preventing delays in the administration of justice. But

[1] *S. C. H.* § 231. Maitland, *Memoranda de Parliamento.*

[2] Fleta, 66.

[3] Pike, 54. Holdsworth, 197-198.

[4] Holdsworth, 174-175.

Parliament only sat at intervals, and it was apparently with the intention of remedying the consequent difficulty found by well-intentioned suitors in getting judgement, that in 1341 an Act directed the election in Parliament of five lords who, in concert with the Chancellor, Treasurer, Judges, and other members of the King's Council, should be empowered in answer to petitions from suitors to direct the Justices. This body thus represented the King in his Council in his Parliament, and could act at all times irrespective of parliamentary sessions. In its definite mention of persons the Act probably gave to the Council a consistency which hitherto it had lacked. At any rate it is to the early years of the succeeding reign that we can definitely trace the separation of the Council and Parliament. In 1383 the Rolls of Parliament make a clear distinction in the direction that 'as to petitions and bills, the king wills that those which cannot be expedited without Parliament be expedited in Parliament, and those which can be expedited by the King's Council be laid before the Council.'[1] Three years later (1386) begin the separate Proceedings and Ordinances of the Privy Council—Concilium secretum aut privatum—as it now came to be called.[2] To complete the separation, the Lords of Parliament, as they called themselves, refuse to allow the Judges to occupy the position of equality with themselves, which those officials had occupied in the old and now defunct assembly of the 'King in his Council in his Parliament,' and while admitting them to the sessions of Parliament, insist that they come there merely to give legal opinions when asked, and not in the capacity of members of the Lords' House in Parliament. It was in pursuance of this view that in 1387 they referred to the Judges the legality of the appeals of the Lords Appellant against Richard II's favourites and ministers, and then rejected the decision to which the Judges came.[3] The reason for this ultimate separation may be found in the growing power of the Commons. By the end of Edward III's reign the form of the House of Commons may be regarded as practically established, and extensive claims to power had been advanced by its members. As a counterpoise, the king on his side felt the need of a more distinctive body of advisers through whom his prerogative should be exercised; while

14 Edw. III. s. 1. c. 5.

[1] Pike, 280, quoting Rot. Parl. iii. 163.

[2] See Nicolas, *Proceedings and Ordinances of the Privy Council.*

[3] Pike, 201.

the Lords must have seen that their hitherto indefinite organization would not long protect the privileges of their order against the formulated claims of the king or the Commons.

But the mere organization of this body of royal advisers had at once set it in antagonism to the national assembly. Already under Henry III the king strove to make the Council into a mere instrument of his will by filling it with his foreign favourites and dependants; and the representatives of the barons had responded by attempts to convert it into a mere committee of the Commune Concilium, by securing for that body a voice in the nomination of its members. When the Commune Concilium gave way to Parliament, complaints against the action of the Council were redoubled. The first attempts to check it were on the lines of the baronial policy under Henry III; for, the appointment of the Lords Ordainers in 1311 aimed at taking the *nomination of members* of the Concilium out of the hands of the Crown. A newer means towards the same end was a *legislative curtailment of the Council's authority*. Among several statutes passed under Edward III with this object, may be noticed especially one of 1352, which, aiming at the power of arbitrary imprisonment exercised by the Council, declared that 'from hence none shall be taken by petition or suggestion made to our lord the king or to his Council, unless it be by indictment or presentment of his good and lawful people of the same neighbourhood,' etc.

By the end, then, of the reign of Richard II the Council had become an organized assembly of royal officials, existing at the pleasure of the king and *ipso facto* dissolved at his death. Like the old and indefinite Curia Regis, it was at once the body of executive ministers and also the supreme court in judicial matters, uniting in itself the now inconsistent functions of the government which suppresses a riot and the court which tries the rioters. Indeed, its legal side was so prominent that out of term time it took cognizance only of such things as were absolutely necessary to be done.

But the Council was not merely the instrument of the royal prerogative. Under favourable conditions it was a check upon the action of the king, 'a curb placed by the aristocracy on the arbitrary exercise of his will.'[1] For it will readily be

Marginal notes:

Attempts to control it.

25 Edw. III. st. 5, c. 4.

Its position as an instrument of the King:

as a check upon the King.
[1] Dicey, *Privy Council*, 29.

understood that certain hereditary officials, such as the Marshal and Chamberlain, would necessarily form a part of every Council; while, although the king was free to exercise a choice among the whole Episcopal body, yet an equally necessary element would be a large number of bishops whose main claim to respect was independent of the Crown. But again, although under Richard II and Henry IV the king's power was sufficient to ensure an annual re-appointment, and to include among the members no less than seven outside the ranks of the nobility; under Henry VI and onwards, appointments seem to have been made for the king's life, and the number of commoners in the Council tended to decrease.[1] Thus the Council imposed stringent regulations on the royal action, partly no doubt to protect the rights of the Crown, but chiefly perhaps to ensure that its members shall be consulted. As a result, no grants or expressions of the royal will were considered valid until there had been affixed to them the royal seal, whether it were the Great Seal of the Chancellor or the Privy Seal in the hands of a lesser official.

[1] Plummer's *Fortescue*, 294, 298.

§ 15. During the early years of the Lancastrians the mutual antagonism of Council and Parliament was temporarily dispelled. From 1400 to 1437 Council occupied that position of a committee wielding power delegated to it by Parliament, to which the larger body had more than once striven to reduce it.[2] By nominating the members of the Council in Parliament, Henry IV seems to have satisfied the extreme popular demand for election of ministers. But after 1437 Henry VI attained his majority, and under the influence of his wife, Margaret of Anjou, he nominated men who were not acceptable to the nation. The succeeding period was that of the Council's highest power; for it was not, as it came to be under the Tudors, overshadowed by the Crown; while the regulations which it had enforced as to royal grants and expressions of the royal will, placed at its disposal the unchecked exercise of the prerogatives of the Crown. It was perhaps owing to this resumption of its power by the Council, that the already growing distinction was emphasized between the Privy and the Ordinary Council. This seems to have become clear during the minority of Henry VI, when it was again performing the additional functions of a Council of

The Privy Council.

Under the Lancastrians.

[2] Plummer's *Fortescue*, 297. *S. C. H.* § 367.

Its power under control.

Under the Yorkists.

Revival of its authority.

Regency. Thus (1) as the administrative body, the Council would include all the great officials of state who were paid and whose regular attendance was demanded; while (2) as the Ordinary Council, it would include judges and other Councillors who would be summoned occasionally and for a special purpose. It is worth while to notice in passing that it was this full Ordinary Council which was really the Star Chamber, and which exercised the judicial side of the Council's authority. The Council had always done its work by committees,[1] but the Privy Council may be regarded as the first permanent committee of the body. This system was much further developed under the Tudor sovereigns, and was rendered necessary by the increased activity of their government.

With the accession of the Tudors the Council entered on a new phase of existence. The period between 1485 and 1640 has been described as the age of government by Councils. After the fall of the Lancastrians the position of the Council underwent a great change; for, owing to the destruction of the power of the nobility in the Wars of the Roses, it 'ceased to be a check on the royal will, and sunk into a body of officials.'[2] But as its independence lessened its powers increased. The political authority which it exercised in the fifteenth century remained untouched; while its legal side was greatly enhanced, and its legislative activity almost superseded that of Parliament itself. Thus (1) every opportunity was seized to *subject outlying parts of the kingdom to the Council's direct control*, as Ireland by Poynings' Act of 1494, and Jersey and Guernsey also during the reign of Henry VII. It was with the same object that special Councils were erected for the government of different parts of England itself. Such were the *Council of the North* (1539), the *Council of Wales and the Marches* (1542), the *Council of the West* (1540), and the *Court of the Castle Chamber* in Ireland which was set up during the reign of Elizabeth.[3] Of similar effect, though older in origin, were the Council of Calais, the Stannary Court and the governments of the Palatinates. The extent of this special jurisdiction may be gathered from the calculation that one-third of England was thus withdrawn from the protection of the Common Law. Again (2) there was a constant attempt on the part of the Tudors to *extend the legislative powers of the*

[1] Plummer's *Fortescue*, 296.

[2] Dicey, *Privy Council*, 85.

[3] Prothero, cx.

Under the Tudors.

Extension of its authority.

Council through the use of Proclamations. These were temporary enactments like the earlier Ordinances, issued by the king with the advice of his Council. They were defined by the lawyers as intended to explain or call attention to ambiguous or obsolete statutes; but the sovereigns did everything in their power to endow them with the full force of parliamentary Acts. But (3) the great aim of the royal policy was to *place the law courts generally under the influence of the Council.* This was attempted in two ways: (*a*) new Courts were erected composed chiefly of Councillors and acting under the supervision of the Council. Such were the Courts of *High Commission*, which will be fully dealt with elsewhere;[1] of *Requests*, formed under Henry VIII as a minor Court of Equity to hear 'poor men's complaints';[2] of *Augmentations*, for dealing with the confiscated monastic property; of *Firstfruits and Tenths*, to administer the Annates and Tenths which were transferred from the Pope to the King; and of *Wards*, set up by Henry VIII for the better exaction of the feudal dues.

[1] pp. 586-588.
[2] Holdsworth, 207-210.

Most important of all was the direct extension of the judicial authority of the Council, which took place through the (*b*) growth of the *Court of Star Chamber*. It has been shown that when, under Henry VI, there appeared a distinction between the Privy or Inner and the Ordinary Council, the judicial functions of the Council were exercised by the larger body. These judicial functions comprised an appellate jurisdiction in civil cases, to the exercise of which no objection was ever made. But they comprised also the jurisdiction of a criminal court of first instance, which, necessary though it often was, formed a subject of constant complaint in Parliament. But during the parliamentary period of Lancastrian rule, Parliament occasionally conferred on the Council by statute criminal powers at first hand. It was, then, going very little beyond what the Lancastrian Parliaments had already done when an Act was passed in **1487**, constituting a new Court composed of seven persons—the Chancellor, Treasurer, Keeper of the Privy Seal, a Bishop, a temporal Lord and the two Chief Justices—which should take cognizance of 'unlawful maintenance, giving of licences, signs and tokens, great riots, unlawful assemblies,' and all offences against peace and order which were too serious to

Its judicial activity.

3 Hen. VII. c. I.

be dealt with by the ordinary local courts.   There seems to be no doubt that this is the court which is shortly afterwards called the Court of Star Chamber.   Its exact connection with the Council is a matter of very considerable doubt.   The jurisdiction assigned to it concerned a class of cases with which the Council would ordinarily have dealt, and it cannot be supposed that the Act which set up this new court was intended to deprive the Council of a portion of its judicial authority.   The powers of the two bodies, therefore, were in these special matters concurrent.[1]   Moreover, no one questions that the two courts remained separate until at least 1529, at which date an Act was passed confirming the jurisdiction of the Star Chamber and adding the President of the Council as an eighth member.   Beyond this date, however, all clue of the connection of the two bodies is lost.   It is generally said that towards the close of Henry VIII's reign, the special work for which the small Star Chamber was created having been accomplished, its separate existence came to an end or, rather, was merged in the general authority of the Council, so that the Star Chamber became what it is thought to have been before the Act of Henry VII, the whole Council sitting in its judicial capacity.[2]   Thus all Privy Councillors were *ex officio* members of the Star Chamber, and since the powers of the Star Chamber rested more upon law than the corresponding powers of the Council, the Council preferred to exercise its judicial functions under shelter of the Act of 1487, and by the addition of the two Chief Justices to the whole body of Councillors for such cases, to seem to keep within the meaning of the Act.[3]   But this could have deceived no one ; for under Elizabeth and the first two Stuarts the Star Chamber exercised a jurisdiction far wider than any conferred by the Act of 1487, although only similar to that of the Council itself before that date.   Moreover, it may well be doubted whether the two bodies were ever regarded as identical.   In the first place, the Privy Council as such still continues from time to time to exercise its old criminal jurisdiction, although in numbers of cases it relegates the trial of offenders to the Star Chamber.   And secondly, it is asserted that 'all contemporary authority on the subject of the Star Chamber points to the inclusion of men whose dignity or learning strengthens the Court, but who are outside

[1] Prothero, ciii.

20 Hen. VIII. c. 20.

[2] Hallam, i. 50-54. Cf. also Busch, *England under the Tudors*, i. 389.

[3] Prothero, cv.

the circle of habitual advisers of the Crown.' In other words, even if all Privy Councillors were *ex officio* members of the Star Chamber, the converse was not the case, and the Star Chamber contained in addition some who were not habitual councillors. Finally, the Long Parliament abolished the Star Chamber on the ground that it had greatly exceeded the powers conferred on it by the Act of 1487, to which it owed its origin. There is plenty of weighty authority to show that this was historically erroneous, and that the Star Chamber existed long before the Act of 1487.[1] But it seems very probable that, by the end of Elizabeth's reign at the very latest, the Star Chamber was a separate body from the Council,[2] and that a distinction was drawn between them 'as to their composition and as to the matters dealt with by the two courts.' Thus it was possible for the Long Parliament, while abolishing 'the court commonly called the Star Chamber,' also to limit the civil jurisdiction of the 'Council table' or Privy Council.[3] We are so accustomed to regard the Star Chamber as an engine of oppression that it is important to notice that its unpopularity was of comparatively late growth. Under the Tudors it did a much needed work as 'a tribunal constantly resorted to as a resource against the ignorance and prejudices of a country jury,' and the verdict of the historian is that 'in such investigations it showed itself intelligent and impartial.'[4] Even under James I it has been pointed out that 'a very large part of the business that came before it arose from suits brought by private persons.' It was probably true that the hatred bestowed upon the Court was due to the use to which the King put it in his quarrel with Parliament and the people, and most especially to its intermeddling in the ecclesiastical disputes.[5]

To return to the development of the Council in its administrative capacity. Under the Tudors the Council was all powerful: there was nothing which it might not do, and in which it might not interfere. Two chief points call for notice. In the first place, it *became a much larger body*, numbering, as we find at the beginning of Edward VI's reign, no less than forty members. This body was divided into six committees for different branches of the Council's work; but one of these, that of the State, seems to have been so much more important

[1] Cf. extracts in Prothero, 175, 401, 408.

[2] Holdsworth, 274-278.

[3] Anson, ii. 98.

[4] Gardiner, vii. 84-85.

[5] Prothero, cvi.

Its administrative work.

than the others, that it probably consisted of the privy as opposed to the ordinary councillors, a distinction which must have increased rather than diminished since the time of Henry VI, and would account for the fact that Henry VIII on many important occasions acted without the concurrence of his Council. The second important point is that *the king acted through his secretaries* in preference to other councillors.

Origin of Secretaries of State.   The office of king's secretary or clerk dates from the reign of Henry III, when its holder formed part of the royal household, and took over some of the work which hitherto had been discharged by the Chancellor and his clerks. At first the office conferred no political influence; but in the fifteenth century its holder was made responsible for the use of the signet. It was under the Tudors that the secretary became a great political officer. Since 1433 there seem to have been two secretaries. They now ceased to be officers of the household: the post was given to men of distinction, who became *ex-officio* members of the Council. Under Elizabeth they were first called Secretaries of State, and one of them became the exponent of the royal will in the House of Commons. When we turn to the Stuarts, we note a manifest though gradual *decline in the authority of the Council*. As far as outward signs went, it was never so powerful as at the beginning of the seventeenth century; at any rate it was never so assertive. But there are manifest proofs that it was unequal to its work, and could not cope with the new difficulties which had arisen from the position taken up by Parliament. Thus, the Council under Charles I reverted to the custom of the Yorkists, and contained a large number of nobility; while a prominent place was given to the bishops. Together with this anti-popular movement went a great decline in administrative talent. The secretaries were no longer men of first-rate ability, such as Thomas Cromwell and Sir William Cecil, or the real advisers of the Crown, but were mere creatures of the king, a Sir John Coke or a Windebank, whom the Commons overrode or ignored.

The Cabinet.   § 16. Meanwhile the numbers of the Privy Council had been growing. The distinction between the effective and honorary members was as old as the Council itself. It was a natural division; for it represented those whom the king chose to consult, and those whom it was impolitic to omit from his counsels. The first body would be composed of the holders of ministerial office; but the latter would claim to be present at the royal Council board. During the political complications of Charles I's reign there are traces that the two bodies were drifting more widely apart. This became increasingly clear when Charles II retained the old Privy Councillors, many of whom had taken part with the Commonwealth. The division of the Council into *committees for purposes of administration* was no new thing. Under Charles I are found at various times an Irish committee (1634), a special committee for Foreign Affairs, and a Scotch committee (1638). Possibly at Clarendon's suggestion this system was revived. The most important of the committees now established was one for Foreign Affairs;[1] and it is to this (which after Clarendon's flight accidentally conferred an undying reproach upon the word 'Cabal'), that the origin of the later CABINET is generally traced. But it seems that there was a further and *purely informal committee* with which the king conferred on his most secret affairs, and which 'was distinct alike from the Foreign Committee, and from the entirety of the Privy Council.'[2] It is, however, important to notice that up to the period of the Treaty of Utrecht all real affairs of state were placed before the *full Council*.

Its origin under Charles II.

[1] Hearn, *Government of England*, 184.

[2] Anson, ii. 102.

But Clarendon's system of committees had not solved the whole question of administration. Indeed, it did not touch the most important question of all, that of harmonizing the relations of the executive and the legislature. The impeachments of Clarendon and Danby, and the king's attempt to shield the latter by the grant of a pardon while the trial was impending, showed the necessity of arriving at some solution, unless at every disagreement recourse was to be had to desperate remedies. It suited the king to assent to a *scheme attributed to Sir William Temple*,[3] by which the Privy Council should consist of thirty members, half of them great officers of State, the other half independent members of both Houses whose joint incomes should equal that of the whole House of Commons. All should be equally entrusted with every secret of State, and the king should do nothing without their advice. The scheme was a compromise between the king's right to appoint ministers and the exercise of

Temple's scheme.

[3] Christie, *Shaftesbury*, ii. 325-326.

parliamentary control by calling those ministers to account. But it was bound to failure; for not only did it reproduce the fault of the constitutional lawyers of the Great Rebellion, and of Cromwell's constitutions, in that it was based upon the idea of a balance of power between executive and legislature; but, practically, the numbers were too large for administration, and nothing secured the unanimity of the members. Moreover, the king was not ready to resign so much of his prerogative as was implied in the continual consultation of this body. He still acted on the advice of a small number of personal friends, of whom Sir W. Temple, inconsistently enough, consented to be one; and before the end of the same year he had dissolved one Parliament against the will of the Council, and another without asking its advice at all.

1679.

The ultimate solution of the question between executive and legislature was only reached at the Revolution of 1688, when the Bill of Rights deprived the king of the undue exercise of his royal prerogative; and the custom of an annual Mutiny Bill and Appropriation Bill ensured the regular summons of Parliament, and rendered it impossible to maintain a body of ministers who were not acceptable to the majority in the House of Commons. But William struggled hard against this conclusion. He not only used every influence at the disposal of the Crown, by the distribution of offices and pensions, to obtain a permanent majority of members favourable to his wishes; but he even himself undertook the management of foreign affairs, and induced the Lord Chancellor Somers to affix the Great Seal to a blank paper, on which was subsequently inscribed the first Partition Treaty with Louis XIV. Lord Somers' consequent impeachment led to the insertion of two clauses in the Act of Settlement [1] designed to secure the responsibility of ministers, which Danby had tried to evade by pleading the royal command, and Somers by claiming the connivance of a Secretary of State. The eighth clause enacted that no royal pardon should be pleadable to an impeachment: the fourth clause, reviving a practice of the fifteenth century, provided that after the accession of the Hanoverians all resolutions of the Privy Council should be signed by the members responsible for them; while, finally, the sixth clause

The
Cabinet
under
William
and Anne.

1698.

[1] *S. C.*
530-531.
Robertson,
90-91.

excluded from the House of Commons all holders of offices or pensions from the Crown. But the two latter provisions were soon proved to be far too stringent. No one would have undertaken the duties and responsibilities of councillorship on the terms proposed;[1] while the exclusion of all ministers would have placed the executive and legislature in hopeless conflict. At the same time some precaution against royal influence in the House of Commons seemed advisable. Consequently, although the fourth and sixth clauses of the Act of Settlement were repealed,[2] two years later the 'Act for the Security of Her Majesties Person, Government, and Succession'[3] incapacitated all persons from sitting in the House of Commons, who should hold either any office created since October 25, 1705, or a pension at the pleasure of the Crown; and required that any member who was appointed to an already existing office, should vacate his seat and subject himself to re-election.

    Such was the result of an attempt to secure ministerial responsibility by legislation. 'Nothing, therefore, but custom, based on practical convenience, has worked out the transition from government by the Crown in Council to government by a Cabinet consisting of ministers indicated by the Commons;—from the legal responsibility of the individual Privy Councillor to the moral responsibility of the collective Cabinet.'[4] This corporate responsibility, which is of the essence of the Cabinet system, came chiefly as a result of the growth of the office of Prime Minister. About the time of Edward I the Justiciar, the royal lieutenant of Norman and early Angevin times, was superseded by the Chancellor as the great political officer of the Crown: and he in his turn gave way under the Tudors to the Treasurer, who was on the whole the chief minister until the accession of the House of Hanover. At the same time no minister, however prominent, had the choice of his colleagues or a decisive voice in measures. Between the Revolution of 1688 and the accession of the Hanoverians there are three instances of a homogeneous ministry, but none of them was sufficiently strong to establish a precedent. For, the Whig Junto was without a leader: Godolphin, under Anne, had for some years to put up with Tory colleagues; and the Tory ministers, who gradually superseded his party, were appointed by the queen without consulting him.

Margin notes:
[1] Hearn, 186.
[2] 1705.
4 & 5 Anne, c. 20.
[3] 1708.
Robertson, 106.
Under the early Hanoverians.
[4] Anson, ii. 104.
1696-1698.
1702-1708.
1710-1711.

Attempts of the king to keep a hold on the Cabinet.

The truth was that circumstances had made the Cabinet 'the motive power in the executive of the country,' so that the king sought every means whereby he might retain at any rate a veto on the action of unacceptable ministers. As he tried to influence Parliament itself by the multiplication of places and pensions and by direct bribes to the members, so he strove to keep the Cabinet in order by *including among its members devoted personal followers of the king*. Thus, from the reign of William III onwards, besides the committees, either permanent or temporary, which did the work now done in the Foreign Office, the Home Office and the Board of Trade, we find not only the whole Privy Council, which was assembled for formal business, but also a twofold Cabinet— an *outer* Cabinet including the great officers of the household, such as the Lord Chamberlain and the Master of the Horse, and non-political officers of State, such as the Archbishop of Canterbury and the Lord Chief Justice ; and an *inner* Cabinet which commanded the confidence of the House of Commons and therefore really settled the policy of the country. It is true that with the accession of the Hanoverians the king disappeared from Cabinet Councils,[1] and a first minister became both necessary and possible. But, as a matter of fact, the withdrawal of his personal influence made it doubly necessary that he should retain an indirect hold over the deliberations of his ministers. Even Walpole, who was perhaps in any modern sense the first Prime Minister, could not nominate his own colleagues, and was obliged for years to tolerate dissensions in his Cabinet ; while the personal interference of George III, exercised in direct and indirect ways alike, placed his ministers completely in the background. The existence of this double Cabinet explains the action of ministers of the eighteenth century in repudiating responsibility for measures carried out by Cabinets of which they were members ;[2] nor is it less easy to understand how the king, by intriguing with the titular colleagues, was able to maintain his own nominees in the Cabinet and to thwart the action of ministers. Burke might declaim as he would against the cabal which had been formed ' to intercept the favour, protection and confidence of the Crown in the passage to its ministers,' and whose members, while not aiming at ' the high and responsible offices of the State,' took

[1] Hearn, 191.

[2] Anson, ii. 111-118.

delight 'in rendering these heads of office thoroughly con-
temptible and ridiculous.'[1]   It was the king himself, and not,
as Burke pretended, a Court faction that was to blame.

Indeed, so long as this personal interference of the Crown
lasted, the growth of corporate responsibility among the
members of the Cabinet was impossible:[2] and it was in any
case against the interest of the Crown.   The ultimate establishment of the principle was due to its compulsory recognition
by the king in a few isolated instances.   Thus, in **1746**, the
Pelhams, who were in office, took a most unpatriotic advantage
of the Jacobite Rebellion, and by resigning in a body forced
the king to admit William Pitt to office.[3]   In **1763** Pitt himself
followed this up by refusing to take office except in a Cabinet
of his own composing, and thus obliged the king to continue
the Grenville-Bedford section of the Whigs in power.   But the
first definite recognition of this corporate responsibility may be
said to date from **1782**, when the second ministry of Lord
Rockingham omitted all titular colleagues and was composed
only of eleven persons, all of whom held high political posts
and were cognizant of all measures taken.   The system of a
double Cabinet was, however, only gradually abolished.   In the
person of the Lord Chancellor especially the king attempted to
maintain a permanent spy upon the other ministers.   Thus, in
1792 the persistent opposition of Lord Thurlow, who had been
Lord Chancellor with one short interruption since 1778, forced
the younger Pitt to offer the king an easily chosen alternative
between his own resignation and that of the Chancellor.[4]   The
first principle dealing with the titular Cabinet was formulated
in **1801**, when Pitt's Chancellor, Lord Loughborough, claimed
to remain, though without office, in the Cabinet of his successor.   Addington met his pretensions with a statement that
' the number of Cabinet ministers should not exceed that of
the persons whose responsible situations in office require their
being members of it.'

But the difficulty lay not only with the king's desire to make
the ministers feel his power, but with the extreme reluctance
of the ministers to submit themselves to the overshadowing
authority of a Prime Minister through whom alone such moral
responsibility could be realized.   Walpole himself definitely
repudiated the position;[5] and even so late as 1806, when

[1] *Thoughts on Present Discontents.*

Establishment of corporate responsibility.

[2] Hearn, 195-197.

[3] Seeley, *Lectures on Political Science,* 281.

[4] Hearn, 200.

Reluctance to acknowledge a Prime Minister.

[5] Morley, *Walpole,* 163.

objection was taken to the appointment of Lord Ellenborough, Chief Justice of the King's Bench, to a seat in the Cabinet, on the ground that he might be at once prosecutor together with the rest of the Cabinet and judge, the other ministers refused to accept this plainly stated doctrine of mutual responsibility. [1]   Indeed, so essential was it before the Reform Bill that the head of the Ministry should possess the confidence of the king, that the real leader of the Government often held a subordinate office, while the First Lord of the Treasury, like the Dukes of Grafton and Portland and the Marquis of Rockingham, were but the nominal leaders.

[1] Campbell, *Lives of Chief Justices*, ii. 451.

It was only with the cessation of corruption and the formation of strong parties over the question of Parliamentary Reform that Cabinet government, as we know it, can be said to have been attained.   The result has been that at any given moment the general direction of the policy of the country is in the hands of a body of men, who are individually the heads of the chief departments of the executive government, and are collectively the nominees of one of their number, the Prime Minister.   He commands the confidence of the majority in the House of Commons and, no matter how successful their own administration, with him they stand or fall.   Thus while on the one side the method by which the Cabinet is formed ensures an unanimity in its advice to the Crown and a secrecy in its deliberations ; on the other side its individual members, as heads of departments, have direct communication with the sovereign. Moreover, the concurrence of the sovereign is necessary for their individual dismissal : although a Prime Minister wishing to get rid of a colleague can practically always force the king's hand by the alternative of his own resignation.   With the final extinction of the double Cabinet, too, the attitude of the Crown towards its ministers has become defined, and it is an accepted principle that the king must neither ask advice outside the Cabinet, nor act within its concurrence, nor refuse his support so long as the ministers retain the confidence of the people.   For, although the legal responsibility of each minister can only be enforced through his position of Privy Councillor, the Cabinet is not the Privy Council.   This body consists of no less than three sets of members—the Cabinet for the time being and members of former Cabinets ; the

Relations of the Cabinet (*a*) to the Crown.

holders of great offices of State unconnected with politics; and eminent men on whom the rank is conferred as a compliment. Thus only in a very general sense can the Cabinet be even called a committee of the Privy Council; for it is unknown to law, its numbers and qualifying offices are indeterminate, and of its deliberations no record is preserved.[1]

The relation of the Cabinet to the Commons has undergone considerable change. Before the Reform Bill a minister who enjoyed the confidence of the Crown could use all those means at the king's disposal to procure a majority in Parliament. From 1832 to 1867, the date of the second Reform Act, ministers did not retire until they had faced the new Parliament and had been definitely defeated. Since 1867, with the exception of the election of 1892, the verdict of the country at the polling booths has been so clear that a Cabinet to whom it has been adverse has not waited for the meeting of Parliament in order to make way for one which will command a majority in the new House of Commons.[2] Such is the Cabinet system as it has worked itself out in two centuries. The lateness of its recognition may be gathered from the fact that Burke is the first writer who mentions it, while the founders of the American Constitution gave it no place in their polity. Meanwhile, certain tendencies may be noticed which are not unlikely to work a transformation in this mode of administration. The Cabinet itself is becoming so large from the increasing number of departments whose heads must be included within it, that the real decision of policy seems to rest with an inner body of the three or four most indispensable members.[3] At the same time, the ever-increasing interference of Parliament with the administration cannot but be viewed with alarm by all who appreciate the necessity of prompt and vigorous action. And this tendency to minute criticism on the part of the Commons intimidates all but the strongest ministers, while the very contrast of his position with that of his colleagues places a popular favourite in an almost dictatorial position. Thus, finally, it is the people and not Parliament, the polling booths and not the lobby, which appoint the Prime Minister and even nominate to him some of his subordinates: and a doubt may perhaps be allowed whether a plebiscite of this character, and even of this size, is not as liable to sudden

[1] Cf. Morley, *Walpole*, 154-160. Gladstone's *Gleanings*, i. 224 et seq.

(*b*) to the Commons.

[2] Anson, ii. 138-140.

[3] Lord Rosebery, *Pitt*, 109. L. Courtney, *Working Const. of United Kingdom*, 115.

I

whims and inconsiderate action as the single chamber which political philosophers and practical statesmen alike deprecate.

The modern departments of Government.

§ 17. Both the existence of the Cabinet and the large number of its members bear witness to the continually increasing subdivision of the functions of Government. From the standpoint of the present day, administrative offices may be divided into three classes. The first of these consists of two great *offices which are now put into commission.* The *Admiralty,* which has succeeded to the work of the Lord High Admiral, is dealt with elsewhere. The *Treasury* [1] has a longer history.

The Treasury.

[1] Anson, ii. 169-175.

The *Treasurer* was originally the custodian of the royal hoard at Winchester. As an officer of the Exchequer he received the accounts of the sheriffs, and appointed officers to collect the revenue.[2] He was, however, subordinate to both Justiciar and Chancellor, until the separation of Chancery from the Exchequer under Richard I removed him from the influence of the latter, and the abeyance of the Justiciarship under Henry III freed him from the former. The separation from Chancery necessitated the appointment of a Chancellor of the Exchequer, with charge of the seal of the Exchequer, which in Exchequer business took the place of the Great Seal of the Chancellor.[3] Under Edward I the appointment of a Chief Baron relieved the Treasurer of the judicial business of the Exchequer. The latter gradually became a great political officer until, under the Tudors, with the more dignified title of Lord High Treasurer, he superseded the Chancellor as first minister of the Crown. The two great holders of the office were Lord Burleigh and his son, the Earl of Salisbury. On the death of the latter, the Treasury was put into commission and was gradually separated from the Exchequer. During the seventeenth century individuals were still occasionally appointed to the office: but since 1714 it has always been in commission. Previous to 1711 the Crown nominated all the Lords of the Treasury: since then this has been the privilege of the First Lord, who, with few exceptions, has himself acted as Prime Minister. The exceptions have been created either by a rivalry in the Cabinet, which caused the real leaders to take subordinate offices under mere figureheads such as Lord Wilmington (1742) and the Dukes of Newcastle (1754) and Portland (1807); or by a desire on the part of the real

[2] *S. C. H.* §§ 122, 126.

[3] *Ibid.* § 237.

1612.

1714.

chief to take a less arduous, as in the case of Chatham, who was Lord Privy Seal (1766), or a more congenial post.   Thus, Fox in 1806, and Lord Salisbury in 1885, 1887 and 1895 preferred the office of Foreign Secretary.

A second class of administrative offices is formed by those Nomina which may be described as *in theory Committees of the Privy* Boards. *Council.* Of these there are five.   (1) The *Board of Trade* finds its origin in two councils for Trade and for Plantations established by Charles II on his accession by commissions under the Great Seal.   They were united in 1672, and extinguished in 1675.   In 1695 this joint board was revived; and [1] Anson, ii. in 1781, on its abolition as both costly and inefficient, its 188-189. place was taken by a committee of the Privy Council.   In these Redlich and two councils may also be seen an anticipation of the office of Hirst, *Local* the Secretary of State for the Colonies.[1]   (2) The *Board of* ii. 312. *Works* succeeded in 1851 to the supervision of public works 1851. and buildings which had been undertaken since 1832 by the administrators of Crown lands, commonly known as Commissioners of Woods and Forests.[2]   (3) The *Local Government* [2] Anson, 193. *Board* was created in 1871, and took over the duties of the 1871. Poor Law Board, of the Home Secretary in respect of local government, and of the Privy Council in connection with public [3] Anson, 194. health.   More recently the County Councils have been placed Redlich and under its central control.[3]   (4) The *Board of Agriculture* was Hirst, ii. 242. formed in 1889, and took the powers exercised in this respect by 1889. the Privy Council and the now extinct Land Commissioners.[4] [4] Anson, 195. (5) The *Committee of Council on Education* was established in Redlich and 1856.   In 1830 the first annual sum granted by Parliament Hirst, ii. 314. in aid of education was administered by the Treasury.   In 1856. 1839 an increased sum was given to the care of a committee of the Privy Council, which speedily became a department and gained permanence by the power, bestowed by statute in 1856, to appoint a Vice-President of the committee who should be under the (not entirely) nominal headship of the President of the Council.   This has prevented the Education Department from becoming independent, and has kept it as a real committee of council.[5]   In all the four previous cases the boards consist [5] Anson, of a head and a small number of high officials.   Thus the 196-197. Redlich and Local Government Board is composed of the Lord President Hirst, ii. 316. of the Council, the Secretaries of State, the Lord Privy Seal and the Chancellor of the Exchequer in addition to its own President. But in all four cases the Board is merely ornamental, and the whole work is done by the respective heads— the Presidents of the Boards of Trade, Local Government and Agriculture, and the First Commissioner of the Board of Works.

The Secretariat. The third class of offices consists of the five *Secretaries of State*. The origin of the office has been already noticed. Until the end of the eighteenth century there were generally two Secretaries of State; although between 1707 and 1746 a third was appointed for Scotch affairs, and from 1768 to 1782 Colonial matters were given to a specially appointed Secretary. After the Revolution of 1688 the work was divided between a northern and a southern department, the latter including Ireland, the Colonies and home affairs. In 1782 the northern department became in name what it had been in reality, the *Foreign Office*; while the southern department as the *Home Office* still dealt with Ireland, the Colonies and some part of the management of the army. In 1794 the exigencies of the War of the French Revolution caused the appointment of a special Secretary of State for *War* to whom, in 1801, was transferred all business connected with the *Colonies*. So it remained until the Crimean War, when the Secretaryships for War and the Colonies became separate. The last addition to the Secretariat was caused by the transference of *India* to the Crown in 1858.[1] Theoretically the division of the secretariat is a mere matter of administrative convenience. Every one of the five is equally capable of discharging the duties connected with any of the four departments other than his own. But the Home Secretary is the principal Secretary of State, and as such has, in addition to the general supervision of law and order within the United Kingdom, certain ceremonial relations to royalty itself.[2] Three secretaryships of a lesser degree of importance may be noted in this place. The Secretary at War lasted from the beginning of a standing army under Charles II until the office was merged in the more recent but greater Secretary of State in 1854.[3] The Irish Act of Union in 1801 made the Chief Secretary to the Lord Lieutenant the principal medium of communication for Ireland, and although recent circumstances have exalted the holder of the office to Cabinet rank, technically the Home Secretary still

1782.

1794.

1854.

1858.

[1] Anson, ii. 166-167.

[2] *Ibid.* 227 et seq.

[3] *Ibid.* 378.

remains responsible for Irish affairs.[1] A separate Secretary for Scotland was only appointed in 1885, but is not, like his temporary predecessor for forty years after the Scotch Union, necessarily a member of the Cabinet.[2]

Two other classes of ministerial officials demand a passing notice. A Cabinet always includes one or two of what would elsewhere be called 'ministers without portfolios,' that is, holders of practically *honorary offices* whom, for one reason or another, it is desirable to place at the centre of the administration. Such are the Lord President of the Council,[3] and the Lord Privy Seal,[4] generally, though not necessarily, members of the House of Lords, and the purely local Chancellor of the Duchy of Lancaster.[5] A second class is formed by the *Law Officers of the Crown*—the Lord Chancellor, a peer and President of the House of Lords (for whom, however, has sometimes been substituted a Lord Keeper, who, although President of the House of Lords, is not a member of it) ; the Attorney-General, who dates back to Edward I ; and the Solicitor-General, originating under Edward IV as the royal adviser in matters connected with Chancery business.[6]

All the officials enumerated above are ministerial; that is, although not all necessarily, and some never, members of the Cabinet, yet they all change with a change in the Government. The necessary members of a Cabinet would seem to be the First Lord of the Treasury and the Chancellor of the Exchequer, the Lord Chancellor, the First Lord of the Admiralty, and the five Secretaries of State. All these, and indeed all ministers, must now almost of necessity sit in Parliament. The last instance to the contrary was Mr. Gladstone's retention of the Colonial Secretaryship for six months in 1846 owing to his failure to obtain the necessary re-election.[7] For upon the various heads devolves the duty of defending their respective departments from criticism in Parliament. The policy of each department is settled by its temporary chief ; but the executive work is done by a large permanent staff, who are admitted partly by patronage, but chiefly by competitive examination, who do not change with the Government, and who represent the specialized knowledge and the traditions of management connected with each individual department. All these officials are by statute excluded from seats in the House of Commons.

[1] Anson, ii. 199.

[2] *Ibid.* 200.

Other changing offices.

[3] Anson, ii. 151.

[4] *Ibid.* 159.

[5] *Ibid.* 197.

[6] *Ibid.* 201.

The Cabinet and the permanent Civil Service.

1846.

[7] *Ibid.* 202.

CHAPTER III

THE LEGISLATURE

Witan, Commune Concilium, and the House of Lords

Origin of
the Witena-
gemot.
[1] Bagehot,
*Physics
and
Politics*,
158.

§ 18. An acute historical observer has told us that mankind owes its freedom from the bonds of archaic custom to the growth of government by discussion.[1] It is, then, to the kind of assembly by which such discussion was encouraged that we must turn in order to discover the principles of national progress. We are wont to regard legislation as the chief work of our modern Parliament; but law is a comparatively late growth in the record of a nation's history. Sir Henry Maine has described the transition from the 'separate, isolated judgements' of a divinely descended king to the customary law maintained by the memory of a religious or political aristocracy, and so to the period when the diffusion of the art of writing suggested

[2] *Ancient
Law*,
chap. i.

the formation of a legal code.[2] It is in the second of these periods that the age of discussion begins; and it is by means of this discussion that the customs are preserved as a useful check on the anarchic elements of the rudimentary stage of life; while they are insensibly but appreciably modified into a means of national advance. The earliest records of the English tribes recognize the existence of government by discussion. The majority of the tribes who came under Tacitus' observation were not under kingly rule; but whether they were monarchical or not, the power was wielded by the tribal assembly, and it is especially noteworthy that, while the *principes* or chiefs care for smaller matters, all important affairs

[3] *S. C.* 56.
c. 11.

are decided in the general assembly which consists of the whole body of free warriors.[3]

In the lapse of centuries the positions were exactly reversed. Connection
What may be called the committee of *principes* developed into between
the WITENAGEMOT, or council of wise men, with whom, in gemot
conjunction with the king, lay the decision of all important and the
matters. Whether any power remained to the general body folkmoot.
of the freemen—the folkmoot, as it was called, is a point of
considerable dispute.   Dr. Stubbs[1] believes that in the small [1] *S. C. H.*
kingdoms of the so-called Heptarchy there was a Witenagemot § 51.
and a folkmoot, and that as each small kingdom became
conquered by a larger neighbour, its Witenagemot disappeared
or was absorbed in that of the greater power, while its folkmoot remained in the slightly altered position of a shiremoot.
Dr. Gneist,[2] on the other hand, is of opinion that, in the [2] *Hist. of*
smaller kingdoms at any rate, the Witenagemot and folkmoot *Eng. Const.*
were practically identical. Mr. Freeman would prolong the i. 99.
council described by Tacitus. 'The ancient Mycel Gemót
was a body in which every freeman of the realm had, in theory
at least, the right to attend in person,' which right, he adds,
'simply died out in practice and was never formally taken
away.' He instances 'the many passages in our early writers
in which very popular language is used, those in which the
gathering of great crowds is spoken of,' and adds, 'there is
nothing wonderful in supposing that the great mass of the
qualified members of an assembly habitually stayed away; it
is much harder to believe that ever and anon crowds of
unqualified persons thrust themselves into an assembly in
which they had no right to appear at all.'[3] Mr. Kemble, [3] *Essays,*
whom Mr. Freeman has followed, collected scattered notices 4th Series,
of over 140 meetings of the Witenagemot between 596 and 444-447.
1066;[4] but nearly all the passages which refer to meetings of [4] *Saxons*
a popular body, are concerned with the election of kings and *in Eng-*
the promulgation of the laws, matters to which the assent of *land,* i.
the populace would wisely be invited. 203-230.
   The rare use of the word Witenagemot seems to show that Compo-
it was not a very definitely formulated body. We generally sition and
hear of the Witan, the wise men, and the description points to the Witena-
a personal rather than an official body. In process of time the gemot.
composition and powers of the Witan may have obtained a more
settled form. The share which they take in the king's grants
of bookland seems to diminish in importance; from necessary

assenters they become merely attesting witnesses.[1] Again, whatever may have been the early custom, their *meetings* were held, at any rate in the later days of Anglo-Saxon rule, at regular times, at the three great Church festivals of Easter, Whitsuntide and Christmas. Finally, the *members* of the ordinary assemblies came to be the royal family, the national officers both ecclesiastical and civil, such as bishops (to whom were added later a number of abbots), ealdormen, and finally *ministri* or royal nominees. These latter would include persons in all kinds of relations to the king, and probably the increase or diminution of the royal power can be marked by an increase or diminution in the number of *ministri* who attest the acts of the assembly. Thus a powerful king would balance the influence of the national officers with a sufficient number of his personal friends. For, although on occasions he might be able to override the decisions of a hostile body, it was strongly in accordance with custom that he should act with and through his councillors. Indeed, although it lay in the power of the Witan not only to elect the king, but even as a last resource to decree his deposition, the authority of the elected king was co-ordinate with that of the electing body. It is possible, therefore, to lay down some general principles as to the powers of the king's advisers in the closing centuries of Anglo-Saxon rule. Thus in *legislation*, the king, following the 'traditional theory of all the German races,' enacted all laws, ecclesiastical no less than secular, with the counsel and consent of his Witan. Until quite the end of the tenth century no *taxation* was required, but the first levies of the shipgeld and danegeld were raised by their authority. As a deliberative and *administrative* body, they were called upon to witness, and thereby nominally at least to assent to grants of land, and to take a definite share in the more momentous questions connected with peace and war. With certain restrictions the purely official members, the bishops and ealdormen, were elected, or more strictly co-opted by the existing members. Finally, in defiance of modern theories of division of powers, this legislative and administrative body acted also as the supreme court of *justice*, whether in the last resort or in cases where otherwise it would have been difficult to bring offenders to justice.

§ 19. The issues involved in the dispute over the composition

of the Anglo-Saxon Witenagemot are simple compared to those The Curia of the Norman and Planta- genet Kings.
which have been raised in connection with the Council of
William I and his successors. Dr. Stubbs has taught us to
believe that the 'plan of the Conqueror was simply to dovetail
a feudal superstructure into the fundamental framework of the
Anglo-Saxon polity.'[1] Thus in pursuance of this plan, while on [1] Preface to *Bened. Abbas.* II. lii-liii.
the one side he perpetuated, among other institutions, the old
English Witenagemot with its qualification of official wisdom;
on the other side he added as a condition of membership the
new feudal status of tenure-in-chief of the Crown. As a result,
the king was able to exercise so much choice among his
tenants-in-chief as is implied in the formula that while all
members of the Witenagemot were tenants-in-chief of the
Crown, all such tenants were not entitled to be numbered
among the Witan. In other words, the Witan remained what
they had previously been—an assembly of Magnates. Nor
did this new feudal title entirely overlay the old qualification
of official wisdom; for, the king from time to time introduced
into the assembly other councillors, such as papal legates and
bishops from his foreign dominions, whose only claim to be
present would rest upon the royal summons; while the English
bishops, though endowed with baronies, claimed their seats
by virtue not of their tenure but of their office. Thus the
Council of the Norman Kings can be said no more to have
been based solely upon tenure-in-chief of the Crown than
is the modern House of Lords upon hereditary peerage;
although in each case the qualification mentioned might well
be quoted as the chief characteristic of the greater number of
the members.

But this view has been subjected to considerable criticism.
In the first place it appears that not only is 'Witenagemot'
not a technical term in Anglo-Saxon times, but the only
authority for the continued use of the word Witan after the
Conquest is the old English Chronicle, the compiler of which
would be led by habit and patriotism to keep the old name.
This may perhaps be granted. In the next point the critics
are at variance among themselves, for while one insists that
the Conqueror's Councils were feudal courts of vassals, and [2] Round, *Anti- quary*, x. 143-147.
therefore from the first must have been composed of all his
tenants-in-chief,[2] another lays so much stress on the great

development of Norman feudalism on English soil as to imply that we cannot argue back from the recognized principles of a later period.[1]   But all those who believe in William's intro-duction of feudal ideas seem to be agreed that under William I Curia Regis—the Norman equivalent for the Witenagemot—was a name applied perhaps exclusively to the great courts held, as the Anglo - Saxon Witenagemot had been held, thrice a year at three definite places, that these assemblies were almost entirely engaged in judicial work, and that the Norman king was far too powerful to be hampered by theories of government.   It is probable therefore that the question of the theoretical composition of William I's Council is of no importance, and in any case would not carry us far.

Its com-position.

If, then, we discard the name Witenagemot and all to which it is supposed to bear witness, we may repeat that William seems to have had a Curia or Concilium whose most usual members would be his tenants-in-chief.   They are described vaguely as barones, optimates, proceres, principes, sapientes ; and beyond the actual holders of ministerial offices—the Justiciar, Chancellor, Treasurer, Chamberlain, Steward and Marshal—to whom may perhaps be added the earls and bishops, they must have been an entirely fluctuating body. Henry I is said to have discontinued the three usual courts ; but although meetings became more frequent,[2] the Council remained an intermittent body, and the only real business for which it was convened seems to have been of a judicial character.   The function which we now especially associate with a deliberative assembly is that of legislation with its necessary accompaniments of discussion and dissent. But this is a comparatively modern idea born of the extreme complexity of life which necessitates the constant readjustment of social relations.   To mediaeval administrators legislation consisted mostly of occasional royal ordinances confirma-tory or explanatory of old law or existing custom.   Cir-cumstances might make it advisable to express the assent of the magnates.   Thus William I and Henry I both act ' communi consilio baronum ' ; but the entire absence of any record of discussion justifies us in regarding the expression as a mere form.   But the time came when *commune consilium* or *concilium* (it is perhaps superfluous to point out that in

[1] *F. and M.* i. 41-87.

[2] *S. C.* 81. Will. Malmesb. iii. § 279. *S. C. H.* § 124.

Latin the meaning is the same) came to be not the advice given in common but the assembly which gave it. At any rate, according to the general interpretation, the words are so used in the celebrated fourteenth article of Magna Carta, which ordains that for holding the 'commune consilium regni' for the assessment of scutages and of any aids other than the three aids mentioned in a previous clause, all tenants-in-chief of the Crown shall be summoned in certain specified ways.[1] [1] S. C. 299. The exact value of this clause in determining the name of the deliberative assembly cannot perhaps be estimated. It may have embodied a word already in common use; it may have stereotyped and given legal authority to one out of many expressions by which the fuller sessions of the Curia Regis were described. For we have seen, in speaking of the evolution of the Privy Council, that it is not until the end of the fourteenth century that the executive and deliberative bodies can be said to have fallen apart. Long before that, however, as Magna Carta testifies, the deliberative side of the Curia Regis had gained a form and a name of its own, although as yet there was little distinction of powers between the bodies which were soon to be distinguished as the 'King in his Council' and the 'King in his Council in his Parliament.'

But the question of the composition of the COMMUNE CONCI- The Com-
LIUM cannot be quite so lightly dismissed. It is often supposed mune
that, in accordance with the policy inaugurated by the Conqueror, Concilium.
the Norman and early Plantagenet kings strove to get rid of feudal influences from the Government, among other ways, by swelling the larger meetings of the Curia Regis until the tenants-in-chief of the Crown were swamped in a general assembly of all landowners.[2] This conclusion seems to be scarcely [2] Cf. S. C. H.
warranted by the scanty evidence produced. It is true that in §§ 123-
speaking of the first great instance of such an assembly—that 124, 159.
at Salisbury, in 1086—the old English chronicler made it include 'all the landowning men whosesoever men they were,' but the other accounts, which contain a more precise enumeration of the classes summoned, stopped short at milites, that is tenants by military service though they may have been tenants of mesne lords; where there is absolutely no proof that the assembly was in any way regarded as a Council.[3] Similar [3] Round,
explanations may be given of the assemblies of 1107 and op. cit.

1116, which have been cited in illustration of the same principle. The instances of Henry II's day (1155, 1177) may be regarded as equally fanciful. It may be that 'the accepted usage' under the first Plantagenet king was a council composed of the whole body of tenants-in-chief of the Crown, and that these were held to include socage tenants as well as those holding by tenure of knight service.[1] The descriptions of such assemblies which are given by chroniclers or in royal ordinances either apply an entirely vague term, such as proceres, sapientes, or enumerate the classes called together. These were the archbishops, bishops, abbots, priors, earls and barons. Now, the only one of these classes about whose position there would be the slightest doubt would be the last. The archbishops and bishops would naturally all come as representatives of the Church and of learning, and were for the most part men who had qualified themselves for their present positions by their work as royal officials. The earls would be a small and a definite number; and the official flavour which seems to have hung about them for more than a century after the Conquest, only gradually gave way to the principle of hereditary succession both to the title and to extensive landed possessions, which necessitated their inclusion in any assembly even when they did not hold an administrative post. The term barones would necessarily include all the classes enumerated; but the abbots, priors and barones, who were otherwise undistinguished, were equally liable to a large and constant fluctuation in their numbers. For in neither case was there any official reason — actual or theoretical — for their presence. The abbots and priors were the heads of wealthy landowning corporations: the barones were tenants-in-chief of the Crown by military service. It was no honour to be summoned to the King's Council; for it meant in many cases a long journey, absence from home at a possibly inconvenient time, and demands for an extra grant of money. It is perhaps a result of this extreme unwillingness to respond to the summons of the king that the king's barons or military tenants-in-chief tend soon after the Conquest to fall apart into two classes. Indeed, Dr. Stubbs thinks 'it may fairly be conjectured that the landowners in Domesday who paid their relief to the sheriff, those who held six manors or less, and

[1] *S. C. H.* § 159.

Distinction between majores and minores barones.

those who paid their relief to the king, stood to each other in
the relation of lesser and greater tenants-in-chief.'[1]   But without [1] *S. C. H.*
committing ourselves to the exact dividing force of a possession § 124, note.
of six manors, we may agree with Dr. Gneist[2] that the extent of [2] *Hist.*
landed possessions did from the first form a distinguishing *Eng.*
mark between two classes of tenants-in-chief of the Crown. *Const.*
These are respectively noted in the ' Dialogus de Scaccario,' i. 289.
attributed to Henry II's Treasurer, FitzNeal, as the holders of
baronies *majores seu minores* ;[3] but the distinction is like that [3] *S. C.* 227.
between felony and trespass in mediaeval law, one to be drawn *Dialog. de*
rather from its results upon the individual than from any exact *Scacc.* 134.
reason for the original distinction.   Thus the holders of the
greater baronies, called by Magna Carta *majores barones*, appear
to have dealt directly with the Exchequer in all their feudal
payments ; whereas the others, whom Magna Carta merely
describes as *omnes illos qui de nobis tenent in capite*, were in the
first instance amenable to the local sheriff.   The distinction
may have been based upon an original difference of responsibility in the matter of the feudal levy : but the general vagueness of the means of definition makes it appear as if the Crown
purposely left a broad border line between the two classes, so
that a number of persons might be placed in one category or
the other according to the convenience of the moment.   Nor
did the directions of Magna Carta immediately clear the
ground.[4]   The Greater Barons, who included the archbishops, [4] *S. C.* 299.
bishops, abbots and earls, were to be summoned to the § 14.
Commune Concilium individually ; ' all those who hold of us in
chief ' were to be summoned in general by the royal sheriffs
and bailiffs.   The individual summons stamped a man as one
of the greater barons ; the smaller tenants-in-chief would
thankfully regard the general summons as an intimation to
stay away ;[5] in the mind of the greater baron, when his order [5] M'Kechnie,
and perhaps when his country was threatened, one summons 296.
would raise a presumption of similar treatment on the next
occasion.   It might be possible to increase the list of the
' majores barones ' : the time could not be far distant when it
would become impolitic to diminish it.

   It is important to inquire how far the chief powers which Powers of
we associate with Parliament were conceived of as residing the Com-
in this somewhat invertebrate assembly which Magna Carta mune
Concilium :

teaches us to call Commune Concilium. If it is possible to trace any development from the even more invertebrate Courts or Councils of the Norman kings, it might be said that such development consisted not so much in the extension of the form of the assembly as in the greater reality and frequency of its action. This, however, must be cautiously expressed. Certainly the kings seem to have consulted their Council on nearly every point, whether it was a definite matter of home or foreign policy, or the state of the kingdom in general. Nor was such (1) *consultation* necessarily a mere form. Normans and early Plantagenets were in a sense equally despotic, and the king would only submit such things as he chose to the consideration of the general Council. Thus there is an almost entire absence of any opposition to or remonstrance against the royal will. A few such cases are indeed recorded, but they seem to have been completely disregarded. Perhaps a more effectual influence over the king was found in the presence of the archbishop, and, especially in secular matters, of the justiciar. At any rate, John writhed under the homilies of Geoffrey Fitz Peter, whom nevertheless he did not venture to dismiss.

(1) counsel.

With this knowledge of both the extent and the limitations of the royal authority, we shall not be surprised to find that in legislation and taxation alike the theoretical power of the Council fell far short of that which it practically exercised; though in moments the practice strove to conform to the theory. Much of the (2) *legislation*, whether in the form of Norman Charters or in that of Plantagenet Assizes, was really of the nature of edicts, declaratory and temporary both in form and force. Yet the kings did not hesitate to claim the advice and assent of their Council. The Grand Assize is set on foot; the Assizes of Clarendon (1166), Northampton (1176), and Woodstock (1184), are all equally issued with the assent or at the advice of the great men of the kingdom. But the amount of real meaning contained in such expressions may be measured by the single recorded instance of initiatory legislation. The Assize of Measures in 1197 was enacted by petition and advice of the bishops and barons. Thus, no doubt, much of this assent to legislation must have been merely formal; but Dr. Stubbs reminds us[1] that if it

(2) legislation.

[1] *S. C. H.* § 160.

had been more of a reality, it would, like much of the judicial power, have become a monopoly in the hands of the barons and their representatives; whereas the real exercise of the legislative power was not taken out of the hands of the king until the people and the barons were united in a common cause.

That some form of application in the matter of (3) *taxation* was observed by the Norman kings seems probable, both from Henry I's description of a certain aid as that 'which my barons gave me,' and from the engagement contained in the Order for the holding of the Courts of the Hundred and the Shire,[1] that in the future he would summon the Courts when his royal needs required it, which may be interpreted as a concession on the part of the king to the necessity of popular consultation. The amount of meaning in these forms may be judged from the usual expression of the chroniclers with regard to Henry II and his sons, that the king *took* a tax. It is true that under John a slight change of form is to be observed. In 1200, John 'demanded' an aid from the whole kingdom;[2] in 1204, a scutage of two-and-a-half marks from each knight's fee is said to have been granted to the king;[3] in 1207 he came to an agreement with his bishops and abbots as to the amount of an ecclesiastical grant, but it is immediately added in the case of the laity that the king 'determined' that every one should give him a thirteenth part of their possessions.[4] This last, indeed, expresses John's real attitude in the matter, and the more constitutional expressions must probably 'be interpreted of the mere payment of the money.'[5] Here at all events there is opposition to the Crown, but it is based throughout on the feudal idea of a voluntary aid from the tenant to relieve the lord's necessities. The result of individual opposition was that important questions were not fought upon their merits, and their solution was thereby delayed. The objection was based upon quibbling grounds—the rights of a class, as when Bishop Hugh of Lincoln refused his assent to a grant for the maintenance of 300 knights, on the plea that the lands of *his* church were bound to render military service in England alone[6]—or the promise of the individual, as when Archbishop Geoffrey of York, in 1201, and again in 1207, resisted the levy of a

(3) taxation.

[1] S. C. 104.

[2] *Ibid.* 272. Rad. Cogges.

[3] *Ibid.* 273. Matt. Par. 209.

[4] *Ibid.* 273. Ann. Waverl.

[5] S. C. H. § 161.

1198.

[6] S. C. 256. V. M. S. Hugonis.

carucage on the plea that *he* had not promised it.   A more hopeful sign of advance is the occasional remonstrance of a class.   Thus, in 1194, the Canons of York refused the fourth part of their moveables for King Richard's ransom ; while in Archbishop Geoffrey's resistance to the carucage he was the mouthpiece of the whole body of prelates.   This change of attitude was doubtless due to the spread of the incidence of taxation from land to moveable goods, from real to personal property ; and it brings in its train the idea that taxation and representation go hand in hand.   But the legal definition lagged here, as usual, behind the actual fact ; for the twelfth article of Magna Carta makes no provision for the levy of a tax on moveables by consent of those who are called on to pay.

1194.

1207.

The last power of the Commune Concilium to be noticed is its function as a (4) *Court of Justice*.   As a matter of historical development this was the earliest and for some time by far the most important work in which the assembled barons took part. We have seen that the formal Curia of the Norman kings met thrice a year, chiefly for judicial work.   But Henry II made the Curia Regis a tribunal of ordinary resort, so that the fuller meetings which answered to the Commune Concilium of the Charter may have been primarily concerned with more strictly political duties.   But this was merely a matter of convenience. The king was as yet scarcely conceived of as the fountain of justice in the meaning of the later law.   In the Curia Regis, no less than in the local courts, the suitors were the judges ; that is, it was the duty of the barones who attended to find the judgement at the king's request.[1]   Thus, however much power might be delegated to bodies, whether temporary, like the itinerant justices, or permanent, like the Courts de Banco and Coram rege, yet there remained a reserve of equitable power to the king and his Sapientes, the representatives of the Anglo-Saxon Witan, the Commune Concilium of the Charter.   It is for taxation that Magna Carta insists that they shall be consulted.   Perhaps it was superfluous to insist upon the judicial functions of the tenants-in-chief of the Crown.   Thus we may agree with a recent author that 'the real fountain of justice was the Commune Concilium Regni,' which afterwards became (as we shall have occasion to notice) 'the King in his Council in his Parliament.'[2]

(4) justice.

[1] *P. and M.* i. 135-136.

[2] Pike, *House of Lords*, 28, note.

§ 20. With the sealing of the Great Charter opens the chief Origin of Parliament, 1215-1295. transitional period in the history of the English Legislature. It is necessary to deal with the constitutional history of the next eighty years more chronologically, and at times in greater detail. From the preceding account of the Commune Concilium two important points should stand out clearly—first, the early and growing separation of the tenants-in-chief into two classes; and further, the indistinct line as yet drawn between the various aspects of the Curia Regis. At the same time it must be borne in mind with reference to the Charter itself, that, while its real importance lay in the fact that it was the outcome of the first national movement in English history,[1] *the provision made in it for the maintenance of national rights was one based on merely feudal considerations.* The *results* of this were most important on the future development of the national assembly. For, in the first place, while the king, or rather the regents under Henry III, no longer summoned any other than tenants-in-chief to the Commune Concilium, the (*a*) minor tenants-in-chief interpreted the general summons to which alone they were henceforth constitutionally entitled, as an intimation that their presence was no longer desired. At the same time the king endeavoured to get rid of baronial dictation by surrounding himself with a body of foreign kinsmen and dependants. The most selfish instincts of the *Majores Barones* were immediately called into play, and their objects were narrowed down to the simple endeavour to get rid of the foreigners who were monopolizing the posts which the barons regarded as peculiarly their own. Thus (*b*) all the early schemes of constitutional reform were oligarchical in character. The king was gradually driven to look elsewhere for support. On the enforced banishment of the foreigners he turned for help to the lesser barons and the shire courts, indignant equally with himself, though for very different reasons, at the oligarchical character of the Government. But a very short experience showed them that Henry was using his new friends merely to recover his own lost power, which would be exercised in the recall of his old allies and foreign friends. This finally provoked the more statesmanlike among the greater barons to put themselves at the head of a party which in a very real sense represented the feeling of the whole nation.

[1] M'Kechnie, 148.

Results of the Great Charter.

K

Prepara-
tion for
Parlia-
ment.

1215-1237.

1238-1265.

1265-1295.

1295-1334.

The time which lies between the passing of the Charter and the completion of a national organization may be divided into four fairly distinct periods.   During the first of these the general interest centres in the struggles with the foreigners ; and the constitutional advance, though interesting and noteworthy, lies below the surface.   The second period contains the schemes of baronial reform, ending in Simon de Montfort's celebrated contribution to the system of national organization.   To this succeed thirty years, during the greater part of which a series of royal experiments culminates in the determination of the elements of which all future Parliaments should be composed.   Then for the next forty years the various classes were trying their strength against each other, with the result that they formed themselves into the two modern Houses of Lords and Commons.

1215-1237.

Divorce of
the minores
barones
from the
Commune
Concilium.

The constitutional interest of the first period lies in two directions.   In the first place, there must be noted the *growing separation between the greater and lesser tenants-in-chief.* This was immediately due to the arrangement of Magna Carta and to the natural burden of attendance, which would weigh all the more heavily on the smaller tenants, now that they found their presence regarded as superfluous.   Meanwhile, the energies of the *minores* were being drawn in another and a more fruitful direction.   We have seen that the important point in the tenure of land was not the status of the holder so much as the performances of services from the land.   Thus many tenants-in-chief, in the acquisition of new estates, became sub-tenants holding of mesne lords.   At the same time alienations, mortgages, and other complications to which the Crusades had given rise, had so split up the old estates and altered their boundaries, that grades of rank, at least among the smaller freeholders, had largely disappeared.   When, therefore, the increased activity of the shire courts which marked the early years of Henry III's reign, threw together the smaller tenants-in-chief of the Crown and the knightly tenants of the greater barons, the two found no difficulty in concerted action.   Their interests were chiefly local in opposition to the more purely class interests of the greater barons ; and the holding of a tenant by knight service would tend to be the same in extent whether he held directly of the Crown or from a mesne lord.

Nor is it without significance for our purpose to note that this increased activity of the shire court was due to the *frequent occupation of the local bodies with matters of taxation.* The assessment and collection of the sums granted by the Commune Concilium were the business of the shire courts ; and the knights appointed for these purposes were habitually *fewer in number* than those who were called into co-operation with the royal officials for judicial business.   Thus, in 1220, two knights were to be elected in each shire to collect a carucage ;[1] in 1225, four knights from each hundred assess and collect a fifteenth on personal property ;[2] in 1232, knights of no specified number assist in the assessment of a fortieth ;[3] in 1237, four knights, for whose appointment no provision is made, take a share in receiving assessments towards a thirtieth from a representative body of each vill.[4] This restriction of number in the persons locally employed, doubtless both suggested the idea of collecting the local assessors into a single body and rendered it possible of fulfilment.   Thus it is not astonishing to find that, when a new central *representative* assembly was called in 1254, the object was to gain its assent to a grant of money.

It is important to trace the growth of the idea of representation by election.   After the Norman Conquest, the feudal theory, which had been foreshadowed in English police arrangements of responsibility, regarded the lord as representing his vassals ; and only on this supposition can the curious expression in a writ of 1237 be explained, that the lords made the grant of a thirtieth 'on behalf of themselves and their villans.'[5]   It is, however, in the jury system that the combination may be gradually traced between the two ideas of representation and election.   The first step in this direction was taken by the Conqueror and his successor in their use of (1) the system of local representatives to gather information.   Henry II extended the system to (2) ascertain the rights and liabilities, judicial and financial, of his subjects through the co-operation of the local courts : while under Richard I these representatives (3) were elected and not merely nominated, as seems to have been the practice in his father's days.   Instances of the whole process will be found in a detailed description of the growth of the jury system.[6]   Curiously enough John was the first to (4)

Activity of the minores barones in local government.

[1] *S. C.* 352.

[2] *Ibid.* 335.

[3] *Ibid.* 361.

[4] *Ibid.* 367.

Union of representation and election.

[5] *S. C.* 366.

[6] Chap. vii.

1213.   summon a representative assembly. In August, 1213, the
king assembled through the sheriffs the reeve and four men
from each vill on the royal demesne to a Council at
[1] *S. C.* 276. St. Albans,[1] for the purpose of assessing the amount of com-
Matt.
Paris, 239.   pensation which he owed to the bishops who at the papal
bidding had excommunicated him, and whose goods had been
confiscated for their pains. Three months later, at a Council
1213.   called to Oxford, but of whose assembly there is no proof,
the counties also through the sheriffs were for the first time
summoned to send four discreet men to speak with the king
[2] *Ibid.* 287. concerning the business of the kingdom.[2]

The effect of these examples was not reassuring. Already,
in 1207, John had violated the practice of his father and his
brother by making no use of a representative local body for
[3] *Ibid.* 283. the assessment of the thirteenth exacted in that year.[3] Magna
Carta took no notice of the representative principle in its
provisions for the grant of taxation, though it extended the
system of election from the jury of presentment to the juries
[4] *Ibid.* 299. used in three of the possessory assizes,[4] a concession which
§ 18.   seems to have been withdrawn in the second re-issue of the
[5] *Ibid.* 345. Carter early in the following reign.[5] But these lapses from
§ 13.   the principle of representation were only momentary. Recognition had been gained of the three ideas which culminated in
the modern Parliament, namely, Representation, Election and
Concentration in a central assembly. Stress of circumstances
in the ensuing period caused the gradual and complete
establishment of these three elements in the modern system
of representative government.

1238-1265.   With 1238 begin the *schemes of baronial reform.* For the
ensuing twenty years these schemes may be said to be characterized by three features or, more correctly, the baronial
demands took three forms. Following the example of earlier
occasions (1218, 1223, 1224) the barons sought from the
Attempted   king or his ministers (i) a *reconfirmation of the Charters* in
reforms
of the   return for a grant of money. In 1253 this was done with such
majores   solemnity that a sentence of excommunication was issued
barones.   against all transgressors ;[6] while in 1254 the demand, coupled
[6] *Ibid.* 373. with the refusal of the bishops and barons to be responsible
for the willingness of the smaller folk to contribute, caused the
Queen and Earl Richard of Cornwall, regents during the king's

absence in Gascony, to repeat the experiment which had proved
abortive in 1213.   The sheriffs were directed to send up to
a Council at Westminster two knights chosen by the county, who
should declare the amount of the aid which their electors were
willing to grant.[1]   A more questionable demand was for (ii) the   [1] *S. C.* 376.
election of the three great officers of state by the Commune Concilium.   But this it was scarcely likely that the king would grant,
and certainly not advisable that the barons should enjoy.   The
demand, however, was not made altogether in vain.   In 1237 the   1237.
barons rejected the indirect hold over the government which
would have followed the control of public expenditure offered
to them by Henry's minister, William of Raleigh.   They either
regarded it as a subtle attempt to raise money more regularly,
or were too stupid to be contented with anything short of a
definite placing of the Crown in commission.   The immediate
effect seems to have been that the Crown was ready to accede
to their utmost desire ; for in 1238 Henry was only prevented
by the refusal of his brother Richard from agreeing to abide
by the decisions of chosen ministers for general reforms.   In
1244 the prelates and barons nominated a committee of twelve   1244.
to place their demands before the king, chief among which was
one for the appointment of ministers.   As the struggle grew
intense this demand became more frequent (1248, 1249, 1255);
and, not satisfied with an attempt to monopolize the central
administration, the barons aimed at securing the appointment of the sheriffs, through whom the king was able to
make his influence penetrate into distant parts of the country.
The most significant and practical demand of the barons
during these twenty years was for (iii) the *regular summons*
to a "Parliament."   The word itself seems to have been
introduced in the course of the struggle, and the chronicler,
Matthew Paris, is accredited with its first use in 1246 for
a general assembly of the legislative body.[2]   The feeling seems   [2] *Ibid.* 328.
to have been growing, that piecemeal representation of the   Matt.
nation in casual assemblies convoked only at the pleasure of   Paris, 696.
the king, was probably accountable for the weakness of the
opposition to the Crown.   The expression of this feeling at
first took the form of refusal to act from want of complete
powers.   Thus in 1253 the clergy used the absence of the
archbishops as an excuse for not deciding in an awkward

matter.   Already in 1249, and again in 1255, the barons, for analogous reasons, assumed a similar passive attitude.

Yet it was very slowly that the barons found their way to the right solution, despite the example of the regents in 1254. For when, in **1258**, the king was compelled by the difficulties arising out of his promises to the Pope, to put himself into the hands of the barons, there was no thought of the extension, so as to include a wider range of persons, of that oligarchical body which had already proved its incompetence to grapple with questions of government.   At the first Parliament in that year, a committee of twenty-four, chosen equally from the Royal Council and the barons, drew up an elaborate *scheme of provisional government*, which came into existence at a second meeting held at Oxford in June of the same year and known to subsequent ages as the Mad Parliament.   Here a list of grievances was presented by the barons,[1] and the scheme called the Provisions of Oxford [2] was ratified.   By this, no less than four committees were appointed, one of which, however, was merely to treat of a temporary money grant.   Of the other three, the first was a committee of twenty-four chosen from either side by an elaborate process of double election, whose work should be the appointment of great officers of State and the redress of grievances.   A standing Council of fifteen was further appointed for the king ; and finally, in order to lessen the troublesome duty of attendance in Parliament, a third committee of twelve was appointed who should meet the Council of fifteen thrice a year as representatives of the nation.   It is not necessary to criticize the scheme at length. It would be hypercritical to note that the powers of the two permanent committees were not accurately defined, and that no provision was made for the filling of vacancies or for the cessation of the scheme.   It is sufficient to point out that, while professing to leave to the king his authority constitutionally restrained, and pretending to represent the nation at large, in reality the scheme placed the executive in the hands of an oligarchy of barons in whose quarrels there was no mediating authority.   It was to the interest of no one except the members of the several committees, that such a method of government should be retained ; and it was not long before their mutual jealousies brought it to an end.

Provisions of Oxford.

[1] *S. C.* 382-387.
[2] *Ibid.* 387-396.

Meanwhile, we must look in another direction for the solution of the problem. It was perhaps the action of the regents in summoning representatives from the shire courts in 1254, that emboldened a body, calling itself the *Communitas Bacheleriae Angliae*,[1] i.e. the knights who found themselves by the action of the barons definitely shut out from the Commune Concilium, to address a remonstrance to Prince, or as contemporaries would have called him, the Lord[2] Edward in October, 1259.[3] This had an immediate result in the Provisions of Westminster,[4] by which remedies were promised for most of the complaints mentioned in the petition of the previous year. Far more important is the fact that it was probably the initiative taken by the knights in this matter which, on the renewal of the quarrel in 1261, suggested to the barons the advisability of summoning three knights from each shire south of the Trent to the autumn Parliament at St. Albans. The king made a similar bid for popular support by summoning the same three to Windsor;[5] but there is no record that either Council was ever held. Three years later Simon de Montfort had won the battle of Lewes, and had taken the burden of government upon his shoulders. In June, 1264, he called together his first Parliament, to which, acting on the precedent of 1254, he had summoned four elected knights as representatives of each shire.[6] They were not, however, given a voice in the formation of the *scheme of government* which followed. This was a matter for the initiated alone. Three electors were, according to one reading, to be chosen by the barons; according to another explanation, self-appointed. These should receive authority from the king to choose nine councillors, of whom three should in turn be always at the Court. All business of State should be done by their advice, and disputes should be decided by a two-thirds majority of either the Council or the three electors; and finally, provision was made for the filling up or the removal of members of the Council.[7] The exact effect of this constitution is a matter of considerable dispute. All writers compare it with the elaborate committees of 1258. On the one side Dr. Pearson[8] and M. Bémont regard its tendency as more oligarchical than that of the arrangements of six years before. 'The constitution of 1258,' says M. Bémont, 'gave all the power to Parliament (i.e. the representatives of the baronial

Simon de Montfort's scheme of government.

[1] *E. H. R.* xvii. 89. Davis, *Eng. under Norm. and Angev.* 453.

[2] Tout, *Edward I,* 12.

[3] *S. C.* 332. Ann. Burton.

[4] *Ibid.* 400-405.

[5] *S. C.* 405.

[6] *Ibid.* 412.

[7] *Ibid.* 413.

[8] *Hist. of Eng.* ii. 252.

[1] *S. de. Montfort,* 217.

party); that of 1264 placed all the authority in the hands of three electors.'[1]   As against this view, Dr. Stubbs and Mr. Prothero maintain that Simon's provision is a distinct development of the scheme of 1258.   'The provisions of 1258 restricted,' says the former, 'the constitution of 1264 extended

[2] *S. C. H.* § 177.

the limits of parliament.'[2]   Mr. Prothero even holds that the three electors resembled the modern Prime Minister, because, once elected, they were dependent on the will of the *Communitas,* in which were included the knights of the shire.[3]

[3] *S. de Montfort,* 289-293. Simon de Montfort's Parliament. 1265.

In January, **1265,** Simon gathered his second Parliament. It was here that the great constitutional advance was made with which his name is especially connected ; for to this assembly were called not only two knights from each shire, but also, practically for the first time, two citizens or burgesses from twenty-one cities or boroughs mentioned individually by

[4] *S.C.* 415.

name.[4]   It is for this reason that *Simon de Montfort has been styled the creator of the House of Commons.*   He is, however, scarcely entitled to the name.   For, in the first place, a very cursory glance at its composition will show that the assembly was merely a parliamentary representation of Simon's own supporters.   Thus, of the barons, who as a body were unfavourable to his cause, only five earls and eighteen barons were summoned ; while of the clergy, who were his staunch supporters, there was a very full and disproportionate number. Again, with regard to Simon's own particular contribution to the making of the national assembly, the representation of the towns was avowedly due to their support of Simon ; and the writ for election was addressed to the mayor of an individual specified town, not to the sheriff for a general representation of all worthy towns in his shire.   And, further, Simon's merit as a great constitution-maker disappears altogether in the serious doubt whether this Parliament of representatives was intended to be permanent.   Indeed, M. Bémont is of opinion that its only object was to sanction the scheme of government established in the previous year, and he points out that, in the

[5] *S. de Montfort,* 231.
[6] *Ibid.* 180.
[7] *Mid. Ages,* ii. 43.

writs of summons for the following June, only prelates and greater barons are summoned and there is no mention of the commons.[5]   Thus, while denying to Simon de Montfort the proud title of 'creator of the House of Commons,' we need not minimize his work by suggesting with Pauli [6] or Hallam [7] that he

borrowed his ideas from Aragon, or with Milman [1] that he was
indebted to Frederick II's Sicilian Constitution, or with a later
writer [2] that he made use of his experience in Gascony. However far we are prepared to go in opposition to his claims, we
may at least believe that his real merit lay in the fact that he
was the clever adapter of existing materials; and—even more
important—that, although a foreigner, he worked from thoroughly
English bases.

From their leading feature the ensuing thirty years may
be styled the period of *attempts at the gradual formation of
a National Council.* Certainly the death of Simon at Evesham
was followed by a pause: for the rest of Henry III's reign
nothing was done in the direction which the example of the
great leader seemed to have indicated. But his work had not
gone by unheeded, and fortunately it was left for a king who
was also a statesman to perfect it. In 1273, even before
Edward's return from Palestine, his regents summoned to
a convention for taking the oath of allegiance not only the
prelates and barons, but also four knights from each shire
and four citizens from each city.[3] This may have been done
in order to ensure the support of the entire nation, doubly
important owing to the prolonged absence of an uncrowned
king; but whatever the reason, the imitation and elaboration of
the assembly harmonized entirely with Edward's own designs.
Of his first Parliament no writs of summons are extant:
but the preamble to its most important enactment describes
it as made, not only by the usual classes of the barons,
but also by 'the community of the realm thither summoned.'[4]
From this mode of expression Dr. Stubbs thinks it 'almost
certain that some representatives of the commons must have
been present.'[5] For the next twenty years Edward seems
to be conducting a series of experiments with the object of
determining in what proportions the various classes, which the
events of the last reign had stereotyped, would most suitably
combine. Thus—to deal in detail with the most prominent
instances—in 1283 he called two representative bodies. In
January, acting on the analogy of the clerical Convocation,
he called two provincial Councils at York and Northampton
respectively. The magnates were absent with the king in
Wales, and the Councils consisted solely of four knights from

[1] *Lat. Christ.* Bk. x. ch. 3.
[2] *Antiquary,* June and Aug. 1883.
1265-1295.
Edward I's experiments.
1273.
[3] *S. C.* 429. Ann. Winton, 113.
1275.
[4] *Ibid.* 450.
[5] *Ibid.* 449.

each shire and two representatives from each city, borough and
[1] *S. C.* 465. 'villa mercatoria' summoned through the sheriff.[1]   To these
were added members of the clergy ; for, the archbishops were
directed to summon through the bishops the heads of the
[2] *Ibid.* 466. various religious houses and proctors of the cathedral clergy.[2]
Judged by the latest standard these Councils were imperfect
bodies ; for, besides the absence of the barons, there were no
representatives of the parochial clergy, and most important of
all in the prospect of future imitation was the fact that it was
not one national assembly.   Later in the same year (September,
1283) was called one body known as the Parliament of
Shrewsbury, or of Acton Burnell, to which, besides the barons,
came two knights for each shire and two representatives from
each of twenty-one cities and boroughs specified by name
and summoned, therefore, not through the sheriff, but by writs
addressed to their own mayors or bailiffs.   The two meetings
of January had been called to make a grant.   This assembly
was brought together chiefly to give national sanction to the
condemnation of the Welsh Prince David.   Consequently
the clergy were entirely left out, and such legislation as there
[3] *Ibid.*
467-468. was seems to have been submitted to the baronage alone.[3]
In **1290**, after the barons had passed the important statute
Quia Emptores, they were reinforced by two or three knights
from each shire for the purpose of a money grant ; but no
[4] *Ibid.*
477-478. representatives were called from the towns or the lower clergy.[4]
In **1294** the parliamentary representation of the clergy was
completed ; for in September of that year the clergy were
summoned, though separately, yet to one assembly embracing
representatives from both provinces.   Thus, besides the bishops
and a large number of abbots, there came deans of cathedrals
and archdeacons in person, and of cathedral chapters one, and
of the parochial clergy two proctors from each diocese summoned through the bishops.   The importance of this assembly
lies in the acknowledgement which it carried with it of the
[5] *Ibid.* 480. need of clerical consent by representatives to taxation.[5]   In
October of the same year came another maimed lay assembly,
[6] *Ibid.* 481. the magnates and four knights from each shire ;[6] but in
1295 for the first time all these various ingredients were
added together in their completest form to make what has
been known to after-ages as the *Model Parliament.*   To this

assembly came the archbishops and bishops, three heads of
religious orders, sixty-seven abbots, seven earls, forty-one
barons, two knights from each of thirty-seven shires and representatives from each of 110 cities and boroughs throughout
the kingdom, a body of rather more than 400 persons.[1]

But although it may be true that, starting from this date,
'a perfect representation of the three Estates was secured,
and a Parliament constituted on the model of which every
succeeding assembly bearing that name was formed,'[2] it was
nearly forty years before the form was really complete.   Mr.
Freeman has shown how purely accidental was the formation of the English Parliament into two chambers rather than
into three or four.[3]   Edward I had in his mind an assembly of
three Estates.   This seems to have been the common form
of which variations are found in the development towards self-
government of nearly every European nation.   'An assembly
of Estates,' says Dr. Stubbs, 'is an organized collection, made
by representation or otherwise, of the several orders, states or
conditions of men, who are recognized as possessing political
power.'[4]   But in England the three theoretical Estates of
clergy, lords and commons never had a chance of combination.
The lower clergy persisted in their attitude of aloofness ; the
knights hovered between the barons and the burgesses.   It
took forty years for those concerned to discover that the clergy
could well be left to their own devices, and that the real
interest of the knights lay in union rather with the burgesses
than with the barons.   At first the various Estates—barons,
knights, burgesses and lower clergy — when they came, sat
each by itself, probably in different parts of Westminster
Hall, and voted its money separately and in different proportions.   But the terms of the grant were of most importance to
the represented and the poorer Estates, who moreover had
been called to Parliament solely for that purpose.   It is not
wonderful, then, that they soon acquired the privilege of
settling the amount of money grants, and the lords acquiesced
in their exercise of this power, as did the king in the abstention of the clergy, because they perceived it was to their own
advantage.   That the separation of the Estates into the two
bodies of lords and commons is not unconnected with the
acquisition of the monopoly in taxation by the latter, would

[1] *S. C.*
484-487.
1295-1334.

[2] *Ibid.* 483.
Change of
Estates
into
Houses.

[3] *Essays,*
4th Series,
442.

[4] *S. C. H.*
§ 185.

appear from the fact that, although Hallam is inclined to date such separation as early as 1315,[1] the first distinct record of a separate session is not found till **1332**, while two years later the various proportional grants of the different Estates, which had settled into an uniform rate of one-fifteenth and one-tenth, became a fixed sum of close upon £40,000.[2]

§ 21. But for the present we must follow the fortunes of the members of the old Commune Concilium. The organization of this body on a feudal model had, as we have seen, been sanctioned by Magna Carta for purposes of taxation. But this was the very duty for which Edward I had formed a Parliament of the three Estates. Meanwhile, the Commune Concilium had acquired a firmer hold on the regulation of every department of government; for, the minority of Henry III had thrown the whole supervision of the administration into its hands, while the most prominent barons would necessarily be members of the Council of Regency. The magnates then, like the clergy, had a corporate existence in a recognized assembly with more or less definite rights, before Edward I placed at their side, and bade them share the most important of their powers with, the representatives of the commons. And not only was it unlikely that they would surrender this position without a struggle; but in the end, although they had to share with the Commons the powers of legislation and general deliberation as well as the first won power of taxation, their descendant—the House of Lords—retains to this day the power of a Court of Justice, which it has never shared with the Commons, but which has descended to it from the days before Edward called the latter to the National Council. The immediate point, then, is the *gradual transformation of the Commune Concilium into the* HOUSE OF LORDS; and we may leave to another chapter the history of the gradual growth of the powers of the House of Commons until the old constituents of the Commune Concilium had become the 'Other House,' or, to use the phraseology of modern political science, a Second Chamber. It may shortly be premised that the distinction between the Commune Concilium and the House of Lords is to be found in the gradual growth and ultimate triumph of the hereditary principle.

The first point, then, which calls for notice is the means by which this hereditary character was generally established. We

have seen that it is idle to discuss the original qualification of
the membership of the Curia Regis. The king summoned
whom he would : except in the case of a very few men of
political ambition, the desire would be rather to evade the
summons than to demand it. But Magna Carta countenances
the idea that in theory the king was to a certain extent bound
by the acts of his tenants-in-chief of all grades, and the king
himself frequently mentions the advice of his barones. Now
the term Baron included all the higher ranks of the feudal
hierarchy, all the majores barones, as well as many others of
less exalted rank ; so that we may accept the definition which
makes it 'perfectly clear that until the end of the reign of
Henry III, at any rate, a Baron was a person holding lands of
the Crown and owing military service to the King.'[1] Not for
a long time yet, apparently not even by the middle of the
fifteenth century, did the term Baron become a title of dignity.
The earls and the holders of other titles as they arose, were in
all documents accorded their special rank : the baron if he
had been knighted, was designated as 'chivaler.' It would be
true to describe him with the author just quoted as 'a person
whose status . . . rendered him liable to military and parliamentary service.'[2] In course of time the liability, as far as
parliamentary service went, became a privilege ; but until that
period was nearly reached it is unprofitable, even if it were
possible, to inquire *whether tenure by barony of itself ever conferred a right to a writ of summons.* Most of the barones
would have asked whether their tenure did render them liable
to the receipt of such a writ, and they caught at the constitutional arrangements sanctioned by the Charter, which after
all may have been largely their own work, as affording them an
excuse for staying away.[3]

But we need not underrate the effect of tenure by barony
upon the development of the House of Lords. In several
directions and until quite recent days we can trace the lasting
influence of rights and claims arising from the idea. A resolution of the House of Lords in 1640, forbade the *surrender
of a barony to the Crown*[4] by grant, fine or any other conveyance, and in 1678 this was clenched by a decision in
a particular case adverse to a surrender by the process of
suffering a fine. The lord's right to prevent a surrender of

(1) Tenure by barony.

[1] Pike, *House of Lords*, 89.

[2] *Ibid.* 95.

[3] See M'Kechnie, 296.

Permanent effects of claims from tenure.

[4] *Complete Peerage*, by G. E. C. i. 293-294. Pike, 269-273.

a dignity to the Crown has been questioned by a recent writer

[1] Pike, 272.

of authority,[1] but there is no doubt about the validity of another resolution passed in 1641 which forbade the *transference of any peerage* from one person to another—a practice which had been occasionally allowed by the Crown.   The only possible foundation for these practices of transference and surrender is to be sought in the continuance of the idea of barony by tenure.   To the same influence must be attributed the power which the heiress of a barony possessed, of *conveying to her husband, although a commoner, a right to the reception of a summons.*[2]   And 'although some royal act of summons, or creation, or both, was necessary to complete the status, the usage was not materially broken down until the system of creation with limitation to heirs male was established.'   Indeed, until an adverse decision in 1580, it was even held that a *tenant by the curtesy of England,* as this right was styled, could retain his seat after his wife's death and, consequently, to the exclusion of his eldest son.

[2] *Complete Peerage,* i. 392-393. Pike, 103-107.

Their late survival.

But it is only within recent memory that the parliamentary claims of barony by tenure have been definitely rejected.   It was not altogether unknown as the basis of a claim to sit in the House of Lords;[3] but it seems to have been allowed as valid in the case of the earldom of Arundel alone, though it was also certainly implied in the descent of the famous Berkeley peerage during the Tudor period.[4]   The early opinions on the question were of doubtful meaning, based on expediency and not on law.   Thus an Order in Council of 1669 definitely took this standpoint: even the judges who were consulted on the case of the barony of Fitzwalter thought that baronies by tenure 'were not fit to be revived,' because they 'had been discontinued many years.'[5]   The conclusions of the Lords' Committee on the dignity of a Peer early in this century were a mere re-echo of this opinion: it was only 'change of circumstances' which had abrogated 'the right of any person to claim to be a lord of Parliament by reason of tenure.'[6]   The matter was finally settled by the judgement of the House of Lords in the case of the Berkeley peerage in 1861, in which claims resting on two striking instances of a devolution of the title were peremptorily disallowed.   There is no need to exaggerate the importance of this decision; but it may be

[3] Pike, 80-81.

[4] *Complete Peerage,* i. 321.

1669.

[5] Cf. Pike, 129-130.

1819.

[6] *Report,* ii. 241.

pointed out that an extensive allowance of this claim, coupled
as it must be with the freedom of alienation characteristic of
the modern land laws, would enable a subject to transfer the
peerage to a stranger, and to 'compel the unwilling sovereign
to receive the homage of a peer so created.'[1]

There is, then, no need to underrate or to ignore the influence of baronies by tenure.   At the same time, the solution
of the question of the general advance towards an hereditary
peerage must be sought in other directions.   It has been seen
that practically it was the *reception of a special writ of summons*
from the king which placed the recipient among the *majores
barones*; so that in this sense alone it can be truly said that
'that estate was a barony which entitled its owner to such
special summons.'[2]   But though the king could and, as we
have seen, did exercise a very wide discretion in the bestowal
of the writ, there would be a certain number of barons, such
as the earls, from whom it could not well be withheld, and a
certain number of great barons just below that rank, in whose
minds one reception of the summons would easily raise presumption of another.   As a matter of fact, it seems that under
Henry III the king's use of the writ did cause dissatisfaction ;
for in 1255 the magnates refused to grant an aid, since all of
their number had not been summoned in accordance with the
direction of the Charter.   It may be, then, that Edward I was
not so great an innovator as is commonly supposed.   Dr. Stubbs
regards the year 1295—the date of the 'Model Parliament'—
as the point of time from which the regularity of the baronial
summons is held to involve the creation of an hereditary
dignity, and so to distinguish the ancient qualification of barony
by tenure from that of barony by writ.[3]   This is probably too
absolute a statement, though we may be justified in fixing 'the
reign of Edward I as the time when the hereditary parliamentary
baronage began, without rigidly ruling that the king could not
after 1295 lawfully refuse a summons to a man who had been
summoned already.'[4]   What Edward I seems actually to have
done was to select a small number who should constantly
receive the special summons, and thus, as Dr. Stubbs points
out, by implication to have put an end to tenure as the sole
qualification for reception of a writ.   But Edward probably
took a further and more important step in the entire divorce of

[1] Lord
Campbell,
quoted by
Anson,
i. 203-204.

(2) Receipt
of Special
Summons.

[2] *S. C. H.*
§ 189.

[3] *Ibid.*
§ 428.

[4] Freeman,
Essays,
4th Ser.,
454.

tenure and summons.   There is considerable evidence to show
that out of even the diminished numbers whom he called to
Parliament, some owed their seats solely to the reception of a
special writ apart from all possible qualification of baronial
tenure.   Thus Thomas Furnival, who was proved in 1326 not
to hold his lands on baronial tenure, was nevertheless summoned
by special writ from 1295 to 1332.[1]   It is because of these
innovations that *Edward I has been called the creator of the
House of Lords*, as much as he is generally acknowledged to be
the creator of the House of Commons.   As a matter of fact
both titles are misleading.   In Mr. Freeman's clear words, ' he
did not create the first elements of either, which existed long
before, nor did he give either its final shape, which neither
took till afterwards ; but he established both in such a shape
that all later changes may be fairly looked on as merely
changes in detail.'[2]   It was the settlement of the hereditary, or
as Mr. Freeman would have us call it, successive character of
the writs of summons, which brought to the front the question
of the nature of this hereditary succession.   A place in the
House of Lords being hereditary, i.e. passing to a successor,
who, on the death of the present recipient, was entitled to the
writ ?   We have seen that the claim arising from a barony
acquired by alienation and not by inheritance was not altogether
unknown.   But a statute of 1382, which, however, has been
supposed to be merely declaratory of the existing custom, has
been interpreted by a recent writer as determining that ' a writ
of summons conferred a right to be summoned upon the heirs
of the first recipient of the writ if only he had obeyed it and
taken his seat.'[3]   On the other hand it has been held that this
legal doctrine did not come into existence until two centuries
later ; that it grew out of prescriptive rights and struggles for
precedence among those who were regularly summoned, and
that the first case of its legal recognition was that of Thomas
Lord De la Warr in the reign of Elizabeth.[4]   In any case
the doctrine was confirmed by two decisions of the House
of Lords in the reign of Charles II, connected with the
names of Clifton (1673) and Freschville (1677).   But whatever the exact meaning of the statute of 1382, it did not
determine who were the heirs.   In discussions of the question,
when it has arisen, contrary arguments have been adduced

[1] But see
Pike,
235-236.

[2] *Essays*,
4th Ser,
455-456.

[3] Anson, i.
192.

[4] Pike,
114-129.

from the egal analogy of succession to property in land. Chief
Justice Coke in the seventeenth century called the right to
a summons a fee simple; but it has lately been pointed out
that it is rather like 'an estate tail created without words of
limitation and incapable of being barred.'[1] The point is, [1] Anson, i.
that the old baronies by writ were so free that they descended 199.
to all lineal, though apparently not collateral, heirs, and even, Pike, 124.
as we have seen, to heiresses who could transmit to their
husbands the presumptive right to the reception of a writ of
summons.

And so things might have continued but for the discovery (3) Letters
of a new method of creation, *by letters patent*, which limited patent.
the hereditary succession of titles to a stricter course of descent,
and ultimately established in the narrowest and most uncompromising fashion the hereditary character of the House of
Lords. Earls had been so created since the reign of Stephen,[2] [2] Pike, 60.
and the new grades of peerage, introduced by Edward III and
his grandson respectively, of Duke (1373) and Marquess (1386),
together with the slightly later Viscount, were from the very
first subject to this method. The creation took place with
ceremonies in Parliament, and the descent of the title was
generally limited to the heirs male of the recipients. In 1387
the method was employed in the case of a simple baron whose
status was for the first time exalted into a definite rank, and
John de Beauchamp, Baron of Kidderminster, became an 1387.
hereditary Lord of Parliament, 'not in virtue of his lands but
of his dignity.'[3] But it was only from the reign of Henry VI [3] Pike, 109.
that creation by patent gradually superseded the old writ of
summons until, by the time of the Tudors, the use of the
latter had altogether ceased as a means of calling new members
to the House of Lords.

There have been many conjectures as to the exact *object*
of the introduction of this new method of creation. Mr.
Freeman thinks[4] that 'one motive was to assert the king's [4] *Essays*,
power of free summons in another shape, after baronies by 4th Ser.,
writ had fully become hereditary,' since by the terms of the 461.
patent the grant could be limited to the lifetime of the recipient
or to succession in any specified line of his descendants.
From a slightly different point of view it has been regarded
as dictated by the desire to limit the peerage in the direct

line of descent; while from the side of the baronage it was encouraged as entirely and finally removing out of the power of the Crown the control of the issue of the summons to the hereditary successors of previous recipients.   The real advantage of the new process was that it simplified all questions relating to disputed titles, since they could mostly be solved by reference to the original patent; while its most important result was that it completed the hereditary character of the House of Lords, defined its limits as an Estate of the realm, and exchanged the old claim of the barons to represent the Commune Concilium for the more modern position of an 'Other House' theoretically equal to the representative body in its powers, but with an inevitable tendency towards the legislative dependence of a Second Chamber.

Life peerages.

It has just been said that one of the advantages of creation by patent has been thought to have been the power which it gave of restricting the rights of peerage to the shortest available time—the period of the life of the grantee.   But Dr. Stubbs believes that 'it is not probable that the Crown ever contemplated the creation, by such single summons, of a barony for life only,' and he conclusively explains away the single or irregular appearance of a considerable number of persons who are recorded among the barons summoned to Parliament from 1295 to 1485.[1]   This seems sufficient refutation of the admissions of lawyers, the conclusions of the Lords' Committee in 1819, and the contention of Mr. Freeman, as to the undisputed right of the Crown in this matter.   'The ancient right of the Crown to create peers for life, never abolished, never seriously questioned,'[2] disappears into the limbo of historic fancies when it is remembered that such questions could not arise until the reception of a writ of summons had grown into a prescriptive right, and that, since that rather vague date, there is no authenticated instance of such a creation.   The apparent exceptions to this rule in the case of peers fall into two classes:[3] they are either grants of higher rank in the peerage, such as that of the dukedom of Exeter to Thomas Beaufort in 1416, or grants of baronies with an express provision that the holder should not sit in Parliament.   Such were the creation of the baronies of Hay in 1606 and (perhaps) of Reede in 1644; and of course the limitation must have been expressed

[1] *S. C. H.* § 428, and note on *Prynne's list.* Cf. also Pike, 376.

[2] *Essays,* 4th Ser., 473.

[3] For instances, see *Complete Peerage,* viii. 94-95.

in the accompanying patent. The creation of peeresses for life under the later Stuart and the Hanoverian sovereigns need only be mentioned in order to omit no point in this particular subject.[1] In the middle of the nineteenth century an attempt was made at the revival, as it was thought, of this ancient prerogative of the Crown. In 1856 Sir James Parke was by patent created Lord Wensleydale for life, and a special clause was inserted entitling him to a writ of summons to the House of Lords. Now, it had been settled by the Lords in two cases under Charles II, that the reception of a writ of summons, if followed by the taking of the seat, constituted an hereditary peerage. It was for this reason that Lord Wensleydale, a son-less man, had been created by letters patent. But the Lords refused altogether to receive him. It was acknowledged that the Crown could create life peerages by patent: the compara-tively recent cases of Lords Hay and Reede, just noticed, seemed to leave no doubt in the matter; but for four hundred years there was no instance of a new life peer in the House of Lords; and if it were lawful to act upon precedents, doubtful at the best and drawn from early stages of the constitution, it would be as much within the competence of the Crown to go behind the Reform Bill and to revive the power undoubtedly once exercised, of issuing writs to unrepresented places, as to change the constitution of the House of Lords by the creation of life peers who should have seats in that assembly.[2]

Now it is necessary at this point to note that, from its earliest existence and except for two short moments in that existence, the House of Lords has contained a number of members who do not owe their position to any hereditary right at all. Until the Reformation the House of Lords contained, in addition to the lay barons, two archbishops, nineteen bishops, a number of abbots, a few priors, and the heads of the religious military orders, namely, the Prior of the Hospital of St. John of Jerusalem in England and, until the dissolution of the Order, the Master of the Knights of the Temple. None of these under any circumstances could claim to sit in Parliament by virtue of hereditary succession. It is, however, necessary to inquire whether they all owed their presence to a similar qualification. Dr. Stubbs has taught us that although as a counterpoise to the lay barons William I endowed the bishops

[1] For instances, see *Complete Peerage*, vi. 474-475. 1856.

[2] Erskine May, i. 295-298.

The Spiritual Estate in Parliament.

Qualifica-tion of the Spiritual Lords.

with baronies, yet 'the bishops and abbots still attended in

[1] *S. C. H.*
§ 123.

[2] *S. C.*
162-163.
Lib. ix. c. 1.

[3] *S. C. H.*
§ 123, note.

[4] Pike, 156.

with baronies, yet 'the bishops and abbots still attended in
virtue of their *official wisdom*,'[1] as they had attended in the
Witenagemot before the Norman Conquest. This position
has, however, been emphatically denied. It is true that
Glanvill, writing after the compact of 1107 between Henry I
and Anselm, allows that while bishops-elect before consecration
are accustomed to do homage, yet an already consecrated
bishop does not do homage for his barony to a new king, but
only takes an oath of fealty.[2] It is true also that the writ of
summons to a council required the presence of a bishop 'on
his faith and love' (fide et dilectione) instead of the 'faith and
homage' (fide et homagio) of the temporal baron. But the
summons of the guardian of the spiritualities of a diocese
during the vacancy of a see which has been quoted in favour
of the official title of the bishop, is surely an argument in the
contrary direction ; for neither the guardian of the spiritualities
nor the vicar-general who might represent an absent bishop,
was the bishop himself; while it has been pointed out that,
from the time of Edward I, when the king required the bishops
as individual advisers, he summoned them as individuals ;
but when he required the assent of the clergy to taxation,
the summons, with the addition of the 'praemunientes' clause
demanding the presence of the lower clergy, was issued alike to
bishops, vicars-general and guardians of spiritualities. With
regard to the abbots and priors Dr. Stubbs himself acknowledges that only 'those who held baronies were summoned,'
and that consequently 'the question is more complicated than
that of the bishops.'[3] On the other hand, to a recent writer
'it is quite clear that they were rightly summoned to Parliament
only because they *held by barony*, and that if they did not
hold by barony, they could claim to be excused as late as the
reign of Edward III.'[4] The same writer goes on to show
that during the fourteenth century, the bishops and abbots,
who must be classed together and indeed were comprehensively described as 'praelati,' not only enjoyed several of the
privileges of peerage but, on one remarkable occasion—the
appeals in Parliament of the Lords Appellant in 1386—claimed
their right, as 'holding of the Lord the King by barony,' to
take part with the other Peers of the Realm in all the business
of Parliament and, since the Canons of the Church forbade

them to take part in the business before Parliament at that moment, they protested that they retired ' saving always the right of our peerage.' But whatever their claims, the spiritual lords could not hold the same position as the lords temporal ; for, since a bishop could be translated from one see to another he could not even be said to hold his lands for life ; he could not of course transmit the lands, much less the dignity, to an heir, and his own punishment for treason or felony had no effect upon the succession to his possessions and office.

But despite the entirely different position, it does not seem impossible that the spiritual lords would have obtained all the privileges which the complete status of peerage carried with it, had it not been for the Canons of the Church and their own obstinate adherence to clerical immunities. The former forbade them to remain when questions of life or limb were under judgement : the latter made them refuse to claim trial by peers when they would have been entitled to it, on the principle that one secular court was as incompetent as another to try churchmen. Even while the prelates themselves were absent from trials of peers, there is evidence both in actual fact and in legal theory that they could be efficiently represented by a proctor acting on their behalf.[1] Moreover, so long as he sat in Parliament, the Prior of the Knights of St. John of Jerusalem enjoyed every privilege of peerage ; while the inferior position in which the spiritual lords generally acquiesced is marked by two utterances from the early years of Henry VIII. The judges decided that a Parliament might be held without any spiritual lords at all ;[2] while, in letters patent issued to the Abbot of Tavistock whose predecessors had once come to Parliament, the king declared the recipient, both in his own person and in that of his successors, to be a Lord of Parliament equally whether he attended or he availed himself of a special provision for occasional absence. And the claims of the spiritual lords to peerage, had they ever desired to repeat them, became more difficult with each succeeding year. The one point common to the spiritual and temporal lords was tenure by barony, and this was rapidly giving way as a title to ' the status of peerage.' For once, then, the lawyers may be taken to have spoken historically when they asserted that the spiritual lords were Lords of Parliament by virtue not of their

Reasons why the spiritual lords did not obtain privileges of peerage.

[1] Pike, 206-218.

[2] Pike, 327.

[1] Cf. Pike, 165-327.

nobility but 'of the ancient baronies annexed to their dignities.'[1]   Moreover, the Reformation changed the whole relative
position of the spiritual and temporal members of the House
of Lords.   The desire of the abbots to escape attendance in
Parliament had resulted in a decline of their numbers from
about sixty under the first two Edwards to an average of
twenty-seven under their successors.   But even so the spiritual
lords were as numerous as the temporal lords.

Position
of the
spiritual
estate in
Parliament
since the
Reforma-
tion.

The dissolution of the monasteries raised the question whether
the summons to the abbots was, like that to the bishops, founded
on their individual or their representative position, and the
adoption of the latter alternative at once cut down the spiritual
lords to half their previous number and, even apart from the
new creations of temporal peers by the Tudor monarchs, left
them in a hopeless minority in the House of Lords.   Not
that the numbers of the spiritual hierarchy remained stationary
at the twenty-one archbishops and bishops who still continued
to represent the spiritual Estate in Parliament.   Henry VIII
himself founded five new bishoprics[2] out of the spoils of the
monasteries.   But despite the steady and, in course of time, enormous increase in population, and the grudging recognition given
to any other spiritual organization outside the bounds of the
national church, no other see was formed until that of Ripon
in 1836.   But in the Act providing for the foundation of the
next new see—that of Manchester in 1847—as well as in
subsequent Acts of the same tenor, a clause is inserted to
prohibit the increase of the number of lords spiritual.   There
are at present in England thirty-five bishops, besides a number
of suffragan bishops, who are spiritually but not officially equal
to diocesan bishops, and have therefore never been eligible for
a seat.   Of this number, the holders of the Sees of Canterbury,
York, London, Durham and Winchester are, by virtue of
their bishoprics, entitled at once to a writ of summons: the
other thirty supply the twenty-one remaining seats in order
of seniority.   To these were to be added from the Act
of Union with Ireland to the disestablishment of the Irish
Church, one archbishop and three bishops of the Irish Church,
all those of each class sitting in rotation for a single session.

[2] Oxford, Peter-borough, Chester, Gloucester, Bristol.

1800-1869.

Abstention
of the

But Edward I had desired that the spiritual Estate should
have a more thorough parliamentary representation than it

lower clergy from Parliament.

could get by the presence merely of its ecclesiastical leaders. We have seen that in 1294 he called representatives of both the cathedral and the parochial clergy to a separate assembly of the spiritual Estate, and that in 1295 he placed them alongside of the two lay Estates. But the clergy, as an Estate, altogether refused to acquiesce in his plans. They already had their own assembly in Convocation, in which they had met for the last seventy years. Now, each archiepiscopal province had its own Convocation, which contained not only the ecclesiastical hierarchy, but also a full representation of the cathedral and parochial clergy. The system of representation in each was slightly different, and mutual jealousies prevented any amalgamation; but it was in Convocation that the clergy were taxed by the Pope and that, with the Papal sanction 'and of their own free will,' they voted their tenths to the king. For this double provincial representation of the clergy Edward wished to substitute one national representation in Parliament; while his outlawry of the clergy in 1296 showed his determination that they should not escape their share of the national burdens. Thus the point for settlement was the assembly in which the clergy should vote their money. On the one hand, the king's desire to carry out his scheme led to the temporary insertion, in the writs to the archbishops, of a special clause 1311-1340. beyond the usual 'praemunientes' clause, enjoining on the fathers of the Church to compel the attendance of representatives from their flocks. But, on the other hand, the clergy voted their grant of money as regularly and at the same time as the other Estates, and at the rate, namely one-tenth, which was paid by the wealthier portion of the community. Consequently, the king was not disposed to complain, and the clergy continued to vote their grant in Convocation until the reign of Charles II, when, by a mere verbal agreement 1664. between Lord Chancellor Clarendon and Archbishop Sheldon, the right of separate clerical taxation, which had become only a form, was surrendered, and the clergy in return took their place among the constituencies of the House of Commons.

But it must be carefully noticed that the clergy did not The lower clergy in Parliament. stand altogether apart from Parliament. For, the higher clergy of course took their place as lords spiritual among the peers; while the special clause added to the writs seems to have produced an occasional response.   Two noteworthy instances occur as a result of Edward II's bid for popular favour against his cousin, Thomas of Lancaster, and the baronage.   Under Richard II, again, there are proofs that clerical proctors occasionally attended the Commons.   Such at least was the position

of Sir Thomas Percy in the Parliament of September, 1397, and such is probably the explanation of the presence of Sir Thomas Haxey in the January Parliament of the same year.

These instances are, after all, but a slight qualification of the general attitude of abstention from Parliament on the part of the spiritual Estate.   And this abstention had important *results.*   For in the first place, as early as the reign of Edward III and onwards to the Reformation, frequent attacks were made upon the Church in the Commons, which their presence would undoubtedly have averted or mollified. Again, under Richard II, in acknowledgement of the attitude which they had taken up, the form of summons to the clergy through the archbishops was slightly changed.   Hitherto they had been called like the Commons, 'ad faciendum et consentiendum.'   Since 1340 there had been temporary alterations, but the form, which has been continued to the present day, became fixed to 'ad consentiendum' alone—a function which could be adequately discharged by absence.   Meanwhile, the clergy had lost the legal right to representation among the Commons ; for one of the earliest recorded cases of interference on the part of the Commons in the election to membership of

their body, is that of Alexander Nowell, of whom a Committee of the Commons reported that, being a prebendary of West-

minster, and so a voter for Convocation, he could not be a member of that House.[1]

§ 22.   We have now examined the qualifications for members of the baronial estate until the earlier methods were absorbed in the general method of creation by letters patent accompanied by a writ of summons.   The hereditary lay members of the House of Lords owe their seats to this double qualification. A writ, once complied with, of itself creates an hereditary title ; the issue of letters patent alone does not entitle to a seat within the House : for infant peers or peeresses in their own right, and even dowager peeresses so long as they remain widows, have all the privileges of their order apart from any

question of a seat in the House of Lords. Thus there may
be peers who are not Lords of Parliament, and it has been
shown that there are Lords of Parliament who are not peers.
But this distinction was the result of a gradual development.
In tracing this development it will be necessary first to mark
the chief steps in the growth of the idea of peerage among the
lay barons, and then to show the means by which the idea was
enforced.

Several passages of the Leges Henrici Primi [1] show us [1] e.g.
that judgement by a man's peers or legal equals was an old S. C. 106.
established principle of English law. Thus a baron would be xxxi. 7.
judged by other barones and not by sub-vassals. But as the Cf. also
administration of the law fell more into the hands of profes- Leg. Hen.
sional judges, many of whom were not of baronial rank, the xxxii.,
barons demanded a more explicit statement of the principle, xxxiii.
and obtained it in the celebrated clause of Magna Carta,[2] [2] S. C. 301.
which forbids a free man to be molested 'nisi per legale judi- § 39.
cium parium suorum vel per legem terrae.' That this had
nothing to do, as is commonly supposed, with trial by jury
will be abundantly clear from the reflection that the business
of the jury is not and never has been to judge, but to find
a verdict. In the expression 'judicium parium' the barons
were practically objecting to judgement by the king's judges
and amercement by the barons of the Exchequer.[3] The same [3] M'Kechnie,
spirit is visible in the demand of the barons in 1233, that 347.
Richard, the Earl Marshal, who had been declared a traitor
by an assembly of the king's partisans and officials, should
have the judgement of his peers, to which Peter des Roches
responded not so much 'contemptuously and with a perverse
misinterpretation of the English law,'[4] as in allusion to the [4] S. C. H.
practice of the royal court, that in England there were no peers § 173.
in the French sense and that the king's justices were the
peers of any man.[5] 'The very title of the "barons" of the [5] M'Kechnie,
Exchequer,' says a writer of authority,[6] 'forbids us to treat 453.
this as mere insolence.' But the barons were striving after [6] P. and M.
more than they were ever destined to get. So long as the i. 393.
court held 'coram rege' was not a separate Court of King's
Bench, but merely a professional committee, which could at
any moment be swollen into a body co-extensive with the
Commune Concilium, no baron could well take exception to

its judgements: but the Exchequer was growing into a law-court and its barons into professional lawyers; and, although this did not come about until long after Magna Carta, yet we may acquiesce in the opinion that the judicium parium 'expresses a claim by the barons for a tribunal of men of baronial rank which shall try even the civil causes in which barons are concerned.'[1] On this point the king never gave way, and, although in a few minor points of procedure the barons were accorded certain privileges, their civil rights, like those of the ordinary freemen, were subject to the decisions of royal judges. But in all charges which could be prosecuted by appeal—treason or felony—and which consequently involved the forfeiture or escheat of land, the barons could with reason demand judgement of their peers.[2] Bracton himself tentatively suggests that since, in cases of treason, judgement by the king or his justices would make the Crown both prosecutor and judge, the cause should be judged by the peers of the accused baron.[3] It has been pointed out that we must not confuse this judgement by peers with the trial of a later date; for, according to the mediaeval method, judgement preceded trial and the trial itself in cases of treason consisted of the ordeal of duellum or battle.[4] Appeal and the resulting battle continued to be lawful modes of judicial procedure until 1819; but appeals in Parliament were abolished in the first year of Henry IV, probably in consequence of the abuse to which they had been put in the quarrels of his predecessor's reign.[5]

But by that time the term Peers, arrogated to their own class by the barons, was obtaining an increasingly exclusive meaning. Thus in 1322 it was 'the Peers of the Land, Earls and Barons' by whose judgement the Despencers were to be banished, and in 1330 Mortimer was adjudged by 'the Earls and Barons as Peers and Judges of Parliament' on the mere notoriety of his misdeeds, to die the death of a traitor. At the same time the Peers took occasion to protest that they were not bound to sit in judgement upon 'others than their equals.' Again, in 1341 a committee of Peers, Bishops and 'Sages of the Law' was appointed (not, as is usually asserted, in connection with the quarrel between Archbishop Stratford and the king[6]) to consider the whole question of judgement by

[1] *P. and M.* i. 152, note.

[2] M'Kechnie, 455.

[3] 119-119 b, quoted by Pike, 173.

[4] Pike, 174, M'Kechnie, 456.

1 Hen. IV. c. 14.

[5] Holdsworth, 189.

1322.

1330.

1341.

[6] Cf. details in Pike, 186-195.

Peers.   The report was to the effect that 'Peers of the Realm
ought not to be arraigned or brought to judgement but in
Parliament and by their Peers,' and despite the dissent of the
legal members of the committee it was embodied in a statute.
The Act, however, was annulled by the king and Council,
and shortly after repealed by a more subservient Parliament.
Thus not only was nothing settled with regard to judgement
by Peers, but in 1387 the Lords seemed to abandon the position 1387.
taken up in 1330, since they claimed as an ancient privilege for
the Lords of Parliament the right of judging, with the king's
assent, crimes against the State in the person of Peers of the
Realm or of others.   They proceeded to carry this into effect
when they overruled the decision of the Judges as to the illegality
of the appeals of the Lords Appellant against five advisers of
Richard II, of whom two were commoners.   This revocation of
their narrow judicial claims did not carry any further consequences with it; for with the introduction of the method of
impeachment by the Commons, the abolition of appeals in
Parliament, and the institution of the Court of the Lord High
Steward, the judgement of the peers became a trial in the [1] Pike,
modern sense, and provision was made for the conviction of chap. x.
all State offenders as well as of the Peers themselves.[1]   *passim.*

But the right of trial by peers was a symptom rather than The doc-
a cause of the establishment of the status of peerage.   For the trine of
cause we must look rather to the development of the *doctrine of* blood.
ennobled blood stigmatized by one great writer as 'historically
a mere absurdity,'[2] but pronounced by another to be not only [2] *S. C. H.*
'no absurdity at all, but one which is perfectly intelligible, § 430, note.
perfectly consistent with itself at all points, and as scientific as Freeman,
anything to be found in mediaeval or even modern literature.'[3] *Essays*,
For it was the outcome of that connection between tenure 4th Ser.
of land and political or official privilege which was of the 464.
essence of feudalism.   Thus until the reign of Henry VIII the [3] Pike,
tenant in fee simple transmitted to his descendants through 141.
his blood 'a capacity of inheritance' which he could only
destroy by conveying away the land in his own lifetime and
thus injuring himself as well as his heirs.   As a natural result,
a conviction for felony or treason corrupted the blood of the
offender, and not only caused forfeiture of any lands which
he had, but also rendered him and consequently his heirs

incapable of inheriting any lands to which they might have a title. But however consistent or scientific the doctrine may have been in its origin, in course of time it became as irrational as feudalism itself. For, the breach between tenure of land and political duty soon began. The statute *De Donis* which permitted entail of lands, left the tenant in tail a mere tenant for life, whose treason could not affect the title of his heirs ; and, although an Act of Henry VIII subjected estates tail like other estates to forfeiture for high treason, yet practically by that time the House of Lords was formed, and the *coup de grace* seemed to be given to the old claims of the blood heirs by another Act of the same reign which endowed the tenant in fee simple with the power within certain limits of disposing of his lands by will. Moreover, dignities could be entailed as well as and apart from lands, though this was a prerogative of the Crown ; and, as in the case of lands after the Act of Henry VIII cited above, while attainder for felony only affected the blood of the individual, a conviction for treason corrupted the blood of the whole family of the offender and deprived him and his heirs of all possession and claims whether of lands or dignities, and on whatever tenure they were held. But until the Restoration it was still possible to maintain in theory that there was a connection between tenure of land and political duty and privilege as expressed by membership of the House of Lords. When, however, tenure by military service was abolished,[1] the two qualifications even in theory parted company. But meanwhile the doctrine of ennobled blood had become so firmly engrafted in the idea of peerage that not only did it outlast the abolition of the feudal tenure to which it owed its birth, but in the years immediately following the Restoration the circumstances under which it could be claimed were still further defined by decisions of the House of Lords. We have seen that to the original method of special summons from the Crown was added, in process of time, the creation of new titles by letters patent. Since this double qualification became common, the House of Lords, by a series of decisions on disputed claims to membership of the House, has gradually concentrated the claims of privilege of peerage in the hands of its lay and hereditary members. Although at moments these decisions seem to aim at the

---

1285.

26 Hen. VIII. c. 13, s. 5.

32 Hen. VIII. c. 1.

[1] Robertson, 2.

limitation of the royal prerogative in the creation of peers, their real object was to assert for the existing members of the House the right analogous to that exercised by the Commons as judges in the validity of elections of members of their own assembly. Thus the House of Lords has at various times laid it down, on the one side, that a documentary record of compliance with a writ of summons constitutes an hereditary peerage; while, on the other side, a peerage cannot be alienated or surrendered to the Crown except by forfeiture for treason; and, going a step further, that the mere issue of letters patent does not confer a title to a seat in the House.

But there was one important class of members whose title to a seat was untouched by any of these decisions. The presence of the archbishops and bishops and, in a less complete sense, of the abbots was coeval with the very existence of the assembly to which they belonged. But the growth of the hereditary principle could not affect them directly; and, so long as they formed the majority of the House, the doctrine of ennobled blood could not in any comprehensive sense become a basis for claims of peerage. But we have seen that their privileges as churchmen were so much more present to the minds of the ecclesiastical members than their rights as peers, that they ceased to urge these latter claims at all. And when the Reformation left the spiritual lords in a hopeless and constantly increasing minority in the House, the lay lords used their advantage of numbers to pass a resolution in 1592 simply denying to the bishops the status of peerage. But this did not prevent the appointment of a committee in 1661, on the restoration of the bishops to the House of Lords, 'to consider of an order in the standing order of this House which mentions the lords, the bishops, to be only Lords of Parliament and not peers, whereas several Acts of Parliament mention them to be peers.' The decision of the Committee does not appear; but the bishops had long ago missed their chance. The chief privilege which they had lost was that of trial by the House of Lords. Yet no one questioned their right to take part in a vote on a bill of attainder, while among the valid Constitutions of Clarendon was one which relaxed the Canon law in allowing them to share in all judicial proceedings up to a point which might involve the decision of a mortal sentence.[1]

Its effect on the status of the spiritual lords in Parliament.

1592.

1661.

[1] *S. C.* 139. § 11.

But the lay lords can perhaps scarcely be blamed for carrying the now firmly established doctrine of ennobled blood to a logical conclusion when, in the impeachment of Danby in 1679, they tried to prevent the bishops from taking part even in the preliminary stages of the trial.

1679.

Effect of the Unions of Scotland and Ireland on the House of Lords.

The resolutions by which the House of Lords defined the status of peerage were by no means adequate to the conditions of the case after the successive unions of the Parliaments of Scotland (1707) and of Ireland (1800) with the English Parliament. The conditions of the two cases, so far as they affected their own peerages, were slightly different. The Scotch peers meet in obedience to a proclamation and elect sixteen representatives of their number, who receive no special summons, but whose election is certified by a return made by the responsible official to the House of Lords: to the Irish peers, on the other hand, on their own application are sent voting papers which they fill up in presence of certain specified local officials, for the election of twenty-eight representatives. Again, the Scotch peers are elected afresh for each successive Parliament, while the Irish peers hold their seats for life. Further, since the Scotch Church was Presbyterian no question arose of representation in the House of Lords: but the Irish Union amalgamated the Churches as well as the Parliaments, and provided that of the four Irish archbishops one, and of the eighteen bishops three, should sit in the House of Lords, not by election but by rotation of sessions, that is, each for a single session according to a definitely prescribed order. Finally, while no provision was made for the necessary retention or extension of the Scotch peerage or for the participation in political life of those peers who were not of the sixteen; in the case of Irish peers the Crown was allowed to create one new peer for every three peerages which became extinct until the number should be reduced to 100, when each extinction of an old title might be supplied by a new creation. Moreover, Irish peers other than the representative peers were allowed to be elected as members of the House of Commons for any constituency of Great Britain, the only disability being that for the time during which any Irish peer so served, his rights and privileges of peerage were entirely in abeyance. Nor was this all. The peerage of Ireland was to be kept at the number of 100 'over and above the number of Irish peers who might be entitled, by descent or creation, to an hereditary seat in the House of Lords of the United Kingdom.'[1] Such a provision was only [1] Pike, possible because, during the century which had elapsed since 366. the union with Scotland, a number of questions affecting the non-representative peers of the incorporated country had been gradually settled. Thus the great disproportion between the number of representative peers and the general body of the Scotch peerage was reduced by the admission of Scotch peers to the peerage of the United Kingdom of Great Britain. For some time the House of Lords offered a strenuous opposition which was met by the elevation of the eldest sons of the Scotch peers to the English peerage, who, in the course of events, succeeded to the Scotch titles of their fathers, but did not thereby vacate their seats in the House of Lords. Finally, 1782. in 1782 the Lords acquiesced in the unanimous opinion of the Judges that the promotion of Scotch peers to the peerage of Great Britain was in no way a contravention of the Act of Union, and all opposition to such creations was withdrawn. Two lesser questions concerned the relations of such peers to the representative peers of Scotland, and it was decided successively,—in 1786, that Scotch representative peers when 1786. raised to the English peerage cease to sit as representatives; and in 1793, that such peers may nevertheless continue to vote 1793. in the election of the representative peers. The only change in the arrangements of the Irish Union has been the dis- appearance from the House of Lords of the representative spiritual lords in consequence of the disestablishment of the Irish Church in 1869. It is important to note the difference 1869. in the probable fate of the Scotch and Irish peerages; for while the latter must of necessity remain at 100, the former will become gradually extinct, or all but its representative members will sit by English titles until the sixteen Scotch representatives, by self-election, if not by actual creation, become hereditary peers of Parliament. At the present moment there are eighty- four peers of Scotland all created before the Union in 1707 : of these fifty-one are peers of the United Kingdom and seventeen have no seat in Parliament. The Irish peerage numbers 176, of whom eighty-five are peers of the United Kingdom and sixty have no seat in Parliament.

Increase
of the
numbers
of the
House of
Lords.

It is interesting, and even not without historical importance, to note the numbers of the House of Lords at various periods. To Edward I's Model Parliament of 1295 there came nine earls and forty-one barons, two archbishops, eighteen bishops, sixty-seven abbots, the Prior of the Hospital of St. John of Jerusalem, and the Masters of the Knights of the Temple and of the Order of Sempringham. Of this number the archbishops and bishops and the Prior of the Knights Hospitallers were alone permanent. As many as 120 abbots and forty priors were summoned at various times, but many of them only appeared once, and under Edward III the normal number sank to twenty-five abbots and a few priors—all generally from the same houses. Yet even so, until the Reformation the number of the prelates was almost invariably slightly in excess of that of the lay barons. At times, under the three Edwards, more than 100 earls and barons are summoned, but their numbers tend to decrease until, under the Lancastrians even with the addition of the holders of the new titles of Duke and Marquis, the lay baronage seldom counts more than fifty members, of whom the simple barons would form a very large proportion. Under Henry VIII not only did the abbots and priors disappear, but the majority in which the lay baronage was now left, was increased by some twenty new creations ; and the growing importance of the status of peerage was marked by an Act regulating the precedence of officers of state and members of the House of Lords. James I began a system of indiscriminate creation of peers, and is reckoned to have added as many as fifty-four new members to the House of Lords, of whom many obtained their titles in return for substantial gifts of money to the Crown. Until the Restoration all peers were in theory tenants-in-chief by knight service of the Crown. The burdens involved in the tenure had long become merely a source of revenue to the king, but their abolition altered the whole character of the peerage, and is considered by some writers to have done away with any claim of the spiritual lords to a seat in Parliament. Henceforth a peerage became even in theory what perhaps it had been for some time in fact, the reward of personal or political service ; while the predominance of the House of Commons after the Revolution brought out the importance of the royal prerogative of creating peers, in producing what may be called a readjustment of the mechanism of the constitution.[1] The result has been an enormous increase in the numbers of the House of Lords. The 139 who were summoned to the Restoration Parliament in 1661 had, by the accession of George I, risen to 168. This gives, however, but a faint idea of the number of peers actually created. Thus the first four Stuart sovereigns called nearly 200 new members to the House of Lords; but since 100 titles in the interval became extinct, their actual addition to the peerage only amounted to 100 members. But it was during the reign of George III, and especially during the administration of the younger Pitt, that the House of Lords was entirely transformed in numbers and character. George III was responsible for 388 new titles, of which 128 were new creations; and of the 388, 140 had been due to Pitt's initiative. Since the Revolution the House of Lords had been regarded as the stronghold of the Whigs, whose political theory opposed to the royal prerogative the divine right of a land-owning oligarchy. Pitt nominated for the honour representatives of all forms of wealth alike—a policy which has been followed by subsequent ministers and has permanently allied the House of Lords with the conservative classes of the country. Finally, by the middle of the nineteenth century the hereditary peers of the United Kingdom had risen to a few short of 400, while at the beginning of the twentieth century their numbers stand at about 500. When to these are added the archbishops and bishops, the representative peers of Scotland and Ireland and the few law lords, the present membership of the House of Lords reaches to about 580.

This vast increase in membership has almost of necessity resulted in a weakening of the sense of political responsibility in individual members of the House of Lords; while the completion of the representative character of the House of Commons has made the body of the electorate increasingly impatient of any check by the hereditary House. Those who do not believe in constitutional cataclysms cling to the necessity of a second chamber. If they are political philosophers, they sketch out an ideal which would create a house of professional and experienced experts, who would

[1] Cf. Bagehot, *Eng. Const.* 229.

Alterations in the House of Lords.

M

prove a far more formidable obstacle to the 'will of the people' than the present hereditary body : if they are practical statesmen, they limit their efforts to proposing modifications of and slight additions to the materials as they already exist. The House of Lords, as we know it, seems, in comparison with the reformed House of Commons, so stable a body that it is difficult to realize that, in ages before our own, modifications in its constituent elements were both carried out and proposed. The *changes actually made* in its membership concerned the spiritual lords. Thus, at the Reformation the abbots and priors were excluded, while for two short moments in the seventeenth century—from the Exclusion Bill of 1642 to the abolition of the House of Lords in 1649, and again from the meeting of Charles II's first Parliament in 1660 to the definite Act of 1661, by which the Exclusion Bill was rescinded—the bishops ceased to be members of the House of Lords. A much longer exclusion from the House was suffered by the Roman Catholic peers. When Elizabeth's oath of supremacy was made compulsory on all members of the House of Commons, 'any temporal person of or above the degree of baron of this realm' was specially exempted, 'forasmuch as the Queen's Majesty is otherwise sufficiently assured of the faith and loyalty of the temporal lords of Her Highness' Court of Parliament.'[1] But in **1678**, in the excitement of the Popish Plot, an Act was passed which extended the requirement of a declaration against Transubstantiation to members of both Houses of Parliament. This caused the exclusion of eighteen Roman Catholic peers. The Act gained the assent of the king as a temporary measure, but it remained on the statute book for a century and a half. In 1791 Catholic peers were restored to their privilege of hereditary councillors of the Crown, but it was not until **1829** that the efforts of Canning and others obtained the repeal of the Test Act, and thus enabled Catholic peers once more to take their seats in the House of Lords.[2]

Among the *attempts to alter the character* of the House of Lords the first place in historical importance is taken by the Peerage Bill of 1719.[3] The jealousy shown by the Whig majority in the House of Lords of any extension of membership of the House, appeared first in its endeavour to prevent

1642-1649.

1660-1661.

5 Eliz. c. 1. sec. 13.

1562.

[1] Prothero, 41. § 14.

30 Chas. II. stat. 2.

31 Geo. III. c. 32.

[2] Robertson, 188.

[3] *Ibid.* 121-123.

e admission of Scotch peers to the peerage of Great Britain,
which would qualify them for an hereditary seat in the House.
But a far greater danger to the Whig majority was the royal
prerogative of creation of peers, which had been used in 1711
to add twelve peers at one stroke to the House, for the purpose
of carrying through the peace with France.   On the accession
of George I the Whigs recovered their ascendency, and in
order to secure it they proposed that, with the exception of
members of the royal family and the case of an extinct
peerage, the peerage of Great Britain should never be increased
by more than six beyond the number at which it then stood.
This barefaced attempt to turn the House of Lords into an
indestructible Whig oligarchy was defeated in the House of
Commons chiefly by the eloquence of Sir Robert Walpole.
Modern politics are familiar with schemes for the reconstruction
of the House of Lords : but apart from the attempts to exclude
the spiritual lords,[1] all of them have for their object the
improvement of its efficiency as a legislative chamber.[2]   It is,
no doubt, peculiarly exasperating to the political party which
claims only a small minority of supporters in the House of
Lords, that measures on which the House of Commons has
spent the better part of a session, should often be thrown out
by the vote of a number of irresponsible persons who at no
other time evince any interest in public affairs.   But it may be
doubted whether an improved legislative second chamber
would not, from its very strength, raise more formidable
questions of practical politics than it had helped to solve.
One thing, however, it might do.   It might open to the young
and ambitious peers a sufficiently attractive field of labour in
the public service to mitigate their loudly expressed desires to
shake off their disabilities and to become eligible for membership of the House of Commons.[3]

§ 23. *The judicial functions of the House of Lords* originated
in the confusion which we have seen originally to have existed
between the 'King-in-his-Council' and the 'King-in-his-Council-
in-Parliament.'   It was in this indeterminate body of Councillors
and Judges that the King exercised both an original jurisdiction, i.e. in the first instance, in criminal charges against
great offenders who were too powerful to be dealt with by
the courts of the sheriff or of the justices in eyre ;[4] and an

[1] Erskine May, i. 300. Pike, 382.

[2] Pike, 383-386.

[3] Cf. Pike, 277. Also cases of Lords Coleridge and Selborne.

Jurisdiction of the House of Lords.

[4] Holdsworth, 188-189.

equitable jurisdiction in civil cases for which the Courts of Common law would find no remedy.[1]   Here, too, he hear cases which were brought up from the lower courts on writ of error, or in which petitions had been presented to him again the judgements of inferior courts.   But Parliament and Counc finally fell apart in the reign of Richard II ; and while Parlia ment kept a large part of the jurisdiction which it had hitherto exercised, its separation from the Council could not but affec it in certain particulars.   Parliament, however, in the judicia sense, had a limited meaning ; for, the term was applied onl to the Lords of Parliament, the representatives of the ol Commune Concilium which grew into the House of Lord Nor was this all ; for, the judges who had been members of the ' King-in-his-Council-in-Parliament,' were not members of the Parliament of the three estates ; but they were none the les required by writs of attendance to be present and give advic when wanted.   The bishops, too, owing to the Canon law whic forbade them to take part in issues of life and death, wer more and more shut out from a share in this important an peculiar function of the Upper Chamber.   Nor did th Commons ever seriously attempt to share or even to rival th judicial functions of the Lords.   In fact, at a very early perio of their career they definitely repudiated for themselves th exercise of any such powers.   In the first Parliament of Henry IV the condemnation of Richard II's advisers by th Lords was followed by a protest of the Commons to the effec that ' no record may be made in Parliament against th Commons, that they are or will be parties to any judgemen given or to be given hereafter in Parliament.'   To this it wa answered that the king and the Lords have of all time had and shall of right have, the judgements in Parliament.[2]

The jurisdiction, then, left to the House of Lords in it separation from the Council may be distinguished as origina and appellate.   The chief original jurisdiction was in connectio with the practice of *Impeachment*.   There were two method by which, in the thirteenth century, persons could be charge with treason—by an appeal which would be decided by battl or by an indictment or impeachment (the two words were a first indistinguishable), the issue of which would be submitte to the verdict of a jury.

[1] Holdsworth 179.

1399.

[2] *S. C. H.* § 303.
(1) Original jurisdic- tion.

An appeal of treason against a baron or a minister would of Early
necessity be made before the 'King-in-his-Council-in-Parliament,' impeach-
until the use to which such appeals had been put in the late ments.
reign caused their abolition by the first Parliament of Henry IV.
But, meanwhile, treason had for the first time been defined by 25 Ed. III.
statute; Parliament and Council had fallen apart; the Lords c. 2.
of Parliament had reduced the judges to the position of 1352.
assessors, and had asserted for members of their body the
privilege of trial by their peers; while the Commons, through
the medium of taxation and petitions, were acquiring a strong
corporate feeling. It was perhaps as a result of this feeling
that in 1376 the Commons of the Good Parliament impeached 1376.
Richard Lyons and Lord Latimer for malversation before
the Lords. Ten years later they used the same method of 1386.
accusation against the Chancellor, Michael de la Pole, Earl of
Suffolk, while in 1397 they so far seem to have formulated the
procedure in such cases as to protest 'before the king in full
Parliament that they intended by his leave to accuse and
impeach any person or persons, as often as seemed to them
good in the Parliament then sitting,'[1] and this protest was at [1] S. C. H.
their request entered as of record on the Rolls of Parliament. § 266.
This method of attack, then, as developed by the Commons,
was aimed against all offenders in high place, whatever their
social rank. These would not necessarily be peers in the
sense of Lords of Parliament; and the Lords at the outset
very nearly defeated the object of the Commons. For, not
content with claiming that *judicium parium* which was claimed
by every Englishman and was especially secured to them by
Magna Carta, at an early stage in their judicial work they 1330.
solemnly declared that the peers were not bound or charged
to render judgement upon others than peers.[2] In 1387, how- [2] Ibid. § 295.
ever, they claimed for the Lords of Parliament the privilege
of judging, with the king's consent, in the case of any very
high crime touching the king's person and the state of all his
realm, perpetrated by Peers of the Realm *with others*. It was
in accordance with this claim that they were ready to impeach
Richard II's favourite, Sir Nicholas Brembre, if the Lords
Appellant had not already made their appeal against him,
and that they actually impeached some of the royal Judges.[3] [3] Pike,
But the methods of trial of peers were as yet by no 200-202.

means settled. The abolition of appeal in Parliament onl applied to charges of high treason: until 1819 a peer coul be appealed of murder in an inferior court, where he woul

¹ Pike, 217.

be tried without any reference to privileges of peerage.[1] A the same time an indictment for high treason in an inferio court would be removed into Parliament; and here, withou any initiative of the Commons, the effect of the old appea was revived in the power of the Lords themselves to declar and adjudge as traitors members of their own body o others who were threatening to disturb the public peace

Attainder.

Such a declaration, when it obtained the sanction of th other estates of the realm, became an Act of Attainder, an act of the legislature pronouncing condemnation without any form of trial. This was a most useful weapon when evidence was defective or rapid action became necessary. Thus, while

1450.

impeachment was revived for the punishment of Michael de la Pole's grandson, William Duke of Suffolk; as soon as the Wars of the Roses begin, the victorious side employs the subservient Parliament to pass Acts of Attainder against the leaders of the other side. In 1459 the Duke of York had been driven to take refuge in Ireland; a House of Commons was assembled on the nomination of the Lancastrian leaders, and through it was passed an Act of Attainder against the heads of the Yorkist party, based on elaborate charges against their recent conduct. In 1461 came the turn of the Yorkists, and Edward IV's first Parliament passed an Act of Attainder against Henry VI, Queen Margaret and a number of noblemen and prominent commoners of the Lancastrian party. But it was not only at moments of great political excitement that Acts of Attainder were found convenient. The Tudor kings habitually used their subservient Parliaments to destroy political or dynastic opponents by this means.

Power of impeachment secured.

1621.

With the revival of the power of Parliament under the Stuarts impeachments were renewed. But here some discrimination is necessary. The earliest cases usually cited are those of Sir Giles Mompesson, the monopolist, and the Lord Chancellor, Francis Bacon, Viscount St. Albans. But in both instances, although the Commons nominally conducted the case, the real accusers were private persons. On the other hand, it was the Commons themselves who impeached

Cranfield, Lord Middlesex, although they were the unconscious 1624.
tools of a political party; and George Villiers, Duke of 1626.
Buckingham. In fact, throughout the seventeenth century
impeachment formed the chief means of getting rid of
political opponents. The Commons, however, found that
this method of attacking their enemies was not unattended
with difficulties. The king might surrender a minister like
Clarendon, who had outstaid his welcome; but to save Bucking- 1667.
ham he would prorogue or even dissolve any number of 1626-1628.
Parliaments in succession, and he would rescue Danby from
the clutches of the Commons by granting him a pardon 1679.
beforehand, which should reduce to a farce the whole work
of the trial.[1] The Long Parliament not only secured itself [1] Robertson,
by statute against a dissolution without its own consent, but 420.
even borrowed from the Crown the method of attainder;
and in the cases of Strafford (1640) and Laud (1641) they
turned the preliminary impeachments into bills of attainder, to
which they forced the king to give his assent. But apart from
this revolutionary procedure of the Commons, the question
whether an impeachment was ended by the prorogation or
dissolution of Parliament was decided in exactly opposite
ways under Charles II—in the negative in the case of Lord 1678.
Stafford; in the affirmative in 1685, in order to procure the 1685.
release of the 'popish lords.' It was not finally settled until
it was settled in the negative in connection with the case
of Warren Hastings. The last method by which the Crown 1791.
could destroy the work of the Commons in an impeachment was taken away by the clause of the Act of Settlement
which forbade any pardon under the Great Seal of England
to be pleaded to an impeachment by the Commons in
Parliament.[2] Again, in one case under Charles II—that of [2] S. C. 531.
Fitzharris—a new obstacle was suddenly interposed in the 1681.
refusal of the House of Lords to entertain the impeachment
of a commoner. There were so many precedents the other
way, including several in the reign of Charles I, that the
Commons were justified in their resolution, 'that it is the
undoubted right of the Commons in Parliament assembled to
impeach before the Lords in Parliament any peer *or commoner*
for treason or any other crime or misdemeanour, and that the
refusal of the Lords to proceed in Parliament upon such im-

peachment is a denial of justice and a violation of the constitution of Parliaments.'[1] Fitzharris was condemned at common law; but immediately after the Revolution the impeachment of Sir Adam Blair and four other commoners gave the Lords an opportunity for reconsidering their position, and the report of a committee appointed to search for precedents was followed by a resolution of the Lords to proceed with the impeachments.

Since the accession of the Hanoverian dynasty both attainder and impeachment have been occasionally employed. Thus the Jacobite Rebellion of 1715 was followed by the passing of Acts of Attainder against a large number of persons concerned, and although an Attainder has been robbed of half its terrors by a recent Act which removes all disabilities from the heirs of an attainted person, an Act of Attainder might still be employed. On the other hand, it is doubtful whether the substitution of moral for legal sanctions, such as is implied in the appointment of a committee of inquiry, has not rendered the process of impeachment obsolete. The triumph of the Whigs on the death of Anne was followed by the impeachment of the Tory leaders, Oxford, Bolingbroke and Ormond. Since then, however, there have been only three cases of its exercise—the Earl of Macclesfield (1725), Warren Hastings (1791-5), and Lord Melville (1804); but none of these were for political reasons, the first and last being for malversation of the public money, while Warren Hastings was charged with misgovernment in India.

It has been thought that the exercise of any *criminal* jurisdiction of first instance apart from impeachment was forbidden by a well-known Act of Edward III, passed at a time when the King in-Council and in-Parliament were still indistinguishable, which allowed no one to be apprehended on petition or suggestion to the Council without due indictment or presentment. But however much the Lords may have applied this prohibition to themselves in general, their representatives in the Long Parliament did not hesitate to assume a criminal jurisdiction of first instance in several cases with which we should not expect to find them dealing.[2] If this was not an usurpation of authority born of a time of political excitement, it may be that the claim to any such criminal jurisdiction came

[1] Robertson, 420.
Pike, 232.

Decline of impeachment.

1870.

1714.

25 Ed. III. st. 5. c. 4.

Original jurisdiction other than impeachment.

[2] Pike, 283.

to an end when the Lords practically resigned the claim which
for a long time they maintained as a court of first instance in
civil causes.   The formation of the Courts of Common Law, the
growth of the equitable power of Chancery, and the development
of the Star Chamber, left little if any need for the action of the
House of Lords in such cases.   But no definite Statute had
deprived them of a jurisdiction which the King-in-his-Council-
in-Parliament had once possessed, and the Peers of the Restoration attempted to revive it.   In 1668, in answer to a petition 1668.
of the plaintiff, the case of *Skinner* v. *the East India Company*
was referred by the Crown to the Lords, who gave judgement
for Skinner.   The East India Company obtained the interposition of the House of Commons, and the matter was turned
into a quarrel over parliamentary privilege.[1]   The king's [1] Holdsworth,
personal interference was necessary to procure an erasure of 180.
the records of the dispute from the Journals of both Houses; Robertson,
but the victory remained with the Commons; for, by never 217-223.
attempting to revive the jurisdiction in dispute, the Lords have
practically admitted that it is not theirs.

It is as a *Court of Appeal* that the House of Lords has (2) Appel-
kept a prominent position in the judicial system of the country. late juris-
In its relations to the Courts of Common Law it merely carried diction.
on the work of the King-in-his-Council-in-Parliament.   It was
a Court of Error from the King's Bench and from an intermediate Court of Error, the Exchequer Chamber, to which
some matters were taken from King's Bench and Exchequer.
A writ directed the judges of those courts to send the records
of the case in question to the King in Parliament, where with
the assent of the Lords spiritual and temporal any error might
be corrected.   But after the House of Lords had formed itself,
there grew up the equitable jurisdiction of the Chancellor—
perhaps, as much as the House of Lords itself, an offshoot of
the comprehensive body of the King in Council in Parliament.
The question of the relations of Chancery to the House of
Lords does not seem to have arisen before the reign of James I,
when there is recorded the first petition of 'appeal' to the
House of Lords against a decision of the Chancellor.   Hitherto
the contest had been between the Chancery and the Courts of
Common Law, but in this very reign the question was decided
in favour of the Chancery, which, flushed with its lately won

victory, not unnaturally resented the attempt of the House of Lords to reduce it to the subordinate position. The matter came to an issue in the case of *Shirley* v. *Fagg*,[1] when, after a lengthy quarrel due to the interposition of the Commons over a matter of parliamentary privilege, the jurisdiction over appeals from Chancery remained to the House of Lords. Moreover, so long as the Court of Exchequer retained an equitable jurisdiction, an appeal by way of petition lay to the House of Lords from the Equity side of the Court of Exchequer, until in 1841 this jurisdiction was transferred to Chancery. So far as England was concerned, after being momentarily threatened with extinction in the Supreme Court of Judicature Act of 1873, the appellate jurisdiction of the House of Lords was saved by the Supreme Court of Judicature Act, 1875, and was for the first time placed on a statutory basis by the Appellate Jurisdiction Act, 1876. Rules made in pursuance of the Supreme Court of Judicature Act, 1875, by the abolition of proceedings in error, have placed Chancery and the Courts of Common Law on the same footing in intermediate appeals, and for the first time recognized the procedure of an appeal in

common law.[2] At the same time the Appellate Jurisdiction Act, 1876 (§ 4), provided for the bringing of every appeal to the House of Lords by way of petition.[3]

Finally, the Act of 1876 introduced a far greater innovation ; for, it authorized the creation of Lords of Parliament, who were neither peers nor yet possessed of hereditary right. Indeed, as they were first planned, their title to be even Lords of Parliament lasted only so long as they discharged the functions of Lords of Appeal for which they were created. But the two Lords of Appeal, now increased to four, have by a subsequent Act of 1887 been permitted to keep their seats for life. The object of these appointments was to increase the efficiency of

the House in the exercise of its judicial functions, and, although in the hearing of appeals every member of the Lords is entitled to be present and to give his vote,[4] a convention dictated by obvious propriety has left the decision in the hands of those members of the House who are past or present holders of high judicial office.[5]

§ 24. It has been truly remarked that the consolidation of the House of Lords has saved the country from the

curse of a noble caste.[1] For, the English peerage differs [1] Freeman, *Essays*, 4th Ser., 493.
from a foreign nobility in that its *privileges attach to the person* and not to the family. In the eyes of the law the children of a peer are commoners in rank, and whatever privileges he may enjoy belong to him individually and in no way extend to them. For in their origin such privileges were due to the membership of an official class. This carried with it a certain social status not sufficiently marked to make its members into a caste, but enough to justify their claim to certain privileges on the ground that the claimants were all peers. Thus, in asserting the right of *amercement by their peers*, the earls and barons of the thirteenth century were claiming no more than what the practice of the king's courts granted to every freeman. But the practical difficulty in the working of this principle was overcome by the king's assertion of the equality of his barons of the Exchequer for this purpose with the other barons. It was on the same ground of membership of an official class that barons were treated in the king's courts in several small ways on a footing different to that of other suitors, and that in the reign of Edward VI, when the curious privilege of benefit of clergy was limited to those actually in Holy Orders, it was saved as well for peers and lords of Parliament; and even when it was abolished for the clergy in 1827, another Act of 1841 was deemed advisable, which should do away with its special applicability to the case of peers. But most of the privileges of peers have been claimed in connection with membership of the House of Lords. Of these the one preliminary to the enjoyment of all the others is that of the *right to a writ of summons*. This was definitely asserted by a committee of the Lords appointed to consider the refusal of a writ to the Earl of Bristol in the reign of Charles I, 1626. and the assertion marks a complete change from the time when attendance in Parliament was regarded as a burden. As to their other privileges, although the Lords are supposed to hold them from time immemorial, and do not therefore, like the Commons, go through the form of petitioning for them to the Crown, yet many are naturally of the same nature as those which will be dealt with in speaking of the House of Commons. There are, however, considerable differences in details. Thus *freedom from arrest*, except on criminal charges, is claimed by

both Houses; but the Lords have never renounced the extension of that privilege to their servants and followers. The parallel privilege of *not being impleaded in civil actions* was by law gradually reduced and finally withdrawn altogether from members of both Houses. The right of *guarding the constitution of their own assembly* is also common to the two Houses; but while the Lords can refuse to allow a new peer to take his seat, who has not fulfilled the usual conditions, it lies in the power of the Crown to decide in all cases of claims to an old peerage, although, as a matter of fact, such cases are usually referred to the House itself. Again, while it is in the power of both Houses to *commit an individual for contempt* of their orders, the House of Lords can pass sentence for a definite term, nor is the prisoner released on the prorogation of Parliament. *Freedom of speech* is no less important to the Lords than to the Commons; and violations of it, though not so frequent as in the Lower House, have been not altogether unknown. Three special privileges the Lords seem to have enjoyed to themselves. In the first place, every individual peer in his capacity of an hereditary councillor of the Crown has the right of personal *access to the Sovereign.*[1] Secondly, until the Lords waived the right by resolution in 1868, they could, unless the sovereign demanded their personal attendance, give their votes by proxy.[2] This custom dates back perhaps to a time when it was important that the Crown should insure in any shape the assent of the barons individually to the money voted and the laws passed by the Commune Concilium. Thirdly, the peers have frequently exercised a right, which apparently it would be equally open to the Commons to assume, of recording a *protest* against any division on the Journals of the House.[3] Finally, in the case of two more strictly personal privileges, Lords and Commons alike have waived their claim to be exempt from appearing as *witnesses* in a law-court; while, since 1870, the privilege of freedom from the necessity of serving on a *Jury* has been secured to the members of both Houses by Statute.

[1] Pike, 252.

[2] *Ibid.* 243.

[3] *Ibid.* 245.

[N.B. Before the arrangements of 1875-6 the only way of questioning the ruling or decision of a Common Law Court was by alleging error apparent on some part of the record of the proceedings, whereas appeals from Chancery were by way of petition for a rehearing and revision or reversal of the whole or any part of the judgement or decree. The result of the arrangements of 1875-6 is that the House of Lords is now the final Court of Appeal from all the Courts (other than ecclesiastical) of the United Kingdom, while the Judicial Committee of the Privy Council is the final Court of Appeal for the rest of the empire and for the ecclesiastical courts. Of both these courts of final appeal the four Lords of Appeal are the nucleus, afforced in the one case by peers, in the other case by privy councillors who have held high judicial office.

The members of the House of Commons.

§ 25. So far we have traced the growth of the legislative body as a whole up to the completion of the form of the *Model Parliament* in 1295. We have then followed the fortunes of the old Commune Concilium, which it superseded, until the members of that assembly, with more definite, if not with actually new qualifications, gradually passed from feudal tenants-in-chief to peers, and their assembly from the House of Lords to the Other House and so to the Second Chamber. The decadence of the House of Lords involves the rise to power of the House of Commons. And the first question to be answered is, who were THE MEMBERS OF THE HOUSE OF COMMONS? It has been shown already that the Estate of the Commons consisted of two distinct parts—Knights of the Shire, and Citizens and Burgesses. Of the *Knights of the Shire*, there were originally and normally two from each of thirty-seven shires, making a body of seventy-four, permanent in numbers though not in individuals. The omitted shires were Chester and Durham, which were counties palatine, and Monmouth, which formed part of the Welsh Marches. Representatives from Wales were called in 1322, and again in 1327—in the former case consisting of twenty-four from North Wales and an equal number from South Wales, summoned through the Justiciar of Wales; in the latter instance coming only from North Wales, but summoned in a similar manner. Wales, however, obtained no permanent status in Parliament until the reign of Henry VIII. Out of the Welsh Marches he, for the first time, formed the English shire of Monmouth and at least four of the shires of South Wales; and from 1536 onwards he summoned two members from the shire and one

Their number for (1) the shires;

1536.

174

from the borough of Monmouth and one member from each
of the twelve Welsh shires, together with one from each of a
group of towns centring round the county town within each
county.[1] A few years later Chester for the first time sent
two members; and, finally, Charles II included Durham,
both shire and city, in the parliamentary system of the
country. Thus the representatives of the shires remained
until the eighteenth century, when the Union with Scotland
added thirty members for the shires, and the Union with
Ireland sixty-four on a like account.

    The first Reform *Act of* **1832** split up several shires
into electoral districts, and increased the number of shire
representatives in England and Wales by sixty-five. The
Representation of the People *Act of* **1867** added forty-four
members for English and Welsh, and three for Scotch shires;
and, finally, the *Act of* **1884** raised the number for England
and Wales to 253, and fixed it for Scotland at thirty-nine, and
for Ireland, which had been untouched in 1867, at eighty-five.

    The *members for cities and boroughs* exhibit much greater
fluctuation in numbers. Under Edward I representatives from
166 were at one time or another summoned; but although
two from each was the orthodox number, sometimes it varied
between one and two according to the size of the borough.
But immediately, for reasons and by methods to be noted
presently, a decline in the number of represented boroughs
is to be marked. Under Edward II the number represented
altogether was **127**: under Edward III it sank further to
ninety-nine, at which it was arrested by the Act of 1382
forbidding the sheriff to omit any city or borough which had
been wont to send representatives. For the next sixty years
the parliamentary boroughs remained at this number. They
were very unevenly distributed over the country. Thus,
between the reigns of Edward III and Edward VI, the three
shires of Lancashire, Hertfordshire and Rutland sent no
burgesses at all; while sixteen others, including Middlesex,
supplied members from only one borough, and seven others
from only two boroughs in each shire. On the other hand, it
is noteworthy that London, though only required to send two
members, nominated four in order to ensure the attendance of
two; and from 1378 onwards the representation required of

Margin notes:
1 Porritt, i.
104-107.

1543.
1673.

1707.

1800.

Effects of
the Reform
Acts.

(2) the
boroughs.

Immediate
diminution
of the
number.

1382-1445.

London was permanently raised by writ to the higher number. Finally, of the twelve shires not already enumerated, Wiltshire had no less than twelve represented, a number which was increased by subsequent creations; Sussex contained nine boroughs, Devon and Dorset seven, and Somerset and Cornwall six apiece. On the whole, with the doubtful exception of Cornwall, the representation in the fifteenth century may be considered as affording a rough index of the relative wealth of the different parts of the country.[1] Thus for the years following 1382 the borough representatives may be placed at 200 in number.

Hitherto one of the methods by which boroughs had escaped their constitutional liabilities had been through royal charter. Under Henry VI for the first time, commencing from 1445, the king by *royal charter* created new parliamentary boroughs. At first these were perhaps not necessarily so much new as renewed representations. Of Edward I's 166 summoned towns, more than seventy had for one reason or another dropped out of Parliament. Edward II added ten on various occasions, and Edward III's only permanent addition was the Cinque Ports, eight in number and each sending two members. Now, by the new method of charter, Henry VI added eight boroughs to the representation of the country, four of them in the already liberally represented Wilts, and Edward IV imitated him by the creation of four more. It is to the Tudor period that we must look for an extensive use of this method.[2] It seems right to think that Henry VIII's additions, including as they did four or five English towns—of which two were Chester and Berwick—Calais and the Welsh county towns, were made with no sinister motives;[3] but when, of Edward VI's creations, together with ten revivals are found fourteen new creations of which eight were in the royal Duchy of Cornwall, it is clear how powerful a means of influence over the House of Commons the use of this prerogative had placed in the hands of the king. It is, indeed, to be read in connection with the narrowing of the borough constituencies, also effected by charter, which was going on at the same time. Further creations of boroughs, then, may be attributed almost entirely to sinister designs. Mary called into existence ten new boroughs and revived two, but to three of these only one member was given. Elizabeth

[1] *S. C. H.* § 433 notes. Porritt, i. 90-91. Its subsequent increase.

[2] For list of places, see *S. C. H.* § 443 note.

[3] Porritt, i. 373.

was responsible for no less than twenty-four new boroughs and seven revivals, most of them unworthy of representation from the beginning.[1]   Under James I eight new constituencies, including the two Universities, were created by royal charter. It is fair, however, to say that royal charter was not the only method of increasing the number of borough representatives. Some towns sent members in compliance with *special statutes*, and some as a result of a granted *petition for the revival of old rights* of representation.   Indeed, under James I, 'there was a strong tendency to revive such ancient and forgotten rights of representation, and the House of Commons resolved, on May 4, 1624, "that a borough cannot forfeit this liberty of sending members by non-user."'[2]   As a result of this resolution fifteen boroughs regained parliamentary representation under the first two Stuarts.[3]   In one way and another, then, 200 members were added to Parliament between the reigns of Henry VIII and Charles II, the last instance of such addition being the grant of two members by royal charter to the borough of Newark;[4] and at the end of the seventeenth century the representatives of the boroughs were over 400 in number.   The Union with Scotland added fifteen members for the boroughs, and that with Ireland thirty-six on a like account.

The Reform *Act of* 1832 made great changes both in the number and the distribution of the borough seats.   Fifty-six boroughs represented by 111 members were absolutely disfranchised; and thirty were deprived of one member a-piece.   Of these 141, the larger proportion were given to English counties (sixty-five), and to the increase of the representation in the other parts of the British Isles.   The rest were distributed among twenty-two hitherto unrepresented large towns which acquired two members each, and twenty smaller towns which should supply single members to the House of Commons.[5]   By the *Act of* 1867, fifty-two seats were cancelled by partial or total disfranchisement of boroughs, of which only twenty were redistributed among towns in England and Wales, either by the addition of an extra member to, or by the subdivision of already existing constituencies, or lastly by the creation of entirely new parliamentary boroughs.   Finally, the *Act of* 1884 cancelled no less than 160 borough seats, which were redistributed almost entirely

1 Porritt, i. 373-376.

2 Anson, i. 124.

3 Porritt, i. 382.

4 *Ibid.* 392.

5 For names, see Robertson, 197-198.

Effects of the Reform Acts.

N

(for only eight new boroughs were created) among already existing electoral divisions, on the totally new principle, except in certain specified cases, of single-member constituencies based upon an attempt at equal electoral districts. The result in numbers is that English boroughs now claim 227 members, to which eleven are to be added on account of Wales, while Scotch boroughs supply thirty-one and Ireland sixteen to the sum total.

That *sum total of the whole House of Commons* has almost steadily increased. A mediaeval House in the fifteenth century contained about 300 members; by the end of the Tudor times it had been increased to 460; and when the royal methods of addition ceased under Charles II, it stood at 513. The Unions with Scotland and Ireland brought it up to 658, a number which, despite its temporary reduction through the disfranchisement of certain boroughs for corrupt practices, remained unaltered by the First Reform Act of 1832, or the Representation of the People Act of 1867. Finally, the Act of 1884 has slightly increased the total number to 670, of which England claims 465 and Wales 30, while to Scotland were awarded 72, and 103 to Ireland.

§ 26. The new principle of an approximation to equal electoral districts, together with the assimilation of the county and borough franchise, has gone far to obliterate the old *distinction between county and borough members.* It was, of course, originally intended that the two classes should represent different interests, namely, those connected with real and with personal property respectively, in other words, land and merchandise, and to the end of the eighteenth century the distinction was maintained in all kinds of artificial ways.[1] But a fortunate and early assimilation of interests, no less than of classes, brought about a close union between the two bodies of representative members. Nor was this unnatural. In the first place, the representative character was common to both classes of members. The number of the shire representatives was fixed, while that of the boroughs fluctuated largely; but the individuals of both bodies were equally subject to change, and at an early stage it became clear that the only hope of making their influence felt with the king and lords lay in the united action of the Commons. In the next

Marginal notes:

Amalgamation of the county and borough members.

[1] Porritt, i. 502-504.

Reasons.

lace, the interests of shire and borough members alike were
local, as contrasted with the distinctly class interest of the
baronage on the one hand, or on the other, of the two bodies
within their own ranks—namely, the lawyers and the merchants
—which in early parliamentary days threatened to consolidate themselves into separate Estates.   These causes of joint
action were further enhanced by the employment of the
same agency—that of the shire court—for the election of both
classes of representatives.   But the ultimate reason of amalgamation is probably to be found in the fact that, almost
from the outset, the social distinction between the two classes
of knights and burgesses was very slight.   Whatever it may
have been originally, it was very soon bridged over.   Wealthy
merchants purchased freehold property and, as members of
the shire court, became liable to distraint of knighthood :
while, owing to the extreme unwillingness displayed by the
higher class to serve in Parliament, valetti or esquires—that is,
men below knightly rank—were elected to serve as knights of
the shire.   Henry III or Edward I had compelled or dis-
trained all holders of the requisite amount of land, no matter
on what tenure they held it, to take up the duties of knighthood on penalty of a heavy fine.   Their object was probably
in part to ensure, for the purposes of local government, a
sufficient supply of men of knightly rank.   But men so shrank
from the burden of attendance in Parliament, which was then
relieved by no known corresponding advantages, that of the
two alternatives they preferred to incur the fine.   The shire
courts were consequently so far compelled to return men of
lower social rank that in 1325, for example, only twenty-seven
members were men of knighty status.

But the Crown did not accept this change without a protest.
In 1340 the writs demanded the election of two '*belted*'
knights (gladiis cinctos) for the shires ; this demand was repeated
at intervals until, after 1376, it became practically a permanent
description.   Yet at first the effect was small ; and in the Good
Parliament which assembled in response to the last-mentioned
writs, only half of the shire members were knights.   Indeed,
whatever effect there was in the intended direction was due
rather to the social importance conferred on knighthood by
the rise of the spirit of chivalry, and also to the gradually

Qualifica-
tions of (1)
belted
knights for
the Shires ;

increasing political importance of a seat among the Commons.
But in any case the return of the wished-for class was very
partial, and in **1445** the Crown yielded the point on which it

23 Hen. VI.
c. 14.

had tried to insist, by assenting to a Statute which required
for the shires the election of either knights or notable esquires
capable of becoming knights, that is to say, of persons in any
case above the rank of yeomen.   At the same time, an attempt
was made to restrain the choice of the electors ; for, not only

1 Hen. V.
c. 1.

was a Statute of 1413 embodied, which required that the
representative should be a resident within the county or
borough which chose him, but it was now demanded that in

(2) gentle-
men born
for the
Shires ;

the case of the shires the representatives should be '*gentlemen
born.*' [1]   This was a distinct attempt to undermine the constitutional principle, so important in the development of English life,

[1] *S. C. H.*
§ 419.
[2] Porritt,
i. 122.

of the legal equality of all freemen outside the small circle of
the actual peerage.   Fortunately it had no especial effect ;
members seem to have been drawn from the same social
class before and after the Statute.   Meanwhile, from the
quiet decision of this struggle there followed two results.   The
amalgamation of the representatives of shire and borough for
joint action was rendered easier, while at the same time the
Crown and Parliament together obtained that upper class
representation which was perhaps the real aim of the king,
and which, down to 1832, formed so definite a feature of our
parliamentary system.

Early weak-
ness of the
boroughs in
Parliament.

Yet despite this harmony and apparent similarity, the
position of the landed gentry was as yet too assured for an
equality in importance to be really possible between the
representatives of both classes of the Commons.   The knights
of the shire were the undoubted leaders.   ' They were,' says
Dr. Stubbs, ' the leaders of parliamentary debate ; they were
the link between the good peers and the good towns ; they
were the indestructible element of the House of Commons ;
they were the representatives of those local divisions of the
realm which were coeval with the historical existence of the
people of England, and the interests of which were most
directly attacked by the abuses of royal prerogative.'   In
short, *it was by the knights of the shire that ' the victory of the*

[3] *S. C. H.*
§ 272.

constitution was won.' [3]   Indeed, until the time of the Tudors,
with one exception (Thomas Yonge of Bristol), no prominent

member of the Commons was representative of a borough.
The reasons for this *comparative insignificance of the burgesses* Reasons.
are important. In the first place the attention of the townsfolk
was concentrated on the internal development of their trade
and organization. It was during the fifteenth century that the
monopoly of power by the gilds was causing the artisans to
migrate into the villages and the journeymen to form gilds of
their own, which gradually resulted in what is known as the
'domestic system' of manufacture. And at the same time
the French wars so diminished commerce and increased
taxation that the towns were seriously affected. Hence the
petitions, under Henry VI and his successors to the middle
of the sixteenth century, for the remission of those portions
of a subsidy which, on the assessment of 1334, should have
been levied from them. Moreover, the external position of
the boroughs was very weak. Their desire to escape the
burden of representation left them at the mercy or manipulation of the sheriff, who could take bribes to omit them or
could appoint his own nominees. But perhaps the chief
influence in the weakening of the boroughs is to be found
in the selfish action of their great men. The merchants
were probably in the main country gentry and members of
the shire courts. As such they lost touch with their fellow
townsmen and, for the sake of their own private gain, were
not unwilling to enter into separate dealings with the king.

Indeed, not only was the power of the Commons thus at
times almost annihilated, but there seemed a *likelihood of the
rise of a separate Estate of merchants*. For, assemblies of
merchants from time to time were brought together for the
purpose of granting supplies of wool to the king apart from
Parliament. Edward I's preliminary attempt at this met 1303.
with failure; but during the early years of Edward III it
became a frequent method of raising supplies which took
the shape of either additional customs or free gifts. By such
private negotiations the king would often renew the grants
made to him in the previous Parliament; and it only remained
for the next Parliament to authorize the taxation which had
been so unconstitutionally obtained. But by the end of
Edward III's reign this method of raising money gradually
ceased. Not only did the Statute of Staples in 1353 regulate 1353.

1362.
1371.

the export trade in wool, but by direct enactment in 1362
and again in 1371, Parliament prohibited such dealings with
the merchants.   These prohibitions would have been evaded
had not the merchants themselves discovered that Edward's
demands on them were out of all proportion to the privileges
which they obtained in return, and had they not therefore understood that their real interest lay in union with the Commons.[1]

[1] S. C. H.
§§ 195, 277.
Their rise
to impor-
tance.

    But meanwhile, their internal decay prevented the boroughs
from taking a prominent part in the affairs of the nation.   I
need not, however, be supposed that they were of no constitutional importance.   We have seen that after 1382 their number
was as fixed as that of the represented shires, and that the
first change under Henry VI heralds a continuous numerical
increase.   Nor was the change confined to mere quantity,
for the adhesion of the towns was an important item in the
victory of the Yorkists.   But more significant are a few facts
to be gleaned from the parliamentary history of the Tudor
times.   Thus, from 1532 to 1536 the Speaker of the House
of Commons was member for a borough, and Henry VIII's
minister, Thomas Cromwell, represented Taunton in Parliament.   The reason for this *change in the character of the
burgesses* lies in the fact that representation was ceasing to be
a burden.   Of this, generally, there are many proofs.   Thus, I
select one which concerns our immediate question, an Act of

1413.

Henry V's reign, already noticed, had attempted to check the
arbitrary manipulation of elections by the sheriff, by enacting

(3) local
residence ;

a *qualification of local residence* for the elected members.   This,
however, if it ever had any effect, speedily became obsolete

1571.

and, so far as regards burgesses, in 1571 it was repealed.   But
for some unexplained reason the Act of 1571 never found its
way on to the Statute book.   The old Act of 1413 remained,
though it was never enforced, and was not finally removed

1774.

from the Statute book until 1774.   The debate over the bill
of 1571 gives us the first reported speeches 'which discuss in
detail the constitution and forms of Parliament'; and it is
noteworthy that one of the chief objections to the repeal of
Henry V's measure was founded on the fear that 'Lords'
letters may henceforth bear all the sway,'—that is, the
Commons practically chose to be the nominees of the Crown
rather than of the Lords.

The opportunities of the Lords had not yet come, but in (Nomination Seats.) this same Parliament the methods were foreshadowed by which they were to establish their future influence. For we find the first instance of the purchase of a seat in the penalties imposed on the Corporation of Westbury for selling its representation to a certain Long, who himself, curiously enough, seems to have kept his seat.[1] The multiplication of '*rotten boroughs*,' [1 Prothero, 132.] as they came to be called, by royal charter, has already been mentioned. To those which were never intended to be other than nomination seats were added towns whose constituencies had been subsequently narrowed, and towns which had come to a stationary condition or had actually decayed. The transference of power from the king to Parliament and the accumulation of great properties which marked the early years of the eighteenth century, placed many of these nomination seats in the hands of noblemen or wealthy commoners. Thus in 1793 the Duke of Norfolk had eleven seats in his gift, the Earl of Lonsdale was answerable for nine members of the House of Commons, and other noblemen for a lesser number. 'Seats,' it has been remarked, 'were held in both Houses alike by hereditary right.' [2] In boroughs of a slightly larger size seats [2 Erskine May, i. 333.] could be obtained either by out-and-out purchase, by the payment of an annual rent, or by a system of individual bribery. The example of Long found ready imitators as the growing commerce brought to the front a new class of ambitious men who had to make local connections for themselves. Such especially were the 'Indian Nabobs,' adventurers who had returned from East and West Indies with ample fortunes, free from party connections, and bent on serving merely personal ends. Their influence reached a culminating point in the early years of the reign of George III,[3] by whom they were [3 Porritt, i. 408-420.] enlisted in the ranks of the 'King's Friends,' a party formed to undermine the political predominance of the Whig nobility. An especially flagrant case of corruption would be punished by temporary disfranchisement by the House of Commons itself. But this was too slight a deterrent, and the sale of boroughs was general and notorious. Indeed, at the election of 1768, it was complained that, owing to the competition of the Nabobs, the general price of boroughs had risen. Not that legislative attempts were wanting, from the time of William III onwards, to check both bribery and the sale of seats ; but too many interests were involved to render such attempts successful ; and even a high-minded man like Sir Samuel Romilly excused while he condemned the system, as the only means by which an independent member could obtain a seat.[1]   The result was that, at the beginning of the nineteenth century, of the 658 members of the House of Commons no less than 487 owed their seats to nomination, of whom 218 in England and Wales alone were returned by eighty-seven peers, and 137 by other individuals of lesser rank.   This system left only a third of the whole House of Commons to be chosen by even the limited constituencies which at that time possessed the franchise.   So far, then, as the two bodies of knights of the shire and burgesses could now be said to represent any particular interests ; while the former were the nominees of the freeholders, — a decently large and independent, but rapidly decreasing body ; on the whole the members for boroughs represented no one so much as the great Whig aristocracy and their commercial allies.

The attempts to correct this by the introduction of a qualification for members seemed to have failed of effect.   The early qualification of residence was fortunately not enforced, though, despite the events of 1571, the law remained unrepealed.   In 1710, after two unsuccessful attempts, a *property qualification* was introduced with elaborate safeguards for its enforcement. It consisted of an estate in land which, for the knight of the shire, should be worth £600, and for a burgess £300 a year. It was, however, ' systematically evaded,'[2] and was perhaps only maintained so long as it was because the extreme reformers regarded its repeal as so essential that moderate men began to fancy there was some peculiar efficacy in its maintenance. Indeed, it survived the First Reform Act, and in 1838 was only enlarged so as to include a similar value in personal property or in real and personal property combined ; nor did it disappear until 1858.

Meanwhile, to the old qualifications, whether of ' belted knights ' for the shires, or of residence or property for knights and burgesses alike, had been added a number of *oaths and declarations*.   These may be regarded as the result of the Reformation or of the Roman Catholic tendencies of the

[1] Porritt, i. 353-364.

(4) property ;

1710.

[2] Ibid. 171-180.

1838.

1858.

(5) oaths and declarations.

Stuarts;[1] and, since the removal of all danger from Jacobite [1] Porritt, i. 145.
invasions, they have been gradually removed or substitutes
have been found for them. At first such oaths applied to
the House of Commons alone. Thus in 1563 the oath of (a) 1563.
supremacy was required to be taken in the presence of the Lord
High Steward before either knights or burgesses could enter
the Parliament-house. To this, in 1610, was added the oath 1610.
of (b) *allegiance*, administered in the same manner.[2] Hitherto [2] Ibid. 127-129.
nothing had hindered Roman Catholic peers from maintaining
their seats in the House of Lords ; but from 1678 this became 1678.
no longer possible ; for these oaths were to be required of both
Houses and should be taken at the tables of their respective
Houses. And if there had been any doubt in the matter, to
these was added a *declaration against transubstantiation*,[3] which [3] Robertson, 82.
was only removed by the Catholic Relief Act of 1829. The
circumstances of the Revolution of 1688 further led to the
imposition of an oath of (c) *abjuration*, repudiating the claims 1701.
of the descendants of James II to the throne, which was
required in 1701 and was enforced by penalties in 1714.[4] [4] Porritt, i. 147-148.
The *object* of these three oaths accompanied by the declara-
tion was *primarily political* and not religious : 'it does not
appear that nonconformists were ever disqualified as such,
except in so far as their religious conviction prevented them
from taking any form of oath.'[5] Until 1829 Roman Catholics [5] Anson, i. 91.
were excluded by the Act of Supremacy, which was then altered
for them, and by the declaration against transubstantiation, 1829.
which was entirely abolished ;[6] Jews were excluded by the oath [6] Porritt, i. 137-140.
of abjuration, which ended with the words ' on the true faith of
a Christian.' By an Act of 1858 this could be dispensed with.[7] [7] Ibid. 140-144.
Quakers, Moravians and other sects were excluded by their
conscientious objection to an oath : an Act of 1833 allowed
them to substitute an affirmation.[8] Meanwhile, in 1858, the 1858.
three oaths of allegiance, supremacy and abjuration had been [8] Ibid. 134-137.
welded into one ; in 1866 the words 'on the true faith of 1866.
a Christian' were omitted in all cases, and the penalties
annexed by the Act of Charles II were partially removed.
The final phase in the matter was due to the conduct of
Mr. Bradlaugh in 1880, who, having refused to take the oath 1880.
and having been adjudged by a Court of Law to be liable
thereby to the statutory penalties, then endeavoured to take the

oath until forcibly prevented by the House, which considered
its forms insulted or at any rate nullified by his conduct.
1888. But the result was the Oaths Act of 1888, which under all
circumstances allowed an affirmation to be substituted for an
oath.

Disqualifications ; (1) Mental. § 27. From the necessary qualifications for a seat in
Parliament we turn to deal with *disqualifications in themselves*.
These depend either on Common or on Statute law, and may
be divided into five classes. In the first class may be placed
those persons who, whether theoretically or practically, are
mentally disqualified for responsible business. Under this
head come those who are technically called *Infants*, as well
as actual imbeciles and *lunatics*. Despite the Common law,
1695. which was confirmed by statute in the reign of William III,
before the First Reform Act it was no uncommon thing for
minors to be elected and often to sit without protest in the
House of Commons, although heavy penalties prevented them
from voting. The most notorious instances were those of
[1] Porritt, i. 223-235. Charles James Fox and Lord John Russell.[1] As to those
who are really mentally unfit, it is to be remembered that *a
member once elected cannot resign his seat*, and that his attend-
[2] *Ibid.* 238, 493. ance can be enforced by a call of the House ;[2] but though
suggested as late as 1882, such a method has not been resorted
to since 1836. The only method, other than dissolution of
Parliament or expulsion from the House, by which a member
can rid himself of his parliamentary duties, is by appointment
(Resignation of a seat in the Commons.) to the stewardship of the Chiltern Hundreds or of certain old
royal manors, which are merely nominal posts, resigned as
soon as their object is effected and now granted as a matter
of course, although in the eighteenth century it was not
[3] *Ibid.* 242-250. uncommon for political reasons to refuse to grant them.[3]
The attitude of the House in this matter was the relic of a
time when members were glad by any excuse to escape attendance, and when such absence might be a serious impediment
to business. Moreover, before the eighteenth century office was
not a disqualification, and members could only get exemption
by permission of the House itself. Thus the House was
inclined to look suspiciously at all pleas of ill health, and
would not declare a vacancy unless the malady could be
[4] *Ibid.* 240. shown to its satisfaction to be incurable.[4] Since 1886 the

matter has become subject to legislation; and continued 49 Vict.
absence of a member, without any call of the House or other c. 16.
method of compulsion, would meet with its due reward in his
rejection on the next occasion when he sought the votes of his
constituents.

A second set of disqualifications is to be found in connection (2) Social.
with certain *classes* of persons. Thus *Aliens*, though originally
allowed to acquire by naturalization the right of sitting in
Parliament, were in 1700 disqualified, and remained so, with
certain memorable exceptions, until an Act of 1870 placed 33 & 34
a naturalized person on the same footing for all purposes as Vict. c. 14.
a British subject. Under the same head come *Peers*. As § 7.
regards English peers no question could arise; and by an
order of the House of Commons made on January 21, 1549,
the sons of English peers were made eligible,[1]—an important 1 Porritt,
witness to the rising influence of the Commons under the i. 123.
Tudor kings. Scotch peers who are not among the sixteen
representatives of that body, are ineligible; and their eldest
sons, who had never sat in the Scotch Parliament, were also
ineligible until the disability was removed in 1832. Irish
peers, on the other hand, who are not among the twenty-eight
representatives, are by the Act of Union allowed to sit for any
constituency of Great Britain. It has been contended lately
that succession to a peerage only renders vacant a seat in the
House of Commons if the new peer applies for his writ. It
has been pointed out in answer, that 'the Peerage is a *status*
involving, among other things, liability to a summons if it be
the Queen's pleasure to issue the writ. It is the *status*, not
the summons, which causes the disqualification.'[2]   2 Anson, i.

Besides social classes there are certain *official* classes to whom 246 note.
this inability to enter Parliament has been or still is extended. 2nd edit.
First among these come the *Lawyers*.[3] It has been noticed Cf. also
already how nearly the merchants in the early days of Parlia- Pike, 239.
ment formed a separate Estate. The lawyers at one time seemed (3) Official.
likely to assume a similar position. Edward I patronized the 3 Porritt, i.
lawyers as much as he courted the merchants, and the possible 512-518.
evil effects of his patronage were only averted by the fact
that the Common law prevented the growth of a legal caste
such as the study of the Roman law encouraged abroad.
But further, in the general difficulty of procuring persons

willing to be representatives, the House of Commons was flooded by common lawyers, the only class who found a visit to London advantageous for their professional interests. Hence came, on the one side, the extreme jealousy shown by the House of Commons towards the action of the Privy Council and of Chancery alike ; hence, also, on the other side, came those complaints of the use to which the lawyers put their parliamentary membership for the furtherance of their own interests, which led in 1372 to a statute, or rather perhaps a parliamentary ordinance, disqualifying lawyers practising in the king's Courts from sitting as knights of the shire. This does not, however, seem to have had the slightest effect. Indeed, when in 1404 Henry IV excluded lawyers by writ from what was consequently known as the 'Unlearned Parliament,' his action met with much adverse criticism, for it was regarded as an interference with the right of free election by the shires.

1372.

1404.

But the same feeling did not apply to the exclusion of that small band among the lawyers, who had risen to be royal *Judges*. As we have seen, they were regarded in a sense as attendants rather than members of the House of Lords, and as such they would be excluded from the House of Commons by the Common law. This was further confirmed by a resolution of the House in 1605 on the ground that they were 'attendants as Judges in the Upper House.' To the English Judges were added the Scotch under George II, and the Irish under George IV. The holders of the newly created judicial posts were disqualified as those posts were created. The sole exception was the Master of the Rolls, until he too was finally excluded by the Supreme Court of Judicature Act of 1873, which disqualified for a seat in the Commons all Judges of the High Court of Justice or of the Supreme Court of Appeal.

1605.

1873.

The same ordinance of 1372, which forbade the election of lawyers as knights of the shire, also excluded *Sheriffs* during their term of office from candidature either for the shire or for any borough within it to which their own precept extended.[1] Practically, however, the restriction was only interpreted to apply to the shire in which the sheriff was the returning officer, and a later resolution of the House has extended the exclusion to all returning officers in this sense. The wholesale

[1] Porritt, i. 123.

local exclusion of the sheriff has been limited by an Act of 16 & 17 Vict. c. 68. s. 1. 1853, by which writs for the cities and boroughs were no longer to be addressed to the sheriff of the shire in which those places were situated.

It seems doubtful whether *Holy Orders* originally rendered their recipient ineligible for membership of the Commons. In 1785 a person in deacon's orders had been admitted by a committee of the House, and the precedents collected by a committee in 1801 have been pronounced inconclusive. We have seen, in the reign of Richard II, the presence of Percy and Haxey who seem to have acted as clerical proctors, but to have been ordinary members of the House, although the latter was certainly in orders of some kind. But in three cases (1553, 1621, 1662) committees of the House of Commons declared clergymen ineligible on the ground that they had a vote in Convocation. In 1664 clergymen were admitted to the electorate, and the old ground of objection seemed thereby removed. The question, however, came up again in 1801 in 1801. connection with the election of the Rev. J. Horne Tooke as member for Old Sarum. While in the doubtful state of the precedents he was allowed to maintain his seat, it was declared by Statute 'that no person having been ordained to the office 41 Geo. III c. 63. of priest or deacon, or being a minister of the Church of Scotland, is capable of being elected,' while the ground of objection now taken was that so many benefices were in the gift of the Crown or of the nobility. To these were added the Roman Catholic clergy by the Catholic Emancipation Act. 1829. But finally, by an Act of 1870, it became possible for any 33 & 34 Vict. c. 91. clergyman of the Church of England legally to divest himself of his orders and so to render himself eligible for election to Parliament.[1]

1 Porritt, i. 125-127.

A fourth and important class of disqualifications comes from (4) Government. *connection with government*, official or otherwise. The agitation against office-holders dates from the Restoration,[2] but no 2 *Ibid.* 4. 205-206. legislation was successful until after the Revolution of 1688. During this period the strength and irresponsibility of the 3 Anson, i. 80; House of Commons made the Crown as anxious to obtain cf. Erskine some influence over its members as the House was to May, i. 369. exclude persons who held office at pleasure of the Crown.[3] Vide Hallam, iii. A beginning was made with Commissioners of Stamps (1694) 192-193.

and of Excise (1699), but these were only preliminary to the sweeping clause of the Act of Settlement (1700) by which, after the accession of the House of Hanover, this ineligibility was extended to *any person who held an office or a place of profit under the king*.[1] But this never came into operation; for in 1705-6 it was, with certain important exceptions, repealed. These *exceptions* form the basis of the law on the subject to the present day. They include (*a*) the holders of any new office created after October 25, 1705, (*b*) the holders of certain specified offices, (*c*) pensioners of the Crown during pleasure, to whom were added under George I pensioners for terms of years.[2] Officers of the army and navy who might receive commissions while acting as members of the Commons, were specially exempted from disqualification:[3] but another clause provides that even the acceptance of one of the old offices vacates the seat of the member who accepts it, but allows him to seek re-election. This originally useful check upon appointments by the Crown is still retained, although it has sunk merely into 'a needless and vexatious delay in the conduct of public business when a new ministry takes office, or a new member is introduced into a ministry.'[4] The principle of disqualification was steadily continued in the cases of both old and new offices and with a distinction between partial and total disqualification. The chief Statutes affecting *old offices* were the Place Bill of 1742,[5] which affected junior officials of the government offices, and Lord Rockingham's Act of 1782[6] for the regulation of the civil list expenditure, which abolished several offices connected with the royal household and generally held by members of Parliament. The existence of over a hundred Statutes on the matter renders it hopeless to attempt an exhaustive summary of the *newly created disqualifying offices*. They have, however, been skilfully summarized into those *connected with the administration of Justice*, such as Judges, Recorders (only for their own boroughs), Registrars, Stipendiary Magistrates; those *representing the Crown*, as Colonial Governors, Court Officials such as were abolished in 1782, or subordinate members of the civil service; those *concerned with the collection of revenue or audit of public accounts;* and those *connected with the administration of property for public objects*, such as Charity and Land Commissioners and

[1] *S. C.* 530-531. 6 Anne, c. 7 [41] s. 24.

[2] Porritt, i. 214.

[3] *Ibid.* 212.

[4] Anson, i. 83.

[5] Robertson, 125.

[6] *Ibid.* 142.

Commissioners of Woods and Forests.[1]   Before passing
away from this subject two important exceptions should be
noticed.   To the old offices existing before October 1705,
whose acceptance henceforth subjected their holder to re-
election by his constituents, have been added a few others
on a like tenure, such as the President of the Local Government Board created in 1871.   A more curious case is that
of the Under Secretaryships of State,—parliamentary and,
therefore, political offices changing with the ministry,—which
are not regarded as disqualifying their holders from seats in
Parliament, because they are not technically considered to
be held of the Crown.

Among those connected with government a powerful class
was composed of great *contractors*.[2]   Their influence, employed
for their own benefit and at the public expense, caused their
entire disqualification in 1782 with a heavy penalty attached to
any violation of the Statute.   But the disability was not held
to apply to subscribers to government loans ; and indeed the
most effectual blow dealt to the wasteful methods of raising
money employed in the eighteenth century, came from the
introduction of a system of close subscriptions which was
the germ of the modern form of contracts by sealed tenders.
This was largely employed by the younger Pitt, and consists
of sealed offers of loans to the government deposited with the
Governor of the Bank of England by a specified day, and
from among which the Chancellor of the Exchequer selects
the most favourable.

The fifth class of disqualifications for parliamentary honours
may be described under the head of convictions for *legal
offences*.[3]   Such, for example, are *bankrupts* who are members
of either House.   By two Acts of 1812 and 1869, confirmed
by the Bankruptcy Act of 1883, a member of the Commons
in this condition does not forfeit his seat for one year, but
meanwhile, unless the disqualification is removed in certain
specified ways, he may not sit or vote.   In 1871 a similar disqualification was extended to members of the House of Lords,
to whom, during the continuance of their bankruptcy, no writs
of summons are issued, although they are not deprived of
the privileges of peerage.   The disqualification of bankruptcy
can only be removed if, among other things, it can be shown

[1] Anson, i. 93-97.

[2] *Ibid.* i. 83. Erskine May, i. 385-389. Porritt, i. 217-219.

(5) Legal.

[3] Anson, i. 83-85.

not to have been due to misconduct. There are, however, other disqualifying legal offences, which involve an action of a criminal character. Such are *corrupt practices* at parliamentary elections, which were met from time to time by the disfranchisement of the borough concerned. The First Reform Act of 1832 momentarily increased such practices by suppressing the very boroughs which were free from bribery because they contained no voters to bribe. But individual examples had little deterring effect; and from 1841 onwards, numerous legislative attempts were made to check the system. Their frequency (1842, 1852, 1854, 1858, 1868, 1883) bears witness rather perhaps to the magnitude of the stake involved than to the inefficacy of legislation in the matter. As far as the candidate is concerned, a conviction for such practices disqualifies him for ever from sitting for the place where the offence was committed, and for seven years from candidature elsewhere. The illegal and unauthorized act of an agent involves merely the first penalty in a minor degree. More important perhaps, though happily not so general, is the disqualification attached to *any one attainted or adjudged guilty of treason or felony* who has not undergone his term of punishment or received a pardon. In the reign of James I, in the case of *Goodwin* (an outlaw who, in defiance of the king's special writ forbidding the election of bankrupts and outlaws as knights of the shire, had been returned for Buckinghamshire in 1604), the Commons pleaded that even if he were an outlaw, a fact which they disputed, there were precedents for persons of that class as members of the House.[1] The modern form of the question turns on the eligibility of a convicted felon. Such were the cases of *Smith O'Brien* in 1849, of *O'Donovan Rossa* in 1870, of *John Mitchel* in 1875, and of *Michael Davitt* in 1882. In the case of Mitchel, the House of Commons declared him disqualified and the seat therefore vacant; and on the re-election of Mitchel, the law courts not only confirmed the previous judgement of the Commons, but awarded the seat to his opponent on the ground that the votes given to Mitchel were, under the circumstances, simply thrown away. Until 1870 there seems, however, to have been some doubt, not so much as to the eligibility of felons who had served their sentences, as to the treatment of such

[1] Prothero, 325-331.

persons by the House of Commons.   It was always possible
that the House would use its power to bring such persons
within the list of those who should be expelled for unfitness.
Such is its method of action in cases of conviction for a misdemeanour which forms no legal disqualification and does
not therefore vacate a seat.   But an Act of that year put it 33 & 34
beyond possibility of doubt that convicted felons who had Vict. c. 23,
served their term or received a pardon, were legally eligible s. 2.
for seats in the House of Commons.

§ 28. From the members we turn to their CONSTITUENTS. The elec-
And here, again, for the sake of clearness it will be well at torate in
first to keep the shires and boroughs separate.   In both cases the Shires.
equally a great dividing line is made by the changes of the
First Reform Act of 1832 : but the subject may fearlessly be
carried across the dividing line in its two separate halves ; for,
the gain will probably be greater than any corresponding loss
from a failure to view our subject as a whole.   The history of
the *electorate of the shire* falls into three periods.   The first of
these runs up to 1430 and is full of disputable points : the (1) Before
second brings us to 1832 and shows us an electoral body both 1430.
simple and certain : the third period has for the present closed
with the Representation of the People Act of 1884, and thus
traces the growth of the franchise which we now enjoy.   The
history of the first period is summed up in the answer to the
question, *Whom did the Knights of the Shire originally represent?*
It has been maintained by several constitutional writers of
authority, that they were the representatives of (1) the minor
tenants-in-chief of the Crown for whom Magna Carta (§14)
required only a general summons ; who in consequence largely
dropped out of attendance at the Commune Concilium ; and
who were thus brought back by a complete representation to
the National Council.   Since there is no question that from
the first the election of knights of the shire was made in
the full county court, these writers are driven to maintain that
tenants-in-chief of the Crown were the only suitors of the court.
As against this view it has been pointed out by Dr. Stubbs
that, if this theory is correct, 'the assembly by which the The mem-
election was made would not be the full county court ; the bers of the
electors would be the tenants-in-chief, not the whole body of Court.
suitors ; and the new system, instead of being an expedient

O

by which the co-operation of all elements of the people might be secured for common objects, would simply place the power of legislation and taxation in the hands of a body constituted on the principle of tenure.'[1]   Dr. Stubbs himself upholds the theory that the knights were the representatives of (2) *the community of the shire as organized in the shire court.*   But what was this organized community ?   It is comparatively easy to show that it did not consist merely of tenants-in-chief of the Crown.   In the first place, it is to be remembered that such a composition would run directly counter to the avowedly anti-feudal policy of the Plantagenet kings, and that knights were elected in the shire courts for numerous local purposes long before they were called to a national assembly.   Moreover, all the documentary evidence goes to confirm this view. On the one side there are notices of the presence of sub-tenants in the shire courts ; on the other side the writs for the election of knights of the shire speak as plainly as words can speak to the participation of the whole shire court ; for in them the sheriff is directed to return two knights to Parliament who have been chosen 'in pleno comitatu, de assensu ejusdem comitatus ; assensu et arbitrio hominum ejusdem comitatus.' Nor does the evidence seem much better for the view that the shire court contained an exhaustive representation of all the people in the shire—freeholders in person, and boroughs and land communities by representation.   It seems much more probable that, whatever the original composition of the shire court may have been supposed to be, by the time that it was called upon to elect representatives to the National Assembly, the duty or burden of attendance had been indissolubly associated with the tenancy of particular acres within the shire. It had become a burden or a service by which a particular tenant held his land.   The evidence for these two rival theories must be examined in connection with the history of the administration of justice.   Here it should merely be noted that at the time when representative knights were summoned to Parliament, the court which elected them was probably a very small and rather miscellaneous assembly.

The knights of the shire, then, were elected by the qualified constituents of the county court.   But the election must have usually taken place in the ordinary monthly, or as it came to be,

[1] *S. C. H.* § 216.

Change in members of Shire Court.

three-weekly court ; for only forty days were allowed between
the issue of the writ and the meeting of the Parliament. Now,
this court was attended only by those who had special business
either as jury, in which case they would be freeholders, or as
parties to a suit. All the more influential members, and with
them apparently some of the smaller freeholders, were exempted
from attendance unless specially summoned either to meet the
king's justices or for the transaction of important kinds of business. At the same time it is noteworthy that the court seems
to have been flooded with persons of less importance than the
proper constituents, and that by the end of Edward III's reign such
persons took part in the election. The *plenus comitatus* had in
fact changed its character, and this was recognized by the first
Act, passed in **1406**, for the regulation of elections of knights of 7 Hen. IV.
the shire ; for by this it was enacted, among other things, 'that c. 15.
all they that be there present (i.e. in the county court), *as well
suitors duly summoned for the same cause as others*, shall attend to
the election of knights for the Parliament.' To this two riders
were shortly added ; for, an Act of **1413** enjoined that the
electors as well as the members should be resident in the shires
and boroughs for which they voted and sat respectively ; while
another of **1432** stipulated that, in the case of shire elections,
the land which gave the vote should be situate in the county.

These last were limiting statutes, and it was in the direction Legislative
of limitation both for members and voters, for shires and limitation
boroughs alike, that the tide of legislation and royal predi- of electors
lection set. The Parliament of 1372 had successfully demanded didates.
the exclusion of sheriffs and lawyers as members. In 1376 the 1372.
Good Parliament, following this example, sought to restrict the 1376.
electorate in the shires, and so the power of the sheriffs,
by a petition that knights of the shire might be chosen by
common election of *the better folk* of the shires. To this the
king replied that they should be elected by common assent of
the whole county. It was perhaps the power placed in the
hands of the sheriff, and at any rate the fear of riotous elections
through the unwieldy and irresponsible character of the electoral bodies, which led to a change of tone on the part of the
king and his advisers. Whatever the reason, the liberal provisions of 1406 were withdrawn by the celebrated Act of **1430**, 8 Hen. VI.
'the first disfranchising Statute on record,' which narrowed the c. 7.

qualification of electors for knights of the shire not only to
freeholders, but to such only as possessed land of the clear
annual value of forty shillings.   The same Act reaffirmed the
condition of residence enacted in 1413 ; and it was followed
two years later by the Act, already quoted, which coupled with
residence the property in respect of which the vote was given.

(2) Be-
tween 1430
and 1832.

Thus the county franchise remained for just four hundred
years, most unfortunate in its exclusion of not only probably
a considerable number of the smaller freeholders—for forty
shillings represented a substantial sum, which has been estimated at between £30 and £40 of present value—but also
of that more important class of emancipated villans and
their representatives, who held land, often to a considerable
amount, on copyhold or leasehold tenure, and who were
quite capable of the responsibility of the vote.   A great
political injustice was committed by this disfranchisement of
a large and increasing number of those interested in land.
But the franchise was not so narrow as we might suppose.
One of the methods by which elections came to be manipulated was the subdivision of freeholds for the purpose of
qualifying additional electors.   This seems to date from the
reign of Charles I.   The door was thus opened for the
manufacture of 'faggot' votes, and very soon the county
franchise was claimed and exercised in respect of any
property which could be construed as a freehold of the
requisite annual value—offices of all kinds, pews in churches,
purchases of land-tax.[1]   But despite this fraudulent increase
of voters, the freeholders in the counties were on the whole
worthy of the trust which was for so long concentrated on
them.   We have already noticed the manner in which early
writers spoke of the yeomen, whether small freeholders or
substantial tenants.[2]   Even in the midst of the general disappearance of small properties which helped to mark the
political influence of the aristocracy after the Revolution of
1688, statesmen still pointed to the county constituencies,
the forty-shilling freeholders, as the most uncorrupt part of
the constitution.   'They represented public opinion,' it has
been said, 'more faithfully than other electoral bodies ; and
on many occasions had great weight in advancing a popular
cause.'[3]   Thus, despite the great and in many cases over-

[1] Porritt,
i. 22-23.

[2] p. 55.

[3] Erskine
May, i.
353.

whelming influence of the nobility, the more moderate among
the early schemes of parliamentary reform—those connected
with the names of Chatham, Wilkes and the younger Pitt—
suggested the disfranchisement of boroughs and the addition
of the seats so gained to the representation of the counties.

The third period in the history of the county electoral bodies (3) Since
is ushered in by the Reform *Act of* **1832**. By that Act the 1832.
old property qualification of a forty-shilling freehold was itself Qualifica-
restricted to occupation or to acquisition by methods other tions of
than purchase, such as inheritance and marriage-settlement; property.
while to it were now added four other *property and non-*
residential qualifications—a freehold for life, however acquired,
of the annual value of £10; copyhold or other land of the
same value; and two sorts of leasehold, viz. of £10 value for
sixty years, and of £50 value for twenty years.[1] The only [1] Robertson,
change made in these qualifications by the *Act of* **1867** was 199.
a reduction of the value of the freehold for life from £10 to
£5.[2] The *Act of* **1884** followed suit with the copyhold and [2] *Ibid.* 425.
leasehold, reducing the former and the first of the leasehold
qualifications similarly from £10 to £5.[3] Thus, besides the [3] *Ibid.* 427.
old forty-shilling freehold narrowed and defined and a leasehold of £50 for twenty years, all other property qualifications
are by the present law reduced to an uniform rate of £5 value.

But, besides adding to the property qualifications, the *Act* of occu-
of **1832** introduced into the county constituencies an entirely pation.
new qualification based upon *occupation*. The right of voting
for members of Parliament was given to the 'tenant of any
lands or tenements for which he should be liable to the clear
yearly rent of £50.' This was known from its introducer as
the 'Chandos' clause, and probably effected its purpose of
strengthening the interests of the landlords. In addition to
this high *rental* value, the *Act of* **1867** created another qualification arising from occupation of any land or tenement of the
rateable value of £12. For these two qualifications the *Act of*
1884 substituted an uniform value of £10, applicable to all
parts of the United Kingdom and to counties and boroughs
alike, but differing in each portion of the kingdom in details
of assessment of value, residence and requisite payment of
taxes. Finally, this last Act added a third qualification to the
county constituencies, that of *residence*, which had been created

in the boroughs by the Act of 1867 and was now merely extended, both in the case of inhabitant occupiers of a house occupied and rated as a separate dwelling, and in the case of lodgers who have resided for a year in lodgings of the clear annual value, if let unfurnished, of £10.

The electorate in the boroughs.

§ 29. Such has been the course of the changes in the *personnel* of those on whom our Constitution has at various times bestowed the privilege of exercising the franchise in the shires. We turn to the more intricate subject of the *constituencies of the boroughs*. There is a difficult preliminary question regarding the actual boroughs which were entitled to send members to Parliament. It has been maintained by those constitutional writers who, in their insistence on the all-importance of tenure, have wished to limit the county constituencies to the tenants-in-chief, that the towns were summoned to send representatives as being in ancient demesne of the

[1] Cf. *Edinb. Rev.* vol. xxxv.

Theory of borough representation.

Crown.[1] It was on this plea that in the early days of Parliament some of the towns tried to escape the burden of representation by asserting that they were not in ancient demesne. The contention amounted to a view that it was as landlord, and not as national sovereign, that the king had summoned burgesses to his councils. The claim, however, had little ground historically, and was disallowed. The long exemption of the Counties Palatine of Chester and Durham shows the respect paid to old anomalies ; but the early representation of the Palatinate of Lancaster prevents any conclusion from these exceptional cases. As to the general question, there seems no doubt whatever that, from the very first occasions when burgesses were brought to the National Councils, they came as representatives of wealthy portions of the country which deserved especial consideration. For, in the first place, the writs summoning representatives of the towns were directed to the sheriffs of each shire, with whom thereby lay the choice of the towns which should be represented. The acts of Simon

[2] *S. C.* 415.
[3] *Ibid.* 468.

de Montfort in 1265,[2] and of Edward I in 1283,[3] in directing the writs to the mayor or bailiff of each individual town, came to be regarded as anomalous. In general the sheriff is directed to return *de qualibet civitate . . . comitatus duos cives et de quolibet burgo duos burgenses*, and not a word is said of demesne ; while, as if to guard against any possible misunder-

standing, the royal writ for the collection of the money granted
in 1296 explicitly states that it was made by an assembly which
included *homines de civitatibus et burgis nostris, de quorumcunque
tenuris aut libertatibus fuerint et de omnibus dominicis nostris*.[1] [1] Palgrave,
Again, the definite distinction and yet amalgamation in the *Parl.*
assembly of these two kinds of towns is illustrated by the *Writs,*
lists of boroughs which were represented in the early Parlia- i. 51.
ments.   From these we find many instances of boroughs, such
as Salisbury which belonged to the bishop, and St Albans
owned by the abbot, which sent members although they were
certainly not in ancient demesne of the Crown ;[2] while, on [2] *S. C. H.*
the other hand, there were many answering to that description § 218 note,
which either (like Pevensey) never, or (like Grantham) not and *Parl.*
till a much later period, were represented in the House of *Writs,* i.
Commons.   In conclusion of this point it may be remarked 34-45.
that a representation of towns in ancient demesne would be
as contrary to the policy of the Plantagenet sovereigns as a
recall of the lesser tenants-in-chief to the National Council in
the persons of the knights of the shire.   The whole tendency
of the royal policy was in favour of national claims as opposed
to those based on merely feudal considerations.

We are now in the position to investigate the constituency The bur-
of any particular borough.   Unfortunately there is far greater densome-
difficulty than in the analogous case of the knights of the ness of
shire, in determining the question *Who elected the members* tation.
for the boroughs ?   The burdensomeness of early representation
is realized most clearly from the action of the towns in connection with their appearance in Parliament.   For, those
towns which were represented were liable for special wages
to their members and to a higher rate of taxation than that
imposed upon the inhabitants of the counties.   The result
was that the towns tried in every way to escape their obligations, and so great was this unwillingness that it became
necessary to appoint *manucaptors* or *bailsmen*, whose duty it
was to see that the elected members presented themselves
wherever the king had appointed that Parliament should be
held, and who were themselves actually provided with power
of attorney to act for an absent member.   But in 1406 the
Act of Henry IV, while it legally popularized the county
electorate, at the same time required that those making the

election should affix their names and their seals to an indenture or writing which should be joined on to and returned with the writ ; and this precaution, although imperfectly complied with, seems at the same time to have checked the sheriff and to have minimized the necessity of manucaptors.

Influences which narrowed the borough constituencies. But so long as representation remained a burden, there were no disputed elections ; the difficulty rather was to procure persons willing to be elected, and thus for some time the question of the exercise of the franchise did not become a matter of dispute. When it did arise as the result of the increasing influence of Parliament under the Tudors, it was settled in a variety of ways, which, however, all concurred in restricting the privilege of the vote according to the custom at municipal elections, or as a consequence of the temporary weakness or strength of the governing body of the town. The process was begun and rendered simple by (1) the increasing grant of charters of incorporation. The early charters had conferred new privileges leading gradually up to entire self-government : while, from the time of Henry VI onwards, their object was the definition of the mutual rights and relations of the townsmen and the organization of corporate bodies for their rule. Among the duties or privileges imposed upon or granted to the corporation was not infrequently the exclusive right of electing the parliamentary representatives of the borough. And in cases where it was not definitely conferred by the charter, the right was often assumed by the governing body of the town, who rested their claim in some way on an interpretation of the charter,[1] and fortified it by (2) the favourable result of a decision by one or other of the various committees of the House of Commons which, from 1604 onwards, tried cases of disputed elections.[2] Indeed, after the rise of parties in Parliament, these decisions were grounded purely upon political considerations. In 1742, Sir Robert Walpole accepted the defeat of the candidate whose cause he was advocating in the Chippenham election petition, as evidence that he had lost his command of the majority in the House, and resigned. And such decisions of the Commons were of importance because ' when once they had declared an election to be invalid on the ground that the votes of a particular class of voters had been accepted or rejected, the right of that class was settled and the

[1] Porritt, i. 43-47, 52-54.

[2] *Ibid.* 539.

custom of the borough fixed.'[1]   This must especially have
been the case after an Act of 1729 had ordained that the
last determination in the House of Commons should definitely
settle the claim to a vote.[2]   And the decisions of the Commons
must have been largely influenced by (3) the existence of that
numerous and, down to the reign of Charles II, ever-increasing
type of boroughs which were never intended to represent anything but the royal power in the House, and in which, therefore,
from the very first the franchise was of the most restricted kind.

The result of these influences will be apparent in a classification of the chief *qualifications* on which, prior to 1832, the
right to a vote within the towns was based.   Of such there
were roughly four, which have been marked off as Tenure,
Residence, Incorporation and Corporate Office.   The qualification of (*a*) *tenure*, which was probably the oldest, was of two
kinds.   The most common form was that of burgage tenure,
which 'was exactly analogous in origin to the freeholder's
qualification in the counties,'[3] and a common form of burgage
tenure connected it, as at Richmond, with the holding of
certain houses, probably in theory those which had contributed
to the ancient *firma burgi*.   No tenure caused so much litigation before election committees, for claims to vote came to be
based upon ownership in such properties as ploughed fields,
as at Old Sarum, or a portion of a salt pit, as at Droitwich,
while women who possessed burgage holdings were allowed to
transfer the vote, which they could not themselves exercise,
practically to anyone whom they chose.[4]   A second form of
the tenure qualification was peculiar to those large towns
which enjoyed the status of a county, and apparently to some
others; and, as in the counties, the franchise was vested in the
forty-shilling freeholders.   These need not, however, have
been very numerous: in Tavistock there were ten; in Gatton
the freeholders together with the next class of voters amounted
jointly to seven in number.   There were, besides, a few quite
anomalous electoral bodies whose rights were based on tenure.
Thus in Cricklade a decision of an election committee in
1685 added to the freeholders, copyholders of lands within
the borough, and even leaseholders for a term of three or more
years.[5]   The qualification of (*b*) *residence* in almost all cases
took the necessary form of the payment of 'scot and lot,'

[1] Anson,
i. 106-107.

[2] Porritt, i. 8.

Qualifica-
tions for
borough
constituen-
cies before
the Reform
Act.

[3] *S. C. H.*
§ 422 end.

[4] Porritt,
33-41.

[5] Quoted
by Erskine
May from
Parl.
Returns,
Sess.
1821-1832,
No. 92.
But see
Oldfield,
Hist. Rep.
sub voc.

that is, a share in the contributions levied from the town for local or national purposes. It was almost a necessity that the voter should be a householder, though exceptions are found. Some of the boroughs with the most populous constituencies, such as Westminster and Preston, belonged to this class. A peculiar case of this qualification of residence is found in the 'pot-wallopers' of Taunton, who are defined as 'all the resident male inhabitants who have obtained a parochial settlement whether they are occupiers of a house or lodgers.'[1] Finally, it should be remarked that this qualification of residence for voters was in the early days of parliamentary representation not only regarded as a matter of course, for 'non-residence,' in the words of a recent writer, 'was not contemplated,'[2] but that the Act of 1413, already quoted, actually required it in the case of electors as well as of members; nor was the Act repealed until 1774. With the third qualification, that of (c) *incorporation*, we reach the chief agency in the narrowing of the borough electorates. The early charters to boroughs, especially in the case of trading towns, not infrequently placed their government in the hands of the freemen of the local merchant gild. Such freedom could, in process of time, be acquired in various ways differing in almost each individual town. They have been summarized as birth, marriage with the daughter or widow of a freeman, apprenticeship or servitude, purchase, or even gift.[3] If it is possible to select in a case where the whole system was so baseless in reason and corrupt in action, the chief evils of this tenure were that, firstly, together with the rights the freeman did not necessarily incur liabilities such as tenure, residence or payment of local taxes; and secondly, in many cases the Corporation had the power of conferring freedom at its pleasure, and used its licence to create freemen, often by the hundred, for the purpose of carrying parliamentary elections.[4] These were the most numerous class of 'faggot' or manufactured votes which were untouched in the boroughs until 1832, although in the analogous case of specially created forty-shilling freeholds in the counties, a legislative attempt was made to check the manufacture in 1712. The last qualification, that of (d) *Corporate Office*, was largely the creation of Tudor charters, often fortified in the eighteenth century by

[1] Oldfield, *Hist. Rep.* iv. 436. Porritt, i. 31.

[2] Anson, i. 100.

[3] *Ibid.* 104.

[4] Porritt, i. 58 et seq.

10 Anne. c. 31.

interested resolutions of the oligarchical House of Commons. For, the inhabitants did not in all cases tamely acquiesce in an interpretation of the charter, which left them at the mercy of a self-elected governing body.   But the prevailing influences were wholly in the direction of restricting the electoral body, and in many instances the continued apathy of the electors permitted of and actually encouraged the direct nomination of the members by the lord of the manor or some local magnate.[1]

[1] Porritt, i. 41 et seq.

It will now be possible to appreciate the full strength of those influences which co-operated to make the representation of the boroughs the pretence which it became in the three centuries preceding the Reform Bill. The narrow constituencies gave every facility either for (i) simple *nomination* of their members, or for the (ii) influence of the voters by *direct bribes*. But there still remained a few towns where the electoral body, being constructed on a liberal basis, was too numerous to be dealt with in either of these methods. In many such, especially seaport and trading places, it was possible to secure the election of candidates of the government by the (iii) *multiplication* of posts in the excise, customs and post office and their distribution among those locally qualified to vote. The ministry of Lord North was said to have created no less than 12,000 of these posts, whose entire number was calculated at a figure between 40,000 and 60,000 out of an electorate of 300,000 persons.[2]   Although it is a bad precedent to disqualify any particular class of men from the exercise of their rights of citizenship, and although such disfranchisement was perhaps the most serious blow that could have been inflicted on government influence at elections, yet a gradually accumulating public opinion imperatively demanded the sacrifice; and from the Revolution onwards, bills for the purpose were constantly introduced until the measure was finally accomplished by Lord Rockingham's Act of 1782, which removed from the electorate all officers connected with the collection of customs and excise.[3] The concession of a popular franchise throughout the country made it safe to restore the right in 1868 to those from whom, on Burke's bold principle of the occasional purifying effect of disfranchisement, it had been so justly taken. There were a few great cities also where

Hindrances to freedom of borough elections.

[2] *Parl. Hist.* xxii. 1337, 1345, quoted by Lecky, iv. 218.

[3] Erskine May, i. 348-349. Robertson, 142.

the electorate was too numerous to be overborne even by the wholesale creation of government votes. But in these the popular candidate, even if successful, was (iv) ruined by the *expenses of the contest*. Many of the reprehensible features in the composition of the House of Commons before 1832 originated in the eagerness and unscrupulousness of candidates, of which constituencies not unnaturally took advantage. Those who were wooing the electors were expected to contribute very handsomely to local needs in all sorts of ways, ranging from the erection of some public building or the freeing of the town from debt to the giving of large orders for local industries. None but rich men had any chance of election in most constituencies.[1] Moreover, while on the one side wages and travelling expenses ceased to be paid as soon as a seat in Parliament became an object of desire, on the other side all election expenses were by custom thrown upon the candidates. The heaviest of these arose from the fact that the poll was kept open for forty days during which there was constant feasting, and every one except the candidate was interested in prolonging the contest to the utmost customary or legal limit.[2] The first limitation to this system resulted from the scandals connected with the Westminster election in 1784. At the election which confirmed George III's arbitrary dismissal of the Coalition Ministry, Charles James Fox was returned for Westminster by a majority of 236 over the Court candidate. But the High Bailiff, who was the returning officer, withheld his return and began a scrutiny into the votes, thus restraining the successful candidate from taking his seat in Parliament. Fox was returned for another constituency; but for a long time the High Bailiff's conduct was defended by Pitt's majority, who refused to order that official to make an immediate return. The iniquity of the whole proceeding at length brought the House of Commons not only to refuse to uphold Pitt in his 'ungenerous conduct,' but to seek a remedy by an enactment of 1785 which limited the poll to fifteen days and closed a scrutiny six days before the day fixed for the meeting of Parliament.[3] In 1853 the poll was further reduced to a single day, and the writs for borough elections to be directed to the returning officers of boroughs,

[1] Porritt, i. 186 et seq.

[2] *Ibid.* 157-165.

25 Geo. III. c. 84.

[3] Erskine May, i. 350-353. Lecky, v. 56-60.

instead of to the sheriff of the county, as hitherto ; and finally
in 1872, the Ballot Act gave legal recognition to an influential
movement in favour of secret voting.[1] Elections both in [1] Erskine
counties and in boroughs were regulated in further details May,
by subsequent legislation, which may be gleaned from any i. 445-447,
modern manual of election law. iii. 454.

We return to the *changes wrought in the borough constituencies
by the three Reform Acts* of the present century. The Reform
Act of 1832, while preserving all *individual* vested rights of the
existing electorate, made a clean sweep of the old anomalous
franchises. The rights of one class, however, were saved—
those of the freemen of such chartered towns as had hitherto
exercised the franchise, though even here the modes of acquiring
freedom were limited to birth and servitude, with the added
qualification of residence in or within seven miles of the
borough.[2] With these restrictions the privilege of freemen has [2] Anson,
survived the reforming fervour of 1867 and 1884. The new i. 108.
qualification introduced by the Bill in the place of those Robertson,
abolished, was an uniform franchise based upon *occupation* of 203.
premises of the annual value of £10.[3] To this single quali- [3] Robertson,
fication the *Act of* 1867 added for the boroughs one based 201.
upon *residence*, whether in the shape of a household franchise
conditional on payment of rates or of a lodger franchise for
unfurnished rooms of the annual value of £10.[4] These quali- [4] *Ibid.* 425.
fications are untouched, except in details, by the *Act of* 1884,
whose great work it was to extend the qualification of residence to the counties and thereby finally to assimilate the
county and borough franchise.[5] [5] Anson,

§ 30. From the foregoing account it will have been abun- i. 108-112
dantly plain that, however clearly Parliament may at times passim.
have expressed the prevailing opinion of the country, it was Outside
not until 1832 that it could exercise any steady pressure in influences
favour of a policy acceptable to the people at large, in opposition liament.
to the wishes either of the king or of the narrow class which
had acquired the franchise. From its very earliest existence,
however, there were influences at work, which, through the
maintenance of the symbols and language of popular government, prevented Parliament from becoming merely the sporting
ground of a close oligarchy. Thus, while in theory elections
were free, the voice of the country was expressed by a small

minority of the people and was constantly overborne by the interests of some few great individuals or of the Crown. Again, by the theory of the constitution, the speeches and votes of individual members were free from outside influence; but in practice they were made and given at the bidding of a few influential persons who had it in their power to make or blast the reputation and the fortunes of the ambitious politician. Circumstances kept apart the theory and the practice of parliamentary government for five hundred years. It is important to examine the working of those influences which, from the first arrangement of Parliament into two Houses down to the eighteenth century, brought about so effectual a separation. It will then be possible to estimate the measures which, during the last century and a quarter, have been either carried out or suggested for realising the harmony between Parliament and the people whom, in theory at least, the House of Commons has always represented.

Influence of the Sheriff.

The earliest and, considering its importance, the most shortlived of such influences seems to have been that exercised on elections by the SHERIFF. Until 1853 the writs were addressed to the sheriff of each shire, enjoining on him to procure the election of two knights for his shire and two citizens or burgesses for every city or borough within the limits of his shire. The whole conduct of the election, therefore, lay in the hands of the sheriff whose sinister designs, where he entertained them, would be rendered com-

Reasons for its exercise.

paratively easy by the *extreme unwillingness of persons to become candidates for Parliament.* The reasons of this reluctance are not far to seek. The summons to Parliament was equivalent to a demand for the grant of taxes; and every

(Desire to escape representation.)

one would be unwilling to face the reproaches of his neighbours for what might be considered undue compliance with the royal demands. And when to this opportunity of incurring popular odium were added the unknown terrors of a distant journey and the inconvenience of absence from a farm or a business, it can be well understood why, in the words of Dr. Stubbs, 'the office of representative was not coveted, and we can imagine cases in which the sheriff would have to nominate and compel the service of an unwilling member.'[1]

[1] *S. C. H.* § 217.

Nor were the *constituencies* any more eager to be represented. For, the members were entitled for their services to *wages* at the rate of four shillings a day for the knights, and two shillings for the burgesses during the parliamentary session, and to a sum for journey money which was usually fixed in the assembly which elected them.[1]   The rate of wages became a settled custom as early as the reign of Edward II, and the sum was collected by the sheriff from all those entitled to vote, on the authority of royal writs *de expensis levandis* which were issued to the members on the last day of the session.   The right, then, to the receipt of wages rested on the Common law, and the fixed sum, though usual, does not seem to have been compulsory. At any rate, although in the case of some few large towns, such as London in 1296 and York in 1483, an increase of wages was sometimes promised, there are other instances, as at Cambridge in 1427, where the constituents bargained with their members to take less.[2]   But under Henry VIII the usual rate was made a matter of legislative grant in the case of the newly enfranchised shires and boroughs of Monmouth and Wales. It was not long, however, before electors took advantage of the increased importance of a seat in Parliament to agree that candidates should serve them for nothing.[3]   Although in isolated cases payment was demanded and obtained, the custom gradually died away.   The last known instance is in 1681, when the Chancellor, Lord Nottingham, gave judgement in favour of a member for Harwich who sued his constituents for his wages.   Thus the payment of members is a lapsed constitutional right ; and when it was moved in the House of Commons in 1870 'to restore the ancient constitutional practice of payment of members,' whatever we may think of the wisdom of the motion, the form was strictly correct.

This desire to escape representation and all its liabilities was common to the inhabitants of the shires and boroughs alike, but it was based on different grounds.   In the case of the *shires* there was no question of the escape of the whole community from the necessity of making an election.   The number of the shires had been fixed long before there was any thought of representation in Parliament ; and although certain shires might and did put off the duty of sending members till a comparatively late period, there was no question of the liability of those which had once received the writs.   Hence the claim of exemption in the shires came in the shape of the *refusal of certain classes*

[1] Porritt, i. 157.

[2] *S. C. H.* §§ 424 and 447 ; and Porritt, i. 155.

35 Hen. VIII. c. 11.
[3] Porritt, i. 153.

1681.

(Method of escaping representation in the Shires.)

to contribute to the wages of the members on the plea that they were not entitled to take part in the election.   There were three such classes—(*a*) *mesne or feudal subtenants*, on the plea that the knights were supposed to represent the tenants-in-chief alone, a theory which has already been shown to have no historical foundation apart from the interest of those who urged it ; (*b*) *tenants in ancient demesne* of the Crown, to whom, on the ground that the king still had the power of taking tallage without leave of Parliament, it seems to have been occasionally allowed ; and (*c*) the *socage tenants* of the county of Kent, who ultimately obtained their exemption.   For, when the Commons attempted to counteract such demands by a petition that the expenses should be levied from all the 'communitates' of the shire, the Crown usually answered by a decision in favour of the local custom.[1]   It was this spirit which animated Edward III in his answer to the petition of the Good Parliament in 1376, that the knights of the shire might be chosen by common election of the better folk of the shire and not merely nominated by the sheriff.[2]

But such a petition discloses the extent of the mischief already at work ; for, the unwillingness of candidates and electors alike, together with the relaxation of the duty of attendance at the local courts, left *the sheriff practically master of the situation.*   He seems to have *used his power in various ways.*   Thus sometimes he would *summon no one especially* for the election or would restrict the notice to a few friends whom he could trust.   This was aimed at by an Act of **1406**, which, while directing that the election should take place 'at the next county court to be holden after the delivery of the writ,' and should be made by all who were present, whether specially summoned or not, required that the signatures and seals of the electors should be placed upon the indenture or writing which always bore the names of the elected members and was joined on to and returned with the writ.   Moreover, these were no longer to go, as heretofore, to Parliament itself, but into the royal Chancery whence the writs were issued. But the provision as to signatures and seals could never have been complied with ; for, the indentures that have been preserved in no case contain more than forty names, which were probably those of the persons to whom special summonses

[1] *S. C. H.* § 216.

[2] *Ibid.* §419.

Methods of its exercise upon the Shires.

7 Hen. IV. c. 15.

had been issued or who had seals to affix, acting as a kind of committee for the rest of the electors. Occasionally, perhaps, it was a mere trick on the part of the sheriff and his friends whereby they complied with the statute without letting go of the power. And this supposition seems borne out by the fact that the returns of the borough members are often found signed and sealed with the same names as those of the knights of the shire.[1]

[1] *S. C. H.* §§ 420-421.

A second method to which the sheriff might resort for the return of his own nominees would be the *deliberate substitution of other names* in the returns for those of the persons who had been properly elected. This could only be met by a petition to the king, the Council or Parliament itself, from a number of those who had made the election. Thus, as a strong though indirect testimony to such action on the part of the sheriff, may be cited the circumstances of the Huntingdonshire election in 1450. The indenture remains with the names of five persons attached, together with a letter signed by 124 freeholders who, fearing that the sheriff intended to make a false return, sent a memorial in which they stated that they, together with 300 more good commoners of the shire, had voted for two certain persons.[2] In this special instance no trick had been attempted; but the terms of the memorial are as striking an illustration as any direct instance of such use of the sheriff's power. But the sheriff had still another method of action; for, taking advantage of the heterogeneous character of the court and the abstention of all members of importance, he would *force through his own candidate* by the appearance of compliance with the necessary forms. For some considerable period the election was made merely by a show of hands, and it was not difficult in a crowded and tumultuous assembly to make the decision go in the way required.[3]

[2] *S. C. H.* § 421, quoting from Prynne, Reg. iii. 156-159.

[3] *Ibid.* § 423.

Legislative attempts to check returns made through these means took two forms. In the first place, the action of the sheriff was subjected to *supervision.* In 1410 it was enacted that the Judges of Assize should inquire into any wrongly made returns, and the sheriff, if convicted of breach of the law, was liable to a fine of £100; while the members unduly returned forfeited their wages. The second method of curtailing the sheriff's power in this matter was by *limitations on the qualifications*

Attempts to check it.

11 Hen. IV. c. 1.

P

1 Hen. V.
c. 1.
both of electors and of candidates.   Thus, by an Act of **1413**
the knights must reside within the shire for which they were
23 Hen. VI.
c. 14.
elected ; while an Act of **1445** restricted the persons chosen to
the class of knights or esquires.   In the case of the electors,
the Act of **1413** required that the electors should also be
10 Hen. VI.
c. 2.
residents ; while in **1432** the freehold in respect of which they
voted must be situated in the shire for which they gave their
8 Hen. VI.
c. 7.
vote.   Two years before had been enacted the important statute
which limited the electorate to the forty-shilling freeholders.
It does not, however, seem to have had any effect on the class
of persons either electing or elected, though doubtless it did
much to check the particular methods of the sheriff's action
which had helped to call it forth.   Nay further, the small
number of names affixed to the indentures may witness to the
influence exercised on elections by the local gentry, in whom
occasionally the sheriffs must have found formidable rivals.
Even more overpowering must have been the interference of
some great local noble.   Certainly in the fifteenth century the
local government or, to speak more correctly, the local means of
control, was almost entirely in the hands of the great nobility,
who either through corruption or intimidation returned their
candidates to Parliament and procured immunity from punishment for their own lawless followers.   In the face of such
obstacles the sheriffs must have been powerless.

Influence
of the
sheriff
upon the
boroughs.
The connection of the sheriff with the *borough* elections calls
for separate treatment.   The unwillingness of the boroughs to
be represented in Parliament came from the fact that such
representation involved the payment of special wages and contribution to the tenth-and-fifteenth at a slightly higher proportion than that exacted from the inhabitants of the shires.

(Methods
of escaping
representa-
tion in the
boroughs.)
The towns tried to escape these liabilities in every way.   The
plea put out by some few that they were *not in ancient demesne*
was, as we have seen, promptly quashed.   It was not easy,
though not altogether impossible, to get emancipation by
charter from the Crown.   A simpler method was to come to
an *understanding with the sheriff* whereby a town dropped
out of representation altogether.   Thus it came about that
many important towns, such as Birmingham and Leeds, had no
representation until 1832, although both were boroughs in the
fourteenth century.

The actual method of election placed an enormous power Methods of its exercise. in the hands of the sheriff. The writs for the election of burgesses were addressed to him, and left in his hands entirely the choice of the boroughs which should be represented; for he was supposed to communicate the writs to such towns in his shire as, by reason of their wealth and position as corporate bodies, were worthy of this extra consideration, and to add his own 'precept' or notice to elect. Now, the sheriff might *omit to send his precept* to a borough. Such an omission was aimed at by an Act of 1382 which forbade the sheriff to 1382. omit any city or borough which had been wont to send members,[1] and, as we have seen, it arrested the downward 1 *S. C. H.* § 296. tendency in point of numbers of the boroughs represented. But, notwithstanding this, it was found necessary by the Act of 1445 to threaten penalties to the sheriff or the mayor to 1445. whose fault the absence of representatives from a borough might be due. But if the sheriff's precept was sent and com- plied with, the election would take place under the conduct of the borough magistrates to whom the precept would be addressed. Thus the actual election would ordinarily be made in the borough court, and the names of the members chosen would be announced to the shire court by the messengers or deputies of the magistrates. Finally, the names of all the representatives from the cities and boroughs which had responded to the sheriff's precept, were placed upon the writ together with the names of the two knights of the shire, and the writ was returned to be verified in Parliament itself or, after 1406, by Chancery. Technically, then, the election of burgesses seems also to have been carried out in the shire court, and the sheriff had an even better chance than in the case of the shire members, of *interpolating in the writs the names of others* than those of the candidates actually elected. The reality of this evil appears in a petition of 1384 from the burghers of Shaftesbury, who demand of Parliament a remedy for the sheriff's action. A more general testimony to the prevalence of this trick is a petition presented by the House of Commons to the king in 1436 against the interference of 2 *S. C. H.* the sheriff in borough elections, especially in the matter of §§ 421- returning the names of members not elected.[2]   423.

Some slight *check* must have been exercised upon the

Attempts
to check it.
1413.
sheriff's power of choice by the application to the boroughs
of the qualification of *residence* for their representatives.
This seems at first to have been generally and rigorously
enforced, and was only evaded when a seat in Parliament
became a post of honour, by the admission of the candidate
to the free burghership of the town which he sought to repre-
23 Hen. VI.
c. 15.
1444.
sent. Further, in 1444 the boroughs were also included in
the Act of 1406, which required that *the electors should add
their names and seals* in an indenture which should be tacked
to the writ. But it must have been the *new charters of incorporation* which for the time dealt an effectual blow at all
outside influence ; for they concentrated the franchise or duty
of election in the hands of a small and select body, which at
first seems to have guarded its new privilege with much care.
To the example of the borough of Westbury in 1571 may be
added the names of Cardigan and Shrewsbury in 1604 ; but
it appears likely that in these cases the fraudulent dealings
' originated in nothing more important than personal ambition
[1] Prothero,
lxiv. 132,
and 331.
and local intrigue.'[1] Thus the creation of ' rotten boroughs '
by the Tudors is as much a testimony to the integrity of the
new electoral bodies in the boroughs as it is a proof that
the Crown did not need to try conclusions with the older
and long established municipalities which sent members to
Parliament.

Influence
of the
Crown.
§ 31. If the influence of the sheriff waned, that of the
CROWN increased and absorbed any powers that remained
to the sheriff in the matter of parliamentary elections. For,
the *action of the Crown upon Parliament* was by no means
confined to the manipulation of elections. It generally began
before the elections were held and continued throughout the
whole session. But the methods employed by the Crown
changed with circumstances. Within our parliamentary life
there have been three periods in which the sovereign definitely
used his powers to obtain a representation of the people which
would at the same time be not unfavourable to the claims
and exercise of the royal prerogative. There are two intermediate periods which in this connection we need only
mention in order to dismiss. From the accession of the
1460-1530.
Yorkist dynasty to the beginning of the Reformation, the
Crown made a bold and fairly successful attempt to dispense

with Parliaments altogether; while from the accession of the 1603-1642. Stuarts to the outbreak of the Great Rebellion the two reigning kings successively took their stand on the prerogative and relied on it to overawe their Parliaments into an attitude of submission and assent. The three periods of influence may be roughly described as those of the Lancastrians, the Tudors and the Hanoverians. During these, as they will be more particularly defined, the efforts of the Crown to procure an artificial harmony with the House of Commons must be separately noted.

The attempts of the kings to control the composition of Methods of the House of Commons seem to have begun almost from the Plan-tagenets the moment when there was a House of Commons to and Lan-control. There is no need to estimate the relative influence castrians. of the Crown and of the sheriff, or even, what might be of greater practical importance, that of the Crown in competition with the great nobility. In some instances the Crown made use of the sheriffs for the furtherance of its own objects : but in general its influence may be said to have been exercised by methods which were at its disposal alone. These methods may be summarized as attempts to alter (*a*) the outward form and (*b*) the internal animating spirit of the House of Commons. Attempts of the first kind took one of two forms. Constitutional custom based on original convenience ulti-mately fixed the number of popular representatives at two respectively for each shire and borough, summoned in both cases through the sheriffs to one single assembly; but, for some time after the summons of what succeeding ages have regarded as the Model Parliament in 1295, the kings did not hesitate to (1) *alter the numbers and details of election and meeting*. An examination of the instances in which the example of 1295 was departed from, would show how far, at any period in its development, the parliamentary system was considered to be binding. Indeed, the name 'Magnum Concilium' is sometimes given by constitutional writers to all assemblies called after 1295, which did not contain the proper constituents of a statutable Parliament summoned in a proper way. But, strictly speaking, the *Magnum Concilium* was the old Commune Concilium subsisting as a Council of Magnates, which, even as late as 1640, the king reserved to himself the right of specially consulting. Such deviations as are now under consideration might more correctly be described as Magna Concilia reinforced by representatives of the popular constituencies. They are found generally in one of three forms. Sometimes, in addition to the Lords, the king summoned only one knight from each shire : at other times, as in 1352 and 1353, the mayors of certain towns would be directed to return one member for the borough ; while the outward form of Parliament would almost entirely disappear in the separation of the proper constituent elements into several bodies meeting at different places. But since the constitutional principle ultimately triumphed, it may be safely asserted that these changes only show that the king dreaded hearing the national complaints, not that he wished to alter the essential features of the national assembly.

With a similar object of influencing the outward form of the House of Commons, the king occasionally (2) *shortened the orthodox time allowed for the conduct of elections*.[1] The usual allowance of forty days between the issue of the writ and its return, dates from Magna Carta. But it was sometimes to the advantage of the local authority acting on the king's behalf, that this time should be shortened. Thus, in 1327 the notice was limited to thirty-five days, in 1352 to twenty-eight days ; while, as an extreme instance, the first Parliament summoned by Henry IV in 1399 had only seven days' notice, and contained, as it was intended to do, the same members as its predecessor.

Under the head of attempts to influence the *spirit* of the Commons come, firstly, some of the (1) *alterations* found from time to time *in the writs of summons*.[2] Interpolations in this spirit were made with two objects ; for they were intended, positively, to secure the election of certain classes such as the 'belted knights' already mentioned, and negatively, to exclude certain classes whose absence for some reason was specially desired. We have seen that a petition of the Commons themselves was taken for the basis of an ordinance in 1372 excluding both sheriffs and lawyers from eligibility for the House of Commons. But in 1350 it was by a clause in the writs of summons issued to the sheriffs

[1] *S. C. H.* § 411.

[2] *Ibid.* § 419.

that directions were given that the persons chosen should not be pleaders and maintainers of quarrels or men who lived by such gains ; while in 1387 public opinion obliged Richard II to withdraw, as contrary to the ancient form and to the liberties of the Lords and Commons, the writs which, with the object of shutting out his enemies from Parliament, directed the election of persons 'in modernis debatis magis indifferentes,' i.e. who had not taken part in the recent quarrels. Nor are parallel instances altogether wanting under later sovereigns.[1] But on the whole the writs remained substantially the same until the form in use at present was substituted by the Ballot Act of 1872.[2]

But if any alteration of the terms of the writ was regarded as unconstitutional, it may have been possible sometimes for a powerful king or minister to (2) *use the influence of the sheriffs and even of the great nobility* to secure the return of a favourable House of Commons. In 1377 John of Gaunt procured the election of a 'packed' House of Commons which reversed all the work of the Good Parliament of the previous year. In 1397 the exclamation of the condemned Earl of Arundel, 'the faithful commons are not here,' points to the same conclusion ; while in 1399, among the charges against Richard II was that of tampering with the elections by directing the sheriffs to return certain persons whom he named.[3]

It will be seen that all the cited instances of undue royal influence over Parliament fall within the reigns of Edward III or his grandson. Not that the royal influence entirely ceased under the Lancastrians ; but the peculiar position of that dynasty, with its purely parliamentary title, caused the kings to be chary of any action likely to provoke popular murmurs ; while their constitutional endeavours only left the way all the more clear both for that manipulation by the sheriff which was met by a series of legislative acts, and for that influence of the great nobility, which only collapsed with their own destruction in the Wars of the Roses. The *Tudors* renewed the regular summons of Parliament because they were possessed of means by which *both Lords and Commons should remain under royal control*. The whole House of Lords could be restrained by the addition of a sufficient number of royal nominees ; and individual peers could be punished for refractory

[1] Hallam, i. 46. Prothero, 280, 441.

[2] Anson, i. 55-56.

[3] *S. C. H.* § 296.

Methods of the Tudors.

conduct by exclusion from the royal presence. Moreover, the Crown still occasionally fell back upon its old policy of (1) *dispensing with a Parliament* for years together. Thus when, despite Elizabeth's prohibition, the Commons insisted on discussing the questions of her marriage and the settlement of the succession, she punished them by omitting to summon Parliament for five years; and again, after 1588, when the disappearance of the long-threatened danger from abroad made the Commons still more demonstrative, Parliament was called only four times in the remaining fifteen years of Elizabeth's reign. At the same time, when a Parliament was held, the Tudors neglected no means of procuring one favourable to the royal wishes. All the Tudor sovereigns courted the prosperous commercial classes by largely increasing the borough representation in the House of Commons. But it was with the object of securing a majority of votes in that House that at any rate Edward VI's ministers and Elizabeth used the royal prerogative of granting charters to (2) *call into existence a number of small boroughs*, later well designated by the epithet 'rotten,' whose only title to special representation was their complete subservience to the royal influence. Somewhat similar motives may have dictated the policy of (3) *narrowing* by the same medium of a royal charter, *the constituencies of the boroughs;* though possibly in the end these swelled the influence of the local landowners rather than of the Crown itself. At any rate, where the king could not nominate he could influence, and the Council under Edward VI had no compunction about sending a circular letter to the sheriffs, now largely removed from the overshadowing influence of the local nobility, ordering them to see that the shires and even the boroughs elected men of learning and wisdom such as should be nominated by the Council. But, although the rival influence of the nobility may now have been exercised rather at the bidding of the Crown than on its own behalf, it was not yet extinct. Thus, in the reign of Mary the Earl of Sussex wrote to the electors of Norfolk and Yarmouth ordering them to vote for his nominees;[1] while in 1571 the abolition of the qualification of residence for burgesses was rejected on the ground that, in the event of such repeal, 'Lords' letters would henceforth bear all the sway.'[2]

1566-1571.

1589.
1593.
1598.
1601.

[1] Hallam, i. 46.

[2] *Ibid.* i. 266-268.

But the influence of the Crown did not cease on the threshold of Parliament. The Speaker, whose office only seems to date definitely from 1377, was the nominee of the Commons, though his election required confirmation by the Crown. Such an official was necessary, not only as chairman of the House, but also as its spokesman in communications with the sovereign. Before the Lancastrian epoch the holders of this office seem to have been generally the stewards or dependants of one or other of the great lords whose factions divided the court. But under the constitutional rule of the Lancastrians, to judge from the long-winded homilies which they inflicted on the king, they must have been really representative of the House of Commons. The Speaker was the medium of communication not only between the Commons and the Crown, but also between the Crown and the Commons ; and it became his business to explain to the House all measures which the Crown wished to lay before the Commons. So important a means of influence was not to be lost, and accordingly we find that the Tudors practically secured for the king the (4) *nomination of the Speaker* with the result that 'the Speaker, instead of being the defender of the liberties of the House, had often to reduce it to an order that meant obsequious reticence or sullen submission.'[1]   Even Sir Thomas More, as Speaker in the Parliament of 1523, found it difficult to be anything except the subservient agent of the king and of Wolsey, and it may well be imagined how far below his level the majority of his successors would fall in efforts to maintain the independence of the House of Commons. But as the Commons grew in strength, the influence of the Speaker was not found sufficient ; and apart from the persuasive efforts of the Star Chamber, Elizabeth considered it necessary to ensure the election of an important royal official, the (5) *Secretary of State, as a member of the Commons*. The fact that this post was held successively by Sir William Cecil, afterwards Lord Burleigh, and by his son, is sufficient evidence of the importance attached by the queen to this method of influencing the House.

But, besides these indirect methods of coercing Parliament, the Crown was always at liberty to (6) fall back upon the prerogative, to issue proclamations, or by use of the dispensing

[1] Stubbs, *Lects. in Mediaev. and Mod. Hist*. 272. Porritt, i. 433 et seq.

power practically to annul the parliamentary statutes, to resort to arbitrary methods of raising supplies which should make it less dependent on a grant from the House of Commons, to single out for punishment members guilty of offensive speeches, or in the last resort to forego the summons of Parliament altogether. But intimidation, amounting to the direct use of force, was a weapon used most carefully, nay, sparingly, by the Tudors in their relations with the Commons. Henry VIII based some of his most unconstitutional actions on the sanction of Parliament ; the Council of Edward VI consented to the repeal of more than one of the harsh measures enacted under his predecessor ; Mary only obtained her desired restoration to communion with Rome by a sacrifice which almost robbed it of all meaning ; Elizabeth, in continual conflict with the Commons and not abating one jot her own rights, yet more than once gave way to the plainly expressed feeling of the House in a manner that served only to endear her all the more to the hearts of her people.

Causes of the Stuart failure to control Parliament.

But the Stuarts brought with them high notions of the prerogative, which led them to regard constitutional forms with contempt. Thus while, in the matter of actual methods, the Stuarts were perhaps mere imitators of their predecessors and not the innovators that they are generally given the credit, or rather discredit, of having been, yet they were for ever challenging Parliament by a definition of the rights of the Crown, and thus provoked counter-definitions as to the limits of a power whose merit it is that it has never been reduced to definition. Thus the indirect expedients of the Tudors for keeping Parliament in friendly relations with the Crown, practically fell into entire disuse. The wholesale creation of 'rotten boroughs' almost ceased with the accession of the Stuarts ; and by far the larger number of those which were created or revived under James I and Charles I owed their privilege to an order of the House of Commons for the issue of a writ on their behalf. Again, all actual interference with the elections or the issue of directions as to who should be elected seems, with one exception,[1] to have ceased. James I and his son preferred to meet their Parliaments face to face or not at all. But the resolute attitude of the House from the very first convinced the Stuarts of the

[1] Prothero, 280.

necessity of occasionally resorting to other means than mere force for making Parliament submissive. But even here, in the measures which they adopted for this purpose, they pitched upon methods which the Tudors would have scorned. In 1614 James, at the advice of Bacon, made an attempt to form within the Commons a party of persons devoted to the interests of the king. But these ' Undertakers,' as they were called, met with complete failure, and the 'Addled' Parliament, as it came to be called, broke up without having enacted a single legislative measure.[1] No happier was the attempt of Charles I in 1626. By a parliamentary ordinance issued in answer to a petition of the Commons in 1372, sheriffs as returning officers had been declared ineligible as members for their own shires. Charles took advantage of this; and, by nominating some of the leading members of the opposition as sheriffs, he hoped to stave off criticism in his second Parliament.[2] But the natural hostility of the opposition was only increased by this obvious attempt to remove its leaders. Nor did the new kings even take the trouble to see that their views were adequately laid before the Commons; for, abandoning the salutary plan of Elizabeth, they placed in the House as exponents of the royal will second-rate politicians and mere mouthpieces of the ministers who in reality directed the royal policy. It is no wonder, then, that the means which these kings preferred were such as overrode and ultimately abolished all constitutional forms whatsoever, or that Parliament ultimately dealt out to them that measure of justice which the kings would fain have inflicted on the Commons.

The Restoration brought back a Parliament much more truly loyal to the Crown than any since the Tudor times, and Charles II was restored unconditionally to the prerogatives enjoyed by his ancestors. But the Rebellion lay between him and the methods employed by his father and grandfather for the maintenance of those prerogatives. When once the fervour of their early loyalty had spent itself, he was forced to have recourse to subtler devices for keeping a hold upon his Parliaments. And yet the old methods did not die without a struggle. In 1674 the city and county of Durham had been summoned for the first time to take their place in the representative system of the country. In 1681 Charles, not to be

[1] Gardiner, ii. 228 et seq.

[2] Ibid. vi. 33.

Methods of the later Stuarts and Hanoverians.

1681.

outdone by Parliament, called out a prerogative which had
been for some little while in abeyance, and by royal charter
enfranchised the loyal town of Newark ; but the attitude of
the Commons warned him not to repeat the act.   Again,
both he and his brother made that assault upon the existing
charters of the boroughs which proved ' the last form of violent
external measures used by the king to affect the representation.'[1]
Charles took care also that the Crown should be adequately
represented in the House of Commons, and he even lent himself
to the formation of a group of members within the House for the
maintenance of the royal influence and the distribution of its
favours.   But all these are as nothing compared with that
gigantic *system of parliamentary corruption* which arose under
Charles II when the loyal feeling of Parliament began to wane.
The Revolution of 1688 practically removed from the power
of the Crown all means of direct and open influence on the
Commons, while it left the Commons a close oligarchy with
increased power and no correspondingly increased responsibilities.   The only means of influence were indirect, and the
low political morality of the time dictated what form they
should take.   For more than a century this gross system lay
like a blight upon the constitution, affecting even the keen party
contest of the reigns of William III and Anne, but flourishing
especially amid the party intrigue and selfish scramble for office
which characterize the early years of the Hanoverian dynasty.
Such corruption was protean in its shapes ; but it is both
possible and instructive to discriminate between the chief forms
which it assumed.

The most gross method was (*a*) the *direct payment* of sums
of money in return for votes given either at the polling booth
by electors or by members in Parliament.   This was chiefly
rendered possible by the general state of the finances and
especially by the fact that there was a portion of the royal
income over which Parliament had no control and which was
therefore specially adapted for use as secret service money.
In the actual traffic over the rotten boroughs the Crown found
formidable rivals in the great nobility ; but yet an estimate
made in 1793 shows that sixteen members of the Commons
were the direct nominees of the Crown, while the secret correspondence of George III and his ministers affords abundant

[1] Porritt, i.
393, 399.

proof of the large sums spent on the direct bribery of 'free and independent' voters at the hustings.[1]   The easier method, however, was to obtain by some heavy bribe, probably other than pecuniary, the support of some of the great borough-mongers; while the ministers of the Crown kept the revenues at their disposal for the purchase of actual votes in Parliament.

A more permanent influence was obtained by (b) the formation of a ministerial party within the House of Commons by the judicious, if wholesale, distribution of *offices and pensions*. Of the gradual disqualification of office-holders for seats in the House of Commons mention has already been made.[2]   It will be sufficient here to summarize the results of the various legislative efforts in this direction.[3]   At the time of the Place Bill of 1742, 200 members of the House of Commons were said to hold Crown appointments of various kinds. That Act only affected the holders of minor offices;[4] but none the less it had a salutary effect in checking a pernicious means of royal influence.   Still, many placemen remained in the House; nor was their influence disguised.   The party of 'King's Friends' succeeded where James I's Undertakers had met with failure, and Burke's indignant tirades in the 'Thoughts on the Present Discontents' took practical shape in a great scheme of economical reform.   In 1780 he proposed the abolition of fifty offices held by members of one or other House of Parliament.   Notwithstanding the opposition in favour of retaining 'the turnspit in the king's kitchen' as a member of Parliament, Lord Rockingham's Act of 1782[5] suppressed a number of offices connected with the royal household which, in the event of their revival, should be considered new offices within the meaning of the Act of 1706 in amendment of the Act of Settlement; in other words, they should disqualify their holders for seats in the House of Commons.   This was 'the last of the statutes which, in creating official disqualifications, had in view the independence of the House of Commons.'[6]   Future disqualifying Acts were chiefly intended to secure a permanent civil service which should be undisturbed in the discharge of administrative routine by considerations based upon the fortune of party politics.   The effect of these Acts has been to reduce the number of placemen in the House of Commons from 270 at

[1] Erskine May, i. 341. Anson, i. 325-327, quoting from Corresp. of Geo. III. with Lord North.

[2] p. 189.

[3] Erskine May, i. 369-375. 1742.

[4] Robertson, 125.

[5] Robertson, 142.

[6] Anson, i. 324.

the accession of the Hanoverians, to less than ninety under George IV. The Reform Act of 1832 had an immediate influence in the same direction. At the same time, there has always been a considerable number of officers of the army and navy who, as having been bred up in feelings of loyalty to the Crown, are regarded by the extremer radicals as the most dangerous type of placemen. But the very knowledge of this loyalty was a dangerous weapon in the hands of unscrupulous politicians, and neither Walpole in the case of the 'Cornet of Horse' Pitt, nor George III in that of General Conway—to mention only the most notorious instances — hesitated to dismiss the holders of these non-political offices for acts and speeches in Parliament. General Conway, however, supplied the last example; and the constitutional temper of Lord Rockingham's first administration put an end to this unwarrantable use of the royal power.

1765-1766.

[1] Erskine May, i. 256-262.

The question of *pensions*,[1] as well as offices, had been dealt with by the Act of Settlement; but its severe provisions had been modified by the Act of 1706, which merely closed the doors of Parliament to those whose pensions were enjoyed during the pleasure of the Crown. To these an Act of the first year of George I added pensioners for terms of years. But none of these provisions could cover the case of secret pensions or of pensions granted to the wives of the royal hirelings. Against such there was no safeguard so long as the system of management of Crown revenues left a sufficient sum of money in the king's hands, which could be applied to such purposes. The history of civil list pensions, apart from the question of a seat in Parliament, is in itself a revelation of the irresponsible waste of money which was characteristic of eighteenth-century government. It was on the accession of Queen Anne that an attempt was made by law to restrain the power of the Crown in granting pensions charged upon its hereditary revenues and whose payment was binding on its successors. The Act which first restrained the alienation of Crown lands, also provided that no portion of the hereditary revenues could be granted away for any term beyond the life of the reigning sovereign. With the accession of George III such pensions became chargeable on the Civil List, and by Lord Rockingham's Act of 1782 their gross amount was considerably restricted.   The Irish pension list, whose history is particularly scandalous, and the Scotch pension list remained untouched by the Act of Anne.   In 1793, in imitation of the English example on George III's accession, the hereditary revenues of the former were exchanged for a fixed Civil List, together with a separate pension list of no less than £124,000.   This sum was reduced in 1813 and again in 1820 to the substantial figure of £50,000. In 1810 the Scotch pension list was reduced by Parliament to £25,000.   In 1830 the three pension lists were consolidated and the amount reduced from more than £145,000 to £70,000.   Finally, on the accession of the late sovereign the right of the Crown to grant pensions was limited to £1,200 a year, and qualifications were stated for such pensions, which would remove them beyond the region of political reward.

A far more subtle method of buying votes than any yet enumerated was (c) the judicious distribution of *shares in loans, lotteries and contracts*[1] among supporters of the government. These were all favourite means of securing a parliamentary majority during the first twenty years of the reign of George III. The scandals caused by the transactions of Bute, of Grafton and of North himself, caused the latter in 1782 to raise a new loan by a system of close subscriptions ; but the deathblow to the waste of public money which had been due to the system of jobbing loans and lotteries, was dealt by the younger Pitt, who developed North's latest device for raising money into the modern form of contracts by sealed proposals from different persons, which were opened in each other's presence and the lowest tenders then and there accepted.   The extravagance of loans and lotteries was only outdone in sheer wastefulness by the grant of lucrative contracts for the public service, a form of bribery which was especially acceptable to the commercial members of the House.   The flagrant abuse of this system during the course of the war with the American Colonies, caused the introduction of a bill to disqualify close government contractors for a seat in the House. This, though at first rejected, was successfully carried through by the second Rockingham ministry in 1782.

An investigation into the sources and the prevalence of

[1] Erskine May, i. 382-389. Anson, i. 324-325.

Why corruption did not destroy public life.

corruption in the eighteenth century leaves us wondering how, in such adverse conditions, public integrity could in any sense be kept alive. It must, however, be remembered that the legitimate prizes were so great as to attract the best ability to the service of the State. Thus, while a parliamentary majority was held together by illegitimate means, the more honourable statesmen, such as Rockingham and both the Pitts, unsparingly condemned the use of such methods, even while they found themselves obliged to acquiesce in their existence. But such condemnation had a wholesome result: it kept alive a standard of public opinion in the matter; it gradually eliminated the grosser methods of corruption, and it prepared the way for a time when political principles should be sufficiently strong to enable a popular minister to dispense with a bought majority, and when the reform of Parliament should put such methods of diplomacy beyond the reach of the most skilful party manager. But in defence of the existing constituencies it should be said that, even before parliamentary reform was obtained, they represented on the whole the most educated classes in the country, and that in moments of popular excitement they proved themselves not unwilling to respond to pressure from outside. Moreover, in Parliament itself the existence of political parties ensured the advocacy of popular measures and their support by popular arguments. Thus the long exclusion of the Tories from power under the first two Hanoverian monarchs turned the defenders of the prerogative into the champions of parliamentary purity; and the equally long exclusion of the Whigs under George III turned the exponents of oligarchical government into the proposers of a moderate, but sufficient, scheme of parliamentary reform. Nor should the growing influence of the press be underrated; for it triumphed in its struggle with the House of Commons over the publication of debates, and together with, and perhaps with more wholesome effect than, the organization of parties, it must have done much to form an intelligent public opinion.[1]

[1] Erskine May, i 390-392. Lecky, i. 450-452.

Reform of the House of Commons,

§ 32. Meanwhile, the question of PARLIAMENTARY REFORM was attracting a continually larger share of the public attention. Since the days of Elizabeth politicians from the monarch downwards recognized the need of getting rid of the ruined and decayed towns, while the records of disputed elections show that local efforts to abolish the existing monopoly in the franchise were frequent from the beginning of the seventeenth century. But no national movement such as culminated in the Reform Act of 1832 was possible until towards the close of the eighteenth century. When it did come it may be said to have gone through four phases. The first of these may be described as preliminary. In point of time it was prior to the French Revolution, and was marked 1st phase by the suggestions of individual statesmen who felt the evils of —to 1790. the existing system. The first of these was no less a person than the elder Pitt who, as *Lord Chatham*, on two separate occasions pointed out the necessity for the amendment of 1766. the borough representation, and as a remedy suggested the 1770. addition of a third member to every county 'to counterbalance the weight of corrupt and venal boroughs.' He ventured to prophesy that, 'before the end of this century, either the Parliament will reform itself from within, or be reformed with a vengeance from without.' It is much to the honour of the notorious *Wilkes* that the next suggestions of parlia- mentary reform are associated with his name. In 1776 he 1776. proposed a bill which came nearer than any of these earlier schemes to the principles which received recognition in 1832. Thus, the disfranchisement of the rotten boroughs, which even Chatham had not felt justified in suggesting, was to be accompanied by an increase of members from London and the large counties, and the enfranchisement of several 'rich, populous, trading towns.' Less merit was attached to the terms of a measure introduced in 1780 by the *Duke of Richmond*, 1780. which took for its basis the principles of annual parliaments, universal suffrage and equal electoral districts. These were three points of the later 'People's Charter,' and outside the (1838.) walls of Parliament were supported by the 'Society for Pro- moting Constitutional Information,' which was founded in the same year by Major Cartwright and joined by members of both Houses. But the bill was proposed in the midst of the Gordon riots, and met with no sympathy in Parliament itself. The last of these preliminary attempts at reform is connected with the name of the younger *William Pitt*, who made no less than three proposals with this object. The first of these was in 1782, during the second Rockingham administration, when his motion for a committee to inquire into the state of the parliamentary representation was rejected by the small majority of 20. 'It has been noticed,' remarks Mr. Lecky, 'that the reformers never again had so good a division until 1831.'[1] Nothing daunted, Pitt returned to the charge in the very next year, and while in opposition to the Coalition Ministry of Fox and North, he advanced a step further by the proposal of three tentative resolutions for measures to prevent bribery, disfranchise corrupt boroughs and increase the county members. But these suggestions, while disappointing to the advocates of reform who were flooding the House with petitions, did not commend them- selves to a Parliament whose conscience had been allayed by Lord Rockingham's late moderate measures, and, in a full house of 450, Pitt's motion was rejected by a majority of 144. The third and last attempt was in 1785, when Pitt had taken his place at the head of the ministry as the nominee of the king. Despite the known hostility of George III, Pitt redeemed the pledge he had so often given, and introduced a comprehensive scheme of reform. By this he proposed (*a*) to distribute among London and the counties and certain large, hitherto unenfranchised, towns, a hundred members gained by the disfranchisement and purchase of small and 'rotten' boroughs: (*b*) to enlarge the county franchise by the addition of copyholders, and (*c*) to compensate the pro- prietors of the disfranchised boroughs to the amount of a million sterling from the revenues of the State. No doubt, Pitt thought that this was the only way out of a great practical difficulty, and he actually applied this method afterwards on a large scale for effecting the Irish Union; but the ardent reformers refused to recognize the vested right of property in the representation, while the king and the rest of the ministry were directly hostile. Pitt was even refused leave to bring in his bill, but by a diminished majority of 74 in a House of 420 members. In 1790, on Flood's motion, and again in 1792 on Grey's motion in favour of reform, Pitt acknowledged that he still entertained an opinion in its favour, although he believed that under the present circum- stances it was impracticable.[2]

In truth, the first phase of the reform movement was at an end. It was no longer a question which depended for its advocacy on individual statesmen. The early stages of the French Revolution made it in England the creed of a party which welcomed the example of a people struggling to be free; while the excesses of the Revolution, together with the sufferings of the working classes in England by reason of the prolonged war, threw the cause of parliamentary reform into the hands of leaders of 'Hampden Clubs' and other democratic associations which found their support among the unenfranchised classes of the nation. Thus a second phase may be said to extend from 1790, when Pitt definitely renounced the cause, to 1797, when an elaborate motion of Grey and Erskine was rejected by a large majority. During these years the proposals of the reformers under the leadership of Mr. Grey were on the lines of those which Pitt had recently formulated, and were supported by the 'Friends of the People,' the most respectable among the political societies which then sprang into existence.[1] After the defeat of Grey's motion the opposition for a time seceded from the House of Commons as a protest against the whole policy of repression for which Pitt was using his huge parliamentary majority. With this episode the reform movement entered on its third and least creditable phase. For twenty-three years it was practically the monopoly of demagogues outside Parliament. Grey and Erskine were called to the House of Lords, and its advocacy in the Commons was left to an eccentric aristocrat—Sir Francis Burdett. To the earlier proposals of the Duke of Richmond was now added the democratic safeguard of the vote by ballot; but frequent motions on behalf of such extreme principles ended by leaving their proposer with one supporter in the House.[2]

The fourth and concluding phase began when Lord John Russell associated himself with the question, and thus restored the leadership in the movement to the Whigs. His first motion in favour of reform in 1820 was followed by others in 1822, 1823 and 1826 on the old lines which had been laid down by Pitt and Grey; but they were all equally rejected by majorities of more than a hundred.[3] The only prospect of success seemed to lie in a change of tactics. The reformers

Marginal notes:

Second phase— 1790-1797.

[1] Erskine May, i. 402-405.

Third phase— 1797-1820.

[2] *Ibid.* i. 405-408.

Fourth phase— 1820-1832.

[3] *Ibid.* i. 410-412.

determined to attack and destroy in detail all those boroughs which could be convicted of gross corruption. Hitherto the few attempts at disfranchisement had failed, although in three notorious cases the guilty electorate was swamped by the addition of all the forty-shilling freeholders in the neighbouring hundred. But now bribery and traffic in seats were to be regarded, not so much as regrettable but perhaps necessary accompaniments of the political system of the time, as serious moral evils which must at all costs be rooted out. In 1820 a preliminary success was gained by the disfranchisement of the Cornish borough of Grampound, and by what has been called the first Redistribution Act its members were transferred to the county of York.[1] This conceded the principle, and the reformers desired to go a step further, and to give representatives so gained to the large manufacturing towns which were without the franchise. With this view, they attacked four notorious cases which had been exposed in the elections of 1826. These were Northampton and Leicester, where the corporations had applied large sums of the corporate funds to support ministerial candidates, and Penrhyn and East Retford where bribery had been employed in the most shameless manner. But the proposals of the reforming party were defeated over their attempts to transfer the seats to Manchester and Birmingham.[2] Had the government conceded these demands, it is possible that the progress of reform would have been postponed for many years. As it was, their rigid opposition caused the resignation of all the more liberal members of the ministry and weakened their ranks for the struggle which now became inevitable.

In 1830 Lord John Russell proposed the direct enfranchisement of Leeds, Birmingham and Manchester, and O'Connell took up the programme of Sir Francis Burdett. But the death of George IV in this year and the consequent dissolution of Parliament brought matters to a crisis. The immediate success of the reform movement may be ascribed to three circumstances. In the first place, the Catholic Emancipation Act of 1829 had so loosened the bonds of party allegiance that politicians were only waiting for some popular cry to form themselves into new parties. Then came the Revolution of 1830, when Charles X's attempts to repress freedom of

Sidenotes:

New Shoreham, 1770. Cricklade, 1782. Aylesbury, 1804.

[1] Erskine May, i. 409.

[2] *Ibid.* i. 413-416.

The final struggle for Reform.

discussion and representative government in France resulted in his deposition ; and the excitement was heightened by the revolt of Belgium from Holland, to which she had been joined in 1815. Finally, the Duke of Wellington, who was Prime Minister, threw down a direct challenge to the country when, in the debate on the address, he declared, in answer to Earl Grey, that 'the legislature and system of representation possessed the full and entire confidence of the country.'[1] A fortnight later the Duke was defeated on a motion of inquiry into the Civil List, and resigned. Lord Grey became Prime Minister, and was of course pledged to a measure of parliamentary reform.   The difficulties to be overcome were enormous—on the one side, the reluctance of the king and the open hostility of the boroughmongers and, through them, of a majority in perhaps both Houses of Parliament ; on the other side, the desires of the more ardent reformers who now looked for an adequate realization of their dreams.   But despite all these, the measure of the government, moderate and yet comprehensive in its provisions, was carried to a triumphant conclusion.   Three bills in succession were introduced.   The first, proposed by Lord John Russell in March, 1831, was only carried through the House of Commons by a majority of one on its second reading, and was defeated in Committee.   Parliament was dissolved, and in a House of Commons full of members pledged to reform, the new bill was passed by a majority of 136, only to be thrown out in the Lords by 41.   A third bill was promptly introduced which remedied some of the objectionable clauses of its two predecessors : thus it retained the number of members of the House at the same total as before, instead of reducing them as was at first proposed.   This bill passed the Commons by a majority of 162, and in April, 1832, its second reading was affirmed by the Lords by 9 votes.   But this was only preliminary to its destruction by amendments moved in Committee.   In fact, the moment had come when either the Lords must give way or the ministers resign.   The king refused to create a sufficient number of peers, and the ministers did resign.   The Commons passed votes of confidence in them : Wellington in vain attempted to form a cabinet, and Grey and his followers returned to office.   The king now put no obstacle to the creation of peers, but at the same time used his personal

[1] Erskine May, i. 417-420.

[1] Erskine May, i. 421-427.

The Reform Act of 1832.

influence to prevent its necessity. The Duke of Wellington also came to the rescue; the opposition peers were persuaded to absent themselves, and the bill was passed.[1]

The details of its provisions have already been described. There were *four chief evils of the old system* which it recognized and met. Eighty-six *rotten boroughs* were wholly or in part disfranchised. Large *town populations hitherto unrepresented* were provided for, and the more populous counties received extra consideration. While the rights of individual electors were saved, the hitherto *restricted franchise*, whether in counties or boroughs, was considerably enlarged, although each was established on a separate basis. One effect of this distinction between the county and the borough franchise must not pass unnoticed. So long as it existed, 'a measure of redistribution was necessarily a measure of disfranchisement. Where a borough ceased to return members, its electors . . . with the exception of those who might possess the county qualification, ceased to be electors at all.'[2] It will be seen that this applies also to the Act of 1867, but not to the Redistribution Act of 1885. Finally, by providing for the registration of electors, the increase of polling districts and the limitation of the days of polling, the Act sought to diminish the *enormous expenses at elections*.[3] These points received further attention from Parliament during the succeeding sessions; but as to general principles the Whigs regarded the Act of 1832 as final, and no further motion for reform was made in Parliament for 20 years.

[2] Anson, i. 126.

[3] Erskine May, i. 427-429.

Reform after 1832.

But the people in general were far from being satisfied. The Reform Act had done nothing except provide 'a remedy for the worst evils of a faulty and corrupt electoral system. It had rescued the representation from a small oligarchy of peers and landowners and had vested it in the hands of the middle classes. But it had spared many boroughs, which were perhaps too small to exercise their suffrage independently : it had overlooked the claims of some considerable places'[4] : and it had not taken the working classes into account at all. From 1838 to 1848 the cause of reform was in the hands of the Chartists, who regarded the establishment of the *six points of the People's Charter* as a panacea for all the political evils of the country, and refused to work with the free-traders, whom

[4] *Ibid.* i. 450.

they stigmatized as 'quacks.' Their six points were the old
proposals of manhood suffrage, annual Parliaments, equal
electoral districts, and vote by ballot, together with two new
suggestions for the revival of payment of members, and the
abolition of the property qualification for members of Parliament, which was merely modified in 1838.[1] The leaders of [1] Erskine
the movement were Daniel O'Connell and Feargus O'Connor, May, ii.
and it was productive of considerable violence in various 407-413.
parts of the country; but it was not until the discovery of
the fictitious names appended to a monster petition presented
to the House of Commons, and purporting to bear more than
five million signatures, that the movement was finally discredited, and the question of the extension of the franchise
once more became a cabinet measure. In the course of the
next fifteen years four abortive measures were proposed, three 1852-1867.
of which were associated with the name of Lord John Russell.
In 1852 he proposed to lower the franchise so as to embrace
classes, especially the most skilled artisans, who had not
been included hitherto. In 1854 he suggested measures for
the representation of minorities and for giving greater weight
to the educated and thrifty classes. These last were imitated
by Mr. Disraeli in 1859 in the government of Lord Derby,
who also suggested the assimilation of the county and borough
franchise.   In 1680, in Lord Palmerston's ministry, Lord
John Russell made his final proposal of reform, in a bill
which, while lowering the franchise, spared all the smaller
boroughs.[2]   [2] *Ibid.* i.
No other governmental measure was proposed during the 450-459.
lifetime of Lord Palmerston, who was known to be unfriendly
to the cause of parliamentary reform. His death in 1865,
and the accession of Earl Russell to the post of Premier,
revived the hopes of the reformers. But circumstances were
unfavourable; reform had not been a moot point at the
previous elections, most of the members were of Lord
Palmerston's opinion, and were not anxious to run the risk
of a dissolution after one session. A bill, however, was introduced by Mr. Gladstone, but a large secession took place
in the party, which was nicknamed by John Bright the 'Cave
of Adullam,' and the ministers carried their proposals by
such small majorities that they regarded it as a defeat and

resigned. Lord Derby was called to office again with his party in a minority in the House of Commons, and the popular disappointment at the failure of the Whigs culminated in a riotous meeting in Hyde Park. Some measure of reform seemed imperatively necessary : the Conservatives introduced their bill, and chiefly owing to the tact of Disraeli who had the conduct of it, the ministry gained the support of the Dissentient Whigs, and in **1867** passed a scheme, stripped of all those provisions and safeguards which had originally commended it to the real supporters of the ministry. Needless to say, this ultimately satisfied a very small section of the House.[1]

[1] Erskine May, iii. 429-439. The Representation of the People Act, 1867.

Besides the redistribution of fifty-two seats gained from disfranchised boroughs, the chief provisions of the Act were the lowering of the property franchise and an addition to the occupation franchise in the counties, and the introduction of the household and lodger franchise into boroughs. By the influence of Lord Cairns provision was also made for the representation of minorities by the addition of a third member for Manchester, Liverpool, Birmingham and Leeds, electors not being allowed to vote for more than two candidates. Partial and unsatisfactory though this measure was in the eyes of reformers, it almost doubled the electorate. The small body of about 300,000 who possessed the franchise before 1832 had risen under that Act to 1,370,000 just before the Act of 1867 came into operation. The operation of that Act raised it to three millions.

1869-1874.

But further legislation was inevitable. Mr. Gladstone's first ministry contented itself with the *Ballot Act* of 1872, which should secure the poorer voters against undue influence by legalizing the system of secret voting. From 1872, however, a motion for the extension of the county franchise became an almost annual proposal, until in his second ministry Mr. Gladstone found himself strong enough to satisfy the utmost aspirations of his most ardent supporters. The two chief notes of the Act of **1884** were the assimilation of the county and borough franchise and a thorough redistribution of seats with some approach to equal electoral districts. No less than two million voters were thus added to the electorate. Thus, of the six points of the People's Charter, a lapse of less than

1880-1885.

The Representation of the People Act, 1884.

forty years had sufficed to accomplish all except two. The property qualification for members of Parliament was abolished in 1858; vote by ballot was granted in 1872, and the last Reform Bill practically provided for manhood suffrage and made a very long step towards equal electoral districts. Annual Parliaments and payment of members alone remain; and while the latter has the support of a large and influential section of the Radical party, the enormous size of the electorate seems to render the former impracticable. *The Redistribution Act, 1885.*

By the Act of 1884 the plain and intelligible principle of 'counting heads' has received such complete recognition that it would probably be impossible, even if it were ever considered desirable, to go back upon it and to attempt to found our system of representation on any other basis. It is thus all the more important to note some of the suggestions which have been made from time to time and have even been embodied in abortive bills, *for the representation of minorities* whether based upon local, social or intellectual considerations.[1] Some of these suggestions were too obviously artificial to be of more than temporary importance. Such were the varieties of what were disdainfully called *fancy franchises*, which found a place in the abortive bills of 1854, 1859 and Mr. Gladstone's measure of 1866, and which were proposed and rejected in the bill of 1867. Their chief object was the recognition, as parliamentary voters, of 'the educated or the thrifty man.' One of the most serious objections to many of them was that it would be easy to create the necessary qualification with a view to an election. A similar objection does not hold in the case of another of these suggestions, the institution of what have been called *three-cornered constituencies*. But this precautionary measure, which was first suggested in the bill of 1854, was actually embodied in the Act of 1867, and was abolished in the Redistribution Act of 1885. The chief objection was that it practically left the majority of voters in the largest cities with one member to represent their views, and thus reduced their power in Parliament to the level of the smallest constituency in the country. A third suggestion in the same direction is, what was originally known from its promoter as, *Hare's scheme*, which gained the warm applause of John Stuart Mill, and which, in a slightly *The representation of minorities.* [1] Anson, i. 134-140.

modified form as *proportional representation*, at one time obtained considerable support. The details are too long for reproduction here. Suffice it to say that a long division sum, with the number of registered electors as dividend and the number of seats to be filled as divisor, will give as its quotient the necessary constituency for an elected member. Voters would be allowed to record their votes in order of preference for all candidates throughout a larger or smaller district as might be thought most practicable. The voting-papers taken at random would be counted until some one candidate had secured the requisite number of qualifying votes. All votes subsequently given for him should then be transferred to the voters' second choice. In this manner, it is contended, all the seats will gradually be filled, no votes will be thrown away in hopeless minorities, all interests will be adequately represented, and the real strength and opinion of the electorate will be satisfactorily tested. It may be doubted, however, whether under any system of reckoning the choice of the voting-papers does not reduce the scheme to a lottery and thereby prevent it from becoming, except in such a rough-and-ready way as the present system provides, a thoroughly trustworthy representation of the country.

CHAPTER V

THE HOUSE OF COMMONS IN ACTION

§ 33. THE history of the form of the House of Commons has now been sketched to its completion, or rather, to the time when it assumed its present shape. This was a necessary preliminary to a study of the far more important point of the growth of the constitutional powers, which has brought the House of Commons to its present omnipotent position. It is primarily as the legislative assembly of the nation that Parliament plays its part in the constitutional system of the country. But the duty of the House of Commons in this respect was originally quite subordinate to its functions in the matter of taxation; while the important share which it now takes in criticism of the executive, was a still later development in its general acquisition of powers. Under these three heads, then,—taxation, legislation and general political deliberation—may be arranged most conveniently all that should be said of the *constitutional progress of the House of Commons.* Now, theoretically and in a general kind of manner, the kings seem to have been willing, almost from the very beginning of Parliaments, to accord to the Commons a participation in the most important powers of government. Thus the Confirmatio Cartarum of **1297,** which followed hard upon the meeting of the Model Parliament, promised in the name of the king with regard to taxation, that 'for so much as divers people of our realm are in fear that the aids and tasks which they have given to us before time towards our wars and other business . . . might turn to a bondage to them and their heirs . . . so likewise the prises taken throughout the realm by our ministers ; we have granted for us and our heirs . . . that for no business henceforth will we take such manner of aids, tasks nor prises, but *by the common assent*

of the realm, and for the common profit thereof, saving the
¹ *S. C.*
496.
ancient tasks and prises due and accustomed.'¹ Even more
definite was the acknowledgement made in the Parliament of
Edward II in **1322** as to legislation, that 'the matters which are
to be established for the estate of our lord the king and of his
heirs, and for the estate of the realm and of the people, shall
be treated, accorded and established in parliaments by our lord
the king, and by the assent of the prelates, earls and barons
and *the commonalty of the realm,* according as hath been
² *S. C. II.*
§ 254.
heretofore accustomed.'² But this was an equality which, in
actual practice and in the prevailing division of Estates, was
worthless. The true position of the Commons was only to be
won gradually, by hard fighting, by use of opportunities ; the
attempt could not begin until the Commons had, as a separate
House of Parliament, acquired a solidarity of form and
interests ; and it was only natural that the first acknowledged
and substantial victory of the Commons should be in that
department in which their help had been first required and
which in the end they have entirely monopolized.

Direct
attempts
to obtain
control over
(1) direct
taxation ;
The leaders of the assembly which had wrung the Confirmatio Cartarum from the representatives of the absent king, had
intended by the words quoted above to ensure the surrender
by the king of all right to direct and indirect TAXATION alike.
But so far as direct taxation was concerned, the king still felt
himself justified in levying, without any special consent, feudal
taxes, such as the three aids and scutage, as well as the old
landlord's tallage on ancient demesne. Consequently in **1340**,
soon after the Estates had arranged themselves in two Houses,
Edward III was forced to consent to a statute which ordained
that ' henceforth no charge or aid should be imposed on the
nation except by common assent of the prelates, earls, barons
and other great men and the commons of the realm assembled
³ *S. C. II.*
§§ 257,
275.
in Parliament.'³ But, although this statute was an answer to
the petitions of the Commons, there is nothing to show that
the power of making money grants was regarded as peculiar
to the representative branch of Parliament. As a matter of
fact, although the statute was intended to preclude every species
of unparliamentary taxation, the king did not hesitate in 1346
to exact a feudal aid at the knighting of the Black Prince, and
that moreover at a double rate ; while under Richard II a scutage

was remitted in 1385 as a tax which the king still regarded as his due when he went to war in person.[1] But the first business of the Commons was to insist on the necessity of their being consulted as a preliminary to any grant of taxation.[2] The usual method seems to have been for the king to send commissioners to each House of Parliament, as he did also to the two clerical Convocations, to lay his demands before them. The Estates and, after the division into two Houses, the Houses then joined in consultation, the result of which was the declaration of the method by which the money should be raised—whether as tenth and fifteenth, wool tax, tonnage and poundage—and of the proportions in which it should be assessed upon the various Estates. At first each Estate voted its grant in a different proportion; but the first advance in the direction of the financial supremacy of the Commons was made when those proportions were reduced to two in number and the difference was based on local and not upon class distinctions. But for the present the grants were still made by the two Houses jointly. It is in 1395 for the first time that the decisive share which the Commons may be said to have gained in the reign of Edward III, finds definite expression in the words of the grant. The money was said to be given 'by the Commons with the advice and assent of the Lords.' This form was repeated in two of the earliest Parliaments of Henry IV (1401 and 1402), and although the form was not always adhered to, the principle of the necessity of participation by the Commons in any such grant, may be said to have received formal recognition in 1407 when Henry IV, in response to a remonstrance of the Commons at his consultation on financial matters with the Lords alone, allowed that neither House should make a report on a grant until both were agreed, and that then the report should be made by the Speaker of the Commons. It is, however, unlikely that this concession 'was at the time understood to recognize the exclusive right of the Commons to originate the grant.'[3] It is enough to suppose that, from the time of Richard II, they were regarded as not merely necessary participators, but as the possessors of the preponderating voice. Indeed, it was not until the reign of Charles I that grants were definitely expressed as made by the Commons alone. In 1625 the subsidies were stated to be granted by 'your

[1] *S. C. H.* § 275.

[2] *Ibia.* §§ 370, 437-438.

[3] *Ibid.* § 370.

Commons assembled in your High Court of Parliament.' The further question of the attitude of the House of Lords towards a money grant must be reserved until the mutual relations of the two Houses are considered.

(2) indirect taxation.

Among the ways by which the first attempts of the Commons to control the grant of direct taxes were evaded, the private dealings of Edward III with the merchants holds the earliest place. This proved to the Commons the necessity of keeping a hand on such indirect means of raising money as were afforded by the Customs, Purveyance and Commissions of Array. But even here the power of Parliament could only be exercised in an indirect manner. Until the Commons were strong enough to enforce it, definite prohibition could have but one effect. The kings would either ignore it altogether, or would find other means of obtaining what they wanted. Thus the only wise policy for the Commons to pursue was, while acquiescing in the fact of a money grant unconstitutionally obtained, to assert the principle that all grants must be sanctioned by their vote. The detailed history of the Customs duties is given elsewhere.[1] Here it is merely necessary to recall that in 1275 the Commune Concilium had granted to the king the customs on wool, woolfells and leather at a fixed rate, to which, under the expressive name of a Maletote, the Confirmatio Cartarum in 1297 forbade any increase. But in 1303 Edward I obtained such increase by private agreement with the foreign merchants ; and in 1353, by the Statute of Staples for the regulation of the foreign trade, Parliament not only acquiesced in the levy of this increased rate from the foreigners, but even turned the Maletote into a parliamentary grant of a subsidy on wool. Towards the end of Edward III's reign the king's frequent attempts to implicate the Commons in his foreign policy, and his continuous demands on them for money to carry on his wars, emboldened them to go further, and in **1362** they obtained an act, which was confirmed in 1371, to the effect that *neither merchant nor any other body should henceforth set any subsidy or charge upon wool without consent of Parliament.* But the increased manufacture of cloth in England appreciably lessened both the custom and the subsidy on the export of wool ; and perhaps in compensation the customs on wine and general merchandise, known

Customs.

[1] Chap. x. 1275.

1297.
Their early settlement.

1303.
1353.

36 Edw. III. c. 11.

1362.
1371.

under the name of tonnage and poundage, were from the
accession of Henry VII granted to the king for his lifetime.

Hallam remarks that from the reign of Richard II to that of
Mary Tudor no addition was made to the established rates
of Customs duties.[1] This may be true of the Lancastrian and
Yorkist kings, but the Tudors began early to use this means
of increasing their revenue. It is noteworthy, however, in the
light of subsequent events, that their interference was covered
by the form of parliamentary sanction. Thus, in 1491, in the
supposed interests of English commerce, the duty on sweet
wines coming from the Levant was largely increased, and in
1532 the importation of French wines was partially forbidden.
Far more important was an Act of 1534 which authorized
Henry VIII 'to regulate by proclamation the course of trade,
even to the extent of repealing statutes in force or reviving
such as might be obsolete, touching the import or export of
any merchandise.'[2] Hence originated the royal right of levying what came to be called 'Impositions,' a right exercised
unchecked by Henry VIII no less than by Mary and Elizabeth.
By this means the Crown was definitely armed by Parliament
with the power of protecting the commerce of the country by
the retaliatory or protective measures which were then in
vogue. Nor was the first use to which James I put this power
any less justifiable than the action of his predecessors. The
Levant Company had agreed to pay Elizabeth £4,000 a year
in return for the privilege, among others, of levying a duty on
currants on all merchants outside the Company who traded in
them. In response to the outcry against monopolies in 1601
the Company surrendered its charter. The Crown thus lost
£4,000 a year and, in order to recoup itself, took over the
duty on currants previously levied by the Company. But the
Company was revived, obtained a patent in 1605 and even
pecuniary assistance from James I;[3] and it was a merchant of
this new Company, *John Bate*, who raised the important
constitutional question of the king's power of taxation by
refusing to pay the duty which he believed to be an illegal
imposition. The government determined to have the case
argued in the Court of Exchequer. The four Barons decided
entirely in favour of the Crown ; Sir Edward Coke and Hake-
will, who was afterwards one of the chief opponents, were at

Their
increase
under the
Tudors
and Stuarts.
[1] i. 42.

[2] Prothero,
lxxiii.

[3] Gardiner,
ii. 2-4.

the time perfectly satisfied, and the Parliament of 1608 acquiesced in the decision. Modern historians have agreed that the Barons' judgement was both unbiassed and in accordance with precedent.[1] It was certain extraneous arguments in which they allowed themselves to indulge, which foreshadowed the strong bias of the judicial bench in the future quarrel between Crown and Parliament : for Baron Clarke held that the statutes assented to by one king did not necessarily bind his successors, while Chief Baron Fleming distinguished between the ordinary power of the Crown which is exercised in accordance with the common law and its absolute power which cannot be circumscribed.[2] Bate's case, then, of itself roused no great feeling. But, in reliance on the decision, the Treasurer, Lord Salisbury, issued the usual Book of Rates embodying the new duties, and James in a commission issued to Salisbury authorizing their levy, clearly claimed the entire right for the Crown. The result was that the popular party in the Parliaments of 1610 and 1614 strongly protested against their levy ; the case was argued against them by the king's supporters, and the ground then taken up was maintained in all the constitutional arguments on either side down to the outbreak of the Civil War.[3] In the later Parliaments of James' reign, those of 1621 and 1624, other matters occupied the attention of the Commons. But the accession of a new king gave the Commons the opportunity for which they were waiting, and they refused to make Charles the usual life-grant of tonnage and poundage for more than one year, pending an inquiry into the illegal customs exacted during James' reign. But even this modified grant was never passed ; for the Bill was read over in the House of Lords, and its course was then stopped by the dissolution. James had taken only the extra sum or imposition without consent of Parliament. Charles did not hesitate to levy Tonnage and Poundage itself when Parliament withheld it, and that he took at the higher rate of his father's impositions. It seemed useless to apply to the judges, and the question only came up again in connection with the Petition of Right in Charles' third Parliament of 1628.

Early in the session a bill for the grant of tonnage and poundage had been introduced, but was put aside by the long debates and negotiations which ended in the king's signature

[1] Gardiner, ii. 5-11. Prothero, lxxv.

[2] Prothero, 340-342.

[3] Gardiner, ii. 70-72, 75-83, 237-241.

The quarrel over Tonnage and Poundage.

of the Petition of Right. One of the four points in this to which the king assented, was that 'no man hereafter should be compelled to make or yield any gift, loan, benevolence, tax, or such like charge without common consent by Act of Parliament.'[1] Some alterations in the incidence of the rates seemed desirable, but Charles refused the temporary bill which the Commons proposed to pass in order to make some provision in the current session. He probably thought that the Commons were putting forward a claim to be the sole originators of the right to levy customs in order that they might compel him to attend to their grievances. The Commons consequently drew up a Remonstrance, the second in that session, in which they gave the lie to their own contemplated action by trying to squeeze into the words of the Petition of Right a prohibition of the levy of tonnage and poundage. 'The receiving of tonnage and poundage,' they declared, 'and other impositions not granted by Parliament is a breach of the fundamental liberties of this kingdom and contrary to your Majesty's late answer to their Petition of Right.' The king was technically in the right when, on proroguing Parliament, he declared that by the Petition he had granted no new, but only confirmed the ancient liberties of the subject, and that as for tonnage and poundage, he did not intend to give away his right to levy it, nor could he in fact do without it.[2] But the Commons' remonstrance was not without effect; for it encouraged the merchants to refuse payment. Charles and his Council, taking their stand on the decision of the judges in Bate's case, ordered the goods of those refusing payment to be seized, and denied them any redress. Two cases in particular came up for trial— that of *Chambers*,[3] in which the judges to whom he appealed refused to interfere with the jurisdiction of the Star Chamber before which he was prosecuted; and that of *John Rolle*,[4] a merchant and also a member of Parliament, in whose behalf the Commons took their stand on the narrow ground of breach of privilege and, in order to punish the royal officers, tried to draw a distinction between them and the king. The defiant and irreconcileable attitude of the Commons in the second session brought about a dissolution; but, before Charles could fulfil his intention, the Commons, with locked doors, held the unwilling Speaker in the chair and passed resolutions

[1] *S. C.* 517.

[2] Gardiner, vi. 222-227. *Const. Docts. Puritan Rev.* 5-9.

[3] Gardiner, vii. 3-7, 82-86, 114.

[4] *Ibid.* vii. 28-35.

1629.

R

[1] Gardiner, vii. 67-76. *Const. Docts.* 16. 1629-1640.

condemning as enemies of the country all who should advise the levying of tonnage and poundage and all who should pay the same.[1] During the eleven unparliamentary years which followed, the impositions continued to be levied with more or less resistance until, in 1641, the Long Parliament passed a Tonnage and Poundage Act conveying these duties to the king for two months only in return for renunciation of all future claim to levy customs and duties of any kind without grant of Parliament.[2]

[2] *Const. Docts.* 88.

At the Restoration the Customs were rearranged and were all granted to Charles II for his life. Finally, James II, on his accession and before the meeting of a Parliament, issued a proclamation for the levy and employment of the Customs just as if they had been granted to him. An excuse for this may be found in the natural derangement of the course of trade which would have resulted from the arrest of goods at the ports until the duties had been voted; but it was perhaps fortunate for James that his first Parliament was enthusiastically Tory and did not hesitate to grant him the Customs revenue of his predecessors, even augmented, for his life.[3] All possible contest between Crown and Parliament over questions of taxation stopped with the Revolution.

[3] Macaulay, *Hist. Eng.* i. 215.

There were *other forms of indirect taxation* more difficult to control because they were less tangible. Such were the old prerogative rights of Purveyance, Commissions of Array and Distraint of Knighthood. The two latter may be easily dismissed. *Commissions of Array*, of which an account will be found elsewhere,[4] only became a means of indirect taxation when the townships on which the troops were levied, were forced to support those troops even though they were used on foreign service.[5] In 1327, in answer to a petition of the Commons complaining of such an infraction of the Statute of Winchester, it was ordained that only in case of invasion should the 'gentz de commune' be called upon to arm themselves at their own expense. Further breaches of the law produced continual petitions, which resulted in an Act in 1352, which was confirmed in 1404, and allowed that except in case of invasion none should go out of their own counties, and that all who went on foreign expeditions should be at the king's charges from the day on which they left their own

Commissions of array. [4] Chap. ix.

[5] *S. C. H.* §§ 280, 373.

25 Edw. III. st. 5. c. 8. 4 Hen. IV. c. 13.

counties. But the abuse was not abolished. Henry V may have raised his victorious army by legal methods, but Edward IV and Richard III used any means ready to their hands. It was not that Commissions of Array were illegal in themselves, but that the method was illegally employed. It continued until the general question between king and Parliament had been settled at the Great Rebellion, when it was superseded by other ways of raising troops, and forbidden by the general attitude of the Commons towards all forms of taxation. *Distraint of Knighthood*, again, had originally fallen on all possessed of land to the value of £20 a year. Elizabeth, James I and Charles I all levied money by this means, and raised the qualifying amount to £40 worth of land. The Long Parliament included this among the many illegal methods of raising money which it abolished. The history of *Purveyance* demands more detailed treatment, and will best be dealt with in speaking of taxation.[1]

Distraint of Knighthood.

[1] Chap. x.

So far an attempt has been made to indicate the dates at which Parliament in general, and the House of Commons in particular, obtained a gradual acknowledgement from the Crown that the grant of all taxes lay with them. But the real control of the Commons in this important matter was gained not so much by direct prohibitory legislation, as by the establishment of three principles whose acknowledgement by the Crown involved a practically complete surrender to the demands of the Commons. These three principles may thus be regarded as *supplementary means by which the Commons obtained a control over the grant of taxation.* In the first place, they stipulated that, before they made their money grant, an answer should be given to the petitions of grievances which they had presented to the king. They insisted, secondly, on the appropriation of these grants to specified purposes; and thirdly, as a natural corollary, that the accounts should be properly audited to ensure that this appropriation had been made.

Indirect methods of obtaining control over taxation.

Hallam[2] has remarked that instead of the 'magnanimous boast that the liberties of England were bought with the blood of our forefathers . . . it is far more generally accurate to say that they were purchased by money.' Indeed, the money question has been a practical solution of otherwise insoluble questions of constitutional rights, and has placed a limit to

[2] *Mid. Ages*, iii. 162.

disputed powers by translating them into a tangible form. From the earliest meeting of Parliament the presentation of grievances became an invariable preliminary to the discussion of a money grant; and, in order to ensure an answer to their petitions, the Commons put off the grant until the last day of the session. It may almost be said that, in the early days of Parliament, constitutional progress really turned on the execution by the Crown of the conditions in return for which the supply had been granted.[1]

For, the supply was practically never refused, while more often than not the promises remained unfulfilled. But with the growing needs of the Crown came the opportunities of the Commons. The feeling that a grant should only be an answer to satisfied petitions, can be first traced in the Parliament of 1339. It was most definitely implied in 1348, and again in 1373; and in the second Parliament of Henry IV, in 1401, a petition on this very point was presented to the king. On this occasion he emphatically refused the demand as contrary to 'the good customs and usages made and used of ancient times,' in other words, as without precedent. But the principle had been definitely formulated as a regular mode of action : it was 'one of the most distinct statements of constitutional theory that had been ever advanced';[2] and the Commons, not to be baffled, soon afterwards adopted the practice of *delaying the grant until the last day of the session.* Indeed, the practical gain of the Commons may be measured by the history of the Lancastrian dynasty; for, the failure of that house was largely due to the fact that while supply was absolutely necessary to the Crown, it had not the strength to carry out the redress which it had promised as a condition of the money granted. Until very recently a relic of this principle, that redress of grievances should precede the grant of supplies, was to be traced in the procedure of the House of Commons. The amount of money which is to be granted to the Crown is considered in the Committee of Supply, into which the whole House of Commons resolves itself for the purpose. But until 1882 it was in the power of any member, on the motion that the Speaker should leave the chair in order that his place should be taken by the chairman of the Committee, to move an amendment relating to any matter

[1] *S. C. H.* § 289.

(1) Redress to precede supply.

[2] *S. C. H.* § 306.

whatsoever. This practice was, however, curtailed by a standing order of the House in 1882.[1]

But the Commons attempted to go a step further, and to ensure that the money granted should be applied to the purposes for which it had been demanded. Already in 1237 one of Henry III's ministers, William of Raleigh, had suggested that the Commune Concilium should appoint a committee with whom the collected grant should be deposited. But the barons refused this most important concession, although in the struggle which followed, one of their chief efforts was to wrest from the king the power of spending the money grants. Under Edward II all the powers of the executive were for a time in commission; but during the period no constitutional principle was established. It was Edward III's squandered expenditure of the supplies so constantly demanded, which first made it an important practical question that Parliament should determine not only the grant, but the way in which that grant should be applied. Nor did the king throw obstacles in the way. As a rule, at the opening of Parliament the members were told the objects for which money was specially needed, and for which Parliament had therefore been called together; and this explanation was often repeated to the Commons alone. It did not follow that the money was applied to the purposes for which it had been demanded of the Commons. Under Edward III no doubt 'the form frequently degenerated into mere verbiage.' Still, the custom was useful; and during his reign a subsidy was often granted on condition of the continuance of the war.[2] Under the Lancastrians, however, there are signs that it was becoming an accepted principle. In 1415, after the victory of Agincourt, tonnage and poundage was granted to Henry V for the rest of his reign, and in 1453, when similarly granted to Henry VI, it was appropriated to the navy.[3] But, like many other constitutional practices, this principle of the appropriation of supplies fell into disuse under the Yorkists and Tudors. It was reintroduced under James I in 1624, when the king himself suggested that the money granted for the succour of the Palatinate should be made over to commissioners nominated by the Commons;[4] it became the custom during the Commonwealth, and under

[1] Anson, i. 270.

(2) Appropriation of supplies.

[2] *S. C. H.* § 287.

[3] Plummer's *Fortescue*, 232. *S. C. H.* § 371.

[4] Prothero, 279.

somewhat curious circumstances gained the recognition of Charles II. In 1665 a large vote had been made, with the proviso that it should be expended on the war with Holland. Clarendon, regarding this as an encroachment on the royal prerogative, offered a strenuous opposition, but Charles refused to support him.[1]

[1] Hallam, ii. 357.

(3) Audit of accounts. But the appropriation of supplies involved the audit of accounts in order to ensure that the intentions of Parliament had been carried out. In 1341 Edward III granted this principle also; but the transitory character of the concession may be gathered from the fact that the Good Parliament of 1376 found it necessary to repeat the demand. On two occasions in the early years of Richard II measures were taken, by the nomination of treasurers, to give effect to the practice; and from the latter occasion treasurers of the subsidies were ordinarily appointed, who should account at the next Parliament for all the money received and paid out. In 1379 the king, or rather his representatives, had actually taken the initiative and ordered the accounts of the previous subsidy to be presented in Parliament.[2] Henry IV made one futile effort to defend his prerogative in this point. In 1406 he met a parliamentary demand for audit with the proud assertion that 'kings do not render accounts'; but in 1407 he thought it better to imitate the example of his predecessor and without further demand to lay the accounts before the Commons.[3] The subsequent history of the principle of audit is to be found in the history of the previous principle of appropriation. Thus, in 1666 Parliament followed up its victory of the previous year by a demand for the appointment of a committee to inspect the accounts of the Treasury. This, however, was prevented by a prorogation; and Charles intended to issue for the purpose a commission which he himself would be able to control. The fall of Clarendon interrupted his design; and in the next year the Commons returning to the charge, forced the reluctant king to assent to a Bill appointing a committee of audit with extensive powers. One of its first results was the expulsion from the Commons of Sir George Carteret, the treasurer of the navy, for issuing money without legal warrant.[4]

1377.

1381.

[2] S. C. H. § 288.

1407.

[3] Ibid. § 371.

1666.

1667.

[4] Hallam, ii. 358-360.

§ 34. The origin of the share of the Commons in LEGIS-

LATION is to be found in the immemorial right of every subject to petition the Crown for redress of any grievance. By Edward I's direction, such petitions were divided into five bundles according as they concerned the Chancery, the Exchequer, the Judges, and the King and Council, the fifth portion comprising those which had been already dealt with. Very soon after the date of the Model Parliament these petitions seem to have been presented to the assembled Parliament, among whose first duties was the appointment of receivers and triers for their consideration. Finally, under Richard II, a division of these petitions was made into three portions, of which one went to the king, another to the Council, while the third was laid before Parliament itself. But they were all the petitions of individuals for redress of personal wrongs ; and their parallel is to be found in the 'Private Bills' of modern Parliaments, Acts for local purposes, such as the regulation of fisheries and the enclosure of commons, or for the authorization of semi-public bodies, such as commercial or railway companies. The authority of the Commons in the initiation of legislation for the public benefit had its origin in the fact that the petitions of an organized and representative body, though not differing in theory from those presented by a private individual, not only dealt with subjects of general interest, but could be emphasized in a manner which necessarily placed them at once upon a different footing. Nor did this method of public petition begin with the Parliament of the three Estates. From the Articles of the Barons which formed the foundation of Magna Carta, on through the Petition of the Barons which resulted in the Provisions of Oxford (1258), to the twelve articles of the Parliament of Lincoln (1301), and the eleven articles of 1309 which led to the appointment of the Lords Ordainers, the same principle was at work. In the last two cases the articles of redress, though probably drawn by the barons, were presented in the name of the whole community : while in all four instances the grievances were chiefly such as affected the classes represented by the Commons. But the attitude of the barons was essentially that of councillors of the Crown. It was only in moments of popular excitement that they assumed the function of petitioners on behalf of the community. The Commons, on the other hand, were essentially petitioners, and they took advantage of every occasion on which they were called together, to accompany and, before long, to preface every grant of taxation with the presentation of a long list of petitions.

Treatment of Commons' petitions by the Crown.

At first there was little or no guarantee that these petitions would meet with any practical result. Even if the king so much as noticed any particular petition, he would give such a verbal and evasive answer as to this day is recorded in the formula 'le roi s'avisera' (the king will think about it), which would be used in any exercise of the royal veto. It was not the question of the Commons' *assent* to legislative acts which was at issue. The necessity, or at least the advisability, of such assent was early recognized. The Act of 1322, which placed the assent of the 'commonalty of the realm' on a level with that of the 'prelates, earls and barons,' no doubt much overstated the fact; but it is not improbable that the Statute *Quia Emptores* was 'the last case in which the assent of the Commons was taken for granted in legislation.'[1] Henceforth their share was at least such as was expressed by the formula 'ad audiendum et ad faciendum' (i.e. assent), which was inserted in their writs of summons to Parliament. But the Commons desired that their petitions should form the foundation of legislation and were thus, unconsciously perhaps, aiming at encroaching upon that initiatory power which had hitherto been a monopoly of the Crown in Council. It was the financial needs of Edward III which gave the Commons the opportunity of making good the first steps in the progress towards legislative supremacy. The king himself started them on their course when he began the custom of declaring at the opening of Parliament, by the mouth of his Chancellor, his readiness to receive the petitions of his people. But this apparent readiness was by itself of little worth. It might at the best lead the king to give *some* answer to his suppliant Commons; but even if he caused their petition to be embodied in the permanent form of a Statute instead of the purely transitory and revocable Ordinance, the duty of drafting the measure lay with the judges, and it was easy for the king to direct them to omit the chief point of the petition, or to insert such a clause as would rob the whole statute of its value.

[1] *S. C. H.* § 224.

Nor did the king stop here. There is only one case of the entire revocation of a duly enacted statute ; but the prerogative power of dispensation was scarcely less effective in nullifying the law of the land.

The Commons attempted to intercept the king at every turn. *The Commons' measures of defence.* They refused to grant supplies until they had received answers to their petitions : they even tried to make the grant upon conditions : they demanded that the royal answers should be formulated in writing and sealed before Parliament was dismissed. The royal method of nullifying enacted statutes was met with no less boldness and ingenuity. The Commons complained again and again of the non-observance of certain statutes, until under Edward III it became a custom to place first on the list presented to the king a petition for the ratification of the Great Charter. With the instinctive feeling that the assertion of principles was in the long run more important than the capture of a momentary advantage, they gave an ' ex post facto' legislative sanction to many of the king's most arbitrary acts. This amounted to a protest in favour of a monopoly of legislative action by Parliament, which the Good Parliament capped by a strong assertion of the power of Parliament alone to repeal a statute once enacted.[1] But none [1] *Rot. Parl.* 368, § 44. of these measures proved really effectual. Indeed, it was *the attitude of the Commons as petitioners* which was at fault, and the only real remedy lay in the discovery of a new method of initiating legislation. To a petition of the Commons against the enactment of statutes without their consent, Henry V replied that 'from henceforth nothing be enacted to the petitions of his Commune that be contrary of their asking, whereby they should be bound without their assent '; but the empty formula only witnesses to the evil for which the Commons were seeking a remedy.[2] This they found in [2] *S. C. H.* § 290. borrowing from the Crown what had hitherto been a royal prerogative of initiating legislation. In order to facilitate the passage of bills which originated with himself and his Council, it seems to have been the custom of the king to present them to the two Houses already drawn up in the form in which they were to appear upon the Statute Book. In order that the time of Parliament should not be wasted, the same privilege was extended to legislation which was called forth by the petitions

of individuals.   In the reign of Henry VI the Commons
adopted the same form for matters of public importance, and
by drawing up their petition 'formam actus in se continens'
(i.e. in the form of a statute) they not only forced the Crown
to submit every proposed alteration in it to their judgement,
but left the king no alternative between acceptance or rejection

[1] *S. C. H.*
§ 440.

of the measure as it stood.[1]   It has been pointed out that this
new method of legislation by Bill 'really laid the foundation
of the omnipotence of Parliament.'[2]   For the first time it drew

[2] Anson,
i. 243.

a strong line between the Executive and the Legislature, and
by transferring to the latter the power of initiation hitherto
enjoyed by the Crown, it formed the first breach in the walls
of that strong administrative fortress whose entire defences
were not captured until the Revolution of 1688.

Hindrances
to the Com-
mons.

(1) Attitude
of the
Lords ;

But it was only the first breach, and that of not very service-
able dimensions.   Time alone could show its value.   For
a long while yet there were hindrances to the complete
exercise of the Commons' power of initiating legislation.
They had not to fear the king alone.   All the other Estates
were jealous.   The *Lords* were not only an estate of the
realm : they were also hereditary councillors of the Crown.
Moreover they had been members of an organized body, the
Commune Concilium, long before the Commons had appeared
upon the scene.   Although occasionally they seem to have
joined the Commons as petitioners, laws were at first enacted
with their counsel and assent ; and for the first century after
the incorporation of the Commons in Parliament, the Lords
must have acted rather as royal councillors, debating the
petitions of the Commons and advising the king as to his
answers, than as an Estate of the realm with at the most only
a concurrent power of initiation with that claimed by the

(2) of the
Clergy ;

representative body.   The attitude of the *Clergy* was also
doubtful.   They had their own organization in Convocation,
with certain powers of separate legislation.   By the middle of
the fourteenth century they alone shared with the Commons
the control of the purse.   Moreover, while the Lancastrian
House posed as the champions of orthodoxy, the Church was
throwing herself more and more under the protection of the
Crown.   There was great cause for fear lest the king should
use the clergy, as he had used the Pope and the body of

merchants, to checkmate the Commons. And, to judge from petitions presented by the Commons in 1344 and 1377, it would seem that the king had occasionally made statutes at the desire of the clergy without submitting them to the approval of Parliament. It is possible also that clerical protests against contemplated parliamentary legislation, although often a matter of form, sometimes influenced a decision of the Commons.[1] But the clergy stood completely apart from parliamentary struggles, and wisely followed the lead of the Commons. As a result, save for an occasional suggestion for the confiscation of their revenues, they were unmolested, and even continued until the Restoration to vote their share of the taxes in their own assembly of Convocation.

[1] *S. C. H.* § 293.

A far more real hindrance to the legislative power of the Commons than any offered by the Lords or the Clergy, came from the necessary attitude of the king. At a time when Parliaments were intermittent it was indispensable that the executive should be armed with powers of temporary legislation. Moreover, before the advent of Parliament, the king with his Council had been executive and legislature in one. All early legislation was intended to meet a temporary emergency. The frequent recurrence of similar circumstances would cause such a temporary enactment to assume a permanent form. Thus there was no reason why in his Ordinances, issued with the advice of his Council, the king should distinguish between the assertion of a general principle and the satisfaction of a momentary need. The only recognition of a difference is to be found in the submission to the formal assent of the Commune Concilium of those more important matters which, under Henry II, were embodied in the form of Assizes. It is probable that the first real attempt to distinguish between temporary and permanent legislation dates from the arrangements made by Edward I for the sorting of petitions, and the existence of this difference was marked by the submission of those of more general interest to the consideration of the assembled Parliament. Then when Parliament itself began to petition, necessarily on matters of national importance, it was impossible to ignore the fact that the legislative power had become something more than a mere stop-gap. The Assizes of Henry II and the Provisions of

(3) of the Crown by (a) Ordinances.

Henry III gave way to the Statutes of Edward I ; but it was entirely against the king's interest to allow any hard-and-fast distinction between the binding force of an Ordinance and of a Statute respectively. Indeed, Edward I seems to have succeeded so well in his endeavour to prevent this, that from his time not only had the royal Ordinances 'been allowed to have very much the same force as the statutes themselves,' but 'until the great enunciation of the right of Parliament in 1322, it might be questioned whether those Ordinances were not laws within the letter of the constitution, and the acquiescence of the Parliaments might be reasonably construed as an admis-sion of the fact.'[1]   It was the extreme shiftiness of the king's conduct in his method of dealing with their petitions, that probably caused the Commons to emphasize the difference between the temporary and the permanent form.   Here, as in the companion matter of taxation, the reign of Edward III supplied the Commons with abundant opportunity ; and the free use of the royal Council to evade the answered petitions of Parliament brought out clearly the essential difference between the king's method of action in his Council and that form of legislation which was soon to be appropriated by Parliament itself.   So long as the Commons remained in the position of petitioners it lay largely with the king whether his answers to the petitions should be couched in the form of Ordinance or of Statute.   In 1363 the Commons themselves chose the form of Ordinance[2] as giving more opportunity for future modification.   On the other hand, when in 1353 the Ordinance of the Staple was sanctioned by a Magnum Concilium which contained an imperfect representation of the Commons, the protests of those who were present forced the king to summon a properly constituted Parliament for the next year in order to convert it into a statute.   The result of these struggles was to deepen the growing distinction between the Executive and the Legislature, and to emphasize the difference between the method of operation pursued by the King-in Council and that which alone was worthy of the sovereign body of the realm, the King-in-Parliament.   Thus while a Statute was 'a law or an amendment of law, enacted by the King-in-Parliament and enrolled in the Statute Roll, not to be altered, repealed, or suspended without authority of the Parliament,

[1] *S. C. H.* § 259.

[2] *Rot. Parl.* ii. 280, § 39.

and valid in all particulars until it has been so revoked'[1]— [1] *S. C. H.* § 292.
in other words, a legislative Act intended to be perpetual in
operation—the Ordinance became essentially the act of an
administrative body, devised to meet a temporary emergency.
How far the upholders of the royal prerogative were still
willing to press the efficacy of this latter power may be judged
not only from a petition of the Commons in 1389, praying
that the Council may not, after Parliament has dispersed,
make any Ordinance contrary to the Common or Statute
law, but also from one of the charges against Richard II,
that he had maintained that the laws were in his mouth
and often in his breast, and that he alone could change and
frame them.

While the Lancastrians were under the dominion of Parlia- Proclama-
ment, their successors did their best to dispense with Parliament tions.
altogether. But in either case the contest between Statute and
Ordinance was unequal. And when Henry VIII began to Under the
appeal regularly to the representatives of the people, he actually Tudors.
employed Parliament itself to wipe out a distinction on the
maintenance of which its whole legislative power depended.
The exact force of the Statute of Proclamations has been 31 Henry
much disputed. It enacted that the king's Proclamations VIII. c. 8,
(as Ordinances were now called), made with the assent of his 1539.
Council, 'should be observed and kept as though they were
made by an Act of Parliament.' A proviso was added to the
effect that such proclamations must not be 'prejudicial to any
person's inheritance, offices, liberty, goods and chattels,' or
infringe the established laws; and this has been construed
as an attempt of the Commons to limit a power which was in
any case certain to be used illegally. However that may be,
the statute was repealed in the first year of Edward VI's reign.
Proclamations, however, were continually used and enforced
by all kinds of penalties, such as fine, imprisonment, and even
labour on the galleys. They were issued by the Council and
their breach was taken cognizance of by the Star Chamber, so
that in reality they created new crimes unknown to the law of
the land. Thus, in *religious* matters, the Council of Edward VI
ordered justices of the peace to 'commit to the galley sowers
and tellers abroad of vain and forged tales and lies': Mary
denounced the penalties of martial law against the possessors

of heretical books: Elizabeth by this method banished Ana-
baptists and Irish from the country. In the *economic* sphere,
Edward's Council regulated the price of provisions; Mary
imposed duties on foreign cloth and French wines, while
Elizabeth prohibited the cultivation of woad, the exportation
of corn and money, and the building of houses within three
miles of London. Already in the reign of Mary the legality
of these proclamations was disputed, and the judges carefully
limited their use to the exposition of existing law. ' The king,'
they said, ' may make a proclamation *quoad terrorem populi* to
put them in fear of his displeasure, but not to impose any fine,
forfeiture or imprisonment; for no proclamation can make
a new law, but only confirm and ratify an ancient one.'

Under the
Stuarts.

But this plain statement deterred neither Elizabeth nor her
successor from the use of proclamations. Indeed under James
they were so numerous—being issued to forbid the election
of outlaws and the inclusion by the sheriff of ancient or

[1] Prothero,
280-281.

depopulated towns in the first Parliament of the reign;[1] to
interfere with freedom of trade by the levy of new customs
duties unsanctioned by Parliament; to prohibit the increase
of London, and to enforce the residence of the gentry in the
provinces—that in 1610 they called forth the remonstrance of
Parliament. In answer, James claimed, in cases of emergency
and during the abeyance of Parliament, the right of issuing
proclamations which went beyond the law. He promised,
however, to consult the judges; and the matter was submitted
to Chief Justice Coke and three others, who, despite the
utmost pressure of the Court, decided (*a*) that the king by
his proclamation cannot create any offence which was not one
before; but he may, for the prevention of offences, admonish
his subjects to keep the law, and the neglect of such proclamation aggravates the offence; thus, they add, if an offence be
not punishable in the Star Chamber, the prohibition of it by
proclamation cannot make it so: while, in answer to the royal
claim to override the existing law, they asserted (*b*) that the
king has no prerogative except what the law of the land allows

[2] Gardiner,
ii. 104.

him.[2] This may be said to sum up the whole question at issue
between king and Parliament in the seventeenth century.
James did not publish the decision; but probably no subsequent proclamations were issued which imposed penalties such

as fine and imprisonment. In some form, however, proclamations were still in use, and so long as the Star Chamber lasted, it did not hesitate to inflict a penalty where none had been legally applied.

But, despite many compensating advantages, it is a weakness of the English Constitution that the executive is only able to act within the limits of the law of the land. If ministers step Their outside the law, they do it at their peril; and moments of modern use. emergency find them shrinking from the responsibility which they incur by intruding into the special province of a most jealous assembly. Thus, in 1766, in what is known as Chatham's Second Administration, the ministers being desirous of meeting beforehand the distress which would be occasioned by the bad harvest, issued two proclamations — one for the revival of certain old economic regulations against forestallers and regraters, which as a reminder of existing law fell within the definition of the judges; another, which directly annulled the existing law for the free export of corn by laying an embargo on all ships laden with wheat. The only defence which the ministers could make was the necessity of immediate action: the proclamations were withdrawn, and Parliament was with difficulty persuaded to pass an Act of Indemnity.[1] Such, [1] Anson. then, is the only method of action possible to an English i. 309-310. minister. He must on an emergency adopt Luther's motto, 'Pecca fortiter' (i.e. break the law boldly), and the safeguard against rash action on his part is the knowledge that his acts must be subsequently covered by an indemnity from Parliament, whose judgement, moreover, will be pronounced after the event.

Perhaps the most subtle hindrance to the legislative power (b) The dis- of the Commons came from the royal claim to dispense with, pensing or even entirely to suspend, the operation of particular statutes. power. The claim was founded on the view of the king as the supreme and sole lawgiver. The maker of the laws, it was argued, could either dispense with their operation in individual cases, or even unmake them altogether. No one questioned the royal right of pardoning a criminal; and if the king could remit a punishment after sentence had been passed, much more should he be able to release a lawbreaker beforehand from the consequences of his act. The philosophical historian might find a justification for the exercise of this power of the prerogative in the hardship which often must have ensued in individual cases from the hastily drawn and crudely expressed statutes of a mediaeval Parliament.   But the whole endeavour of the Commons was, as we have just seen, to substitute the King-in-Parliament for the King-in-Council as the supreme legislative body ; while all the available evidence goes to prove that the power of dispensing with the laws in individual cases was used rather to forward the private aims of the king and those who could influence him, than to remedy the inequality of the laws in the interest of justice.   In one of the four Parliaments of 1328 the Statute of Northampton restricted the royal prerogative of dispensation.   But yet, in 1330, in 1347, and again in 1351, the Commons petitioned against the use of this power for the issue of charters of pardon, or rather of license beforehand, to a large number of common malefactors. Indeed, these petitions stand side by side with those against the sale of writs in Chancery and the extended jurisdiction of the Council.   Another Act, of 1390, prohibits the indiscriminate grant of pardons.   But the exercise of this necessary right was a matter of discretion, which could not be regulated by statute. Accordingly, the law courts set to work, and the great judges of the Lancastrian time drew a distinction between *mala in se* or violations of divine law such as murder and robbery, in which cases they denied the royal power of dispensation ; and *mala prohibita* or crimes created by statute, where they thought the king's power to hold good.   They further denied the law-fulness of the power when exercised against common law crimes, i.e. those in which the original common law had been confirmed by statute, or against the rights of individuals or corporations.   In short, the king's prerogative was unable to set at nought the moral law, or to pardon one man for an offence against another.   The king could only use his power to excuse an injury against himself or an illegal act from which no one had derived any harm.   But when political questions were concerned the majority of the Stuart judges set aside these subtle distinctions, and decided the whole matter from the standpoint of divine right.   Thus in the case of *Thomas v. Sorrell* 'the king in the interest of trade granted a dispensation from penalties provided for his benefit,'[1] and the

1674.

[1] Anson, i 315.

judges rightly upheld the royal prerogative on the ground that no third party had received an injury.[1] But they equally upheld it in the test case of *Godden* v. *Hales*. Here a Roman Catholic officer pleaded a dispensation from James II for his omission to conform to the requirements of the Test Act, and the judges based their decision on several grounds [2]—that the kings of England were sovereign princes ; the laws were the king's laws, it was therefore an inseparable part of his prerogative to dispense with particular laws in particular cases : of the need of such dispensation the king was the judge ; and finally, this was an ancient remnant of the prerogative of the king and could not be taken away from him, since it was not a power given him by the people. It is a marvellous testimony to the self-restraint of the authors of the Bill of Rights that, instead of denying the dispensing power altogether, they contented themselves with a condemnation of its illegality 'as it hath been assumed and exercised of late,' and with a declaration of its future invalidity unless Parliament had made provision for such power in the terms of the statute so violated. As a result, apart from the licence of Parliament itself, the only lawful dispensations are such as may have been granted before James II and were not covered by the words of the Bill of Rights. Cases of these are so few as to be of no practical importance.[3]

But if the philosophical historian could discover some justification for the exercise of the dispensing power, he would find nothing to urge in favour of the claim to suspend the operation of a statute in the case of a whole class ; for this was nothing else than an abolition of the law. Yet the exercise of this power was by no means unknown. The earliest instance was probably the omission from the reissue in 1216, of those financial and constitutional clauses of the Great Charter which were among its most valuable provisions. But the circumstances were exceptional. It is in connection with religious questions that this prerogative has in almost every instance been employed. This was the method by which the Pope obtained an occasional relaxation of the statutes in which an angry Parliament prohibited papal taxation ; while, after the Reformation the Stuart kings used it to shield the Roman Catholics from the penal laws.[4] Under James I and his son Parliament made frequent remonstrances. But their foreign

[1] Robertson, 229.

[2] *Ibid.* 248.

[3] Anson, i. 314-316.

(c) The suspending power.

[4] Cf. Prothero, 422.

S

policy as well as their natural inclinations dictated their line of conduct to these kings, and the results of their leniency were not serious.   It was under the later Stuarts that the power assumed dangerous proportions.   Charles II's Declarations of Indulgence had to be withdrawn; but James II, acting on the opinion of his prerogative set forth by the judges in *Godden* v. *Hales*, not only issued a Declaration by which he 'immediately suspended . . . the exercise of all and all manner of penal laws ecclesiastical, for not coming to church, or for not receiving the sacrament, or for any other nonconformity to the religion established,' but he even commanded that it should be read in the parish churches.   The trial of the seven bishops who petitioned against it, and their triumphant acquittal, sounded the knell both of James' tenure of the throne and of the interpretation which he had put on the royal power; and the first clause of the Bill of Rights condemns as illegal 'the pretended power of suspending of laws or the execution of laws by regal authority, without consent of Parliament.'[1]

§ 35. The attempt of the Commons to obtain control over the two most important functions of government—the enactment or amendment of laws and the assessment of taxes— practically involved an interference in every department of the executive.   The extent to which this was carried may be gathered from the subjects of the numerous petitions which were presented by every Parliament to the king.   Despite their many merits, we may set aside the Articles of the Barons in 1215, and the Petition of the Barons in 1258, as being largely occupied with old grievances arising from the undue exercise of feudal rights and the influence of aliens on the Crown.   The best early instances of petitions of national importance are to be found in those presented in the Parliament of Lincoln in 1301, the Parliaments of 1309 and of 1341, and above all in the Good Parliament of 1376.   An analysis of the hundred and forty petitions which emanated from the latter seems to prove that no point of national administration was considered as outside its supervision.   The directly feudal grievances have disappeared; but it is still, and for a long time remains, necessary to protest against the abuses of purveyance, the jurisdiction of the Courts of the Steward and the Marshal, the method of appointing sheriffs.   The presence of the

1662.
1672.

[1] Anson, i. 317-319.

Control of the general administration by the Commons.

Commons has placed in the forefront some comparatively new questions, such as the Pope's interference in the National Church, the freedom of election to Parliament, and all matters connected with the regulation of labour.   A general survey of the petitions seems to show 'that the government was ill administered rather than that any resolute project for retarding the growth of popular freedom was entertained by the adminis-trators.'[1]   And herein lay the danger of the situation.   It has been remarked that 'half the struggles of the Middle Ages originated in the uncertainty of the line drawn between the executive and the legislative.'[2]   For, the king had been trained to regard the country as a property to be administered for his own benefit ; while the legislature sought a real instead of merely theoretical power.   Consequently, while the king resented any interference with his prerogatives, Parliament, not knowing where to stop, claimed such purely executive functions as the election of ministers, the regulation of the royal house-hold and of its own summons.   The struggle resolved itself into a contest for the sovereign power in the State.

[1] *S. C. H.* § 262 end.

[2] Cf. *Ibid.* § 295 end.

But in fairness to the Crown it must be said that, however minutely the Commons inquired into the details of adminis-tration, they *shrank from direct responsibility*.   This may be illustrated in two departments.   The last point on which a popular assembly would be qualified to judge would be in questions of *foreign politics*.   Nor were the Commons asked to do so, until Edward III, in want of their money, sought to implicate them in his warlike projects.   At first they were lavish in their grants and seem to have been prepared to share the responsibility for war with the king.   In 1338 Edward asserted that his expedition was made not only with the assent of the Lords, but at the earnest request of the Commons. This may have been the turning-point ; for in the very next year the Commons declared that they were not bound to give advice on matters of which they had no knowledge.[3] In 1348 they made their ignorance and simplicity a plea for declining to express an opinion, and referred the king to the advice of the great and wise men of the Council.[4]   In 1354 they replied to a request for their opinion on the pending treaty, that 'whatever issue the king and the Lords might please to take of the said treaty would be agreeable to them.'[5]

(1) Foreign politics.

1339.

[3] *Rot. Parl.* ii. 105, § 11.

[4] *Ibid.* ii. 165, § 5.

[5] *Ibid.* ii. 262, § 58.

Under Richard II they pursued a similar course, in 1382, referring the question of an expedition to the Lords,[1] and in 1384 trying to make out that the French war was a personal quarrel of the king.[2] But the grudging nature of their supplies, and the attempts to establish the principles of appropriation and audit, sufficiently proved the distrust of a warlike policy which Edward III's extravagance had implanted in them.[3] Under the Lancastrians the changed position of Parliament made the Commons bolder in the matter of accepting responsibility. They supported Henry V's war as loyally as their predecessors in the early years of Edward III. They joined in the ratification of the treaty of 1416 between Henry and the Emperor Sigismund, and in the treaty of Troyes in 1420; while in 1446 they consented to the repeal of that article in the latter which required the assent of Parliament to any treaty of peace between the two kings.[4] Foreign politics were among the subjects with which the Tudor and Stuart sovereigns forbade Parliament to meddle. There was much to be said for this prohibition; but it was the anti-national attitude of the Stuarts which forced Parliament to take part in a discussion for which they were of necessity insufficiently provided.

(2) The law courts.

A second illustration of the timid conduct of the early Commons is found in their attitude towards *judicial matters.* A celebrated article of Magna Carta (§ 40) had made the king promise that he would not ' sell, deny or defer right or justice.' It was in their desire to maintain this that the Commons found their justification for the review to which they subjected the action of the law courts. The king, moreover, invited their participation in judicial questions; and it became very usual for the Chancellor, in opening Parliament, to demand on behalf of the Crown the advice of the Estates as to the best means of maintaining the public peace. In response to this request the Commons, from the early years of Edward's III's reign to the dark days which preceded the Wars of the Roses, never ceased to point out in their petitions the administrative abuses which stood in need of reform—the indiscriminate sale of writs in Chancery for the authorization of all kinds of illegal acts; the interference of the Privy Council with the ordinary course of the law; the extension of the jurisdiction of the Courts of the Steward, the Constable and the Marshal beyond the limits imposed on them by the Articuli super Cartas (1300); the attempted revival of the old feudal jurisdictions supported by the extensive practices of livery and maintenance; the corrupt conduct of the judges of assize and the sheriffs. These complaints were not coupled with demands for new legislation; they were merely petitions that the existing laws should be justly administered. But the Commons never aimed at direct judicial authority.[1] It seems as if they shrank from the responsibility which it would entail; for, although instances are to be found in which the Commons listened to the complaints of individuals against great officials, the fact that most ministers were peers necessarily gave their trial to the House of Lords, while the Commons' attitude of petitioners determined their part in an impeachment to be that of accusers before the natural judges. Indeed, on the deposition of Richard II, the Commons once for all repudiated for themselves the position of judges. Once or twice subsequently, in moments of passion, as in the case of *Floyd* (1621), whom they ordered to pay £1000 and to be put in the pillory for expressing delight at the defeat of the Elector Palatine;[2] and again in the case of *Mist* (1721),[3] a printer whom they committed to Newgate for publishing a journal in which some hope was expressed for the restoration of the Stuarts, the Commons have violated their own principle, and have arrogated to themselves the functions of a law court. Otherwise, their judicial authority has been exercised merely in cases of breach of privilege, which will presently demand notice.

The supervision of the Commons over the general administration was of little effect so long as they were unorganized and the ministers were in every sense the servants of the Crown. It was not until the discovery of the method of Cabinet government that a real and effective supervision of the administration was secured. It remains to be proved whether the present system of minute interference does not impose an impossible burden on the ministers to whom it is applied, and deprive them of that sense of personal responsibility which is necessary to draw out all the greatest qualities of a first-rate administrator.

§ 36. The progress of the Commons was threatened from two sides. We have already noticed the methods by which

margin notes:
[1] *S. C. H.* § 295.

[2] Hallam, i. 360-362. Prothero, 337-339.

[3] Hallam, iii. 279.

The Commons.

protect themselves against the Crown, by

the *Crown* sought to preserve a subservient Parliament. The Commons fortified themselves against these insidious attacks, partly by trying to provide for regular meetings of Parliament, partly by the assertion of privileges without which no member was able to act freely. No less necessary was it for the Commons to define their position in relation to the *House of Lords*. The two Houses had plenty of common interests, but the older and socially superior body struggled to maintain its political position.

(1) Fixing the meeting of Parliament.

The *time of year* at which Parliament should meet was governed by non-political considerations. It was a combination of three determining causes. The charters of Anglo-Saxon Witenagemots are dated at the *great Church Festivals* of Christmas, Easter and Whitsuntide, a custom which was imitated by the Norman kings in their three crown-wearing seasons at Winchester, Westminster and Gloucester respectively. But one of the chief duties of the Commune Concilium was the decision of judicial matters, and since the *legal terms*, derived from the Roman division into 'dies fasti' and 'dies nefasti,' had been made to coincide with the festivals of the Church, this custom was maintained; while the lawyer element which early predominated in Parliament, ensured the continuance of so convenient a time. But the greatest determinant in the Middle Ages was the *Harvest*, during which the schools and law courts were closed, and not only was Parliament prorogued or adjourned, but even civil war was suspended.[1]

[1] *S. C. H.* § 409.

Duration of Parliament.

All other matters connected with the summons of Parliament rested with the king and his councillors. Thus, although the assembly was ordinarily held at Westminster, special circumstances often caused its summons elsewhere, as when the Scotch wars made it convenient for the king that Parliament should meet at York. As a matter of fact, most of the great towns were chosen in turn, but there was always some temporary reason for a deviation from London.[2] Again, in 1258 the Provisions of Oxford had directed the calling of three Parliaments every year.[3] These were baronial councils for discharging the judicial functions of the Commune Concilium, and as such they were maintained by Edward I. But for the summons of a Parliament of the three Estates this was far too often. For while, on the one side, the Commons

[2] *Ibid.* § 412-414.
[3] *S. C.* 392.

felt representation to be a burden and regarded frequent summonses merely as frequent demands for money, the king, though he wished to get the money as often as he could, yet did not care to hear the grievances of the assembled nation more often than he was obliged. Thus, while at ordinary times it was with the greatest difficulty that any one could be induced to undertake the function of a member of Parliament, in moments of popular excitement demands were made for annual assemblies, and the provision of the Ordinances in 1311,[1] followed by Acts of 1330 and 1362, established annual Parliaments as the rule. But how little the king felt himself bound by these enactments, is clear from the numerous exceptions to this rule. Under Edward III was discovered the expedient of voting supplies for two or three years together; while, as Parliament advanced in power, a wealthier class of persons was willing to be returned as members. They were not in such haste as their poorer predecessors to return to neglected businesses; sessions could become longer and prorogations could be more frequent. Thus more business was despatched; larger supplies were voted; and it was not so necessary to call Parliament every year. The Acts of 1330 and 1362 provided for the summons of more than one Parliament, if necessary, in the course of the same year. In 1328 no less than four assemblies had been called. In 1332 and in 1340 Parliament came together three times within the twelve months, and twice in 1334 and again in 1352. But as each assembly was preceded by a fresh election, and as the members were paid according to the number of days on which the Parliament sat, these frequent sessions were so unwelcome as to occasion a petition in 1380 from both Houses that they should not be called together again for a year.[2]

On the accession of the Yorkists the occasional intermission of Parliament passed into a regular practice, and was only rescinded when Henry VIII desired the co-operation of the people in his religious changes. Under Charles I the evident intention of the Crown to return to the custom of the Yorkists, produced the Triennial Act of the Long Parliament (Feb. 1641). This provided that if the king neglected to summon a Parliament for three years after the meeting of the last Parliament, the Chancellor or, failing him, the peers or, in the

[1] *Rot. Parl.*
i. 285, § 29.
4 Edw. III.
c. 14.
36 Edw. III.
c. 10.

[2] *S. C. H.*
§§ 296, 410.

Triennial
Act.
16 Car. I.
c. 1.

event of their neglect, the sheriffs and mayors might issue writs, and if all officials failed in this duty, the electors themselves should proceed to choose representatives ; while, except with its own consent, the new Parliament might not be prorogued for fifty days.[1]   The Act was repealed after the Restoration ; but a desire was expressed that Parliament should not be intermitted for more than three years at a time.   The experience of the reign of Charles II showed that a prolonged Parliament might be as mischievous to public liberty as no Parliament at all : for the 'Pensionary Parliament' sat for seventeen years.   Yet the authors of the Bill of Rights contented themselves with the assertion that 'for the redress of grievances, and for the amending, strengthening, and preserving of the laws, Parliament ought to be held frequently.'[2]

So long as the Crown retained the right of summoning Parliament, the intermission of the Assembly could be dealt with only indirectly ; but in 1694 a second *Triennial Act*[3] put a limit to the existence of any individual Parliament : while in May 1716 this limit was further increased by the *Septennial Act*.[4] Numerous have been the attempts in the present century to effect its repeal ; some, like those of the Chartists, in favour of annual Parliaments, some with a view to the modification of the present length.   Custom has reduced the time to an average of about six years' duration, and the apprehensions roused by the coming election take off almost another year from the effectiveness of the work done by the House of Commons.   Until 1696 the demise of the Crown put an end to the existing Parliament ; but an Act of that year provided that it should continue for six months after the death of the reigning monarch, while an Act of 1797 revived the old Parliament for six months in the event of the monarch's death just after its dissolution.   Finally, by the Representation of the People Act (1867), no dissolution of Parliament is necessary at future demises of the Crown.

§ 37.   The second method by which the Commons have tried to protect themselves against the direct attacks of the Crown, is the assertion and maintenance of PRIVILEGES OF PARLIAMENT. Since the reign of Henry VIII it has been the custom, at the commencement of every Parliament, for the Speaker to demand from the Crown on behalf of the Commons a confirmation of

[1] Gardiner, *Const. Docts.* 74-84.

1660-1677.

[2] *S. C.* 525, § 13.

[3] Robertson, 83.

[4] *Ibid.* 117.

7 & 8 Will. III. c. 15.

37 Geo. III. c. 127, s. 34.

30 & 31 Vict. c. 102, § 51.

(2) Asserting privileges of Parliament.

'their ancient and undoubted rights and privileges.' [1] But these privileges are not regarded as in any sense depending on a grant from the Crown ; and an assertion of the attitude of the House in this respect still survives in the custom of taking the first reading of some Bill before it enters on the discussion of the speech from the throne. The Speaker then claims in particular for the members of the House 'that their persons and servants might be *free from arrests* and molestations ; that they may enjoy *liberty of speech* in all their debates ; may have collective *access to his Majesty's royal person* whenever occasion shall require : and that all their proceedings may receive from his Majesty *the most favourable construction.'* [2] But beyond these privileges the House has acquired certain rights necessary for the proper maintenance of its dignity, but not claimed in words from the Crown. These have been most carefully enumerated as the right to *provide for its own constitution ;* the right to *exclusive cognizance of all that takes place within the House ;* and the right of *inflicting punishment for breach of privilege.'* [3] Many of these will be found to include lesser rights which, in process of time, have grown out of them.

Of the first set of privileges—those demanded by the Speaker —two are purely formal. 'The most favourable construction' has been described as 'not a constitutional right but a personal courtesy '; for while, on the one side, the Crown can take no notice of anything said or done inside the House, on the other side the right of freedom of speech affords sufficient guarantee against any active interference with members of the Commons. But it does not follow that in the days of the greater personal influence of the Crown, this demand was useless. Again, although 'the right of access to the Crown' is only enjoyed collectively by the whole House, yet those members of the Commons who are Privy Councillors, are as much entitled to a personal audience of the monarch as are the peers themselves.

Far different was it with the first two rights claimed by the Speaker. The claims made under the heads of freedom from arrest and liberty of speech were in course of time considerably extended. Thus, the recognition of *freedom from arrest* has been dated back to a law of Æthelberht [4] at the end of the sixth century, while Cnut certainly extends his special

Side notes:

[1] Prothero, lxxxvii.

[2] Erskine May, *Parlt. Practice,* 57. Anson, i. 148.

[3] Anson, i. 162 et seq.

Formal privileges.

Freedom from arrest.

[4] *S. C.* 61.

[1] *S. C.* 74.
Extension
of the
privilege.
protection over those going to and from the 'gemot.'[1]   Indeed, it was a necessary precaution to ensure the safe arrival and departure, and the regular attendance of members.   But the extent of the privilege was most indeterminate.   In the first place, it is mere prescriptive custom which has fixed the time spent ' eundo ' or ' exinde redeundo ' at forty days each.   Such

1847.
was allowed in the case of Mr. Duncombe, and has been indirectly confirmed by several Acts of Parliament.   But the Lords claim only twenty days ; and there are cases in the sixteenth century which seem to show that only twenty days or even fewer were then thought sufficient for the Commons. In the next place, from its earliest recognition the privilege seems to have been held to *include the servants and the estates*

5 Hen. IV.
c. 6.

11 Hen. VI.
c. 11.
of members.   This extension was confirmed by statute in the particular case of *Richard Chedder*, a member's servant who had been assaulted, and generally in an Act of 1433.   It was also applied to *exempt* those who claimed it *from legal arrest* and from being impleaded in civil suits.   The former was asserted in the cases of *Clerk* (1460), *Atwyll* (1477), *Ferrer* (1543), *Martin* (1587), and *Neale* (1594), members, and those

[2] *S. C. H.*
§ 452.
Prothero,
128.

[3] Prothero,
320-324.
1 Jas. I.
c. 13.
of *Lark* (1429) and *Smalley* (1575), servants.[2]   Finally, the celebrated case of *Sir Thomas Shirley* (1603) was followed by the first distinct legislative acknowledgment of the right of freedom from arrest.[3]   The privilege of *not being impleaded in civil suits* seems to have been acknowledged as early as 1290 ; and, despite some instances to the contrary, it was successfully claimed as a prescriptive right in the case of Atwyll, quoted above, and was maintained either by writs of ' supersedeas,' such as those issued by Edward II in 1314 to stay all actions against members in their absence, or in the seventeenth century by a letter of the Speaker to the judges to the same effect.   Members sometimes waived the privilege, and the law courts did not always let it go unquestioned ; but it was sufficiently obnoxious to the course of justice to necessitate its removal by legislation.   A series of statutes, commencing

12 & 13
Will. III.
c. 3.
10 Geo. III.
c. 50.
in 1700 and ending in 1770, first allowed actions to be begun against any person entitled to privilege in the principal courts of Common law and Equity at certain times, such as a dis- solution, prorogation or an adjournment for more than fourteen days.   They then extended this right of trial to all courts of

record, and finally not only allowed any action to be tried *at any time* against privileged persons, but withdrew from their servants the privilege of freedom from arrest and imprisonment, saving it only for the persons of the members themselves.[1] Yet to this day the Speaker claims immunity for the servants of members, and it has been conjectured [2] that it might still be asserted for servants in actual attendance on members at the House. Until 1853 the Speaker also claimed immunity for the *estates* of members ; but the Commons wisely waived the right, and the word was for the future omitted from the demand. It is perhaps a natural extension of the privilege which releases out of custody for a civil action, a member elected while he is under restraint. Finally, privilege of Parliament was held to include freedom from the necessity of obeying a subpoena to serve as a *witness*, and from the liability to *jury* service. The first claim does not seem to have arisen until the end of the sixteenth century ; [3] it was only with some difficulty established, and has now been waived : the latter has been more willingly allowed by the law courts, and now rests upon an Act of 1870.

Side by side with these extensions should be set certain *exceptions* to the privilege. Thus freedom from arrest has never been held to apply to a member charged with *treason, felony, or breach of the peace.* It is limited to misdemeanours and civil causes. This was laid down by the judges in Thorpe's case [4] (1453), and was recognized by more than one resolution of the House itself (1675, 1697). Again, by an Act of 1849, *bankrupt* members were exempted from arrest during the period of their privilege ; but by the Bankruptcy Act of 1869 this temporary protection was withdrawn. In 1763, in the teeth of a decision of the Court of Common Pleas, both Houses resolved, in the case of Wilkes, that 'privilege of Parliament does not extend to the case of writing and publishing *seditious libels*' ; [5] and this seems to have carried with it the principle 'that privilege is not claimable for any indictable offence.' Finally, the privilege has been held not to extend to a member committed for *contempt of court.* The point was for some time doubtful, but was decided in the negative by a Committee of Privileges appointed to consider the case of Mr. Long Wellesley in 1831, and their opinion has been confirmed in a number of subsequent cases.[6]

[1] Anson, i. 150-151.
[2] Erskine May, *Parlt. Practice*, 8th ed., 65 note.
[3] Instances in Prothero, xc. and 129.
33 & 34 Vict. c. 77, § 9.
Exceptions.
[4] Pike, 249.
12 & 13 Vict. c. 106.
[5] Robertson, 302.
[6] Anson, i. 149.

Means of
enforcing
the privi-
lege.

1453.

[1] *S. C. H.*
§ 451.
Pike, 248-
250.

[2] Prothero,
127.

1604.

1625.

Freedom
of speech.

Its two
forms.

The assertion of a privilege was of little use unless it was backed up by adequate means of protection and enforcement. Such means were of various kinds. At first, in the case of members actually under sentence, in order to avoid undue injury to the plaintiff, it was usual to pass special statutes authorizing the Chancellor to issue writs for their release : while, if a member was merely awaiting his trial in custody, a writ of privilege issued from the Chancery was deemed sufficient. In the exceptional case of *Thomas Thorpe*, the Commons even called in the assistance of the House of Lords. But in 1543, in the case of *George Ferrer*,[1] the Commons asserted their own authority, refused a writ of privilege offered them by the Chancellor, and through their serjeant successfully demanded the prisoner's release. They seem still to have had occasional resort to Chancery ; but before the end of Elizabeth's reign occur several cases by which the Commons must have considered that they had finally asserted for themselves not only the privilege of freedom from arrest but the means for enforcing it.[2] Nor did they stop here : for, in order to safeguard it, they began the custom of appointing a standing committee of privileges at the opening of each session. But these precautions proved insufficient, and the privilege itself was only finally secured by an Act of Parliament passed in 1604 in consequence of the dispute over the arrest of Sir Thomas Shirley. Hitherto the Commons had enforced the privilege by a writ issued in accordance with the Speaker's warrant. But the Act of 1604 together with a subsequent declaration of the Commons, 'that the House hath power when they see cause to send the serjeant immediately to deliver a prisoner,' made a writ of privilege unnecessary ; and it has become enough either to procure a decree of release from a judge of the court in which the member was sentenced, or for the House merely to issue its warrant or order for the same purpose.

Freedom of speech is the keystone of the arch of parliamentary privilege, the one without which all other privileges would be valueless. It is in fact a natural and necessary adjunct of any popular assembly. It was claimed by the Speaker only from the reign of Henry VIII onwards ; but it had already been acknowledged by the Crown, and was subsequently confirmed

alike by decisions of the law courts and Acts of the legislature.
More than one question was involved in the claim.   In its
barest form, freedom of speech denoted the right of (1) *exemption from punishment for words uttered in debate*.   The need
of the privilege was shown from the conduct of Edward I
towards Henry Keighley, the spokesman of the Commons
in the Parliament of Lincoln; of John of Gaunt towards 1301.
Peter de la Mare, the 'prolocutor' of the Good Parliament; 1376.
and of the Yorkist party to the Lancastrian Thomas Thorpe,
the Speaker in 1453.[1]   Owing to political reasons, the effort [1] *S. C. H.*
of the Commons in the last case completely failed; but § 451.
already, in the case of *Haxey*, they had vindicated their 1397.
right; for Henry IV, with the advice and assent of the
Lords Spiritual and Temporal, entirely reversed the judgement
passed at the instigation of his predecessor for the prisoner's
reflections in Parliament on the royal household.   The principle
received further confirmation in the cases of *Thomas Young*
(1451)[2] and *Richard Strode* (1512),[3] the latter of which was [2] *S. C. H.*
followed by an Act[4] condemning as utterly void, both in the § 451.
case of Strode and of all members of the present and future [3] Anson, i. 147.
Parliaments, legal proceedings 'for any bill, speaking, reason- [4] 4 Hen.
ing, or declaring of any matter or matters concerning the VIII. c. 8.
Parliament, to be communed or treated of.'   But this statute
afforded no protection against the interference of the Crown,
and while the Tudor sovereigns seem to have done everything
to encourage and to assist the acquisition of many other
privileges by the House of Commons, the privilege of freedom
of speech was just the one which they 'could not afford to [5] Prothero,
recognize.'[5]   xciv.
   The claim by the Speaker appears first in 1541; but with the
growth of the power of the Commons there arose an important
question — political rather than constitutional, but involving
some important cases — concerning (2) *the class of subjects
which it was allowable for Parliament to discuss*.   This will be
dealt with in the next chapter.   Here it is necessary to note
that while, on the one side, Elizabeth in 1571 prohibited the
Commons from meddling with any matters of state except such
as were propounded to them,[6] and followed this up in the Par- [6] *Ibid.* 119.
liament of 1593 by telling the Speaker, when he petitioned for
the usual privileges, that liberty of speech meant merely the

Prothero, 125. right of saying yes or no to questions laid before the House ;[1] on the other side, in the Parliament of 1587 Wentworth, in indignation at these attempts to gag the House, asked 'whether this Council was not a place for any member of the same, freely and without control, by bill or speech, to utter any of [2] Ibid. 123-124. the griefs of the Commonwealth ?'[2]   The attempt of the Crown to enforce its views led to the cases of *Strickland*[3] (1571), who [3] Ibid. 119. introduced a bill for reforms in the Book of Common Prayer, and was forbidden to attend Parliament, until the strongly expressed feeling of the Commons caused Elizabeth to withdraw the prohibition ; of *Cope* (1587), committed to the Tower for introducing ecclesiastical reforms, and of *Peter Wentworth*, who was imprisoned no less than three times (1576, 1587, 1593) for persisting in the discussion of subjects unacceptable to the Queen.   Under the Stuarts both sides began to formulate their claims.   Thus, at the end of the first session of the Parliament of 1621 James imprisoned Sir Edwin Sandys, a previous offender.   To the remonstrances of the Commons James, while declaring that Sandys was not imprisoned for any misdemeanour in Parliament, took occasion to say that he thought himself 'very free and able to punish any man's misdemeanours in Parliament as well during their sitting as [4] Ibid. 310. after ;'[4] and that he did not intend to let the power lie idle. The Commons answered in a Petition claiming, as they had [5] Ibid. 288. claimed at the very beginning of the reign,[5] freedom of speech as their ancient and undoubted right and an inheritance received from their ancestors, without which they could not freely debate nor clearly discern of things in [6] Ibid. 311-312. question before them, nor truly inform the king.[6]   To James' rejoinder that these privileges were derived from the grace and permission of his ancestors and himself, since most of them had grown from precedents which showed rather [7] Ibid. 313. a toleration than inheritance,[7] the Commons answered with [8] Ibid. 313-314. a famous Protestation[8] in which they shortly declared that the liberties, franchises and privileges of Parliament were the undoubted birthright and inheritance of the subjects of England ; that the arduous and urgent affairs concerning the king, state and defence of the realm and other such matters were proper subjects and matter of counsel and debate in Parliament, and that in the handling and proceeding of those businesses every

member of the Houses of Parliament had and of right ought
to have freedom of speech to the fullest possible extent without
any fear of impeachment, imprisonment, or molestation except
from the House itself.[1] James dissolved Parliament, tore the
protestation from the journals of the House of Commons, and
meted out various punishments to the chief offenders. The
last instance of the direct violation of this right was in the case
of *Sir John Eliot* and eight others who were imprisoned by the
Privy Council at the end of Charles' third Parliament in 1629.
The details of the case are full of interest, but are too long for
reproduction here. Suffice it to say that the prisoners denied
the jurisdiction of the Star Chamber in matters which had
arisen in Parliament, and Charles, finding he could not sustain
the position that the alleged offences had taken place during
the adjournment, allowed the case to be taken before the
Court of King's Bench. The prisoners still resisted the jurisdiction of any court in any, except capital, offences committed
in Parliament, and refused to plead. But the judges of the
King's Bench declared that all twelve judges had agreed that
offences committed in Parliament could, after the dissolution,
be punished in another Court. They further maintained their
own jurisdiction on the ground that the issue did not lie
between the Crown and Parliament as a whole, but between
the Crown and some private persons; and that a member of
Parliament, by committing sedition, made himself incapable
of pleading privilege. Judgement was of course given against
the prisoners.[2] This judgement was subsequently entirely
condemned—in July 1641 by a resolution of the Long Parliament, in 1667 by a resolution of the Long Parliament of the
Restoration, in 1668 in a judgement on a writ of error of the
House of Lords; while, finally, the Bill of Rights removed
all doubt about the matter by affirming 'that the freedom
of speech, and debates or proceedings in Parliament, ought
not to be impeached or questioned in any court or place out
of Parliament.'[3]

It was perhaps natural that privileges of Parliament, like
most other rights, should be first vindicated and then extended,
until they threatened to lose all basis in reason. The Revolution of 1688 assured to the Commons liberty of speech as
against the arbitrary interference of the Crown. But it was

[1] Gardiner, iv. 261-262. Prothero, 313-314.

1629.

[2] Gardiner, vii. 90-96, 108-119.

[3] *S. C.* 525, § 9.

Extension of the privilege.

the victory of an oligarchy which hastened to share its spoils by the exclusion of all outside influences from admission to the House. These influences could come through two channels—the presence of strangers at the sittings of the House, and the publication of the debates in the House. The Commons of the eighteenth century went about to protect themselves from

(1) Exclusion of strangers from debate.

both these dangers. The custom of *excluding strangers from the debates* was probably at first dictated by convenience, for as late as 1771 a stranger was counted in a division.[1] It was no doubt maintained in order to exclude royal spies, and was thus a

[1] Anson, i. 156 note.

[2] For earliest case, *vide* Prothero, 133.

valuable adjunct to the larger privilege of freedom of speech.[2] After the Revolution the dominant party in Parliament found it a useful weapon for preventing the words of a member of the opposition from being carried beyond the walls of the House. In the middle of the eighteenth century it was fashionable to attend the debates of the House; but any member could draw attention to the presence of strangers, and the Speaker was then forced to order their expulsion. Matters reached a crisis in the corrupt Parliament which met

1770.

in 1768. In 1770, on a motion relating to preparations for a war with Spain, the Lords (who in this respect were no better than the Commons), despite the protests of Lord Chatham and others, cleared their House of strangers, thus excluding among others several members of the Commons who were waiting at the bar to bring up a bill. These returned to their own House, and, in retaliation, obtained the exclusion of all strangers, including peers. The only peers thus treated were Chatham and his associates, who had withdrawn in disgust from the Lords and sought a refuge below the bar of the House

[3] Erskine May, ii. 27-33.

of Commons.[3] Both Houses continued for some years to enforce this exclusion, which ended, in the case of the Commons, in a conflict with the press. Strangers were, however, gradually readmitted, though it was only in 1845 that the standing orders

[4] *Ibid.* ii. 55.

of the House of Commons recognized their presence.[4] The revival of the practice of exclusion led to a discussion of the process by which it was enforced; and in 1875 it was resolved that the notice of the presence of strangers in the House should under ordinary circumstances be followed by a vote of the

[5] Anson, i. 156.

House, without debate or amendment, on the question of exclusion.[5] The right of individual members in the matter has been thus curtailed; and the position of reporters, in whose behalf the question was raised, is left to the results of the contest over *the publication of debates*.

Since such publication on a large scale could only be achieved through the press, the prohibition to print the debates of the House for the general information can only date from a time when the press had begun to be a recognized power. But even then Parliament was willing to waive its rights in the matter for the purpose of gaining popular support. Thus, in 1641 the Long Parliament, while for the first time prohibiting, without leave of the House, the publication in print of speeches made in the House, itself undertook such publication under the title of 'Diurnal Occurrences in Parliament.' Acceptable speeches of individuals were also printed by its order; but the private publication of his speeches by an opponent like Sir Edward Dering was punished with the utmost severity. Again, in 1680 the Commons directed the printing of its votes and proceedings under the supervision of the Speaker in order to prevent the inaccurate reports circulated in pamphlets and in the private letters of members to their constituents. But the prohibition still continued, and with the increased jealousy of outside interference which followed the Revolution, it was maintained by frequent resolutions and the punishment of offenders. But the continued and ill-concealed violation of the privilege led to a resolution of the House in 1738 condemning as 'a high indignity and a notorious breach of privilege' the publication of any account of its proceedings. This engendered extra caution in the reporters, and the speeches were assigned to fictitious persons in an imaginary assembly. In 1771, however, under the instigation of Wilkes, all precautions were thrown to the winds, and intentionally inaccurate speeches were reported in the daily newspapers under the nicknames of the members. The result was a series of attacks by the Commons on the printers and publishers, which led to the cases of *Wheble*, *Thompson* and *Miller*. The two former were collusively apprehended in the City of London and discharged by two Aldermen, one of whom was Wilkes. Miller gave the messenger of the House into custody for assault and was upheld by the Lord Mayor, who committed the prisoner for attempting to arrest any one in the City without a warrant backed by a City magistrate.

(2) Restrictions on publication of debates.

T

The House committed to the Tower the Lord Mayor and the
other Alderman, who were members. Wilkes refused to
attend, and finally was left alone. But, despite the order of
the House to the contrary, the messenger was indicted, and
only escaped through the interference of the Attorney-General
while the House made no further attempt to assert its privilege
Until 1834, however, reporters were surrounded by difficulties
They were not allowed to take notes, and were liable to be
crowded out through want of space or to be excluded with
other strangers. But after the destruction by fire of the old
Houses of Parliament, separate galleries were provided for
them. Since then, the House of Commons has facilitated
the publication of its proceedings for the information of the
electors, and has been followed at an interval by the Lords
Thus, in 1836 the former began the custom of recording
and publishing daily the votes of every member — a plan
which the Lords adopted in 1857. Again, since 1839 the
Commons, and since 1852 the Lords, have published the
names of all members sitting upon select committees together
with the evidence taken before them; while in 1835 the
Commons directed that all their papers should be freely and
cheaply sold.[1]

[1] Erskine
May, ii.
34-60.

Limits to
privilege of
freedom of
speech.

Although the House has asserted its privilege by the occa
sional commitment of those who have libelled its members in
an individual or a corporate capacity, yet the information
supplied by the press is so minute and its comments are so
unrestrained, that it is not easy to appreciate the *limits* to the
violation of this privilege. For while, on the one side, the
reports of parliamentary proceedings are both made and pub
lished on sufferance; on the other side, such publications are
equally with any others *amenable to the ordinary law of libel*.
This is true of the publication either of a full debate by a
newspaper, of an individual speech by the speaker, or of
parliamentary papers printed for general distribution by order
of the House. With regard to *newspapers*, however, it was
decided by the Court of Queen's Bench in the case of *Wason*
v. *Walter* that an honest and faithful report of a debate in
Parliament exempts the proprietor of the paper 'from legal
responsibility, though the character of individuals may inci
dentally be injuriously affected.'[2] But since the parliamentar

1868.

[2] Robertson,
403.

privilege itself forbids the report of a debate, the publication of his *speech by an individual member* is in no way covered by it ; and the printed speech is treated by the law courts as unconnected with any proceedings in Parliament. Thus, while in the case of *Lake* v. *King* it was held that a member was not liable for otherwise libellous statements in papers circulated among the members themselves ; at the same time, the case of *Creevey* decided that the corrected report of the speech of a particular member was not privileged, which contained 'reflections injurious to the character of an individual.' Finally, the House of Commons found itself, with regard to *papers published by its order*, in the position of the individual member.[1] In the case of *Stockdale* v. *Hansard* (1836) the Lord Chief Justice and, on reservation, the Court of King's Bench, successively decided that an order of the House of Commons was not sufficient justification 'for any bookseller who published a parliamentary report containing a libel against any man.' The Commons endeavoured to support their printer, Hansard, by an assertion of their privilege ; but a lengthy quarrel was only ended by an Act which provided that all legal proceedings in such cases should be stayed on the production of a certificate that the paper in question was printed by order of either House of Parliament.[2]

§ 38. The second set of privileges to be noticed—those not claimed by the Speaker—have for their object the assertion of the dignity and independence of the House of Commons. For this purpose it was necessary, in the first place, that the House should secure the *right to provide for its own constitution.* This right, when translated into act, has included the power of issuing writs for filling vacancies among the members ; the immediate application of legal disqualifications ; and the trial of disputed elections. Writs for the election of members of the Commons were originally issued from the Chancery and, when filled up, were returned for verification in Parliament itself, while complaints against any particular return were heard by the king with the aid of his Council or even of Parliament. The Act of 1406 directed that the return to the writ should be made on an indenture signed and sealed by all who took part in the election. Hence-

Marginal notes:

1813.

[1] Erskine May, ii. 78-82.

3 & 4 Vict. c. 9.

[2] Anson, i. 160.

(1) Regulating the constitution of the House by

7 Hen. IV. c. 15.

forth the returns were made into Chancery; and although the Act of 1410 gave the inquiry into undue returns to the justices of assize, the king still seems to have reserved to himself, with the help of the Lords or the judges, the consideration of the validity of the return. The growing power of the Commons under the Tudors caused them to claim the exercise of this power for their own House. The first point which they made good was the *declaration of incapacity* to be a member of the House. This was asserted in the case of *Alexander Nowell* (1553), who, being a member of Convocation, was disqualified for a seat among the Commons.[1] It has been exercised, without any reference to a Court of Law, in the case of persons attainted of treason or felony, who by the Common law are incapable of being elected to Parliament. Such was the action of the House in the cases of *Smith O'Brien* (1849), *O'Donovan Rossa* (1870), *John Mitchel* (1875), and *Michael Davitt* (1882).

Side by side with this right may be placed the *expulsion* for conduct which the Commons have considered to be unworthy of a member of their House. Of this the earliest instances were *Arthur Hall* (1581),[2] for publishing a book 'derogatory to the authority of Parliament'; and *Dr. Parry* (1584),[3] for branding a bill against the Jesuits with the epithet 'bloody.' Among the numerous cases which have occurred in the course of the last three centuries, the most celebrated are those of *Sir John Trevor*, the Speaker (1694), for taking bribes; *Walpole* (1711), for peculation in office; and *John Wilkes* (**1764**), for being the author of a seditious libel.[4] In the last case Wilkes was re-elected no less than three times, and the House, having begun by declaring his election void and so creating a new disability of their own devising, ended by pronouncing that the votes given to him were thrown away, and that his opponent, who was in a hopeless minority, was duly elected (1770).[5] Wilkes was elected to the next Parliament (1774), took his seat without further opposition, and ultimately in 1782 obtained from the House a reversal of its former acts against him.[6] The *result* of this and many other cases is that, whilst the House is perfectly at liberty to expel a person whom it accounts unworthy to be a member, such expulsion not only lasts merely for the current Parliament, but it merely vacates the seat and does not create a disqualification

Margin notes:

11 Hen. IV. c. 1.

(a) declaration of incapacity to sit.

[1] Hallam, i. 275.

(b) expulsion for unworthy conduct.

[2] Prothero, 131.

[3] Hallam, i. 274.

[4] Robertson, 302.

[5] *Ibid.* 333.

[6] *Ibid.* 336.

to sit again, which is beyond the province of the House of Commons. The practical difficulty is that the constituency may continue to re-elect the expelled member to the vacant seat, and so for a period may disfranchise itself.[1]

The conduct of the House of Commons in the case of Wilkes was made possible by its possession of the *right of trying contested elections.* This right was first distinctly asserted in the case of the *county of Norfolk.* Owing to some informality in the first election, a second writ was issued by the Chancellor. Whereupon the Commons, despite Elizabeth's assertion that the matter belonged to the Chancellor, held an inquiry and declared the first election good.[2] But it was only after the stubborn resistance of the Commons to James I in the matter of the Buckinghamshire election, known as the case of *Goodwin and Fortescue* (1604),[3] that the Commons definitely secured an acknowledgement of their right to take cognizance of all disputed returns. This right received the sanction of the Court of Exchequer Chamber in the case of *Barnardiston* v. *Soame* (1674), of the House of Lords in 1689, and of the Courts of Common Law in the cases of *Onslow* (1680) and *Prideaux* v. *Morris* (1702); while it was taken for granted in a statute of 1696 which declared the illegality of a double return to a writ. But the temptation to extend the right proved irresistible; and in the case of *Ashby* v. *White,* followed by that of the *Aylesbury men,* the Commons attempted to adjudicate upon a strictly legal point—the qualification of an elector.[4]

Disputed elections were at first tried by select committees specially nominated, but these were superseded by a permanent Committee of Privileges and Elections, nominated by the House and composed of Privy Councillors and eminent lawyers.[5] This was gradually enlarged by the addition of all Privy Councillors and a large number of lawyers; until after 1672 it became an open committee of the whole House, in which all members were allowed to have a vote.[6] In special cases a disputed election was heard at the bar of the House itself; and in the time of Speaker Onslow the confidence which he inspired in suitors caused this to become the usual custom. But in the midst of this fluctuating and incompetent tribunal all sense of justice was lost. Each disputed

[1] Anson, i. 167.
(c) trying disputed returns.
1586.

[2] Prothero, 130.

[3] *Ibid.* 325-331.

7 Will. III. c. 7.
1703.
1704.

[4] Robertson, 271.
Methods of trying contested elections.

[5] Prothero, 117.

[6] But cf. Porritt, i. 538-539.
1727-1761.

election became a trial of party strength, and members voted for the candidate who professed the same political opinions irrespective of the wishes of the constituents or the merits of the case. The best-known instance is that of the Chippenham election petition, in which the defeat of his candidate was considered by Walpole as equivalent to a vote of want of confidence. In **1770** the *Grenville Act*,[1] named from its author, attempted a remedy for this scandal. The decision of disputed returns was to lie with a committee. From forty-nine members chosen by ballot the petitioner and the sitting member were to strike out names alternately until the number was reduced to thirteen. To this number each party should add one nominee, and this committee of fifteen was empowered to take evidence on oath, and to decide the matter without any appeal back to the House. This Act, at first temporary, became permanent in 1774; but it had little effect in curing the old evils. The preliminary ballot became a party matter, and each side struck out its political opponents, while both concurred in omitting all the ablest men. The committee was thus both 'partial and incompetent.' Sir Robert *Peel's Act* in **1839** reduced its number to six, and a subsequent Act to five, nominated in each case by an impartial body—the general committee of elections. But no satisfactory solution was reached until **1868** when, by an entire change of principle, the Act of Henry IV (**1410**) was revived, and by the *Elections Act*[2] the trial of disputed elections was transferred to the judges of the High Court of Justice, acting as servants and nominees of the House of Commons. To them in the first instance the petition of the aggrieved party is presented. The trial is heard in the neighbourhood whose representation is in question, the decision is reported to the Speaker, and the House takes action thereupon.

The second of the privileges acquired by the House, but nowhere expressed in words, has been described as the *right to the exclusive cognizance of matters arising within the House.* This involves, in the first place, the power of the House to punish its own members, which has been asserted in the cases of *John Storie* (1548),[3] for violent language ; *Copley* (1558), for speaking disrespectfully of Queen Mary ; *Peter Wentworth* (1576),[4] for discussing matters which Elizabeth had forbidden ;

[1] Anson, i. 165. Porritt, i. 540.

[2] Anson, i. 160.

31 & 32 Vict. c. 125, amended by 42 & 43 Vict. c. 75,

(2) Exclusive cognizance of everything within the House.

[3] Hallam, i. 271-274.
[4] Prothero, xciii.

Arthur Hall and Dr. Parry, already mentioned; together with all the numerous cases of expulsion for various offences committed inside the House. The extent of this power may be judged from the fact that the law courts have frequently declared that they will take cognizance of nothing short of a criminal offence committed within the House or by its order. Thus, in the case of Eliot already mentioned, who was convicted by the Court of King's Bench, among other things, of an assault on the Speaker, the House of Lords, in reversing the decision in 1668, chose the ground that one of the offences, seditious speeches, was not within the province of the Court of King's Bench. They avoided an expression of opinion on the act which did fall within the competence of a Court of Common Law, and silence would seem to imply acquiescence in such a view.[1] Within recent years the attitude of the law courts in the matter has been most clearly laid down in the case of *Bradlaugh* v. *Gosset*, in the course of which Mr. Justice Stephen declared that he knew of 'no authority for the proposition that an ordinary crime committed in the House of Commons would be withdrawn from the ordinary course of criminal justice.'[2] At the same time, the same judge asserted that the House had the exclusive power of interpreting a particular statute (the *Parliamentary Oaths Act*, 29 & 30 Vict. c. 19) 'so far as the regulation of its own proceedings within its own walls is concerned; and that, even if that interpretation should be erroneous, this court has no power to interfere with it directly or indirectly.' A distinction was thus clearly made between acts done in the House itself, and those 'rights to be exercised out of and independently of the House.'

Limits of the privilege.

[1] Anson, i. 171.
1884.

[2] Robertson, 412.

A clear understanding of this principle would have saved more than one conflict between the House of Commons and the law courts. For, not content with the exclusive cognizance of all that went on within their walls, the Commons have been inclined to extend their privileges and to claim for themselves the exclusive power of determining their extent. The reason is obvious. A confirmation in the law courts of a privilege asserted by the Commons may be reversed on an appeal to the House of Lords; while its rejection by the court leaves the Commons with the sole alternative of a similar

Conflicts between the Commons and the law courts, over

appeal. In either case one House becomes the judge of privileges claimed by the other. The Commons have preferred to carry matters with a high hand. They have drawn up resolutions of their right to the privileges in question; they have prohibited suitors, and have committed the judges and executive officers to prison for contempt. But the judges have maintained an even course throughout. While admitting the necessity of receiving resolutions of the Commons with all due respect, they have regarded it as their main business to interpret the law. No resolution of one branch of the legislature can lay claim to the binding force of a statute. Thus no act, in itself illegal, can be legalized by the authority of the House of Commons, for 'it is necessary, in answer to an action for the commission of such illegal act, to show, not only the authority under which it was done, but the power and right of the House of Commons to give such authority.'[1] These were the principles maintained in the two celebrated cases of *Ashby* v. *White* and *Stockdale* v. *Hansard*. In both cases the Commons tried to assert by a resolution what they conceived to be a violated privilege, and to force the law courts to pay heed to it. In the first case, the real question was mixed up with a quarrel over the jurisdiction in error of the House of Lords, and the matter was only ended by the prorogation of Parliament.[2] In the second case, the contest between the Commons and the law courts continued until an Act was passed to protect parliamentary papers from the ordinary law of libel.[3] The contemporary case of *Howard* v. *Gosset* shows that the law courts were influenced by no capricious motive in their quarrel with the House; for, a judgement against the serjeant-at-arms for executing the Speaker's warrant with undue severity, was unanimously reversed when the Commons resolved to test its legality by an appeal to the Court of Exchequer Chamber. A similar appeal in the former case would probably have resulted equally in a verdict for the House of Commons. As it was, the Courts maintained their point and clearly established the principle that 'they will not be deterred from upholding private rights by the fact that questions of parliamentary privilege are involved in their maintenance; and that, except as regards the internal regulation of its proceedings by the House, Courts of Law will not hesitate

(i) extent of Commons' privileges.

[1] Patteson, J., in case of *Stockdale* v. *Hansard*.

1703.

[2] Anson, i. 176, 180.

1839.

[3] *Ibid.* 177, 180.

1842.

to inquire into alleged privilege, as they would into local custom, and determine its extent and application.'[1]

Nor has the question of the extent of its privileges been the only cause of contention between the House of Commons and the law courts. The natural result of the right of the House to exclusive cognizance of matters arising within it, is the *power of inflicting punishment for breach of privilege*. This may be visited either upon a member or upon some one outside the House. Until 1666 it often took the form of a fine, but this has fallen into disuse. The modern forms are—expulsion in the case of a member; and admonition and commitment to the custody of the serjeant-at-arms or to prison, which are applicable to all offenders. It is the limits of this power of commitment which have been called in question by the law courts. The power itself was originally based on the contention, vehemently upheld in the case of Goodwin and Fortescue, that the House of Commons was a Court of Record. But Lord Mansfield denied that the Journals of the House were matter of record; and since the Commons gave up the right to determine disputed elections, the claim has lost all meaning. The law courts have themselves maintained this power of the House to punish for breach of privilege in the cases of *Alexander Murray* (1751) and *Burdett* v. *Abbott* (1810),[2] on the ground of its necessity for maintaining the dignity of the House. But when the Superior Courts of Law have been called on to examine into a return made to a writ of Habeas Corpus which has been sued out by a prisoner committed by order of the House, they have applied to the matter those principles which guide them in their conduct towards each other. Thus, in both the cases just noted, it was held by the judges that if the commitment was alleged to be for contempt without specifying the precise act, the law courts would not inquire further into the matter,[3] for they had no means of judging of the question. In the earlier case of *Paty*, the majority of the judges practically went still further, and refused even to take cognizance of any act which the House of Commons chose to describe as a contempt; but the two later decisions have made it clear that a specification of the act for which a prisoner had been committed by the Commons, would justify the law courts, in their opinion, in inquiring into its

[1] Anson, i. 182.

(3) Punishment for violating privileges.

(ii) limits of power of commitment.

[2] Robertson, 359.

[3] *Ibid.* 366. 1705.

[1] Anson, i.
182-183.

truth and justice.[1]   Otherwise the individual would have no protection against an arbitrary vote of the House.

Relations of the Commons and the Lords.

§ 39.   The relations of the House of Commons to the Crown have been defined largely by the legal provision for the meeting of Parliament in the Triennial Act, and by the gradual assertion of parliamentary privilege.   Equally important is it, in considering the growth of the Commons, to consider their attitude towards the remaining branch of the legislature—the House

Their original attitude.

of Lords.   It has been pointed out already that the original difference in the position of the two Estates came from the fact that the Lords had a position in the organized body of the Commune Concilium with fairly defined rights and powers. The exact force of this difference may be illustrated from three sides.   In the first place, the *wording of the writs of summons* to Parliament would show the part which the Crown intended that each estate should play in the new assembly.   Thus, while the Lords were generally summoned by the formula 'tractaturi vestrumque consilium impensuri,' the presence of the representatives of the Commons was desired 'ad faciendum et

[2] *S. C. H.*
§§ 417, 419.

consentiendum.'[2]   In other words, the Commons were not called together with the other Estates for deliberation and advice, but merely in order that they might strengthen the resolutions of the king and the Lords with their presence and their supposed assent.   Again, the *form of the enactment of laws* originally stated that they were made with the 'counsel and consent of the Witan,' and the same form continued to the end of the thirteenth century with the substitution of the word 'Barons' for Witan.   The early parliamentary form expressed the equal 'consent of the prelates, earls, barons and commonalty of the realm.'   But this theoretical equality of the Commons meant nothing, while it displeased the other Estates; and in the first year of Edward III the share of the Commons was

[3] *Ibid.*
§ 293.

more modestly and truthfully expressed as 'petition.'[3]   Under Richard II the equality of the Commons in legislation is again expressed; but under Henry IV the formula again mentions the

[4] *Ibid.*
§ 441.

'request' or 'prayer of the Commons.'[4]   Lastly, in the *grant of taxation*, each Estate at first voted its proportion separately. But soon after the Estates had definitely separated off into two Houses, the method of grant begins to assume a common form; and the greater importance of the Commons in this parti-

cular is acknowledged in the formula that all grants are made ¹ *S. C. H.*
'by the Commons with the advice and assent of the Lords.'[1]   § 438.

But as the power of the Commons grew, the actual changes Change
in the relations of the two Houses were far wider than any- in their
thing expressed by the traditional formulae.   Until 1872 the attitude.
writs of summons to Parliament remained substantially the
same as in the fourteenth century.   The Lords were still
called 'to treat and give their council,' the Commons 'to do
and consent to' what is ordained by the Common Council.
Now, however, while the summonses to the peers remain the
same as always, the Ballot Act has provided for the Commons 1872.
a shortened form which does not commit itself to the part
which the elected members are supposed to play in the
assembly.   Meanwhile, all the three chief powers which had
descended to the Lords from the Commune Concilium were
in one way and another challenged by the Commons.   An
examination of the disputes in each case will show clearly
the change in relations which, in the six centuries of their
existence, the two Houses have undergone.   The Commune
Concilium was organized by Magna Carta solely for purposes
of *taxation*.   But it was for this very purpose that Edward I Commons
included the representatives of the Commons in the National monopolize
Assembly ; and although from an early period grants of money Taxation.
were said to be made by the latter, it was only very gradually
that the Lords surrendered all claim to a voice in the regulation of supplies.   The first step in the ultimate monopoly of
the Commons in all matters relating to taxation was taken in
1407.   The king consulted with the Lords as to the necessary The Lords
amount of the supplies to be raised, and then summoned deprived of
the Commons in order to communicate to them the decision (a) initia-
of the Lords.   But when the Commons in alarm complained tion.
of this derogation to their liberties, Henry, who had acted
in mere carelessness, immediately gave way and, in an Ordinance called the 'Indemnity of the Lords and Commons,'
while asserting the right of each House to deliberate by itself
on the state of the realm, he promised that 'neither House
should make any report to the king on a grant made by the
Commons and assented to by the Lords, or on any negotiations
concerning the grant until both houses were agreed, and that
then the report should be made *in manner and form as*

[1] S. C. H.
§ 315,
quoting
Rot. Parl.
iii. 611.
[2] Porritt, i.
548 et seq.

(b) amend-
ment,
1671.

[3] Robertson,
422.
1678.

hath hitherto been accustomed, that is, by the Speaker of the Commons.'[1] But although the right of *initiation* was gone, the Lords still claimed the power of interfering with money bills by amendment or rejection.[2] The right of *amendment* was denied by the Commons in two resolutions in the reign of Charles II. In the first they asserted 'that in all aids given to the king by the Commons, the rate or tax ought not to be altered':[3] and they followed this up by an elaborate summary of their whole claim 'that all aids and supplies, and aids to his Majesty in Parliament, are the *sole* gift of the Commons; and all bills for the granting of any such aids and supplies ought to *begin* with the Commons: and that it is the undoubted and sole right of the Commons to direct, limit, and appoint in such bills the ends, purposes, considerations, conditions, limitations and qualifications of such grants: which ought *not to be changed or altered by the House of Lords.*'[4]

[4] *Ibid.* 422.

But the Lords still retained the right of altogether rejecting a money bill. They were, however, so chary in the use of this power that the Commons took advantage of their forbearance, and by the process of 'tacking' on to a money bill another bill whose rejection by the Lords was a foregone conclusion, they left to the Lords the unwelcome alternative of passing the obnoxious bill or of rejecting the necessary supplies.

(c) re-
jection.

In 1702 the Lords not unnaturally stigmatized this practice as 'unparliamentary and tending to the destruction of the constitution of this government.' The right of *rejection* was suffered to be in abeyance until 1860, when it was exercised upon a bill for the repeal of the paper duties which formed part of the financial arrangements assented to by the Commons for the ensuing year. This not only upset the calculations of the ministers, but was regarded by the Commons as an invasion of their privileges; and, while unable to alter matters for that session, they drew up for future guidance a series of resolutions which affirmed the sole right of the Commons to grant aids and supplies to the Crown; the jealousy with which the Commons regarded even the sparing use of the power of rejecting money bills exercised by the Lords, since it affects the right of the Commons to grant the supplies, and to provide the ways and means for the service of the year; and finally, the sole power of the Commons to impose and remit taxes and to frame bills of supply that their right as to the matter, manner, measure, or time, may be maintained inviolate.[1] These resolutions are careful not to deny the abstract right of the Lords to reject money bills; but they are intended 'to guard for the future against an undue exercise of that power by the Lords, and to secure to the Commons their rightful control over Taxation and Supply.'[2] This, however, is to be done by the Commons framing their money bills in such a way as to render impossible the exercise of the right of rejection. As a practical outcome of these resolutions, in the next year the Commons included all the proposed financial measures in one bill; and, as amendment was out of the question, the Lords were constrained to accept the whole proposal, since they were not prepared to adopt the only alternative of rejection.

> [1] Robertson, 422.
>
> [2] Anson, i. 267.
>
> 1861.

The power of the Lords in *legislation* has remained a much greater reality than their power in taxation. It was under Henry VI that the Commons asserted their equality in this respect with the other Estates of the realm, by substituting the form of bill for that of petition which they had hitherto employed. Thus from 1445 laws begin to be enacted 'by authority of Parliament'; and from the beginning of Henry VII's reign no further mention is made of petition or request;[3] while the general formula which exists to the present day, expresses 'the assent of the Lords Spiritual and Temporal, the Commons in Parliament assembled, and the authority of the same.' But, except in the matter of money bills, a strict equality has been maintained between the two Houses in legislation. The Lords, equally with the Commons, possess the right of initiative and the power of rejecting or amending a bill which is sent up to them from the Lower House. There are only two methods of overcoming the dead-lock which otherwise ensues on the refusal of one House to accept the amendments of the other. The first is a *conference* between appointed members (called Managers) of both Houses. This was a common custom, especially for the settlement of the money grant, in the last quarter of the fourteenth century. It took the form of a selection of a number of the Lords, either by their own House or even by the Commons, to confer with the whole body of the Lower House. But the

> Commons' share in Legislation.
>
> [3] S. C. H. §§ 439-441.
>
> Methods of overcoming opposition of the Lords.
>
> (I) Persuasion.

Lords were tenacious of their position and seemed inclined to resent the dictation of the Lower House. Thus, although in 1377 the Commons selected the committee of Lords with whom they would confer, in 1378 the Lords described this conference of a select number with the whole House of Commons as a novelty, and preferred the discussion by a committee on either side. Again, in 1381 they resented an application from the Commons to know the opinions of the prelates, barons and judges separately, since it was the practice of Parliament for the Commons to lay their advice before the Lords. Neither was the king particularly favourable to this procedure. In 1383 Richard II attempted to nominate the committee of Lords who should confer with the Commons; and in 1402 Henry IV allowed the conference as a great favour, but his own concession in the matter of taxation five years later (1407) practically conceded the point.[1] Since then, conferences have been frequently held between select committees of both Houses, and for a long time it was customary that the number of the Commons nominated should be double that of the Lords. Conferences were either *formal*, in which case they limited themselves to the reading of reasons for its disagreement drawn up by the committee of the objecting House; or *free*, when they took the form of a debate for the purpose of arriving at some compromise or agreement. But free conferences are almost entirely discredited. None were held between 1740 and 1836, and there has been no instance since the latter date: while in 1857 even formal conferences were superseded by resolutions of both Houses in favour of messages, unless a conference should be specially demanded by either side.[2]

The second method of overcoming a disagreement between the two Houses is the *coercion* of the House of Lords. In theory this can be effected by a *creation of peers*. It was by this means that the Tory government of Harley and St. John succeeded in forcing the Treaty of Utrecht through the Whig House of Lords. It was a threat of resort to this means that among other things brought the Lords to reason on the occasion of the first Reform Bill. An eminent writer has characterized this power of creating peers as the 'safety valve' of the constitution,[3] but although we need not go so

[1] *S. C. H.* §§ 293, 436.

[2] Anson, i. 258-260. Porritt, i. 557-561.

(2) Coercion.

1711.

[3] Bagehot, *Eng. Const.* 229.

far as to regard it with another distinguished author as 'not only unconstitutional but absolutely illegal,'[1] it seems more consonant with modern feeling and common sense to hold 'that to introduce a number of persons into the House of Lords for the sole object of determining a vote on a particular occasion is a use of legal powers which nothing could justify but imminent risk, in the alternative, of public danger.'[2] A more effectual and constitutional method of overcoming the resistance of the House of Lords is by a *dissolution* of Parliament and an appeal to the constituencies to endorse the action of their representatives in the House of Commons. Such was the action taken in the case of the Reform Bill, but then not recognized by the Lords in its full significance. Since then, however, and largely in consequence of that bill, the relative power of the two Houses has undergone great change, and the opposition leaders in the House of Lords, in considering the bill for the disestablishment of the Irish Church, gave way on the express ground that, when the country has once decisively spoken, the Lords no less than the Commons should feel that they hold a mandate to carry out the wishes of the constituents. The only way in which the Lords can assure themselves of the clearness of that speech, is by holding out until an appeal has been made to the electorate. In this way they act as the guardians of the rights of a temporary or accidental minority.

But not only have the Commons monopolized the right of granting taxes and forced the Lords to acknowledge the necessity of accepting laws at their command: they have even interfered with the exercise of that *judicial* power, a share in which they themselves were the first to repudiate. The causes of such interference have been twofold. In the first place, the Commons have been led by sheer *jealousy* to resent what appeared to them to be an invasion of their privileges. Thus, in the case of *Shirley* v. *Fagg*, the question at issue touched the claim of the Lords to hear appeals from the Court of Chancery; and the sole reason for the interposition of the Commons was the fact that the original decision of Chancery had been given in favour of a member of their House. Considering the motive of the Commons it is not a matter for regret that the Lords made good their claim.

[1] Hearn, *Govt. of England* 177.

[2] Anson, i. 261.

1869.

Commons' interference in judicial action of the Lords called for by (1) interference with privileges. 1675.

1703-4.

Again, in the case of *Ashby* v. *White* and the succeeding cases, the Commons considered that the Lords, in hearing an appeal in error from the decision of the Court of Queen's Bench on the question of Ashby's right to vote, had unwarrantably interfered with a privilege—that of deciding the qualifications of electors—which the Commons quite wrongly claimed for themselves. They even went so far as to commit the other electors, who followed Ashby's example, for breach of privilege, and refused to allow any reference by writ of error to the judgement of the Lords. But the Commons have not always been actuated by such unworthy motives in questioning the jurisdiction of the Lords. They were called upon to

1668-9.

take part in the case of *Skinner* v. *the East India Company*,

(2) excess of jurisdiction.

partly perhaps because some members of the Company were also members of the Commons, but chiefly because they were petitioned by the Company and therefore felt themselves obliged to uphold the rights of individuals against an usurped jurisdiction. The quarrel was not fought out to a conclusion ; but the Lords gave way and practically admitted not only their own mistake, but the justice of the Commons' conduct in the matter. The Commons were equally successful in their con-

1681.

tention arising out of the case of *Fitzharris*, whom they had impeached for a capital offence and whom, as being a commoner, the Lords refused to try. There were numerous precedents in favour of the Commons' contention, the latest being those of the judges and royal servants who had been

1640-1.

impeached by the Long Parliament ; while all constitutional lawyers were agreed in regarding an impeachment as an exceptional mode of trial. In the matter of Fitzharris the Commons protested against the refusal of the Lords as a denial of justice and a violation of the constitution of Parliament, declaring that it was 'their undoubted right to impeach any peer or commoner for treason, or any other crime or

[1] Robertson, 420.

misdemeanour.'[1]   Fitzharris was tried at common law ; but the Lords acknowledged the untenability of their attitude by never again questioning the right of an impeached commoner to a trial in their court.

CHAPTER VI

THE EXECUTIVE AND LEGISLATURE IN CONFLICT

§ 40. THE growth of the power of the legislature has been
dealt with at some length. It is necessary, however, to traverse
much of the same ground from the side of the executive. It
has been seen that until the petitions of the Commons became
the means by which legislation was initiated, it is merely *Struggle of*
complimentary to talk of any assembly as the Legislature. Up *the execu-*
to the date indicated, then, constitutional history is chiefly *tive against*
concerned with THE STRUGGLES OF THE EXECUTIVE AGAINST *tive ten-*
THOSE PROVINCIAL AND DISRUPTIVE FORCES which are so *dencies of*
characteristic of early English history. The settlement of the
English tribes took a century and a half to accomplish. For *450-600.*
the next two hundred years England was divided among *600-800.*
a number of small kingdoms : and the only semblance of
unity came from the organization of the Church and the
more or less acknowledged supremacy of one of the greater
princes.[1] How soon this would have led on to a more *[1] Trans. R.*
substantial union, it is impossible to determine; for the *Hist. Soc.*
Danish invasions introduced a new element of disruption. *xiv. 222.*
The real unity of England may be said to date from Ælfred's *(1) provin-*
consolidation of Western Mercia with Wessex, which was *cial feeling;*
followed by Eadward the Elder's conquest of all England
south of the Humber together with his shadowy supremacy
over Northumbria. But the difficulty of swift communication *under the*
made even this restricted area too great to be governed from *Anglo-*
one centre; and although in 954 Northumbria also was *Saxons,*
incorporated within the English kingdom, it was only as an
addition to those ealdormanries which Eadward the Elder's
son and successor, Æthelstan, had found himself compelled
to establish. Thus the last century of Anglo-Saxon history is

U

a time of strong contrast. On the one side stood the king, already as strong, in what may be called his *material strength,* as the elimination of all royal rivals, the maintenance of an extensive thegnhood, and the spread of the practice of commendation could make him. But with the acquisition of a right to the title of King of the English his *personal dignity* became much exalted. Its limits may be measured by the promises made by the king to the people at his coronation, that he would do their will although he was their lord, and by the continued exercise of the Witan's power of deposition. For the present, the king shared with other lords the advantages to be derived from the imposition of oaths of fealty and the maintenance of a law of treason. But it was probably this enhancement of the personal dignity of the Crown which caused Æthelstan and his successors to assume the imperial titles of Imperator and Basileus.[1] A practical comment on such titles may be found in the commendation of the princes of the Welsh, Danes and Scots to Eadward the Elder and the bestowal of Cumbria and Galloway by Eadmund on Malcolm, the son of the Scotch king, and (more doubtfully) that of the Lothians by Eadgar on Kenneth II. Alongside of this personal assumption ran an increase of *official position,* which gradually transformed the king from representative of his people and the guardian of law to lord of their land and the source of all justice. On the other side stood the great ealdormen, who, whether the descendants of the old royal houses, or related to the West-Saxon royal family, or the nominees of the reigning king, equally represented the *strong provincial feelings* which had been fostered by the separate and mostly antagonistic existence of 400 years. Except under a very strong king they could manipulate the Witan ; while locally their action could and often did paralyze that of the Crown. Indeed, the division into ealdormanries was rather a change of name than of fact. Whatever was the outward form, the disruptive spirit characteristic of feudalism was abroad in England in a far stronger measure than it ever was after the Conqueror had done his work ; and in a much more real sense than ever after the Norman Conquest, the king realised the feudal position of 'primus inter pares.'

The Anglo-Saxon kingdom had altogether succumbed to

[1] Freeman, *Norm. Conq.* i. 548 et seq.

924.

945.

that provincial feeling which had made her rulers powerless against Danes and Normans alike. William and his successors determined at all costs to remedy this 'centralization without concentration' which had placed them where they were. Fortunately, two reasons made this possible as it had not been possible before. Firstly, the Normans, as a small band of strangers among a hostile population, were obliged for the sake of military discipline to submit to restraints which they would otherwise have refused. Thus, while the tenure of land was on the feudal condition of specified military service, William abolished the great provincial earldoms and enhanced the power of his own representative, the local sheriff. Secondly, the presence of a common foe caused the English people at length to draw together. The king perceiving, with the instinct of a statesman, that they were unable to organize themselves, did everything to win their confidence. Thus he went out of his way to maintain as much of the old constitution as he could understand or profitably use. He solemnly confirmed Eadward the Confessor's laws, and encouraged English institutions. The *local courts* of shire and hundred were a counterfoil to the feudal and manorial jurisdictions. The *fyrd* was, in theory at least, the nation in arms. The old *oath of fealty*, which was enforced on all landowners without distinction of tenure at the famous meeting of Salisbury in 1086, was a denial of the exclusive claims to their tenants' services made by the feudal lords.[1]

under the Normans.

[1] Jenks, *op. cit.* 93.

Meanwhile, a new power had arisen which was as inimical to the aims of the Crown and the growth of nationality as that of the baronage itself. The Anglo-Saxon Church had on the whole acknowledged only a somewhat shadowy supremacy on the part of Rome. Consequently, despite the efforts of Dunstan's party of reform and the introduction of foreign bishops by Eadward the Confessor, England remained ecclesiastically provincial. The clergy sat in the secular courts and connected themselves by marriage with the local gentry. William's work was to bring the English Church into harmony with the ecclesiastical discipline and thought of Western Europe. The prevailing sentiment of the Church demanded such a separation between things ecclesiastical and things temporal as was implied in the celibacy of the clergy, which, to avoid a great outburst

(2) claims of the Church;

William I's ecclesiastical policy.

of feeling, Lanfranc only gradually introduced; and in the establishment of distinct ecclesiastical courts, which fell in with William's idea of using the Church as a counterpoise to the feudal barons. He accordingly made the bishops hold their lands on baronial tenure, and by an Ordinance gave them tribunals of their own.[1] At first sight it seems as if, in striving to correct the centrifugal tendencies of Anglo-Saxon institutions and of feudalism, the Conqueror had merely substituted one kind of disruption for another. But it must be remembered that the Church was 'the sole depository of mental and moral authority,' and that it was only by such isolation from the world of the feudal baron that its full effect as a civilizing agency could be felt. Anselm and Becket, either or both, may have been fighting for their order rather than in the general interest of the nation; but behind the actual subjects of their contest lay that principle of appeal to some other standard than brute force, which the whole existence of the clerical order represented. Yet none the less was the Church inimical to the growth of nationality. William tried to provide bulwarks against the interference of Rome. He not only exercised the power implied in the direct appointment of bishops and their investiture with the ring and crozier, but he also refused homage to the Pope, and issued, in the form of a declaration of old customs (Consuetudines), four prohibitions of the exercise of important ecclesiastical powers without leave of the Crown. But this policy depended for its success on the harmonious working of the local heads of Church and State: for, when the throne fell to a less statesmanlike monarch, the archbishop would be bound to fortify himself and his order by an appeal to that clerical immunity from lay jurisdiction of which William I himself had laid the foundation; and, in the last resort, to that very papal influence which it was the interest of king and bishops alike to exclude. Moreover, this close alliance between the heads of Church and State, while for a time moralizing the action of the State, tended inevitably to feudalize all ecclesiastical relations. Bishoprics became the reward for temporal service: the feudal passion for exemptions and special jurisdictions helped the growth of clerical immunities. Stress was laid on rights rather than duties, and it was this weakening of the inherent feelings of responsibility which

[1] *S. C.* 85.

Its results.

enabled William II and his minister, Ranulf Flambard, to deal with the property of the Church on the principles which they applied to the fiefs of lay barons. The futility of Anselm's continued protests led him finally to betray the nationality of the Church, which as a foreigner he had never valued, and to seek counsel from the Pope.

The two forces, then, which threatened to circumscribe the growth of the executive, were the provincialism of the feudal baronage and the cosmopolitanism of the Church : the one, (3) feudal-with the aid of the rest of the nation, the king crushed : with ism. the other he found it more advantageous to come to terms. For a century the baronage struggled in arms against the 1074-1174. Crown, generally finding a leader among the members of the royal family. Their chief strength lay in those continental connections which enabled them to enforce their own appeal to arms by a rising in the foreign dominions of the English king. Henry I attempted to sever the Norman and English barons by confiscating the estates of rebellious Normans on this side of the Channel. But the twenty years of anarchy Henry I's associated with the name of Stephen, destroyed the good and effect of this and other measures directed to the same end. Henry II's anti-feudal Henry II went steadily to work on the lines laid down by his policy. grandfather. On the one side, he *undermined the feudal position and privileges of the barons.* Henry I's Coronation Charter[1] not only renounced the feudal tyrannies in which [1] *S. C.* 100. William II had indulged, but even enforced on the great lords a similar conduct towards their vassals. The same king probably also began that system of scutage, or acceptance of payment in lieu of personal service, which destroyed the principle of the feudal army. Henry II continued this, and even transferred the feudal tenants so disarmed to the ranks of the fyrd ; while he included the feudal jurisdictions in the judicial system of the country, by enforcing in the Assize of Clarendon the supervision of his sheriffs and justices. On 1166. the other side, Henry I and his grandson both strove to counteract the influence of the baronage by the *formation of a strong central government.* This was begun by Henry I's great minister, Bishop Roger of Salisbury, in his organization of the machinery of the Exchequer. He created his own staff out of the 'novi homines' or new official nobility who were planted upon the lands of the North left desolate by Henry's father. Out of these were taken the sheriffs, who summed up the local administration ; and the barons of the Exchequer, who went round, although in irregular fashion, to watch over the conduct of the sheriffs and to listen to any local complaints that might be preferred against them. Henry II carried this organization further. In the absence of law and amidst the conflict of customs, he made the custom of the king's court prevail over all others until it gradually hardened into the Common law of the land. He continued the creation of an administrative class to whose members he finally entrusted all the sheriffdoms. By thus making the sheriff a mere official of the Crown he kept a constant connection between the central and the local government ; and, not content with that, he subjected him to the supervision of frequent royal commissioners, travelling now in the capacity of barons of the Exchequer, now as justices on circuit. It was the attempts of Henry II to curb the baronial privileges which drove the feudal barons to their last insurrection in 1174. The fidelity of the king's officers and the sympathy of the people gave the victory to the king, and inflicted on English feudalism a wound from which it never recovered.

Their partial success.

Henry's complete success daunted the barons too much for them to attempt anything more while he lived ; and his successor occupied them in the Crusade and his French wars.

1204.

But it was the loss of Normandy which really placed the feudal baronage beyond any hope of recovering their position ; for it forced them to decide whether they would be Normans or Englishmen, and taught them for the first time that they had interests in common with the people. Their momentary championship of the popular cause at Runnymead led to their control over the administration during the minority of Henry III.

1215.

But this only sufficed to show their selfishness and incapacity. Their patriotism was founded on nothing deeper than hatred of the foreign favourites of the Crown. They sought to secure the appointment of the sheriffs and the ministers, while they obtained for themselves exemption from attendance at the popular courts and essayed to conduct the administration by committees of jealous barons who neither did anything themselves nor allowed anything to be done. Henry III's only attempt at influencing the baronage was to concentrate all the great titles by marriage in the members of the royal family. The later Anglo-Saxon kings had treated the ealdormen in a similar manner. But this was never a solution of the difficulty. Certainly a small party, headed by Simon de Montfort, rose superior to the interests of its class. But, as in the contest which procured the Charter, this was a momentary divergence from their general line of conduct.

Edward I had to go to work in a way very similar to that of his great ancestors, the first two Henries. The institution of scutage and the loss of Normandy had done their work, and the feudal army no longer gave any cause for fear. But the feudal jurisdictions had grown from appropriation of royal rights; and Edward's issue of writs Quo Warranto was directed to the establishment of the difference between manorial rights which could be left to the lords; and feudal rights as such, which were now treated as usurpations of the regalia. The *barons* were still, however, too strong to be overborne. Edward preferred, therefore, to *attack them indirectly*. Setting before himself as a principle 'the elimination of the doctrine of tenure from political life,' he began by diminishing the importance of a feudal status. For this purpose he perfected the measure of Distraint of Knighthood, begun by his father, which made knighthood a mere question of income; and he emphasized the sufficiency of the royal summons apart from tenure as a qualification for the membership of the royal Council. But he could go no further in his direct attacks upon the barons; for, the people were insufficiently organized, and the Church with its foreign ties could not be depended on. He had, therefore, even to bribe the great barons into acquiescence with his general schemes by allowing them to share in the advantages of that land legislation which, by the statute De Donis, established entail; by De Religiosis, prevented the alienation of lands to the Church; and by Quia Emptores, put an end to the losses which accrued to the superior lords through subinfeudation.[1] But the real force which was counteracting the power of the barons, was *the continued development of a strong central government.* Henry I's measures had been retarded by the anarchy of Stephen's reign, Henry II's by that of the reign of John. The long strife of

Edward I's anti-feudal measures.

1278.

[1] But see *P. and M.* i. 318.

his father's time emboldened Edward I to strengthen the Crown by every method at his disposal. For purposes of administration he formulated the Concilium Ordinarium, and made it more than formerly dependent on the Crown. He further simplified and defined both the provincial jurisdiction of the judges in the Statutes of Westminster I (1275), Gloucester (1278), and Westminster II (1285); and the work of the Courts of Common Law by the Statute of Rhuddlan (1284), and the Articuli super Cartas (1300).

Formation of a national legislature

But Edward's great work was the incorporation of the people in the government by the completion of the form of the National Parliament. This popular participation had been the strong portion of the Anglo-Saxon system which William I had continued. He retained the local organization for the administration of justice, in the courts of shire and hundred; and for internal defence, in the liability of all freemen to the fyrd. Both were placed under the sheriff, whom the abolition of the local earldom left as the sole representative of the central government in the provinces. Every precaution was taken, while strengthening his local power, to keep this official in proper subjection to the royal administration. Henry I and his grandson both appointed royal officials to the post, and subjected them to the supervision of other officials. Part of their duties were made over to other specially-appointed persons. Their tenure of office was limited. But chiefest of all, the people were enlisted on the side of orderly government; and in nearly every department of business the sheriff found himself under the necessity of relying on the co-operation of a representative body of the neighbourhood. William I had already used the system of witness by local committees in compiling the Domesday Book. Under Henry II, the same system was gradually applied to the needs of civil and criminal justice, and even to the assessment of taxation. The establishment of trial by jury did away with the earlier and more conjectural methods of compurgation and ordeal. The extension of the principle of local representation to the region of taxation, led directly to the formation of a National Parliament. The principle was first applied indirectly. By the Assize of Arms in 1181 the old fyrd was reorganized on the basis of differences in individual wealth, and each man's liabilities were determined by a jury, that is, a sworn committee of his neighbours. The liability lasted on ; and the force itself, placed under its own constables and supervised by special justices, settled into the position of a local police. Meanwhile, with the increase of commerce and wealth, the levy of taxation on personal property was becoming as usual as it was profitable. This called for the continual activity of juries elected in the local courts, in which the greater barons were no longer present. But the larger part of this personal property was to be found in the boroughs on which the kings from Henry I onwards had, sometimes from an enlightened policy, but oftener in return for a substantial sum of money, bestowed the powers of self-government. Both classes—representatives of shires and of boroughs alike— owed their summons before the king to a series of accidents ; but if the Charter was to be a real guarantee against royal tyranny, something more was needed than a baronial council disposed to hold the crown in commission. Thus Edward's early recognition of this, which ended in the creation of the 'Model Parliament,' was followed almost immediately by the 1295. great Confirmation of the Charters, to which subsequent 1297. generations so frequently appealed.

§ 41. From the definite establishment of a legislative body Relations apart from the executive, the struggle of the executive against between the disruptive tendencies of feudalism gives way to the question the execu- of THE RELATIONS BETWEEN THE EXECUTIVE AND THE LEGIS- legislature. LATURE. This now becomes the central feature of English constitutional history. From Edward I onwards, the King-in- Council and the King-in-Parliament tend to fall apart. The king preferred to act through his Council, but was obliged occasionally to act through the larger body. In 1322 Edward II assented that all the affairs of the country should be 'treated, accorded and established in parliaments by our lord the king, and by the consent of the prelates, earls and barons, and commonalty of the realm.' Edward III's continual necessities were the occasion for the acknowledgement of all kinds of powers as residing in the Commons ; but, at the same time, Early pre- the reiterated petitions of Parliament against the action of the dominance Council show that the executive was all-powerful, and that executive. the grant of extensive powers carried with it no real authority

beyond an occasional opportunity of hampering the government. Nor did the extraordinary prosperity of Parliament
under the Lancastrians tell a really different tale. The powers
won early in the fifteenth century were little more than
a repetition of those which had been partially acknowledged
by Edward III. The confirmation which they obtained under
the Lancastrians, was the result of a reaction following on
Richard II's attempted despotism. To the factious Lords
Appellant Richard opposed all the discontented classes in the
kingdom, whether Lollards or unenfranchised peasants, who
had participated equally in the Peasants' Revolt of 1381. The
division of his enemies enabled Richard to use Parliament
for effecting his purposes; and a carefully packed House of
1398.   Commons made the king independent of further supplies by
giving him an income for life, and delegated its authority in
the matter of petitions to a small committee of both Houses
which the king could easily influence.

The Revolution of 1399 has often been compared to that of
1688, for they both represented in one aspect a conservative
and orthodox reaction. Henry IV came to the throne as the
champion of the Church against the Lollard tendencies of
Richard's court, and as the upholder of constitutional govern-
Triumph   ment against Richard's despotism. But in another aspect,
of the   the accession of the Lancastrian dynasty meant *the triumph*
legislature,   *of the legislature over the executive.* For, Henry's title was
1399-1437.   merely parliamentary. He was thus doubly pledged to the
maintenance of constitutional rule; and it is not difficult to
understand the meaning of the extraordinarily full privileges and
powers which were obtained by Parliament from the Lancastrian
kings. Thus (1) control over taxation was secured through
1407.   the establishment of the power of the Commons to initiate
1401.   money grants, of the principle that redress should precede
supply, of the appropriation of supply and of the audit
of accounts. To this was added (2) control over legislation, partly through the influence which Parliament possessed
in the nomination of the Council, but chiefly through the
substitution of the form of bill, or actual wording of the
subsequent statute, for the old petition. The germ of parliamentary privileges is found in the assertion of (3) freedom of
speech. But all these were of little account compared to the

maintenance of (4) ministerial responsibility. In moments of extreme aggravation the legislature had sometimes demanded the right of electing the chief ministers. This had been enforced by the capital punishment of the obnoxious minister and, under Edward III, by the practice of impeachment. These were, however, heroic remedies. The circumstances under which the Lancastrians came to the throne, established a sounder method. The election of ministers was impracticable; but up to Henry VI's assumption of the government in 1437, the Council was little else than a committee of parliamentary nominees; for, the king nominated its members in Parliament, which more than once felt itself justified in passing what amounted to votes of confidence in the ministers. The influence of the Commons extended even to (5) direct control over foreign affairs, a power which they had definitely rejected when offered from sinister motives by Edward III and Richard II, but one which under the changed conditions they did not hesitate to wield.

But this triumph of the legislature over the executive was *far too premature*. It was useful as affording precedents to a future time; but, at the moment, the extensive rights enjoyed by the Commons were a hindrance to constitutional growth; for they only served to hide the insurmountable obstacles in the way of efficient government. In the fourteenth century, the chief obstacle to the progress of the Commons had come from the jealous attitude of the king who, as the bonds of parliamentary control were drawn tighter round him, used all indirect means of loosening the threatened pressure. In the fifteenth century, owing to the peculiar position of the Lancastrian dynasty, this influence was usurped by the nobility. The Commons could protect themselves by procuring legislation against the unlawful action of the sheriff, and could maintain a theoretical control over the nobility in the supervision of the Council; but unassisted by the weak executive, they were powerless against that enormous local influence which, upheld by the practices of livery and maintenance, defied royal judges and sheriffs, and revived the old feudal evil of private war to an extent unknown in England since the anarchy of Stephen's time.

The cause is to be sought in the history of the preceding

Its failure.

Causes of the failure.

century. The success of the royal policy in abolishing all privileges connected with the feudal status, had been largely counteracted by two measures :—Henry III accumulated the great titles within the royal family, while Edward I was compelled to share the advantages of his land legislation with the greater barons. As a consequence, the nobility concentrated upon itself, and became an intermarrying and exclusive caste. Since land could now be both freely alienated and also tied up in entails, estates were accumulated in the hands of a few great owners. Thus all disputes between individual nobles were enhanced by the fact that they gathered up at once the special bitterness of family feuds and the petty and hereditary jealousies which spring from neighbours' rivalries. But further than this, the growing practice of entails prevented the younger son from obtaining any settlement upon his father's lands. He was compensated by the creation of small sinecure offices of state and by the appropriation of all lucrative ecclesiastical posts. In other words, the great nobles, not content with disposing of their own extensive patronage, usurped much from the Crown, sometimes in return for bribes (a system of traffic termed 'brokage'), sometimes merely in order to extend their local influence.[1]

From three sides might this influence have been checked ; but, despite the addition of the Lancastrian inheritance, the *Crown* was impoverished by the large grants which it had to make as hush-money to the nobles. It was, consequently, unable to deal severely with great offenders who had the power of opening at any moment the question of its right to the throne ; while its attempts to found its claim upon a brilliant foreign policy ended, after a momentary success, in an ignominious failure which brought about the very rivalry which that policy was intended to avert. Nor was the *law* any more capable of restraining the nobility. The early part of the fifteenth century was a time of great legal advance. Chancery was developing its procedure and the common-law judges were pronouncing judgements which would be cited for many generations. Yet the administration of the law was full of the most flagrant abuses ; for, writs of all kinds, even royal writs interfering with the course of justice, could be readily purchased ; and the nobles did not scruple either to

[1] Plummer, *Fortescue*, 336.

ntimidate the local courts or to ignore adverse decisions of
 superior tribunal. *Parliament* was no less powerless to aid ;
or not only were the Commons wanting in permanence and
nemselves an oligarchy, split up by religious differences and
ubject to the influence of the nobles ; but their supervision
f the executive was little short of dictation—a function for
vhich their want of a wide experience entirely disqualified
hem. The whole position has been summed up in the phrase
hat *Constitutional progress had outrun administrative order.*
t does not help us much to say that the Lancastrian rule
vas constitutional, thereby meaning that in its strongest
noments it attended to legal forms and acted in harmony
vith Parliament ;[1] for, the real power lay not with king or
Parliament, but with an oligarchy of nobles, whose local and
amily quarrels made government impossible at home and
.broad alike.

[1] Cf. *S. C. H.* 363.

§ 42. It is not unfair, however, to call the Lancastrian era
a great constitutional experiment.' The triumph of the legis-
ature which was its key-note, was of short duration. Already
n 1437 the executive, in the shape of the Council, had freed
tself from the trammels imposed on it during nearly forty
years ; and on the accession of the Yorkist dynasty, strong in
he possession of hereditary claim and successful on the battle-
ield, it obtained an authority which it had not wielded since
the creation of Parliament. Nor was this only because Parlianent as an institution had met with complete discredit. It
nad certainly failed as an active engine of government, and it
was becoming increasingly less representative of the interests
of the nation. Without, therefore, exciting any popular
commotion, Edward IV began the policy of *dispensing
with Parliament*, which his successors for a while continued.
The later fifteenth century was everywhere a time of much
social reconstruction. The two great mediæval bonds of
Feudalism and Catholicism were both relaxed. The intense
local spirit of the first and the universal claim of the last
were both giving way to the rising claims of nationality in
State and Church alike ; and in the midst of this transition
every one looked to the monarchy as the one stable power.
In England, as elsewhere, a succession of able sovereigns
answered the call upon them, and used their opportunities to

Triumph of the executive, 1437-1588.

1461-1529.

build up a strong executive. The first need of the government was (1) *a great treasure*, doubly necessary if there
was to be no recourse to Parliament. The poverty of the
Lancastrians had been in no small degree responsible for their
failure. This was gradually remedied. Edward IV shared
in the commercial enterprise of the time; Henry VII revived
obsolete royal and feudal rights: Henry VIII confiscated the
monastic property; all three kings raised loans and benevolences in the place of regular taxes. It was scarcely less
important that the Crown should surround itself with (2)
a subservient nobility.   The power of the old nobles was
destroyed successively by the Yorkist and the first two Tudor
sovereigns by repressive legislation, such as the statutes of
Fines and of Liveries, by confiscations, and by systematic
executions. The Reformation did away with the abbots, the
least national element in the House of Lords, and bound the
bishops to the side of the Crown. Edward IV had roused
the discontent of the old nobility by raising his wife's relations
to the House of Lords. By the side of the subservient
bishops Henry VIII placed a number of lay nobles whose
chief claim to distinction was their official connection with
the Crown. But the kings did not stop here. Yorkists and
Tudors alike sought to make their system of government
acceptable by the adoption of (3) *a popular policy.*   Edward IV
threw himself into the literary and commercial movements of
the day, and was especially popular among the burgesses.
Richard III tried to secure his precarious crown by promoting
a mass of acceptable legislation in the only Parliament which
he called. Henry VII gave to the country the peace and
security which above all things she desired. Henry VIII
gratified the pride of his people by raising England once more
to a position of importance in Europe. But this abeyance of
parliamentary government was a policy of expediency, whose
continuance was rendered practically impossible by Henry
VIII's personal extravagance and his extensive foreign policy;
while the rise in prices consequent on the influx of precious
metals from America, increased expenditure without necessarily raising the amount of the revenue. The means at
the disposal of the Crown, which were consistent with the
maintenance of popularity, were entirely insufficient apart

rom parliamentary grants. The king, therefore, preferred to ummon Parliament with regularity, and trusted to the influnce at his command to (4) *manage* it in a way favourable to is designs. The Crown was aided by the popular approval f its religious policy; and the extent of its success may be neasured by the numerous and swiftly alternating changes 1 which Parliament acquiesced.

But whether the Crown practically dispensed with Parlianent or manipulated it, the executive dealt in the same way ith any of those constitutional checks upon its power, in hich the Lancastrian kings had been obliged to acquiesce. 'hus, the exclusive parliamentary right of taxation was set at ought by the levy of forced loans and benevolences; the rant of monopolies in all kinds of articles; the increase of ustoms; and the infliction of heavy fines by the Star Chamber. o less was the exclusive parliamentary right of legislation verridden by the extensive use of royal proclamations; while ie freedom of the individual as secured by none but a legal rrest and a speedy legal trial, became a mere farce before ie widely-extended sphere of action assumed by the Council; ie inclusion of all kinds of offences under the head of eason; the unwarrantable use of martial law; and the inmidation of juries by heavy fines in the Star Chamber for erdicts adverse to the interests of the Crown.

But despite the careful and unscrupulous management of ie Crown, Parliament did not sit down patiently while all ie rights which gave any meaning to its existence were thus hittled away. When first left face to face with the Crown s opposition was, as might be expected, small and very ccasional: but this is all the more striking from the contrast ith the usual subservience of its attitude. Thus, under *Ienry VIII*, Wolsey's demand for a large subsidy of £800,000 y an income tax of one-fifth payable over five years, caused n unprecedented debate of a fortnight's duration, and in the nd the royal supporters had to be contented with a somewhat maller subsidy.[1] Again, on two occasions Parliament excused he king from the repayment of the loans which he had conracted. In 1529 this licence applied to all the outstanding pans of the reign; and in 1544, to those of the two preceding ears together with the re-surrender by the lenders of all those

Side notes:

1529-1603.

The executive under the Tudors.

The legislature under the Tudors.

1523.

[1] Brewer, *Henry VIII*, ii.

21 Hen. VIII. c. 24.

35 Hen. VIII. c. 12.

which the king had repaid.   These can scarcely be construed
as other than instances of parliamentary subservience.   But
from these it is necessary carefully to discriminate two other
statutes which outwardly bear marks of the same spirit.   The
Act of 1539 which endowed the king's proclamations with the
force of law, and that of 1544 which allowed the king to
nominate his successor, were both statutes of limitation; for
the first statute, dealing with a power which would in any case
be used illegally, excepted any proclamation that was prejudicial to a subject's property or person, and the second
limited the royal power of nomination to the successor of
Henry VIII's three children, whose rights were thereby
assured.   The Council of *Edward VI* found it necessary
to make concessions, and the Statute of Proclamations was
repealed.   The weakness of the king and the divided state of
his Council encouraged Parliament; and in 1552 a House of
Commons whose elections had been controlled by the Council,
rejected a bill including new crimes under the head of treason,
and substituted a more moderate measure containing a safeguard in the requirement of two witnesses to a charge of
treason.   Even *Mary's* enthusiasm met with a substantial
check from the opposition which she encountered from Parliament.   Her Spanish marriage—the first subject of disagreement—could only be carried out after Parliament had been
dissolved and Wyatt's rebellion suppressed.   The Commons
offered no opposition to the reconciliation with Rome; and
not only did Mary's second Parliament restore the Church to
its position previous to the Reformation, but even Cardinal
Pole was suffered to land in England.   This, however, was
only after considerable contention and on the clear understanding, unpalatable as it was to the queen, that the holders
of the monastic lands should be confirmed in their possession
of both the land and the impropriated tithes.   *Elizabeth* had
to meet a House of Commons emboldened by previous
victories and permeated with the Puritan spirit which martyr-
dom and contact with foreign reformers had rendered aggressive; but during the early years of the reign the serious
danger in which the country lay, caused its members to stay
their hand and to mingle courtesy with their boldest remonstrances.   Elizabeth on her side redoubled the efforts of her

31 Hen.
VIII. c. 8.
35 Hen.
VIII. c. 1.

1553-4.

1554-5.

predecessors to maintain a hold over Parliament. But these only served to postpone the inevitable trial of strength between an overweening executive and a tenacious legislature; and the disappearance of foreign danger on the defeat of the Spanish Armada, practically brought to an end the armed **1588.** truce which had hitherto existed between the Commons and the Crown.

The establishment of the Reformation in England had threatened to unite the Catholic powers of France and Spain against her. Consequently, under the Tudors *foreign politics* had assumed an inordinate importance. These now sank into **Transition** the background. At the same time, the conversion of tillage **from** into pasture and the consequent displacement of the villan **Tudors to** population; the cessation of the French wars and the break up **Stuarts.** of noble retinues, which let loose a number of vagabonds trained to no occupation but that of arms; the enclosure of common lands and the transference of monastic property; the influx of precious metals from America, and the debasement of the coinage by Henry VIII and the ministers of his son—all these had raised *social questions* of the utmost magnitude which had gradually been set at rest. The buccaneering expeditions on the Spanish Main and the formation of numerous trading companies had drawn off the more restless spirits; the intro-duction of new manufactures by the Flemish and Huguenot refugees had given work to the industrious; the consolidated Poor Law dealt alike with the vagabond and the impotent poor; while the revival of an efficient system of local govern-ment under the centralized administration of the Justices of the Peace, secured that order in everyday transactions which is so essential for the encouragement of trade and manufacture. Other questions were now to occupy the national attention. The speculations of the Renaissance on the origin of Society, and the doubt thrown by the Reformation on the place of authority in religion, both contributed to bring to the front *constitutional and religious questions.* Is authority, whether in State or Church, republican or monarchical? Is it, in secular affairs, based upon a voidable contract; or upon indefeasible and inalienable right? Does the divinely appointed form of Church government reside in bishops or in a board of presbyters? The answer of the Tudors to these questions

X

had been most decisive. The royal prerogative and the royal supremacy went hand in hand. The Commonwealth of England was administered by the king and his officers, whether members of the Council or bishops. Parliament was only summoned to discuss such matters as the Crown chose to lay before it: when it stepped outside this limit, the Crown exercised a right of interference. What else at the opening of each Parliament was the meaning of the Speaker's request from the Crown for freedom of speech; and was not the king able to dissolve Parliament when he would? In her theory of ecclesiastical government Elizabeth went strangely near the maintenance of the Church as a department of State; and her threats to contumacious bishops seemed to betray her concurrence in the belief of the councillors of Edward VI, that the rulers of the Church held their power and dignity entirely at the pleasure of the Crown.

Struggle between the executive and legislature, 1603-1642.

§ 43. The Tudors, then, bequeathed to their successors a strong executive; and the uses to which the Stuarts put it were merely imitations of Tudor precedents. There was the same overriding of parliamentary legislation by proclamations and dispensations. For parliamentary grants were substituted loans and benevolences, monopolies, increased customs, obsolete royal and feudal rights. Perhaps the only great novelty was the addition of a subservient bench of Judges to the means employed by the Tudors for invalidating individual liberty. If, then, in their acts the Stuarts were mere imitators of their predecessors, it is important to understand why their government failed where that of the Tudors had been conspicuously successful. Something must no doubt be attributed to the different political and social conditions of the two epochs. Those changing conditions and disturbing circumstances which had made the people acquiesce in an arbitrary royal power as the one guarantee of order, had passed away. The Tudors had held it as long as they reigned, only because they were ever regardful of popular opinion. They had been content to enjoy the reality of power, and had not cared to reduce its claims to definition. But the Stuarts were not Englishmen, and did not understand English modes of thought. Their whole foreign policy is a sufficient proof. The Spanish Marriage was peculiarly abhorrent to the English nation;

Causes of the struggle.

yet it was the centre of James I's foreign policy. No less unsympathetic was their religious policy, and James' principle of ' no bishop, no king,' so identified the Church with monarchy, that it well-nigh perished in the Great Rebellion. The truth was that the Stuarts had no traditions of rule to maintain ; and in default of them, they fell back upon definitions of those rights of royalty, which they found that their predecessors had enjoyed. Unfortunately, in their case the current theory of kingship by divine right received a great confirmation from the circumstances of James' accession ; for, his acceptance in England contradicted both the Statute law by which Henry VIII had given preference to the descendants of his younger sister Mary ; and the Common law of the land which forbade an alien, as James was, to inherit land in England. Everything, then, converged to make James and his son take up an anti-national position. The remonstrances of Parliament were met by definitions of the royal prerogative, which in their turn challenged Parliament to fall back upon the privileges won by the Commons in the days of the Lancastrians. As the need for tact increased, so the amount of tact which royalty displayed, diminished ; and at a time when the rising power and independence of the Commons made them increasingly sensitive under any save the most punctilious treatment, the Crown paraded its prerogative and sought to overawe Parliament by riding roughshod over its most elementary rights. All those means by which the Tudors had kept a friendly legislature, were abandoned ; the Stuarts always forced matters to a crisis, and tried to obtain their own way by dictation and by punishing their opponents.

But we must carefully discriminate. Neither Tudors nor Stuarts denied a place to Parliament in the English Constitution. James himself repudiated one of the Canons of 1606 in which a too subservient Convocation asserted that resistance under any circumstances to the established authority was unlawful ;[1] and he also suppressed Dr. Cowell's *Interpreter*, which asserted that although it was politic to make laws by consent of the whole realm, ' yet simply to bind a prince to or by those laws were repugnant to the nature and constitution of an absolute monarchy '[2] such as he had previously asserted England to be. The attitude of the first two Stuart kings on

Character of the struggle.

[1] Gardiner, i. 289.

[2] Prothero, 410.

the question of the relation of the Crown to Parliament, is fitly depicted in James' letter to the Speaker of the Commons in 1621, in which he informed the House that its members were not to be permitted to meddle with matters of government or with ' mysteries of State.'[1]   The king's ministers draw out this position in detail.   Northampton tells the Commons that their members were only intended to express the wants of the counties and boroughs for which they sat;[2] and Bacon, when carrying the king's prohibition to discuss the impositions, explained to the indignant House that it might always discuss matters which concerned the interest of the subject, enforcing his position by precedents from Elizabeth's reign.[3]   In fact, the Tudor and Stuart theory turned the House of Commons into a kind of royal commission for the collection of information on any subject which the executive chose to submit to its consideration. This is at any rate an intelligible position, though it ill suited the rising aspirations of the popular representatives.   It followed, without much difficulty, that the kings drew a distinction between certain subjects in which Parliament might participate, and certain others with which it had nothing to do.   Thus, the quarrels over *taxation* and *legislation* did not turn on the question whether the exclusive right belonged to the king, but where the line should be drawn defining the powers respectively of king and Parliament.   The right of Parliament to grant subsidies and to make statutes was not called in question ; but the right was being practically annulled by the prerogative powers of levying impositions and issuing proclamations.   On the other hand, there were three great questions in which the king denied that Parliament had any right to exercise a voice. *Foreign policy* came under the head of ' mysteries of State,' demanding study and secrecy : *Ecclesiastical affairs* were matters for the royal supremacy : *Ministers* owed their appointment solely to the king and were so entirely his servants that Charles I constantly declared that he and not they must bear all responsibility for what had been done.   The actual subjects of contention do not so much matter here.   What is of extreme importance is the general attitude of the two parties.   The fault of the Commons was that they tried to carry into practice the theory of the constitution as a balance of powers.   The king's political theory was sounder ; for, it started from the recognition

[1] Prothero, 310.

[2] Gardiner, i. 353.

[3] *Ibid*. ii. 71.

of the fact that in every constitution there must exist some authority armed with the power of saying the final word in a discussion. In the Tudor times this had been the king; after the Revolution of 1688 it became the Parliament. The epoch of the Stuarts represents the transition from one to the other, when executive and legislature were measuring themselves against each other, and the anti-national action of the Crown in its religous and foreign policy convinced the people of the danger of leaving it unchecked. But the only substitute for the king which the leaders of the people had as yet to offer, was a House of Commons 'unguided by any Cabinet and undisciplined by any party ties.'

§ 44. In any crisis the theory of a balance of powers between executive and legislature leads straight to civil war as the only arbiter; and on this occasion there was nothing to check the natural evolution of events. From 1642 to 1660 the English Constitution was practically in abeyance; but the expedients which were evoked to fill the void, formed no unimportant element in the future development of the constitution. For, in the first place, the period of the Commonwealth was distinguished by an attempt to change the whole current of English history. As things have worked themselves out, we have a constitution which contains no fundamental laws, unalterable by the three Estates in Parliament assembled, but leaves that body the legal sovereign with control of the executive. But had the constitutions projected under the Commonwealth been permanent, the development of our system would have been hampered, if not checked, by fundamental laws, and the sovereignty would have reposed in a written constitution; while the executive and legislature would have existed independently of each other, as in the United States at the present day. In the second place, Cromwell was perhaps chiefly hindered by his conservatism. For he fell back on old expedients, and tried, as far as might be, to reproduce the old constitution without those links of historical association which had bound its several parts together, and with that balance of powers which his training in the ranks of the parliamentary party had led him to regard as the ideal. Thus the *Instrument of Government* set up an executive of a Protector and Council with co-ordinate authority, and a Parliament of one chamber independent of the

Constitutional lessons of the Commonwealth, 1642.

Negative lessons.

1653.

[1] Gardiner,
*Const.
Docts. of
Puritan Rev.*
314-325.

[2] Cf. Gar-
diner,
*Cromwell's
Place in
History*,
96-99.

1656.

[3] Gardiner,
*Const.
Docts.*
334-350.

Positive
lessons.

Council, unable on the one hand to alter the constitution, and on the other hand to be itself adjourned or dissolved for five months without its own consent.[1]   The refusal of the assembly elected under this scheme to accept it without comment, put an end to Cromwell's first attempt at parliamentary government.[2]   He next tried to conciliate a large section of public opinion by a return to the three constituent elements of the old constitution.   The opposition of the army forced him to lay aside his intention of accepting the Crown, though the *Humble Petition and Advice* gave him power to appoint his successor.   The House of Lords, however, was to be restored as the 'Other House,' and a number of old and new members were summoned by the Protector with the intention that future vacancies should be filled by the House itself.[3]   But this was merely playing at constitutional government.   The Protector was not the historical monarchy, and commanded no traditional reverence; the real Lords refused to sit with their spurious fellows, who moreover comprised so many of Cromwell's chief supporters that the Commons were left without sufficient control.   Hostile criticism of the new constitution, especially of the powers of the 'Other House,' was only ended by a summary dissolution; and Cromwell reigned supreme until his death.   The truth probably was that there were too many antagonistic elements at work to endue any brand-new constitution with stability.   At the same time, it was a lesson of no small value to future reformers, that neither was England willing to dispense with the framework of her constitution, nor could that framework subsist apart from its historical antecedents.

But the period of the Commonwealth bequeathed other experiences scarcely less valuable than the two already noticed. The abolition of the monarchy deprived the executive of those revenues which, like the feudal incidents, had no meaning apart from the Crown.   The expedients which were substituted for them, borrowed as they mostly were from the Dutch, gave hints of which the government of the Restoration was not slow to avail itself.   Again, Cromwell's principles of toleration, though imperfect and one-sided, were the first definite attempt logically to carry out the teaching of the Reformation, and, like all principles of liberty, when once allowed, were difficult to go back from. Finally, the constitutions of the Commonwealth, with all their disregard of historical antecedents, gave an example of comprehensive representative government, which it took nearly two centuries for the country to realize. The Chamber set up by the Instrument of Government contained not only 400 members from England, Wales, and outlying districts, but 30 from Scotland and 30 from Ireland in addition. There was a redistribution of seats in England and Wales, 261 members being given to shires and 139 to boroughs, and most of the petty boroughs were disfranchised and their seats given either to shires or to large unrepresented towns. The franchise in the boroughs was left to custom which had always regulated it; but in the shires it was altered from the freehold of the annual value of forty shillings—the qualification since 1430—to a real or personal estate of £200.[1] We have to wait until the middle of the eighteenth century before any statesman even suggested so far-reaching a scheme of parliamentary reform, and until 1832 before anything parallel to it could be carried out.

[1] Gardiner, *Const. Docts.* 314 *et seq.* §§ 10, 18.

For, Cromwell failed to establish any permanent system of government; and on his death all the classes to whom the maintenance of law and order was more important than liberty, combined to restore the ancient ways. The Stuarts came back amidst a royalist reaction which seemed to arm them with every power for outdoing even the most arbitrary courses of their predecessors. For, not only was the position of the Crown theoretically unchanged, and the whole of the Tudor constitution in Privy Council, Parliament, local government and royal supremacy restored; but the Crown was tied by no conditions, and Charles' reign was dated in a significant manner from his father's death. The Church not unnaturally preached passive obedience to a race of kings who had suffered so much in her cause. Even Parliament followed in the same direction. It abolished the Triennial Act, contenting itself with a recommendation that Parliament should be called at least once in three years; it passed an Act against tumultuous petitions, thus circumscribing one of the most indefeasible rights of the people; and in view of the Militia Bill of the Long Parliament, it asserted that legislative authority could never be exercised without consent of the king, which was a practical endorsement

The settlement of the Restoration.

of the doctrine of non-resistance ; and that the sole command of the armed forces had ever been vested in the king alone, and that neither House of Parliament could pretend to it or could lawfully levy war offensive or defensive against the king.   It was the continued existence of this same spirit which later on in the reign caused the rejection of the Exclusion Bill, in which the majority in Parliament faithfully echoed the national voice; and which under James II formed the most plausible excuse for the opinions of the judges as to the dispensing power of the royal prerogative.   It was also in the exercise of this theoretically untouched royal prerogative that both Charles and James used the dispensing power to issue declarations of indulgence to Catholic and Protestant dissenters, and that James at his accession collected tonnage and poundage before it had been granted to him for life in the usual way by Parliament.   Yet there is no need to under-estimate the results of the Great Rebellion.   The executive was deprived of some of the most prominent means of oppression. For, Parliament, while restoring the royal power of calling and dissolving the legislature, and leaving the appointment of the judges in the king's hands, not only abolished feudal tenures and incidents together with purveyance, thus taking away from the Crown a large and oppressive source of prerogative revenue ; but it also refused to contemplate the revival of the Star Chamber and the Court of High Commission, leaving as the only method of procedure in extraordinary cases a bill of pains and penalties, in other words, the action of Parliament itself.

Constitu-
tional
results of
the Great
Rebellion,
1660-1688.

§ 45. The great Rebellion, then, did not definitely solve the question of the relations of the executive and legislature to each other.   All that it can be said to have done in this respect is to have shown that certain solutions, such as the abolition of hereditary monarchy and hereditary aristocracy, were unacceptable to the country.   Its work was negative rather than positive.   The proper adjustment of relations was yet to be found.   For, the king still governed nominally by means of the Privy Council, of whose harmony with Parliament there was no guarantee.   But despite the still unsettled condition of this all-important question, Charles II and his brother had only themselves to thank for the final catastrophe. In their relations with Parliament they profited by experience ;

and in nothing can the results of the Great Rebellion be better appraised than in the difference of the methods employed by the later Stuarts in their assault upon constitutional liberties, from those by which their predecessors had provoked the Civil War. Thus, there was no attempt at *legislation without consent of Parliament.* The only use of such a power was in the Declarations of Indulgence which, however, professed to be by virtue of the royal supremacy; and Charles withdrew them in response to the remonstrances of Parliament, while James sought to fortify them with judicial decisions. Nor was there any attempt at *taxation without consent of Parliament.* For, on the one side, Parliament strengthened its control over the finances by the acquisition of the clerical 1664. claim to vote separate supplies, by the confirmation of the 1666. principle of the appropriation of supplies, and of that of the 1667. audit of accounts. On the other side, the king preferred to sell himself to France. James' only violation of this principle in the collection of ungranted customs was perhaps justified by its necessity for the continued prosecution of the trade of the country. Even *ministerial responsibility* to Parliament was acknowledged by the king in his surrender of Clarendon, and in the inability of his pardon to save Danby from impeachment.

But here the attention of Charles II and James II to the Causes of lessons of the Great Rebellion ceased, and in their *violation* the Revolu-*of the liberty of the subject* they rivalled the most indefensible tion. acts of their predecessors; while in their quarrels with the Church they threw away the one weapon with which their father had honourably if obstinately refused to part. The (1) Insecur-acts of the early Stuarts had demonstrated the incompleteness ity of of the safeguards of individual liberty. Something was done liberty. to remedy this fault under Charles II. In **1670** a decision of Chief Justice Vaughan practically ended the personal responsi- Bushel's bility of the jury for their verdicts. A few years later the Case. efforts of Lord Shaftesbury procured the partial safeguard of the Habeas Corpus Act. But these measures by themselves 1679. proved of small assistance. By an attack upon the borough corporations the king was able to obtain the nomination of juries which would give their verdicts for the Crown. The scope of the Habeas Corpus Act was very partial; for, it applied only to criminal charges, and contained no provision to ensure a true return from the gaoler. But the Stuarts had other methods of striking down their victims. The censorship which they maintained over the press muzzled the most formidable engine of free discussion : the indefiniteness of the treason laws enabled them to condemn on the most paltry evidence such opponents as Lord Russell and Algernon Sidney. But even these would have been of little avail to the Crown unless the appointment of the judges had enabled both Charles and James to maintain an entirely subservient bench. The devotion of the interpreters of the law to the royal cause removed the last safeguard against the capricious tyranny of the executive ; while the maintenance of a military force despite all the care of Parliament to reduce it, and especially under the Roman Catholic officers whom James forced into its ranks, formed no slight guarantee against any opposition to the designs of the king.

(2) Attack of the Crown on the Church. But the two later Stuart kings committed the capital error of quarrelling with the *Church*, and thereby not only alienated their strongest supporters, but cut away from under their own feet the powerful argument of divine right in which their predecessors had entrenched themselves. The Restoration had been the work of the wealthier classes, who sought to draw tighter the existing bonds of orderly rule. They desired, therefore, to strengthen Parliament and the Church. The **1661-1679.** Long Parliament of the Restoration, as it was called, in its fervent Anglicanism found itself at one with the minister Clarendon. In their common desire to use the Church as a defence against Roman Catholics on the one side, and democratic Puritans on the other, the Commons set themselves to give its members a monopoly of the temporal power. **1661-1665. Corporation Act. Act of Uniformity. Conventicle Act. Five-Mile Act.** The series of enactments known as Clarendon's Code aimed at banishing Presbyterians from the government of boroughs and the possession of benefices, and depriving them of the ministrations of their preachers. Charles' intrigues with France necessitated similar protective legislation against the Roman Catholics ; and in 1673 Parliament passed the Test Act which in 1678 was extended from office-holders to all members of Parliament of both Houses ; and thus for the first time peers were excluded from the House of Lords on accoun f their religion. Not content with these safeguards, the arliamentary party led by Shaftesbury introduced the Exclu-on Bill; but pressing it on from sinister rather than truly atriotic motives, they met with a well-deserved check. But 1e Church scarcely needed this additional safeguard to make er the exclusive body which Parliament was helping her to ecome. Indeed, so much was this the case that the Puritans o longer claimed, as they had under James I, to be within er pale, provided they could obtain certain modifications in er ceremonial. Laud's clear demonstration of the incom-atibility of Anglicanism and Calvinism had done its work. 'rom Nonconformists, or persons who objected to conform to ertain ceremonials, the Puritans had become Dissenters from 1e whole attitude of the Church. The Church could no longer retend to be entirely national. It was the established form f religion, and the Puritans now stood outside and demanded oleration. The first person to answer that demand was the ing, and that king a Stuart whose father had risked his life or the maintenance of the Church. Charles II, a Roman Catholic probably from the beginning of his reign, hoped to btain his point by combining the cause of the Roman Catholics with that of the Dissenters. He had promised berty of conscience in the Declaration of Breda; but despite 1e favourable attitude of the king, the Savoy Conference 1661. etween Anglicans and Presbyterians failed, and Parliament egan to restore the Anglican Church in renewed strength. Charles accordingly fell back upon the royal power of dis-ensation; and in 1663, and again in 1672, he published Declarations of Indulgence. Parliament, however, compelled im to withdraw them both, and answered the second with he Test Act. Nor did a Comprehension Bill in 1668 meet vith a different fate. James set to work more resolutely. He e-established the High Commission Court with Jeffreys at its 1ead; he attacked the two Universities, the strongholds of Anglicanism; and he issued two Declarations of Indulgence. n the first of these he allowed public worship to the Roman Catholics as well as to the Dissenters, who, however, entirely ejected it. His command that the second should be publicly ead by the clergy, produced the petition of the bishops against it, seven of whom were tried for libel and, despite the

precautions taken with judges and jury, were acquitted. I
the whole history of the time between the Rebellion and th
Revolution nothing is more significant than the fact th
the strength of the earlier Stuarts thus became the weakne
and the ultimate cause of the fall of the later Stuart sovereign

Triumph
of the legis-
lature
secured by.
¹ S. C. 523.
§ 46. If proof were required of the unwritten nature of th
English Constitution there could be none better than th
afforded by the Bill of Rights.[1]   There was no attempt to defin
the fundamental bases of the constitution.   It seemed to tak
for granted that these were sufficiently known ; and it limite
itself to a declaration of the various points in which they ha
been violated by the action of the late king.   So far as it cor
cerned the action of the Crown, the whole document professe
to be merely a declaration of the law as it stood.   The impor

1588-1689.
ance, then, of the Bill of Rights, as of Magna Carta, mu
not be sought so much in its individual provisions, as in th
change of situation to which it bore witness.   It marks th
end of the struggle between the executive and the legislatur
which had lasted for just a century ; and it signalizes th
victory of the latter by stamping as illegal many of thos
modes of action by which the executive had striven to ignor
or override its wishes.   But there was nothing in the Bill c
Rights itself to prevent the recurrence of all those modes c
unconstitutional action which had caused the struggle.   Fc
the real safeguards we must look to the history of the followin
years.   One thing, however, the Bill of Rights accomplishec
By its declaration of the sovereignty of William and Mary
broke the line of succession ; and although, with regard for tende

(1) break
in succes-
sion ;
consciences, it spoke of them as succeeding to the thron
rendered vacant by the imagined abdication of King Jame
yet by this very act it consigned the doctrine of divine right t
the grave of shattered ideals.   The close connection of Mar
with the late king concealed at the moment the full force of thi

1701.
declaration.   It was only when the Act of Settlement went o
to nominate the line of the Electress Sophia of Hanover to th
ultimate succession, that it appeared how entirely the right t
the throne depended on parliamentary recognition.

(2) settle-
ment of
revenue ;
Meanwhile, Parliament had forged other fetters for the Crowr
In settling the *Revenue*, which was granted for the king's lif
a distinction was drawn between the expenditure for the civ

government and the money voted for the maintenance of the armed forces of the Crown. For, the Bill of Rights had declared the illegality of a standing army in time of peace without consent of Parliament; and the legislature refused to make any provision for military discipline except for the ensuing year. The king, therefore, had only a limited revenue at his disposal; and the recommendation of the Bill of Rights that 'Parliament ought to be held frequently' was assured by the necessity of annual sessions imposed upon the Crown if it wished to obtain the means of maintaining and governing the army. By these means the provision aimed against the levying of money for the Crown 'by pretence of prerogative' was effectually safeguarded. It was no less important to circumscribe the royal right to override parliamentary legislation. The Bill of Rights condemned the royal claim to suspend the laws, and the late developments of the claim to dispense with them. But the grossly abused power of dismissing the judges (3) appointwas left to the king, until the Act of Settlement prescribed that ment of from the accession of the House of Hanover, though their judges; mode of appointment remained untouched, the tenure of their seats should be dependent—not on the whim of the Crown, but — on their own good behaviour, of which Parliament became the critic.

But the action of Parliament, to be effectual, must be organized. If it wished to usurp the position of the king, it must evolve some effectual substitute. The abolition of the Crown had been shown to be out of the question. The direct responsibility of the sovereign involved nothing short of a revolution at each disagreement between Parliament and the Crown. It was necessary, therefore, to interpose some (4) Cabinet responsible organization over which Parliament could maintain govern- a permanent control. But Parliament itself did not represent ment. one prevailing opinion. The struggle over the Exclusion Bill under Charles II had caused politicians to range themselves into two parties according as they supported or opposed the indefeasible right of hereditary succession. The Whigs, to whom William owed his throne, hoped to monopolize all power; but the new king endeavoured, though with less reason, to maintain the high prerogatives of his predecessors, and himself conducted the administration of the government.

It became all-important to remove both the individual responsibility of the king, and the ability of the ministers to shelter themselves for their acts behind his commands.   The only possible solution of the question was to make the minister responsible to Parliament.   In his desire to enlist all England in the war with France, William chose his ministers indifferently from both the political parties.   But he lay under the necessity of obtaining the consent of Parliament for all his acts.   In order, therefore, to bring as much influence as possible to bear upon Parliament, he was obliged to take all his ministers from members of either House, and ultimately to secure the support of that one of the two parties which was most numerously represented in the House of Commons.   Thus without in the least degree relaxing his own power of choice, the wish to carry on the French war with greater energy led William to fill all offices with members of the Whig party who were eager for its prosecution.   The same reason led Anne to assent to the desire of Godolphin and Marlborough for a number of Whig colleagues ; while the wish for the conclusion of peace brought about the substitution of an equally complete body of Tory ministers.   Thus, although the appointment of ministers still remained very practically with the Crown, it had to be exercised with some regard to the party which held the majority of votes in Parliament.   It is true that a parliamentary majority could be more or less manufactured ; but in moments of national crisis the worthlessness of these means of influence was frequently demonstrated ; so that the Crown not only could not afford, but did not venture to ignore the evident wishes of the nation.   The history of *Cabinet Government* is dealt with elsewhere.   Here it is necessary to notice that in it lay the solution of the question between the legislature and the executive ; that under William III and Anne the solution had advanced a very little way ; for, accident and not principle had occasionally called into existence a number of ministers of homogeneous opinions, who entirely repudiated any corporate responsibility.   This corporate responsibility, which is of the essence of Cabinet government, only came into being when George I for obvious reasons absented himself from the discussions of his ministers.   The system was only gradually worked out to its modern perfection ; but long before the

1696-1698.

1708-1710.

1710-1714.

personal action of the Crown was eliminated, it was recognized that a close harmony between the ministers and the majority in Parliament was necessary; while the clumsy method of punishment by impeachment of an individual minister gave way to the less severe but equally effective withdrawal of parliamentary support from an unpopular ministry.

The full effect of these safeguards in preventing an undue extension of the power of the executive may be realized from an examination of the present use of the royal prerogative. The prerogative has been described as 'the discretionary power of the Crown.' But inasmuch as the Crown acts solely by advice of its ministers, the royal prerogative is a reserve power in the hands of the Cabinet of the day, and its use is regulated by those conventions of the constitution which are meant to stand between the several members of the sovereign body of the Crown in Parliament and a breach of the law. This may be illustrated in detail. Among the methods which William III employed to keep the executive authority in his own hands, was the use of the royal *veto* on bills which had been accepted by both Houses of Parliament. He could no longer bully the Commons as the Tudors and early Stuarts had done, and in the state of popular feeling his method of influencing them indirectly met with only qualified success. Consequently, his use of the veto on no less than four occasions—a bill for securing the independence of the judicial bench (1692);[1] a triennial bill (1693);[2] a place bill (1693);[3] and an election bill (1696)[4]—exceeded any previous example. Nor did after-events make it less unique; his successors forged new means of influencing Parliament, and, except indirectly, dared not oppose the constitutionally expressed wishes of the nation. Thus, with the single exception of a Scotch Militia Bill in 1707 the veto of the Crown has not been used in the British Isles for nearly 200 years, although its exercise is not altogether unknown in matters which emanate from colonial Parliaments. Here there is practically no scope for the personal discretion of the Crown. Nor in the old prerogative power of *summoning Parliament* has anything been left to the Crown. The Triennial Act, which William vetoed, was passed in 1695; and, while the law henceforth demanded a Parliament at least once in three years, the necessity of obtaining supplies for the

Results on the royal prerogative.

[1] Macaulay, *Hist. of Eng.* iii. 219-220.
[2] *Ibid.* iii. 410.
[3] *Ibid.* iv. 49.
[4] *Ibid.* iv. 148.

army ensured annual sessions.   This period of three years was extended to the seven of the present time by the Septennial Act of 1716.   The legality of this measure has been often questioned.   For, the Parliament which passed it, in fear that a general election so soon after the accession of the Hanoverians might be fraught with danger, applied its provisions not only to future Parliaments but to the existence of the sitting House. This was no doubt a breach of the confidence of their con- stituencies on the part of individual members and an unpre- cedented use of the powers of Parliament as a body ; but since the law courts could take no cognizance of the action, it was not illegal, and indeed its enactments had been cited as the most conclusive proof of the omnipotence of the sovereignty of Parliament in the English Constitution.[1]   Both these weapons, then, have for some time been removed from the armoury of the executive.   Far otherwise has it been with the Crown's *power of deciding when Parliament shall be dissolved.*   A dis- solution of Parliament has been described as an appeal from the legal to the political sovereign, from the ministry and Parliament of the day to the constituencies which exercise the rights of the people.[2]   Since the Revolution of 1688 there have been periods, such as the reign of William III, when Cabinet government was as yet imperfect, and the early years of George III during his struggle with the Whig oligarchy, in which the king used this power of dissolution as a threat.   But as soon as the system of administration by a homogeneous Cabinet was established, a dissolution only became a means of ascertaining whether the ministry in power commanded the confidence of the people, and the king was only justified in exercising his prerogative if he had reason to believe that the original harmony between Parliament and people had been broken.   Thus, in 1784, when George III took the first pretext for dismissing the Coalition Ministry of Fox and North, and maintained the younger Pitt as his minister for three months in the face of a hostile Parliament, his ultimate use of the power of dissolution was entirely justified by the large majority returned to the next Parliament in support of William Pitt.   And when in 1834 William IV dismissed Lord Melbourne in favour of Sir Robert Peel, and dissolved Parliament in the hope which proved to be vain, that the country would return a majority for his new

[1] Dicey, 45.

[2] *Ibid.* 361.

minister, the justification of his use of the royal prerogative lies in the king's belief that the old Parliament had lost the confidence of the constituencies.

The prerogative for which the king fought most strenuously, was his *power of the choice of ministers;* and even after he had been compelled to relinquish the system of an inner and an outer Cabinet or the practice of keeping one royal spy in the person of the Lord Chancellor, he attempted to exercise a choice amongst the nominees of the dominant party. Thus, by his demand of certain pledges, George III drove the Ministry of All the Talents to resignation in 1807. The dismissal of Lord Melbourne in favour of Sir Robert Peel has just been noticed. In 1839 Peel, though possessing the confidence of the country, was unable to assume power because the Queen refused to part with the ladies of the bed-chamber who were near relatives of the outgoing ministry. But the Reform Act had made it impossible for the Crown to uphold its ministers in the face of a hostile Parliament. The elections of 1841 went strongly in favour of Sir Robert Peel; a compromise was arrived at, and the Tories came into office. But although the Crown has thus practically surrendered the power of the choice of ministers, it still plays an important part *in the conduct of administration.* Its right to be consulted was definitely asserted when, in 1851, the Queen concurred with the Prime Minister, Lord John Russell, in the dismissal of the Foreign Secretary, Lord Palmerston, who had given assurances of friendship to the French Government when the Cabinet had decided to maintain a neutral attitude. And there are moments when the personal discretion of the Crown may assume an inestimable importance. For, in the absence of any one definite head of the dominant party, it becomes incumbent on the sovereign to choose between the rival candidates for leadership. Of the influence of the long experience of an individual sovereign something has been said already. It may be noted, in conclusion, that this divorce of the ornamental and the practical heads of the English admini- stration relieves the real guide of the executive of half his work, and removes from the competitors for power the men of second- rate ambition even if of first-rate ability, who are attracted by the benefits to be obtained from the highest office rather than by a feeling of devotion to the public service.

Y

The English system of law.

§ 47. THE English system of Jurisprudence is the one in Western Europe which is most purely of native growth. In France, Italy and Spain the influence of Roman law on native custom was far larger than even its most ardent champion believes it to have been between the Tweed and the English Channel. Thus in England the distinction between *Common law and Equity* takes a peculiar form. An historical investigation will make comparatively clear a practical difference which legal definitions have found it impossible to determine.

The earliest form of the *Common law* of the land was in the shape of local, tribal or national customs, which have given it the name of *Customary* law. But, for their validity, such customs demanded judicial recognition, whether the judge was the body of free suitors or an individual representative of the royal authority; and such judicial recognition was obtained by means of three sets of courts—(*a*) national, those of the Hundred and Shire, (*b*) private, those of the Thegns and of Lords of Manors, (*c*) municipal, those of the chartered and privileged Boroughs.

(A) National Courts. Hundred.

The smallest administrative division recognized in the arrangements of our mediæval constitution was the *Hundred*. The question of its origin is one of the most obscure points in English history. No mention of the name is found on English soil until the 'Ordinance of the Hundred,' a document which at the earliest is assigned to the reign of Eadgar. It may be that the language of the Ordinance must be interpreted as presupposing the existence of the district with which it deals; but this would not necessarily lead us to look for its origin in a very remote past. And yet *the commonly accepted theory*

Theories of its origin.

322

seeks to connect this governmental arrangement of the tenth
century with a division which the Roman historian, Tacitus,
writing eight centuries earlier, notices as existing among the
German tribes.   According to his account, every Civitas or
Tribe was divided into a number of Pagi, and each Pagus contained a number of Vici; but the organization centred round
the division of the Pagus which supplied its presiding chief with
a hundred assessors when he sat to administer justice, and was
responsible for a contingent of a hundred men when the tribe
went out to war.[1]   Of the Pagus we hear no more.   In fact, [1] *S. C.*
if the tribes of which Tacitus speaks were the ancestors of the 56-57.
tribes which conquered Britain, we get no authentic informa- §§ 6, 12.
tion of them for five hundred years.   But, meanwhile, the
records of the kindred tribe of the Franks in their new home
in Gaul in the fourth century, tell of the existence of the *Mallus*
—the ordinary court of justice—composed of all fully qualified
landowners of the district under the presidency of an officer
called Centenarius: while two centuries later the laws of the
Frankish kings Childebert and Clothair[2] mention the local [2] *Ibid.*
division of the *Centena* which possibly formed the basis of 69, 70.
the contemporary police system in Gaul.

So far as it relates to the history of the hundred before our
English records begin, this chain of direct evidence has been
most ingeniously broken in every link.   By a masterly analysis Coulanges'
of the few sentences in which Tacitus speaks of the system of criticism
justice among the Germans, M. Fustel de Coulanges has shown ordinary
that it is at any rate probable that the princeps who adminis- view.
tered justice with the aid of a hundred comites, was an itinerant
judge appointed by the national assembly and taking round
with him, after the fashion of all Roman Judices, a chosen
band of freemen (plebs as distinguished from principes) who
acted as his council and, in the absence of documents,
personally attested his decisions.[3]   No less ingeniously does [3] *Recher-*
M. de Coulanges explain away the analogy of the Mallus. *ches sur*
There is nothing to show that it was an assembly, or that *quelques*
a system of popular judgement prevailed.   It was a tribunal *d'histoire,*
in which justice was rendered by the royal officer, and to it 361-371.
were amenable not only the Franks but also the Romano-
Gallic inhabitants.[4]   The judge in the Mallus was the Comes; [4] *Ibid.*
and for administrative purposes he appointed officials who are 398-402.

called by various Roman names. Among these is found the centenarius, who perhaps at first was a military officer—the equivalent of the centurio—and was then turned into a civil official with powers of police.[1] The centenarius may well have existed before the centena, the division over which he is supposed to have presided, and of whose existence there is no evidence earlier than the eighth century. The edicts of Childebert and Clothair are copies of the ninth century; the names of the kings to whom the edicts are assigned are purely arbitrary; and the centena seems to be a personal division for purposes of police.[2]

The presumptive *evidence for the early existence of the hundred* on English soil is to be found in three directions. In the first place, the scanty collections of Anglo-Saxon dooms or laws which we possess, from the very first contain references to some subdivision of the tribal kingdoms. Thus, the Laws of Hlothære and Eadric, kings of Kent, under date about 680, speak of the summons of an offender to a *Methel* or a *Thing*;[3] from the Laws of Wihtræd, also king of Kent at a slightly later date, we hear of a presiding official called a Reeve; while the contemporary Laws of Ini of Wessex make several references to shire, shireman and reeve.[4] The earliest extant Landbocs or Charters afford a second line of evidence in their mention of 'regiones'[5] which local knowledge and ingenuity have identified with modern hundreds. Finally, attention has recently been called to a document of a date perhaps as early as the seventh century, now known as the Tribal Hidage, which divides at any rate the Midlands into districts composed of varying numbers of hides;[6] and the general accuracy of the evidence gains striking confirmation from the notices of local place-names and divisions to be gathered from the writings of the earliest English historian, Bede. It does not follow, however, that the name 'hundred' as yet denoted an organized area of administration, although there already existed some administrative unit which was to be represented later by the hundred of history.[7] And this may be the meaning of some of those numerous names of local divisions which remain to this day, and whose origin is as hard to decipher as that of the Hundred itself. Thus, in two shires, below the hundreds come subordinate divisions—in Kent the *Lathes*, an organized

[1] *La Monarchie Franque*, 224-225.

[2] *Ibid.* 11-95.

[3] *S. C.* 61.

[4] *Ibid.* 61-62, §§ 8, 36, 39.
[5] H. Adams in *Essays in Anglo-Saxon Law*.
[6] *Trans. R. Hist. Soc.* xiv. 188-230. Chadwick, 263-268.

[7] Chadwick, 241-248. Cf. also Jenks, *op. cit.* 164.

judicial division superseding the hundred in that capacity; in Sussex the *Rapes*, a mere geographical expression no doubt originating in the roping or measuring out of the land at some time perhaps not previous to the Norman Conquest. In the Anglian districts we get *Wapentakes*,[1] corresponding in organization to the hundred, and sometimes existing side by side with it. These are found in Durham, Yorkshire, Lincoln, Nottingham, Derby, Rutland and Leicester. In two of these — Yorkshire and Lincoln — above the Wapentakes comes the division of the *Trithings or Ridings*. But these may be regarded as local peculiarities; whereas in all parts of England are found the remains of subordinate divisions which go by the name of *shires*. Such were all the administrative subdivisions of Cornwall as late as the twelfth century, many districts of Yorkshire, and in Domesday the divisions of the city of York itself. 'It is not impossible,' says Dr. Stubbs,[2] 'that the original name of the subdivision immediately above the township' (which we are now learning to call the tun or vill) 'was scir or shire, a term of various application.' In confirmation of this he points out that in Ælfred's translation of Bede a diocese was a bishop's scire; while, further, the Anglo-Saxon translation of the Gospels (St. Luke xvi. 2) calls the stewardship of the unjust steward his 'grœfscire.'[3]

One other theory deserves more than a passing notice. Among the earliest rights which a tribal chief would claim would be that of sustentation at the expense of his subjects. In course of time this vague right would take the shape of a fixed tribute, rent or tax: in early days it is impossible and unnecessary to distinguish. As a result, perhaps the country would be 'plotted out according to some rude scheme to provide the king with meat and cheese and ale.'[4] Such a scheme would probably be based on the existing unit of the hide. This is the measure of assessment disclosed by Domesday. In the early period of the settlement in Britain the vills and even the individual tenements would have been more homogeneous in size than they afterwards became. Hence the system of assessment in hundreds of hides disclosed by the 'Tribal Hidage' would have been comparatively easy. The hundred hides may have been composed of multiples of an earlier unit of five hides,[5] or, by

[1] Chadwick, 245-248.

[2] *S. C. H.* i. § 45.

[3] *Ibid.* i. § 48.

[4] *Domesday*, 351.

[5] Round, *Feudal England*, 97.

what has been compactly called 'the method of subpartitioned provincial quotas,' the larger district may have been divided up in smaller round numbers into sub-districts.[1] It does not particularly concern us here whether the number at which any given sub-district was rated, was distributed, perhaps in terms of five hides, among the component vills. The hides, the original settlements, might split up, and in the hands of new owners might form different combinations: but unless they became altogether exempted or the number of their assessable hides was reduced by royal favour, these districts would continue for all time to be rated at a definite number of hides irrespective of their actual size. Thus it is quite *possible that the hundred originated as an unit in the assessment* of the obligations of the freemen towards the king and that it was adapted to other purposes as need arose. Whether the hundred or some smaller area were the primary unit, Domesday probably worked only upon the existing measures of assessment.

Two questions now arise, namely, how do we account for the extraordinary variations in the size of the districts to which the name Hundred was afterwards attached; and, to what do we attribute the introduction of the name at all? A conjectural answer may be attempted. During the early period of the settlement of the English in Britain no administrative district was needed between the primary social unit of the tun—which, to avoid confusion, with Professor Maitland we may call the vill—and the political unit of the Tribe or Folk. Perhaps even the area of the vill was, in the earliest settled parts, as large as one or more of the historical hundreds.[2] At any rate, all over England are found groups of villages bearing one common and one distinguishing name, as if to denote that they had all once formed part of an united organization. Population would be scattered, and yet the scanty numbers would at first forbid too wide an area of settlement. But when on the one side population increased, while on the other side the successful chief grew into the king, and conquest enlarged the boundaries of his kingdom, not only would the machinery of central government expand, but some intermediate organization would also become necessary. This latter could be supplied in two ways. In

Marginal notes:

[1] *Domesday*, 450.

Suggested origin of the Hundred in England.

[2] *Surnames of Eng. Villages*, Archaeological Rev. iv. 235. Cf. also Chadwick, 254-261.

the first place, the already existing agricultural units of tun or vill, especially such as were royal property, might form the nuclei of administrative districts. In the earliest settled parts of the country the population would be thickest; and although no single vill would be likely to contain a hundred households, that number might well occupy a very modest space, while the small size of the existing divisions would be no drawback to their adoption for governmental purposes. But in the north and the midlands the population was so sparse that these administrative divisions would have to be artificially created; and, while being modelled on those in the south in respect of organization, in size they would tend to approximate to the larger of the existing divisions. Or the history of the continental hundreds, as M. de Coulanges reads it, may have been reproduced in England, and separate portions of the country where population had for some reason concentrated, may have been gradually shorn off from the surrounding districts and organized apart. Perhaps in either of these cases the name 'Shire' might have been applied to the resulting district: it seems probable that there was no technical name. But this became necessary as the smaller heptarchic kingdoms with their ready-made organization were absorbed into Wessex; for, two stages of local administrative machinery now existed, and it was important to distinguish between them. Why the term shire was appropriated to the larger division of the small kingdoms and their administrative analogues, we cannot tell; but, as a probable result, the landbocs or charters of later date than the reign of Ecgberht cease to allude to the regiones and other Latin equivalents for which the common English form was the word 'shire.' Finally, to the smaller administrative subdivision might be applied the name which, their connection with Frankish lands would teach the English kings, was the analogous division on the other side of the Channel, namely, the Centena or Hundred. William of Malmesbury, writing of course after the Norman Conquest, has preserved for us the tradition that Ælfred instituted among other things the arrangement of the land into hundreds. Historians have come to treat this as a mere piece of gossip. But if, with Mr J. H. Round, we may argue back from the evidence of Domesday,

we may believe it not impossible, though perhaps somewhat
improbable, that it was Ælfred or one of his immediate
predecessors or successors who, in imitation of Frankish usage,
introduced as an area for the assessment of taxation the
division of the hundred on which, two centuries later, the
calculations of liabilities in Domesday were apparently based.
However that may be, it is from the reign of his son, Eadward
the Elder, that we get what many would regard as the first
unmistakable evidence of the administrative hundred.   One
of his dooms ordains that 'every reeve have a gemot always
once in four weeks,'[1] of which the clause in the Ordinance of
the Hundred determining 'that they meet always within four
weeks,'[2] seems a mere confirmation.   Moreover, when Eadward's
successor, Æthelstan, demands that 'there be named in every
reeve's manung (i.e. district) as many men as are known to be
unlying that they may be for witness in every suit,'[3] a very
natural interpretation connects this with a doom of the reign
of Eadgar which bids that 'witness be appointed . . . to every
Hundred.'[4]   In conclusion, probably we shall not be very far
wrong if we accept the Ordinance of the Hundred as emanating
from Eadgar, and regard it as a consolidation and universal
application of a system of local administration already at work
in most parts of the country.   The remains of the Danelagh
north of the Humber had only just been extinguished in the
reign of Eadred : the division of England between Eadred's
sons had only just been healed by the death of Eadwig :
Eadgar had at his side a statesman of extraordinary ability.
Between them king and archbishop issued laws regulating the
shire-gemot and the burh-gemot, the relations of the local
courts to the Crown and the general police system of the
country.   The Ordinance of the Hundred takes its place as
part of a great scheme for the consolidation of justice and
police throughout the land.

As to the kind and the method of the administrative work
done by the hundred we have the scantiest evidence.   Its
business was evidently transacted in a monthly court, and the
officials responsible for its conduct seem to have been a deputy
of the sheriff, who presided, and the hundred-man of the
Ordinance of the Hundred[5] or hundredes-ealdor, mentioned
elsewhere in Eadgar's Laws, who was perhaps 'the convener

[1] *S. C.* 64, c. 11.

[2] *Ibid.* 70. § 1.

[3] *Ibid.* 66.

[4] *Ibid.* 72, supplement, cap. 3.

[5] *S. C.* 70. §§ 2, 45.

and constituting functionary of the court.'[1] Whether, however, we believe this latter official to have been the elected representative of the freemen, as is often supposed, depends partly on our view of the *composition of the hundred court* in pre-Norman times. The evidence generally quoted comes from the 'Leges Henrici Primi,' which are now believed to be a contemporary but unauthorised attempt of a Norman lawyer to bring up to date the Anglo-Saxon dooms.[2] Here it is stated that the local courts should contain bishops, earls, barons, vavasores (perhaps tenants by knight service), the reeves of tuns or vills and other lords of lands, together with a string of evidently local officials who may perhaps be classed in pairs as sheriffs (vicedomini, vicarii), officers of hundreds (centenarii, aldermanni), and officers of royal franchises (praefecti, praepositi).[3] This would be an exhaustive enumeration of all landholders and officials within the district; and the principle would apply as much to the hundred court as to the shire court. Another clause adds that a freeholder by his presence represents all his demesne lands (in the broader sense), but that his steward can lawfully appear for him—which would often be necessary for a lord with wide possessions. Finally, it is said that if both lord and steward had to be away, the reeve, priest and four of the more substantial men of the vill might appear and answer for all who had not been summoned by name to the court. The next clause especially applies this provision to the hundred court.[4] This evidence has been quoted at length and perhaps somewhat out of place, because upon it and practically it alone has been based the whole structure of popular representation and popular justice in the local courts before the Norman Conquest. But what is the real value of such evidence? It is unauthoritative; it is not even contemporary, and its purport is something quite other than is generally supposed. The priest, reeve and four men of each vill were not ordinary attendants at the local courts; they came under special circumstances. Nay, further, whether we believe that they came at all even in the days of Henry I, depends on the view which we take of the document whence our information is derived. It may have been a record of previous custom; it may have been a mere speculative exercise of a Norman lawyer who only half understood his subject.

But the point on which stress should be laid is that, on the most generous hypothesis, the evidence cannot be extended beyond a century or so before the Norman Conquest. The system of popular representation and popular administration of justice in the local courts cannot, so far as our evidence goes, be said to have existed in the Anglo-Saxon courts before the days of Eadgar ; and then the evidence does not bear upon its face any proof of a really popular organization of the local courts. Finally, it is generally said that although 'the judges of the court were the whole body of suitors,' yet for convenience sake 'a representative body of twelve seems to have been instituted as a judicial committee of the court.'[1] But this is a generalization which is based upon extraordinarily little evidence. A law of Eadgar certainly ordains that in every hundred twelve witnesses shall be chosen before whom all commercial transactions shall take place.[2] But the evidence chiefly relied on is a law of Æthelred[3] which commands that the twelve senior thegns should join the sheriff in presenting the criminals of the district for trial ; but the use of the word Wapentake seems to make it only too probable that the ordinance referred merely to the northern shires—an interpretation which is in harmony with the record preserved in Domesday of the twelve hereditary lawmen of Lincoln.[4] Nor perhaps is the evidence much strengthened by the solitary reference[5] in the large number of extant landbocs or charters to the presence of 'all the eldest thegns' in the shire court. We can, therefore, assert little or nothing about the work of the local courts before the Norman Conquest. And one consideration may encourage us to think that fresh evidence on the point would only lead us further from such generalizations as we had hitherto accepted. The origin of grants of freedom from the jurisdiction of the local courts will be discussed more appropriately as an introduction to the history of the manorial court ; but here attention may be drawn to the fact that Domesday records cases in which the jurisdiction of the hundred court itself was in private hands. In Worcestershire, the sheriff reported that there were no less than seven out of the twelve hundreds in which he had no authority. The grants of Anglo-Saxon kings on which long after the Norman Conquest the abbots of the greater

[1] *S. C. H.* § 46.

[2] *S. C.* 72.
[3] *Ibid.* 72. iii. cap. 3.

[4] But cf. Chadwick, 246 note.
[5] Kemble, *Cod. Dipl.* iv. 137.

monasteries sometimes based a claim to a similar jurisdiction, no doubt were often forgeries; but they may be taken as indicating a belief in the existence of such rights. Thus it is possible that from their first formation or recognition, some of the hundreds were under an individual thegn exercising powers delegated to him by the central authority, and that the exercise of private jurisdiction which was afterwards considered the result of a special grant, was thus an original form of local organization.

Much of what has been said of the hundred applies also to the history of the *Shire* or, as it came to be called in Norman times, the County. It seems probable that the shire organization began in Wessex. The south-eastern shires have each a definite history: Sussex, Surrey, Kent, Middlesex, and Essex at one time or another formed independent kingdoms with rulers of their own, and were all ultimately absorbed by Wessex. The western shires offer a very different problem. Hampshire and perhaps Berkshire formed the nucleus of the kingdom, but Wiltshire, Dorset, Devon, and Somerset are conjectured to have been the early settlements of separate branches of the West Saxon folk. It is no question of separate dynasties. From the beginning there was only one royal family in Wessex. But in all the English kingdoms, the free use of a royal title—subregulus and others—even as applied to persons who have no definite kingdom, may point to a primitive idea that the kingdom was a family possession, and that every male member of full age could claim a share in the royal rights and estates.[1] It may have been in order to avoid the constant quarrels which resulted, that the West Saxon kings created as sub-kingdoms for their relatives the shires of a later date.[2] By the ninth century all the southern shires except Cornwall existed, each with its own ealdorman. The shires of Mercia were of later growth. Nothing could be done with English Mercia so long as it remained under its own semi-independent ealdorman with a council of its own. But when these disappeared in the reign of Eadward the Elder, in order to prevent its again becoming a separate kingdom, Mercia was divided up. Early Mercia had been composed of five separate settlements of Anglian folk which Penda had drawn together into his formidable kingdom and these Arch-

The Shire or County.

[1] Chadwick, 298.

[2] *Ibid.* 288.

bishop Theodore had organized into four bishoprics.   There
was also the early West Saxon kingdom of the Hwiccas on
one side to work upon, and on the other side the once great
East Anglian kingdom, while, finally, the Danish organization
of the five boroughs, each the centre of an administrative
district, was one that could be bodily taken over, and, moreover, could be extended to English Mercia.   The newly
formed shires, no doubt reproducing in many cases old
divisions, would thus centre round one of the many boroughs
which had sprung into existence all over the country during
the recent Danish wars.   The shires north of the Humber are
easily explained, for they were late in their formation, and
they represented divisions already stereotyped before they
were worked into the general administrative system of the

Its Court.
country.   The dissimilarity of origin both as to time and
circumstances of the various shires made no difference in the
methods of their administration.   On this point little need
be added to what has been said already in speaking of the

[1] *S. C.* 71,
cap 5.
hundred.   Eadgar directs[1] that the shire court shall be held
twice a year, that the bishop and ealdorman shall both be
present, and that ecclesiastical as well as secular justice shall
be administered.   The presence of the sheriff was no doubt
taken for granted, since he was probably the convener of the
court.   These three officials will, each in his place, deserve a
detailed description.   For the moment it must be enough to
trace the history of the ealdorman.

The ealdorman—usually described as dux in the Latin
charters—may be the equivalent, and the representative of
the subregulus of an earlier time.   Towards the end of the
Anglo-Saxon period, when he had ceased to be necessarily a
member of the royal house, he may have been nominated by
the king and Witan in conjunction.   In early days he was a
member of either the ruling dynasty in Wessex or a dependent
royal house.   Thus he was one of the greatest officials in the
land.   As such he was entitled to many privileges.   A high
compensation was due to him under the head of borgbryce
or mundbryce (breach of his surety or protection), for burg-
bryce or violation of his house, and for manbot or murder of
a dependent.   The value of his own life as denoted by the
wergild was probably double that of the ordinary thegn.   It

is possible that there were estates attached to the office, and
Domesday seems to suggest that 'the third penny,' that is a
third part of the profits of jurisdiction within his government,
also went to him, for he was the military and administrative official within his sphere of jurisdiction. In the former
capacity he commanded the local fyrd, while as a civil official
he was the executor of the laws, and the protector of the weak
within the shire.[1] Perhaps the original West Saxon shires each   [1] Chadwick,
had an ealdorman. But when the country came to be con-   chap. v.
solidated by the work of Eadward the Elder and his successors,
the shires seem to have been grouped together into provinces;
and from Æthelstan onwards the number of administrative
officials who bore the title within the English districts did not
exceed seven or eight. It may be that this was a concession
to the strong local feeling which dated from heptarchic times;
but, although most of the names of the old kingdoms reappear,
their boundaries seem to have been shifted constantly, and
there is some evidence that the divisions made were artificial
and based upon an unit of hundreds of hides. On this
principle it may be that most of Wessex was divided in the
days of Eadward the Elder into three approximately equal
districts, and that the application of a similar principle to the
midlands after the conquest of the Danelaw yielded three
others, each of the six forming a group of 120 hundreds and
being reckoned at 12,000 hides.[2] Any conjectural method of   [2] *Ibid.*
division presents difficulties. The Anglo-Saxon Chronicle tells   chap. vi.
us that Cnut divided the kingdom into four earldoms. The
word jarl, transformed into the modern earl, was the Danish
variant of the old English eorl. It is used interchangeably
with ealdorman to denote the provincial administrators.
Cnut's act thus appears to be little more than a development
of the policy of his English predecessors. But whatever was
the object of these divisions, the work of Ælfred and Eadward
the Elder was utterly undone by their successors. Indeed, the
last century of early English rule, from the accession of Eadgar   959-1066.
onwards, is merely a record of the struggle for power of rival
ealdormen. Not that the kings neglected measures of precaution. In anticipation of the policy which proved so fatal
to the later Plantagenets, they sought to connect the ealdormen
by marriage with the royal family. Again, they recalled into

existence old divisions such as that of Northumbria into Bernicia and Deira ; or they separated off from the greater provinces smaller governments, such as the Hwiccas and Magesætas from Mercia. As a third means they secured the appointment of royal favourites and even of foreigners who should be dependent on the king alone. Such were, under Æthelred, his favourites Ælfric who was placed over the Central Provinces, and Eadric Streona over Mercia ; under Cnut, the Danes, Eric in Northumbria, Thurkil in East Anglia, and, most important of all, the semi-Dane and royal favourite, Godwine, in Wessex. But none of these measures were effectual. Provincial feeling was for the present far too strong, and the success of Godwine's family is sufficient proof of the risk incurred by a policy whose original object perhaps had been the easier administration of the united kingdom by the guarantee of ancient customs, laws, and liberties.

Changes produced by Norman Conquest. § 48. Among the measures adopted by the Conqueror for retaining the old English constitution, so far as he could understand it, was the maintenance, if not the revival, of the national courts of hundred and shire. Nor was this a mere pretence. The ill-doings of William II, however they affected the local courts, evoked from his successor an additional promise of the recognition of old customs in the matter. The compilation called ' Leges Henrici Primi ' professes to show us the courts with the same constituent elements as before the Conquest : and these courts continued to use the old procedure of witness, compurgation and ordeal. But the very different atmosphere engendered by the Norman rule was bound to work changes in the ancient system, and ultimately, as events proved, to supersede and thus destroy it. The most important and far-reaching of these changes may be grouped under four **(1) Disappearance of the earl.** heads. In the first place, the earl disappeared from the court. William I and his son created few earls, and the old official idea still so far remained that each title was necessarily connected with a county or a group of counties.[1] But **¹ Round, *Geoffrey de Mandeville*, 191-193, 273, 320.** everything else in connection with the new earls showed the purely personal character of the title. Thus it is most probable that at first the dignity was not hereditary. The positive mention of hereditary succession in the only extant charter of creation of Stephen's reign, perhaps points to the

exceptional nature of the grant.[1]   Again, whatever the prerogative of the old official earl, the endowment of the third
penny of the pleas of the shire seems to have belonged in
the first instance only to the earls of Danish shires; in all
other cases it was a matter of special grant; and evidence
of Henry II's reign shows that often it was withheld.[2]   The
analogous endowment of the third penny of the revenues
of the county borough which has often been confused with
the share of the county pleas, was even more occasionally
granted.[3]   In neither case had the earl a claim.   Occasionally
we find demesne lands apparently annexed to the title, and
sometimes the king would grant to the earl the royal demesne
lands within the shire.   In such a case the king would also
allow the earl to act as his own sheriff or to nominate the
sheriff and so to control the shire court.   And the height
of the earl's ambition and independence would be reached
if he also obtained for himself the right of acting as local
Justiciar in his own shire.   But scarcely any, if any, of these
privileges belonged to the earl as such.   Few earls had all
of them, while some of them were possessed by other barons.
Those few earls who did enjoy them have been ranked by
later historians as Earls Palatine, and the name is generally
applied to the Earls of Chester and Kent and the Bishop
of Durham.   But there is little reason for treating these
three as exceptions.   The title of Earl Palatine is used in
Norman times only to denote the Viceroy or chief Justiciar.[4]
Odo of Bayeux occupied no exceptional position as Earl
of Kent.   The Norman Bishop of Durham had apparently
no more privileges than the Archbishop of York.   The Earls
of Shropshire and Hereford, Cornwall, and Surrey, and the
holders of the hundreds of Richmond and Holderness who
were not earls at all, probably enjoyed as many prerogatives
as the Earl of Chester.   But many of these were relatives
of the Conqueror, and he and his sons did not hesitate to
reduce the power of a too troublesome noble.   The forfeiture
of Kent by Odo of Bayeux under William I, and of Shropshire by the powerful Robert of Belesme under Henry I,
showed the limits of these extensive grants.   But Durham
and Chester were both frontier earldoms, and in neither case
did the king dare to diminish the power of the holders.

[1] Round, *Geoffrey de Mandeville*, 53, 242, 440.

[2] *Ibid.* 289, 293. *Dialog. de Scac.* 203-204.

[3] Round, 289-290.

[4] Davis, *England under Normans and Angevins*, 519.

The privileges of Durham date from long before the Conquest,[1] and must have been among the earliest grants of bookland of an extensive kind. These were confirmed by the Conqueror and his successors, and Domesday significantly omits all notice of the lands of St. Cuthbert, wherever they are situated. Chester was held by the family of Hugh Lupus of Avranches until 1237. It was granted to Simon de Montfort, the king's brother-in-law : then it was kept for sons of the king until in the reign of Richard II it was erected by Act of Parliament into a Principality which should go, like Wales, to the king's eldest son. Chester was not included in the representation in Parliament until 1536, nor Durham until 1672. Even then Chester continued to retain its palatine jurisdiction until 1830, while Durham, though the temporal jurisdiction was taken over by the Crown in 1836, has kept its separate Court of Chancery to the present day.[2] In course of time we find other instances of the enjoyment of extensive 'jura regalia.' Alongside of Chester and for the same reason, there grew up the Lords Marchers of Wales. Their territories covered the border counties and the whole of South Wales. The Act of 1536 which took away their jurisdiction enumerated no less than 137, but the chief of them were the Earls of Shropshire, Gloucester, Hereford and Pembroke, and the Lords of Brecon and Glamorgan, and the extinction of their privileges led to the division of South Wales for the first time into counties on the English model. Less important cases of extensive jurisdiction are those of Hexhamshire under the Archbishop of York, which retained its privileges until 1571, and the Isle of Ely which was governed by its Bishop until 1538. The Stannary courts of Devon and Cornwall should come under the same head. Their special jurisdiction dates from the reign of Richard I, but since the reign of Edward III the Duchy of Cornwall and the Stannary jurisdiction have been vested in the eldest son of the king. The Stannary jurisdiction has been gradually abolished within the last century, but the Duchy of Cornwall still retains its separate organization.[3] The greatest of all the Palatinates was the Duchy of Lancaster, which was given by Edward III to his cousin the Earl, or Duke as he shortly

[1] Holdsworth, 12.

[2] *Ibid.* 50-54.

[3] *Ibid.* 55-61.

afterwards became. In the person of Henry IV the Duke of Lancaster became also king; but it was not until the attainder of Henry VI that it was definitely united to the Crown as such, and even this union, though confirmed by an Act of Henry VII, left it 'under a separate guiding and governance from the other inheritances of the Crown.' Thus in the counties of Chester, Durham and Lancaster, which alone are of importance, the king's writs did not run: the sole administration of justice lay with the earl in whose name writs were issued, and offences were punished as against his peace. They all had Courts of Common law and separate Chanceries, the judges of which were appointed by the earls until 1536, when many of the special privileges were curtailed by Statute. The Chancery Courts of Durham and Lancaster still exist; but the Courts of Pleas at Durham and of Common Pleas at Lancaster were abolished by the Supreme Court of Judicature Act of 1873.

27 Hen. VIII c. 24.

The removal of the earl from the shire court left the way free for the advancement of the sheriff to supreme power in local matters. Originally the sheriff had been the representative of royal interests and especially the steward of the royal demesne in his own shire. His constant presence made him also the judicial president of the court and the ordinary administrator of the law. Thus the items for which he was accountable to the king consisted not only of the rents from the tenants of the demesne, but also of the profits of justice, especially such as arose from the Pleas of the Crown or cases reserved for royal judges, and of all those royal rights, such as the right to treasure trove, which grew with the growth of the royal prerogative. In many cases the sheriff farmed these profits, that is, he paid a lump sum into the Exchequer as representing what he levied from the shire;[1] but the opportunities for extortion given by this system caused the wealthier portions of the shire to seek to make terms with him or to escape altogether from his control. The intimate connection between the sheriff and the Crown makes the rise of the king's power an index to that of the sheriff. Thus after the Conquest, although the sheriff was called *vice-comes* by the Normans, he was in no sense dependent, like the French and Norman bailiffs, on the Comes or earl. In fact

(2) Supre-
macy of
the Sheriff.

[1] M'Kechnie,
374-375.

Z

the office conveyed so much power that, under the first two Norman kings and again in the early days of Henry II, it was sought by powerful nobles and ecclesiastics, who often paid large sums for the post, and occasionally succeeded in making it hereditary.   A very little advance in that direction would have reproduced the great provincial governments of the pre-Conquest era.   Henry I attempted to remedy the mistake of his father and his brother by appointing to the shrievalties resident justices superior to the sheriffs and members of the newly formed Exchequer; but these last were weak or even too much in league with the 'barones scaccarii' who audited their accounts; so that such appointments formed no efficient check upon extortion.   On the other hand, when, after the Inquest of Sheriffs in 1170, Henry II found it necessary to remedy the mistakes of his early days, he repeated his grandfather's method of appointment, but took care to keep separate the individuals who filled respectively the offices of sheriff and of justice.   The appointment to the office of sheriff was generally for a term of years, though it was revocable at the royal pleasure : and the *duties* of the office may be described as fourfold.   In the first place, now that the earl was gone, upon the sheriff fell the *military* duties of summoning and superintending the equipment of the lesser tenants-in-chief and of leading the forces of the local fyrd.   In *judicial* matters, as the local 'Justitiarius regis' he still presided in the shire court.   As a *police* officer, he raised the Hue and Cry and supervised the arrangements of the Frankpledge; while to his earlier *financial* responsibilities was added the collection of the feudal dues of the lesser tenants-in-chief of the Crown.

Extent of his jurisdiction.

And while the sheriff climbed into a position of supremacy in local affairs, the special sphere of his jurisdiction not unnaturally tended to increase in importance.   This came about in three ways.   In the first place, the value of the hundred as an administrative division was seriously weakened.   We have already seen that, in Anglo-Saxon times, the grants of 'sake and soke' exempted those who were subject to them from attendance at the court of the local hundred.   The circumstances of the Norman Conquest multiplied the rights of private lords, and, in many hundreds, the great extension of manorial jurisdiction under whatever name must have left few to attend the local court. At the same time the hundred was made responsible for the Presentment of Englishry, and to it was extended a liability for other police penalties for which the vills were primarily answerable. And even where the hundred court continued to be held, its jurisdiction — both criminal and civil—was enfeebled. The new police regulations introduced by the Conqueror set up a machinery which could be conveniently applied to the purposes of criminal justice in a court which came to be known as the Sheriff's Tourn. The introduction of the possessory assizes by Henry II and the enormous importance assumed by them, transferred to the shire court the most important class of civil cases in mediaeval law, and left to the hundred only the hearing of small actions of debt and trespass. For this purpose the bailiff held, under Henry II apparently every fortnight, and under Henry III every three weeks, a small court which came to be known as the *Curia Parva Hundredi*. But this court was not strictly regarded as inferior to the shire court; it simply entertained a different class of cases.[1]

Meanwhile, the necessary activity of the shire court so enormously increased that the old six-monthly meetings appointed by Eadgar's Law were quite insufficient. Even as early as the reign of Cnut, the king provided for a more frequent meeting in case of need.[2] In the Ordinance which restored the local courts to their condition before the Conquest, Henry I reserves to himself the right of summoning them for royal business oftener than the usual number of times, which a passage in the 'Leges Henrici Primi' interprets as still twice a year for the shire courts.[3] This very infrequent meeting of the shire court has been accounted for on the ground that before the Conquest most of the judicial work was done in the hundred court, and that preliminary steps in judicial procedure may have been taken in non-compulsory meetings of the shire court which would be held as preparatory to the solemn half-yearly meetings at which all suitors were obliged to attend.[4] Equally probable is it that after the Conquest 'the increase of business under the new system of writs and assizes . . . involved the frequent adjournment of the court for short terms,' or that 'the gradual withdrawal of the more important

[1] *P. and M.* i. 544.

Meetings of the Shire Court.

[2] *S. C.* 73, cap. 18.

[3] *Ibid.* 105, vii. 4.

[4] *P. and M.* i. 526.

suits' increased 'the number of less important meetings for the convenience of petty suitors.'[1]   Whatever the reason, the Charter of 1217 witnesses to the custom of frequent sessions by appointing that the shire court shall meet not more than once a month, and even less often where such has been the custom.[2]   Thus in the thirteenth century, if not earlier, the name shire or county court, as perhaps it should be called, seems applicable to no less than three kinds of meetings—a monthly court, a half-yearly court which was distinguished as the Great or General Counties, and a specially convened court with an unusually large number of suitors to meet the itinerant justices when at long intervals they came to hold a general eyre.   Of the suitors to these various assemblies something will be said presently ; but after, no less than before the Conquest, they were the judges or dooms-men of the court, that is, they found the customary law. Their numbers, however, would often be limited.   As will be seen in speaking of their qualification, the suitors of the local court would ordinarily be a small body ; in any given case some of them might not be peers of the parties and so would be unable to take part in the judgement ; while for the transaction of the ordinary business there seem indications of the appointment of a small committee of the whole body called 'buzones,' possibly as denoting the 'men of affairs' (besoin).[3]

But the shire court was concerned chiefly with civil cases, and the real influence of the sheriff came to be exercised in his half-yearly journey through the separate hundreds when, as royal commissioner, he disposed of the small criminal cases which could be most easily dealt with in the places where the deeds were committed.   It is to be remembered that a great many of the hundreds both before and after the Norman Conquest were in the hands of private lords ; and if such lords added to their powers in those districts the right of taking View of Frankpledge, the sheriff was practically excluded from the exercise of all authority within the bounds of that hundred.   The court which he held in those hundreds to which his power extended, the *Sheriff's Tourn and Leet* (Turnus Vice-comitis), though it was often called the Great Court of the Hundred, was a branch of the shire court; but being held by virtue of royal commission, unlike the shire court it

[1] *S. C. H.* § 163.

[2] *S. C.* 346, § 42.

[3] *P. and M.* i. 540, Maitland, *Pleas of Crown for County of Gloucester*, Introd. xxiv.

The Sheriff's Tourn.

was a royal court of record, that is, its cases could be quoted as precedents. It seems likely that this court originated in the Assize of Clarendon in 1166. The first clause directs that inquiry shall be made separately by the judges and the sheriffs in each county and hundred through the agency of twelve men of the hundred and four men of the vill concerning the commission of misdemeanours.[1] But we know that one of the chief duties of the tourn came to be the maintenance of the frankpledge. Now, the frankpledge existed before Henry II; but the procedure of the presentment of criminals for trial by a jury of the neighbourhood was introduced by him, and not unnaturally it has been conjectured that the easiest method was to use the already existing machinery for this latter purpose. Thus 'the duty of producing one's neighbour to answer accusations (the duty of the frankpledges) could well be converted into the duty of telling tales against him.'[2]

[1] S. C. 143.

[2] Maitland, Introd. to *Select Pleas in Manorial Courts*, xxx–xxxvii.

The procedure of the Sheriff's Tourn[3] needs a detailed description. There were present before the sheriff representatives from each police district whether vill or tithing. From the former came the reeve and four men, from the latter the tithing man. In places where both systems prevailed, both sets of representatives would come. In addition to these there would be a jury of twelve freeholders to do duty for all the freeholders in the hundred, who probably in theory should have been present. Before these representatives of vills and tithings the sheriff placed a set of inquiries called 'the articles of the view,' different in different places and at different times. The object of these was threefold—to see that the proper working of the system of frankpledge was kept up; and to get accusations both against those suspected of serious crimes so that they might be kept in safe custody until the next visit of the royal judges; and against those accused of all kinds of minor offences which the sheriff himself was empowered to punish summarily by amercement. The answers of the representatives of vills and tithings took the shape of presentments; the names of those presented were laid before the twelve freeholders, and those accusations which they endorsed were dealt with according to the gravity of the offence. Finally, the sheriff as sole judge decided whether a suspect

Its procedure.

[3] *P. and M.* i. 515, 546. Maitland, *Select Pleas,* xxviii–xxxiv.

should be kept for the king's judges or should be let off with an amercement; but in the latter case he did not settle the amount which was to be paid. Two or more suitors of the court were chosen for the purpose at the opening of the court, and took an oath that they would do the work justly.

(3) Direct intervention of the Crown by

The last class of changes wrought by the altered circumstances of the Conquest in the local courts, came from the active interference of the Crown in provincial administration. This took three principal shapes. (1) It will be seen presently that in their criminal code the Anglo-Saxons had reached the point at which all except the most serious crimes could be

Monopoly of criminal justice.

atoned for by payments of various kinds. Criminal justice was thus a source of revenue; and when the king was asserting his position as supreme judge in the land, an additional incentive was given to his desire to reserve certain classes of cases for trial by himself or his officers alone. It is in Cnut's Laws that we first find a list of what came afterwards to be

[1] M'Kechnie, 359.

called Pleas of the Crown.[1] It included a comparatively small number of offences, consisting chiefly of acts involving or likely to involve serious breaches of the peace, and of neglect of military duty; and these were cherished quite as much for their saleable value as for the special power with which they endowed the royal authority. Even after the Norman Conquest the kings did not hesitate to grant away all kinds of important rights of jurisdiction; but the mere fact that the powers granted grew more extensive with the lapse of time, shows that the claims of the king were rising until they included the right to prohibit the exercise of any criminal jurisdiction except such as had originated from an express

[2] *P. and M.* i. 563-564; ii. 451-452.

royal grant.[2] When these powers had not been granted away they were exercised at first by the sheriffs, for a time after the Conquest in some parts by local justiciars, then by specially appointed officers called Coroners, and finally they were reserved for the hearing of the king's judges in their circuits.

(2) It is only in quite modern times, since the Judicature Act of 1875, that there has been any strict system of appeal from court to court recognized in English Common law. But

Evocation of causes.

the evolution of the system of writs enabled the king to offer remedial justice to all his subjects who would pay for it. Even in Anglo-Saxon times a litigant could 'forsake' the proposed doom or judgement of the local court by charging with falsehood the doomsmen who uttered it. With the introduction of a system of writs a litigant could obtain a writ of false judgement by which the sheriff or other official of a local court was bidden to send before the king's justices four suitors of the court bearing a record of the proceedings of the case in question. If the facts of the record were disputed, battle might ensue between the complainant and the champion of the local court: if they were admitted, there would be a question of law for the judges to decide. False judgement would lead to amercement. Again, actions begun in seignorial courts and in a lesser degree those begun in shire courts could be removed before judgement for hearing by the Curia Regis. Even actions that had been heard by the itinerant justices who were regarded as part of the Curia Regis, could be evoked before one of the central courts which during the thirteenth century became permanent at Westminster; and the errors of the judges would be corrected. Even the ecclesiastical courts were subject to the interference of the Crown; but after the failure of the direct attempt to supervise them by the Constitutions of Clarendon, the safest method of asserting the royal power was by the issue of prohibitions to the ecclesiastical judge to meddle with any particular suit.

(3) But there were smaller and less pleasant ways by which the extent of the royal power could be brought home to the suitors of the local courts. Every offender was regarded at first as a self-constituted outlaw whose life and property lay at the mercy of the king.[1] But the king found it more profitable to allow the offender to condone his offences by the payment of a sum of money, which was known as an amercement.[2] A great number of such payments came to be fixed sums; but the kings were always interested in declaring that offenders lay 'in misericordiâ suâ,' so that they could adapt the penalty to the position and wealth of the culprit. It was, however, regarded by the people as a hardship, and Henry I promised in his charter that a penalty of the kind should be moderate;[3] and in his charter to the citizens of London, that it should not extend beyond the citizen's *were* of a hundred shillings;[4] but a greater safeguard lay in the

Arbitrary amercement.

[1] M'Kechnie, 336.

[2] *Ibid.* 345.

[3] *S. C.* 101.

§ 8.

[4] *Ibid.* 108.

custom sanctioned by Magna Carta (§ 20) by which amercements were 'affeered,' that is, the sum to be paid was fixed
by a small committee of a man's social equals. It was this
clause which also prevented the imposition of a fine in the
modern sense; but imprisonment was indefinite in Common
law, that is, 'during the king's pleasure,' and the judges
devised the method of passing sentence of imprisonment and
then allowing a prisoner to make an end (finem facere) of
the matter by paying a sum of money. Imprisonment was
a troublesome and unsafe method of dealing with offenders :
a sentence of imprisonment, therefore, became merely a method
of inflicting fines without violating the Common law.[1]

§ 49. The second class of courts through which the Common
law of the land was administered, were those of the English
thegns and of the later lords of manors. The origin of
private jurisdiction in England is a much disputed point.
The Anglo-Saxon terms which denote it—sake and soke—
are practically never found as a formula before the reign of
Eadward the Confessor; and while we may reject Kemble's
explanation of their late appearance, that 'they were so
inherent in the land as not to require particularization'[2] in
the grants made by the kings, there is little consolation in
Dr. Stubbs' remark that they 'occur almost universally in
Norman grants of confirmation, as describing definite immunities which may have been only implied, though necessarily
implied, in the original grant, and customarily recognized
under these names.'[3] Many writers have tried to explain the
two words.[4] One (it does not much matter which) may mean
the right to the jurisdiction itself : the other, the right to the
amercements arising from it. Dr. Stubbs concludes that it is
' an alliterative jingle which will not bear close analysis '; and to
this explanation Professor Maitland appeals in evidence of the
antiquity of the phrase.[5] There is no doubt about its meaning
when it appears : it carries with it the jurisdictional powers of a
manorial court. Two explanations of its late appearance have
been offered. Mr. Adams notes that the word 'soke' appears
before its companion and that the earliest extant charters contain
grants of the pecuniary profits of justice which otherwise would
have gone to the king. He explains that the jealousy of the
magnates towards the king prevented the amelioration of

[1] *P. and M.*
ii. 512-517.

(B) Private
jurisdic-
tions.

Their
origin.

[2] *Cod. Dipl.*
i. xliv.
[3] *S. C. H.*
§ 73.
[4] Ellis,
*Introd. to
Domesday,*
i. 273.
Kemble,
Cod. Dipl.
i. xlv.
S. C. H.
§ 73 note.
Adams'
*Essays in
A.-S. Law.*
Maitland,
*Select
Pleas,* xxii,
and *Domes-
day,* 84-85.
[5] *Domesday,*
266.

the law and thereby encouraged a resort to the arbitration of the lord in preference to the national courts. Such arbitration would be conducted according to the judicial forms in use in those courts. Then, from the continent came the idea that the administration of justice was no less a possession of the king than the land and offices of which he had been wont to dispose ; and Eadward the Confessor's additional grant of ' sake ' conferred on the arbitration of the lord the status of a legal court. It seems doubtful, however, whether the meaning of the terms ' sake and soke ' would have been lost so soon after the Conquest, if the rights which they expressed had been formulated so late, and as the result of a definite royal grant : Professor Maitland points out that the formula, of which this jingle is the indispensable part, appears at the time when royal writs were taking the place of the Latin charters. Such writs were less formal than the charters, and under Eadward the Confessor they were usually written in English. The first fact may well lead us to think that many of the early writs have been lost : the second would explain the appearance of the formula in question. In any case there seems ground for believing that the origin of private jurisdiction is to be sought [1] long before the eleventh century.[1]

We have seen that grants of bookland transferred to the grantee the right to certain or, in extreme cases, to all of those dues which would otherwise have been paid to the Crown by the inhabitants of the land which was the subject of grant. Now, among these transferred rights was often included one which practically made over to the grantee the right to the wites or penalties due to the king in compensation for crimes committed on the granted land. In view of the fact that ' even in the days of full-grown feudalism the right to hold a court was after all rather a fiscal than a jurisdictional right,' [2] we may easily believe that the question how the dues should be collected was a matter of comparative unimportance. The grantee might use the existing machinery of the neighbouring local court for their exaction : even if the ' superiority ' given him extended over the whole district from which suit was due to the court, it did not alter the method of procedure. His steward took the place of the local bailiff, but the suitors still remained the judges of the

[1] Vinogradoff, 214.

[2] *Domesday*, 277.

[1] Vinogra-
doff,
193 : 216.

court.   Such lords might be the 'landricas' mentioned in the
laws of the last century of Anglo-Saxon history.[1]   Domesday
records many Hundreds of which the soke was in the hands of
private lords.   But the lord might set up a court of his own.
In this case he was merely regarded as owning the soke of
a certain portion of the hundred, and those who did suit at
his court were naturally exempted from attendance at the
local court.   Here was *the beginning of seignorial jurisdiction*.
By the time of the Norman Conquest these private courts
were becoming too numerous to be regarded as separately
organized portions of the hundred.   But it was the Norman
lawyers who simplified the confused relationships of Anglo-
Saxon days by consolidating landownership with jurisdiction
over all the inhabitants.   So far we have been speaking of the
holders of bookland—the great churches and monasteries, and
a few of the greatest thegns.   The jurisdiction bestowed on
them was of the most extensive kind : in some cases even the
'trinoda necessitas' was not excepted from the grant.   True the
grant does not extend to the 'botless' crimes : the king retains
in his own hands the highest criminal jurisdiction.   But in
reserving for himself the cognizance of certain specified classes
of offences as pleas of the crown, Cnut appears to be trying
to draw a line before it is too late, beyond which such grants
shall not be carried.   But the feeling of the time is too strong
for him.   The only way to repress violent crime is to arm
with the fullest authority the person of supreme local influence.
Hence Cnut himself is found granting away the very jurisdiction which he has just reserved for the Crown.   The result was
that although the grants of 'sake and soke' denoted powers
which were exclusively in the king's gift, apparently they would
have left the Anglo-Saxon king with no jurisdiction of any
kind except in the last resort.[2]   Moreover, the owners of these
great 'superiorities' not only loaned out portions of their land,
but even delegated jurisdiction to others.   The two did not by
any means go together ; a man might hold his land of one
lord and be in the soke or jurisdiction of another.   Many such
owners of soke would not be in a position to hold a court of
their own : there was no necessary connection between the
holding of a 'manerium' and the exercise of jurisdiction over
its inhabitants.   Such an owner would generally content him-

[2] *P. and M.*
i. 563.

elf with claiming his wites and other dues through the local
hundred court. But meanwhile, in its intense anxiety to cope
with violent crime, especially with theft, the law was making
the lord increasingly responsible for the appearance if not the
actual conduct of his men. Thus, much of what was meant
by seignorial power was being rapidly consolidated just before
the Norman Conquest. Perhaps, after all, the simplification
of relationships undertaken by the Norman lawyers was no
such gigantic task as is usually supposed. At any rate it was
very soon carried through.

After the Norman Conquest the questions connected with
private jurisdiction alter in character. Under the Anglo-Saxons
such jurisdiction perhaps implied the right to hold a court,
but did not necessarily result in a court, much less in any
classification of courts. But now that the possession of a
manor was held to imply a court, subinfeudation meant the
existence of a hierarchy of courts. In the language of the
Norman lawyers, the old owner of bookland was now possessed
of an Honour, that is, of an aggregate of manors. The lawyers
tell us that, although a manor necessarily carried with it the
right to hold a court for its inhabitants, even if the manors
which formed an Honour were contiguous, there was no common
court ; justice in England was strictly manorial, bound up with
the possession of a manor, and was in no sense feudal, exercised over tenants who did not hold of a particular manor.
But this is an historical accident. Legally there was nothing
to prevent an honorial court on this side of the English Channel.
Nor is proof lacking that such did exist.[1] The Leges Henrici
Primi surely contemplate such a court when they tell us that
a lord can compel the attendance at his court of a tenant who
resides in a remote manor belonging to his Honour. About
a century later, the Petitions of the Barons in 1258[2] take for
granted a threefold gradation of courts—those of the *proximus
capitalis dominus feodi*, the *superior capitalis dominus*, and the
alter superior. But it is true that in England such a gradation
of courts was rare, so rare perhaps that the lawyers could
afford to ignore it. The reason for their rarity is to be found
in the all-pervading character of the royal courts. By means
of Pleas of the Crown, of the monopolization of questions
about freehold through the use of writs, of the actions of

The effect of the Norman Conquest on their development.

[1] *Select Pleas,* xlii-lii. *P. and M.* i. 573-574.

[2] *S. C.* 386, § 29.

[1] *S. C.* 404,
§ 16.
Cf. 386.
*Petition of
Barons,*
§ 29.
[2] Vide
below,
p. 377.
[3] *Select
Pleas,*
lii–lx.

assize and, more definitely, by the legislative limitation both
of appeals from a lord to an overlord in the Provisions of
Westminster (1259),[1] and of the competence of local courts
by the interpretation of the Statute of Gloucester (1278),[2] the
feudal courts were left practically at the mercy of the royal
judges.[3] It is, then, substantially true to say that in England
there was no classification as in France, of *haute, moyenne* or
basse justice, and no gradation of courts to stop the application
of the remedies of a growing Common law.

Distinction
between
Court Leet
and Court
Baron.

Nor, probably, was there at first any classification of rights.
An immense variety of franchises or grades of rights and
powers were exercised by the private courts ; but these were at
first the result of gradual accumulation, they were used in
the mass, and little thought was given to the titles by which
they were acquired or held. Some differences, however, were
gradually established. Thus, the rights already described under
the name of sake and soke, and in Latin as Halimote or

[4] *S. C.* 106,
ix. 4.

Hallmoot,[4] that is, the right to a *libera curia*—not a court of
freeholders, as is usually supposed, but one which is the lord's
own—were contrasted with powers which fell under the head

[5] *Select
Pleas,*
xvii–xx.

1278.

of jura regalia.[5] Of these the most important was View of
Frankpledge. But this too was exercised by private lords, until
they were brought to an explanation of their claims by the
issue of Edward I's Writ *Quo Warranto.* The investigations
under this writ established the doctrine that the only possible
warrant for the exercise of the Regalia was an express royal
grant ; in order to prevent the landowners from being deprived
of powers which they had exercised ever since they held their
lands, the king conceded in 1290 that continuous possession
of a franchise from any date before the coronation of Richard I
should be considered sufficient answer to the inquiry Quo
Warranto. This distinction was emphasized in the gradual
separation of the manorial court into a Court Leet and a Court
Baron. The Court Leet was, as the lawyers assert, a police court
exercising royal franchises as a court of record ; but it did not
exist as a separate court until ' the stringent quo-warranto-ing,'
which began in the reign of Edward I, gradually brought out
a distinction between the strictly manorial and the royal
franchises. The Court Baron was a civil court and not a court
of record. The explanation of the lawyers—that it was the

Curia baronum or court of the freeholders—has two fatal flaws. In the first place, no such expression is known to occur in a description of the court, and moreover there is no evidence that freeholders as such were ever styled *barones*.

A similar process of gradual separation can be traced in the purely manorial franchises. The hallmoot or lord's court was attended by freemen and villans alike. Often the freeholders by themselves would have been too few to form a court; for, although there are even a few cases of manors without any freeholders at all, there are many in which the number could be counted on the fingers of one hand. Again, in the rolls of the manorial courts no distinction is made between cases affecting freemen and those in which villans are concerned; while, since even the villans had *judicium parium* or the right of trial by their equals, they would scarcely have objected to a jury formed by those who, though fellow members of the manorial court, were their social superiors. But the introduction of the new procedure with its important accompaniment of a jury of recognition, drew out the distinction between the free and villan tenants. The lord's courts eagerly adopted the new procedure, but with this difference in its application—that, while they could force their villans to take the oath required from Recognitors, the free tenants were in the matter beyond their reach. Thus for the trial of villans' claims even as against the lord there could be, as in the king's courts, a judge and jury which could administer the 'custom of the manor'; but the freeholders could appeal to the royal courts, and their claims were protected not only by the judgement of their fellows, but by the law of the land. There followed the gradual separation of the court dealing with the freemen, the Court Baron (whatever the derivation of the term), from the Court Customary which took cognizance of the affairs of all tenants less than freeholders.

Distinction between Court Baron and Court Customary.

We may summarize the history of the manorial courts as follows:—a lord starting with the grants of 'sake and soke,' gradually accumulated and discharged by means of the same court, a variety of powers. But in time there grew up a distinction, on the one side, between those powers which he exercised as representative of the king and those which in

Summary.

feudal theory were regarded as inherent in his position of lord of a manor; on the other side, between the mediatorial power which the lord exercised in connection with his free tenants and the judicial authority wielded over his villans. Thus the one original court fell into three courts, and the lawyers introduced and elaborated all kinds of principles which had no existence in the thirteenth century.

The municipal courts will be dealt with more fitly under the head of local government.

§ 50. But these three separate kinds of courts—national, manorial and municipal—represented the application of three several kinds of custom. If this custom was to be harmonized and consolidated into law, it needed the steady, persistent action and the regulative force of one set of universally recognized tribunals. Thus it came about that these various local courts were superseded by the action of courts and judges whose power emanated from the king and that 'the concentration of justice in the king's court, the evolution of Common law were but one process.'[1] The reason for this supersession of the local courts is to be found in the superior justice administered by the royal courts. This may be illustrated from a detail study of the three following points —the introduction of a new method of procedure by the use of writs and of trial by jury; the regulative influence of the Itinerant Justices; and the protection afforded by the establishment of the three Courts of Common Law at Westminster.

[1] Maitland, *Bracton's Note Book*, Introd. 5. Cf. also *Social England*, i. 277.

Classification of crimes.

In ancient law there was little or no distinction between crime and tort or civil wrong. It did not matter whether the offender had slain his fellow or removed his neighbour's landmark. In either case the community as such assumed the same attitude towards him. He had committed a breach of the peace or mutual understanding on which the civil life of the tribe was based. If he committed the worst crimes he was regarded as having put himself outside the common peace and as an *outlaw* to whom no mercy should be shown. Or in some cases it became the business of the family of the injured man to exact the vengeance in a *blood-feud* which would last for successive generations. For lesser faults the offender could generally *atone by a money payment*, and thus buy back the peace which he had broken. Such crimes were bot-worthy or emendable, as opposed to botless crimes which exposed the offender to outlawry or the blood-feud and, later, to actual *punishment*.[1] But it must be remembered that the machinery for imprisonment was of the very roughest kind : the only perfectly safe punishment for any criminal was death, and here the Church interfered to secure for the sinner as long a time as possible for repentance. Nevertheless in England, under the great kings of the West-Saxon line, the laws were concerned rather with the punishment than with the emendation of offences, until the disorder produced by the Danish invasions and the position of the Danish kings enabled the Church to use an effectual influence in legislation. Thus by the time of the Norman Conquest outlawry was still the punishment for some of the worst crimes ; the blood-feud, if it ever existed in Anglo-Saxon law, had disappeared chiefly owing to the exertions of King Eadmund, and by far the greater number of offences had a pecuniary mulct attached to them. In fact there gradually grew up an elaborate tariff regulating the price to be paid according to the offence and the station in life of both victim and offender ; and the knowledge of this must have formed no small part of the legal education of the time. Nor was this all : the compositions to be paid consisted of two distinct parts — the *man-bot* which went to the lord of the injured party or, if a life had been taken, in the shape of wergild to his relatives or his lord ; and the *wíte* which was paid to the king or other owner of jurisdiction as the representative of the community whose peace had been broken by the defender's act.[2] Finally, to raise to a maximum the unworkableness of the whole system, a considerable variation from district to district is found between the offences severally regarded as bot-worthy and botless, and no modern code will give us the clue as to the category in which any particular crime will be found. The result was that the old system became so cumbrous as to be unworkable : besides the wer and wíte all kinds of other payments might be incurred by an offender—to the lord of the injured man, to the owner of the house or the manorial jurisdiction within which the offence had been committed. A payment under such a number of different heads was so large that only rich men could afford to pay. The whole system became intolerable as well

[1] Cf. Jenks, *op. cit.* 100-105.

[2] *Ibid.* 105-108 ; 107-109.

as unworkable, and at the beginning of the twelfth century

[1] *P. and M.* ii. 447-460.

it seems to have suddenly disappeared.[1] In its place there arose a system in which outlawry was nothing more than a piece of judicial procedure to secure the presence of the defendant; a few crimes marked off as *felonies* [2] placed the life

[2] *Ibid.* 463-465.

of the offender at the king's mercy, while other offences, both

[3] *Ibid.* 510.

civil and criminal, which were technically known as *trespasses* [3] and represented the later misdemeanours, were amended by

[4] *Ibid.* 511-513.

money penalties at the discretion of the judge [4] in place of the wites, and by damages [5] assessed by a tribunal instead of

[5] *Ibid.* 521-523.

the bots.

Methods of judicial procedure.

Such being the classification of offences we are in a position to understand the methods of judicial procedure by which suspected offenders were put to the test. The leading characteristic of all early judicial procedure is the close attention paid to compliance with set forms of action and speech. The business of a court of justice was not to judge—that is, to weigh the merits of the case—but to see that the proper forms were duly observed; and the trial consisted of an attempt on the part of one of the litigants to fulfil the form prescribed by the court. Thus by a kind of method which we have come to associate with a work of Mr Lewis Carroll, the judgement preceded the trial. It would, therefore, be more correct to speak not of a trial but of *proof*, and to say that the judgement of the court determined the mode of proof and which of the parties to the suit should be subjected to it.[6] Thus the earliest

[6] *Ibid.* 596. Thayer, *Development of Trial by Jury*, 9. M'Kechnie, 101-103.

modes of proof were one-sided, and it was often a matter of considerable importance to a litigant that the proof should or should not be awarded to him rather than to his adversary, since some prescribed forms would be easy and others difficult to fulfil. As a matter of practice the proof was generally allotted to the defendant; but there were means by which the plaintiff could sometimes obtain it, when it was to his advantage to do so.[7] The various stages in the procedure were as follows.

[7] *P. and M.* 599-600.

The two parties to a suit appeared before the court. The plaintiff made his charge in set phrase, any mistake or omission in which would cause the loss of his suit. This had to be accompanied either by a foreoath, i.e. a confirmatory oath on his own part; by the production of two witnesses, sometimes called his secta or suit, to the bona fides of his complaint, though at this stage they were neither put on oath nor examined; or finally, by the exhibition of the injury of which he complained. The defendant answered also in set phrase, and at first contented himself with a merely formal denial of the charge, which at a later date was technically called a 'Thwertutnay,' a downright No.[1] If the proper formulae had so far been complied with, the court pronounced the 'medial' or intermediate judgement, that is, appointed the proof or 'law.'[2] Of this there were several kinds. The party to whom the proof was allotted might be called upon merely to produce a charter, or he might be put to one of two severer tests both of which were appeals to the supernatural. The first of these was the various forms of the well-known (a) *Ordeal*. The earliest mention of the Ordeal in England is at the end of the ninth century, and its somewhat benighted appearance, together with the fact that the later formulae used in connection with it are copied from Frankish sources, has led to the conjecture that the Church managed for some time to keep outside the recognized law a mode of proof which came so directly from heathen sources. Later, however, she adopted certain forms of it, and invested them as far as possible with a Christian air. The chief forms used in England were the ordeal of water, in which the accused was thrown bound into the water and considered guilty if he did not sink; and the ordeal of fire, in which he was required to walk over, or to handle, bars of red-hot iron, and the mark of the iron after three days' interval was held to prove his guilt.[3] The second mode of proof consisted of (b) *Oaths* of various kinds. In very rare instances the man himself would be put on his oath, and in the later laws official witnesses and others who had been solemnly taken to witness at the time of the occurrence, would be required to swear to a set formula. But by far the most usual mode of this kind was the Oath of *Oath-helpers*, who at a much later date and by a term 'borrowed by legal antiquarians from ecclesiastical sources,' came to be called 'Compurgators.' Probably at first these would be kinsmen who might have an interest in the suit which would involve a blood-feud; but they ultimately became mere 'witnesses to character' chosen sometimes from among persons designated by the court or the opponent, sometimes simply from

[1] *P. and M.* ii. 602-606.

[2] M'Kechnie 430.

[3] *P. and M.* ii. 596-597.

2 A

neighbours. They swore merely to their belief in the truth
of the oath already taken by the party for whom they appeared.
The number which he had to produce was determined by the
court, but there seems some evidence in favour of a normal
number of eleven or, with the principal, twelve in all.   Until
the establishment of the jury this was by far the most popular
form of proof, and came to be known familiarly as 'Wager
of law.'[1]   It was one or other of these modes of proof that
the court allotted to one or other of the parties to the suit.
The Ordeal would be reserved for serious charges ; the oath of
oath-helpers would be the mode in ordinary cases ; while in a
few special instances the matter would be left to sworn first-
hand witnesses.   Finally, the judgement of the court in the
matter of the proof to be allotted, was followed by the *Wager*—
that is, the party to whom the proof was awarded gave security
that he would fulfil this judgement or 'make this law.'   Then
if he failed in the allotted test, either at ordeal or by the
non-production of the necessary number of oath-helpers or
witnesses, he would at once be punished as a perjurer.   Such
punishment would generally consist of confiscation of goods or,
for the more serious offences, forfeiture of life.

[1] *P. and M.*
ii. 598-599.

Changes
in judicial
procedure
made by
the Nor-
mans.

§ 51. These modes of procedure long survived the Norman
Conquest.   The Normans had practically no written law of
their own, nor was there much that they could borrow from
their neighbours.   In many ways they had not reached, in their
development of methods of government, any further stage than
had been attained by the race which they came to rule.   But if
they were not originators, they were among the most assimila-
tive people whom the civilized world has seen.   Thus they
accepted, probably because they were already used to, the
greater part of the old English law, and we are told that a
careful study of the history of the eleventh and early twelfth
centuries would incline a reader to doubt 'whether in the
sphere of law the Conquest is going to produce any very large
permanent changes.'[2]   Some additions, however, it did make,
the importance of which it would be impossible to underrate.
But this was mostly a work of time, and it is perhaps impossible
to determine how much of the resulting changes was due to
direct Norman initiative, and how much to a combination of

[2] *P. and M.*
i. 57.

circumstances, many of which had nothing to do with the fact
that the Normans had conquered England.

The first of these additions which demand our notice was
a new method of judicial procedure, the absence of which,
however, from the Anglo-Saxon courts, says Dr. Stubbs, 'is far
more curious than its introduction from abroad.'[1] This is the
trial by battle (duellum), which was only the Ordeal in another
form, but a bilateral ordeal.   It could be used in criminal and
civil cases alike.[2] In *criminal* charges it only applied to the class
of cases described as felony.   The term *felony* was originally
used to denote crimes which consisted of a breach of what
may be called the feudal bond ; but, perhaps because a conviction of felony caused the felon's land to escheat to the lord,
it was to the advantage of the magnates to extend the meaning
of the word ; so that in the course of the twelfth century it came
to include all crimes for which no bot or money compensation
could be paid.[3]   In the course of another century some seven
or eight definite crimes came under this head ;[4] but since both
omissions and inclusions were different to those of modern
law, it is only possible to define the felony of the twelfth and
thirteenth centuries by a description of its legal effects.[5]   Thus,
a felony was any crime which could be prosecuted by appeal,
that is, an accusation in which the accuser must offer battle as
a mode of proof ; and which involved as the punishment the
escheat of his land to his lord, the loss of his goods to the man
whom he had wronged, and the forfeiture of life or limb.   The
prosecutor or appellant, then, in a criminal charge stated his
case and offered to prove its truth *by his own body*.   The
defendant had to accept the offer, and the court awarded
' wager of battle.'   In *civil* suits — the chief of which in
mediaeval times were suits about land—the demandant, as he
was called, offered battle *by the body of a champion* who was in
theory a witness to the seisin of the land in question, but in
practice a professional pugilist hired for the occasion, and it
was the champion of the tenant whom he had to fight.   The
duel took place at the appointed time before the judges, and
was fought with well-defined and not very deadly weapons.
The burden of proving the charge lay upon the appellant and
the demandant respectively ; and the case went against them
if before nightfall the appellant or the champion of the

(1) Intro-
duction of
Trial by
Battle.

[1] *S. C. H.*
§ 99.

[2] M'Kechnie,
418.

[3] *P. and M.*
i. 284-286.
[4] *Ibid.* ii.
476-498.

[5] *Ibid.*
i. 464.

demandant had not made their adversary cry ' that odious word '
—craven—which so far deprived the vanquished of his civil
rights that as an infamous person he could never again appear
as a witness in a suit.   The convicted felon of course was
hanged ;[1] but the defeated appellant or demandant equally, as
perjurers, were heavily fined.   But the English were tenacious
of their old methods of proof : a trial by battle at first found no
favour in their eyes.   Freedom from it was among the privileges sought by the chartered boroughs,[2] and it may have been
this dislike which led Henry II to extend the method of inquest
and assize.   William I in introducing it had made its acceptance
optional by an English defendant ;[3] but its unpopularity wore
away, and by the end of Henry II's reign it had become one
of the chief modes of trial in the king's courts.[4]   Despite the
penalties attached to the use of a professional, schools of hired
pugilists existed, and many of the local courts kept in their pay
a champion who would represent them in the numerous claims
which might arise in the course of litigation.   But the duellum
gave way before the universal adoption of the system of trial
by jury ; although it remained as a legal mode of procedure
revived from time to time, until the use to which it was put in
the celebrated case of *Ashford* v. *Thornton* in 1819 caused its
abolition by Statute.[5]

The other noteworthy additions made by direct Norman
influence to English judicial procedure were more than mere
additions; for they were the means of working an entire revolution
in the old pre-Conquest methods.   The first of these was such
an extension of the use of *writs* that practically the Normans
may be said to have introduced them.   Before the Conquest,
except in cases of appeal and the trial of Pleas of the Crown,
the king rarely interfered with the local courts.   And even
after the Conquest, in the desire to preserve the ancient constitution, the Crown was content to leave to the local courts
the power of first instance or preliminary trial.   The original
writs, therefore, had no connection whatever with the relief that
was sought; they were merely a general direction from the
royal court to do right to the plaintiff.   But as the king's
authority became recognized, a writ came to be the only
appropriate commencement of a civil action at law, and, until
late in the reign of Henry II, a particular writ to suit each case

[1] M'Kech-
nie, 418.

[2] *S. C.* 108.

[3] *Ibid.*
84, § 6.
[4] But see
M'Kechnie,
419.

59 Geo. III.
c. 46.
[5] Neilson,
*Trial by
Combat.*
Thayer,
op. cit. 39-46.

(2) Extension
of the use of
Writs.

was framed in the Chancellor's office and, on demand, was issued therefrom to the sheriff. When the case was decided, the sheriff's duty was to return the writ with the judgement endorsed upon it; this was registered by the Chancellor's clerks, and the collection of such writs formed one main foundation of the Common law in civil cases. These clerks who furnished the appropriate writ to a plaintiff were called Masters. They were ecclesiastics and doctors of civil law, that is, the old Roman law. They would consequently resort to the principles of Roman law to fill defects in the English Common law. But the tendency was towards a definition of the Common law. Thus, while in the earlier thirteenth century the king's power to make new writs was unquestioned, ' as the struggle for Parliament drew near and Henry III forced on the struggle by attempting to govern without a Chancellor and other ministers, the complaints of new and illegal writs grew loud, and the general principle was drawn into debate.' [1]   In the first place, the Provisions of Oxford made the Chancellor swear ' Ke il ne enselera nul bref fors bref de curs sanz le commandement le rei e de sun cunseil,' that he would seal no writs excepting ' writs of course ' without the commandment of the king and of his council. [2]   These brefs de curs, brevia de cursu, or ' of course,' were writs framed to meet ordinary cases of continual recurrence, and they could be had for a moderate price by an intending plaintiff. [3]   It was to these writs that no addition could now be made without consent of the king and council. But, secondly, the action of the judges made it almost impossible for the Chancellor's clerks to innovate in the forms of writs ; for, the judges assumed the right of deciding on the validity of the writs on which actions before them must be founded. An attempt to remedy this was made in the Statute of Westminster II, § 24, which allowed the issue of writs ' *consimili casu*,' that is, in like case, falling under ' like law ' to one already in existence. But the judges so completely ignored this power of the clerks that ' henceforth the Common law was dammed and forced to flow in unnatural artificial channels. Thus was closed the cycle of original writs, the catalogue of forms of action to which nought but Statute could make addition.' [4]

We have seen the formal nature of early procedure—the

[1] Maitland, *Bracton's Note Book*, Introd. 6.

[2] *S. C.* 389.

[3] M'Kechnie, 461.

[4] Maitland, *Bracton's Note Book.*

(3) Trial
by Jury.

statement in set phrase of the plaintiff's case, the denial in equally set phrase of the defendant which came to be known as the 'Thwertutnay.'   Nor did this formal part of the defendant's answer disappear from the pleadings ; but in course of time and as the science of pleading became elaborated, it was thrust into the background, and the real answer was contained in an adaptation of the *Exceptio* of Roman law.   This is defined as ' a plea of a countervailing right,'[1] that is, the defendant does not deny the plaintiff's statement, but argues that special circumstances, which he proceeds to mention, do away with its applicability in this particular case.   But the introduction of the exception practically amounted to a destruction of the old simple method of procedure ; and it only assumed importance in connection with the second great innovation in legal procedure which we owe directly to the Normans—the use and spread of the system of trial by jury.   The origin of the jury has been a matter of much speculation.   Dr. Stubbs enumerates some nine or ten different theories, of which the only common principle seems to be the use of an oath in judicial procedure. Dr. Stubbs himself favours the view that the system was derived directly from the capitularies or charters declaratory of law issued by the kings of the Franks, who in their turn may have adopted it from the code identified with the name of the Emperor Theodosius.   The first use of the jury was for cases in which the royal interests were concerned.   The *missi* or itinerant officials of the monarchs of the house of Charlemagne were instructed to inquire into fiscal and judicial matters in the district courts by the aid of sworn witnesses representing the evidence of the neighbourhood.   The system was continued in France, where, however, it was not developed and was soon forgotten ; and in Normandy, where also it retained a comparatively primitive form.   In both these countries, though used primarily for royal or ducal purposes, permission was by special favour obtained for its adaptation to the concerns of Churches and even of private persons.

The system was introduced into England at the Norman Conquest, and only in England was it much developed.   It had no connection with the doomsmen or suitors of a local court whose business was 'to make a judgement,' that is, to declare the customary law ; nor with the oath-helpers who

[1] Moyle,
Justinian,
594, 653.

Its origin.

A.D. 435-438.

The
' Assize.'

swore to a set formula; nor with the frankpledge which was a permanent institution; nor, except by analogy, with the twelve senior thegns about whom we know so little.[1] But throughout the Norman period it remained an exceptional mode of procedure. It was thus that in 1086 Domesday was compiled from information supplied chiefly by the priest, reeve and six villans of each vill.[2] There are also a few instances under all the Norman kings of the use of this method in judicial cases, but always as a matter of royal favour where the rights of private individuals, or especially of monasteries, were concerned.[3] These were all regarded as acts of the shire court: the method of selecting the jurors is not clearly laid down; but in all probability they were chosen by the sheriff, perhaps by rotation from a list or according to their nearness to the place or their presumed acquaintance with the business to be done. Already under Henry I some of the characteristic difficulties of the system are apparent. There is a body of *judices* and *juratores* which, if merely synonymous terms, are at any rate to be distinguished from the *minuti homines* who were also obliged to attend the local courts. Again, the numerous fines recorded in the earliest extant Pipe Roll (31 Henry I), 'pro defectu recognitionis,' show that there was great reluctance to attend the courts and consequently a scarcity of qualified jurors. It is to Henry II that we must look for the establishment of that inquest by recognition as part of the settled law of the land, which finally resulted in the modern form of trial by jury. But for the present we must not speak of a jury (jurata).[4] Hitherto the process in which this sworn body of neighbours was employed, had been an *Inquisitio*, an inquiry. Now that its use was becoming common, stress was laid rather upon the work of the sworn men, and the process was described as *Recognitio*, the answer. But the word that was most often used in this connection, was the very confusing word *Assize*.[5] It denoted at least three things—an assembly, the ordinance of such an assembly and, what is most important in tracing the development of the jury, a particular remedial method of judicial procedure. For, the neighbours summoned to take part in the inquiry, themselves came to be called the Assize.[6]

A clear appreciation of Henry II's remedies by Assize

[1] Stubbs, E. E. H., 168, and S. C. 72.

[2] S. C. 86.

[3] Thayer, 50-53.

[4] M'Kechnie, 163.

[5] Ibid. 320, note.

[6] S. C. 57-59.

depends upon an exact knowledge of the meaning of a word which we have had frequent occasion to use without precise definition—the word *Seisin*.[1] Now, seisin, as we have seen, means possession, and in English law it is contrasted with 'jus' or right. It did not always follow that the man in possession of a tenement was the man who ought to be there. But further, it must be pointed out (though it seems a virtual contradiction of our definition) that all ownership was practically possessory. The law never attempted to decide ownership as against all the world ; it only decided between the two litigants in court, of whom the successful one might subsequently be ousted by a better claimant. Finally, as the law developed, rights took a concrete shape ; they came to be regarded as incorporeal things not essentially different from so corporeal a thing as land. The term 'seisin' was applied to the right to services from land, no less than to the land itself; and the same legal actions as availed for recovering possession of a tenement could be used by owners who were denied the services due from that tenement.

Armed with this knowledge we shall not misunderstand the ordinary division of these means for the ascertainment of rights of possession or remedies for the deprivation of them, into (1) proprietary and (2) possessory actions.

(1) *Proprietary actions*.[2] Hitherto any question regarding the right to ownership of land held by any free tenure, would have been begun in the lord's court and was decided by battle. But Henry II made it a principle that no man need answer for his free tenement, that is, that no freeholder's tenure should be called in question, without a royal writ directing an inquiry into his title. A claimant, therefore, or demandant, as he was technically called, had to obtain from the king's court, as represented probably by the Chancellor, one of the original or originating writs known as the Writ of Right (*breve de recto tenendo*). This would bid the lord of the tenement, on pain of removal of the matter into the king's court, to do him right, that is, to secure him in possession of the disputed tenement. Armed with this writ the demandant appeared in the manorial court, claimed the land as his right and inheritance because he or some ancestor was seised of right, and offered battle by the body of a champion who was in

theory a witness to the original seisin. The man in possession, called the tenant, would deny the claim and either accept battle or put himself on the Grand Assize. If he chose the latter alternative, the demandant would have to get an auxiliary writ bidding the lord choose four knights of the shire, who should in turn choose twelve knights of the neighbourhood in which the disputed tenement lay. These would be required to answer before some of the king's judges whether from their own personal knowledge the demandant had a better claim than the tenant; and according to their verdict the land in dispute would be adjudged to one party and his heirs and abjudged for ever from the other party and his heirs.[1] But it was probably more usual to remove the case straight away into the king's court. This would be done by another writ—'Praecipe quod reddat'[2]—and the duty of summoning the assize would devolve upon the sheriff. The indiscriminate use of this last writ was naturally much disliked by the holders of private courts, and Magna Carta[3] attempts to stop its applicability to them. Meanwhile, however, other circumstances had determined that the remedial measures begun by a writ of right should practically fall into abeyance. For, this mode of procedure was not regarded with favour even by the class whom it was designed to aid. In the first place, it was a very tedious process. A man was not lightly to be abjudged from a free tenement. Thus all kinds of precautionary measures were permissible, which in the hands of unscrupulous men became mere means of delay. The choice of the assize might be a lengthy proceeding; for, the members chosen by the sheriff might be challenged on all kinds of grounds, and were able themselves to urge all manner of excuses for non-attendance; while in his answer to the demandant's claim the tenant was allowed to plead exceptions. Nor was this the tenant's only advantage; for in the mode of procedure the choice was open to him between trial by battle and by assize. As a remedy Henry II instituted, perhaps by degrees, a more summary method of procedure to be adopted in certain cases, which are generally distinguished as the petty or possessory assizes.

(2) *Possessory actions*.[4] The advantage of this new method was that it could always be applied to a new case with royal permission; but as a matter of fact it was only established in

[1] M'Kechnie, 322.

[2] *Ibid.* 406-410.

[3] *S. C.* 301. § 34.

[4] Maitland, Introd. to *Rolls of the King's Court, Richard I* (Pipe Roll Society): *P. and M.* i. 123-127; ii. 46-62.

a few cases ; and of these, four especially may be enumerated as those in common use. (a) The Assize *Utrum* was an attempt to limit by confirming the claims of the ecclesiastical courts in dealing with land held by the Church. The Constitutions of Clarendon [1] direct that the preliminary determination *whether* a disputed tenement is held by lay or eleemosynary tenure is to be in the hands of the king's justiciar inquiring through the sworn evidence of the neighbourhood. The narrowing down of the definition of eleemosynary tenure soon deprived this assize of much meaning. Far more important was the Assize of (b) *Novel disseisin.* This was established by the Assize of Clarendon and was used to determine whether, since some recent date mentioned in the originating writ, the holder of a certain tenement, here called the defendant, had unjustly and without judgement, that is, without legal proceedings, disseised or dispossessed the plaintiff of his free tenement. Scarcely less important was the Assize of (c) *Mort d'ancestor* which was established by the Assize of Northampton [2] in order to determine whether since some definite date the person whose heir the plaintiff claimed to be, died seised as of fee, that is, holding the land by a title which, if good, would descend to his heir. Finally, in litigation about advowsons or the right of presenting to an ecclesiastical benefice, there already existed a special proprietary action begun in the king's court by writ of right of advowson. Here also Henry instituted a possessory action, the Assize of (d) *Darrein presentment,* by which a sworn committee of neighbours was used to ascertain who made the presentation on the last occasion, so that he or his lawful heir should present now. All these possessory assizes had certain features in common. In the first place, their mode of procedure was summary. They were not taken into the lord's court at all, but began at once before the king's judges. In accordance with the original writ the sheriff himself summoned the twelve men to form the assize ; they need be not knights, but merely freeholders, for the matter to be decided was not so important as in the Grand Assize ; while, finally, not nearly the same number of grounds for challenging the members nor excuses for their non-attendance were allowed as in the Grand Assize. And, secondly, this method of procedure by assize lays so much stress on the necessity

[1] *S. C.* 139. § 9.

[2] *Ibid.* 151. § 4.

of a legal remedy for wrong-doing, that it seems to us almost to defeat its own end, namely, the accomplishment of justice. For in a case of Novel disseisin self-help, or the forcible ejection of the intruder, might only be attempted within four days of his intrusion, although in Mort d'ancestor the limit was longer in order to allow the news of the ancestor's death to reach an absent heir. But at the end of these periods the man in possession obtained a lawful seisin, and could defend himself by a writ of novel disseisin against even the lawful heir. Finally they confer upon the person to whom seisin is given the coveted option of deciding whether the question of absolute ownership should be settled if at all by the hated duellum or by recourse to the tedious process of the Grand Assize.[1]

But before the actual assize had been appointed for a proprietary action or had been sworn under a possessory action, in course of time a very important act was often interposed, with which is intimately bound up the development of the jury. To the claim of the demandant in a proprietary action and of the plaintiff in a possessory action the tenant and defendant respectively might reply by pleading an 'exceptio,' a special plea or reason why the assize should not be held; and he might offer to submit this plea to a jury or, as the phrase was, to a verdict of the country. The other party, on pain of losing the case, would be bound to accept the offer. As a matter of fact, this question which had arisen out of the pleadings, would probably be submitted to the twelve men summoned for the assize; but it is important to notice that the assize and the jury represented a different idea. The assize originated in a royal writ, the jury in the consent of the parties : the assize was summoned before the defendant's case was heard, the jury were summoned to answer a question of fact which it had been agreed to submit to them.

The 'Assize' and the Jury.

In theory, then, it was only by mutual consent of both parties that a jury was employed : but the judges seem to have found means of compelling an unwilling suitor to submit to the test. And as the old Thwertutnay of the defendant became a mere form and the real point at issue was contained in the exception, the assize gave way entirely to the jury. Now, the early jury, no less than the assize which they superseded, were

The Jurors as Witnesses.

required to answer from their own personal knowledge. But it has been pointed out[1] that it is not quite true to say in the usual phrase that the 'jurors were witnesses'; for if their 'veredictum' had once become 'testimonium,' the judges would have treated them like modern witnesses, they would have been dealt with separately, and the court would have discussed the divergent testimony of the twelve. But apparently, in direct opposition to the theory of their functions, the jury, as distinct from the assize, very soon seem to have been expected, when summoned, to make inquiries about the facts to which they had to testify, 'to collect testimony . . . weigh it and to state the net result in a verdict.'[2] Moreover, for some purposes from the very first, actual witnesses (e.g. to a deed) were mingled with the jury in their deliberations, although generally it was only the jury who testified in open court: while, as further aids, charters and documents were exhibited to the jury, witnesses were occasionally examined before them, the judge charged them at the beginning of the trial in order to keep them to the point in their verdict, and then the counsel on either side addressed them in perfectly unsupported statements of fact.[3] But from the middle of the fourteenth century witnesses and jury began to be sharply separated off, and unanimity on the part of the jury was required; while in the fifteenth century witnesses began to testify in open court. For a long time, however, the old idea of testimony from personal knowledge hung about the jury. 'A man,' says Professor Maitland, speaking of the end of the Middle Ages, 'who had been summoned as a juror, and who sought to escape on the ground that he already knew something of the facts in question, would be told that he had given a very good reason for his being placed in the jury-box.'[4] Thus as late as 1543 we find a statute requiring six out of the twelve jurors to be inhabitants of the particular hundred concerned, it being intended that these should inform the others.[5]

Meanwhile the method of ascertaining royal rights by the evidence of the neighbourhood had been adapted to the purposes of criminal justice. The system of frankpledge had already set up a number of small mutually responsible bodies under the eye of the sheriff. It is perhaps not unlikely that to Henry II occurred the brilliant idea of turning the

[1] *P. and M.* ii. 619-620.

[2] *Ibid.* 622.

[3] *Ibid.* 625-626. Thayer, chap. iii. passim.

[4] Maitland, in *Social England,* i. 291.

[5] Thayer, 90 et seq. The Jury of presentment.

already existing machinery for 'producing one's neighbour
to answer accusations' into a machinery for 'telling tales
against him.'[1]   In other words, the same court held by the
sheriff twice a year through the hundreds and consequently
called his Tourn, was used both to take View of Frankpledge
and to receive presentments of suspected criminals.   We can
only notice the earliest recorded instances of the application
of a jury of presentment.   The sixth article of the Constitutions
of Clarendon[2] seems an attempt on the part of Henry II to
check the arbitrary judgements of ecclesiastical courts upon
laymen by a provision for the appointment of a kind of jury
consisting of neighbours of the accused empannelled by the
sheriff, on whose presentment the ecclesiastical judge is allowed
to act.   Nothing further is heard of the jury in ecclesiastical
courts.   On the other hand, the first clause, practically the
preamble, of the Assize of Clarendon[3] provides that twelve
men of each hundred and four of each vill shall swear that
they will answer truly whether any man is reputed to have
been guilty of murder, robbery or suchlike heinous offence.
Ten years later the Assize of Northampton[4] extended the
subjects about which inquiry should be made, and directed
that such inquiry should be carried out both by the judges
and by the sheriffs, that is, in the judicial eyres or circuits and
in the local court which came to be called the Sheriff's Tourn.
The composition and procedure of this latter court will be
described elsewhere.

A session of the justices in eyre was only an enlarged
edition of the sheriff's tourn.   There were assembled before
the judges all officials of the shire, the hundreds and the
liberties, and all who were bound by their tenure to do suit at
the shire court; together with twelve men representing each
hundred and chosen by two or four knights who had been
nominated by the bailiff of the hundred; and, finally, the
reeve and four men from each vill.   These representative
members of hundred and vill were all sworn to speak the
truth, and then a set of questions, known as the Articles of
the Eyre and drawn up by the king's councillors, was delivered
to them in writing to be answered by a certain day.   But,
meanwhile, they privately handed in their list of suspects
whose escape could thereby be prevented by an order of arrest

[1] Maitland,
Introd. to
Select
Pleas in
Manorial
Courts, ii.
xxxiv.

[2] S. C.
138-139.

[3] Ibid. 143.
1166.

[4] Ibid. 151.
1176.

Procedure
before the
itinerant
Justices.

from the judges. On the appointed day the juries of the hundreds appeared with such of the presentments of the vills in writing as they 'avowed' or endorsed. But the judges further questioned them orally and compared their answers with the written statement which they had just handed in and with the rolls of the sheriffs and coroners on which were recorded the presentments of the tourns and inquests. For any inconsistency of statement the jury was amerced, and since some of the statements to which they had to swear might date from the last eyre—an interval of perhaps seven years—such amercement was frequent. In fact, the procedure degenerated into an extortionate absurdity. But, in any case, the chief business of the eyre seems to have been to amerce through the jury the communities which they represented, and which on the confessions of their representative jury had neglected their police duties by failing to present or to arrest suspected criminals.[1]

[1] *Pleas of Crown for County of Gloucester*, Introd. xxiii-xliv. *P. and M.* ii. 641-652. Holdsworth, 113-115.

The development of the Petty Jury.

So far the procedure continued fairly uniform from generation to generation. It was only the graver crimes—the felonies—about which the juries seem to have been called upon to witness before the judges. But in the procedure after the presentments had been made, early in the thirteenth century a great change has to be noted. At first the judges, having received the presentments of the jurors of the hundreds, would put on oath the representatives of the four vills nearest to the one of which each presented suspect was an inhabitant; and in each case in which they endorsed the presentments of the man's own vill and of his hundred, the accused proceeded to the ordeal. But in 1215 the Fourth Lateran Council practically abolished the ordeal by forbidding the clergy to take part in it, and owing to the peculiar relations of England with the Pope at the beginning of Henry III's reign, the decree took effect sooner in England than in any country of Western Europe. The only procedure now at hand was the procedure which was developing itself out of the assize, namely, a resort to the verdict of the country by a specially empannelled jury. But we have seen that submission to the verdict of a jury was purely optional, a matter of mutual agreement between the two parties to a suit. Consequently the accused might not put himself upon the country ; and, in their lack of any other procedure, the judges

resorted to all kinds of expedients in order to force him to
submit. At last the Statute of Westminster I (§ 12) ordained 1275.
that notorious felons who refused, should be kept 'en la prison
forte et dure' (in strong and hard prison) as refusing the common
law of the land. This led to the development of the barbarous
peine forte et dure [1] by which a recalcitrant was gradually starved [1] Thayer,
or crushed by a load of iron into submission or death. The 74-80.
point of such obstinate resistance was that an unconvicted
criminal saved for his family the land which, on his conviction
for felony, would have escheated to the lord or, if his offence
was treason, would have been forfeit to the king.[2] But if the [2] M'Kechnie
accused did put himself upon the country, the jury of the hundred 395-400.
which had hitherto only presented him as suspect, were now
asked to pronounce definitely on the question of his guilt. It
would not be unreasonable for them to acquit him, for their presentment was made only on common rumour and might well
have been made in order to save themselves from an amercement if the rumour reached the judges from elsewhere. But if
they found him guilty, the representatives of the four neighbouring vills were again put on oath, and sometimes to them was
added the jury of another hundred. If the verdict of these
numerous unconnected bodies was unanimous the prisoner was
sentenced. Thus the jury to which his fate was submitted might
number as many as forty-four persons ; and, since there is seldom
any record of difference of opinion among them, it has been
supposed that the unanimity was somewhat fictitious, and that
trial by jury was trial by common repute.

The further development of trial by jury is more important
in the history of our law than in that of our constitution, nor
as yet can we at all clearly trace the steps which ultimately led
to the modern system of indictment by grand jury and trial
by petty jury.[3] All that we can say for certain is that, in the [3] Holds-
first place, there arose a not unnatural idea that a man's worth,
indictors would not try him impartially, and a statute of 1352 156-161.
forbade them to try him at all ; then, the disuse of the presenting jury for the further trial involved the disuse of the four
neighbouring vills which had corroborated their evidence ;
and finally, the elaborate character of the old judges' eyres was
altered, and the indictment of the sheriff's tourn and the
inquests of coroners became sufficient to put a man upon

his trial without any further presentment by the hundred jurors.

Survival of
old methods
of pro-
cedure.

But notwithstanding the universal establishment of the jury system, all the old methods of procedure died hard.   Certainly the local courts of hundred and shire never assimilated trial by jury and, for this reason among others, decayed with the decay of compurgation and ordeal.   But compurgation was not abolished by statute until 1333, and trial by battle only disappeared in 1819.   Even the ' peine forte et dure ' remained a legal method until 1772.[1]   The difficulties and dangers which beset the jury in its development towards its modern form, will be dealt with in speaking of the violations of the liberty of the subject in comparatively modern times.   There remains to be noticed shortly another early use to which Henry II and his immediate successors put the sworn representatives of hundred and vill, namely, as a committee of assessment for *financial* purposes.

[1] Holds-
worth, 155.

The Jury of
assessment.

So long as taxation was based exclusively upon land, the witness of Domesday might be a sufficient guard against undue exactions.   But when merchandise, moveables, or personal property were called on to contribute to the Exchequer, an owner's liabilities were not so easy to determine.   In the first instance the payer's own return would be accepted ; but in cases of doubt or dispute recourse was had to the evidence of his neighbours as to his probable expenditure ; and this could be judged from the standard of life which he maintained. This method was applied on the first occasion indirectly, in order to determine the weapons which under the Assize of Arms (1181) every freeman was to keep at hand.[2]   Its first direct use was for the Saladin Tithe, a tenth part of every one's rents and moveables, that is, income whether derived from land or merchandise, which was voted for the Third Crusade.[3] The success of the system led to its application in 1198 to determine the liabilities of land,[4] and thus to an assessment which should supersede the now antiquated record of Domesday.   But the use of these juries of assessment is intimately connected with the history of representation, and the gradual formation of Parliament entirely did away with their employment for this purpose.

[2] S. C. 155.

[3] Ibid. 160.

[4] Ibid. 257.

The Itinerant
Justices.

§ 52. But neither writs nor jury would have been of much

importance or avail without the constant, regulative action of the *Itinerant Justices*. The great weakness of the early English constitution was that want of intimate connection between the central and the local government which effectually prevented all concerted action. The greater kings were aware of this fatal defect and took measures to remedy it. Thus Ælfred, perhaps in imitation of the ' missi ' of the Karolingian Empire, investigated cases of injustice through ' fideles ' or royal messengers : while for the same purpose Eadgar and Cnut held the Witan thrice a year at stated times and places, an example which was imitated by the first two Norman kings. But this was not enough. The enormously increased activity of the central government after the Norman Conquest caused the formulation of an elaborate financial system. After 1086 Domesday became the authority on which all landed property was rated ; but changes in the ownership of land, the formation of new forests and the cultivation of waste land made it necessary constantly to modify the previous assessment of any individual owner. Under William II such questions were referred to the shire court. But the sheriffs themselves required supervision. For this purpose Henry I sent through the country officials of the newly-formed Exchequer, who should assess the revenue, and take the exclusive cognizance at any rate of the pleas of the crown out of the sheriff's hands. Not content with that, in some cases he even seems to have appointed resident justices superior to the sheriff for hearing such pleas. But as yet the system was most inefficient. The sheriffs themselves were much too powerful to be interfered with. Their posts were in many cases hereditary and threatened to fall into the hands of a few great men, each administering a large cluster of shires. Moreover, the visits of the new officials were extremely irregular and were concerned rather with financial than with judicial business ; while, finally, the private jurisdictions of the great feudal lords were left intact.[1]

Nor for the first twelve years of Henry II's reign (1154-1166) is there proof of the beginning of a better system. After the disorders of the late reign Henry moved tentatively along the path of reform. From 1156 at intervals of two or three years the great officials, Justiciar, Chancellor and Constable, held pleas alone or together in most of the shires. But the

Their origin.

Beginning of the system.

Under Henry I.

[1] *S. C. H.* § 127.

Formulation of the system under Henry II.

2 B

1166.

circumstances of Henry's quarrel with Becket gave an impulse to popular reform, and from the date of the Assize of Clarendon (1) the visits of royal officials to the provinces became frequent and, before long, regular. The Assize of Clarendon was carried out by two of the king's ministers assisted by the sheriffs; in 1168 and again in 1170 four barons of the Exchequer held pleas in various shires: while in 1173 the principle of circuits was introduced, and in 1176 the Assize of Northampton was carried out by three judges in each of six circuits into which the country was divided, some of whom were at the same time sheriffs and barons of the Exchequer. But this combination of offices was coming to be unusual. The sheriffs of Henry's early years were great local magnates holding pairs of shires, apparently for life, and both oppressing the people and hindering the work of the king's judges. But in 1170 the complaints of their conduct encouraged Henry to issue a strong commission of inquiry composed of barons and of clergy not already occupied in administrative work. The Inquest of Sheriffs resulted in (2) the dismissal of a large number of the acting sheriffs, in whose place were substituted trained officials drawn from the same class as the justices; although as a rule care was taken to place the two offices in the hands of different individuals. Moreover, (3) the judicial aspect of the journeys of these royal officials into the provinces gradually assumed more importance and prominence than the financial aspect; and this change would no doubt be aided by the introduction of the taxation of personal property, which transferred the details of assessment to sworn representatives of each district. And finally, (4) by the Assizes of Clarendon and Northampton all judicial and administrative power was being gathered up into the hands of the king's representatives;

[1] *S. C.* 144. § 11.

for by the former[1] no private franchise was to exclude the sheriff, and by the latter the pleas of the crown were practically taken out of the hands of the sheriff whose local interests were too strong, and were entrusted entirely to the justices to whom the sheriffs should act henceforth as police officers and subordinate administrative officials.

The growth of a body of professional judges.

But, meanwhile, Henry's various measures of reform had rapidly increased the amount of judicial business which had to be done in the king's name. The intermittent and somewhat indefinite Curia Regis, of which in theory all the itinerant justices were members, no longer sufficed for the purpose. There was need of some more permanent arrangement; and permanence in administrative work brings with it the opportunity for professional training and the cultivation of a professional pride. To attain this permanence Henry seems to have tried a series of experiments, until in 1178 he chose two clerks and three laymen out of the eighteen persons acting as itinerant justices at the time, and appointed them to remain at the king's court as a kind of permanent nucleus of a central judicial body; although the king and his councillors were still to exercise an equitable jurisdiction in the last resort.[1] How little of the professional stamp as yet hung about the king's judicial officials is clear from the fact that the rest of the eighteen do not seem to have gone on acting as judges, but probably resumed subordinate places in the Exchequer; while, for a long time to come, with the professional judges on their circuits were associated knights of the shire—country gentlemen who were occupied in numerous branches of local administrative work. In fact the itinerant justices were not necessarily members of the central Curia at all, and could be summoned before it to bear record of their acts; but each body of justices would usually include one or two professional judges. In any case they went as the king's representatives, and their court was everywhere Curia Regis, though their authority was probably defined by the words of a temporary commission.[2]

[1] *P. and M.* i. 133.

[2] *Ibid.* 134-135.

The chief of these judicial commissions were:—(*a*) *that of the Peace.* This was the oldest and most important, and was the primary duty of the royal judges; but with the increase of order in the country it was given over entirely to inferior magistrates of the first instance or primary resort, whose history will be traced under the head of Justices of the Peace. Commissions (*b*) *of Gaol Delivery* were preliminary investigations to prevent the oppressions of local magnates, and were generally made over to local commissioners. Those (*c*) *of Oyer and Terminer* were for the purpose of hearing and determining criminal cases, such as treason, felony and trespass. (*d*) *For taking the Assize* large numbers of commissions were issued annually, and were heard by a professional judge who could

Their commissions.

choose his own local assessors.   Finally, (e) *Nisi prius* was
not issued as a special commission until the Statute of Westminster II in 1285.   It was intended to relieve the pressure
of the commissions for the assize.   Two justices, with the aid
of one or two knights of the shire, were to take all assizes
thrice a year at Westminster, and the juries empannelled for
such cases were to be sent up to Westminster *unless, before* the
day fixed for trial by the judges there, the itinerant justices
had come into the county.[1]

The history of the jury is paralleled in that of the itinerant
justices.   Under Edward I those commissions which still
remained in the hands of the justices, were gradually amalgamated.   Already, in the early days of the system, there had
been some attempts in that direction.   Thus by the Assize of
Northampton, criminal and civil actions, superintendence of
the procedure of a criminal jury, together with more miscellaneous duties, were given to one and the same set of
commissioners ;[2] while in 1194 to the commissioners were
given not only civil and criminal cases, but also the collection of tallages and all crown dues.[3]   These, however, were
isolated instances.   More permanently, though at considerable
and irregular intervals, such as five to seven years, a circuit
for all pleas would be instituted in the shires.   For each shire
two or three of the professional judges were commissioned
together with a prelate, baron or knight of the shire.[4]   Under
Edward I this method became permanent.   Thus, in 1293 the
kingdom was divided into four circuits with two judges to
each who should take the assizes and should be on duty
throughout the year.   Their power did not cease with the
special temporary commission.   The ordinance of 1299 was a
step further in the same direction ; for it enjoined that justices
of assize, if laymen, should also act as justices of gaol delivery.

§ 53.   But while the king's commissioners were travelling
round the country, there were gradually being organized three
central courts through whose influence the Common law was
reduced to one uniform system prevailing over all local and
class peculiarities, so that in its turn it might be a bulwark
against the encroachments of the Crown.   We have seen that
in 1178 out of the eighteen acting itinerant judges, Henry II
selected five to be continually with him.   According to *the*

[1] *P. and M.*
179-180.
Cf. also
*Select
Pleas of
Crown,*
Introd. xxi.

Their con-
solidation.

1176.

[2] *S. C.*
151-152.
[3] *Ibid.*
259-261.

[4] *Pleas of
Crown for
County of
Gloucester,*
Introd. xxi.

The three
Courts of
Common
Law.

usual theory,[1] the members of this court were changed from time to time, but were all chosen from the officials of the Exchequer: the business which came before them was that which at a later date was referred to the three Courts of Common law, that is, either 'placita quae sequuntur regem,' criminal or civil cases which touched the king's rights and revenue, or 'communia placita,' cases of private litigation in which the king intervened as supreme arbiter and judge. From this court difficult cases were referred to the King in his Council,[2] and such cases included questions of revenue as well as legal matters of a more general nature.

But the position of this body of judges was extremely vague, and probably this theory should be largely *qualified*. A recent writer[3] has produced evidence to show that these five judges who were appointed to be permanently at the king's court for the sake of hearing 'all the claims and plaints of the people,' were the origin not, as is generally supposed, of the later Court of King's Bench, but of the later Court of Common Pleas which, in accordance with a provision of Magna Carta, became fixed at Westminster.[4] It seems difficult, however, to identify this professional judicial committee with either of these later Courts of Common law. For some time after 1178, what has been aptly called the 'dualism' of the king's court must be regarded as more or less of an accident. Thus, during the absence of Richard I the distinction between the five judges and the general body of the king's councillors altogether disappeared. Under John the dualism reappeared; for we find not only that a certain number of judges were sitting in banco at Westminster, while others were hearing pleas 'coram rege' wherever the king happened to be; but that even when the king was at Westminster, the two bodies of judges did not necessarily coalesce. Moreover, suitors would be summoned either before the justices of the bench sitting at Westminster or 'before us wheresoever we shall be in England.' But as yet all judicial arrangements were so entirely subservient to the king's will that two courts cannot be said to have existed. For, either body was competent to hear alike common pleas and pleas of the crown; the two sets of judges at any time might and sometimes did coalesce, while individual judges were not permanently assigned to one or other division. Thus it

[1] *S. C. H.* § 163.

[2] *S. C.* 197. *Dialogus* I, c. 8, and 152, § 7.

[3] Pike, 31.

[4] Maitland, *Select Pleas of Crown*, Introd. xiii.

[1] Maitland, *Select Pleas of Crown,* Introd. xvi-xvii.

may be said that 'the king's court of John's reign shows no cleft, though it does show a well-marked line of cleavage.'[1] Magna Carta (§ 17) said that common pleas should not follow the king but be heard in a fixed place; and this clause was repeated in the reissues of 1216 and 1217. This meant that some permanent tribunal should be appointed in a definite place to which private litigants could bring their cases with some assurance of finding judges to hear them. But for the present the injunction was needless. For during Henry III's minority the dualism disappeared, and there was only one judicial body of the justices of the bench sitting at Westminster to hear all kinds of cases and supervised by the Council of Regency. Then, when Henry came of age, in imitation of his predecessors he began to make progresses and to do justice in person with the aid of his judges and members of his Council.

Court of Common Pleas.

[2] M'Kechnie, 308-317.

1234.

But in **1234** a very definite step in organization may be marked.[2] It was probably during the last years of Henry II that the pleas heard in the king's court began to be enrolled; and from the justiciarship of Archbishop Hubert Walter (1194-1198) it became a frequent, though not as yet a regular practice. Now, on the dismissal of Stephen Segrave, Hubert de Burgh's successor in the justiciarship, no justiciar was appointed and, instead of all the pleas heard before the king's judges being entered on one set of 'de banco' rolls, those heard by the judges with the king, the 'placita quae sequuntur regem,' were entered on separate 'coram rege' rolls. Thenceforth there were two distinct sets of plea rolls, those of the bench being drawn up terminally, those of the cases heard 'coram rege' annually as if uninfluenced by legal terms. Each body had also a different process to compel the attendance of suitors. The justices of the bench wanted little more to turn them into the more modern Court of Common Pleas: but

[3] *Select Pleas of the Crown.* *Bracton's Note Book.* *P. and M.* i. 177-179.

this did not happen until the reign of Edward I, when the judges of the court obtained a permanent organization under a Chief Justice of their own, and they were no longer allowed to hear pleas of the crown in any shape.[3]

Court of Exchequer.

Meanwhile, the old Exchequer had completely changed its form. At first, with its membership of all the great officers of State, it was merely 'a phase of the general governing body of the realm.' But it gradually tended to become 'partly a judicial tribunal, partly a financial bureau.' Early in Henry III's reign the Justiciar and Chancellor ceased ordinarily to attend, and the Treasurer became president of the court; while its seal was put in the keeping of a new, special Chancellor of the Exchequer, and men were definitely appointed to be barons of the Exchequer, that is, as permanent officials of the court. Its chief work was to collect the king's revenue; but it was empowered by the king and council to redress the grievances of any petitioner against the action of the Crown. As yet, however, it was not regarded as a law court; for if a question of general law was involved in any matter that came before its officers, they were told to associate with themselves the king's judges for the purpose of deciding it. But the barons of the Exchequer had devised certain summary methods of procedure for the collection of money due to the Crown. It was probably the desire of suitors to avail themselves of these methods that encouraged the barons to entertain what were really common pleas.[1] This was checked by a clause in the Articuli super Cartas in 1300; but as a kind of compensation we find that a Chief Baron was appointed, and suitors were sometimes expressly allowed to go to the Exchequer in order that they might have the benefit of those summary processes. As a consequence, the Exchequer was more and more confined to the work of a court of law standing side by side with the Court of Common Pleas.[2]

[1] M'Kechnie, 316, and note.

[2] P. and M. i. 169-172.

There remained the court held 'coram rege,' which before very long ceased to imply the necessary presence of the king. But, for some time after 1234, its work continued to be indistinguishable from that of the King's Council itself, and it thus possessed a jurisdiction in error over the Common Bench, which it retained even when formed into a separate court. For before the end of Henry III's reign the ordinary work 'coram rege' seems to have been done by a committee of professional judges under a definitely appointed Chief Justice; and, while the Common Bench continued to remain *the* Bench in an especial sense, under Edward I this committee began to be distinguished as the King's Bench. But as yet it was not a separate body; for at any moment the committee

Court of King's Bench.

could be afforced by the presence of the king and any or all of his councillors, ecclesiastical or lay; nor was there any distinction in the class of cases which could be heard by the ordinary or by the afforced court. In 1290, however, the afforced court obtained its own rolls, and the cases heard before it, as opposed to the cases heard before the professional committee, were entered on the Parliament Rolls. Then, before long the term Parliament came to be appropriated to the meeting of the three Estates, and the Parliament Rolls became the records of those meetings. Finally, the King in Parliament when acting as a law court, came to be the House of Lords; the King in Council became a court of final equitable appeal and also a court of first instance in extraordinary cases, keeping no roll or record of its pleas or cases.[1]

[1] Maitland, Introd. *Memoranda de Parliamento.*

Thus out of the old Curia Regis on its judicial side there had been evolved (1) three Courts of Common law—King's Bench, Common Bench or, as it was afterwards called, Common Pleas, and Exchequer; and (2) two supreme courts —the House of Lords and the King in Council.

Courts of Exchequer Chamber.

The distinction between the authority of these last two courts will be noticed elsewhere. Here it is important to note the creation of two intermediate courts of error whose origin is connected with the later history of the Court of Exchequer. A careful distinction must be made between them. The barons, most tenacious of their privileges, claimed the right of amending all errors in their judgements in the Exchequer itself, and, consequently, unlike the Common Pleas, successfully evaded the claims of the King's Bench to hear such cases. This, however, would not have been altogether satisfactory, and in 1357 a statutable court was created, composed of the Chancellor and Treasurer who should associate with them the justices and other learned persons for the purpose of hearing appeals in error against the decisions of the barons of the Exchequer. This was known as the Court of Exchequer Chamber, and remained a separate court until 1830.[2] But it was only as a Court of Common law that the Exchequer was amenable to the intermediate court. Apparently under the Tudors, in imitation of Chancery, it developed a jurisdiction in Equity, and in many kinds of cases it exercised an equitable jurisdiction concurrent with that of Chancery until all such

31 Edw. III. stat. 1, cap. 12.

[2] Holdsworth, 107-108.

jurisdiction, except in so far as it was concerned with matters of revenue, was transferred to Chancery by statute in 1842. Meanwhile, like Chancery itself the Exchequer on its equitable side was amenable to the correction of its errors by the House of Lords. More than two centuries later another court, which also came to be known as the Exchequer Chamber, was created by Act of Parliament as an intermediate court of error between the King's Bench and the House of Lords, by which could be avoided the delays incidental to the existence of a court of final appeal whose sessions depended on the political needs of the sovereign.[1]

§ 54. Before passing on to the results of the concentration of justice in the royal courts, it is necessary to deal shortly with a class of prerogative courts through whose agency the royal power must have been widely spread. The *Forest Courts* were a creation of the Conquest. A forest was not necessarily a waste place, nor did it always belong to the king : on the contrary, it was generally private property and was often thickly populated.[2] The basis of the royal claim upon the forests is difficult to determine, especially as none was recognized either by the law or by the owners of property. The struggle between king and nation over the extension of the area of the forests lasted for more than two centuries. The general course of it was as follows. William I afforested or made the New Forest. Henry I, by consent of his barons, kept the forests which his father had made ;[3] and Stephen surrendered Henry I's additions.[4] By Magna Carta John surrendered all which he himself had added ;[5] while Henry II surrendered all additions made since the accession of Richard I, and submitted to a perambulation which should determine the boundaries.[6] The limitation of the forests was the last point upon which Edward I gave way ; but, by the Articuli super Cartas, he was obliged to submit to a restraint similar to that which had been placed upon his father.[7] The attempt of Charles I to revive the forest jurisdiction was met by an Act of the Long Parliament limiting the forests to their old boundaries. The administrative offices were abolished in 1817, but the forests though much diminished still exist, and are administered as part of the Crown lands by the Commissioners of Woods and Forests.

1585.

[1] Pike, 292-294.

Forest Courts.

[2] Inderwick, *The King's Peace.*
Pearson, *Historical Maps.* 1066-1300.

[3] S. C. 101. § 10.
[4] *Ibid.* 120.
[5] S. C. 297. § 47.
[6] *Ibid.* 348. § 1.
1300.

[7] *Ibid.* 446 ; *Statutes of Realm,* i. 136.

For all dwellers within this expansive forest area there were a special law and a special set of courts. The earliest *forest law* is one attributed to Cnut,[1] which is merely a confirmation of the rights of landowners. The first code of forest laws is the Assize of Woodstock drawn up under Henry II, and recording the severities of his grandfather.[2] By it, the forest jurisdiction was extended (§ 9) over the clergy by connivance of the papal legate, and (§ 11) over the whole population of the shires at the summons of the Master Forester. Richard I went even further ; for he demanded that the whole population should come as a matter of course before the itinerant justices of the forest.[3] This, however, was withdrawn by Magna Carta (§ 44), which also provided (§ 48) for the abolition through inquest by jury of all evil customs of the forest.[4] The result of this provision was that Henry III's ministers issued a separate Charter of the Forest,[5] in which the punishments decreed against offenders were much milder than those of Henry II's Assize. Thus, while in the Assize (§ 12) for a third offence an offender forfeited freedom or life, by the Charter (§ 10) no one should lose life or limb. Again, whereas the Assize (§§ 3, 7) restricted the rights of private owners within their own forests, the Charter (§§ 9, 12, 13) promised to these same owners a confirmation of their rights.

The administrative machinery of the forests was singularly complete. At the head stood the permanent Forest Justiciar or Chief Forester, one for the whole country until 1238 when one was appointed to each of two provinces divided by the river Trent. To each group of forests there was a separate warden, either an hereditary official or appointed by the king, and often also holding the constableship of the royal castle which was an accompaniment of any large forest. Under him came the permanent foresters or gamekeepers, who were the cause of much petty oppression, and a series of committees formed of knights—four verderers for each forest appointed in the shire court, doing a work analogous to that of the coroners and responsible directly to the king ; twelve Regarders in each shire who made tours of inspection every third year in order to answer a series of questions called the chapters of the Regard and dealing with all possible encroachments on the royal rights, and four Agistors who

[1] *S. C.* 74. § 81.

[2] *Ibid.* 157-159.

[3] *Ibid.* 258 ; R. Hoveden, iv. 63.
[4] *S. C.* 302. M'Kechnie, 511-514.
[5] *S. C.* 348-351.

met with the verderers and foresters in the Swainmotes held thrice a year for the purpose of regulating the pasturing of swine and cattle in the woods.[1] Transgressions of the forest law were dealt with by a series of courts. The lowest of these was (1) the Court of Attachments or Woodmote, held every forty days by the verderers to receive the presentment of suspected offenders against the vert and venison, who had been attacked or arrested by the Foresters. (2) The Court of Inquisitions, at first a special enquiry held whenever a forest offence was discovered, some time in the thirteenth century became a general court of inquiry held at regular intervals. Here were bound to appear the officers of the forest together with the reeve and four men from the neighbouring vills, and it was their duty to 'keep' pleas, that is to receive indictments of all offences committed in the forest, which they handed on to (3) the Court of the Forest Justices in Eyre, which at a later date was known as the Court of Justice Seat. This was the only court with the power of punishing any except the most trivial offences within the forest jurisdiction. But it was held only at considerable intervals—perhaps once in seven years—and not very regularly. All forest officials, all landowners within the forest, the reeve, and four men from each township were assembled by the sheriff. The Justices, among whom was included the Master Forester, punished chiefly by amercements those who were presented by the juries in the courts below.[2] These profits of justice were the most valuable part of the revenues derived from the forests.[3]

In this manner a large portion of the country must have been withdrawn alike from the action of the Common law and from the influence of private lords. The best parallel is to be found in the prerogative courts of Tudor and Stuart times, which are said to have dominated as much as a third of the whole country.

§ 55. So far we have been dealing with the reasons which led to the gradual concentration of justice in the royal courts. It is necessary now to consider the results of this most important change. They may be grouped under the three following heads—(1) the decay of the local courts; (2) the change of the Common law to a written law; and (3) the rise of the jurisdiction of Chancery.

[1] M'Kechnie, 485-489, and 491.

[2] M'Kechnie, 489-490. Holdsworth, 341-345.

[3] Dial. de Scac. p. 141.

Results of concentration of justice in King's Courts.

Con-
stituent
members of
the local
courts.
It is usually asserted that the Conquest made no difference in the constituent elements of the local courts. We have already seen that the earliest evidence for their composition— a passage in the Leges Henrici Primi—points to the presence of only a limited number of suitors in these courts. Corroborative evidence to the same effect may be afforded by another somewhat mysterious passage in this document which tells us that the king's *judices* are the *barones* of the county, whereas the *villani* and others of lesser rank were not to be reckoned among the number.[1]   Moreover, under Henry I, from elsewhere we get a distinction between the *judices* and *juratores*, and the *minuti homines*.[2]   Finally, the sworn committee of neighbours who developed into the jury, are always spoken of as *legales homines*, as if to mark them off from other men.   Such hints as these might make us hesitate before we accepted the usual account of the exhaustively representative character of the local courts.   But the cartularies of manors in the thirteenth century and the Hundred Rolls drawn up in 1279 seem to afford overwhelming evidence that the suitors at the local courts must have been a very limited body.   Thus, on nearly every manor are noted tenements whose holders ' defend ' their lands by attendance at the local courts, that is, the suit to the local courts is mentioned in the same list with the various personal duties and payments which constituted the rent by which the tenant held his land.   This method of representation in the local courts may have originated in the collective liability of the vill to which the passage already quoted from the Leges Henrici Primi may bear witness ; and it may owe its existence in point of time to the revival of the local courts by Henry I when, it has been thought, that ' the duty was conceived as being incumbent . . . on all freeholders who or whose overlords had no chartered or prescriptive immunity ; but that it was also conceived as being, like the taxes of the times, a burden on the land held by those freeholders.'[3]   Whatever the origin, the result seems perfectly clear.   Each local court, whether county, hundred, or even manorial, is entitled to a fixed number of ' suits,' the number of which could not lawfully be increased by subdivision of the holdings or in any other way.   The question as to who should actually discharge the due suit, would be a matter for a bargain

[1] *S. C.* 106, xxix.

[2] Pipe Roll, 31 Hen. I.

[3] Maitland, in *E. H. R.* iii. 420-421.

between lord and tenant ; but when once fixed it would tend
always to be incumbent on the holder of a particular tenement.
So carefully is the requisite suit provided for that certain tenants
are bound in respect of their holdings to attend regularly at
every or at each alternate meeting of the monthly or three-
weekly shire court, certain others at the half-yearly court of the
shire or of the sheriff's tourn, and others even at the specially
full court convened to meet the justices in eyre.[1]   The result [1] *P. and M.*
was that the local courts, though not large in number of suitors, i. 526-531.
were composed of very miscellaneous elements ; for, the persons
on whom the duty was laid might be drawn from any class of
freeholders.   It may be for this reason that men were able to
regard the local courts as representative assemblies and to
speak of them as being the counties and hundreds.[2]   But [2] *Ibid.*
even this small number of suitors to the local courts was 534.
further reduced by the legislation and the practice of the
thirteenth century.   For on the one side the Statute of Merton 1236.
allowed every baron to appear by proxy ; and the Statute of
Marlborough exempted from the sheriff's tourn all above the 1267.
degree of Knight unless they were specially summoned ; while
the grant of the privilege of their own View of Frankpledge
removed the boroughs from the same assembly.   Again, it was
perhaps the burden of the work and the danger of corruption
that led to the limitation of the jurors for assizes to freeholders, Stat. West.
first, of twenty shillings', and then, of forty shillings' annual value. II. c. 38.
On the other side, some landowners, chiefly religious bodies, 2 Hen. V.
gained exemption from attendance at the local courts for them- c. 3.
selves and their tenants ; while others succeeded in 'subtracting'
or withholding their suit, a practice which after a time made [3] *Ibid.*
such abstention into a prescriptive right.[3]   523.

   Together with this denudation of the local courts went Decline of
a diminution of the power of the sheriff.   This may be dated the sheriff's
from Henry II's great Inquest of Sheriffs in 1170, and may authority.
be traced in the four departments of the sheriff's work.   Thus,
(1) his *military* authority was lessened when scutage practically
did away with the levy of the minor tenants-in-chief ; while
the Assize of Arms in 1181 placed in the hands of the justices
the duty of superintending the armaments of the local fyrd.[4] [4] *S. C.* 155.
Under Henry III, chief constables were appointed for every § 9.
hundred, and a petty constable for each vill,[5] who generally [5] *Ibid.* 372.
1252.

combined the duties with that of bailiff or reeve. Finally, by the Statute of Winchester view of armour was to be held by two constables in every hundred and franchise, and defaulters should be presented to the sheriff.[1] Yet the sheriff's power was not altogether destroyed. Until the appointment of a Lord Lieutenant under the Tudors, he remained the local leader of the shire forces. Those of the lesser barons, too, who did not pay scutage, were mustered under him ; and even the greater barons occasionally were entrusted to him rather than to the Constable and the Marshal who usually convened them. A remnant of the sheriff's military authority appears in his later duty of 'pricking' for Commissions of Array. As (2) a *judicial* officer, the sheriff was gradually deprived of all his more important work. In the first place, (*a*) special officials were appointed, to whom were allotted duties which naturally would have fallen to the sheriff. Such were the *Coroners*, who, by the judicial instructions of 1194, were to be elected by the people to 'keep' the pleas of the crown and generally to look after royal interests.[2] Under Edward I they were specially charged with the holding of inquests in cases of unusual death ; but for some reason they were probably found inadequate, for their duties did not develop. Such, again, were *Justices of Trail Baston* instituted under Edward I and occasionally appointed in later times, who were a kind of Court Martial for disorderly periods and districts ; but on account of their summary methods of procedure they met with much opposition.[3] A third kind of such officials were the *Conservatores Pacis*, of whom as Justices of the Peace much will need to be said in another connexion. But (*b*) the sheriff was actually and by direct legislation deprived of portions of his power. Thus, the directions issued for the Judicial Iter of 1194 laid down that no sheriff should be justice in his own country ;[4] while Magna Carta forbade the sheriff to 'hold' pleas of the crown.[5] Again, (*c*) the sheriff was made amenable to the Itinerant Justices. For, while the Assize of Clarendon charged the sheriff and the justices equally with the work of receiving presentments from hundred and vill,[6] by the Assize of Northampton this duty was committed to the justices alone.[7] Similarly, at first the sheriff had a hand in the appointment of Juries of Assize ; but by the directions of 1194 the jury to act on the eyre was to be chosen by the shire court.[8] Yet the

---

Margin notes:

1285.

[1] *S. C.* 471. § vi.

[2] *Ibid.* 260, § 20. M'Kechnie, 370. Holdsworth, 45-46.

[3] Year Book, 14, 15 Ed. III (R. S.) xxxvi.

[4] *S. C.* 260. § 21.
[5] *Ibid.* 300. § 24. M'Kechnie, 361-363.
[6] *S. C.* 143. § 1.
[7] *Ibid.* 151-152.
[8] *Ibid.* 259.

sheriff retained some traces of his former position. Thus, for a long while the tourn continued to be held to receive present-ments and to conduct preliminary examinations of persons charged with crimes. Having ceased to be judges, the sheriffs remained presidents of a number of small local courts which could accuse, although they could not try. This power, how-ever, was used for purposes of extortion, and a law of Edward IV deprived them of it. There remained to them merely the duties of arresting suspects and of exacting penalties adjudged by the courts. As (3) a *police* officer, the sheriff's power received an irreparable blow from the lapse of the View of Frankpledge, which robbed his tourn of its most characteristic duty; and from the appointment of constables in the hundreds and vills. He was, however, the person to whom royal writs, such as those for distraint of knighthood, continued to be addressed; and to him were prisoners entrusted until the coming of the Itinerant Justices. Lastly, his (4) *financial* duties also threatened to disappear; for, first the assessment of taxes, and then their collection, were made over to special commissioners; while the charters of boroughs removed them in many points from the sheriff's control. But the sheriff could not be altogether dispensed with. He still raised the ferm of the shire and collected the tallage of unchartered towns: he was concerned with purveyance, and for some time helped the special com-missioners in the collection of the taxes. Thus, though deposed from the supreme place which he had occupied before 1170, the sheriff still retained numerous shreds of his ancient powers. Indeed, his continued importance is attested by the struggle over his appointment in the contests of the thirteenth century, and by the influence which he exercised in the two following centuries as returning officer over the election of members to Parliament.

1 Edw. IV c. 2.

While the courts were thus dwindling in the number of their suitors, and while the sheriff was being docked of one piece of authority after another, the actual competence of the courts themselves was gradually reduced. The extension of pleas of the crown and their transference from the sheriffs to the coroners and then to the Itinerant Justices, was only the natural corollary to the organization of the judicial body. But the employment of writs, followed by the remedy of the assize,

Decline of com-petence of the local courts.

gradually made the king's court a court of first instance for all England, and practically withdrew from the private courts all valuable jurisdiction over freeholders. The courts, however, continued to exist. But in 1278 the Statute of Gloucester was interpreted to mean that no action for more than forty shillings could be tried in a local court. This limitation of competence told alike on the national and the feudal courts ; and, while the part taken by the shire courts in the election of parliamentary representatives gave them a new lease of life, the feudal courts entirely disappeared, leaving only the manorial court with jurisdiction over customary tenants.

6 Edw. I.
c. 8.

Fixing of
the Com-
mon law.

The second great result of the supremacy of the royal courts was a strong impetus towards the fixing of the form of the Common law. Up to the time of Edward I the Common law was definitely an unwritten law ; and, although it never entirely ceased to be so, yet it was tending to take a settled form. The causes of this important change were—(*a*) the establishment of Parliament as the one proper organ of legislation, which prevented the unauthorised development of procedure by the issue of new writs ; (*b*) the establishment of a series of precedents by judicial decisions which were considered to have an authority binding on succeeding judges almost equally with acts of the legislature. To these may be added (*c*) the growth of a class of professional lawyers, as is proved by the publica-tion of such authoritative law-books as those associated with the names of Glanvill, Bracton, ' Fleta ' and Britton ; and (*d*) the formulation of the Courts of Common law.

The Common law of England may thus be said to consist of three elements :—(1) *Lex non scripta* or *customary law*. Such customs date from remote antiquity ' whereof the memory of man runneth not to the contrary,' and, in order to obtain recognition, they must have existed continuously. A second element is formed by the (2) *Lex scripta* or *statute law*, in which the duty of interpretation devolves on the judges who are guided by various recognized rules or canons of con-struction. To these may be added (3) *maxims drawn from approved legal authorities*. In deciding a case for which no precedent could be quoted, the judges at first would listen to arguments drawn from Roman law. This put into the hands of the common-law judges a power of innovation and expansion. But in the reign of Richard II they refused to allow such pleadings for the future ; and with the banishment of Roman law from the courts this power ceased, until competition with Chancery caused the common lawyers once more to adopt those principles by whose application Chancery had thriven.

§ 56. In sharp contrast to the methods and sources of the Common law stands the legal system of the CHANCERY, which owes its power to the deliberate refusal of the common lawyers to meet the growing needs of a developing society by measures for the continuous development of their procedure.

The Chancellor first appears in England under Eadward the Confessor. He was the chief secretary, head of the king's chaplains and keeper of the royal seal. The name was derived from the *cancelli* or screen behind which he worked. Owing to the literary qualifications of the office, in early days it was always in the hands of an ecclesiastic.[1] It was not until the abolition of the justiciarship that the Chancellor became the great political official which he remained until the days of the Tudor sovereigns. But, meanwhile, his legal position was considerable ; for he was the head of the office from which were issued the writs through whose operation the royal justice overrode the private jurisdictions.[2] From the time of Edward I the advance of the Chancellor's power was continuous until (α) under Edward III the Chancery was established as a separate court ; (β) under Edward IV it became a separate jurisdiction ; (γ) under James I it established its right to hear cases on writ of error from the common-law courts, and (δ) by the time of Lord Eldon the Chancellor's 'discretion' had become practically fixed within recorded precedents.

The establishment of Chancery is generally ascribed to an Ordinance of Edward I in 1290 by which petitions were delegated to be dealt with by the courts which they concerned. Among these mention is made of the Chancellor. But this was probably no novelty. The Chancellor at first exercised his jurisdiction in the King's Council, of which he was the president ; but as yet he had no monopoly in the application of the royal prerogative of grace, much of which was carried out by the king in person.[3] Under Edward II the Chancellor seems to have begun to sit regularly for judicial business. A

Chancery.

Early history of the Chancellor.

[1] *S. C. H.* § 121.

[2] Jenks, 141-145.

Chancery becomes a separate court.

[3] Kerly, *Hist. of Equity,* 27.

large and important part of this was concerned with petitions whose claims affected the royal rights, and this became the chief portion of the Chancellor's common-law jurisdiction. Under Edward III the Chancery was fully established as a separate court with its seat at Westminster. In 1350 all such matters as were of grace, that is, such as involved the exercise of the king's prerogative of grace, were referred to the Chancellor. Thus the Chancery, as a formulated court, exercised two kinds of powers—(i) as a court of ordinary jurisdiction ; for, the king could at his pleasure sue either there or in the common-law courts in any case to which he was a party : (ii) as a distinct court for giving relief in cases which required extraordinary remedies. But two important provisos must be made. In the first place, although petitions now began to be addressed to the Chancellor direct, yet matters of grace did not come exclusively to him. A close connection continued between him and the Council of which in these matters he seemed to be the official representative and acting committee. Secondly, although Chancery had a procedure of its own, yet it often adopted common-law procedure in matters outside its ordinary jurisdiction, and the special procedure in cases falling within it ; while, since the Chancellor never had authority to summon a jury, matters of disputed fact were transferred to be tried in the King's Bench.

Chancery gets separate jurisdiction. Thus although the Chancery was a distinct court, the jurisdiction of the Chancellor was not as yet a thing enjoyed by himself in his court alone. But the practical settlement of the Common law, for reasons already stated, caused continual failure of redress, especially when the plaintiff was poor and unable to pay the fees for obtaining the original writs. Thus the encouragement came from two sides. On the one hand, *individuals* applied for help to the Chancellor because the special procedure of his court enabled him to give remedies for wrongs which the Common law did not recognize. This procedure consisted of (i) a power, borrowed from the Council, of compelling the attendance of a defendant under penalty, by what was hence called the Writ of Subpoena, and (ii) the power, borrowed from the Canon law, of examining the defendant upon oath. But, on the other hand, the *Commons* who had begun by complaining strongly of the Chancellor's growing jurisdiction, finding that it could not be extinguished, tried to regulate it. Not only was it recognized by an Act of Richard II's reign as a distinct and permanent court, but Parliament even delegated matters to the Chancellor as the person who should redress wrongs for which the Common law gave no remedy. Two important results followed from this double encouragement. By the enforcement of Uses of which the common-law courts refused to take cognizance, a vast mass of business was attracted to the court, and there was formed and administered in Chancery a distinct code of laws by which the enjoyment and alienation of property was regulated on principles very different from those of the Common law. Moreover, instead of remaining a kind of acting committee of the Council, by the reign of Edward IV the Chancellor himself conducted the business of his court and formulated its decrees.

17 Ric. II. c. 6.

But with the establishment of the Chancellor's separate jurisdiction, the Courts of Common law took the place of Parliament as plaintiffs against the action of Chancery. And this on two grounds. (1) In the first place, the common lawyers joined issue with Chancery on the *kind of law* which was administered by that court. Now, although high legal opinion can be quoted in support of the view that the Chancellor was guided merely by personal discretion in his judgements; yet beneath such discretion are to be found two leading principles which, in some degree or other, he made the source of his decisions. The first of these was (*a*) *the Roman law*, which included the dictates both of *equity* as set forth in the Civil law (especially since the refusal of the common lawyers to allow its efficacy in their courts), and those also of *conscience*, which had been a monopoly of the Canon law until the lay lawyers succeeded in removing from the ecclesiastical courts the cognizance of all such cases where laymen were concerned. Henceforth Council or Chancery alone could hear such cases. To this should be added (*b*) *Precedents*, especially after the commencement of the publication of Year Books or reports of adjudicated cases. Of these the first instance in Common law comes from the reign of Edward I ; while the earliest Chancery reports date from Henry V. But it is to the Tudor times and to the development and concentration of the legal functions

Chancery and the Common Law Courts.

of the Chancellor that we have to look for the full growth of this force. The changes made in the law of property by the Statutes of Uses (1535-6) and Wills (1540), and the changes made in its possession by the dissolution of the monasteries, rendered necessary the appointment of a regularly trained lawyer to the Chancery. Thus Wolsey's successor was Sir Thomas More. But owing to the ignorance of the Civil law displayed by these non-ecclesiastical Chancellors, precedents assumed such an increasing importance that, under Elizabeth, they began to be authoritatively published ; and the extent of their influence may be measured by the fact that, under Charles I, the Chancellor refused to interfere in a case because there was no precedent to guide him.

(2) A much more serious cause of complaint against Chancery was its desire to *supervise the judgements of the Courts of Common law.* This it attempted to do by the issue of *injunctions* prohibiting plaintiffs from proceeding with actions at common law, or of *executions* on judgements obtained at common law in cases where the legal claims seemed to be against equity or conscience. So long as the Chancellor was a great political official, the protests of the common lawyers were ineffectual ; but under the Tudors, while the position of the Chancellor was reduced, the Common law was strengthened by the introduction of new remedies in competition with Chancery, and by the abolition (through the Statute of Uses) of much of the Chancellor's early jurisdiction. In James I's reign, therefore, the common lawyers determined to bring matters to an issue. Two notorious swindlers, named *Glanville* and *Allen*, who had obtained judgement by fraud in the common law-courts, had been punished in Chancery. Chief Justice Coke persuaded the culprits to indict the prosecutors and their counsel for 'praemunire,' because they had called in question a judgement of the King's Court. But, on the appeal of the Chancellor, the king referred the matter to the Attorney-General, Bacon, and other lawyers, who decided in favour of the Chancellor's power.[1] Henceforth, down to the Judicature Act of 1873, recognition was given to the right of the Chancellor to grant injunctions against suits at law and against the enforcements of judgements obtained in the common-law courts.

But the position of Chancery itself from this time underwent

[1] Holdsworth, 246-250.

a considerable change. Hitherto there had been no regular Changes in appeal *against the decisions of the Chancellor.* The only course Chancery. open to suitors was a petition to Parliament or the Crown, until the case of *Shirley* v. *Fagg* established the right of such 1675. appeal *to the House of Lords.* At the same time, the friends of the Common law did everything in their power so to ameliorate the condition of the Common law as to lessen the reasons for the interference of the Chancellor. Two most important results were obtained—(1) owing to the action of two great Chancellors, Lords Hardwicke and Eldon, *the Chancellor's* 1736-1756. *discretion was placed within definable limits.* From the time of the latter 'the development of equity was effected ostensibly and, in the great majority of cases, actually by strict deduction from the principles to be discovered in decided cases, and the work of subsequent Chancery judges has been, for the most part, confined, as Lord Eldon's was, to tracing out these 1801-1827. principles into detail and to rationalizing them by repeated review and definition.'[1] (2) Owing also to the obstinate [1] Kerly's refusal of Lord Eldon to surrender any branch of equitable *Hist. of* jurisdiction, the great improvement in the remedies given *Equity,* by the Common law made the jurisdiction of Chancery no 182. longer supplementary to, but merely concurrent with that of Cf. also the Courts of Common law. As a consequence, the reform *Ancient* of Chancery procedure in 1833, followed by that of the *Law,* 69. Common law in 1852 and 1854, ended finally in *the fusion of Common law and Equity* by the first Judicature Act of 1873. The result of this and subsequent supplementary Acts has been to consolidate all the existing superior courts into one Supreme Court of Judicature, consisting of two primary divisions—(a) the High Court of Justice consisting of three subdivisions—Chancery; Queen's Bench; Probate, Divorce and Admiralty: (b) the Court of Appeal from the decisions of the judges of each of these subdivisions.

CHAPTER VIII

POLICE AND LOCAL ADMINISTRATION

Early
System of
Police.

§ 57. IT is difficult to carry our minds back to a time when every one who was not a blood relation, either real or supposed, was an enemy with whom no terms should be kept; or even to the comparatively late period when the peace or guarantee for order lapsed on the death of the king from whose sanction it was supposed to emanate, until the election of his successor. This 'peace' has been defined as the primitive alliance for mutual good behaviour, a breach of which ipso facto outlawed the transgressor until he had taken measures to repair it.[1] It seems to have consisted of three grades. For, firstly, there lay upon the land the *frith* which it was the duty of the local courts of hundred and shire to maintain. Besides this there was the *grith* or special protection under the guarantee of some powerful individual, such as was obtained by commendation. But even beyond these we find mention of a *mund* or personal guardianship, such as a lord would exercise over his household and immediate dependents. According to the closeness of an individual's relations to the guardians of the peace, the protection which he could rely on would increase in effectiveness. Thus the growth of commendation, which was so prominent a feature of the waning Anglo-Saxon monarchy, would result in the gradual substitution of the king's or thegn's grith for the old national frith which was too vague to afford adequate security in dangerous times. The old courts and their officials remained; but the law which they applied would tend to emanate from the king and witan rather than to remain a mere declaration of national customs by the local courts. This transition was not completely effected until after the Norman Conquest: yet in the last century of Anglo-Saxon

[1] *S. C. H.* § 72.

390

rule there are sufficient indications of the direction in which things were tending. Thus Æthelstan's laws mention the king's *oferhyrnes* or a special penalty to be paid for contempt of the royal jurisdiction:[1] under Eadmund we find an oath of fealty;[2] and so great was the desire to obtain justice at first hand from the Crown, that both Eadgar and Cnut were obliged to enforce resort in the first instance to the local court.[3]

These were means of protection for the weak and the innocent. More than one device was necessary in order to secure the guilty. The first in point of moral force and the least modern in idea, was an attempt to bind men's consciences and to enlist them on the side of order, by the universal *enforcement of an oath for the maintenance of peace*. Thus Eadmund's Oath of Fealty demands 'ut nemo concelet hoc (i.e. treasonable feelings) in fratre vel proximo suo plus quam in extraneo.'[4] Cnut desires 'that every man above xii years old make oath that he will neither be a thief nor cognizant of theft.'[5] Nor did this method die out at the Conquest; for in 1195 knights are assigned or appointed to exact a similar oath from all above the age of fifteen years.[6]

Doubtless a more effective way was the promotion of a comprehensive *system of suretyship and registration*. Now, in the earliest organized communities the basis of any such system is naturally the family. But how define the family? What may be called the current theory seeks the foundation of kinship among the Teutonic races in a power analogous to the Roman 'patria potestas.' According to this the father exercised an absolute power over all his male children and his wife, and over his female children until their marriage, when they exchanged his authority for that of the head of the family which they entered.[7] But this is far too absolute a statement. The importance of these family groups in early Teutonic law arises from the joint responsibility of all their members; for, wrong done to or by an individual member is the concern of all the group. But these groups were not mutually exclusive. In England it is abundantly clear that marriage did not sever the bond between the woman and her kinsfolk. In this the Leges Henrici Primi, late though they are, may be regarded as sufficiently indicative of English

---

[1] *S. C.* 66. § 20.

[2] *Ibid.* 67. § 1.

[3] *Ibid.* 71, cap. 2, and 73, cap. 17.

Oath for maintenance of the peace.

[4] *Ibid.* 67. § 1.

[5] *Ibid.* 74, cap. 21.

[6] *Ibid.* 264.

Suretyship and Registration.

(a) Responsibility of the Kindred.

[7] Maine, *Ancient Law,* 135 et seq.

custom, and several passages show that her blood kinsmen were responsible for a married woman's misdeeds, that they received her wergild, and even that her husband could not remove her away from the neighbourhood of the kinsfolk without giving them security that he would treat her well. Again, in the important test of the wergild a man's paternal kindred share in the payment or the receipt with his maternal kindred in the proportion of two to one, while in the absence of kin on the father's side a law of Ælfred allots a two-thirds share to the maternal kindred.[1] Thus every person was a member of two maegthe or family groups, though not in equal degree. But it does not follow from this that these groups were not organized.[2] There is no trace of a head of the kin on English soil; but, so far as place names can take us, the original settlements seem to have been made by kinsfolk, and the Anglo-Saxon laws contain numerous traces of the continued use of the family tie in the last resort. Thus a law of Æthelstan ordains that the kin must find a lord for a lordless man.[3] But on the whole it remains true that the political importance of the tie of kindred is prehistoric. The permanent responsibility which, we have seen, did not lie upon the family, was otherwise provided for. In early German law a lord was absolutely responsible for the acts of his slaves, and probably a householder would have to answer for the free inmates of his house. But the lord's free tenants were not so kept in check; though possibly he might have to produce them in court to meet an accusation. It has been thought that the Anglo-Saxon laws show an attempt on the part of the lords to get rid of this liability. Thus a law of Æthelstan[4] allows them to substitute for such liability the duty of keeping their men in groups, each of which should be jointly responsible for the production of all its members. It may be that in this enactment is to be found the much disputed origin of the system of Frankpledge.[5]

The Laws of Eadward the Confessor speak, in connection with the tenmannetale or frithborg, as it is called elsewhere in England, of a system of mutual responsibility founded on a division into numerical groups of ten.[6] But this whole account may be regarded as utterly apocryphal. The date of the compilation has been placed at about 1130, and it is said

[1] *S. C.* 63. § 27.

[2] Cf. *P. and M.* ii. 239.

[3] *S. C.* 66. § 2.

[4] *Ibid.* 66. § 7.

[5] *P. and M.* ii. 528.

(*b*) Mutual responsibility.

[6] *S. C.* 77.

to represent 'private work of a bad and untrustworthy kind.'[1]
Apart from this, however, there is plenty of evidence for the
existence of responsible groups among the Anglo-Saxons. We
have already noticed a law of Æthelstan's day, which would
affect the rural districts, the estates of great lords. But this
may have been preceded by the regulation of similar groups in
the few burhs or towns of which the country as yet could boast.
We find mention of gilds in Ælfred's day ; and in Æthelstan's
time the document known as the ' Judicia Civitatis Lundoniæ '[2]
provides for the division of the inhabitants of London into
bodies of ten or twelve who are associated together for some
public obligations : while a law of Æthelstan provides that any
one thrice failing to attend the gemot (possibly the shire moot)[3]
is to pay the 'king's oferhyrnes' which he has thereby incurred,
and is to be put in borh by the chief men of the burh.[4] Similarly Eadmund provides that all suspects are to be brought ' sub
plegio.'[5]   These may be tentative attempts at police supervision applied to special places and special persons. Under
Eadgar, as we might expect, these regulations are given a more
general application. Thus, every man 'both within the burhs
and without the burhs' is to have a borh which is 'to bring
and hold him to every justice,' and to be responsible for his
non-appearance.[6] This provision is repeated by Æthelred
with a special application to the case of freemen, and with
a renewal of the old law that every lord shall be answerable for
his own household.[7] Finally, Cnut enacts that every freeman
be brought into a hundred and into a tithing, and that every
one be brought into a hundred and in borh,[8] a distinction
which is borne out by the division of the hundred in the Leges
Henrici Primi into tithings and lord's pledges[9] or, as they are
called in another passage, free pledges.

All this evidence seems to make it probable that an arrangement by groups for police purposes was of comparatively early
origin. A doubt seems to hang about the meaning of the
word ' borh' : but although there are passages in which we seem
almost forced to give it a personal application, analogy and
later actual use make it probable that the word denotes some
kind of mutually responsible group or organized police district.
We have seen that Cnut's laws rank it alongside of the tithing.
Now, the name *tithing*[10] would seem to suggest that it was part

[1] *P. and M.* i. 81.

[2] *S. C.* 67.

[3] Cf. *Domesday*, 185.

[4] *S. C.* 66. § 20.

[5] *Ibid.* 67.

§ 7.

[6] *Ibid.* 71, cap. 6, 72, cap. 3.

[7] *Ibid.* 72, cap. 1.

[8] *Ibid.* 73, cap. 20.

[9] *Ibid.* 105, § vi. 1, and 106, § viii. 2.

Frank-pledge.

[10] *Select Pleas in Manorial Courts*, xxx. *P. and M.* i. 554-558.

of the same system as the hundred.   When the larger organiza
tion for police purposes was described as the hundred, to the
smaller may have been applied the cognate term tithing.   Thus
in the south of England where perhaps these divisions were
first applied, they were *geographical*, and the tithing corre
sponded to a vill or part of a vill.   It is possible also that the
tithing took the place of the lord's original liability and, there
fore, comprised exactly the same area, namely, the manoria
vill.   But when the system came to be extended to parts of the
country where the lord's influence was not so strong, it would
rest on a different basis.   Thus over a large part of England
the tithing is found to denote a *personal* group of ten or twelve
individuals headed by a chief-pledge or tithing-man.   But in
either case it was the duty of the township to see that its
inhabitants were in frankpledge : when any one of them was
accused of a crime and was not forthcoming, if he was a member
of a tithing, the group was amerced ; but if he was not a
member, the township itself suffered.   This system of mutua
responsibility was enforced in two ways—by amercements for
failure of duty, and by periodical inspections which are though
to be as old certainly as the reign of Henry I.   The Assize
of Clarendon placed them in the hands of the sheriff; but
probably from the first in a large number of cases the right
was claimed and exercised by lords of manors.   The cour
held for the purpose, called the sheriff's tourn and perhaps the
manorial court leet, was apparently attended by the reeve and
four men where the tithing and vill coincided, and by the
chief pledge of each tithing where several such divisions were
contained in a vill.   In this court, as we have seen, has been
found the origin of the jury of presentment.   But it is to be
noted that this system of police supervision was not by any
means universal.   In the first place, there were severa
parts of England where it did not exist at all,—for example
probably nowhere in the ancient kingdom of Northumbria
while in the thirteenth century both Westmoreland and Shrop
shire claimed to be free of it.   Secondly, in the thirteenth
century, the legal authority of the time states that every male
of twelve years whether free or serf ought to be in frankpledge
with certain exceptions.   These are great lords, knights, clerks
freeholders, and those in mainpast, that is, in the household o

another.   But as a matter of fact, although in some boroughs—
for example, Norwich—freemen were in frankpledge, in some
shires a man's free status is given as the reason for his not
being in frankpledge ; while, further, we find that those who
were so enrolled were unfree, placed where they were by the
lord or his steward without any means of resistance on their
part.

Alongside of the frankpledge grew up the *Murdrum*.   For Murdrum.
the better protection of the Normans William I ordained that
in the case of a murdered man his lord should either produce
the homicide or pay as much of the large sum of 46 marks of
silver as he was able, the residue being made up by the
neighbouring hundred.[1]   By interpretation of the lawyers this   [1] *S. C.* 84.
came to mean that the burden of proof that the murdered man   § 3.
was not a Norman should lie upon the hundred in which the
corpse was found : otherwise the heavy fine should be exacted.
But here, as elsewhere, exemptions from its operation were
granted to favoured districts.   In the case of both Frankpledge
and Murdrum the institution was maintained solely as a method
of extorting money, long after it had lost any basis in reason.
This is the meaning of a clause added to the Charter in its
second reissue under Henry III, by which the sheriff is forbidden to hold his tourn more than twice a year or to seek
opportunities, other than those enjoyed by his predecessors
under Henry II, for taking View of Frankpledge.[2]   But further,   [2] *Ibid.*
the Barons complain in their Petition (1258) at the Parliament   346.   § 42.
of Oxford, that the sheriffs, at both annual tourns, require the
personal attendance of earls and barons who hold lands in
several districts and counties, and fine them heavily if they
do not come.[3]   Accordingly, the Provisions of Westminster   [3] *Ibia.*
(1259) release from ordinary attendance all of the rank of 3   384.   § 17.
barones, excuse them from liability in any district except that
in which they live, and enjoin the observance of the appropriate clause of the Charter.[4]   In the same way, the author of   [4] *Ibid.*
the *Dialogus de Scaccario*, writing in the reign of Henry II,   402.   § 4.
alludes to the intermingling of the free classes in the country,
which makes it impossible, a century after the Conquest, to
distinguish a Norman from an Englishman ;[5] yet we not only   [5] *Ibid.*
find the liability to the Murdrum still existing, but its use pressed   201-202.
in the most unjustifiable manner.   Thus in their Petition of

1258 the Barons again complain that, although in the tim
of dearth men are found dead from want of food, the distric

¹ S. C.
385. § 21.

is fined before the justices '*tanquam de murdro.*'¹ The system
may still have been found a useful check on violence or an ai
in the detection of crime ; for, the Provisions of Westminste
content themselves with enjoining that such fine should onl

² *Ibid.* 405.
§ 22.

be exacted in the case of those feloniously slain.²

Both these methods, although sufficiently tenacious, woul
die out or be superseded in course of time. The sheriff'
tourn and the private leet gave way to the reign of the justice
of the peace. But the idea of responsibility did not altogethe

Regula-
tions about
Vagrants.

disappear. For, meanwhile, in the case of casual stranger
whom the mediaeval law regarded with the utmost suspicion
responsibility was enforced on all who harboured them fo

³ *Ibid.*
145, § 16 ;
151, § 2 ;
375, § 4 ;
and 471,
§ 4.

more than a day.³ Doubtless such vagrants would almos
entirely consist of fugitive villans from the manors ; so that
although, on the one side, a lengthened residence in a chartered
borough was allowed, perhaps in the interests of the borough'
privileges, to confer the boon of freedom ; yet nothing must be
done to aid such restless movement. Thus by the Assize o
Clarendon the sheriff is to keep a register of all who have lef
their own shires, and if they are not to be found, their chattel

⁴ *Ibid.*
145. § 18.

are forfeit to the king.⁴ Again, a sojourner for more than one
night (§ 16) may be detained until he can find bail, or, in the
milder terms of Henry III's legislation, unless his host wil

⁵ *Ibid.*
375. § 4.

answer for him,⁵ a precaution which does not seem to have
been necessary in harvest time. The Black Death gave ar
enormous impulse to this wandering spirit, and led to strong
and afterwards discriminative legislation, the application o
which was entrusted chiefly to the holders of the new office
of justice of the peace.

Watch and
Ward.

The final regulation to be noticed is the provision made for
the detection of actual fugitives from justice. In the first place,
in Anglo-Saxon times, the duty of the modern police constable
seems to have been shared by all members of the fyrd, and,
however much or little this may have meant, no further or more
effective arrangements are found until the reign of Henry III.
In a writ of 1233 for the conservation of the peace, provision
is made for the regular nightly guard at city gates of at least
four men who shall detain strangers and give the alarm in the

ase of fugitives.[1]   The importance attached to the punish- [1] *S. C.* 362-363.
nent of a defaulting watcher is shown by his being subjected
ot to the sheriff but to the Itinerant Justices.   Writs of 1252
nd 1253 repeat and confirm these regulations, and bring them
nto connection with two important institutions—the Assize of
\rms or maintenance of the fyrd, and the Hue and Cry or
ncient method of pursuit of criminals.[2]   In a subsequent [2] *Ibid.*
hapter it will be pointed out that the fyrd was the basis of 371-372 and
he duty of watch and ward.   The *Hue and Cry* dates back to 375.
.adgar's Ordinance of the Hundred, where regulations are laid Hue and
.own for the pursuit of criminals by the entire population from Cry.
ne hundred and even one tithing to another.[3]   The same [3] *Ibid.* 70.
.ability of all to help in the arrest, which to this day forms part
f the common law of England, was applied to the boroughs
.y Æthelred.[4]   Possibly the duty of local presentment and the [4] *Ibid.* 72.
ormation and liability of the frankpledge may have obscured § ii. cap. 6.
his use of a *levée en masse* as a means of direct arrest.   But it
eappears under Richard I in connection with the oath for the
reservation of the peace.[5]   Under Henry III, in the writs [5] *Ibid.* 264.
.lready quoted, the duty is primarily entrusted to the special
igilatores or appointed watchers : twenty years later a special
 officer, the constable, is added for this very purpose.[6]   Finally, [6] *Ibid.* 372.
he whole mediaeval police system, on its active and aggressive
ide, is drawn together in Edward I's Statute of Winchester, 1285.
y which provision is made for the Assize of Arms (§ 6), the
resentment of offences (§ 1), the responsibility of the hundred
§ 2), the maintenance of watch and ward, and the levy of hue
nd cry (§ 4).   The Assize of Arms is to be carried out by the
constables ; the sheriffs raise the hue and cry and keep suspected
criminals, and the justices maintain a general and coercive supervision over the entire arrangements.[7]   [7] *Ibid.*
                                                          470-474.
   § 58. With the decay of the sheriff's power fell the system
of police of which he had been the centre.   The official who Justice of
ultimately succeeded to his place was the *Justice of the Peace*, Justice of
under whom the units of administration were the shire or the Peace.
county and the parish.   The hundred as an administrative
unit simply disappeared, and, together with the name, the
only survival of its old functions was, until lately, its liability
for damages in the event of a riot within its bounds.
   The origin of the Justice of the Peace is to be found in Origin of
                                                          the office.

Richard I's proclamation of 1195 which appointed or *assigned* knights to receive from all above the age of fifteen the oaths for the maintenance of the peace.[1]   Occasionally, under Henry III (1230, 1253, 1264), similar appointments were made.   Under Edward I there were elected in the shire courts —in 1277 *custodes;* and in 1285, to carry out the Statute of Winchester, *conservatores pacis.*   Under Edward III the system was finally established.   In 1327 the conservators of the peace were again assigned or nominated by the Crown, thus definitely becoming royal commissioners and losing all connection with the shire court.   Hitherto these officials had had merely executive power, 'they were little more than constables on a large scale.'[2]   But in 1328 for the first time they were entrusted with judicial functions; for, in connection with the execution of the Statute of Winchester, they were authorized to examine and punish evil doers.   In 1330 these magistrates might take indictments for trial before the justices of gaol delivery, and persons so indicted might not ordinarily be bailed by the sheriff.   It was an important advance in 1344 when they were made a permanent staff of royal *custodes pacis*, ready, in case of need, to be appointed 'with other wise and learned in the law' to judicial functions.   Thus these guardians of the peace had become a permanent body endowed on occasion with the duty of judges.   Finally, in 1360 'a lord and three or four of the most worthy, together with some learned in the law, were authorized to seize, examine and punish, by common or statute law, or according to their best judgement, all disturbers of the peace ; on complaint in the king's name, to hear and determine felonies, or on suspicion to arrest and imprison all dangerous persons, or to take surety for their good behaviour.'

There were now two bodies existing side by side, the shire court and the justices; and during the next century the powers of the former were gradually transferred to the newer organization.   We have seen that all the more substantial suitors of the shire court had gained exemption from attendance, and that the sheriff's judicial powers had been made over to the Itinerant Justices.   The shire court remained for the election of coroners, verderers and knights of the shire ; but to the justices sitting in quarter sessions were transferred not only all the *criminal* jurisdiction which remained to the shire court in

[1] *S. C.* 264.

1 Edw. III. st. ii. § 16.

[2] Stephen, *Hist. Crim. Law*, i. 112.

18 Edw. III. st. ii. § 2.

34 Edw. III. c. 1.

His gradual supersession of the Shire Court.

ıe fourteenth century, but even the right to hear and determine
ıe pleas of the crown.   Indeed, all crimes and felonies, except
ˉeason, were by their commission conferred upon the assembled
ıstices, until Quarter Sessions became a serious rival to the
tinerant Justices or, as they were now called, the Judges of
ʌssize.[1]   But after the Tudor period it became customary to
ˌeserve cases involving capital offences for the Judges of Assize ;
lthough the jurisdiction of Quarter Sessions in such matters
ˉas not abrogated until 1842.   Again, although essentially
ˑriminal tribunals, Quarter Sessions had originally a limited
ıuthority in *civil* suits, which during the sixteenth century had
ˌeen increased, until here too the power of the justices
ˌecame practically coordinate with that of the Assizes.[2]   This,
ˌowever, was a weak point and, in the present century, led to
he establishment of the so-called County Courts.   But an
ˌqually important side of the powers of the general body of
ˌstices dealt with local administration.   Quarter Sessions
ˌecame the executive and *administrative* body for the shire.[3]
ʌll the old local officials became the servants of the justices
ˌnd often their nominees.   The sheriffs themselves, the
ˌonstables[4] and manorial bailiffs were forced to attend their
ˌrders and to execute their degrees : the coroner was made
ˌnswerable to them.   Again, they took the place of the sheriff
ˌnd their sessions the place of the shire court, as the medium
ˌf communication between the Crown and the people.   All
ˌetters from the Council were addressed to them, and under
he Stuarts they were used as the agents of government in the
ˌemands for purveyance, benevolences, forced loans and ship
ˌoney.   They were also the *fiscal* board of the shire, with the
ˌuty of assessing, levying and superintending the expenditure
ˌf a county rate.   And finally, their general administrative
ıuthority touched such important matters as the settlement
ˌf wages[5] and of prices, the enforcement of laws against
ˌecusants and nonconformists,[6] the maintenance of bridges,
ˌoads for the most part, prisons and public buildings of all
ˌinds.   Indeed, from the first the justice seems to have
ˌssumed the position which has been aptly described as that
ˌf 'the State's man-of-all-work.'

   Thus was gradually consolidated that monopoly of the upper
lass in administration, that local rule of the landed gentry,

[1] Prothero, 145.

[5] & 6 Vict. c. 38.

[2] *Ibid.* 76, 90, 96.

[3] *Ibid.* Index sub voc. *Justices of the Peace.*

[4] *Ibid.* 146, 148.

[5] *Ibid.* 48.

[6] *Ibid.* Index sub voc. *Recusants.*

which foreigners rather than native writers have noted a
so characteristic of the modern English constitution.[1] In
origin and theory the justices were mere delegates of the royal
power, appointed perhaps originally by the king, then under
the Tudors by the Chancellor, and at present by the Crown
on the recommendation of the Lord Lieutenant of the shire
though removable for misconduct by the Chancellor. Up to
the middle of the fifteenth century the qualification for the
office was vaguely stated as worthiness or sufficiency ; but in
1440 the appointment of men of small estate who used the
office merely for purposes of extortion, caused a definite requirement of lands or tenements to the value of £20 a year, the
original amount of a knight's fee. Three centuries later this
was raised to £100 in land or houses except in the case of
certain individuals exempted by exalted birth or legal training.
Originally and in accordance with statute, a fixed payment of
four shillings a day during sessions was made to the justices
while under Elizabeth the Statute of Apprenticeship allowed
them five shillings a day for their work in connection with the
statute.[2] Now, however the duty is entirely honorary. The
object of all later statutes was to place the office in the hands
of men who would not need payment, and who would, therefore,
presumably be above taking bribes. As a proof of this, the
Act of 1360 had said nothing about numbers : but in 1388
was imposed a statutable limit of six justices besides the Judges
of Assize, who were always included in the commission. But
this restriction was soon disregarded. Towards the close of
Elizabeth's reign no less than fifty-five are enumerated in
Devonshire alone. The smallest counties now contain many
more than six ; while the most numerous magistracy—that of
Lancashire—reaches to more than 800. The whole number
must be little short of 20,000 ; but considerably less than half
of these are ' active ' justices who have taken the requisite oaths
and received from Chancery the necessary writ of power. The
extent of the jurisdiction entrusted to the justices was only
gradually determined by a number of individual statutes which
conferred on them special powers. In this way by the time of
Elizabeth [3] the commission of the justices had become so stuffed
with the substance of these individual statutes that it was confused and often unintelligible ; so that a writer feared lest the

[1] E.g. Dr. Gneist and M. Boutmy.

Appoint-
ment and
qualifica-
tion.

18 Hen. VI. c. 11.

18 Geo. II.

12 Ric. II. c. 10.

[2] Prothero, 53.

12 Ric. II. c. 10.

1592.

[3] Ibid. 144-147.

backs of the justices would be broken by these 'not loads but stacks of statutes.' The result was that, in **1590**, Sir Christopher Wray, Chief Justice of the Queen's Bench, drew up a new form of commission, which remains practically unaltered to the present day.[1] In this is recognized the double capacity of the justices as administrators, by the authority given them to execute all statutes for the maintenance of the peace without enumerating such enactments individually; and as judicial officers, by the power conferred on any two justices to hear and determine, by the oath of good and lawful men of the county, a number of offences enumerated in the commission. This latter power at first depended on a provision that one of the justices (quorum) who heard such cases should be of a select number whose names were expressly repeated in the document because they were, as the statute of 1360 had demanded, 'learned in the law.' In consequence of this clause it was, until comparatively lately, customary to omit a few names from those of the quorum 'for the sake of propriety.' Now, however, all the commissioned justices are included, so that the expression has entirely lost its meaning. But it is to be noticed that, despite the apparently complete character of this commission, it was considered necessary to confirm by definite statute powers long exercised by the justices. Thus, in earlier days the power of preliminary inquiry, though exercised almost from the institution of the office, was not conferred by statute until 1554. Again, the law gave the justices no other authority for the apprehension of offenders than was by the Common law inherent in every constable and, indeed, in every private person. It has been suggested that the power to issue warrants of arrest was the outcome of the old duty which lay upon local officers of starting the hue and cry. However that may be, such power of arrest and examination has now been regulated by a series of statutes beginning from the reign of George I. A foreign writer[2] has remarked that the most characteristic trait of this new jurisdiction is its utter independence of a feudal origin. It is a revocable delegation, not a dismemberment, of the judicial authority of the Crown. The possession of landed property is not in theory, though it is in practice, the basis of the power of a justice of the peace; but the limits of his

[1] Prothero, 147-149.

[2] 1 & 2 Phil. & Mary, c. 13.

[3] Boutmy *Eng. Const.* (trans.) 114.

jurisdiction are quite independent of such a consideration, which, on the other hand, was of the essence of feudal authority. It is only to be expected, therefore, that the development of the office of justice of the peace is chiefly to be traced to the period of the definite break-up of feudal jurisdictions. It is to the time of the Tudors, then, that we must look for the reconstruction of English local government on the ruins of the sheriff and the manor. But on the one side, the shire remains the unit of jurisdiction. Thus under Henry VIII a new official, a Lord Lieutenant, was appointed to take up the military duties of the sheriff. He was, and is generally, like the old ealdorman, a local nobleman, and also *custos rotulorum*, or keeper of the records, in which capacity he is the head of the justices for the county. In 1871, however, his military duties were taken away and revested in the Crown. In the same way the justices were appointed for the whole shire, though convenience decided that for ordinary purposes their activity should be limited to their respective neighbourhoods. But it was not until 1828 that such division was recognized by statute. Again, even within a narrower limit there are certain duties which can be performed by a single justice. It is necessary, therefore, in speaking of the justices of the peace, to distinguish between the powers of the single justice, of Petty or Special Sessions, and of Quarter or General Sessions.

Powers of a single justice.

As an administrator, *the single justice*, in his primary capacity of conservator of the peace, can issue warrants of all kinds, can give orders to police constables for the preservation of the peace and, on extreme occasions under the so-called Riot Act, can himself intervene. On him also has been laid an immense variety of police regulative duties, the number of which can only be adequately realized from practical knowledge. In his second capacity of judge, the justice acquired the duty of the sheriff in his tourn of conducting preliminary examinations of persons charged with crimes and felonies. Of this

1 Edw. IV. c. 2.

the sheriff was deprived in 1461 and, as we have seen, the justices used the power long before it was conferred on them by statute in 1554. The further power of hearing and determining minor criminal cases without the aid of a jury was wholly the creation of statutes. It grew up in a curiously accidental fashion. Statute after statute prescribed that this

or that petty offence might be punished sometimes by one
justice, sometimes by two or more; but very seldom was the
slightest hint given as to how, or when, or where, the case
was to be tried.   Only in the present century have we begun
to think of the summary jurisdiction as normal, and to regulate
by general statutes the mode in which it must be exercised.
There are traces of this power even under the Tudors, but it
was chiefly used by the justices in their capacity of 'mere
police or administrative agents.'   But gradually a regular procedure was developed, helped by the definite authority
conferred by statute, until in 1879 such authority was reduced
to cases which did not involve more than a fortnight's
imprisonment or a fine of twenty shillings.

But, in the majority of cases, matters to be dealt with out
of Quarter Sessions were entrusted by statute to two or more
justices.   A meeting for this purpose was known as *Petty*
Sessions; while, if there were duties to be performed at fixed
times, the meetings for their discharge were called 'special
or special petty sessions.'   In practice, however, the two were
amalgamated.   This answered roughly to the old hundred
jurisdiction, and may be paralleled by the more recent attempt
to make the divisions for such sessions correspond with the
modern poor-law union.   In this way the justices, though
nominally appointed for the whole shire, now discharge a great
portion of their work in the petty sessional division in which
they reside; and have for that division a court-house, a chairman and a regularly constituted 'bench.'   The duties of the
magistrates in petty sessions are very like those which the
single magistrate is competent to discharge, but apply to cases
which an individual has no power to touch.   The justice is
mostly of a penal kind, involving the infliction of fines or
imprisonment.   So far as it is summary, it is dependent
entirely upon statute; but the extent of it may be judged from
the fact that more than 700,000 cases are annually so decided;
while, even in matters accounted truly criminal, the cases so
tried in every department of justice outnumber those to which
a jury is applied.   But the court has also a real civil jurisdiction in certain limited cases which need not here be specified.
Of these even the recently formed County Courts have not
robbed it.   A very large portion of its power was administrative,

Petty
Sessions.

especially by way of supervision, though this was seriously
curtailed by the creation of County Councils. Thus, to the
justices in petty sessions was given the important power of
granting licences of all kinds,[1] much of which they still retain,
while in their hands rested the appointment of all manner
of local officials, overseers of the poor and of highways, parish
and county constables and others.

Above the petty and special sessions tower the *Quarter
Sessions* consisting, in theory, of all the justices in the shire,
although any two may hold a legal session. Of the *quorum*
mention has been made. In 1362 it was enacted that the
justices should make their sessions four times a year, and
in 1388 this was confirmed and enforced, if necessary, by
penalties. Under Henry IV provision was made for other
meetings of the same body, and these were in contradistinction
called General Sessions. These distinctions, however, are of
no importance; for, powers given to the justices by statute
may in almost every case be exercised indifferently in both
assemblies. The high powers which Quarter Sessions exercised
until recently have been already noted. But although the
justices have been deprived of power of life and death, of the
trial of offences involving penal servitude for life, of many of
the more serious misdemeanours, such as perjury, forgery
and others; yet three-quarters of the criminal trials still take
place in borough and county sessions, so that they exercise
a very real, though diminished, power. Such cases are of
course tried with a petty jury on presentation by the grand
jury. But the Quarter Sessions also hears without jury appeals
from the summary jurisdiction of individual magistrates or of
petty sessions. Perhaps enough has been said already as to
the administrative work of the Quarter Sessions. It is sufficient
to repeat that until lately it formed a general court of appeal
on all fiscal and regulative matters connected with the shire.
But the Act establishing the *County Councils*, which came
into force in April, 1889, while leaving to the justices of the
peace 'their judicial authority together with the general
execution of certain licence laws, and a share in the
management of the county police,' transferred to a more
or less popularly-elected body, called a County Council,
almost all the general administrative functions, such as the

---

[1] Cf. Pro-
thero, 102,
187, 264.

Quarter
Sessions.

36 Edw.
III. st. 1.
§ 12.
21 Ric. II.
c. 10.

County
Councils.
51 & 52
Vict. c. 41.

control of local finance, of pauper lunatic asylums, of re-
formatory and industrial schools, of county buildings and
property, the jurisdiction over weights and measures, roads
and bridges, and the appointment of many county officers,
such as the coroner.[1]   Other officials, such as the clerk of
the peace and the chief constable, are appointed, and the
latter, together with the county police force, is supervised,
by a joint committee of the Quarter Sessions and the County
Council.

[1] Redlich and Hurst, ii. 64 et seq.

It has been noticed that the weakest point in the position
of the justices was their limited jurisdiction in civil cases.
Indeed, up to 1846, justice in such cases 'was, as a rule, only
to be obtained at Westminster, or by means of an action begun
at Westminster and tried under a commission of assize on
circuit.'[2]   During the last century a remedy was attempted by
'the occasional and sporadic creation of little courts, courts of
conscience or courts of requests: about a hundred of these were
erected as now this town, now that, made its voice heard.   In
general a body of unpaid commissioners, of local tradesmen or
the like, was empowered to adjudicate without jury upon very
small debts.'[3]   The first general remedy was an Act of 1846
which divided the country into circuits, to each of which was
assigned a separate judge.   These circuit divisions had no
reference to the counties, so that the title of County Courts is
an entire misnomer.   Moreover, each circuit is divided into
districts, and each district has a separate court.   At first courts
were limited to the recovery of small debts; but their
jurisdiction has been gradually extended by statute until they
now form a real relief to the judges of the High Court.   The
judges of these courts are appointed and are dismissible by
the Lord Chancellor.   Appeals from their decisions go to the
High Court and, with the leave of the judges there, to the
Court of Appeal, and finally to the House of Lords.

So-called County Courts.

[2] Anson, 449.

[3] Maitland, Justice and Police, 23.

Apart from this general system, and existing before it, are
some twenty-seven *local courts of record*, each with a history of
its own.   Such are the Chancery of the Duchy of Lancaster,
the Lord Mayor's Court in London, the Hundred Court of
Salford, the Liverpool Court of Passage, the Tolzey and Pie
Poudre Court at Bristol, beside those in a few other chartered
boroughs.[4]

[4] For list, see Holdsworth, 309, and note.

Control
over
Justices
of the
Peace,

Finally, it is to be noticed that the multifarious duties which, before 1889, were imposed on the justices, brought them under the supervising control of the Privy Council, Home Office, Board of Trade, and Local Government Board when these latter departments were created; while in their judicial capacity they have been amenable to the Court of King's Bench and, since 1873, to the High Court of Justice. This control is exercised in three ways. By a writ of *mandamus* the High Court can order the justices to hear cases which are within their jurisdiction; by writ of *prohibition* it can prevent them from interfering in matters beyond their province; while by writ of *certiorari* it can call up any case in which there has been, or there is danger of, a failure of justice.

Vill or
Township.

§ 59. In speaking of the local courts whose business it was to administer the common law, no mention was made of the division which Dr. Stubbs calls 'the unit of the constitutional machinery, the simplest form of social organization.'[1] It has been usual with modern historians to call this division the Township; but the only evidence at our command would lead us to give this name to the inhabitants and not to the district itself.[2] The English name for the latter was Tún; but to avoid the confusion which would arise from the use of a word with so definite a modern meaning, it will be convenient to adapt the Latin equivalent—Villa—and to call it VILL.[3] Whether this represented a free village community or, as the Latin equivalent implies, the estate of an individual owner, is a matter of considerable dispute. At any rate, it seems practically certain that there is no direct evidence for the existence of a court belonging to the vill. And herein lies the great difficulty in speaking of the vill; for as soon as we get evidence of it, we find it being treated as an unit of public law and yet apparently without any organization of its own.[4] The only organization is that of the manor, and although *vill and manor* were often spoken of as if they were interchangeable terms and, in the majority of cases, may originally have coincided, yet when our records really begin, they were *by no means necessarily identical.*[5] For, until the Statute Quia Emptores the creation of new tenants would cause incessant change in the boundaries of particular manors; while, as soon as a centralized system of government was fairly established, the creation of new vills

[1] *S. C. H.*
§ 39.

[2] Ashley,
*The A. S.
Township*
in Quart.
Journ.
Econ. viii.
345.

[3] *P. and M.*
i. 550.

[4] *Ibid.*
554.

[5] *Ibid.*
596.

1290.

without permission would have subjected the whole administrative arrangement of the country to constant alteration.
Thus in the south of England a vill would often contain several
manors, each with its separate court; and even in the north
where the manors were so large that the position was exactly
reversed, the vills were kept apart in the action of the manorial
court which managed the business connected with them.
But it is further to be remarked, though here we are on more
disputable ground, that it is *not at all certain that the vill and the*
parish corresponded. It is usual to regard the parish as merely
the ecclesiastical side of the vill, and as having supplied in its
vestry for lay purposes the organization which was wanting to
the vill. It has, however, been lately asserted that until the
time of the Tudors it was a purely ecclesiastical district, and
that there is no earlier proof of its use for purposes of civil
government.[1]

But in any case the vill was an unit of public law, that is,
upon it were laid both duties and liabilities. As to its *duties*[2]—
the priest, the reeve and four men of each vill had to attend
a number of local courts—the ordinary courts of hundred
and shire, the sheriff's tourn and the special court held at
long intervals to meet the king's judges on circuit: again,
upon the vill lay the duty of seeing that all its members who
were liable were in frankpledge and, if it corresponded to
a tithing, of being responsible for any of its members who
were suspected of crime; moreover, as a police district the
vill was responsible for the arrest, the pursuit and the safe
custody of all suspected malefactors, while finally, as an unit
for the Assize of Arms, it was expressly endowed with a
constable and obliged to keep arms ready for use. But this
was a comparatively late addition to its *liabilities;*[3] for already
it was bound, as a district, to contribute to fines and amercements, such as the Murdrum, and under this pretence it was
often subjected to the unlawful exactions of the sheriff or the
bailiff of the hundred. It was probably a result of this liability
that the inhabitants of the vill — the township, for so we
may justifiably use the word—came to be treated as a body
capable of being amerced for the commission of common
misdeeds. But if vill and manor did not as a rule coincide and
yet the vill is the recognized unit of public law, while the manor

[1] *P. and M.*
i. 548, 603;
cf. also
Maitland
on *Survi-*
val of
Archaic
Communi-
ties in Law
Quart. Rev.
ix. 227.

[2] *P. and M.*
i. 550-552.
Duties and
liabilities
of the
township.

[3] *Ibid.*
552-553.

has the organization, it becomes important to ascertain *how these duties and liabilities of the vill were apportioned* among its inhabitants.[1]   The most important duty to be provided for was that of supplying representatives to the various local courts.   This seems to have been arranged between the various manors of which the vill was composed, each supplying one or more of the four men who were required to go, and the reeve being the reeve of one of the manors; while within each manor the duty was discharged in the same way as the duty of ordinary suit to the local courts—by a definite tenant or tenants who occupied their holdings by virtue of such suit of court.   A much more difficult matter would be the allotment of financial liabilities whether permanent or accidental.   But for all such purposes each vill seems to have borne a definitely known relation towards the hundred, as did each hundred towards the shire.   Then within each vill the share of the vill was permanently apportioned among the various manors; though this was only a private arrangement of the lords of the various manors, and the men of the vill would probably be 'jointly and severally' liable for the whole sum charged upon it.   In course of time this method even extended to the taxation of movable property and, instead of a fresh assessment on each occasion by a few chosen inhabitants, the sum at which the whole vill was rated had become fixed, a proportion of that sum was demanded and it was apportioned among the various inhabitants.

Meanwhile, it was the vill and not the manor, which formed the ecclesiastical unit of the parish.   At whatever date we may believe the vestry to have arisen, it was apparently the first assembly of the vill as such; so that with the decay of the manorial system and in the reconstruction of local government under the Tudors it is not wonderful that the vestry became endowed with civil functions.   Thus, owing to the decay of the sheriff's tourn and the private leets, duties, such as the maintenance of the roads and bridges, were placed upon a new basis. Hitherto the neglect of the local court in such matters was met by its indictment and presentment before the King's Bench or the Itinerant Justices.   Under Henry VIII the General Sessions of the Justices of the Peace were placed for this purpose on a level with the other two.   Under Mary a

[1] *P. and M.* i. 600-604.

The Vestry.

22 Hen. VIII. c. 5, § 1. 2 & 3 Phil. & Mary, c. 8.

surveyor of highways was to be elected by the vestry, who could levy on all individual owners in the parish a rate in kind, such as the loan of a cart or actual manual labour, for the repair of the local highways. In course of time this became commuted into a money payment. The manner of assessing and levying this and all parochial rates (for the parish now became the unit of local taxation) was copied from the Church rate. This, as being originally a voluntary contribution for the maintenance of the building of the church, needed the consent of the parish assembled in vestry meeting. The earliest instance of such levy is in the reign of Edward III. The basis for these grants seems to have been the Christian household in proportion to the amount of its possessions. From the first no distinctions were made between owner-ship and occupation, residence and non-residence. All other parochial taxes tended to conform to this model and were assessed upon this basis, whether it was the highway rate already mentioned or the even more important poor rate.

It is as the *unit for the management and relief of the poor* that under the Tudors the Parish assumed the greatest prominence. Something has been said already of the early laws of vagrancy. The reason of their severity is to be found in the supposition of mediaeval life that every man was a member of a group, whether family, gild or manor, and it was the duty of that group to relieve his wants. The vagrant poor were composed of two classes—*professional beggars*, such as the friars, who would not be included among those seriously in want ; for, 'where mendicancy was no disgrace, alms-giving was likely to be considered the most necessary and the most ordinary of the virtues' : and, secondly, *valiant labourers* wandering about in search of work. Neither were these among the needy classes. 'The vagrancy of the times did not imply the distress of the labourers, but their prosperity. The scarcity of labour allowed of high wages, and the vagrant labourer of the time seems never to have been satisfied, but was always wandering in search of still higher wages.'[1] The class of the really destitute, then, was very small. It must have consisted merely, in the towns, of craftsmen who could not procure admission into a gild ; and in the country, of the small,

Parochial Relief of the Poor. (1) Before 1601.

Mediaeval Poverty.

[1] Toynbee, *Industrial Revolution*, 97.

1349.

though growing, class of free but landless labourers. The Statute, or rather Ordinance, of Labourers which first deals comprehensively with this vagrancy, has nothing to do with the maintenance of the poor. It was called for by that restlessness of the 'valiant labourer' which resulted from the scarcity of labour after the Black Death, and thus its object was to deal with the able-bodied vagrant by forbidding the bestowal of alms, fixing his wages and preventing him from migrating. Indeed, all the efforts of mediaeval legislators in the matter aimed at enacting a 'vagrancy law and not a poor law.'[1] It is under Richard II that we find the first recognition of a distinction between the impotent and the able-bodied poor.[2] The Act of **1388** seems to prove that society had outgrown the organization of the old social and economic groups. The increase in the class of real paupers necessitated a new attitude on the part of the State towards the individual ; in future the communication between the two must be direct, not through the medium of groups which were no longer self-sufficient. For the present this new relation extends only to regulated permission. An able-bodied man who was out of work might get leave to migrate elsewhere if he could obtain a definite engagement : the impotent were to remain where they were at the time of the passing of the Act ; and if the inhabitants were unwilling to support them, they were to go to other towns within the hundred or to their birthplace, and there to abide for the remainder of their lives.

During the next two centuries able-bodied pauperism became one of the most serious features of English social history. 'In the sixteenth century,' it has been said, 'the "beggars" became a positive terror to quiet folk . . . In the rural districts the inroads of beggars resembled those of tramps in parts of America to-day.'[3] The chief reason was, no doubt, the transformation of large portions of arable into pasture to meet the growing demand for English wool. The full effect of this would not appear until the cessation of the French wars removed the greatest outlet for the energies of the surplus and restless portion of the population. Scarcely less effective in this direction would be the break-up of the retinues of great nobles which had formed so important a feature of the fifteenth century, by Henry VII's legislation and the

[1] Ashley, *Econ. Hist.* I. pt. ii. 340 ; and *Report on Poor Laws* (1834), 4.

[2] Cunning-ham, *Eng. Ind. and Com.* i. § 120. 12 Ric. II. c. 7.

Growth of Poverty.

[3] Ashley, *Econ. Hist.* I. pt. ii. 351.

action of the Star Chamber; the change in manufacture from the gild system working for a local market, to what has been called 'the domestic system' supplying the whole of Western Europe, and bringing with it 'additional danger of glut and cessation of employment, owing to the greater fluctuations of demand';[1] the rise in prices which followed the spread throughout Europe of the precious metals obtained from Mexico and Peru. It was not that methods of alleviating poverty had been wanting in the Middle Ages, nor that those methods had decayed. Even when that portion of the tithes which had originally been set apart for the relief of the poor and impotent had been otherwise bestowed, there were ample means for the relief of all existing poverty and want—the alms-giving of great persons like prelates and nobles, and of great corporations like monasteries and gilds, to say nothing of the more permanent relief afforded by the numerous hospitals —'the most characteristic form of mediaeval charity.' And although the work of the monasteries and gilds has been most unduly exaggerated, it was not so much that they had decayed as that they were quite unable to meet the distress which had grown up in spite of them.[2] The indiscriminate alms-giving has, with some exaggeration, been attributed to the mediaeval belief in the efficacy of charity for the soul of the donor irrespective of its object; but it was quite sufficient to raise and maintain a whole army of shameless idlers, whose very existence would cause the deserving poor to suffer in silence rather than to add themselves to so disreputable a crew; while there would be drawn into its ranks all the honest in intention but weak of will, who would find it easier to beg than to seek a precarious livelihood.

For a century and a half the principles of the Act of 1388 were maintained and, in such legislation as took place, merely amplified. On the one side, such Acts as those of 1427 and 1495 merely brought the Statute of Labourers of 1349 up to date by fixing the wages which were to be given to artisans and agricultural labourers respectively. On the other side, another Act of 1495 requires impotent beggars to go to the hundred where they were best known, or had been born, or had last dwelt, and not to beg outside the limits of such district. Finally, in 1531 the justices are required to assign

[1] Ashley, *Econ. Hist.* I. pt. ii. 352-356.

[2] *Ibid.* 313, 328.

Early legislative attempts to check it.

6 Hen. VI. c. 3.
11 Hen. VII. c. 22,
11 Hen. VII. c. 2.

22 Hen. VIII. c. 12.

to the impotent poor an area within which they may beg, while the able-bodied vagrant is to be whipped and sent back to the place where he was born or had last lived for three years, and there he is to put himself to labour. Five years later the futility of these measures caused a change of principle, and the Act of **1536** attempted to suppress indiscriminate alms-giving and licensed begging by directing the formation of a common fund in each locality, to which alone all voluntary alms should be given, and out of which the impotent should be relieved. It also showed an appreciation of the possible difficulty of the able-bodied in finding work by directing that not only, as in previous Acts, should such be sent to a place upon which they had some kind of claim through birth or a certain residence, but that these alms should also be employed by the local authorities in keeping them to continual labour. Any who still begged were to be punished with degrees of severity varying from a whipping and an incision on the right ear up to a felon's death for the third conviction.

27 Hen. VIII. c. 25.

During the next sixty years the law was developed both as regarded the *impotent* and the able-bodied. As regards the former, an Act of 1547, 'the offspring of terror,' directs that they shall be forcibly conveyed from constable to constable until they are brought to the place in which the former Acts required that they should dwell. The attempt of the Act of 1536 to put an end to promiscuous alms-giving was now supplemented by the direction that each curate should exhort his parishioners every Sunday to help in relieving the needy who had a claim upon the parish. The law gradually advanced from exhortation to compulsion. Thus in 1551 a book was to be kept with the names of householders and of the impotent poor, and two collectors were to be annually appointed, who, at a certain time, should persuade persons to contribute. Those who proved unwilling should be first exhorted by the minister and churchwardens, and then reasoned with by the bishop· But this was not enough. In 1563, if the bishop failed, the justices of the peace at Quarter Sessions were compulsorily to assess the recalcitrant householder at his due amount, and to enforce payment by imprisonment;[1] and finally, in 1572 the justices were to make a direct assessment, and to appoint overseers of the poor who should relieve the minister,

Gradual consolidation of the Poor Laws.
1 Edw. VI. c. 3.

5 & 6 Edw. VI. c. 2.

5 Eliz. c. 3.

[1] Prothero, 43-44.
14 Eliz. c. 5.

churchwardens and collectors of their responsibility in the matter.[1]

The treatment of the *sturdy beggar* was not so satisfactory. By the Act of 1547, such an one refusing to work was to be branded, adjudged the slave of any one who should demand him, and punished with death for a second attempt at flight. Even the impotent person who could do a certain amount of work for his own support and refused to do it, might be punished 'with chaining, beating, or otherwise.' This terrific Act was repealed in the next year so far as regarded the sturdy vagabond. But the Act of 1572, although enjoining that rogues and vagabonds shall be set to work out of the surplus of the collections made for the impotent poor, yet directs that to the idle the same severe punishments should be meted out, ranging from whipping to death, according to the frequency of the offence.[2] In 1576 a new departure was made in the licence given to the justices to establish Houses of Correction in every county, and to provide a stock of materials on which the unemployed should be set to work.[3] Unfortunately, however, these Houses of Correction seem to have been closed in most parts of England before the end of the century, possibly because the vagabondage with which they had been intended to deal had, with the increase of employment during Elizabeth's reign, ceased to be a social danger.

The two later Acts of 1597 and 1601 were practically limited to consolidating the provisions of previous Acts. Thus, as regards the *impotent poor*, while the Act of 1597 merely completed the legislation in favour of compulsory assessment by allowing the distraint of the goods of those who would not pay,[4] the Act of 1601 merely repeated the provisions of previous Acts with regard to the appointment of overseers by the justices, the provision of a stock to set the poor on work, the binding of children as apprentices, and even the building of houses on the waste for the poor to inhabit.[5] Again, with regard to the *vagabond*, the Act of 1597 enjoins his punishment by whipping in the first instance, by relegation to the parish on which he has some claim, and finally to the House of Correction or to the common gaol, while dangerous persons were to be disposed of outside the country. This was practically repeated in the Act of 1601, the compre-

[1] Prothero, 70.

[2] *Ibid.* 68-71. 18 Eliz. c. 3.

[3] Prothero, 73.

[4] 39 Eliz. c. 3.

[5] Prothero, 97. 43 Eliz. c. 2.

[5] Prothero, 104. 39 Eliz. c. 4, 5.

hensive object of which has been described as the desire 'to provide work for those who could work, relief for those who could not, and punishment for those who would not.'[1]   The *parochial chargeability* of the poor had only been gradually recognized.   In the earlier Acts the hundred was generally chosen as the responsible unit for relief; but the Act of 1536 imposed a fine on the parish which should not relieve its impotent poor; the Act of 1547 directed the curate to exhort his parishioners to relieve the needy born in the same parish; the Act of 1551 laid the duty of collection and demand upon parochial officers.   The Act of 1572 imposed the burden on the jurisdiction of the justices; but the Act of 1597 returned to the parochial limit, which was maintained in the Act of 1601.

[1] Cunningham, *Eng. Ind. and Com.* ii. 61.

It has been generally acknowledged that this last Act lays down the principles on which a sound Poor Law should be administered, and that it was the perversion of these principles —partly from motives of self-interest, partly from mistaken kindness—which led to the disastrous developments of the next two centuries.   The steps in this downward course must be briefly noted.   In the first place, the fear of the wealthier parishes that they would become chargeable with the needy whose own parishes could not sustain them, caused a stricter definition of this chargeability.   The question of 'settlement' had been dealt with first in the Act of 1572, and the justices were directed, if the parishes in which the poor aged and impotent persons were found were unwilling to provide for them, to settle such persons at 'meet and convenient places' within their district, and to appoint a weekly sum for their support.[2]   But this was far too vague.   Until the Act of 1662, say the Commissioners of 1834, 'there seem to have been only two statutory grounds of settlement—birth, and residence, first for three years, and afterwards in some cases for one.'[3]   This Act allowed the removal of any stranger within forty days back to his own parish where he had obtained a settlement (which was now defined as a continuous residence of forty days), unless the new comer could give sufficient security that he would never become chargeable to the new parish.[4]   A man was thus removed, not because he had fallen into hopeless poverty, but on the chance that some day he might so fall.

(2) 1601-1834.

Departure from the principles of 1601.

The laws of settlement.

[2] Prothero, 70.

[3] Report, 84.
14 Car. II. c. 12.

[4] Robertson, 428.

Furthermore, by an Act of James II the 'forty days' was to be reckoned from the time when the migrant gave notice to the overseer of his residence in the parish.   Critics of the Poor Law have been unable to find language strong enough to condemn the laws of settlement.   One author has described them as consummating the degradation of the labourer by making him a serf without land.[1]   'The iron of slavery,' says another writer, 'entered into the soul of the English labourer.'[2]   In fact, although the mischief of which it was the cause may not be underestimated, the system could not work in all its rigour, and certain relaxations were allowed.   By an Act of 1691, 'derivative settlements' were allowed through payment of taxes for a year, serving an annual office, hiring for a year, and apprenticeship.   Again, in 1696, a further modification allowed the grant of a certificate of acknowledgement of settlement, under which safeguard the holder of it could migrate to a district where his labour was required, the new parish being assured that he would not become chargeable to it and, therefore, not troubling to remove him back until there was absolute need.   Finally, in 1795, the removal of persons from any parish was forbidden, until they were actually in need of support.[3]   At the same time, although the law was thus relaxed, the fixed principle which caused the refusal of all permanent relief to labourers who had no settlement in the parish, and also to settled labourers who should reside elsewhere, acted as a very efficient check upon migration.   But the derivative modes of obtaining a settlement were retained; and churchwardens and overseers, in their anxiety to prevent the acquirement of such settlements, appealed to the law courts and spent, in constant litigation, a large portion of the money which should have been devoted to the relief of destitution.

Nor was this the only fault to be found with the method of expenditure.   The Act of 1691 complains that churchwardens and overseers of the poor, by means of their unlimited power and upon frivolous pretences, but chiefly for their own private ends, give relief to what persons and number they think fit, by which means the rates for the poor are daily increased.   As a remedy the Act directs the keeping of a register with names and dates, which shall be examined annually by the vestry; and that, beyond the persons then allowed, no relief shall be

1 Jac. II. c. 17.

1 Thorold Rogers, *Work and Wages,* 433.

2 Fowle, *Poor Law,* 63.

3 Will. & Mary, c. 11. 8 & 9 Will. III. c. 30.

36 Geo. III. c. 23.

3 Report, 85.

Increased power of Justice in administration of relief.

given 'except by authority of one justice, or by order of th
bench of justices at Quarter Sessions.' The effect of this wa
practically to *supersede the overseer by the justice* in the grantin
of relief. The practice arose by which justices ordered relie
at their own discretion and without the knowledge of th
parish officers. The result was most fatal to the maintenanc
of the original principles of the poor law. The position of th
justices has been described as 'that of charitable gentlemen t
whom the oppressed poor could appeal against the tyrann
of the overseers.'[1] At the same time, the feeling, faithfull
reflected in Parliament, was prevalent, that the State shoul
ensure sufficient subsistence to the working population. A
the beginning of George III's reign this led to much legislatio
in favour of the unrepresented people; but it was not unt
1795, and then only in an informal manner, that the principl
was embodied in all its naked simplicity. The rise of price
consequent on the French war was bearing so hardly on th
poorer classes that the Berkshire magistrates at Speenhamlanc
near Newbury, declared that further allowances were necessary
and, while recommending farmers to increase their labourer
wages in proportion to the price of provisions, and themselve
drawing up a scale of relief upon this basis, they promise
to grant assistance to every poor family in proportion to it
numbers. This *Speenhamland Act of Parliament*, as it cam
to be called, was speedily imitated in many parts of Englanc
It definitely established the principle of a right to relief in
dependent of work done. It made it more profitable to b
idle than to work, and increased the rates to so vast an exter
that they threatened in some cases to exceed the whole rent
large tracts of land, in consequence, went out of cultivatior
There were other parallel methods of obtaining relief—no les
than six such were discovered by the Commission of 1834—
most of which had for their object the employment, whethe
real or pretended, of the labourers by the farmers and othe
ratepayers at the expense of the parish.[2]

This whole system of outdoor relief was legalized by th
abrogation of the *Workhouse test*. During the closing year
of the seventeenth century, workhouses had been erected a
Bristol and several other large towns, and were used as a tes
of destitution. The success of this experiment led to th

passing of an Act in 1722 by which parishes were allowed to unite and provide workhouses, and 'no poor who refused to be lodged or kept in such houses should be entitled to ask or receive parochial relief.' This seems to have met with immediate success; but the humanitarian feelings of the time contributed to discredit it. In 1782 'Gilbert's Act,' attributing the increased expenditure to the misconduct of the overseers, provided for the voluntary formation of Unions in each of which the workhouse should be supervised by paid guardians under the control of the justices. None but the impotent should go to the workhouse, but suitable employment should be found for the able-bodied near their homes.[1] Sixty-seven Unions were thus formed. In 1796 this was followed by the entire abolition of the workhouse test; for, in parishes which had not accepted Gilbert's Act the overseers were empowered to give relief in cases of sickness or distress at the applicant's own home, even though the applicant refused to conform to the Act of 1722 and enter the workhouse as a sign of destitution.

The final violation of the Act of 1601 which requires notice was concerned with the administration of the *law of bastardy*. An Act of 1572 had thought it sufficient, in dealing with this unpleasant subject, to enjoin that, in order that the support of illegitimate children should not defraud the aged and impotent poor of their relief, the justices should place the burden of such a child's support upon its parents. Subsequent legislation made an attempt to punish the parents. Thus, under an Act of James I, the mother was to be imprisoned with hard labour. Two centuries later the sentimental feeling of the time turned the tables on the father, and by two Acts of 1809-10 a woman was actually allowed to fix the fatherhood of her as yet unborn child on any man, who was thereupon imprisoned until he should indemnify the parish against all charges connected with his reputed offspring. The result was most disastrous to morality. The mother could ruin any man against whom she bore a grudge, while she herself not only lived comfortably on the allowance which the supposed father was compelled to make, but was the better off in proportion to the profligacy of her conduct, and was even 'considered a good object of marriage on account of these weekly payments.'[2]

(marginal notes:) 9 Geo. I. c. 7. 22 Geo. III. c. 83. [1] Robertson, 429. 36 Geo. III. c. 23. Law of bastardy. 18 Eliz. c. 3, § 2. [2] Report 96.

2 E

Results of
departure
from prin-
ciples of
1601.

The working of this deteriorated system may be briefly summarized.   The local overseers, a set of ignorant and unprincipled men, who were only in office for short periods varying from two to six months, were entirely overridden by the justices, philanthropic country gentlemen who generally had no local knowledge and were not specially interested in keeping down the poor-rate.   For, the rate was levied on houses and on tithe.   It consequently fell most heavily on small householders, such as the independent labourer, and on the tithe-owners, whether clergymen or local landlords.   But the pauper could appeal from the overseer to *any* justice, and would consequently choose the weakest or the most charitable within his reach.   Since 1795 the justices employed the power

5 Eliz. c. 4.

given them by the old law of 1562 to fix what they considered should be the minimum of a labourer's fair wage, and undertook to supplement it in proportion to the number of his family.   The farmers being the chief employers of labour welcomed the system ; for they either diminished wages to the minimum allowance of the justices, with the knowledge that it would be made up to their labourers from the rates ; or they dismissed their own men in favour of the paupers whom, in accordance with arrangements in vogue in many places, the parish compelled them to employ or at any rate to support. And thus the honest labourer was driven out of work, or at best had to accept in the minimum wage a less sum than was paid to the rate-aided pauper ; while marriages were recklessly made, the pauper going, as it has been said, straight from the church to the overseer ; and every encouragement was given not only to incontinence, but to immorality of the most flagrant kind.

From as early as the middle of the seventeenth century onwards, many suggestions were made for remedying the evils which arose from the maladministration or the violation of the Act of 1601 ; but no legislative measure of improvement was passed until early in the present century.   In 1819, in accordance with the report of a Committee of the House of Commons, the power of the justices in the direct administration of relief was intercepted by the permissive establishment of *select vestries* which alone could order permanent relief in such places as established them.   But their members were drawn from the same class as the overseers; they were irresponsible, and made use of their power to attack the tithe-owners, lowering wages and increasing rates in order to swell the burden upon tithe.

§ 60. One of the first acts of the Reformed Parliament was to subject the whole system of poor relief to the searching investigation of a strong committee, whose report formed the The modern foundation of the *Poor Law Amendment Act of* 1834.[1] In Poor Law. its main provisions this Act attempted a reversion to the principle of 1601, and acknowledged the duty of the State to provide for its destitute citizens. The organization for this purpose was centred in a board of three Poor Law Commissioners appointed for five years. Their first business was to divide the country into administrative districts. Large towns and extensive and well-populated parishes remained as separate districts; but rural parishes, varying from twenty to thirty in number, were grouped into separate Unions, as these districts were everywhere called. This formation could only proceed slowly, partly because Parliament refused to allow the voluntary Unions, formed under Gilbert's Act of 1782, to be dissolved except with their consent, and their continued existence much interfered with the new grouping of many districts; partly because each Union was to support a so-called Workhouse, and these buildings took time to erect. England is now divided into about 650 Unions, the division having been made without any regard to previous areas of local government and inaugurating a confusion in local administration which has been only slightly removed by the Act for the establishment of County Councils in 1889. The Central Board appoints Assistant Commissioners (who, since 1847, have been called Inspectors), and audits the accounts of each Union. The Unions themselves are administered by Boards of Guardians, unpaid officials elected by the ratepayers of each parish in number according to the size of the parish. But each parish while contributing, not according to its rateable value but according to its expenditure in poor relief, to a common fund for the maintenance of the officers and workhouse of the Union, retained the chargeability for its own poor. The workhouse was intended as a test of destitution, and owed its name to the intention of the framers of

1 Robertson, 430-431.

the Act, that it should be used for setting able-bodied paupers to work in the manner provided by the Statute of 1601. For, outdoor relief was to be gradually abolished; and ten years after this Act a final order was issued that 'every able-bodied person . . . requiring relief . . . shall be relieved only in the workhouse of the Union.' The aged and impotent alone were exempted from the operation of this rule.

Its development.
This is not the place to praise or to censure a departure from the principles laid down in 1834; but of the fact of such a departure there can be no doubt. Here it will be enough merely to chronicle the changes in administration or practice that have taken place in the last sixty years. In the first place, at the expiration of their five years, the Poor Law Commissioners successfully defended themselves against a host of malicious attacks; and, after having had their powers annually renewed from 1839 to 1842, they were further reappointed for five years. Hitherto the Commissioners had been independent of Parliament; but now that the reforms had been carried through, it was thought better to make them into a ministerial department. Accordingly, in 1847, a Poor Law Board was formed, consisting of a number of great officials of State headed by a President with whom the whole work of the Board really lay. In 1871, the desire to bring the Poor Law administration more into connection with local government caused the Board to be merged in the newly constituted and more extensive Local Government Board. In the second place, a series of statutes from 1846 to 1865 transferred the chargeability of the poor from the parish to the Union, and substituted a short residence of a year for all other methods of obtaining the settlement which constituted a claim for relief upon the Unions. In the third place, outdoor relief, instead of becoming extinguished, largely exceeds in the number of its recipients the use of the workhouse as a limit and test of destitution. It is round this question of the advisability of outdoor relief that the battle between Poor Law reformers and philanthropists chiefly rages. The relaxation in the original intention of the Act has been the result of two exceptions allowed by the Commissioners. Outdoor relief might be granted in the case of either the aged, who were defined as all over sixty years of age; or, by a subsequent

order, the able-bodied who, through special circumstances affecting themselves or their families, were unable to work. The latter class of cases rested entirely on the discretion of the guardians. Owing to the irregularity of their attendance, the administration of the Poor Law in this respect—the sole point in which the initiative is left to the local bodies—is most capricious. Not only do Unions differ in the amount of outdoor relief allowed, but in the same Union, on successive days of meeting, two sets of guardians may attend imbued with diametrically opposite opinions on the advisability of outdoor relief. In any case, the way of escape allowed by the Central Board out of the rigid interpretation of the Act of 1834 has been seized upon by the guardians; and the recipients of outdoor relief steadily grew until their numbers were six times as great as those of the inmates of the houses. Considerable pressure from the Central Board has since reduced the proportion to three to one; but the question is still a long way from solution, and there is a tendency among a class of politicians to gain popularity by advocating a large scheme of outdoor relief. One result of the system has been to increase the expense of the relief administered in the workhouses, which, originally built on a large scale, are now half tenanted, and yet are obliged to maintain a staff suitable to the size and possible requirements of the building. Finally, the original intention of the workhouses has been completely lost sight of, and they have become the permanent abode of the thriftless and the unfortunate, and the temporary accommodation of the tramp. In fact, the two points upon which all critics of the Poor Law would be agreed, are the want of moral classification among the inmates of a workhouse, the absence of which allows the unfortunate to be contaminated by contact with the thriftless; and its total inability to deal with the 'casual pauper' who remains, as he has been described, king of the situation, doing no work, subsisting upon mistaken private charity, and only taking refuge in the workhouse when driven by absolute need.

The division of the country into Unions by the Act of 1834 formed a bad precedent for the extension of local government to other purposes. Although for the purposes of the Education Act of 1871 the Parish was chosen on the whole as the

New areas of local administration.

unit, and although for sanitary purposes by the Act of 1872 the Union is the common area of administration and the Board of Guardians are the sanitary authority; yet in the course of the century there were formed Highway Boards and Urban Sanitary Districts, which might or might not correspond with any existing local area.[1] Much of this confusion has been removed by the creation of County Councils in 1889, of which there are sixty for administrative counties and sixty-two for county boroughs mostly with a population of over 50,000. To these bodies are entrusted powers taken partly from Quarter Sessions, partly from the highway and sanitary authorities.[2] In 1894 the system of local government was completed by its extension to the smaller area of the parish.[3] In all rural parishes there was set up a primary assembly called a Parish Meeting consisting of all electors to Parliament or the County Council. In parishes of 300 inhabitants and more or, under certain conditions, in those of an even smaller population, there was established in addition a representative body called a Parish Council. Small parishes are allowed to group themselves under a common Parish Council, and large parishes can be grouped into electoral wards. In the former case each parish, and in the latter case each ward, has a separate Parish Meeting. The powers of these bodies are partly old, consisting of the civil duties of the vestry, the power hitherto belonging to the justices of the peace of appointing overseers of the poor, and certain duties and powers hitherto discharged by the churchwardens, overseers and guardians. To these have been added new powers, the chief of which perhaps are exercised in connection with allotments and parochial charities of a certain kind. It should be noticed that very stringent limits are placed upon the power of these bodies to levy a local rate.[4] The extent of the application of this scheme of local self-government may be gauged from the fact that there are nearly 7,000 parishes with Parish Councils and about 6,000 more which are not of sufficient size to be compelled to resort to any administrative machinery more elaborate than an annual Parish Meeting.

§ 61. Tacitus tells us that the German tribes 'abhorred walled towns as the defences of slavery and the graves of freedom.'[5] It is in the towns of the provinces that the

[1] Cf. Chalmers, Local Government.

[2] Robertson, 434-435.
[3] Jenks, An Outline of English Local Government.

[4] Robertson, 435-437.

Boroughs.
[5] Hist. iv. 64.

advocates for Roman continuity have hitherto found their chief examples. But while recent students seem to deny such continuity even in the towns of Gaul, the ingenuity of a few enthusiasts has never gained currency for a Roman origin of English BOROUGHS. Unhampered, then, by any ambiguous account of a previous organization, we may proceed to ask why certain spots in the country gradually became separated from the surrounding districts and acquired an organization and privileges of their own. In some sense, no doubt, 'the burh of the Anglo-Saxon period was simply a more strictly organized form' of the vill.[1] But the power of self-government which it soon acquires puts it on a plane with the administrative areas of the hundred and shire; and the later interest of the history of the borough is concentrated on its development into a corporation, an ideal person in the eyes of the law, *universitas* in contradistinction to the *communitates*, the organized groups of individuals known as the shires, the hundreds, the vills.[2]

[1] *S. C. H.* § 44.

[2] *P. and M.* 472, 660.

In its origin 'the burh was the fortified house and court-yard of the mighty man—the king, the magistrate or the noble,'[3] and from an early date the law protected it against the attacks of the marauder. Ine ordains[4] that the violation of a king's or bishop's house (*burg-bryce* is the name of the offence) shall be atoned for by the huge payment of 120 shillings, and that of other classes likely to have burhs, in proportion. A law of Ælfred to the same effect carries the penalty as low as fifteen shillings for the burh-bryce of a six-hynde man, that is, of one whose 'wergild' is 600 shillings. This looks as if every substantial thegn in a technical sense might be said to inhabit a burh. But of the burhs which grew into boroughs the origin is to be sought in more than one direction. In most cases they must have grown up spontaneously[5] according as need or convenience caused the assembling of a miscellaneous population round some existing centre. Such would be the administrative centre of the king's palace or a farm under a royal reeve, or the ecclesiastical centre of some monastery or shrine. The old Roman cities would have the substantial advantage of containing good material for building already collected. Moreover, men would be inclined to congregate at such convenient places as were formed by the

[3] *S. C. H.* § 44.

[4] *S. C.* 62. § 45.

The Anglo-Saxon Burh.

[5] But see *Domesday*, 219.

fords or the furthest navigable points of rivers, the crossing of Roman roads, harbours or estuaries. Such spots may or may not have been fortified. The presence or absence of defences would be a comparative index of the state of civilization reached by that portion of the country. The superior culture of Wessex and Kent may confine these origins to their numerous boroughs. In the midlands and in the west, where Danish or British pressure was constant, the boroughs may have had a more definite military purpose. But even here the point to be ascertained in any given case is whether the borough grew out of a previously existing vill, that is, whether it was agricultural in origin or, like Henry the Fowler's creations in Germany, it was planted down in a vacant spot purely in accordance with military needs.[1] This at least seems certain — that boroughs existed in England before the coming of the Danes. But it is no less certain that the Danish settlements gave a great impetus to trade, and so to the foundation of new boroughs.

For, it was primarily as places of trade that boroughs originated : a study of the mint marks on Anglo-Saxon coins shows that they clustered chiefly about the trades routes of the time.[2] Thus it is probable that every borough, whatever its origin, would contain a market and be the residence of at least one moneyer. It is not so probable that every borough had a gild. We know little about the Anglo-Saxon gilds, although much has been conjectured. The 'voluntary associations for mutual support,' known by that name all over western Europe, were evidently familiar to the English as early as the ninth century, if not before. The most common form, so far as evidence takes us, was the Cnihts-gild found in London, Winchester and Canterbury.[3] The Cniht was probably a *knabe* or lesser thegn. The extant statutes of four other Anglo-Saxon gilds (Abbotsbury, Cambridge, Exeter, Woodbury) reveal the object of these associations as partly social—to form a bond of fellowship among those who have no kindred—partly religious, to ensure prayers for the souls of the members after death. The Judicia Civitatis Lundoniae [4] of Æthelstan's reign with their mention of frith-gegildas are ordinances imposed from above, perhaps upon already existing voluntary associations : [5] they are not the statutes of a gigantic

[1] *E. H. R.* xii. 774.

[2] *Ibid.* xi. 759.

[3] Gross, *Gild Merchant*, i. 183-188. *Domesday*, 191.

[4] *S. C.* 67.

[5] Gross, *Gild Merchant*, i. 178.

gild. In none of these cases was the gild to be identified
with the administrative organization of the borough.

The form of that organization varied. A law of Æthelstan
lays upon the chief men of the burh the duty of coercing
a persistent absentee from the gemot.[1] Eadgar definitely
ordains that a burh-gemot shall be held only thrice in the
year, whereas a shire-gemot shall meet twice, while apparently
the hundred gemot is intended to come together every month.[2]
Probably therefore the burh-gemot was a matter of special
grant. Again, it was a safeguard to honest traders that only
such transactions should be held valid as had taken place
before witnesses. Thus Æthelstan ordains that 'no man
buy any property out of port over xx pence,' and that what
anyone buys within must be on the witness of the port-
reeve or some other credible person.[3] Eadgar, including the
assemblies of hundreds and wapentakes with burhs as places
where buying and selling might proceed and requiring the
maintenance of a body of sworn persons who could act as
witnesses, fixes the number of such a body as xxxvi for burhs,
but considers xii enough in the case of small burhs and
hundreds.[4] The lesser number in the case of hundreds can
be explained on the ground of fewer transactions. Small
burhs must have possessed some simple form of organization :
perhaps it did not differ substantially from the organization
of a vill. Even in the case of the greater burhs we hear of a
port-reeve and a wic-reeve, never of a burh-reeve. These names
are only to be explained on the hypothesis that, whatever the
original meaning of the word, the primary object of a burh
was to serve as a place of trade or a centre of administration and not as a military post. In several boroughs of the
Danelaw we hear of twelve lawmen[5] or judices.[6] They seem
to have been men of position and privileges, which descended to
their heirs. Probably they were the witnesses and doomsmen
required for the transaction of business in the local courts ;
but although their number connects them with the requirements of Eadgar's law for smaller burhs and for hundreds,
the places where they appear are among the most important
in the country. In many cases these owners of heritable
jurisdictions would be tenants of the king ; but in Chester
at any rate the king's tenants lived side by side with those

[1] S. C. 66.
§ 20.

[2] Ibid. 71.
§ 5.

[3] Ibid. 66.
§ 12.

[4] Ibid. 72.
§§ 4, 5.

[5] Lincoln,
Stamford,
Cambridge.

[6] York,
Chester.

[1] *S. C.* 87.

[2] *S. C. H.*
§ 131 ;
cf. also § 44.

[3] *Domesday,*
178-180.

[4] Ballard,
*Domesday
Boroughs,*
11-31.

[5] *S. C.* 90.

[6] Ballard,
op. cit. 51.

of the earl and the bishop.[1] London is generally allowed to have been 'a bundle of communities, townships, parishes and lordships, of which each has its own constitution,'[2] but London has a wic-reeve or a port-reeve, and there is no reason why it should not have been able to boast as much central ized authority as many other boroughs. Similarly there is no reason to suppose that London was the only borough which grew by the coalescing of communities or estates which, though contiguous, held their lands of different lords. The 'tenurial heterogeneity of the burgesses' which is apparent in the Domesday record, is explained most easily on the hypothesis of some such origin. In other cases the originally free alodial proprietors of an important vill may have commended them selves individually to different lords, ecclesiastical as well as lay : while the same result would be produced by gifts of houses or lands within the borough from the king or other lord. There is another explanation of this 'tenurial hetero geneity'[3] which may apply to the circumstances of the boroughs in the west and north. Military strongholds must often have been artificially created, and while the duty of burh-bot as part of the trinoda necessitas exacted from every landowner maintained the walls of these and other burhs, a permanent population may have been provided by laying upon the great thegns of the surrounding district the duty of main taining a certain number of houses within the burh.[4] Thus it comes about that these houses—*murales mansiones* they are called at Oxford[5]—are often reckoned as belonging to a manor which lies at a distance from the borough. How far these imported inhabitants were military in character is matter for conjecture. In any case this part of their duties would soon be lost in the mercantile pursuits for which the security of a walled town would give ample opportunity. Whatever the origin, the character of the population, the method of administration and the aims of the inhabitants would all tend to become identical with those of the dwellers in the more peaceful boroughs.

All evidence seems to show that from an early period the members of the administrative council—the burgesses, lawmen judices—whatever the name, were an aristocratic body.[6] Now the essence of burghership comes to be burgage tenure, and

ourgage tenure is practically heritable tenure at a money rent.
It may have come about in different ways : the trader who
settled in the burh would pay a money rent to the king or
some other lord : the representative of the great neighbouring
landowner and his liability, might hold by a rent which would
represent 'commuted wall-work.'[1] The payment of these
rents gave the first opening for the advance of the burh in
the direction of self-government. For, it was here that there
began the practice of letting out the burh to farm. The
sheriff through whom the payments would be made, would
accept a lump sum from the burgesses or from the reeve. The
tolls from the market and the wites from the moot would be
similarly treated, and the whole would make up the ferm
of the burh—*firma burgi*—which would constitute an important part of the profit of the sheriff out of which he
recouped himself for the sum, the ferm of the shire, for which
he was held accountable to the royal Treasury.[2] Then, when
the Danegeld began to be imposed the burhs no less than
hundreds were assessed at a round sum as if each contained
a certain number of hides. In this case, as when the sheriff
farmed the burh to its burgesses, writers have been inclined
to see the existence of corporate responsibility for the geld and
corporate enjoyment of the profits. It is possible, however,
that in the case of the geld the sum due was repartitioned afresh
at each exaction among the holders of the burgage tenements,
while the profits were divided annually, or even immediately
exhausted, at a *bytt-fylling* or some similar festive meeting.
Had it been otherwise, could we really attribute corporate
action and the possession of property to the burgesses at the
first mention of their recognition as a body to be dealt with by
the sheriff, the peculiar organization of the burh would have
been accomplished and there would be little more to investigate
in its history. It is probable that as yet the body of burgesses
did not appreciably differ from the community that assembled
in the hundred or the shire courts. Such responsibility as
there was, was a joint and several responsibility : each burgess
was regarded by the sheriff as having agreed with him for the
payment of the whole sum of the ferm or the geld due from
the borough.[3]

The Norman Conquest affected the town in three im-

[1] *Domesday*, 200.

[2] *Ibid.* 204.

[3] *Ibid.* 206-208.

Effect of
the Norman
Conquest.

portant ways. (1) The boroughs all came to be regarded as in some lord's demesne. This placed the burgesses—the holders of the burgage tenure, the suitors of the burh-gemots—in the semi-dependent position of villan tenants, and was soon made to carry with it, over and above the annual firma burgi, an occasional payment known as Tallage, which might be exacted by every lord from the towns in his demesne. (2) At the same time, the few existing towns suffered severely; for, the civic population recorded in Domesday fell from 17,000 to 7,000. This was due to the long resistance which the Danish portion of the population is said to have offered, and to the clearances made by William in order to obtain sites for castles for military purposes. And yet this diminished number of burgesses was made responsible for the same firma burgi.

[1] *S. C.* 84. § 4.

(3) To crown their misfortunes, although a law of the Conqueror[1] made all Frenchmen settled in England in the days of King Edward to be at scot and lot (i.e. to take their share in taxation) with the other inhabitants according to the law of England; yet this very distinction seems to imply that the much greater number of foreign artisans who followed in the wake of the Conquest itself, occupied an exceptional position.

Efforts for
Self-
govern-
ment.

The efforts of the towns in the direction of self-government had for their first object the acquisition of freedom from the judicial and financial control of the sheriff, and their success is recorded in the charters which they won from the kings or their lords.[2] These may be dealt with in two groups. The first comprises those charters granted by the Norman kings. Of these Henry I's grant to London[3] is as much more important as it is in advance of any other in the privileges won. The first object of all towns was the definite settlement of their firma; and some, such as Chester,[4] had gained this even before the Conquest. This in itself had a twofold object and result—to get rid of the interference and arbitrary assessment of the sheriff, and to shake off the theory of villenage: for the customs of Newcastle show an established distinction between a burgess and a villan.[5] After the settlement of the ferm, London gained the election of its own sheriff and justiciar.[6] This was far in advance of anything yet gained by other towns, and its object was not only that the citizens might be amenable to the jurisdiction of their own courts and magistrates alone, but,

[2] *S. C. H.* § 131.
[3] *S. C.* 108. Round, *Geoffrey de Mandeville,* 356.
(1) Under the Normans, 1066-1154.
[4] *Ibid.* 88.
[5] *S. C.* 112.
[6] M'Kechnie, 285 et seq.

n the case of London, that even pleas of the crown, which
were in an ordinary case specially exempted, might be kept by
its own officer.   A not unnatural corollary to this grant of
jurisdiction was freedom from the hated Norman innovations
of the liability to the payment of *murdrum* and of procedure
by way of *duellum* or trial by battle.[1]   Again, it was no small [1] *S. C.* 111.
privilege that the burgesses should be freed from the indefinite
exactions of the king which went by the name of *scot and lot*,
or from the oppressive *Danegeld*.   Lastly, while other towns,
such as York and Beverley,[2] gained freedom from tolls [2] *Ibid.* 110.
throughout their respective shires, to London alone was it
granted that such freedom should include the whole of
England.

The charters granted to towns by the Norman kings call
for two general remarks.   In the first place, the London Charter
became a model to smaller towns for some time to come.
Thus, the charters of Richard I to Winchester and to Lincoln,[3] [3] *Ibid.*
and that to Northampton [4] under John, will be found practically 265-266.
to correspond in the detailed privileges granted, with those [4] *Ibid.* 310.
which London gained from Henry I.   And, secondly, it is
clear that, in a smaller way, the charters of certain towns
became a model for the other towns in their district.[5]   Thus [5] Gross,
the Archbishop of York grants to Beverley the same privileges I. App. E.
as the citizens of York already possess ; the burgesses of $E.\ H.\ R.$ xv.
Hartlepool [6] gain from John the liberties and laws enjoyed by 74.
Newcastle : while the same king grants to Helston [6] the liberties Cunning-
and customs of Launceston. ham, i.
§ 76.
[6] *Ibid.* 313.

Under the early Plantagenet kings the charters to towns
grow far more frequent and full.   To begin with, they contain (2) Under
a grant of those privileges, often much extended, which London the early
had already obtained — the settlement of their firma ; the Plantage-
election of their own bailiffs together with (though this point nets,
is not yet generally conceded) special provision for pleas of 1154-1191.
the crown ; the maintenance of such old rights of jurisdiction
as were implied in the grants of sake and soke, toll, team and
infangenthef, together with freedom from the innovations of
the murdrum and duellum, and from various kinds of fines
of which many were the mark of villan tenure ; and finally,
freedom from tolls, not only over England, but throughout
the king's dominions generally : and with this was generally

combined the power of reprisal for any tolls unjustly levied.
This growth in the privileges of boroughs was largely due to
the overriding of feudal claims by the king.   When he allows
that the citizens of London 'non placitabunt extra muros
civitatis pro ullo placito '[1] he is ignoring the claims of the lord
of certain tenements inside the borough to the suit of those
tenants whose tenements are often attached to the court of
some distant manor.   In the same way, when he recognizes
that residence for a year and a day within a borough shall
confer freedom on the unreclaimed villan, he is treating the
whole borough as if it were a manor in the ancient demesne
of the Crown.[2]   The serf is not actually free, but no one
except the king shall have jurisdiction over him.[3]

There was much, however, to be done before the boroughs
could be called self-governing communities, free from outside
influence.   Many of the smaller boroughs remained in the
hands of some mesne lord, who sent his steward to preside in
their courts and exacted tallage from the burgesses.   Even the
greater boroughs had to put up with seignorial jurisdictions
within their walls.   Nor did the king in the least intend
that the privileges granted to the boroughs should hinder the
general administrative system of the country.   The courts of
the manorial lords, the Church and the boroughs alike should
be subjected to royal supervision.   'The group of burgesses
was a franchise-holder in a land full of franchise-holders, and
had to submit to the rules which governed the other possessors
of royal rights.'[4]   Thus they continued to be amenable both
to the king's court and to the sheriff of the shire.   The
jurisdiction of the borough court was a limited one.   In
civil cases a proprietary action for a burgage tenement could
only be begun by the king's writ of right, while the criminal
powers of the borough magistrates were confined within the
very moderate limits which the royal lawyers came to allow
to the old grants of sake and soke with their accompaniments.
Moreover, not only had the borough to appear by twelve
representatives before the justices in eyre to make presentments
of all that went on within the borough,[5] but the king's commissioners would sit in the borough itself to hold gaol deliveries
and even eyres.   Again, in matters of taxation, the payment
of the firma burgi gave to the burgesses themselves the right of

[1] S. C. 108.

[2] Ibid. 112, 166.
[3] Ibid. 167.

[4] P. and M. i. 652.

[5] S. C. 358.

evying the burgage rents, and often of taking the tolls for their
market and the amercements arising from their court. Yet
they were themselves as a body liable to be fined or amerced
in the shire court or before the king's judges; and to the
sheriff was entrusted the duty of collecting from them that
arbitrary aid (auxilium burgi) which had grown into the
Tallage;[1] while they might not even levy any occasional
local rates without the royal leave. Finally, the sheriff supervised the military array of the burgesses: he saw that they
among others had been sworn to arms[2] and summoned them
all, when necessary, to the field.[3]

And in nothing that the boroughs had yet gained are we
justified in seeing that idea of corporate capacity of possession
or liability which constitutes the essence of a modern borough.
When the king grants that the burgesses and their heirs shall
hold their tenements in free burgage, it is a privilege that
applies severally to each individual burgess. Even when he
grants that the burgesses shall hold the borough to farm, it
is to the burgesses as a body of individuals that he grants it,
and in no sense does the grant mark them off from the neighbouring hundreds which are farmed by their respective bailiffs.
Again the amercement of a borough does not point to corporate
liability; for when the money has to be paid, it is levied from
a few of the leading burgesses who are left to recoup themselves through the agency of the borough court. The fact
was that before the idea of incorporation could arise there
must be a distinction between the property of the individual
burgesses and the common property of the borough as such.
True the borough already possessed privileges—franchises as
they should be called; and it is in connection with their
possession that the corporate idea slowly emerges; for, the
franchises of any of the other communities of the land were not
of such a nature as needed active assertion and maintenance.
But the most valuable of its franchises consisted of tolls which
could be divided up among the individual burgesses. It was
not until towards the close of the Middle Ages that they
became endowed with land. This was due to the generosity
of individual burgesses and the gifts, by king or lord, of the
meadows over which the burgesses had hitherto exercised
common rights of pasture. There was no need to apply the

[1] S. C. 444,
Matt.
Westm.
430.
[2] S. C. 371.
[3] Ibid. 359.

The begin-
ning of the
corporate
idea.

1279.
15 Ric. II.
c. 5.

prohibitions of the Statute of Mortmain to boroughs until more
than a century after its first promulgation.   It would be im
possible to say that in the eyes of the law the borough became
a corporate body at any given moment in its history.   The
employment of a common seal would do much to emphasize
the unity of the borough in the eyes of strangers : the constant
interference of the king ending in the grant of a charter bestowing
new privileges, would serve to distinguish it from the hundred
or shire which owed their existence not to definite grant, bu
to immemorial recognition.   Then the citizens of London took

1191.

advantage of Richard I's absence to gain recognition of their
foreign-born *Communa*—'a thing which neither Richard no
his father,' exclaims the indignant chronicler, 'would ever have

[1] *S. C.* 252.
Ric. Divis.
p. 53.
[2] Round,
*Commune of
London,* 222
et seq.

allowed.'[1]   This was a government by a mayor and a small
aristocratic body who came to be known as aldermen.[2]   The
sheriff or sheriffs who since the charter of Henry I had farmed
both London and the whole of Middlesex, now took a sub
ordinate position as 'merely the financial' representatives o
the citizens.   And when Magna Carta granted to the 'barones'
of the city of London the right of electing their Mayor ever

[3] M'Kechnie,
286-287.

year, the Communa became an established fact.[3]   In itself i
can scarcely be said to have established the corporate idea
As far as London was concerned, it probably gave to the some
what heterogeneous collection of communities an unity which
they had hitherto not enjoyed.   But many other borough
hastened to obtain the same form of government, perhaps
aiming at the extensive privileges which gave London it
unique position.   But, that these privileges were not essentia
to a borough is proved by the fact that Winchester had to wai
until the reign of Edward III before it got even the permanen
settlement of its firma burgi, while Norwich, one of the firs
cities in the kingdom, had no mayor until the beginning of the
fifteenth century.

The Muni-
cipality and
the Mer-
chant Gild.

Now, the establishment of the Communa was the victory o
an oligarchy.   The burgesses as a body or as represented by
the doomsmen of the burh-gemot were the aristocracy of the
town.   With the definition of burgherhood as occupation of one
of the old burgage tenements, they need no longer be afraid
of arbitrary additions to their number from outside.   While
therefore, they closed their ranks on the one side, on the

other side they took upon themselves to confer the rights of burghership on outsiders and so helped to get rid of the position which they had hitherto occupied as 'a mere group of joint tenants or co-owners.' The important part played by the merchant gild in this change has caused much misunderstanding among both lawyers and historians as to the relations between the merchant gild and the governing body in mediaeval towns.[1] The early charters granted to boroughs frequently contain mention of the merchant gild. Thus, Henry II grants to Lincoln 'its own gild merchant of the men of the city and of the other merchants of the county, as they had it in the time of his predecessors,'[2] and to Oxford, 'its own merchant gild . . . so that no one who was not of the gildhall should carry on any merchandise in the suburbs, except as he used to do it in the time of' Henry I.[3] In their charters to Winchester both Henry II and Richard I speak of 'our citizens of Winchester of the merchant gild';[4] while Richard, without any mention of the merchant gild, grants to the citizens of Lincoln in an especially full charter, freedom from tolls throughout England. To the same purpose John unites in one grant the gild, the hansa and freedom from every kind of toll.[5] It seems difficult to interpret these otherwise than as an identification, by authority, of the members of the merchant gild and of the borough court. Of course some places—and those of considerable commercial importance—never had a merchant gild. In London there are but slight traces of its existence; in Norwich there are no traces at all.[6] In other important towns the gild and the governing body became practically identical.[7] But as a rule the organization of the gild would be separate from that of the governing body of the town. For, the object of the merchant gild was clearly defined. It would be twofold, the one exclusive—to get for the gild-brethren a monopoly of trade in the town and the privilege of trading in other towns;[8] the other inclusive—to let all within the gild share in all advantages of trade, and to secure help for its members in sickness or misfortune.[9] Thus the inducements to join the gild would be the possession of a commercial status which membership with such a body would give, and the possibility of procuring better terms of foreign trade by combination. With regard to the member-

[1] Gross, *Gild Merchant,* I. chaps. v. and vi.

[2] *S. C.* 166.

[3] *Ibid.* 167.

[4] *Ibid.* 166, 265.

[5] *S. C. H.* § 165.

[6] Gross, I. 21 note, and 116.

[7] *Ibid.* I. 66, 75.

[8] *Ibid.* I. 37-43.

[9] *Ibid.* I. 49.

ship of the gild, it is important to note that (1) not even all the
burgesses in the town would belong to it ;[1] while in many towns
there were classes, like the Jews and Flemish weavers, who held
their privileges by direct grant from the crown, and would
thus claim to be independent of the gild.[2]   Again (2) in some
towns there were members of the gild who were not burgesses,
such, for example, as burgesses of other towns and sometimes
even neighbouring monasteries and lords of manors.[3]   At the
same time, at any rate in some towns, membership of the gild
must have been fairly comprehensive, so as to include men
in a very humble way of business ; for, while the towns were
mainly agricultural, not only was the gild widely spread (we
know of 150 towns which obtained the privilege in the twelfth
and thirteenth centuries), but it contained, even in the small
town of Totnes, as many as 200 members.[4]

§ 62. As a general rule, however, the Communa and the
merchant gild were equally aristocratic institutions.   Thus it
is not surprising that the establishment of the former was
followed immediately by the outbreak of violent quarrels in
London.   In 1196 William Fitz-Osbert, on behalf of the poorer
citizens, complained that they were made to bear an undue
proportion of the burden of the taxes : but the riot which he
led only ended in his death.   This was but a foretaste of the
quarrels which arose from the relations between the merchant
and the craft gilds.   The latter were associations of all artisans
who were engaged in a particular industry in a particular town.
They came into existence a century later than the merchant
gilds, that is, in a few cases in the twelfth century ; but in the
following century they were to be found in all branches of
manufacture and in every industrial centre.   They were first
formed, perhaps, like the merchant gilds, by foreigners, chiefly
weavers, of whom a great stream came after the Conquest
from Flanders under the protection of Queen Matilda.   For
this reason, no doubt, even when the craft had spread to the
native English, weavers were for a long time excluded from
any position in the towns, and craft gilds were regarded with
suspicion.   Those which were formed without the royal sanction
(adulterine gilds, as they were called) were heavily fined, though
not necessarily suppressed.   A century later, under Edward I,
these organizations were encouraged as a counterpoise to the

[1] Gross, I. 69.

[2] *Ibid*. I. 70, 108.

[3] *Ibid*. I. 66-68.

[4] *Ibid*. I. 90-93.

The Craft Gilds.

ising oligarchy in the towns. In many cases that oligarchy was co-extensive with the merchant gild, and an important question arises as to the connection of the merchant and craft gilds. We are met by two entirely opposite views. On the one side it is held[1] that the craft gilds were formed in self-defence out of the landless, and consequently unenfranchised, artisans to resist the oppression of the merchant gild, armed as it often was with the powers of a municipality. On the other side it is urged that civic quarrels were not, as such a view would imply, between capital and labour, but between burgess and alien.[2] Few towns would possess a sufficient number of merchants to form an organization of wealth for the oppression of the craftsmen. Moreover, the regulations of the crafts insist on good work, and there is little in them that would protect the members from outside oppression; while the approval of the town magistrates was needed for their recognition and enforcement. Thus it seems more likely that craft gilds were formed with the approval and encouragement of the magistrates for the regulation of industry in particular branches.[3] But whichever of these, if either, may have been the origin of the craft gilds, by the end of Edward III's reign citizenship came to be bound up with membership in one of the crafts, until the decline of the gilds at the end of the sixteenth century.[4] It has been usual to believe that an Act of 1545, which was re-enacted and enforced in 1547, confiscated to the king the property of the gilds on the plea that a great portion of their wealth was spent in superstitious uses; and that thus at one sweep disappeared 'the benefit societies of the Middle Ages.'[5] It has, on the other hand, been shown that the intention of the Acts of 1545 and 1547 was very different, and that the sole result of the latter, which alone took effect, was to vest in the king, as rent-charges, all sums of money hitherto devoted to the maintenance of any religious service or establishment; that the gilds were close corporations whose funds benefited few besides the families of the members; that there is mention of several gilds and recognition by statute of their officers for the discharge of public duties in the reign of Elizabeth, and that the practical disappearance of the gilds was due to economic causes, such as the introduction of new industries and the spread of the

[1] By Professor Ashley and, more cautiously, by Dr. Stubbs.

Their relation to the Merchant Gild.

[2] Drs. Cunningham and Gross.

[3] Gross, I. chap. vii.

[4] *Ibid.* I. 124, note.

Causes of their decline.

[5] Thorold Rogers, *Work and Wages,* 346; *Econ. Interp. of Hist.* 367. Cf. Cunningham, *Eng. Ind. and Com.* i. § 149.

'domestic' system of manufacture. The London gilds, which were treated in no respect differently to the rest, have alone survived, not because they were too rich to be touched, but because they were more than gilds of artisans, that is, they were wealthy corporations whose civic duties survived the disuse of those economic functions for the discharge of which they had been called into existence.[1]

[1] Ashley, *Econ. Hist.* vol. i. pt. ii. 139-155. Growth of oligarchy in the towns.

There seems sufficient proof that at its first establishment local self-government was founded on a tolerably wide basis. Evidence drawn from such unconnected places as Hereford, Ipswich and Beverley, seems to show that citizenship could be easily obtained and that the bailiff or other local magistrate was elected by the whole community. The great change which did away with this popular government was due partly to the growing inequalities of wealth, partly to that important feature of the Middle Ages—the disinclination for duties of any sort unless they were accompanied by some manifest advantage. Thus we find in the fourteenth century, equally, for example, in Scarborough and in King's Lynn, a recognized distinction between the rich, the middle class, and the poor (*divites* or *potentiores*, *mediocres*, *pauperes* or *inferiores*); and thus, following the example of London, already noted, complaints are found at Stamford (1260), Gloucester (1290), and Oxford (1293) of the unjust taxation of the poor by the rich. In short, it must be owned that 'the few well-to-do persons of the community who aspired to fill public positions were not prompted by any love of fame or glory. They had in mind a far more practical and unworthy end—namely, to manipulate the financial system of the borough in such ways as to promote their own interests by putting burdens on other people's shoulders.'[2]   But this was only the beginning of the end. The oppressions and usurpations of the richer citizens did not pass without protest from their poorer fellows. Sometimes an appeal was made to the Courts of Common law, sometimes resort was had to arbitration; while occasionally, as at Bristol in 1317, a serious popular outbreak was the result. But on the whole, the indifference and poverty of the mass of citizens gradually gave the victory to the wealthy few.[3]   Thus it early became the custom for a body of twelve or twenty-four to be annually elected as a committee of the whole community of

[2] C. W. Colby, *Eng. Hist. Rev.* v. 645.

Examples:—

[3] Mrs Green, *Town Life in 15th Cent.* II. chap. x.

citizens. Now, in the case of Winchester, early in the reign Win-
chester. of Edward I, the two bailiffs who existed side by side with the mayor were elected, one by the committee, the other by the general body of the people. Under Henry VI, a century and a half later, the committee had practically usurped the nomination of both officials, leaving to the general body of citizens the empty right of confirmation. It only needed the grant of charters of incorporation from the crown to legalize the custom and confirm the power to the oligarchy which had usurped it. A few towns had obtained, by Act of Parliament, a recognition of their local customs ; but Henry VI began the easier and more common form of royal charter for this purpose. Thus at Leicester, in 1464, Edward IV Leicester. recognized a body of twenty-four mayor's brethren and a common council of twice that number. Three years afterwards this latter body obtained the election of the mayor. In 1484 the former committee became aldermen and divided the town into twelve wards, merely for police purposes ; while in 1489 the mayor, the brethren and the common council formed themselves into a close corporation, and their position 1 S. C. H. was assured to them both by Act of Parliament and by royal § 488. charter.[1] In Exeter, again, the *commune concilium* of the city, Exeter. which had once consisted of the whole body of the freemen— the *tota villata* as it is elsewhere described—was narrowed down to a body of twenty-four, in whose hands was placed the election first of the aldermen (1288), then of the mayor (1347). During the century and a half which followed, this narrow committee was transforming itself into a permanent self-elected body until the charter of 1497 practically confirmed the privileges which it had monopolized. The charter of Charles I (1627) only added to its powers. But in Exeter, unlike the majority of corporate towns, the election of members of Parliament never fell into the hands of this exclusive corporation. It remained with the whole body of freemen.[2] [2] Freeman,
Exeter.

The last development in municipal government which calls for notice, was the constitution of some of the largest towns as counties, with sheriffs and a shire jurisdiction of their own.[3] [3] S. C. H.
iii. § 488. This involved the final banishment of the sheriff of the shire from interference in their concerns. Henry I's charter had Boroughs
made into already given this privilege to London ; but not for more than Shires.

200 years did any other town attain it. Edward III gave
it to Bristol in 1373, Richard II to York in 1397. In the
fifteenth century it became more common, and, finally, about
eighteen towns procured the privilege, the majority of whom

retain it to the present day.[1]

Such were the corporations which formed the stronghold
of the Whigs when that party came into existence, and which
on that account, were attacked successively by Charles II and
his brother James II. The details need not detain us; for, the
new charters granted were drawn on even narrower lines than

were those which they superseded. It was not until the Reform
Parliament that any change was made, and the Municipal
Corporations Act of **1835** 'provided a uniform constitution for
all boroughs to which it applied, based on the model of the
best municipal corporations.' This consisted of a council
composed of the mayor, aldermen, and common councillors.
The councillors are elected by all ratepaying residents of
either sex for three years, a third retiring annually; and their
number is fixed at the time of incorporation. The aldermen
are in number one third of that of the councillors, by whom
they are appointed for six years, one half retiring triennially by
rotation. The mayor is elected annually by the council from
among the aldermen or councillors. Finally, the Municipal
Corporations Act of 1882 made this constitution compulsory,
and an Act of the following year abolished all municipal
corporations which did not come within the provisions of
the Act of 1882. The three hundred existing boroughs of
England and Wales are regulated by this Act.

The judicial constitution of boroughs varies greatly.[2] The
Act of 1835 did away with the judicial authority of the aldermen and with the elected justices of the peace. In their
place in every borough there were naturally two justices of the
peace, the Mayor and the ex-Mayor. But besides these, most
boroughs of any size have a separate commission of the
peace which includes the county justices together with some
additional justices of their own. Further, it is possible for
a borough to have a court of Quarter Sessions under a trained
lawyer called a Recorder, and a Stipendiary Magistrate for a
practically similar purpose. The whole judicial organization
of the town is subject to the supervisory control of the High
Court of Justice.

CHAPTER IX

LIBERTY OF THE SUBJECT

§ 63. THE freedom of the individual is the peculiar boast of the English people. Other nations endow their citizens with political privileges as extensive as our own : but few possess in the same degree that immunity from petty official tyranny which makes daily life in the British dominions freer than perhaps anywhere else in the civilized world. To the subjects of many European governments this personal liberty is guaranteed by an article of the written constitution under which they live. But the English constitution rests on no such written basis ; and consequently this right, ' which consists in the power of locomotion, of changing situation, of moving one's person to whatsoever place one's inclination may direct, without imprisonment or restraint, unless by due course of law,'[1] *exists nowhere in English law as a stated principle*, except perhaps in a well-known article of the Great Charter. In other words, it is *secured indirectly*, ' by the strict maintenance of the principle that no man can be arrested or imprisoned except . . . under some legal warrant or authority, and . . . by the provision of adequate legal means for the enforcement of this principle.'[2] It is not, however, to be supposed that mediaeval England, except perhaps in degree, was more exempt than other nations from that ' ferocity of the times and the occasional despotism of jealous or usurping princes ' which overrode all securities for liberty and, in too many countries, made government only another name for systematized oppression. A contempt for even the legal rights of individuals is no uncommon mark of that kind of rule by a despot or a privileged class, which was most prevalent in the Middle Ages. Kings, nobles, and even Parliament when it took upon itself judicial

Personal liberty.

[1] Stephen's *Commentaries* (11th ed.), i. 149.

[2] Dicey, 195.

439

functions, only too frequently sacrificed the claims of individual right to their own desires or interests. And yet, in England at least, the means of securing this individual liberty of the freeman were coeval with the Common law. How it was secured in early times, except as against actual enslavement, is not very clear; but with the introduction of the system of procedure by writs, methods of redress against unlawful detention were abundantly provided. No less than four

Secured by issue of writs.

such writs seem to have been framed. The first was (a) the writ *de odio et atia*. The original purpose of this writ had been to afford protection against malicious accusations of homicide. An innocent man, appealed of this crime, could procure this writ from the chancery on the ground that his appellant acted 'out of spite and hate,' and this plea would be submitted to a jury of recognition whose affirmative verdict would put an end to further proceeding, and so to the threatened duellum. But between the request for the writ and the verdict of the recognitors the accused might be kept in prison without privilege of bail, and this writ came to be used primarily for the further purpose of releasing upon bail those who had committed homicide in self-defence or by misadventure. Meanwhile John's abuse of the writ, by exacting the payment of exorbitant sums, had led to the clause in Magna Carta which provided that 'this writ of inquest of life or limbs'

[1] *S. C.* 301. § 36.

shall be granted free.[1] The accused had still to appear before the king's judges when they visited the neighbourhood. The danger of course was lest a packed jury should show favour to a culpably guilty prisoner, and several Acts of Edward I's reign show doubt in the minds of the legislative body as to the possibility of guarding against this evil. The writ seems

[2] M'Kechnie, 420-425.

to have become obsolete as appeals went out of fashion.[2] (b) The writ of *mainprize* or *manucaptio* commanded the sheriff to take sureties, called *mainpernors*, for the appearance of the prisoner and to set him at liberty; while (c) the writ *de homine replegiando* bade the same official to replevy or repledge, that is, deliver a prisoner from custody 'in the same manner that chattels taken in distress may be replevied,' on bail being given for his subsequent appearance.

Writ of Habeas Corpus;

But all these remedies fell into disuse or were superseded by the still existing (d) writ of HABEAS CORPUS. Of this there

seem to have been no less than five variations the chief of
which was the *Habeas Corpus ad subjiciendum.*[1] This form of
the writ is not of privilege, but of right existing at Common
law, and, therefore, cannot ordinarily be withheld. Originally
it might be demanded from the Court of King's Bench by
a prisoner or his friends, and could be addressed to any
person, whether an authorized gaoler or not, who detained
another person in custody, commanding such detainer 'to
produce the body of the prisoner with the day and cause of
his caption and detention, to do, submit to, and receive,
whatsoever the judge or court awarding such writ shall direct.'
This might seem an effectual method for ensuring a prisoner
against wrongful or arbitrarily prolonged detention. But,
despite its apparent simplicity, it was many centuries before
the full and efficient working of the writ was finally secured.
In the first place, on a statement of a prisoner's case by himself or his friends, the writ as being of right could not
ordinarily be withheld by a judge; but Sir Edward Coke,
when Chief Justice in 1616, denied it to a man imprisoned
for piracy, whose own statement seemed to establish the truth
of the charge against him. But there was a much more
important class of cases which threatened altogether to anni-
hilate the action of the writ. The deeds or misdeeds of an
English official, whether Prime Minister or parish constable,
are amenable to the ordinary law of the land, administered by
the ordinary courts; and the plea of official duty affords no
excuse for the performance of an otherwise illegal act. But in
France and many other nations of the European continent,
members of the administration are protected in the discharge
of their official duties by a particular law administered by
special courts, which legalizes acts unlawful for a private individual. The disadvantages of the English system for enabling
the government by prompt action to check at its beginning
a threatened disturbance of public order, have often been
pointed out. Here it is necessary to notice that the English
government has not always acquiesced in this interpretation
of the law. The strong executive of the Tudors and early
Stuarts was based upon a theory of the law similar to that
of the French *droit administratif.*[2] The formulated Stuart
theory, upheld by the decision of the judges, as to the

[1] Law Quart. Rev. viii. 164. Jenks on Early Hist. Hab. Corp.

How evaded.

[2] Dicey, 326-329.

extraordinary power of the prerogative, or in other words
the discretionary power of the Crown, claimed the right o
committing individuals to prison and retaining them ther
without the need of any further return to a writ of Habea
Corpus by the gaoler than that the prisoner was retained b
special command of the king, *per speciale mandatum regis.*   Bu
this claim to a power of practically indefinite imprisonment wa
contrary not only to the spirit of Magna Carta which provide
that no free man should be taken or imprisoned or otherwis
penally dealt with unless by lawful judgement of his peers an
by the law of the land;[1] but also to the letter of a mor
explicit Act of 1351-2 which, aiming directly at the exercis
of extraordinary powers by the Council, enacted that no on
should be taken by petition or suggestion to the king unles
it be by indictment or presentment or by writ original at th
Common law.   The exercise of this power of commitmen
even by a single councillor, led to a formal complaint fron
the judges in 1591 addressed to the Chancellor, Sir Christophe
Hatton, and the Treasurer, Lord Burleigh ; which, howeve
while enumerating examples of illegal commitments, acknow
ledges that a committal 'by Her Majesty's special command
ment, or by order from the Council board, or for treaso
touching Her Majesty's person,' is sufficient return to a wri
of Habeas Corpus.   It may be that, in this acknowledge
ment of the power of the Council, the judges were only con
templating the alternative of bailing a prisoner or of remandin
him back to prison.   But the Council did not hesitate t
wield this power in a way that amounted to an entire refusa
of trial to a prisoner committed *per speciale mandatum regi*
The admission of Chief Justice Anderson and his fellow judge
in 1591 was used to justify the decision of the judges in th
celebrated case of *Darnell* or *the Five Knights.*   A number c
persons had been imprisoned by the Privy Council for refusa
to contribute to a forced loan : five of them applied to th
Court of King's Bench for a writ of Habeas Corpus ; the gaole
made the return that they were confined *per speciale mandatu*
regis, and the case of one of the prisoners, named Darnel
was argued out before the assembled judges.   The plaintiff
counsel did not deny the right of the Council to commit t
prison ; but they asserted that the cause of commitment mus

[1] *S. C.* 301.
§ 39.
25 Edw.
III. st. 5,
c. 4.

Darnell's
Case.

1627.

be named in the warrant in order that the Court might decide
whether the charge was one in which bail was allowed or
not; whereas the prisoner had been committed merely at
the special command of the king. It was defended by the
Attorney-General on the ground that reasons of state might
make a definite charge inexpedient in political cases. This,
however, had nothing to do with the matter. It was well
known that the real cause of imprisonment was not the necessity of collecting scattered evidence of some deep conspiracy,
but the refusal of the prisoners to contribute to a loan the
levy of which they regarded as illegal and the legality of
which the king dared not put to the test before the common-
law courts. This the judges sufficiently recognized; for,
while giving judgement for the Crown, they refused to leave
on record the assertion that the king need not specify the
cause of commitment.[1] As a direct answer to this decision
the Petition of Right, rehearsing that, in violation of Magna
Carta and of the Statute 25 Edw. III, certain of the king's
subjects had been detained by the king's special command
alone, prayed that for the future no such imprisonment
should be allowed.[2] Yet this very definite prohibition did
not prevent the committal of Sir John Eliot, Selden and
others, at the special command of the king, on the general
charge of 'notable contempts and stirring up sedition against
the king and government'; nor did it even prevent the judges
from delaying to find it bailable and thereby prolonging the
imprisonment for two terms and a long vacation. Finally,
the Act of the Long Parliament which abolished the Star
Chamber, provided that every one committed by the king
himself or by the Council collectively or individually, could
claim from the King's Bench or Common Pleas, without delay
upon any pretence whatsoever, a writ of Habeas Corpus; and
that within three days the Court should determine upon the
legality of the commitment and act accordingly.[3]

But if a direct refusal of the writ, even to important prisoners
of state, was thus forbidden, there were many ways which had
always existed, of evading the action of the writ. Early
attempts of the Commons under Charles II to remedy some
of these defects, failed through the opposition of the Lords;
but matters were brought to a head by the case of *Jenkes*,

[1] Gardiner, vi. 213-217. 1628.

[2] Gardiner, *Const. Docts.* 2-3. 1629.

16 Car. I. c. 10, 1641.

[3] Gardiner, *op. cit.* 111.

a London citizen committed by the King in Council for what the government chose to interpret as a seditious speech at the Guildhall. So many difficulties were thrown in the way, including the refusal of the Lord Chancellor and the Lord Chief Justice to grant a writ in vacation, that it was many weeks before the prisoner was finally released on bail.[1] Three years later the efforts of Lord Shaftesbury procured the passing of the *Habeas Corpus Amendment Act*, 1679, which embodied in a statute the right hitherto based but imperfectly upon Common law, and remedied some of the most important defects in the administration of that law. Thus (1) although practically no excuse justified a judge in refusing a writ, the detainer, whether a lawful gaoler or not, was not bound to produce his prisoner until a second (called *alias*) and even a third writ (called *pluries*) had been issued. The statute enacted as a remedy that every prisoner on a criminal charge, except one of treason or felony, could obtain a writ, and must be produced for trial within twenty days of its issue; while no person once delivered by *habeas corpus* should be recommitted for the same offence. This was enforced by heavy penalties both from gaoler and judge. But further, since a person charged with treason or felony would still be left at the mercy of the judge who had no right to inquire into the truth of the charge made against him, a subsequent clause of the statute provided that every prisoner on such charge must be tried at the next gaol delivery, or else released on bail, unless the witnesses for the Crown could not be produced in time; while, in any case, if still untried after the second gaol delivery he could claim his discharge. (2) A second grave defect in the working of the writ had been made clear in the case of Jenkes. No court, except the King's Bench, was accustomed to issue these writs, and it was a question whether during vacation, which comprised a large portion of the year, they could be issued at all. The statute met this difficulty by providing that all the superior courts might issue the writs; while in vacation a single judge of any such court was armed with the same authority. (3) A third set of provisions was aimed against a custom which had become common under Lord Clarendon, though not unknown to his predecessors, of transporting prisoners to the Channel Islands or elsewhere

[1] Hallam, iii. 10-11.

Habeas Corpus Amendment Act, 1679.

out of the operation of the law. The Act forbade, except under certain specified circumstances, the transference of a prisoner to Scotland, Ireland, Jersey, Guernsey, Tangiers or any place beyond the seas; while it provided that the writ should run in the counties palatine, cinque ports and other privileged places.[1]

[1] *S. C.* 517-523. Robertson, 46-54.

But, with all its merits, this Act was far from conclusive. Indeed, the history of the Habeas Corpus Acts has been instanced as an apt illustration of 'the predominant attention paid under the English Constitution to *remedies*, that is, to modes of procedure . . . by which to turn a merely nominal into an effective or real right.'[2] For 'they are intended . . . simply to meet actual and experienced difficulties'; and consequently, it is not to be wondered at that a century and a half elapsed before the machinery for securing protection against unlawful imprisonment was finally perfected. Thus (*a*) the Act of 1679 fixed no limit to the amount of bail that might be demanded. This was remedied by the clause of the Bill of Rights in 1689, which declared that 'excessive bail ought not to be required,' the precise amount being left to the discretion and honourable motives of the judge on a review of the charge and the rank of the prisoner. More lasting defects were (*b*) the application of the writ merely to commitments on criminal charges, and (*c*) the absence of any provision against the allegation of a false charge or, as it was technically called, a false return, by the gaoler. These were corrected by an Act of 1816, which extended the action of the writ to non-criminal charges and authorized the judges to examine into the truth of the facts alleged in the return to the writ with a view to bailing, remanding, or even discharging the prisoner.[3] It should be noticed, in conclusion, that by a subsequent Act the action of the writ outside England has been limited to those colonies or foreign dependencies of the Crown whose courts have no authority to issue the writs or to ensure their execution.

[2] Dicey, 207.

Its defects remedied.

56 Geo. III. c. 100.

[3] Hallam, iii. 14-15. 25 & 26 Vict. c. 20.

But the writ of Habeas Corpus is important not merely for the efficacy with which it secures the liberty of the subject. It '*determines the whole relation of the judicial body towards the executive.*'[4] For, since all officials from the highest to the lowest are amenable to the ordinary law of the land, the

Its Constitutional importance.

[4] Dicey, 208.

duty of issuing and enforcing this writ arms the judges with
the power of reviewing and hampering even to the point of
vetoing the action of the executive; for they may fail to find
such action in accordance with the letter of the law. Two
illustrations of this position must not be omitted. In the first
place, notwithstanding all their claims of extra-legal power,
the Tudors and the Stuarts were not so blind to the general
reverence of Englishmen for their Common law as to refuse
the assistance of the lawyers; and the conflicts of the seventeenth century over the position of the judges were due to
the fact that, while the reforming Royalists such as Bacon
and Wentworth regarded them as the best instruments of
conservative innovation, the parliamentary party held them
as the exponents and defenders of the ancient liberties
enshrined in the Common law. Thus the question of *judicial
independence* became part of the larger question of the maintenance of national rights, and even an inquiry into so technical
a subject as the proper return to a writ of Habeas Corpus
contained in itself an assertion, on the one side, of the need
of a strong executive, and, on the other, of the permanent
importance of the maintenance of popular rights. A second
illustration of the connection between the executive and the
judicial bench may be drawn from the procedure in the
so-called *Suspension of the Habeas Corpus Act.* In times of
political danger it has been found expedient to pass temporary,
generally annual, Acts suspending the action of the writ of
Habeas Corpus in the case of persons charged with certain
specified crimes such as treasonable practices. It is important
to understand that there is *never anything like a general
suspension of the action of the writ in all cases.* Such
temporary suspensions were fairly frequent in the troubled
times which succeeded the Revolution of 1688, and again in
the Rebellions of 1715 and 1745, and during the intermediate
Jacobite conspiracy of 1722,—in all about nine times up to
the last of these dates. For the next fifty years no measures
were taken to suspend the operation of the law; but then,
in the apprehensions occasioned by the course of the French
Revolution, Parliament under the guidance of Pitt took the
hitherto unprecedented step of renewing for eight years in
1794-1801. succession an Act which withdrew the benefit of the writ

from all those charged with conspiring against the person and government of the king.[1] But the power of the judicature in restraint of the executive was never more triumphantly acknowledged than in the means taken by the ministers of the day to defend themselves against any legal liabilities which they might have incurred during the suspension. For, the withdrawal of the application of the writs to persons charged with certain crimes does not preclude persons falsely charged from redress at the hands of their accusers when the suspension has been removed. On the expiration of this Act in 1801, and again on the occasion of the next suspension in 1817,[2] the executive sought to protect itself by procuring from Parliament Acts of Indemnity, that is to say, 'retrospective statutes which free persons who have broken the law from responsibility for its breach, and thus make lawful acts which when they were committed were unlawful.'[3] The limitation to this otherwise formidable and irresponsible power of the executive, which equals, if it does not surpass that wielded by the most despotic of the Tudors or Stuarts, is found in the authorization of Parliament, a body ever jealous for the maintenance of individual liberty. Since 1817 there has been no suspension of the Habeas Corpus Act in England, although unfortunately the history of Ireland has a different tale to tell.[4]

§ 64. But besides the attempts to set at nought or to evade the action of the writ of Habeas Corpus, there were other methods of undermining the liberty of the individual, 'remnants,' as they have been called, 'of a jurisprudence which had favoured prerogative at the expense of liberty.'[5] Among such was a power, employed by the Secretary of State and based upon certain parts of the Acts for the regulation of the press, by which *general warrants* were issued for the apprehension of the unnamed authors, printers and publishers of a particular obscene or seditious libel. This practice grew up with the Acts after the Restoration, but survived the expiration of the Acts themselves in 1695. It was a very ready means for the exercise of much petty tyranny both in the seizure of persons and of papers; but it was continued, inadvertently perhaps or, more probably, on the ground of usage, until the whole question was raised both in the law courts and in

[1] Erskine May, iii. 12-15.

[2] *Ibid.* 16-17.

[3] Dicey, 218.

[4] Cf. Erskine May, iii. 19 note.

Methods of violating the liberty of the Subject.

[5] Erskine May, iii. 2.

(a) Issue of general warrants;

Parliament by a series of cases, the chief of which are associated with the name of Wilkes. In 1763, for the punishment of those who had so freely criticised the utterances of the government in No. 45 of the 'North Briton,' the Secretary of State (Lord Halifax) issued a general warrant[1] for the apprehension of the authors, printers and publishers, together with their papers, the execution of which was personally superintended by Wood, the Under-Secretary. Under this warrant forty-nine persons were arrested, including the editor, John Wilkes, and a printer named Leach, but including also many perfectly innocent persons; and the whole proceedings were conducted with much arbitrary violence. The first action which resulted was that of several printers who had been arrested, against the messengers by whom the arrest was made, in which Lord Chief Justice Pratt, better known by his later title of Lord Camden, held that the warrant was illegal,[2] and the printers obtained damages. *Wilkes* himself brought actions against both Lord Halifax and *Mr. Wood*.[3] From the latter a jury at the direction of the same Judge gave Wilkes £800 damages; and when in 1769 his action against *Lord Halifax* was brought to an end, no less than £4,000 damages were awarded.[4] Meanwhile, in 1763, the printer *Leach* had also obtained a verdict with damages against one of the messengers named *Money*; and, on appeal to the Court of King's Bench, the judgement was upheld by Lord Mansfield.[5] Finally, in 1765, in the case of *Entick* v. *Carrington*, Lord Camden condemned the issue by the Secretary of State of a general search-warrant which placed all the books and papers of a specified individual at the mercy of the messengers who conducted the search.[6] From the law courts the matter was taken into Parliament; and the decisions of Lord Camden in the Common Pleas and Lord Mansfield in the King's Bench were followed by resolutions of the House of Commons, promoted by the Ministry of Lord Rockingham, which condemned as illegal general warrants whether for the seizure of persons or of papers. The refusal of the Lords to concur in a Declaratory Bill to this effect was of no moment in the light of the unanimous decisions of the law courts.[7]

For some time the state of certain departments of the law itself can only be described as a direct encouragement of gross violations of personal liberty. In cases where contempt

Case of Wilkes.

[1] Robertson, 300.

[2] *Ibid.* 309.

[3] Lecky, iii. 73-75.

[4] Erskine May, iii. 2-6.

[5] Robertson, 314.

[6] *Ibid.* 316-330.

1766.

[7] *Ibid.* 313.

of court had been committed, not merely by disrespect such as could be atoned for by an apology, but by failure to comply with their decrees through inability to pay the costs of an unsuccessful suit, the courts of equity thought nothing of relegating such unfortunate litigants to imprisonment for life. Indeed, the case of *debtors* in general was such as to encourage a considerable amount of petty tyranny. In the eyes of the law the person of the debtor was the property of his creditor until the debt was discharged; and the debtor, therefore, however solvent, was liable at any moment to arrest and detention in a prison whose horrors have become traditional. There was no distinction between the fraudulent and the unfortunate debtor; and both alike, if insolvent, were condemned to a lifelong imprisonment. From time to time in the course of the eighteenth century several small measures of relief were passed; but the first general measure really dealing with the subject was the Insolvent Debtors' Act of 1813, which distinguished between crime and misfortune by allowing an insolvent debtor to get his discharge by giving an account of all his debts and property. But until 1827 Crown debtors were exempted from the operation of this Act. In 1838, arrest for debt, which had been limited by previous Acts, was abolished in all but a few specified cases, and the lands of the debtor were for the first time allowed to satisfy the claim. It was a natural corollary to the distinction recognized in 1813 that, by the Bankruptcy Act of 1861, fraudulent debt was treated as a crime.[1]

And if the law treated English citizens so harshly, it was not likely that aliens would find much favour in its eyes. The institution of *negro slavery* had never been recognized by English law; although for the colonies or plantations, as they were commonly called, it had been legalized by several statutes. Although more than one English Judge had pronounced a pious opinion in favour of the freedom of a negro on English soil, yet the status of a colonial slave in England had never been called in question until the case of James Sommersett in 1772.[2] He was a negro who was arrested for refusing to return to his master's service. A writ of Habeas Corpus was obtained and in the discussion of the case before the Court of King's Bench, Lord Mansfield, ignoring arguments drawn from the legal existence of villenage in England, pronounced

(b) life imprisonment of debtors;

53 Geo. III. c. 102.

[1] Erskine May, iii. 25-35.
24 & 25 Vict. c. 134, § 221.

(c) negro slavery;

Sommersett's Case.

[2] Erskine May, iii. 36-39.

[1] Robertson, 342.

definitely that slavery in England was illegal.[1]   But despite the efforts of Wilberforce and his friends, and the promises of Pitt, the slave trade and the institution of slavery continued to be recognized in our colonies, until the unceasing efforts of Charles James Fox were crowned with a well-merited success which he himself did not live to see, and the trade in negroes was absolutely forbidden to subjects of the British Crown.[2]

1807.

[2] Ibid. 167-170.

(d) restrictions on foreign settlers.

With regard to *foreign settlers*, who came to England of their own free will, foreign merchants and Jews were under the special protection of the Crown, which exacted heavy tolls from them as a licence to trade, but at the same time granted them extensive privileges.   From Edward I to the Commonwealth the Jews as a body had disappeared from England ; but the policy of Edward III had encouraged the settlement of Flemish artisans, and from the time of the Reformation there was a constant stream of religious and political fugitives into the country, who brought with them some of the best blood and industry of France and the Netherlands.[3]   As the Crown had extended an especial protection over all foreigners, so it reserved to itself the right of expelling them from the country ; but this power was not exercised after the early years of Elizabeth's reign.   During the period of their residence in England all foreigners enjoyed the same personal liberty as British subjects : but by the Common law they were unable to acquire land, to hold any public office or even to exercise any civil rights.   The only methods by which they could become English subjects were by denization under the king's letters patent, or by naturalization by Act of Parliament ; and even those who did not undergo either of these processes were given a safe asylum against the persecutions of foreign governments.   The first departure from these generous principles of treatment was due to the alarm of the French Revolution.   In 1793 the *Alien Act*, which remained more or less in force until 1826 and was renewed for a short period in 1848, placed foreigners under a strict surveillance, and required that they should be registered and should live in certain specified districts.   Yet even at this period the general principle of repudiating the dictation of foreign governments as to our conduct towards dwellers on English soil was maintained, and Napoleon's

[3] Cf. Lecky, i. 188-192.

arrogant demand that all adherents of the old French monarchy should be removed out of British dominions was met with a flat refusal. In 1844 a further step was taken in the passing of Mr. Hutt's *Naturalization Act*, which enabled aliens, on a certificate from the Home Secretary or on taking the oath of allegiance, to acquire all the rights of a natural born subject short of eligibility for membership of Parliament or the Privy Council. This has been further amended and extended by the Naturalization Act of 1870. Finally, the protection afforded to foreigners has been somewhat modified by the signature of *Extradition treaties* with the United States in 1842, with France in 1843 and subsequently with most of the civilized nations of the world, by which each of the contracting parties agrees to surrender to the other criminals of that other nation found within its jurisdiction. Even during the excitement caused by the arrogant demands of Napoleon, the English government did not refuse to satisfy the latter's complaints of the attacks made on him by the press, but prosecuted for libel on Napoleon a refugee named Jean Peltier. Despite Mackintosh's able defence, he was pronounced guilty, though the renewal of war with France precluded the necessity of calling him up for judgement.[1] England has, however, steadily maintained her policy of granting an asylum to political refugees as such, which, despite occasional abuse, such as the plotting of the Orsini conspiracy against the French government in 1858, has brought to our shores and domiciled among us, often for long years together, most of the advocates of individual liberty and self-government.[2]

§ 65. There has been occasion already to notice the similarity between the ideas which animate the governments of continental Europe and those which the Tudor and early Stuart sovereigns endeavoured to realize. The parallel extends to the *duties of the administration towards the expression of opinion*. The Tudors and their imitators, the first Stuart sovereigns, no less than the French or Belgian government of to-day, considered in all good faith that it was the duty of the administration to regulate 'the utterance and formation of opinion' whether religious or otherwise. It was this consideration which in their opinion justified them in the maintenance of institutions and of a system which, if it could have

[1] Erskine May, ii. 333-334.

[2] *Ibid.* iii. 50-59.

Freedom of opinion.

Methods of repression.

been carried out, bade fair to cut off all intellectual advance, and was, even in its imperfections, a formidable engine of tyranny over individuals and classes. The system was centred in that judicial committee which has gained undying infamy as the *Star Chamber*. This body exercised a supervision not only over great offenders who might have set at defiance the ordinary Courts of Common law, but even over the petty details of private life which affected no one but the parties concerned. Indeed, it carried the principle of paternal government to a ridiculous excess, and arrogated to itself the duties of a public censor.[1] It will easily be seen that, however excellent was the intention which underlay such action, the temptation and opportunities of individual oppression were as irresistible as they were manifold. The exaction of heavy fines often for what were little better than imaginary offences ; the arbitrary power of arrest which was exercised by each Councillor as well as by the whole body ; the intolerable interferences in private quarrels whether concerning persons or property ; the methods of procedure by personal examination of the prisoner and by torture, both equally alien to the spirit and practice of the Common law, all combined to render the abolition of the Star Chamber one of the best possible guarantees for the assurance of individual liberty.

But if, after the downfall of this instrument of oppression, the executive did not still consider itself in the same degree as heretofore responsible for the guidance and control of popular opinion ; yet it still deemed necessary certain measures of precaution which, though never to this day entirely dispensed with, have diminished with time, the increase of stability, and the removal of anticipations of treasonable outbreaks. The most arbitrary proceedings of the Star Chamber were based upon the evidence,—if not of written papers often of a private nature, or of common rumour,—at best of *spies and informers* who were not confronted with the prisoner whom their charges were to condemn. But the disappearance of that tribunal, followed as it was by a long period of political unrest, did not allow government, even if such had been its wish, to dispense with the aid of these useful auxiliaries. The system continued until the present century, when the trials of those who took part in the disturbances of the period 1817-

Marginal notes:

(*a*) Control of Star Chamber ;

[1] For instances, vide Dicey's *Privy Council*, 105-112, and the authorities there quoted.

1641.

(*b*) use of spies and informers ;

1820 furnished proofs that the conspirators had actually been urged to violence by the emissaries of the government, and the ministers who were responsible incurred an odium due rather to the system than to their particular use of it; while the formation of a body of detective police has done away with the necessity of employing such agents.[1]

[1] Erskine May, iii. 39-44.

The organization of the Post Office placed in the hands of an unscrupulous government another necessary but tempting means of interfering with individual freedom. Perhaps it was not unnatural that the State in its capacity of post-master should object to facilitate the correspondence of those who were plotting its destruction; and from the very first the foreign mails seem to have been carefully searched. Cromwell by an Act, and Charles II by a proclamation, reserved to the representative of the government *the right of opening letters;* and finally, by an Act of Anne's reign, which has been confirmed by later statutes, the Secretary of State was armed with a power of issuing warrants for this purpose. Nor was the power suffered to remain idle; and while it was exercised for public purposes in 1722, 1745, and at other times of political danger, statesmen in office were not above making use of their privilege to incriminate their political opponents. In 1844 the avowal of the Secretary of State, Sir James Graham, that he had used this power, produced a great uproar throughout the country, which he only quieted by proposing the appointment of a secret committee to examine into the law on the matter. The committee, which contained many of the leading statesmen of both political parties, not only entirely justified Sir James Graham's conduct, but also recommended no alteration of the law. The Secretary of State, therefore, to this day retains his former authority to open letters.[2]

(c) the power of opening private letters;

[2] Erskine May, iii. 44-49.

But in the sixteenth and seventeenth centuries, by far the most important method of influencing public opinion was the strict *censorship* which was exercised *over all printed matter.* At first this censorship was placed in the hands of the Church; but after the Reformation it became part of the prerogative of the Crown, who appointed the licenser and granted a monopoly of printing to London and in a restricted measure to the two Universities, under the supervision of the Stationers' Company, the Archbishop of Canterbury and the Bishop of

(d) censorship of the press;

[1] Prothero, 168-172. Hallam, i. 238-239.
[2] 23 Eliz. c. 2. Prothero, 77-80.
[3] Hallam, i. 206. Prothero, 442.
[4] Prothero, 223-224.
[5] Hallam, i. 206.

London.[1]   Under Elizabeth special statutes armed the judges with the power, through the verdicts of subservient juries, of punishing the publication of anything approaching to the expression of seditious opinions.[2]   Under these statutes sentence of death was passed upon *Udall* (1591) for an alleged libel on the bishops;[3] *Barrow* and *Greenwood* (1586) for the writing of seditious books;[4] and *Penry* for a suspected connection with the Martin Marprelate tracts.[5]   But since the supervision of all opinion, whether spoken or written, was part of the royal prerogative, not least among the duties of the Star Chamber was its work in the suppression of all unlicensed political discussion.   Under the first two Stuarts the opposition excited by their misgovernment kept the members active.   The severe punishments of heavy fines, mutilation, whipping, imprisonment or banishment, which were inflicted for various Puritan publications upon *Leighton* (1630),[6] *Prynne*,[7] *Burton*,

[6] *Ibid.* ii. 37. Gardiner, vii. 144-151.
[7] Gardiner, vii. 329-334.
[8] *Ibid.* viii. 226-233.
[9] *Ibid.* viii. 248-249.
[10] Prothero, 394.

Bastwick (1637),[8] and *Lilburne* (1638),[9] were merely specimens of the exercise of the prerogative of the Crown through the Council in this respect.   The actual restrictions on the liberty of printing were drawn tighter by an ordinance of the Council.[10] But the overthrow of the Star Chamber did not mend matters ; and the severe restrictions imposed by the Long Parliament upon printing, produced the strong plea for freedom in Milton's ' Areopagitica.'   After the Restoration the Licensing Act of 1662 placed the whole control of the press in the hands of the government, and the regulations were very similar to those which had been in vogue under Elizabeth.   From 1679 to 1685 the Act was suffered to lapse ; but a decision of the judges armed the Crown with precisely analogous powers at

[11] Hallam, iii. 2-5.

common law.[11]   The Act, however, was revived on James II's accession, and lasted until 1695, when it was finally suffered to expire ; and with its expiration ' a censorship of the press

[12] *Ibid.* iii. 166-168. Erskine May, ii. 243.

was for ever renounced by the law of England.'[12]

But a theoretical freedom is compatible with very serious practical restrictions ; and the direct control over the press was succeeded by such serious impediments to free criticism and expression of opinion as were offered by the imposition of

(e) stamp duties ;
10 Anne, c. 19.

a stamp duty on newspapers and advertisements, and a vigorous execution of the laws of libel.   The first Stamp Act of this kind was imposed in 1712 and was found so successful both as a means of revenue and as a check on the publication of cheap papers, that by the end of George II's reign the amount of the duty had been quadrupled.[1] In 1819, by one of the 'Six Acts,' the duty was extended to leaflets and tracts which had hitherto been considered too slight to be called newspapers, but which were widely circulated.[2] But the Reform Act of 1832 was naturally followed by a change of attitude on the part of the administration towards fugitive criticism. The duty on advertisements was reduced in 1833 and abolished in 1853; and a similar fate befell the stamp on newspapers in 1836 and 1855 respectively. The last hindrance to the multiplication of cheap newspapers was swept away by the abolition of the duty on paper in 1861.[3]

Perhaps a more serious impediment to freedom of discussion was really formed by *the partial administration and the iniquitous interpretation of the Law of Libel.* Under William III and Anne party feeling ran so high that any one who insulted the dominant party was treated as a libeller, and the whole influence of the government was used to procure his punishment by a sentence of the law courts. The effect of so potent a weapon at a time when political discussion was unusually active can easily be imagined. Under the first two Georges the contempt of a government which had more efficacious means at its disposal, caused it to treat the libellous utterances of its opponents in the press with unusual tolerance. But meanwhile, the judges had been maturing that perverted reading of the law which was not slow to declare itself on the increase of political discussion which marked the accession of George III, and in support of a government which determined to gag the expression of adverse opinion. This interpretation, gradually evolved as circumstances called it forth, consisted of three propositions, each of which may be identified for convenience sake with the particular case which established it. Although the chief interest of the trials which arose out of the publication of No. 45 of the 'North Briton' turned rather on the question of the legality of general warrants; yet in the trial of the printers Lord Mansfield had laid it down (1) *that it was the province of the judge alone to determine the criminality of a libel.*[4] This left to the jury merely the determination of the comparatively immaterial issue of the fact

[1] Erskine May, ii. 245.

[2] *Ibid.* ii. 359.

[3] *Ibid.* ii. 380-382.

(*f*) law of libel.

[4] Hallam, iii. 169. Erskine May, ii. 253.

of its publication, which in the majority of cases would not be disputed. This reading of the law was accepted and enforced by all the judges with the sole exception of Lord Camden. The juries, however, not unnaturally resented an interpretation which practically removed the sole remaining security for freedom of the press; and in indirect ways they endeavoured to escape from it. Thus in the trial of *Woodfall*, the original publisher in the 'Public Advertiser' of Junius' celebrated 'Letter to the King,' the jury, with a clever perception of the real meaning of the judge's charge and to his infinite annoyance, found the defendant 'guilty of printing and publishing only.' In the contemporaneous case of *Miller*, on the same charge, the jury practically challenged Lord Mansfield's doctrine which transferred the trial from the jury to the judge, by a verdict of 'not guilty.' In fact, this interpretation of the law was strenuously combated both in Parliament by such authorities as Lords Chatham and Camden, Sir G. Savile and Burke; and in the law courts by Erskine in his defences of the Dean of St. Asaph (1779) and of Stockdale (1789).[1] But common sense and equity alike were bound to triumph. In his earlier days Charles James Fox had defended Lord Mansfield's interpretation. But in **1792**, chiefly by his advocacy and despite the opposition of the majority of the judges and leading exponents of the law, the *Libel Act* was passed.[2] By this the right of the jury to determine in a case of libel upon the guilt of the whole matter was distinctly affirmed; and a dangerous weapon of attack upon the liberty of the subject in the free and legitimate expression of opinion, was removed. But if this was the most insidious of the judicial interpretations of the law, the other two were no less subversive of the real spirit of individual liberty. In 1731, on the trial of a certain *Franklin* for a libel in the 'Craftsman,' the judge had strongly ruled (2) *that falsehood was not essential to the guilt of a libel*, and had refused to allow the production of any evidence tending to prove the truth of the statements which formed the ground of the accusation.[3] This was merely to bring into conformity with the Common law the action of the judges since the Revolution, which condemned the expression of any opinion adverse to the government of the day. Again, in the case of *Almon*, a bookseller who was tried for selling a reprint

1770.

[1] Erskine May, ii. 253-260.

[2] Robertson, 156.

[3] Hallam, iii. 169 note.

1770.

of Junius' 'Letter to the King,' Lord Mansfield added to his other interpretation a proposition (3) *that a publisher was criminally responsible for the acts of his servants;* and this was soon interpreted to mean that the publication of a libel by a servant was conclusive proof of the connivance of the master.[1] Both these propositions were accepted as the reading of the law for sixty years after the first interpretation had been exploded by the Libel Act. The period which followed 1792 was one of strong reaction; and the repressive measures of a government which was not unnaturally but, as the event proved, was unnecessarily alarmed at the threatened outbreak of popular opinions, for a time at least suspended many of those safeguards of individual liberty which had been already secured. Thus it was only in 1843 that Lord Campbell's *Libel Act* allowed a defendant to plead in excuse the truth of an unfavourable criticism and its publication for the public benefit; and a publisher to prove the publication of a libel without his consent.

[1] Erskine May, ii. 252.

6 & 7 Vict. c. 96.

The liberty of the press was thus placed upon its present footing. Unlike the law of many European nations, in England freedom of discussion does not rest upon the guarantee of an article in the constitution. There is no censorship of the press; and misuse of the press is punished by the ordinary courts. Thus such punishment is only inflicted for statements which shall be proved to be a breach of the law. In other words, the law of the press is merely part of the law of libel: the offence consists in its publication, and all concerned—whether writer, publisher, or printer—are individually and equally liable. 'Freedom of discussion in England,' it has been pithily said, 'is little else than the right to write or say anything which a jury, consisting of twelve shopkeepers, think it expedient should be said or written.'[2]

[2] Dicey, 231.

§ 66. Until comparatively recent times, one of the most formidable menaces to individual liberty came from the connection between the executive and the judicial body. The necessity for a separation between these two powers was so little understood, that it was by no means uncommon for an official, whether a member of the Council or a sheriff, to judge an offender against an order which he had himself issued. In the eyes of a bureaucratic government, this method had the

(*g*) dependence of the judges on the Crown;

advantage of ensuring for its members immunity from any legal consequences which their arbitrary acts might have incurred.   And even the establishment of a more highly organized system of administration has only very gradually recognized the distinction between the executive and the judicial powers.   The Lord Chancellor still forms part of every Cabinet : until little more than a century ago the Chancellor of the Exchequer from time to time exercised judicial functions early in the present century the Lord Chief Justice Ellenborough was a member of the ministry of 'All the Talents.' The connection of the judges with the House of Lords has been noticed in an earlier chapter.   They were regarded as councillors of the Crown in judicial matters, and the defenders of the royal prerogative, or as Bacon described them, as 'lion under the throne.'   Nor was this position questioned until the use which the Stuarts made of the judges in their attacks upon individual liberty, withdrew from Englishmen the protection of that Common law in which had lain their boasted security from national oppression.   Indeed, no small portion of the strength of the Stuarts rested on the fact that, in the majority of cases, the kings had on their side the technical interpretation of the law.   Yet, although the decisions of the law courts were quite subservient to the wishes of the Crown, there was so much opposition to the Crown among the lawyers, that in 1628 Charles I contemplated excluding them from Parliament, as in 1626 he had excluded some of the country gentry by making them sheriffs.   This marked difference in the sentiments of lawyers who were in office and those who were not bound by an official position, is easily accounted for.   In its desire to exalt the authority both of the law and of the court which administer it, the legal profession naturally tends to reverence, perhaps unduly, the supposed source of the law. But while, on the one side, the lawyers, if left to themselves, naturally looked at the king through the medium of the Common law, the judges and legal officials would be as much disposed on their part to regard the law through the medium of the king.   To lawyers out of office, then, the law was the first consideration, and its guardianship the most sacred trust of the royal prerogative : the judges and others who were appointed by the king, and held office only

1806.

The judges under the Stuarts.

during his good pleasure, gave their first thought to the interpretation of the royal will through the medium of the existing
law, and were thus not infrequently led to give decisions both
prejudicial to individual liberty and subversive of the plain
teaching of the Common law.   Thus it is carefully to be borne
in mind that, without the exercise of any undue influence
on the part of the Crown, the judges were prepared to give
decisions favourable to the prerogative or even to the known
wishes of the monarch.   Of this there were two noteworthy
instances at the very beginning of the quarrel between the
Commons and the Crown.   In 1606, in the celebrated case
of *Bate*, the judges distinguished between the ordinary and
extraordinary prerogative of the Crown, attributed to the latter
the right of levying the customs, for the refusal to pay which [1] Prothero,
the prisoner was being tried, and defined it as a power which 340-342.
the Commons could in no way diminish.[1]   In the case of Gardiner,
Calvin, or, as it should more rightly be, Colville, in accordance ii. 5-6.
with the strong desire of the king and in the face of a Parlia- 1608.
ment unwilling to legislate on the matter, twelve out of fourteen
judges decided that Scotch *post-nati*, i.e. those born after the
accession of James I to the English throne, were natural-born
subjects of the English Crown.[2]   This position of the judges [2] Gardiner,
as, in a very real and important sense, servants of the Crown, i. 334, 356.
may be illustrated in three ways.   (1) At the present day, the Prothero,
government, when in doubt as to the legality of a proposed 446.
course of action, takes the advice of the law officers of the
Crown—the Attorney-General and Solicitor-General for the
time being.   The government of the seventeenth century in
a similar predicament consulted the judges.   The result was
that the judges were often called upon to take part in cases in
which they had already pledged themselves by the expression
of an extra-judicial opinion.   Thus they were called upon to
give such opinions, under Elizabeth, as to the legality of
commitments by council, with a result already noticed : under
James I, as to the legal power and limits of proclamations,
when, however, the judges, under the leadership of Coke,
pronounced a decision adverse to the Crown :[3] and similarly [3] Gardiner,
under Charles I, as to the binding force of the Petition of ii. 104.
Right, which they proceeded to explain away ;[4] and as to the [4] *Ibid.*
legality of the levy of ship-money, in which they fully upheld vi. 294.

[1] Gardiner, viii. 94.

the action of the Crown.[1] (2) Until the time of the Stuart the dismissal of a judge for political reasons had been an event of infrequent occurrence, and throughout the reign of Elizabeth not a single instance is to be found. But with the

[2] Ibid. iii. 25.

dismissal of Chief Justice Coke by James I in 1616[2] the judges were given cause to realize that they held office at the king's good pleasure, nor were they allowed to forget it In 1626 Chief Justice Crew was dismissed for refusing to

[3] Ibid. vi. 149.

acknowledge the legality of forced loans:[3] in 1630 Chief Baron Walter met with a like fate for questioning the lawfulness of actions taken against members of the House of

[4] Ibid. vii. 113.

Commons for their conduct in the House;[4] while in 1634

[5] Ibid. vii. 361.

Chief Justice Heath's opposition to ship-money caused his summary removal from the bench.[5] These are only the more prominent instances of the use of a power which, so long as it existed, was too tempting to leave unemployed. For, the Restoration still left the appointment of the judges entirely in the king's hands ; and the removal of other means of influence made it doubly necessary that Charles II and his brother should have a subservient bench. Thus under Charles II, three Lord Chancellors, Clarendon, Shaftesbury, and Bridgeman (who was, however, only Lord Keeper), three chief justices, and six judges were dismissed, notoriously for political reasons. James II used his authority even more arbitrarily ; for in three years he had purged the bench of no less than twelve judges who had refused to aid him in his schemes ; and, more thorough in his methods than his predecessor, he set himself to break the power of the gentry by systematically striking off the lists of justices of the peace those who were not sufficiently complaisant

[6] Gneist, Const. Hist. ii. 298-302 and notes.

to his wishes.[6] But (3) in the Star Chamber the Tudors and early Stuarts had an instrument for keeping the Courts of Common law in subservience. Among other ways of effecting this, the members of that body did not hesitate to use their extra-legal authority for the purpose of reprimanding the judges who might have given a decision adverse to the Crown or had refused to submit to the royal dictates. Thus, in the case of *Commendams,* as it is called, the judges, under the leadership of Coke, refused to obey the royal command to stay their judgement until they had spoken with the king. The rest of he judges were forced to submission by the Star Chamber, nd Coke's obduracy was punished with dismissal.[1]

Indeed, the one great exception to the ordinary attitude of he Stuart judges was *Sir Edward Coke*. In his early days he ad sought advancement by subservience to the Crown ; and, s Attorney-General, he conducted the case against the con-pirators of the Gunpowder Plot. In 1613 he had been made Chief Justice of the King's Bench. But what he valued more han high position or royal favour was the Common law, of which he was the most learned exponent of his time. He was n no sense a statesman, but a lawyer pure and simple, and, ike the common lawyers of the day, most pedantic in his reatment of the law. In the three years during which he was t the head of the Common-law courts he made it his endeavour a) to bring all the courts in England under the Court of King's Bench, and (β) to set up the twelve judges as arbiters between the Crown and the nation. His attempt to gain hese two objects brought him into collision with three powerful odies. The issue of prohibitions laid upon (i) *the ecclesiastical ourts* the preliminary burden of proving that cases which came before them lay within their jurisdiction. By his use of prohibi-ions Coke fell foul of those courts in the cases of *Fuller*[2] and *Sir William Chancey*.[3] The Statute of Praemunire forbade appeals to any other court against sentences obtained in the king's courts. By premising that the king's court meant the Courts of Common law alone, Coke attempted, in the cases of *Glanville* and *Allen*,[4] to twist this statute into a bar to the claim of (ii) *Chancery* to find a remedy in cases in which the decisions of the Common law had been manifestly erroneous. The king, however, came to the rescue, and, by the advice of the Attorney-General Bacon, who was Coke's professional and political rival, he confirmed the claim of Chancery. But Coke did not scruple to quarrel with (iii) *the Crown* itself. He had a particular dislike to the extra-judicial opinions demanded of the judges ; and in 1610, in the matter of the Proclamations, he gave a decision adverse to the Crown ; while in 1611 he opposed the attempt which the king made to put an end to the practice of prohibitions. In 1613 the king transferred him from the headship of the Common Pleas to that of the King's Bench, a technical promotion whose loss of salary

[1] Gardiner, iii. 13-23.

[2] *Ibid.* ii. 40.
[3] *Ibid.* ii. 122.

[4] *Ibid.* iii. 11.

made it a real punishment.   But Coke's new position only
spurred him on to the accomplishment of the two object
which he had set before himself.   In the case of *Peacham* he
not only objected to an attempt of the Council to intimidate
the judges by the 'auricular taking of opinions,' that is, by the
practice of consulting them individually, but his adverse decision
forced that body to leave the trial to the ordinary process of
the Common law.[1]   Finally, his refusal to submit to the royal
wishes in the case of *Commendams* filled up the measure of
his iniquities, and in 1616 he was dimissed from the King's
Bench and the Privy Council.   He entered Parliament and
became the leader of the legal party in the opposition, thus
identifying the popular cause with the maintenance of the law
He had a chief hand in the drafting of the Petition of Right
but death removed him some years before the outbreak of the
Civil War.

This power of intimidation through the Council was denied
to the later Stuarts, but they 'packed' the bench with a shame
lessness as well as a success which left them no cause to regret
the loss of other means of influence.   Charles II and James II
took every care to appoint fit instruments for the work in hand
The most unscrupulous was appointed Chief Justice at a critical
moment—Scroggs, with a view to the trials arising out of the
Popish Plot; Pemberton, in order to condemn Lord Russell
Saunders, to annul the charters of the boroughs : while James,
in all methods more violent than his predecessor, employed
his subservient bench to legalize that dispensing power, which
in Charles' hands had twice failed, for the admission of Roman
Catholics into the army.   This was the result of the decision
in the collusive action of *Godden* v. *Hales*.[2]   The state to
which the bench of judges was thus reduced may be gathered
from the fact that, after the Revolution, all the ten judges who
were then in office, were summarily dismissed.

The Revolution removed the means of some of the worst
excesses of the Stuarts; although for the removal of others,
equally important, the haste with which the Bill of Rights had
been drawn up, forced the country to wait for some years.
Among these was the appointment and tenure of the judges,
which at length found mention in the Act of Settlement.   Here
it was provided (§ 7), that, after the accession of the Hanoverian

[1] Gardiner,
ii. 273.

1634.

[2] Hallam,
iii. 60-63.

1700.

ne, 'judges' commissions be made *quamdiu se bene gesserint*, The judges since the Revolution of 1688. nd their salaries ascertained and established; but upon the ddress of both Houses of Parliament, it may be lawful to emove them.' In two particulars, however, these important fficials still remained personally attached to the Crown : their ommissions ceased on the death of the reigning sovereign, and art of their salary continued to be a charge upon the Civil ∟ist. Both these hindrances to the complete independence of he judges were removed on the accession and largely by the ersonal initiative of George III.[1] The judges were thus freed [1] Robertson, 140. rom all those sinister influences which in the seventeenth entury had made them the most powerful allies of the xecutive in its inroads upon personal liberty. But the uthority of the Crown did not thereby lose a chief support in ts contests with social disorder. The whole previous training f the judges places them upon the side of existing authority, nd the omnipotence of precedents in the English law courts s a formidable barrier to anything approaching violent inno- ation. During the alarms caused by the progress of French evolutionary principles, the sternest upholder of authority ould not have accused the judges of any undue predilection or liberty of opinion; and the repressive measures of the egislature were only too well seconded by the severe sentences f the judges on all prisoners charged with seditious acts or peeches. The chief victims between 1792 and 1794 were— n England, Thomas Paine for his book 'The Rights of Man'; nd in Scotland, Thomas Muir, the Rev. Fyshe Palmer and Villiam Skirving, the secretary of a society calling itself 'the Convention of the Friends of the People' in Edinburgh, who vere all three condemned to varying terms of transportation. But public feeling revolted from this severity, and when the uries, which had at first been in complete harmony with he judges, began as their only alternative to acquit political risoners, a lull followed in indictments for political offences.[2] [2] *Ibid.* ii. 280-311. The measures of the legislature proved sufficient to repress ll attempts at unlicensed association for political purposes; out the freedom of the press was more difficult to curb. Here too, however, the judges came to the rescue of the government, and from 1799 to 1811 the laws of libel were administered in a way that left little to be desired by those

[1] Robertson, ii. 331-336.

in authority.[1]   The subject need not be pursued further
Similar feelings animated the conduct of the judges in the
trials which resulted from the renewal of social disorder

[2] *Ibid.* ii. 348-363.

between 1817 and 1820;[2] but the complete vindication of
authority on the one side, and the infusion of a milder and
more sympathetic spirit into the legislature on the other
have combined to render unnecessary any such accumulation
of harsh laws backed up by severe judicial sentences, as those
which so unhappily characterized the last half of the long reign
of George III.

It remains to be briefly noted, in this connection, that it is
only comparatively recently that trial by jury has formed a real
safeguard to the liberty of the individual.   It has been seen
that for a long while the jury did not cast off the character of
witnesses in favour of its modern form of judges of fact.   The
members of a jury, then, found themselves assailed by two
dangers.   They, no less than the judges, were liable to
(a) *summons before the Star Chamber* for verdicts contrary to
the wishes of the executive, and were severely punished if they

(h) liabili-
ties of the
jury.

refused to reconsider what they had done.   Thus, in 1554
when Sir Nicholas Throckmorton was acquitted of treasonous
participation in Wyatt's rebellion, the jury was heavily fined

[3] Hallam, i. 49.

and imprisoned.[3]   A more legal, though not less iniquitous
restraint upon a juryman was (b) *a personal responsibility for
his verdict.*   By a writ of attaint the verdict of a jury in civil
cases was liable to review at the hands of a fresh jury of
twenty-four.   In so far as the first jury were regarded as
witnesses, a reversal of their verdict convicted them of perjury
and the members were punished with imprisonment while their
lands and goods were held forfeit to the king.   The writ of
attaint was not legally abolished until 1826 : when, however, the
jury lost their character of witnesses it fell into disuse.   But
until the decision of Chief Justice Vaughan in the case of

1670.

Bushell, the jury were considered amenable to legal penalties

[4] Hallam, iii. 9.

for their verdict.[4]   Yet for some time it seemed as if the jury
had only escaped from the Star Chamber to fall into the hands
of the judge.   Charles II attempted to secure the condemnation
of his political opponents through juries manipulated by sheriffs
in the royal interest.   He did indeed so obtain the execution
of Lord Russell and of Algernon Sidney, while it was only by

a timely flight that the leader of the opposition, Shaftesbury, saved himself from a similar fate. But all the intimidation exercised by the judges was ineffectual to force the jury to subservience. Despite the careful selection of the jury, the seven bishops were acquitted. Indeed, after the Revolution the judges discovered that their only avenue to complete control over a prisoner's fate lay in a perverse misreading of the law. Such must be the explanation of the extraordinary interpretation of the law of libel.[1] The undue severity exercised by the [1] p. 455. judges in the political trials of the revolutionary period, were at last met by the juries with the same courage with which their predecessors had met and finally vanquished the judges' reading of the libel laws : and sentences of acquittal in the cases of Miller (1770), Hardy and John Horne Tooke (1794), and Hone (1817)—to mention but a few of the most prominent— were a conclusive proof that the surest guarantee for individual liberty would not be sacrificed by those to whose best interest it was that it should be maintained inviolate.

§ 67. One of the most serious dangers which from time The Army. to time threatened the individual liberty of Englishmen, came from the undue use and extension of the principles of MILITARY SERVICE. This may be described conveniently in connection with the history of the methods employed at various times for the defence of the country against foreign attack. The land forces may be said to have been based on one or other of three principles—(1) homage ; (2) allegiance ; (3) pay.

Although not the first in point of time, the principle of (1) The *homage* may be most conveniently dealt with first of all, Feudal because, unlike the other two, it has entirely disappeared out Levy. of the arrangements of a modern military force. The most effective part of the Anglo-Saxon military arrangements was that which represented the *Comitatus* described by Tacitus— the dux or leader with his comites or band of noble youths,[2] [2] *S. C.* 57, who on the conquest of Britain developed into the king and §§ 13, 14. the body of landowners. They had formed the professional army with which the chief had carried out his conquest, and grants of land had been given them in recognition of their past services and with the understanding that similar service would be continued.

2 H

Before the
Norman
Conquest.

But as the personal element in the relations between king
and thegns dwindled away and as thegnhood extended, the need
of some new basis for a reliable military force would be felt.
Now, the great work of the Norman Conquest was to simplify
the complicated relations of Anglo-Saxon life by 'territorializing'
them all, that is, by binding up all duties and services with
the possession of land.   But it seems quite possible that the
territorializing of what is often considered the most important
of such duties—that of military service—had begun long
before the invasion of William.   A document assigned to
the first half of the tenth century tells us that even a ceorl
could attain to thegnhood if to the possession of five hides
of land he added special service to the king.[1]   The five hides
may denote the unit of military service.   There is much mention
of it in Domesday in that connection.   On the other hand
we are told of thegns who had other thegns under them owing
military service to the Crown :[2]   there is evidence that the king
sometimes allowed his ecclesiastical tenants to compound for
the military service which was due from their lands, and the
lord seems even to have been allowed to exact a fine from
a tenant who refused to obey the summons to the host.   All
this looks like an incipient feudalism.   It would be very much
to the king's advantage that the service of the great thegns
should be settled in amount, and that they should be re
sponsible for the service of the smaller folk.   Things might
be tending in this direction : the king's charters might even
occasionally contain stipulations for definite military service.
But we have no real warrant as yet for saying that military
service and the tenure of land were inseparably connected
that 'the land was being plotted out with five-hide-units,' that
the 'five-hide rule obtained throughout a large part of England,
or that ordinarily 'in the eleventh century the king could only
ask for one man's service from every five-hides.'[3]

This territorializing of the military service was, however
quickly completed by William I in his introduction of the
FEUDAL LEVY.   Lands were definitely granted out by the
Conqueror on condition that their holders should discharge at
least part of their obligations by military service.   The unit of
service was the knight's fee, but the obligations of individual
tenants-in-chief of the Crown varied from the liability for

After the
Norman
Conquest.

[1] *S. C.* 65.
Cf. *E. H. R.*
xii. 490.

[2] *S. C.* 65,
§ 3, 'the
king's " ut-
ware."'

[3] *Domes-
day*, 156,
159, 295.

appearance in person or by deputy, to responsibility for a large number of fully equipped knights. It does not seem that the number demanded by the king bore any strict relation to the size of the tenant's estate.[1] The materials at our disposal prove the existence of a number of estates which, while differing widely in size, bore the same liabilities for military service.[2] Thus it seems likely that this service was arbitrarily fixed by the king when he granted the estate, perhaps, as has been suggested, in terms of an unit of five knights. In any case, the amount of the service was a bargain between the tenant-in-chief and the Crown, and the tenant-in-chief alone was responsible for the performance of the service due from his estate. Moreover, seldom, if ever, did he enfeoff or make permanent provision for the full number of knights for which his estate was liable : the balance of the service due remained charged on his demesne, and the Assize of Arms imposed on him the obligation of keeping in stock the proper equipment for the temporary doers of that service.[3] Over the size of this feudal levy there has been much dispute. The legend of Ordericus Vitalis,[4] that the Conqueror provided for a force of 60,000 knights, and the more sober calculation of Stephen Segrave in the thirteenth century, which fixed it at 32,000, may be dismissed as equally improbable. On the one side, it has been thought[5] that not even the officials of the Exchequer were able to fix the number of existing knights' fees, and that the ascertainment of this was the chief object of Henry II's inquiry in 1166, of which the few extant returns form our earliest authority for the organization of the feudal host in England. But on the other side, it has been pointed out that such ignorance on the part of the Crown officials was impossible on the supposition of an original bargain between the tenants-in-chief and the Crown, and that what Henry II really desired to ascertain in 1166 was the number of knights' fees which had been created on each estate.[6] More probable conjectures, of which the proofs are too long to give here, have placed the available number of knights at between five and seven thousand.[7]

From the very first establishment of the feudal force the kings seem to have realized the difficulties inseparable from its existence, and to have made every effort to modify and

[1] *S. C. H.* § 96.

[2] Round, *Feudal England,* 247 et seq.

[3] *S. C.* 154. § 1.

[4] *Ibid.* 82.

[5] *S. C. H.* § 161, and *S. C.* 146.

[6] Round, *Feudal England,* 237.

[7] *Ibid.* 292.

Its disadvantages.

gradually to destroy it.   The Oath of Salisbury withdrew from every English subtenant all excuse for obedience to the ordinary feudal rule of following his immediate lord in preference to the overlord.   Despite this precautionary measure, the events of Stephen's reign showed that the existence of the feudal levy was highly (*a*) *dangerous* to the Crown.   Moreover, the limited term of the service proved it to be (*b*) *ineffective for foreign warfare*.   For, a large part of the time would be consumed in journeys ; a considerable portion of the levy consisted of ecclesiastics whose constant opposition limited the service ; while the division to which the enfeoffed knights' fees were often subjected rendered it difficult to get full service even of the limited amount, since the owner of a half fee was only liable for half the usual service.   As to the whole question of *the liability of the mediæval army to foreign service*, it is to be noted that, under William II and even at a later date, the obligation was taken to include the fyrd or national militia ;[1] that scutage, or the commutation for personal service, applied to bishops who could have no foreign fiefs, and to simple knights who would be mostly of English birth, so that no difference was made between home and foreign service.   It is true, however, that the introduction of scutage might be construed as implying a doubt whether service could be demanded of Englishmen in a land where they had no fiefs.   But in 1177 earls, barons, and knights crossed the Channel for Henry II against France.[2]   And if there had been doubts or even (*c*) *quarrels over the foreign service* under Henry II and Richard I, the doubts were set at rest and the quarrels consequently increased by the loss of Normandy in 1204 ; for, while the new nobility of Henry II had never boasted of possessions out of England, the king's excuse for claiming service in his lands on the other side of the Channel was now entirely taken away.   Thus the pleas put out by the feudal tenants as an excuse for not rendering service, took two forms. (1) Sometimes they claimed that their tenure did not include service abroad.   This was urged by Bishops Hugh of Lincoln and Herbert of Salisbury to Richard I's demand in 1198 for a force of 300 knights to serve him for a year in Normandy ;[3] and by the northern barons in 1213 when they refused to follow John to France.[4]   On the other hand, the barons who led the

[1] *S. C.* 93, Flor. Wigorn.

[2] *Ibid.* 131 ; Ben. Abb. i. 160.

[3] *Ibid.* 255 ; R. Hoveden, iv. 40 ; and V. M. S. Hugonis, 248.

[4] *Ibid.* 277 ; Rad. Cogges, 872.

opposition to Edward I which ended in the confirmation of
the Charters, refused to go to Gascony while the king himself
went to Flanders, since (2) their service abroad only meant
personal service with the king.[1]

It is small wonder, then, that the kings attempted to
modify the organization of the feudal levy. The effect of
(i) the *Oath of Salisbury* has been already mentioned. The
anarchy of Stephen's reign spurred his successors on to
further efforts. The first attempt to get rid of a large portion
of the feudal force was by (ii) *Scutage*. This was a payment
in place of personal service, at a varying but definitely determined rate, and is generally said to have been first applied
by Henry II in 1156 to the Church lands held on military
tenure, in order to ensure in some form a service to the performance of which constant difficulties were raised by those
from whom it was due. In 1159 it was extended to the
agrarii milites, as they are termed by the chronicler.[2] The
advantage of this was that, while the king thus got rid
of the most cumbersome and discontented portion of the
feudal levy, he procured for himself a sum of money with
which he could hire mercenary troops for his foreign wars.
It seems possible, however, that scutage originated earlier
than the reign of Henry II. Domesday contains notices of
payment in lieu of military service, whether the payment was
made to a substitute[3] or direct to the Crown. Moreover,
since a great baron rarely provided by definite enfeoffment for
the whole of the service due from his estate, he must have
found substitutes for that portion of it which remained charged
upon his demesne. It has been conjectured that scutage
represented the sum paid to such substitutes, which there is
much reason to suppose was paid as early as the reign of
Henry I to the king instead. The forty days' service required
of a feudal tenant bears a definite relation to both the marc
and the pound, in varying rates of either of which scutage was
afterwards exacted. It does not seem idle to suppose that
the substitute's probable pay of 4*d.* or 6*d.* a day for forty days
gives the clue to the amounts exacted under the name of
scutum or shield-money.[4] The history of scutage as a tax
is pursued elsewhere. Another device employed by Henry II
for lessening the numbers of the feudal levy was the application

[1] *S. C.*
440 ;
W. de
Heming,
ii. 121.

Attempts
to get rid
of it.

[2] *Ibid.*
129,
Rob. de
Monte.

[3] *Ibid.* 91,
*Customs of
Berks,*
line 7.

[4] Cf. *Ibid.*
175,
line 24.

to it of the principle of a (iii) *Quota*. In 1157 he called on
every two knights to supply a third, who should thus be at
his service for four months.   In the same way Richard I, in
1194, summoned a third part of the knight service of the
kingdom,[1] although in 1198 his attempt to obtain a force of
300 knights for a year on the same principle was defeated by
the resolute attitude of the two bishops.   In 1205 John provided
himself with a tenth part of the full feudal force equipped by
the abstention of the remaining nine-tenths;[2] while, under
Henry III, the year 1234 furnishes an instance of a similar
service.   The principle was carried even beyond the feudal
levy.   For, the kings did not hesitate to (iv) *confound the
feudal force with the local fyrd*, whether by rendering the
holders of knights' fees liable to the Assize of Arms, by imposing the system of quota alike on the fyrd and the feudal
tenants, or by summoning the two bodies, for both of which
the sheriff was in the main responsible, to meet at the same time
and place.   The last method to be noticed aimed at the dis-
armament of the feudal force by a measure that practically
amounted to its degradation.   (v) *Distraint of knighthood* was
a measure by which all holders of a certain quantity of land,
irrespective of the tenure by which they held it, were forced
either to take upon themselves the duties and responsibilities
of knightly tenure or to pay a heavy fine.   It may be that
its primary object was the degradation of the knightly body
by the wholesale introduction into it of those who had no
pretensions to gentle birth.   But it equally served the purpose
of swelling the royal coffers with the feudal dues of those
willing and the fines of those unwilling to accept the dignity thus
thrust upon them, and of increasing the number of persons
who would be eligible as knights of the shire in Parliament.
The earliest instance of a levy of this kind is in 1224, and
others occur under Henry III;[3] but it seems doubtful whether
they referred only to tenants-in-chief of the Crown or were
intended to include tenants of other lords.   Under Edward I
however, all such doubt is removed.   In 1278 the sheriffs are
directed to force the knightly rank upon all holders of land
worth £20 a year, ' whosoever tenants they are' (*de quocunque
teneant*).[4]   The reluctance of the freeholders to undertake
this burden is probably accountable for the early fluctuation

[1] S. C.
254;
R. Hove-
den, iii.
242.

[2] *Ibid*. 281.

[3] S. C. H.
§ 239 for
references.

[4] S. C.
457.

in the qualification. In 1285 this is fixed as high as an estate of the annual value of £100. But, until the time of the Tudors, an estate of £20 seems to have been the distinguishing mark of an esquire who wanted nothing but his own willingness or the command of the king to advance him to knightly rank. The increase in general wealth and the fall in the value of money probably account for the advance of the qualifying sum by Elizabeth to an estate of £40, at which rate both James I and Charles I imposed the obligation. It was abolished by the Long Parliament; and the destruction of feudal tenures on the accession of Charles II removed all possibility of its revival. It must be borne in mind that these efforts of the Crown to rid itself of the feudal levy were by no means systematic. The feudal force was still occasionally called out in full numbers when the king took the field in person; but these various endeavours to suppress it were practically crowned with success. For, chiefly by their means the minor tenants-in-chief of the Crown became blended with the general body of freeholders; the caste spirit provoked by feudalism, after a moment's glorification under the name of chivalry, sank under the discredit which attached to that spurious form of military enthusiasm; and with the general decay of feudal obligations into a mere means of raising revenue, new and more efficacious methods were found of providing for the defence of the country. The last occasion of the summons of the feudal levy was as late as Charles I's Scotch war in 1640.

§ 68. The earliest principle on which military service was based was that which, with the establishment of monarchy, came to be known as (2) *allegiance*. Tacitus describes the fighting force of the German tribes as the nation in arms organized according to *pagi*, each of which sent its hundred warriors to the host.[1] In Anglo-Saxon times we find mention of a threefold duty which lay upon every freeman. This included *burh-bot* or maintenance of local fortifications, *bric-bot* or repair of bridges, and *fyrdung* or duty with the FYRD, a national militia which seemed to carry on the system described by Tacitus.[2] The service was enforced by a heavy penalty for neglect, called *fyrdwite*,[3] which varied, according to the rank of the offender, from forfeiture of his land to a moderate fine.

(2) The National Militia.

[1] *S. C.* 56. § 6.

Its original organization.

[2] *Ibid.* 73, c. 26.

[3] *Ibid.* 62, c. 51.

After the settlement of the English the fyrd may have sunk into neglect; but the spasmodic character of the Danish invasions led to its revival, and Ælfred organized it into two halves, alternately for active service and as a reserve. But as society became more complicated, or as equipment became more elaborate and costly, the original liabilities became contracted. By commendation or otherwise a simple freeman could so compromise his freedom and its obligations that he could escape his duty altogether or lay it permanently on another; while whole towns and even shires were able to compound for the duty by a fixed amount in men or even in money.[1] Among the old English institutions retained by the Conqueror, the fyrd held a chief place. He and his successors kept it as a balance to the feudal class, and relied on it in their struggles with the Norman barons.[2] William II, however, did not scruple to use it as a means of extortion also. In 1094 Ranulf Flambard summoned the troops to Hastings for an expedition to Normandy and then fleeced them of their journey money, leaving them to make their way home as best they could.[3] But the new system of government inaugurated by the Conquest brought out *two principles* in connection with the position of the fyrd. William I's action in the Oath of Salisbury bound it definitely to the Crown by (a) an *Oath of Allegiance* which superseded all feudal or other ties. Thus, in the language of the lawyers, liege homage was due in England to the king alone, whereas on the continent it could be exacted by every lord who had land to bestow. Again, although William II and, in great emergencies, some of his successors, thought themselves justified in using the fyrd for foreign warfare, the accepted theory limited its use to (b) *defensive* war alone. Certainly it was often called out for Welsh and Scotch wars, but, without any undue wresting of language, these might be regarded as wars of defence. It was put to its legitimate use in such contests as the victory of Archbishop Thurstan over David of Scotland at the battle of the Standard or Northallerton, and the defeat of William the Lion at Alnwick in 1174. On both these occasions it was called out to repel invasion.

It must have been partly at least as a tribute to the past usefulness of the fyrd that Henry II, in 1181, gave it a more

[1] *S. C.* 90 (Oxford), 91 (Berks).

1088-1101.

[2] *Ibid.* 92, 96.

[3] *Ibid.* 94.

1138.

Its reorganization.

definite organization in the *Assize of Arms*. All freemen (§§ 1-3) were to possess arms of a quality differing according to their wealth, and their liabilities (§ 9) were to be assessed, if necessary, by a sworn jury of their neighbours. It is noticeable that this liability attached itself to all, even to feudal tenants, while villans (§ 12) and Jews (§ 7) were specially omitted.[1] The next century witnessed three important developments in the system : (a) *villans were included* in the liability ;[2] instead of the whole available force, (β) sometimes only a *quota* was called out, as in 1231 when a writ was issued to the Sheriff of Gloucester for the equipment of 200 men at the expense of those who were not called out :[3] (γ) the fyrd *was connected with the police system*, and was organized under a constable for that purpose.[4] The double and, in earlier days, inseparable duties of military service and of police in its various departments had always been incumbent on the freemen of the country in their local organizations. Henceforth the latter tended to become their chief employment, and the *Statute of Winchester* under Edward I summed up the position of the fyrd after all these changes, further organizing the whole system in the matter of equipment and placing it under the superintendence of appointed justices.[5] Indeed, the military duties of the fyrd were already being rendered useless by the employment of new methods of raising troops. The duty of service in the fyrd, combined with the custom of making use of a quota of the troops, whether feudal or national, at the king's disposal, led to the granting of *Commissions of Array* to royal officers for the forcible levy or impressment of a specified number of men. Thus, in 1282, Edward I had commissioned a certain William de Butiller to 'elect'—that is, to press or pick—1000 men in Lancashire. Henceforward the use of this method of raising troops becomes frequent, with the variation that sometimes, as in 1294, the numbers of the men to be impressed were not fixed beforehand. Under Edward I men thus impressed were taken into the royal service and paid by the king: but under Edward II commissions of array became a grave national abuse and a heavy item of indirect taxation ; for, the counties and townships where the troops were levied, were forced to pay their wages and to supply them with better arms than the Statute of Winchester required. The result was so convenient

[1] *S. C.* 154-156.

[2] *Ibid.* 371.

[3] *Ibid.* 360.

[4] *Ibid.* 372.

1285.

[5] *Ibid.* 470-472.

to the king that Parliament had to return again and again to the attack of the abuse. An Act of 1327, repeated in 1352 and confirmed in 1404, established the principle that except in cases of invasion such troops should not leave their counties, and then only by acquiescence of Parliament and at the expense of the Crown.[1] This, however, by no means stopped the evil. Commissions were issued frequently under the Tudors and the early Stuarts; and it was their object 'to organize but not actually to bring into the field, the national militia.' When called out the troops received from the Crown wages and 'coat and conduct money,' that is, for uniforms and travelling expenses.[2]

1 Cf. p. 242.

2 Prothero, cxx.

The modern Militia.

Meanwhile, the old obligations of the fyrd had not been extinguished. They were revived in the reigns of Edward VI and Queen Mary. By a statute of 1550, amended by another in 1558, the mustering of the national militia was taken away from the sheriff and given to a new officer, the lord-lieutenant of the county; while the contributions of persons of property were carefully regulated. The effect of this, however, was short-lived; for under James I the repeal of the Statute of Winchester did away with the special obligation to possess arms, though not of course with the common-law obligation of defence; and the want was supplied by the collection of provisions and magazines of arms into one place in each county. One of the first acts of the Long Parliament was to condemn commissions of array or the compulsory impressment of soldiers to serve outside the country, as illegal, 'save in case of necessity of invasion or by reason of tenure.' They went even further; for, the two 'Army Plots' whereby the king attempted to use the army which had been raised for the Scotch war, for the purpose of overawing Parliament, led the Commons to secure for their own nominees the command of the local forces. It was proposed, therefore, that Parliament should take into its own hands the nomination of the lords-lieutenant who should obey the orders of the House of Commons, and for two years should be irremovable by the king. Despite Charles' refusal, they proceeded to carry this into effect, and were thus guilty of as great illegality as the king who, notwithstanding the Act of the previous year, levied troops by commissions of array. The first motion of the Restoration Parliament was

1642.

a declaration that any Act was invalid without the king's consent, and that the sole command of any force by land or sea, or of the national militia, was in the hands of the Crown. At the same time, provision was made by statute for keeping up the militia as a national force; and it acquired a great popularity, not only on account of its strong local connection, but because it was regarded as emphatically the army of the nation as opposed to the regular troops who formed particularly the army of the Crown. The king appointed the lords-lieutenant with the power of nominating officers and with the general control of a force in which the liability to service now rested upon property. It became in fact a local force officered by the local gentry, manned by their tenants, and controlled in the county itself. Both socially and constitutionally it enjoyed an unique position. But during the first half of the eighteenth century the continued maintenance of the standing army caused the militia to fall into neglect, and on its reorganization in 1757 considerable changes in detail, though not in the local principle, were introduced. The power of the central authority was increased; for, to the Crown was given a veto on the appointment of officers; the number of men to be raised was settled beforehand and apportioned to each district, and the choice was to be made by ballot; while, instead of special exemption as hitherto, the militia at times of service was liable to the Mutiny Act. At the same time, to the Crown was given the important power, with the ultimate sanction of Parliament, of embodying or specially calling out the militia in case of apprehended invasion or of actual rebellion. The force was embodied on several occasions previous to 1815 : but the large numbers of men which were drafted from it into the army, especially during the Peninsular war, did away with much of its peculiar character as a defensive force. After 1815 the militia fell into decay, and in 1829 the ballot was suspended. But in 1852 the force was placed upon its modern footing; and during the Crimean War and the South African War it has done excellent service at home and abroad, in garrisons and in the field. Enlistment has now become voluntary, though resort might be had to the ballot if the numbers fell short of those fixed by Parliament. The new army system inaugurated in 1871 removed the control of the militia from the lords-lieutenant and vested it in the Crown through the Secretary of State; the money voted for the militia forms part of the army estimates, and not, as formerly, a separate grant; while the regiments themselves are reckoned as battalions of the regiments of the line, which take their name from and have their headquarters in the respective counties.

The modern Volunteer force.

But the readiness of the nation to accept the obligations of the ancient fyrd is not to be measured by the number of enlistments in the modern militia. The 'citizen armies' which a system of conscription has given to many European nations, find their counterpart in the British *Volunteers*. Societies for national defence can be traced as early as the Tudor times, and are still represented in the Honourable Artillery Company of London. The trained bands of the City, which were so prominent during the Civil Wars and the Commonwealth,

[1] Firth, *Cromwell's Army.*

probably come under the same head.[1] But the first general formation of a volunteer force came when the American War of Independence had almost denuded Ireland of her usual garrison, and a threatened invasion from France led the government to accept for the defence of Ireland several voluntarily enlisted corps, which soon numbered over 40,000 men. This organization became political, and played no unimportant part in procuring Irish parliamentary independence and in the establishment of what is known as 'Grattan's

[2] Erskine May, iii. 311 et seq.

Parliament.'[2] The Napoleonic wars gave another occasion for the formation of large corps of volunteers in England as well as in Ireland. But, with the exception of some cavalry called *Yeomanry*, these were disbanded on the conclusion of peace. The present volunteer force owes its origin to the danger which threatened England from the attitude of France and the United States at the time when her hands were occupied with the Indian Mutiny and the Chinese War. In 1859 there was revived an old Act of 1804, which empowered the Crown to accept the services of corps of volunteer troops; and a new Act of 1863 allowed the sovereign, with the ultimate sanction of Parliament, to call them out for service on any apprehension of invasion. As the force became permanent its ranks were filled not merely, as at first, with the well-to-do, but with the artisan class; voluntary subscriptions were not sufficient for its maintenance, and Parliament voted a regular grant which forms part of the annual Army Estimates. By an Army Order issued in April 1901, the existing Yeomanry and the Imperial Yeomanry raised in connection with the South African War have been merged into one force bearing the name of the Imperial Yeomanry. The present organization of the volunteers is governed by the Regulation of Forces Act passed in 1881. 44 & 45 Vict. c. 57, § 9.

§ 69. Thus in the formation of a modern army the old obligation of tenure has altogether disappeared; while that arising from allegiance has been revived in a voluntary method which has practically staved off any necessity for the full legal enforcement of the original obligation. But, for the defence of the country in the first instance, and practically for all offensive warfare, all other methods of raising troops have been abandoned in favour of the principle of (3) *Payment.* The first mercenaries in England were Cnut's Huskarls, a Danish body-guard of several thousand men. In fact, at first all hired soldiers were foreigners. William I's army at Hastings was a volunteer mercenary army drawn from almost every part of Western Europe; and in 1085 his troops which repelled the invasion of the Danes consisted of *solidarii*, footmen and archers from France and Brittany. Again, Henry I took into his pay many of the Flemings who had survived the First Crusade. Indeed, the foreigners introduced in one way and another by the Norman kings formed the mainstay of the armies of both Stephen and Matilda. But by the treaty of Wallingford provision was made for the removal of all such aliens from England, and their banishment was one of the most popular acts in Henry II's restoration of civil government. For the next century or more the kings fought their wars abroad with mercenaries hired with the proceeds of scutage — Henry II with men from Brabant, Wales, and Galloway, to whom Richard I added Basques and Navarese, many of such troops being outlaws or returned Crusaders. On two occasions only were they brought to England—in 1174, when a body of Flemings was landed to repel invasion and was withdrawn after a month; and in 1213, when John raised a mercenary army against the barons and, despite the prohibition of Magna Carta,[1] retained them in arms for the later struggle. This time they were not so easily disposed of, Mercenaries.

1153.

[1] *S. C.* 302. § 5.

[1] S. C. H. § 162.

for it was only with the expulsion of Falkes de Breauté in 122.
that the last of them disappeared.[1]   But the desire of the king:
to rid themselves of the feudal levy, the increasing restriction
of the fyrd to duties of police, and the dislike of the English
people to the presence of foreign troops, all combined with
the longer duration of wars to force the king to seek new
methods of supplying himself with an army.   These were
found in the semi-feudal retinues of the great lords, who
agreed to supply the king with bands of men at a fixed rate

[2] Ibid. § 474.

of pay.[2]   It was with an army formed chiefly in this manner
that the battles of the Hundred Years' War were fought.   But
the nobles' retinues were broken up by the legislation of
Henry VII; and the Tudor sovereigns relied upon com
missions of array and, for personal defence, upon a small
permanent body called Yeomen of the Guard.

The modern mercenary army.

The modern army owes its beginning to the great Civil
War.   In 1645 the parliamentary forces were organized on
a definite basis, and in 1653 the Instrument of Government
provided for a standing army of 30,000 men.   When this
army was disbanded at the Restoration, the king managed to
retain as guards a small body of about 5,000 troops, including
Monk's Coldstreams and some cavalry, which he hoped to
make the nucleus of a force to aid his schemes of despotism
But one legacy of the rule of Cromwell and his Major Generals
was an intense national antipathy to a professional army.
Consequently, in 1667, when the king hastily raised 12,000
troops for the Dutch war, the Commons unanimously resolved
to request him to disband them on the conclusion of peace.
Again, in 1673, when levies were raised for the second Dutch
war, Parliament voted the maintenance of any troops other
than the militia to be a national grievance; and in 1678,
when 20,000 troops were enrolled on the pretext of a French
war, supplies were granted only on condition that these should
be disbanded.   James II, nothing daunted by these evidences
of popular feeling, set to work to provide himself with a reliable
force.   While, on the one side, he tried to suppress the militia
by dismissing all lords-lieutenant whom he could not trust, and
by disarming the propertied classes who formed the body of the
force; on the other side, he increased the numbers of the
standing army, and placed it under officers on whom he could

rely.   Monmouth's rebellion gave him an excuse for raising
new regiments; and into these, on the strength of the judicial
decision in *Godden* v. *Hales*,[1] he introduced Roman Catholic   [1] Robertson,
officers.   On the pretext of a London riot, which had been   245-248.
provoked by the open celebration of Roman Catholic rites, he
placed these troops in a permanent camp on Hounslow Heath.
But popular feeling was so strong that even this army expressed
delight at the acquittal of the seven bishops; and on William
of Orange's advance a large portion of it deserted James.
Considering the uses to which Charles and James had designed
to put their army, it is not wonderful that the Bill of Rights
declared the maintenance of a standing army in time of peace
to be illegal.   Peace, however, did not come till the treaty of
Ryswick, when Parliament voted the reduction of the army to   1697.
7,000 men.   But the long war which occupied almost the
whole of Anne's reign, the danger from the Jacobites during
the earlier years of the Hanoverian dynasty, the Austrian
Succession and the Seven Years' wars, the war of American
Independence and the long struggle with Napoleon, all necessitated the existence of a large standing army, and, by accustoming
the people to its presence, removed from their minds the old
apprehensions of danger.   Meanwhile, the measures taken for
its maintenance and discipline were such as removed all sting
implied in the old taunt that it was the king's army.   The
method of appropriation of supplies dictated the financial
clauses of the *Mutiny Act*,[2] on which the legal status of the   [2] *Ibid.* 58-61.
army depended.   With few and insignificant exceptions, this   1689.
was (1) an annual measure authorizing, among other things,
the maintenance of a certain specified number of troops and
providing the necessary funds.   This Act is the strongest constitutional guarantee for an annual parliamentary session; for
without it the maintenance of an army becomes illegal, and by
it Parliament retains a hold on the armed forces of the nation.

But the Mutiny Act or, as in this particular it has been   Martial
called since 1881, the Army Act, provides also for the   law.
discipline of the army by special and appropriate methods.
(2) *Martial law*, or the summary discipline of military service,
was originally enforced by the Court of Chivalry, presided over
by the Earl Marshal or the Lord High Constable, the officers
responsible for the ordering of the feudal array in the field.

But as the feudal host was in theory an army of occupation, the jurisdiction of this court extended to offences committed in time of peace as well as during actual service. As the Courts of Common law became organized in the hands of trained lawyers, the frequent complaints made against the arbitrary action of this court caused its restriction by statute, and under Richard II the powers of its officials were defined and limited to time of war. During the Wars of the Roses martial law was used by both sides for the speedy punishment of prisoners, and they were subjected to all kinds of strange legal systems by such learned ruffians as Tiptoft, Earl of Worcester, who is said to have tried his victims by the law of Padua. Under the Tudors the Court of Chivalry fell into disuse; for after the death of the Duke of Buckingham the office of Constable was revived merely for a coronation, and the court continued to be held before the Earl Marshal for civil cases only, passing in time into the modern College of Heralds. But the want of a summary military tribunal was corrected by the issue, in time of war or rebellion, of Articles of War whose administration was entrusted to specially constituted bodies of persons. Thus, those who had taken part in the Pilgrimage of Grace and in Sir Thomas Wyatt's rebellion were so punished. Under Elizabeth this mode of summary punishment was put to more dubious uses. In 1573 the Queen was with difficulty dissuaded from applying it to a fanatic named Burchell who had attempted the life of Sir John Hawkins. Again, in 1588 a royal proclamation subjected to martial law all introducers of Papal bulls into England; while in 1595 Sir Thomas Wyllford was appointed Provost Marshal of London for the purpose of so punishing some riotous apprentices. It was in accordance with this prerogative power of decreeing martial law that Charles I not only billeted the troops he had raised for the Spanish War on those who had refused to contribute to his forced loans, but issued a commission to certain persons to apply such summary remedies for restraining some disorders of which the troops were guilty. Thus, while Elizabeth applied it to civilians, Charles did not scruple to use it in time of peace. The Petition of Right condemned both the billeting and the use of martial law. But martial law had come to mean little more than the suspension of the Common law during a rebellion

1521.

1536.
1554.

1628.

in favour of some more summary mode of trial. With the advent of a standing army a new problem presented itself. Acting on the analogy of the old royal authority to issue Articles of War, Charles II and his successor added Articles which regulated the punishment of soldiers by the civil courts in time of peace. But something more than this was necessary, otherwise desertion would be little more than a breach of contract, and a blow given to an officer would fall under the head of a common assault. Accordingly, when the Mutiny Acts for the first time definitely authorized the maintenance of an army, ministers contented themselves with merely supplementing the right always exercised by the Crown of issuing Articles in times of war; mutiny and desertion were made punishable with death, whether the troops were on active service or not. In 1715 the Mutiny Act of that year gave the Crown the right of issuing Articles in time of peace, and this right lasted until 1879, when these Articles were drawn together into a code of military law which, with amendments, exists to the present day.

The result of the Mutiny Act and its successor, the Army Acts, is to provide a special code of law applicable to a special class of persons in a special part of their relations with their fellow men. It is important to realize that a soldier is not exempt from, and therefore does not lose the protection of, the Common law. He has been aptly likened to the clergyman, in that he incurs 'special obligations in his official character, but is not thereby exempted from the ordinary liabilities of citizenship.'[1] In French law it is a fundamental principle that every kind of offence committed by a soldier must be tried by a military tribunal. In England, on the other hand, the soldier is in a twofold position as (*a*) citizen and (*b*) soldier. (*a*) In his former and original capacity he is subject to the same liabilities both criminal and civil which any civilian would incur, and he is amenable to the Courts of Common law. The extent of this liability is clear from two well-known cases of the last century. During the riots which followed Wilkes' election to Parliament in 1768 the mob pelted the magistrates and troops. Before leave had been given to fire, a man was shot, and at the coroner's inquest the verdict of wilful murder was brought in against the soldiers.[2] It is immaterial to the

Legal position of the soldier.

[1] Dicey, 290.

[2] Lecky, iii. 133.

present argument that they were acquitted on their trial. Again, in 1780, when the question of the legality of using the military in the suppression of the Gordon riots was raised in the House of Lords, Lord Mansfield defended it on the ground that the troops had been called in as citizens employed to preserve the laws and the constitution; for, a soldier did not by enlistment lose his citizenship.[1] But such a double position could not possibly be maintained if it involved a conflict of jurisdictions between civil and military courts. As it is, the connection between the courts is quite clear. Enlistment is a civil proceeding which, since 1694, has taken place before a justice of the peace; it is the business of the civil courts to determine whether any individual is subject to the jurisdiction set up by the Mutiny Act; while any excess of jurisdiction on the part of military courts would be met by the issue of a writ of Habeas Corpus and the discharge of the prisoner from custody. (b) The soldier's exceptional capacity may now be dismissed in a few words. Although even the plea of acting under orders does not excuse him in the commission of a criminal act which is tried by the civil courts, on the other hand there are certain classes of acts which by the special position of the soldiers are exalted from slight misdemeanours into serious crimes. These would include, besides all negative acts or neglect of military rules, such positive breach of discipline as would be implied in an assault upon an officer.

It has been said that enlistment is a civil proceeding: in other words, it is a contract between the Crown and the individual who takes service in the army. Thus the standing army of the last two centuries is a mercenary force. But the prerogative right of impressment, which may be regarded as little else than a compulsion to fulfil the old obligation of every freeman, has never been abolished. Its use for soldiers was condemned by the Long Parliament except in cases of sudden invasions, and the only violation of this Act was an authorization by Parliament, during the American War of Independence, of the impressment of all 'idle and disorderly persons,' in whose behalf no one was disposed to complain of the breach of individual liberty involved. Ready enlistment in time of war and the formation of a volunteer force have hitherto rendered unnecessary any extensive recourse to this

[1] Erskine May, ii. 276.

Methods of raising an army.

(1) Impressment.

1779.

prerogative right. It may be remarked in conclusion, that, since the Act of 1641, any force raised by this method in time of national danger would have to be disbanded as soon as the danger which made it lawful has passed away. It affords no means of maintaining a standing army.

A standing army, then, is one raised by voluntary enlistment (2) Voluntary enlistment and sanctioned from year to year by Parliament. Enlistment is a contract, but it has not always been made by the same people. The first volunteer mercenary armies of Englishmen were raised by contract between the king and some of the great nobility; and even after the army became a permanent force, this method of recruiting was for a long time sustained. An individual officer with a commission as colonel was authorized to raise a regiment of a certain strength : he made his own terms with the recruits, and paid them out of his share of the sum voted by Parliament for the support of the army. This system was employed as late as the Crimean War: but, meanwhile, in 1783 the Crown took over the duty of recruiting and, consequently, of paying the troops direct. As to the *length of service*, from the first parliamentary recognition of a standing army the contract made by the soldier was for life unless he was discharged by the Crown. But in 1847 the period of service was for the first time limited to a maximum term of twenty-one years. A minimum term was also appointed within which the soldier could get his discharge only by payment of a sum of money, and it is this minimum limit which has been chiefly curtailed by the subsequent Enlistment Acts of 1870 and 1879.

No more apt illustration could be given of the suspicion Government of the army. which originally attended the maintenance of a standing army than the provision made for its management. This 'exhibited a medley of conflicting jurisdictions,' the result of which was that 'the soldier was fed by the Treasury and armed by the Ordnance Board : the Home Secretary was responsible for his movements in his native country : the Colonial Secretary superintended his movements abroad : the Secretary at War took care that he was paid, and was responsible for the lawful administration of the flogging which was provided for him by the Commander-in-Chief.'[1] Thus the modern War Office has [1] Anson, grown from the gradual amalgamation of (*a*) the *Ordnance* ii. 375.

Board, controlled by the Master General of Ordnance, who in the eighteenth century was the chief adviser of the government in all military matters ; (*b*) the office of the *Secretary at War* which began with the standing army under Charles II, and the holder of which until 1783 was responsible to the Crown alone ; in 1793 the establishment of the office of General Commanding-in-Chief divided the control of the army between a permanent military and a permanent civil authority; while in 1794 the appointment of a special Secretary of State for War over-shadowed, but did not extinguish, the older official; (*c*) the Commissariat, which was a department of the Treasury. The first great change in the control of the army was due to the Crimean War. In 1855 the Secretary of State for War was relieved of the Secretaryship for the Colonies, which had in 1801 been added to his duties ; the Secretary at War was amalgamated with him, and the two other departments were placed under him. But this absorption of offices entailed too much work on the Secretary of State. In 1870, the work was apportioned among three departments—Military, Ordnance, and Finance. Then in 1888 the Surveyor-General of Ordnance was abolished, and his work distributed between the Military side under the Commander-in-Chief and the civil side under the Financial Secretary. Further, in 1895 there were set up both an Army Board consisting of the heads of the Military Departments, presided over by the Commander-in-Chief, and a War Office Council under the Secretary of State, for considering special subjects. But the power of these two boards was both ill defined and extremely limited. In 1901 a Committee of business experts outside the War Office reported in favour of co-ordination of authorities. In accordance with their recommendations, the two bodies were welded into one War Office Board as a permanent and integral part of the War Office. A further step in the same direction was taken in 1904, when the Commander-in-Chiefship was abolished and an Army Council was created by Letters Patent, to which were handed over the powers of the Secretary of State for War and of the Commander-in-Chief.

The Navy. § 70. In striking contrast with the feeling long entertained in the country about the army, the maintenance of the NAVY has never roused any jealous suspicion among Englishmen at large. And yet the actual amount of interference with the freedom of the individual which has been based on the plea of the maintenance of the navy, has been greater, or at any rate more striking, than any which the exigencies of the army produced. Two such will at once occur to the reader—the levy of ship-money in the reign of Charles I, and the employment of press-gangs, whose deeds in the last century are so notorious. But Englishmen were proud of their navy, and knew it to be necessary for the defence of their shores, their commerce, and their colonies; so that, although the adoption of other methods has rendered resort to such measures unnecessary, up to the present moment no law like the Act of the Long Parliament forbidding impressment for the army except in the case of grave national danger, protects the sanctity of our homes from the invasion of the press-gang. The *means by which the navy has at various times been manned* fall under three heads—(1) the duty laid upon the Cinque Ports; (2) hire or forcible impressment of both ships and men from the mercantile marine at other ports; (3) voluntary enlistment to serve on ships provided by the Crown.

It is to be remembered that there was no permanent royal navy until the time of the Tudors. The sovereign possessed a few vessels which answered the purpose of the present royal yachts; for they were intended only to take the king to and fro between his various dominions. And if there were no ships much less was there any permanent staff of seamen. Even for some time after the foundations of a royal navy had been laid, the ships were laid up in dock in time of peace and entrusted to the guard of a few caretakers. But at a time when no ship could leave a harbour unless she were armed with sufficient strength to resist attack from pirates, it only needed the organization of a system which could be put in force at need, to procure for the Crown a very adequate supply 1349. of both ships and men. Thus at the siege of Calais by Edward III, of the 730 ships said to have been employed, with nearly 15,000 men on board, only 25 were royal vessels, bearing the meagre equipment of 419 men; while the fleet which met the Armada at a time when the English navy had really been begun, consisted of 176 vessels and 15,000 men, out of which only 34 ships and 6,000 men belonged to the royal service.

The first attempt at such organization by the Crown was an application of obligations analogous to those of the feudal levy. Ælfred, to whom, among other things, the foundation of the English navy is ascribed, found it so difficult to procure sailors at home that he had to man his ships with Frisian mercenaries. One of his successors seems to have laid the obligation of providing a vessel upon an estate of a certain size, and Æthelred may have merely systematized this method when he directed that every 300 hides of land should furnish a ship. That this obligation was incumbent not only on the seaboard districts, is sufficiently clear from the mention of Wiltshire and Worcestershire in this connection. This system, however, did not outlast the Norman Conquest, although it is probably responsible for the custom which prevailed long after, by which ships from the same counties went into battle side by side. Nor does there seem to have been any arrangement before the Conquest for procuring sailors to man the ships. Both wants were provided by William I's incorporation of the (1) *Cinque Ports*. These were originally the five ports of Dover, Hastings, Hythe, Romney and Sandwich. To these were subsequently added the 'ancient towns' of Winchelsea and Rye; and gradually a number of other places, both on the coast and even inland, some of them corporate towns, were attached with the title of limb or member, to one or other of the chief ports. This powerful corporation possessed all the apparatus of self-government under a lord warden, who for some time was the nearest approach in England to an admiral of the seas. He held his Court of Chancery, now abolished, in St James' Church at Dover; he presided over the Shepway or local parliament held near Hythe, which heard appeals from the minor courts of each port and beyond which there lay an appeal to the Court of King's Bench. Over this he still in theory presides, as well as over his Admiralty Court; he is, moreover, the Governor of Dover Castle and the nominator of all Justices of the Peace for the liberties of the Cinque Ports. Below the Shepway came two courts—the Court of Brotherhood, composed of the mayors of the seven chief towns and a number of jurats and freemen from each; and the Court of Guestling, containing,

1008.

1191.

(1) Obligations of the Cinque Ports.

in addition, the mayors, bailiffs, and representatives of the corporate members. These conducted all the business relating to the supply of ships. For, in return for the privileges involved in this organization, each member of the corporation was bound to furnish a fixed number of ships and men to serve the king without pay for fifteen days in each year. In the thirteenth and fourteenth centuries this liability had become fixed at fifty-seven ships, of which Dover provided the lion's share of twenty.[1] It is probable that, until the formation of a royal navy under the Tudors, the contingent from the Cinque Ports formed the nucleus of any English force upon the sea, and that for some time later it continued to be an appreciable element in all naval armaments.

[1] Social England, i. 412.

But the force of the Cinque Ports alone does not account for the large number of ships mentioned as taking part in all early English naval warfare. King John is said to have equipped a fleet of 500 ships; Edward III won his victory at Sluys with a fleet of 300; Henry V transported his army to France in no less than 1,500 vessels. Indeed, although no other ports seem to have owed definite sea-service to the Crown, yet in time of war they were always liable to have their (2) *shipping put in requisition*, whether by hiring or impressment, for the needs of the state. By this means, until the formation of an adequate royal navy, first the contingent of the Cinque Ports and then the scanty ships of the navy itself were supplemented. It was, no doubt, largely for this reason that from the time of Edward III onwards much trouble was taken by the king to encourage merchant shipping. Edward imitated his father in proclaiming himself 'Sovereign of the sea,' and, for the protection of commerce from pirates, endeavoured to organize some form of fleets sailing under convoy of ships of war. Under Richard II the first Navigation Act was passed with the object of encouraging English shipping by giving to home merchants a monopoly of the carrying trade. Henry IV and Henry VI appointed guardians for the coast.[2] Henry V built a few large ships, and invited the merchants to follow his example. Edward IV began the system of commercial treaties with foreign nations. All the chief requisites of ship-building, such as timber and hemp, were carefully guarded from waste, and their cultivation was enjoined. Nor was the

1340.

(2) Impressment of merchant ships.

1381.

[2] Plummer's Fortescue, 235-238.

manning of the fleet a difficult task. Everything was done by the legislature for the development of the English fisheries, because they were regarded as the best school for the training of seamen. Indeed, the Parliament of Edward VI went so far as to enforce what has been styled a ' Political Lent,'[1] or the eating of fish on so many days in each week, in order to create a demand which the Reformation had done much to destroy. The statute was re-enacted by both Elizabeth and James I, the legislature on all three occasions carefully guarding itself against any supposed religious object in the enactment.   The seamen so trained were liable to be pressed for the royal service ; but their engagement only lasted for the term of the current war. This matter of the impressment of seafaring men on the outbreak of a war has been the subject of many statutes from the days of Richard II down to those of George III, and of one judicial argument in the reign of Charles II.[2] In every case its legality has been placed beyond dispute, and indeed the Crimean War was the first occasion on which the fleet was manned without recourse to impressment. The formation of a *naval reserve* will probably prevent the employment of any such measure in the future.   Early in the eighteenth century, if not before, suggestions and attempts were made for the registration of all seafaring men who could be summoned to serve in case of need ; but no system was set on foot until 1859, when a naval reserve was formed of those officers and men of the mercantile marine and of fishermen who are willing, in consideration of a small retaining pay, to undergo a certain number of days' annual training on board a war-ship or at a naval battery. These, together with the coastguard, the seaman pensioner reserve, and the royal naval artillery volunteers, form a body of over 40,000 men who are at the disposal of the Admiralty in the event of war. The two former bodies consist of professional sailors who have served a term in the royal navy ; the last are the naval counterpart of the army volunteers. Ships, as well as men, are at the disposal of the government in case of need ; and since about the beginning of the present reign, either by contract or by register, the Admiralty have had an option, which they have not been slow to use, of engaging a certain number of suitable vessels for the service of transport or other warlike need.

1548.

[1] Cunningham, *Eng. Ind. and Com.* i. 499.

[2] Cf. Robertson, 344.

The foundation of the royal navy has been variously attributed to Ælfred, John, Edward III, and Henry V. But the efforts of none of these sovereigns in this direction were permanent. Both Richard I for his crusade of 1190, and John for his contest with Louis of France and the barons, acquired royal vessels in addition to the contingent of the Cinque Ports, and manned them with mercenaries mostly of English blood : while Henry V built a fleet which the neglect of his successor suffered to decay. All the earliest efforts of the executive seem to have been devoted to the provision of an organization which could be brought into effectual use in time of war without burdening the Crown with the expenses of a permanent fleet. But until the fourteenth century there was no permanent organization for naval affairs, and commanders were appointed whenever it was necessary to collect a fleet. The nearest approach to an organization was that of the officers of the Cinque Ports. But in 1306 Edward I, having instituted a system of coastguard, divided up the coast between three admirals, for whom his grandson substituted one Lord High Admiral (1360).[1] It was, perhaps, the establishment of this organization which caused Edward II to claim for the English king the dominion of the sea, a position to which Edward III's victory at Sluys for a time gave some valid claim. Further, Richard I had issued ordinances for the administration of his crusading fleet ; but it is the regulations of Henry V which form the origin and basis of the present Admiralty law. It is to the early days of the Tudors that we must ascribe the real beginning of a (3) *permanent royal navy*. Henry VIII established the dockyards at Deptford, Woolwich and Portsmouth, and appointed commissioners to superintend the civil part of the naval administration. But the ships which he and his successors maintained, were manned by the old methods as occasion required, and no permanent body of officers or men was maintained in time of peace. The exigencies of the Commonwealth caused the formation of a standing fleet, as well as a standing army ; and the excellence of the material at the disposal of the government was shown by the success of the Commonwealth in its contest with the Dutch, who then possessed the finest navy in the world. With the reign of Charles II the royal navy becomes a permanent institution

[1] *S. C. H.* § 243.

, 1340.

(3) Voluntary enlistment.

of the country. The exertions of the Lord High Admiral, the Duke of York (afterwards James II), and Samuel Pepys as Secretary to the Admiralty, resulted in the establishment for the first time of a system of half-pay, by which a permanent staff of officers and men was retained in time of peace. To the same period is to be ascribed the first parliamentary recognition of the navy by a vote for its maintenance and by a provision for its discipline under which the first Articles of War for the navy were promulgated. These, with amendments, are embodied in the Naval Discipline Act, which since 1866 provides permanently for the navy, as the Mutiny Act and Army Act have over the same period provided for the army. To the same persons is due the organization of the Admiralty in four departments. On the death of Queen Anne's husband, Prince George of Denmark, the office of Lord High Admiral was replaced by the Admiralty Board, and was revived only in 1827, when it was held for a short time by the Duke of Clarence, afterwards William IV. The Navy Board, Victualling Board, and Treasurer of the Navy represented respectively the professional, the commissariat and the financial duties in connection with the naval organization of the country. In 1832 the two boards were abolished, and in 1835 the office of treasurer also disappeared. The whole work is now done by the Admiralty Board, consisting of a First Lord who, as a cabinet minister, is supreme, four naval lords, a civil lord, a financial and a parliamentary secretary,—all of whom change with the government—and a permanent secretary. The First Lord alone is responsible for all that is done, and he apportions the business among the members of the board. But the Admiralty Board is jointly at the head of the navy, and the First Lord has no necessary professional adviser.

§ 71. Such are the most important methods by which from time to time in the course of English history, individual liberty has been imperilled or violated. Others, such as the undue extension or the indefinite interpretation of the law of treason, are dealt with elsewhere. In conclusion, the fulness as well as the limitations of this individual liberty may be illustrated by the history of the practices of (*a*) the presentation of public *petitions*, (*b*) the holding of public *meetings*, (*c*) the formation of public *associations*. Their appositeness consists in the fact

1708.

Popular methods of influencing the administration.

(1) Petitions.

that *it is by these three methods that the nation outside Parliament endeavours to influence the executive in some particular direction.* After the establishment of Parliament the subjects of such petitions seem to have been confined to the redress of private grievances. The exciting political events which led up to the Great Rebellion began the modern system of petitions, whether addressed to the king or to Parliament, on matters of public interest. The demonstrations by which the presentation of some of these petitions was accompanied, led immediately after the Restoration to the passing of an Act against tumultuous petitions, by which no petition to the Crown or either house of Parliament for the alteration of matters established by law in Church and State should bear more than twenty signatures without the approving cognizance of a certain number of specified officials ; and no petition should be presented by a body of more than ten persons.[1] In 1680, when the political feeling in the country showed itself in the presentation of numerous petitions to the Crown for the meeting of Parliament, the petitioners were by a royal proclamation threatened with the penalties of the Act, and counter-petitions were encouraged from those who 'abhorred' the disloyal designs which underlay the wish for the calling of Parliament.[2] Such a use of the Statute inhibited all petitions except such as might be pleasing to the Crown ; and accordingly, the Bill of Rights declared that 'the subject has a right to petition, and that all commitments and prosecutions for such petitions are illegal.' But the Revolution was the triumph of Parliament and of the narrow oligarchy then represented in the House. Whigs and Tories alike resented the attempt to exercise any outside influence upon their deliberations ; and, although it was some time before Place Bills put a check on the power of the Crown, the Commons did not scruple to use their privileges for the purpose of excluding the influence of the people from the so-called house of popular representatives. The most striking instance of the use of this power was the case of the *Kentish Petitioners* in 1701. The Tory ministry in power was withholding supplies for a war begun by the Whigs. The grand jury and many of the freeholders of Kent, indignant at this unpatriotic conduct, petitioned that the loyal addresses of Parliament might be turned into bills of supply. The

13 Car. II. c. 5. 1661.

Hallam, ii. 329.

[2] *Ibid.* ii. 442.

petition was with difficulty presented ; it was voted scandalous, insolent, and seditious ; and five of the petitioners were imprisoned until the end of the session.[1] It is small wonder then, that general petitions were little used ; for, those unacceptable to the majority, such as the petitions from the City of London in 1690 and from a number of clergy, lawyers and doctors in 1772 for a relaxation of some of the religious disabilities of the day, were summarily rejected. It almost seems a judgement on the action of the Commons that the first question on which an extended system of petitioning was invoked, was that of parliamentary reform. In 1779 the freeholders of Yorkshire, to the number of 8,000, began a movement which spread into many parts of the country and produced forty petitions in that year, and three years afterwards fifty more, all concerned with the reform of the House of Commons. It was the movement for the abolition of the slave trade, beginning with a petition of the Quakers in 1782 and continuing until the Emancipation Act of 1833, which, in the number of petitions presented, first rivalled the exertions of modern days :[2] but it was not until towards the end of George IV's reign that the principle of attempting to influence Parliament through the carefully expressed manifestoes of men of ability and local authority, gave way to the present democratic practice of counting heads, and produced those monster petitions whose influence has been so largely discounted by the frauds which were employed in their concoction. Of these the most celebrated was the petition of the Chartists in 1848, which purported to bear no less than five million signatures.[3] It would seem as if the extension of the franchise had naturally removed the object of petitions, and that their use would therefore cease : for they afforded one of the few means by which the unenfranchised classes could express their opinions on public matters. However that may be, the tide of petitions has flowed steadily on throughout this century, reaching for many years in succession an annual average of considerably more than ten thousand. The liberty allowed to petitioners is so unrestrained that the House of Commons permits them practically 'to express anything short of an intention to break the law or a contempt for the body to which they appeal for redress.'[4] This enormous development

[1] Hallam, iii. 271-272.

[2] Erskine May, ii. 62-68.

[3] *Ibid.* ii. 410.

[4] Anson. i. 350.

n the use of petitions soon entailed a change in the procedure
of the House of Commons. Hitherto the presentation of a
petition was followed by a debate on its contents. A con-
tinuation of this practice would have absorbed the whole time
of the House. It was accordingly resolved by standing orders
of 1842 and 1853 that, while a debate might be raised on
any petition which disclosed matters requiring an immediate
remedy, in ordinary cases the member presenting it should limit
himself to a statement of its contents, the places or persons
whence it emanates, and the number of signatures attached.

Petitions are in many cases the outcome of *public meetings,* (2) Meet-
which are often held for the purpose by *political associations.* ings, and
All three forms of expressing and crystallizing public opinion (3) Asso-
took their rise about the same period. The oligarchical ciations.
Parliament of the eighteenth century, which used all means
to shut out the influence of the people, was bound occasionally
to bend before the storm of public opinion. In the early
part of the century this was marshalled by the newspaper
press. Thus, in 1733 Walpole, although commanding a
majority in Parliament, was forced to withdraw his excise
scheme in deference to the clamours of the people ; in 1754
Parliament was intimidated into a repeal of the Act for the
naturalization of the Jews, which had been passed a short
while before ; and in 1763 Bute was by the same means
driven into an involuntary retirement. It was, however, with 1768.
the agitation produced by the case of Wilkes and with the
interference of the Commons with the rights of electors in
the Middlesex election, that the real history of public meetings
and associations begins. Of these latter some of the most
important were the Protestant Association formed for the
repeal of the Catholic Relief Act of 1778 and leading to the
Gordon Riots in 1780 ; the Slave Trade Association for
the abolition of the slave trade, and the direct predecessor of
the present Anti-Slavery Society ; the Revolution Society to
commemorate the Revolution of 1688 ; the Society for sup-
porting the Bill of Rights, which was the outcome of the
Middlesex election ; the Society for Constitutional Information formed in 1780 to forward the cause of Parliamentary
Reform ; and the London Corresponding Society and the
Society of the Friends of the People, both of which were the

[1] Erskine May, ii. 266-284.

1795.

[2] *Ibid.* ii. 319-330.

1799.
1819.

[3] *Ibid.* 353-359.

1820.

1830-1844.
1838-1848.

result of the early movements of the French Revolution.[1] From 1792 onwards the repressive measures of the government drove many of these societies to secrecy, and 'association degenerated into conspiracy.' This was met by two Acts— one to prevent seditious meetings, and another to suppress by name certain societies, including the extreme London Corresponding Society which gave its name to this Act.[2] These were for the time effective; but the renewed agitation, chiefly from social causes, which followed the cessation of war, was again met by a proclamation against seditious meetings enforced in what is known as the 'Manchester Massacre,' and by one of the 'Six Acts' which prohibited any meeting of more than fifty persons without notice and permission. The operation of this, however, was limited to five years.[3] But the disgust occasioned by the Cato Street conspiracy showed that all serious danger had passed away. In 1824 the repeal of the Combination Laws, which had practically forbidden all associations of working men for the purpose of securing better wages, did much to satisfy the superior members of the class which had contributed most, and perhaps most justly, to the social discontent of the previous period. The extraordinary success, on the one side, attained by the Catholic Association in the Catholic Emancipation Act of 1829; by the widespread agitation in favour of parliamentary reform in the Act of 1832; and by the Anti-Corn-Law League in 1846, together with the failure of O'Connell's agitation in favour of the repeal of the Irish Union and of the Chartist Movement, showed both the impossibility of successfully coping by repressive measures with movements that command a widespread sympathy, and the inevitable failure of an organization which appeals to one class or section of the community alone. The laws which govern the formation of political associations relate chiefly to the demand from their members of oaths or engagements unsanctioned by the law. The right of public meeting is limited by such laws as regulate individual liberty of speech and person. Thus, all meetings are legal until some illegal act has been committed; while no magistrate or official has any power to prohibit a meeting by proclamation merely because he is aware that the holding of it will lead to a breach of the peace. This affords merely another illustration of the truth that the

English law takes account only of a man's actions and not of his intentions. The absence of any power to take cognizance of the latter is no doubt in many ways a cause of weakness to the executive; but it finds ample compensation in the increased security which is thereby given to the liberty of the individual.

CHAPTER X

REVENUE AND TAXATION

Early distinction between revenue and taxation.

§ 72. It has been shown already what an important part is played by questions of money in the development of the English Constitution. For, it was the king's desire to obtain grants from his subjects in the most convenient manner possible, which led to the first summons of representatives of the Commons to Parliament; and it was the constant necessities of the king that gave the Commons the opportunity of gradually establishing the dependence of the Crown upon Parliament, not only in questions connected with grants of money, but in all other matters whatsoever. From the outset it is convenient to distinguish between revenue and taxation. The king was provided with regular means, whether in the shape of lands or of privileges convertible into money, by which the royal dignity could be sustained and the ordinary functions of government carried on. The earliest attempts at taxation are connected with the invasions of the Danes, and take the shape of special levies to meet special and temporary emergencies. With the increase of the necessary functions of government comes a corresponding increase in the need for extra supplies; but it is only very gradually that the grantors discover that the duty of assent, carrying with it of necessity the opportunity of refusal, has placed a most effective weapon in their hands. The constant cry of mediaeval times 'that the king should live of his own' (*que notre seigneur le roi vive de soen*), must not, however, be misconstrued. Not only did the ever-growing activity of government make it more and more impossible to meet increasing expenses with a stationary or even diminishing revenue; but 'no patriotic statesman dreamed of dispensing altogether with the taxation which gave the nation an un-

496

varying hold on the king whether he were good or bad.'[1]   The [1] *S. C. H.*
desire which underlay the demand was no more than that in § 274.
time of peace the revenue should suffice for the ordinary
expenditure of government.   Indeed, so long as the personal
government of the monarch lasted, Parliament clung to the
view that taxation was an exceptional method of supplying
the needs of administration, perhaps chiefly called for by the
advisability of meeting in each year the expenses of that year.
But experience proved that taxation must be annual ; and
while Parliament used the necessity of an annual grant as
a means of keeping a hold upon the course of government, the
superior facilities for borrowing enabled the Crown to meet
extraordinary expenditure by loans.   Thus, whereas during
the time of personal government ordinary expenses were met
by the revenue and extraordinary charges by intermittent
taxation, the establishment of the omnipotence of Parliament
at the Revolution of 1688 inaugurated an era in which the
ordinary expenses of government were met by regular taxes
annually granted ; while for extraordinary burdens government
had recourse to loans, the interest on which became an annual
charge.   Posterity was thus burdened with a large share in
the payment of the current expenses, on the specious pretext
that they were incurred partly in its interests.

The ancient hereditary REVENUES of the Crown may be
grouped under two heads : (1) *land,* which included rents and
dues of various kinds ; (2) *the exercise of the royal prerogative,*
which took the shape of numerous fees and fines.   In the
course of time, to these were added others, such as (3) the
feudal dues after the Norman Conquest, (4) the *Post Office* at
the Restoration, and (5) the *hereditary revenues of Scotland and
Ireland.*   By far the most important of these have been the The Crown
Crown Lands.   It does not seem likely that in the early days Lands.
of kingship the holder possessed any lands by virtue of his
title.   As a great thegn he would doubtless have extensive
estates in folkland : as king he would enjoy those gradually
growing rights to various dues off all the lands of the kingdom
which, when 'booked' to church or thegn, constituted the
somewhat rare tenure of bookland.   With the consent of his
Witan the king would even 'book' land to himself, and thus
perhaps make provision for his own young children whom the

succession of his brother to the throne might otherwise leave insufficiently provided for. But at the Norman Conquest, or at any rate by the time of Domesday, the whole country in theory passed into the estate of the Crown. Then the royal demesne was composed of those estates which in theory had not been granted away by the Crown. In the record of Domesday these comprised over 1,400 manors. Nor does his booking away of other lands seem to have deprived the king of the oldest of the royal rights over them—the ' feorm-fultum ' or right of sustenance for himself and his court on their progresses through the country. The king of Anglo-Saxon times may be regarded as a great landowner, moving from estate to estate and living on the profits. The Norman and Plantagenet kings were equally ubiquitous; but their rents were taken largely in money, and the right of sustenance became the excuse for the hateful claims to purveyance and preemption. These will be mentioned later. For the present it must be remarked that, as soon as a discrimination begins to be made between items of expenditure, it is a recognized principle that *the personal expenditure of the court should be met out of the revenues from the royal demesne lands.* And at first sight it would seem that this must have provided a more than adequate source. For not only did the rules of escheat and forfeiture supply a constant means of replenishing, if not of extending, the demesne lands of the Crown; but from time to time individual kings made large additions. Henry IV brought with him the Lancastrian inheritance which even to the present day has remained apart from the general estate of the Crown.[1] By his confiscation of the lands of those monastic houses which were connected with foreign orders (alien priories, as they were called), Henry V afforded a valuable precedent both for Wolsey's destruction of some of the smaller monasteries and more especially for the sweeping act of Henry VIII. But fortunately for the liberties of the nation, almost from the first the kings gave away with one hand what they had grasped with the other. From the time of Stephen onwards the accumulations and confiscations of the first three Norman kings were bestowed with lavish bounty on the royal favourites. As a consequence, the royal demesne diminished rather than increased, and, meanwhile, the expenses

[1] Anson, ii. 304.

which it was intended to cover grew continually. Under
Edward I the maintenance of the royal household cost
£15,000. Under Edward III £25,000 was devoted to this
charge out of a total expenditure of £150,000. Under
Richard II, with a slightly diminished revenue, the amount
rose to £45,000, and yet the king severely resented the
remonstrance which was in consequence presented by the
Commons. Under Henry IV the Lancastrian inheritance
was whittled away in bribes to the great nobles who had
recognized his title; and while the general revenue still
declined, the court absorbed more than £50,000. It is
not difficult to understand the constantly recurring cry that
'the king should live of his own.' And the reason of his
inability to do so was rightly understood: for in all the
popular risings of the Lancastrian and Yorkist times, such
as those of the Percies in 1403, of Cade in 1450, and of
Robin of Redesdale in 1469, this demand was coupled with
complaints against the royal councillors for mismanaging and
misappropriating the royal revenues.

The Crown did not seem capable of protecting itself in the
matter, and several devices were resorted to in the interests
of the true dignity and independence of the sovereign. It
was not that the country grudged supplies to its rulers or
wished to interfere unduly with their actions. A king who
ministered to the glory of the land might go a long way in
the direction of unconstitutional taxation before any serious
dissatisfaction would arise. The complaints against Henry III,
Edward II, and Richard II were far more vehement than
even against the wasteful Edward III. But the people were
persuaded that the Crown was rich; and, if in time of peace
the means ordinarily to hand did not suffice to cover the
expenses of government, the blame was laid on the extravagance of the royal household and the rapacity of the ministers
and favourites, whom there were no means of checking by
a proper audit. Thus 'the extravagance of the court was
really only . . . a colourable ground of complaint against an
otherwise intolerable administration.'[1] But the evil was a
serious one in itself, and attempts were made to meet it by
stringent remedies. Setting aside the various devices—by
election, oath, and sale of office—for ensuring the responsi-

[1] S. C. H. § 285.

[1] *S. C. H.* § 286.

[2] Plummer's *Fortescue*, 279-280. *S. C. H.* § 284.

[3] *Ibid.* § 285.

bility of ministers in the general conduct of the administration,[1] we may notice (*a*) the numerous attempts at *resumption* of the royal demesne.[2]   This was undertaken by so strong a ruler as Henry II, and in Henry III's reign the barons coupled it with the banishment of his foreign favourites.   The first definite action of Parliament was in 1450, when, in order to recruit the slender resources of the Crown, an Act of Resumption annulled all grants of royal demesne made since the beginning of the current reign.   This was repeated in 1455 and four times under Edward IV; but owing to the number of exemptions allowed from the operation of the Acts, the general effect seems to have been small.   A more important, though not for some time more successful, method of restraint had for its object (*b*) the *limitation* of the king's power of alienating the royal revenues in the future.[3]   The first attempt at this is found in the Ordinances of 1311 which forbade any gift of land or crown property of any kind without consent of the Ordainers.   The barons went even further,

1315.

and subsequently put the king on an allowance of £10 a day. Edward III's device of promoting and rewarding his favourites with the apparent approval of Parliament, prevented any attempt at regulation until the last year of his reign; but on the accession of Richard II the projected reform of the

1376.

Good Parliament was abandoned; and, despite the appointment of numerous commissions of reform in Parliament, nothing was done in the new reign.   Among the charges against Richard was one of alienating the royal estates; and on the accession of Henry IV several legislative attempts were made to check the power of the Crown in this respect. But these failed; for the courtiers made their own arrangements with the king, and the grants were filled with 'non obstante' clauses.   But, as in earlier days the numerous forfeitures and escheats had saved the Crown from complete poverty, so now the same result was produced by the royal ventures in trade and the revival of obsolete rights to which Edward IV and Henry VII had recourse, and more especially by the enormous confiscation of monastic property.   But the lavish and probably politic grants of Henry VIII, followed by the frequent sales, profitable under Queen Elizabeth and necessary under Charles I, together with the prodigality of

Charles II, left the Crown as poor as ever. At length William III's unnecessary generosity to his personal friends seemed to call for the interference of Parliament; and under his successor it was provided that no future lease of the crown land should be granted for more than thirty-one years or the duration of three lives. Had this rule been put in force immediately after the Restoration, the entire Civil List of Queen Anne might have been provided out of the land revenues of the Crown.[1]

[1] Erskine May, i. 230.

§ 73. Together with extensive landed possessions the Crown enjoyed a number of *fees and fines levied in exercise of the royal prerogative*. Among such was the king's share, as guardian of the peace, in the *profits of justice* in the local courts. In early days these, together with the rents of the royal demesne lands, were farmed by the sheriff of each shire. Under the head of fines may be enumerated the early *fyrdwite*[2] for non-attendance at the mustering of the local militia, and *oferhyrnes*[3] for contempt of court; while with the Normans there was introduced an extensive system of composition for offences which left the offender at the mercy of the king. Under the same general head may be ranged the numerous payments for appointments to offices, which amounted to a sale or at best a fine to ensure the good behaviour of the holder, and the grant of privileges and exemptions of all kinds, such as charters to towns, the tolls of markets, fords and ports; while the sum total was swollen by the addition of such minor and miscellaneous profits as would arise from the produce of wrecks, the claim to treasure trove, the right to work mines or at least to a royalty on their proceeds.

Fees and Fines.

[2] S. C. 62.
[3] § 51. *Ibid.* 66. § 20.

The greater number of these rights were enjoyed by the Crown without any kind of protest. There was, however, one class of these privileges which was especially obnoxious to the people. These were comprised under the general term *Purveyance*, and were connected with the commissariat of the Court on its journeys through the country. Originally, this duty of *hospitium* had been discharged by voluntary gifts to the chief on his journeys; but the constant demands on this score may have caused such commutation of the liability as is described in the frequent claim to a 'firma unius noctis.' Yet no commutation could deprive the king of his undefined right

Purvey-ance.

of exaction to meet unexpected necessities.   The wants of the
Court as it moved were supplied by purveyors who would
occasionally obtain what they needed by simple seizure or
caption, but more commonly by *preemption* or compulsory
purchase at prices fixed by the purveyors themselves.[1]   The
value and consequent oppressiveness of the right are proved
by the constant legislation by which the Commons strove to
check its exercise.   In the first Parliament of James I it was
declared that there were thirty-six statutes in restraint of
the right.   Of these no less than ten were passed under
Edward III, by the last of which the use of purveyance was
limited to the personal wants of the king and queen.[2]

The future history of purveyance is bound up with that of
the *Feudal Dues*.   The history of the gradual fixing of the
relief has been already traced.   It has also been shown that
the levy of feudal aids was early limited to three occasions.
But, that this was a restriction on the general right is proved
by the twelfth clause of Magna Carta, which forbids the levy
of any aid other than the three usual aids without consent of
the Commune Concilium, and at the same time enjoins that
even these three should be 'reasonable.'[3]   The vagueness of
this epithet was corrected in the Statute of Westminster I,
which fixed the aids exacted on the occasion of the knighting
of a son and the marriage of a daughter at twenty shillings for
each knight's fee.   In the Confirmatio Cartarum the king was
made to repeat the promise of the Charter itself ; and a more
stringent provision was embodied in a statute of **1340** to the
effect that the various classes of the community should not
' be from henceforth charged nor grieved to make any aid or
to sustain charge if it be not by common assent of . . .
Parliament.'[4]   But whatever may have been the view of the
Commons, the king did not regard it as within their power, if
indeed it was within their meaning, to curb his feudal rights ;
for not only did he exact an aid for the knighting of his eldest
son, but, in direct defiance of the Statute of Westminster I,
he took it at twice the usual rate.   But the feudal aids were
passing away as methods of raising money.   For more than
a century and a half after the Black Prince no king's eldest
son was knighted in the lifetime of his father, while on the
marriage of Henry IV's eldest daughter to the Duke of

[1] M'Kech-
nie, 386-
389, 392.

[2] 36 Edw.
III. c. 2.

Feudal
Dues.

[3] *S. C.* 298.
1275.

1297.

[4] 14 Edw.
III. st. 2.

1346.

Bavaria no claim to a feudal aid was made. The aids were, however, useful weapons in the hands of a rapacious king for obtaining extra grants from his subjects. For this purpose they were revived by Henry VII, who, although his eldest 1503. son was just dead and his eldest daughter Margaret was already married to the king of Scotland, levied by consent of Parliament an aid which produced more than £30,000, and which was paid by socage and copyhold tenants as well as by those of knightly rank. The other feudal payments had continued to be exacted, and brought in an appreciable annual income to the Crown. Henry VIII, acting on the hint given by his father, systematized all the feudal rights of the Crown under a special Court of Wards. It did not matter that the feudal army had completely disappeared, and that with it had gone every reason for the maintenance of such a Court. But other influences were at work to destroy a system which was at once antiquated and obnoxious. The permanent revenue of the Crown was seriously reduced by the fall in the value of silver, which followed the opening of the American mines. The financiers of the seventeenth century had, therefore, to discover some source of revenue which would yield a regular income sufficient to meet the continually growing needs of government. The first which occurred to them was a commutation of the old royal and feudal rights of the Crown, which were so lucrative and yet so unmeaning. These rights included purveyance and the feudal dues, each of which needed separate treatment. In the case of purveyance the Commons desired merely to do away with the illegal extensions of the system ;[1] whereas in the case of [1] Cf. the feudal dues they aimed at destroying a whole system which, Prothero, while it lasted, was strictly within the letter of the law. The 124, 340. first debate on the matter in the first Parliament of James I[2] [2] *Ibid.* 291. was quashed by the Lords, who denied that the feudal rights concerned any but themselves. But in 1609 James took an aid for the knighting of his eldest son, 'which amounted to a tax of five per cent. on the yearly value of all land held of the king, whether by military tenure or by socage.'[3] The [3] *Ibid.* lxxi. irritation that must have been caused by 'its concomitant inquiries and opportunities for extortion and jobbery' brought matters to a head. A renewal of negotiations ended in an

agreement for the surrender of the royal claims, including
purveyance, in return for a fixed sum of £200,000 a year.[1]
An exception, however, was made in the case of the three
occasional aids which might still be taken at a fixed rate.
But before the agreement became law both parties had
changed their minds. The king thought that he would not
gain much by the bargain, while the Commons feared the
addition of so large a sum to the royal revenue. Consequently,
the Great Contract, as the bargain was called, fell through,
and it was only at the Restoration that feudal tenure and all
that it involved, together with purveyance and its accompaniment preemption, was finally abolished, and other means
were found of increasing the royal revenues.

The first of these means was an *excise on beer and other
liquors*, which was avowedly intended to take the place of
the surrendered royal and feudal dues. It has been usual to
stigmatize the selfishness of the landowners who thus substituted for the feudal dues which fell only on themselves,
a class of taxes which fell upon the general public. But apart
from the political inadvisability of alienating the landowning
interest from the newly established government, it is to be
considered that the tax which was at first projected, a general
land-tax, would have been offensive to the socage and copyhold
tenants who had not been liable for feudal dues ; while a tax
levied under a different name from those lands alone which
had paid feudal charges, would have borne unfairly on those
who had bought the lands under the Commonwealth on the
understanding that all such liabilities had been abolished.[2]
The general history of Excise will be dealt with under the
head of Taxation. Here it shall be said merely that this
excise was made part of the hereditary revenue of the Crown ;
in 1736 it was commuted for a fixed sum of £70,000, and at
the accession of George III it was merged in the general
revenue of the country.

In 1663, to this excise were added the revenues of the *Post
Office*. This had been set on foot by James I for the convenience of English merchants corresponding with foreign
countries, and was made available by Charles I for the trans-
mission of internal correspondence in England and Scotland.
During the Commonwealth it became a source of revenue, and

[1] Prothero, 295, 299.

Substitutes for feudal dues.
(a) Excise on beer.

[2] Rogers, Econ. Interp. of Hist. 154.

(b) Post Office.

1635.

n 1659 was farmed out for £14,000. At the Restoration it
was organized by statute and obtained the monopoly of letter
carrying for hire, the profits of which were made part of the
hereditary revenues of the Crown. It was at first farmed out
or £21,500, but the profits rapidly increased. At the end of
William III's reign it brought in £75,000; under Anne and
George I this had risen to over £90,000; and, while in 1710
he proceeds were divided between the king's Civil List and
general expenditure, after 1760 the whole was merged under
he latter head.

§ 74. Such were the hereditary revenues of the Crown after
he Restoration. To these were added certain grants of the
nature of taxes for the life of the reigning king, such as the old
tonnage and poundage now reorganized, and a new temporary
excise on wine at the same rate as the hereditary excise.

With the proceeds of this hereditary revenue and these
permanent taxes the king was still expected to keep up the
royal state, the civil government, and all that was necessary
for the defence of the kingdom in time of peace. In fact this
was the true Civil List. The items under this head at the *The*
disposal of Charles I had realized an average annual sum *modern*
of one million pounds, and experience had proved it to be *Civil List.*
insufficient. It was calculated that the sources set apart at
he Restoration would raise the sum total to £1,200,000.
At first they did not yield so much; but eventually, owing
to the improvement in trade and a better management of
the customs, they so far passed the estimates that James II
enjoyed from these sources an average income of £1,500,000.
But after the Revolution the use to which Charles II and
his brother had put the money granted caused Parliament,
practically for the first time, to attempt some definite limitation
to the personal expenditure of the Crown. Thus the sources
of income set apart at the accession of William and Mary
were calculated to produce £1,200,000; and of this the
hereditary revenues and the excise duties, together estimated
at £700,000, were appropriated to the civil expenditure of
the Crown. This included not only the personal expenses
of the Court, but the salaries of ambassadors, judges, and the
civil service generally, together with all current pensions. It
seems, however, that the sovereigns, being thus circumscribed

in their revenue, refused to consider themselves obliged to restrain their expenditure within the amount appropriated to the Civil List.   Thus, down to the accession of George II these sources realized an average of £700,000 a year; but both Anne and George I respectively applied to Parliament to discharge more than one million pounds' worth of debts.   The Civil List of George II was guaranteed at a minimum amount of £800,000; for, any deficiency in the usual sources was to be met by a parliamentary grant: but even with this increase Parliament was called on to release the king from a debt of £450,000.   But with the accession of George III Parliament for the first time obtained acknowledgement of its power of direct control over the personal expenditure of the Crown.   Hitherto, since the Revolution, Parliament had guaranteed to the Crown certain branches of revenue which were calculated to produce an adequate income.   Now George III surrendered the crown lands, the excise, and the Post Office in return for a definite sum of £800,000 a year, which in 1777 was raised to £900,000.   But out of this were still paid the salaries of ambassadors, judges, and civil servants, annuities to members of the royal family, and pensions for public services.   At the same time, there remained at the absolute disposal of the Crown certain other sources of revenue, such as the hereditary revenues of Scotland and Ireland.   Yet this did not preclude occasional applications to Parliament for the discharge of debts which during the reign amounted to £3,500,000.

Subsequent reform was in two directions.   On the one side, most of those sources of revenue which remained beyond the control of Parliament were surrendered by the Crown; on the other side, the sum voted by Parliament was gradually relieved of all burdens except those immediately connected with the maintenance of the personal dignity of the monarch.   The first step in this direction was taken by Lord Rockingham's 22 Geo. III. Act of 1782, by which the Civil List was divided into eight c. 82. classes and the expenditure was to be according to a prescribed order.   It was a natural step to transfer such of these classes as did not concern the personal estate of the Crown, to the Consolidated Fund, out of which, since 1787, the expenses of the civil government of the country are defrayed.   This was of course accompanied by a 'pro tanto' diminution of the sum voted to the Crown. Thus in 1816 various payments to members of the royal family were so disposed of. Again, on the accession of William IV, the vote of a smaller Civil List of £510,000 was accompanied by the withdrawal of nearly all public charges, except a pension list of £75,000 and a sum for secret service of £23,000. At the same time, George IV's surrender of the hereditary revenues of Ireland and of all that the Crown still kept under the same title from England, was followed by William IV's surrender of the hereditary revenues of Scotland and some smaller sources of independent income. On the accession of Queen Victoria, the Civil List was reduced to £385,000 distributed under six heads of expenditure, but for the present king it has been raised to £470,000. The sole extra expense with which it is now charged is a diminished pension list from which fresh annual grants may be made of no more than £1,200. The sole extraneous source of income at the disposal of the sovereign is the Duchy of Lancaster, which has been jealously kept apart from the crown lands. This now yields about £60,000 a year. At the same time, it is noteworthy that the crown lands themselves, which at the time of their surrender produced little more than £6,000, now add no less than £450,000 to the revenue of the country. It is probably no exaggeration to say that these apparent encroachments, even upon the private expenditure of the Crown, have in reality added to its true dignity and more than ever conciliated the confidence and affections of the people.[1]

[1] Erskine May, i. 232-247.

§ 75. The earliest form of TAXATION was probably the *Danegeld*. It was levied first in 991 by Æthelred at the suggestion of Archbishop Sigeric and with consent of the Witan, and then at intervals up to the reign of Eadward the Confessor, by whom it was abolished. It was revived by William I in 1084, and remained a frequent exaction for about eighty years. It was a land-tax taken, under the Anglo-Saxons, at the rate of two shillings on every hide. William I not only robbed it of its meaning by making it a regular levy, but trebled the amount which in future levies was generally taken at six shillings on the hide. It was a crushing burden on the smaller folk, and substantially helped both to reduce the pre-Norman ceorl to the post-Conquest villanus and to the universal

Early forms of taxation.

establishment of a manorial system.   Now, according to the
feudal theory of taxation, the taxpayer made a voluntary offering
to relieve the temporary necessities of his lord, and thus his
promise of the tax bound only the individual who made it.
Hence all opposition to taxation was at first personal.   It is true
that Henry I speaks of 'the aid which my barons gave me'
and, in his order for holding the local courts, promises to
summon these courts if his necessities require it.[1]   Thus some
form of grant may have been observed ; but there is no account
of any definite vote of taxes or of a discussion over a money
grant until the end of the reign of Richard I.   The feudal
theory of taxation also involved the necessity of its levy upon
land.   The unit was the somewhat indefinite hide ; and since
the chief object of Domesday had probably been to obtain
a basis for the fair assessment of the danegeld, in cases of
dispute Domesday formed the evidence of the liabilities of
an estate.

[1] *S. C.* 104.

Changes
under
Henry II.   The reign of Henry II inaugurated new principles in taxation
as in so much else.   In the first place, the exemptions claimed
by the Church lands from the liabilities of feudal tenure
were met by levying from them a commutation for personal
service in the form of scutage.   Secondly, the basis of feudal
taxation in general shifted from the hide, which had been
common to feudal and national taxation alike, to the more
special ratings on the knight's fee ; while, under Richard I,
even for national levies upon land the hide gave way to the
more definite carucate of a hundred acres.   Finally, the
growing wealth of the country suggested the accumulated
merchandise as a fit subject for taxation.   Thus personal
property no less than real property became contributory to the
needs of the state.   These changes produced two results.
The witness of Domesday had become insufficient as a method
of ultimate assessment ; and thus, while the feudal taxes were
left to the statement of the individual, for personal property
and even for real property in the carucage, the returns of the
individual payer were liable to be submitted to the decision
of a small committee or jury of his neighbours.   Again, the
first departure from the individual theory of taxation was
Class taxa-
tion.   made in the application of special taxes to each separate class
of the community.   Thus by the Charter of Henry I the

feudal class had been exempted from every demand except personal service [1]—an exemption, however, which only applied to the levy of special aids and not to the ordinary feudal dues. They were brought under contribution by an extension of the levy of scutage. Again, from all landowners would be required the donum, auxilium or carucage which had taken the place of danegeld ; and upon the same principle tallage was levied on all burgage tenants. The application of the principle of class taxation was an important step in constitutional advance ; for, it encouraged the growth of a system of estates, each responsible for its own particular burden and distinguished by the interests of its own particular class.

It has been shown elsewhere that the full number of knights whom a great estate had to furnish, was seldom to be found enfeoffed or provided with the requisite amount of land. For those which were not enfeoffed but remained, in the technical phrase, 'charged on the demesne,' the lord had to provide substitutes. It has been thought that *scutage* may have represented originally the sum paid to a substitute for a knight, and thus the royal demand involved merely a change in the mode of payment—to the king instead of to a substitute. However that may be, there were reasons why the kings should wish to get rid of the feudal levy, and even the Norman kings may have begun the system of taking payments in lieu of personal service. Traces of such a payment are found as early as the reign of Henry I, although there seems to be no definite mention of it until 1156. In that year Henry II prepared an expedition to Wales, and met the unwillingness of the great ecclesiastical tenants to supply military service, by the demand that they should pay instead, at the rate of twenty shillings on each knight's fee for which service was due. In 1159 the same principle was extended to the *agrarii milites*, as the chronicler describes them.[2] This time the rate of payment was two marks from each knight's fee, and the number thus compounded for seems to have been 1280. Since the service was still exacted from *capitales barones* this would represent only a small portion of the whole available levy.[3] Now, on strictly feudal principles, as between the king and his tenants-in-chief there could be no commutation of military service. The tenant-in-chief had either

[1] *S. C.* 101. § 11.

[2] *S. C.* 129. Rob. de Monte.

[3] Round, *Feudal England*, 280.

to appear with his contingent when summoned, or after the campaign to pay whatever fine the Barons of the Exchequer imposed upon a man who by his disobedience had merited the penalty of forfeiture. Thus the tenant-in-chief of the Crown did not pay scutage, but an amercement for neglect of duty. We have seen that the means by which the military liability of a great tenant-in-chief was actually discharged, were a matter of private arrangement on his part. But in England at least military service was a royal duty, and on this plea the Crown passed over the lord and took a scutage from the actual tenant-in-demesne by knight-service. But the scutage was not raised until the campaign was over, and the rate at which it was taken would probably be governed by the market price of men hired to do the service due from knight's fees which remained 'on the demesne.' The tenants, who found military service a great burden, made this practice of the king the foundation for a claim to pay scutage as their right rather than to serve in person. Their lords were gradually forced to assent, to hire substitutes to do the duty and to obtain permission from the king to recoup themselves by the levy of a scutage. Often, however, perhaps in a case where the tenant-in-chief had made default, the king would amerce the tenant-in-chief and take a scutage from his tenants by knight-service.[1] It seems probable, then, that scutage applied to three classes of persons—to the smaller tenants-in-chief of the Crown by knight-service, to the actually enfeoffed tenants by knight-service of tenants-in-chief, and to the whole military service of the ecclesiastical tenants-in-chief who found it increasingly expensive to hire knights. On the other hand, the great tenant-in-chief of the Crown—the baron proper—would himself go or be heavily amerced, and would take his proper contingent, which would, however, consist entirely of soldiers hired for the particular occasion.

[1] *P. and M.* i. 245-254. M'Kechnie, 86-93: 275-276.

The rate of scutage seems to have varied from ten shillings, the demand in 1189, to three marks (i.e. forty shillings) from each knight's fee, and this larger sum became frequent under Henry III and the usual rate taken under Edward I. Meanwhile, John's exaction of no less than ten scutages for abortive expeditions led to the provision in Magna Carta[2] that no scutage should be taken except by leave of the 'Commune

[2] *S. C.* 298. § 12.

'Concilium regni.' But in the second reissue of the Charter by the barons under Henry III it was withdrawn in favour of a provision for taking scutage as it had been taken under Henry II.[1] But with the disuse of the feudal levy scutage tended to disappear. In process of time estates had been broken up, and the original liability for knights' fees had become divided. The trouble of collecting increased, while the excuse for it was slighter: at the same time new methods of taxation had been found more productive and less obnoxious to those on whom scutage would have fallen. The result was that, although the liability to scutage was only abolished with the abolition of feudal tenure, yet after the reign of Edward I there are only two traces of it—in 1322 after Edward II's victory over his rebellious barons at Borough-bridge, when it was taken in the shape of amercements imposed on those who had refused to serve in the army defeated at Bannockburn; and in 1385 when Richard II in view of an expedition remitted scutage as if it were a tax which he considered the king might still levy when he went to war in person.

There was no levy of danegeld after 1162.[2] But there were occasional taxes called in general terms 'dona' or 'auxilia,' and raised by separate negotiation between the officers of the Exchequer and each community of payers. These dona were reckoned, like danegeld, upon the hide. But the hide was a vague measurement; for since it probably comprised only cultivated land, the area of assessment must have shifted continually, and the evidence of Domesday must have become increasingly untrustworthy. In 1194, therefore, the place of the hide was taken by the more definite measurement of the carucate or ploughland of 100 acres. Like its predecessors, the new *carucage* was intended to fall on the whole landowning class, and the rate was first fixed at the old amount of two shillings on each carucate.[3] But the amount was variable; for in 1198 each carucate paid five shillings[4] and in 1200 three shillings.[5] Meanwhile, in 1198 an important change took place in the method of assessment, and for the statement of the individual payer was substituted the sworn evidence of a local jury. Carucage may be traced into the early years of Henry III, after which it seems to have disappeared.

1217.

[1] *S. C.* 347.
§ 44.

1661.

Land-owners.

[2] Round, *Feudal England,* 497.

[3] *S. C.* 254; R. Hoveden, iii. 240.
[4] *Ibid.* 257; *Ibid.* iv. 46.
[5] *Ibid.* 272; *Ibid.* iv. 107.

Royal
demesne.

Together with the danegeld from the country was exacted the Auxilium burgi from the towns. This continued under the more common name of *Tallage*, and formed an occasional tax nominally extending in amount to one-tenth of the goods of those entitled to pay. But the towns were regarded as in the demesne of some lord ; and while they all contributed their share to the ferm of the shire, the king could only levy the further impost of tallage on such as were in the ancient demesne of the Crown. For the claim to take this tax seems to have rested on the plea that the inhabitants of towns were holders by villan tenure. Thus other lords had in this matter the same rights as the king, and the only restraint on their power seems to have been the understanding that they should not tallage their lands unless the king tallaged the demesne of the Crown. Some foreign expedition seems to have been considered necessary as an excuse for the levy, and the demand of a sum from London was followed by a visit of the itinerant justices to the other towns in ancient demesne, which were assessed on the basis of the grant obtained from the metropolis. The name 'tallage' first appears under Henry II, and the tax was continued under his successors.[1] It was perhaps the only tax which John did not exact oppressively ; for he desired to win the support of the tenants of the crown lands against the barons. The barons, however, seem to have desired to limit the royal right of tallage, but to have failed in their attempts ; for among the articles presented for the king's signature at Runnymede, the one restricting the levy of scutage or aid to the permission of the Commune Concilium, demands a similar restriction in the case of tallages and other exactions from the citizens of London ;[2] while in the corresponding clause of the Charter, as it was actually confirmed, all mention of the tallage disappears.[3] Under Henry III tallages were frequent, but the oppressiveness seems often to have been lessened by exacting them, like the later benevolences, only from the richer citizens. Tallage, however, followed the taxes already mentioned, and gradually fell into disuse. It is sometimes supposed to have been forbidden by the Confirmatio Cartarum ; but the Latin version of that document, which bears the significant title *De tallagio non concedendo*, although it was treated by the judges in the

[1] M'Kechnie, 278-284.

[2] *S. C.* 293. § 32.

[3] *Ibid.* 298. § 12.

1297.

Hampden case under Charles I as a statute, was merely a chronicler's *résumé* of the intention of the French document. In view of some of his later answers to remonstrances from Parliament, it even seems doubtful whether the king considered that the comprehensive statute of 1340 included tallage among its prohibited methods of taxation. However that may be, there are only three known occasions after 1297 on which a tallage was imposed:—by Edward I himself in 1304, when it met with no complaint; in 1312, when it was strenuously but vainly resisted by London and Bristol; and in 1332, when Edward III accepted in its place a grant of a tenth-and-fifteenth from Parliament.[1] The fact was that [1] *S. C. H.* the changed method of taxation consequent on the formation § 275. of a Parliament of Estates, removed any claim of the king or of the lords to levy such special contributions from the towns in their demesne. For, after 1283 separate negotiations by officials of the Exchequer with the various tax-paying communities practically ceased in favour of a general grant made in Parliament;[2] and the principle of tallage only afforded an [2] *Ibid.* extra plea to those towns which, in their desire to escape § 222. representation, vainly tried to urge that they were not in ancient demesne of the Crown. Thus, after the summons of representatives of the boroughs to Parliament the king's retention of tallage was an illogical proceeding, if, as seems natural, he desired to levy a tax upon the whole burgher population and not merely on that portion of it which dwelt on the royal demesne.

§ 76. The disappearance of these class taxes of a feudal National era brings us to the period of national taxation. At the outset taxation. it will be convenient to note two temporary methods of taxation which never passed beyond the stage of experiment. In the last Parliament of the important reign of Edward III the 1377. king's ministers suggested to the Commons, as one among several alternative methods of taxation, the levy of a groat on every hearth. Ultimately both Parliament and Convocation granted a *poll-tax* of a groat a head on all persons over sixteen years of age, and this form of taxation was repeated in 1379 and 1380, with the important difference that in both cases it was graduated. Thus, in 1379 the scale descended from the Duke of Lancaster, who paid ten marks, down to the poorest person, whose contribution was a groat; while in 1380 the maximum difference between payers was on the much smaller proportion of sixty groats to three.[1] It was this latter levy which formed at any rate the excuse for the Peasant Revolt of 1381 ; and consequently, this method of taxation practically[2] disappears until after the Restoration. It was exacted on three occasions under Charles II, and regularly after the Revolution from 1689 to 1698. The last grant ran until 1706, after which the tax was not renewed. It was not a popular tax, although under Richard II it had served the useful purpose of bringing home to every individual in the kingdom the misdeeds of the royal ministers.

[1] Dowell, *Hist. of Taxation,* i. 93-99.
[2] *Ibid.* iii. 3-4.

Nor was the similar levy of the *hearth money* any more successful. The principle had been long familiar in the payment of Peter's Pence. This was a tax of a penny on every hearth, which from the beginning of the tenth century formed an annual contribution to the Pope, but which at some period before the thirteenth century was compounded for a lump sum of rather more than £200. The suggestion that Parliament should apply such a tax in 1377 did not meet with favour ; nor is there mention of it until after the Restoration, when, from 1662 until the Revolution, a levy was made of two shillings on every hearth or stove. The inquisitorial nature of the tax, which would necessarily lead to the domiciliary visits of the collectors, no doubt accounts for its unpopularity and consequent discontinuance after the Revolution.[3]

[3] *Ibid.* iii. 165-167.

The more permanent forms of national taxation may be divided under the two heads of *direct,* that is, paid immediately by the contributor ; and *indirect,* that is, falling only ultimately on the person who is intended to pay it. Under the first head will be mentioned successively the various attempts made from the fourteenth to the eighteenth centuries to levy a tax on all real and personal property in the country. This required for its efficiency a constant reassessment, a difficulty which was no doubt the reason why the Tenth-and-fifteenth, the Subsidy, and the Property, or rather Land Tax, each in turn became settled at a fixed amount and levied on an old assessment. Thus with the lapse of time they decreased in value, and after attempts to supplement them, they were abolished in favour of more productive methods. The Property Tax still drags

Levied directly.

out an unpopular existence under the more appropriate name of the Land Tax; but for the last century the real direct tax has been the Income Tax. First among the indirect taxes stand the Customs with their long, intricate, and interesting history; to them, since the Restoration, has been added the Excise; and since the Revolution, Stamp duties of multifarious kinds—although both these include payments which come under the head of direct as well as indirect taxes.

The germer of national as opposed to feudal forms of taxation must be looked for in the reign of Henry II. The growing wealth of the country and the close contact with the continent induced Henry to attempt to bring under contribution incomes which were derived from other sources than land. Indirectly this attempt was made as early as 1181, when, by the Assize of Arms, all freemen were directed to have in their possession arms corresponding to the amount of their income.[1] The first instance of a direct contribution on this basis is the Saladin Tithe of 1188, in which a tenth part *reddituum et mobilium*, that is, of rents from land and of income from merchandise, was levied from every one in support of the third crusade.[2] It was not until all the financial resources of the country were called out for the payment of Richard I's ransom, that the justiciar, Hubert Walter, Archbishop of Canterbury, first applied this method of taxation for national purposes.[3] In 1193, besides the payment of the aid by the tenants-in-chief of the Crown, one-fourth not only of their rents, but also of their 'moveables,' was demanded from clergy and laity alike. In fact, whatever may have been Henry II's intention in its first devising, this tax, when it emerged as a regular form of levy, consisted of fractional parts, varying from one-fourth to one-fortieth levied on rents from land and incomes from personal property. As the fairness of an individual return could scarcely be expected in the computation of personal property, the assessment was made by a sworn committee of neighbours. But on the other hand, the undue pressure of a tax so jealously guarded from evasion was mitigated by the allowance of numerous exemptions. The exemptions applied sometimes to goods of a particular class, but latterly and more rationally to the possessors of all goods below a certain value. Thus, while from the collection of a thirtieth in 1237 were excepted all goods applied to eccle-

Tax on Moveables.

[1] *S. C.* 154. §§ 1-3.

[2] *Ibid.* 160.

[3] *Ibid.* 252; R. Hoveden, iii. 210.

siastical uses, horses used for various purposes, the precious metals and household utensils ;[1] in 1276 the exemption applied to all persons not having goods of the value of fifteen shillings.[2] The history of the grant of the tax may be divided into four periods. For the first century of its levy it was negotiated separately with each shire by the officials of the Exchequer. After 1290 it became a grant made by the assembled Parliament; but until 1334 each Estate voted its own liabilities and in a different proportion to the rest. For the purpose of money grants, these Estates were often four— clergy (who, however, actually voted their share in Convocations), lay barons, knights of the shire, and burgesses. But the knights and burgesses coalesced, and, as being the poorer and more numerous portion of the taxpayers, claimed the right of deciding the amount of a grant. The old distinction between Estates gave way to a new distinction based on the difference between town and country or, roughly, between real and personal property ; and while the ordinary proportion granted for dwellers outside a chartered town was one-fifteenth, one-tenth was the settled share of inhabitants of a parliamentary borough. A further change followed almost immediately upon the acceptance of these rates ; for, in consequence of the rigid exaction of the tenth-and-fifteenth in 1332, it was arranged that a further increase should be avoided by taking the contribution of each community for the future at the actual amount for which it had been assessed in that year. Thus the *tenth-and-fifteenth* became a fixed sum of about £39,000 ; and Parliament granted it as such, sometimes voting two or more tenths-and-fifteenths, sometimes adding a half tenth-and-fifteenth. Now, not only had the tenth-and-fifteenth become a fixed sum ; but during the fifteenth century it tended to decrease in amount. From the early years of Henry VI onwards, Parliament in voting the supplies seems to have found it necessary to grant remissions of definite sums, and to specify for exemption particular towns. Thus in 1433, £4,000 were remitted from the tenth-and-fifteenth voted, and Great Yarmouth and Lincoln were mentioned for exemption. Sometimes the list included a larger number of towns, of which some were wholly, but others only partially, exempted. The effect of these remissions has been minimized

[1] *S. C.* 366.
[2] *Ibid.* 431 ; Ann. Winton. 120.
1193-1290.
1290-1332.

Tenth-and-Fifteenth.

1332-1514.

by calling them 'no more than the reduction to a regular
system of a practice which had prevailed in an irregular and
uncertain fashion before;'[1] but it seems scarcely true that
'the amount was not a large one,' and in any case, the
reduction of such occasional remissions to a system would
permanently decrease the sum total on which calculations of
grants were based.[2] The result was that the tenth-and-
fifteenth by no means represented the taxable capacity of the
country. It had been originally intended that there should be
periodical re-assessments of the property subject to the tax;
but this design had been frustrated by the practical commutation of the tax and by the exemptions granted to particular
communities. Under the now antiquated assessment the
decaying grant must have fallen most unfairly and capriciously;
and it was natural that with the return of prosperity the Tudors
should at any rate attempt to find some regular method of
supplementing it. This was found in the subsidy, which for
more than a century ran side by side with the old tenth-
and-fifteenth and gradually superseded it. The last instance
of the old form of taxation is in 1624, the last Parliament of
James I.

The first instance of the grant of a *Subsidy* is in 1514, when,
to supply the deficit caused by Henry VIII's expedition to
France in the previous year, the Commons granted a general
subsidy of sixpence in the pound. The amount varied from
time to time; but the usual rate became 2*s.* 8*d.* in the pound
or two-fifteenths on moveables, and 4*s.* in the pound or two-
tenths on the yearly value of land.[3] The subsidy, however,
followed the same course as the tenth-and-fifteenth. In
order to keep it a fair levy a periodical re-assessment would
have been needed. But 'Englishmen have apparently always
objected to inquisitorial levies based on attempts to find
out what their actual possessions amount to, and greatly
prefer to pay a fixed sum.'[4] Consequently, before the end
of the Tudor era a subsidy came to be based upon the
payments made at the last levy; and, although it was never
reduced so completely as the tenth-and-fifteenth, to a definite
amount irrespective of the value of the property of which it
was supposed to be a proportion, yet a subsidy came to denote
a sum of about £80,000. It was levied on all kinds of

[1] Ashley, *Econ. Hist.* vol. i. pt. ii. 51.

[2] Cf. Dowell, i. 111.

1514-1624.

Subsidy.

[3] Prothero, lxxxi.

[4] Cunning-ham, *Eng. Ind. and Com.* i. 548.

property and was raised under the superintendence of royal commissioners and not, like the tenth-and-fifteenth, by collectors appointed by the local member of Parliament. But although every precaution was taken to make it comprehensive, the actual amount tended to decline. For, such assessment as there was seems to have been carried out in so unfair or at the best so careless a manner that poor and wealthy paid a like amount. Meanwhile the clergy continued to tax themselves apart, although after 1533 their grant had to be confirmed by the Crown in Parliament. During the Commonwealth the subsidy was abandoned in favour of more lucrative modes of raising money, and on its revival at the Restoration the lay and clerical subsidy together did not amount to more than £70,000. Whether this was the reason or not, the subsidy disappeared as a method of taxation, and by an informal agreement between the Chancellor and Archbishop Sheldon of Canterbury the clergy waived their privilege of voting their supplies separately in Convocation.

1664.

It has been shown that royal revenues had not only proved inadequate under Charles I to meet the growing expenses of government, but that at the Restoration they were deliberately diminished by the surrender of the feudal incidents. Among the methods resorted to for their increase, two—the poll tax and hearth money—were of merely temporary interest. But meanwhile, the Commonwealth, borrowing largely from the Dutch, had introduced expedients which, despite the bitter outcry raised against them by the royalists on the ground of their excessive severity, were adopted at the Restoration by the ministers of Charles II. The chief of these expedients were the excise and the monthly assessments. Of these the *Assessment*[1] was merely the Tudor subsidy levied in the strictest possible manner: for, the sum required was settled and demanded month by month, the occupier was responsible for the payment, a proportion was assigned to each district and was taken on an official assessment of the actual value of a man's possessions. The result was a general pressure which fell more severely on all owners of property in the country than the most unconstitutional levies of the Stuart kings. No doubt the consequent discontent was partly accountable for the reaction which ended in the Restoration :

Monthly Assessment.

[1] Dowell, iii. 72.

but the best testimony to the ability of the parliamentary methods of finance is found in their subsequent adoption by the royalists. The assessment took the place of the subsidy; but a short experience seemed to show that, however well it might succeed as a temporary method, the continual re-assessment was a difficult matter. The assessment became careless; it was complained that personal property, which would of course be the more difficult to estimate, did not pay its fair share of the whole; and thus, although the amount produced was certainly greater than that yielded by the subsidy, it was not so much greater as to encourage the financiers of the Revolution to be content with it as a permanent method.

Indeed, the last levy of the assessment was in 1691; and in the next year came the last attempt 'to lay a fixed and permanent charge upon all property, real and personal.' This Property Tax, as it was intended to be, was a subsidy of 4s. Land Tax. in the pound on land, offices, and personal property. But the assessments still continued so careless that the yield of the tax decreased with each year, until in 1697 the ministers, falling back on the assessment of 1692, calculated that the rate of 1s. in the pound on that assessment would produce nearly £500,000, and thus turned the Property Tax, like the tenth-and-fifteenth and the subsidy before it, into a fixed sum. To make the likeness complete, this sum was apportioned among the towns and counties at a definite amount. This last attempt at the taxation of all property contained every element of injustice. Provision had originally been made for the assessment of personal property and offices in order that their owners should contribute to the fixed amount; but since personal property is continually shifting, while the value and ownership of land can be ascertained at any moment, and since it had been provided that any deficiency should be. met by an extra levy on the land, the death of the original payers of quotas on personal property was followed by the levy of the whole sum from the land alone. The intended Property Tax thus became the *Land Tax*. But even as a land tax it was unfair; for, despite an attempt at the Restoration to adopt the carefully made assessment for the levy of ship-money, the usual basis of assessment was that made under the Commonwealth, in which the devotion of the home counties to the parliamentary cause placed the burden of the tax on them. This they continued to bear, despite the fact asserted by an influential writer at the end of the seventeenth century, that the northern and western parts of England had grown proportionately wealthier since the Restoration.   From 1697 to 1798 the Land Tax fluctuated between 1s. and 4s. in the pound, being calculated to produce half a million of money for every shilling rated.   But in **1798** Pitt fixed it at a perpetual rate of 4s. in the pound, thus making it a permanent charge upon the land ; and as such it remains to the present day.   The rate is levied on the old assessment of 1692 ; but by a provision of Pitt's Act much of it has been redeemed.   At the same time, the charge upon personalty which had fallen into complete disuse, was made a separate tax annually granted ; but it produced so little that in 1833 it was repealed.   The tax on offices, which was also a part of the original grant of 1692, was not finally abandoned until 1876.[1]

[1] Dowell, iii. 81-91.

Income Tax.

By this time it must have been evident to financiers that the perpetual re-assessment necessary for the direct taxation of property presented insurmountable difficulties.   Direct taxation, therefore, takes a different form, and Pitt inaugurated the *Income and Property Tax*, so familiar at the present day.

A precedent for such a tax was to be found in the fifteenth century.   We may set aside as irregular the cases of 1382, when the 'landowners' taxed themselves on the plea of the poverty of the country,[2] and of 1404, when the lords temporal granted a special tax of five per cent. from all those whose incomes were over 500 marks a year.[3]   But in 1435 and again in 1450, a graduated tax on incomes derived from fixed sources formed part of the ordinary parliamentary grant.   In the former year the rates were 6d. from incomes between £5 and £100; 8d. from those between £100 and £400, and 2s. on all those above that amount.[4]   In 1450 the taxable unit was lower, being 6d. on all between 20s. and £200, 1s. between £20 and £200, and 2s. on all above £200.[5] There seem to be no farther instances of this tax until Pitt imposed it in **1799**.   Now, while leaving incomes under £60 entirely free, he made it a graduated tax on those between

[2] Dowell, i. 104.

[3] *Ibid.* i. 106.

[4] *Ibid.* i. 113.

[5] *Ibid.* i. 316.

1799-1815.

£60 and £200, and a tax of ten per cent. or 2s. in the
pound on all incomes above £200. After the Peace of
Amiens the tax was repealed by Addington; but on the 1802.
renewal of war in the following year it was revived at the
rate of five per cent. on all incomes of £150 and beyond.
The sources of income were now classed under five separate
schedules, and the yield of the tax was about six millions
a year. It continued and was increased from time to time
until 1815, when the close of the war once more removed
the excuse for its imposition. But in **1842**, when Sir Robert
Peel took office after a series of deficits, some strong financial
reforms were necessary. These chiefly took the shape of
a gradual reduction of the heavy and multifarious customs
duties. It was necessary to help the government to tide over
the time until the anticipated increase of trade should give
back to the revenue in other ways the amount of customs so
surrendered. For this purpose Peel revived the Income Tax
at 7d. in the pound for a period of three or perhaps five years,
allowing total exemption on all incomes under £150. But
in 1845 the tax was renewed for another period, and, despite
the repeated assertions of its temporary nature by successive
Chancellors of the Exchequer, it has never been repealed.
Until 1888 the rate varied almost from year to year, rising
as high as 1s. 4d. in 1855-6, and falling as low as 2d. in the
pound in 1874-5. From time to time slight changes have
been made in the amount of incomes subject to abatement
or exemption from the tax. Thus from 1863-71 all incomes
under £100 a year were exempt; while from incomes under
£200 an abatement of £60 was allowed, and the tax was
taken on the remaining £140. In 1872 the abatement was
extended to £80 out of incomes under £300; in 1876
exemption was extended to incomes under £150 and an
abatement of £120 to incomes under £400;[1] in 1894 the [1] Dowell,
exemption was raised to incomes of £160, and two scales of iii. 92-112.
abatement were allowed; while, finally, in 1899 four scales
of abatement affected incomes under £700 a year.[2] At its [2] Cf.
original re-imposition in 1842 the intrinsic unfairness of a tax Table in
which treated precarious and certain incomes alike was widely *Whitaker's*
felt; but in view of the necessity of doing something quickly *Almanack.*
to restore the revenue to a healthy state, and on the under-

standing that the tax was only to be a temporary expedient, the objections were not pressed. It has now become practically permanent, but not until 1894 was anything done towards the realization of a scheme advocated by many politicians and economists, of a graduated income tax.

Levied indirectly.

§ 77. The history of indirect taxation opens with the intricate and often obscure *Customs* duties. A twofold origin has been

Early history of the Customs Duties.

assigned to this important portion of the revenue. On the one hand, the Customs are generally regarded as the toll which the king, as representative of the nation in its intercourse with foreign countries, exacted from merchants in return for his protection, and as a licence to carry on their trade un-

[1] Dowell, i. 75.

molested.[1] A slightly different view has made the Customs the counterpart to Purveyance, springing from the prerogative right of prise or arbitrary seizure of supplies with the double object of relieving the royal wants and watching over the

[2] Hubert Hall, *Customs Revenue of Eng.* i. 58-62.

native commerce.[2] Nothing, however, turns on the origin of these dues. In either case these tolls or prises in kind were probably arbitrary in amount; and their history is that of their commutation for money payments or for definitely limited amounts of the article on which they were levied. It is to be noted at the outset that, unlike our present system, duties were levied on goods exported as well as on foreign goods brought into the country. By the opening of the thirteenth century custom or agreement between the king's officers and the merchants had fixed these commutations. On the export of wool and leather, the staple commodities of the realm, a toll was taken of half a mark (6s. 8d.) on each sack or on 300 woolfells (i.e. fleeces or untanned hides), and a mark on a last or load of tanned hides or leather. On the import of wine the duties levied on native and on foreign merchants differed. From the former was taken the *Recta Prisa* which, comprising the forfeiture of one or two casks from each cargo according to its size, practically amounted to a payment of one-tenth. But the alien merchant had to pay in money, and from him a toll was taken on each cask of the cargo at no settled rate. Beyond wool, leather and wine, all other articles, whether of import or export, still remained subject to the royal right of prisage, and were arbitrarily seized by the king's officers until they were redeemed by the traders, often at a ruinous cost. Sometimes it seems that even a licence over and above the settled toll was paid by an individual trader for leave to export or import a particular cargo. But all rates above the ordinary rates were known as *mala tolta;* although, with the curious tendency of all mediaeval financial trans- actions to stereotype themselves, even this illegal impost was generally taken in the shape of an advance of the ordinary rate to 40*s.* or three marks on the sack of wool. The attempts of the nation to check the arbitrary power of the Crown in the matter of the customs began with Magna Carta, when the *antiquae et rectae consuetudines* in all their vagueness were allowed, and all *mala tolta* were forbidden.[1] This does not, however, seem to have had much restraining influence; and in 1275, in the first Parliament of Edward I, the *Magna aut antiqua custuma* on wool was settled at the rates mentioned above, and granted to the king as part of his ordinary revenue. Henceforth any maletolte became unconstitutional. The Confirmatio Cartarum attempted to check the royal right of arbitrary prisage by a clause which forbade, without consent of the realm, the levy of any aids, mises or prises except those already settled.[2] Henceforth it was not possible for the king, without flying in the face of Parliament, to place arbitrary dues upon English merchants. But nothing had been done to interfere with the exercise of the royal prerogative in its dealings with foreigners. To this the king now turned; and in 1303, by the *Carta Mercatoria* conveying certain privileges to foreign merchants, Edward I obtained their assent to the *Parva et nova custuma.* These included an increase of fifty per cent. in the customs on wool and leather; so that an alien henceforth paid 10*s.*, where a denizen or native merchant paid 6*s.* 8*d.* To this was added a settled duty of 2*s.* per tun on imported wine, which went by the name of *butlerage* or *tunnage,* and 3*d.* per pound of 20*s.* on all other imported and exported merchandise. This was the origin of *tunnage* and *poundage.* In 1309, probably in answer to popular demands, the latter were suspended; for, it was thought that with the right of the king to extra dues would disappear the privileges of the Carta Mercatoria. But meanwhile the native merchants had refused to assent to the levy of the higher rates, and con- sequently they remained subject to the antiqua custuma as far

[1] *S. C.* 301. § 41.

[2] *Ibid.* 495. § 6.

1297.

as it was settled, together with the exercise of the royal right of prisage so far as the Crown could still exact it in accordance with its old prerogative.

Parliamentary control of Customs.

But the events of the reign of Edward III forced Parliament to great efforts in the curtailment of the royal prerogative of taxation. The control of the customs was as important as, and far more difficult than, the attempt to keep a hold on the direct methods of taxation. But the underhand dealings of the king with the merchants made it imperatively necessary that something should be done. The Commons were shrewd enough to see that, although the king cared not to guard the theory of his prerogative power so long as he possessed the substance of kingly authority, yet the unsupported authority was only such as each individual king could make it ; and when the theory had been yielded, Parliament had but to bide its time in order to make good the substance of power. Indeed, by his attempt to gain their sanction and, consequently, their money, for his foreign enterprises, Edward III himself provoked them to the attitude which they adopted. Without, therefore, combating the king directly, Parliament was careful to sanction after they had been taken, the loans which he had raised by agreement with the merchants, and thus at every opportunity to assert the position that all taxation should be authorized by the representatives of the people. Thus it was not until half a century after the king had first levied the nova custuma from alien merchants, that Parliament gave its sanction to the levy. The Statute of Staples [1] passed without protest from the king. But the popular leaders went further, and in some important matters forestalled him. When the foreign wars of Edward began, it was not improbable that he would have imitated his grandfather by the levy of a maletolte. To prevent such a course Parliament made him a definite grant, at the old rate of the maletolte, in the form of a *subsidy on wool and leather*. The first instance of this grant was in 1341 at the rate of 40s. alike on the sack of wool, 300 wool-fells or a last of leather; and from the time of the Statute of Staples this became one of the most regular means of supply, Parliament forcing the king to allow by statute in 1362, and again in 1371, that no subsidy should be placed upon wool without its consent. It was, indeed, an extra tax

[1] 27 Edw. III. st. 2. 1353.

on wool over and above the rates of the magna custuma already granted as part of the hereditary revenues of the Crown. But, not content with this, in 1373 Parliament proceeded to revive the nova custuma under the name of *tunnage and poundage* at the rate of 2s. per tun on wine, and 6d. per £ on merchandise not already bearing fixed custom. By this means it was imposed on English as well as foreign merchants. Both these were specific grants, in contrast to the antiqua custuma which was the parliamentary regulation of the ordinary exercise of the royal prerogative.[1] The remaining history of both branches is soon told. As England took to manufacturing her own raw material into cloth, the ancient customs on wool, together with the subsidy on wool, decreased in amount. Thus, whereas under Edward III these customs had reached the imposing sum of £68,000; under Henry VI, in 1448, they had shrunk to £12,000. The customs, therefore, lingered on while the subsidy died out; for cloth rather than wool became a chief article of export. Tunnage and poundage were granted to the Crown for short periods, but on the accession of Henry VII they became a grant to the king for his lifetime, and so continued until the first year of Charles I. Meanwhile, the old wine duties on denizens known as prisage, and on aliens known as butlerage, remained in the hands of the Crown, and were usually farmed out to subjects. They were even exempted from the consolidated customs duties of the Restoration; and it was not until 1803 that they were turned into annuities to be paid to the persons to whom the Crown had farmed the original duties. The whole position of the customs duties at the end of Edward III's reign will best be gathered from a short summary of the difference in the payments exacted from native and from foreign merchants respectively. Thus, on *wool and leather*, while they might both have to contribute to an extra subsidy of 40s., ordinarily the native paid the antiqua custuma of 6s. 8d. as against the nova custuma of 10s. on the part of the foreigner. On *wine* while they both were equally liable to tunnage, the recta prisa of the native was probably more than balanced by the butlerage to which the alien was subject. Finally, on *merchandise* the Englishman was the victim of poundage alone; the foreigner was bound by the extra levy of the nova custuma, which added to his duty 3d. per pound on general merchandise.

[1] *S. C. H.* § 277.

In early days the case of the foreign merchants was very hard. Certainly they were welcomed by the king and the nobility, who, as the chief landowners, were interested in encouraging the export of English wool. But they were regarded with great suspicion by the people, and their position was subjected to numerous restrictions. The foreigners were not only liable to higher rates of customs than the native merchants, but they paid in money and not in a percentage of their goods. Moreover, in every country the possession of an abundant treasure was becoming an object of desire. Consequently, in payment for their imports foreign merchants might take no money out of the land, but only English goods. The home merchants were further protected by the prohibition of all retail trading to aliens. Finally, for police purposes, foreigners were restricted as to the time and place of residence, for they were bound to lodge with citizens who would be responsible for their good behaviour, and to depart as soon as their goods were sold ; nor were they free from reprisals for the bad debts of their fellow-countrymen. Under such conditions it was impossible for foreign trade to flourish. Merchants trading with England formed themselves into two societies for mutual protection. Of these the earlier was the *London Hanse* consisting of seventeen towns mostly from Flanders and North-Western France, formed with the twofold object of freedom of trade with England and monopoly of the English trade abroad. But although this organization lingered on until the fifteenth century, it was completely overshadowed by the more important body of the *Teutonic Hanse*, which, starting under the auspices of Cologne and with its centre on the Rhine, was swallowed up in the larger political organization led by Lübeck and clustering round the Baltic. Championed by this powerful body and favourably regarded by the king, the merchants obtained a gradual relaxation of their disadvantages. By the Carta Mercatoria, in return for the extra payments of the nova custuma, many of these disadvantages were withdrawn. Foreign merchants were allowed to engage in retail trade in certain specified goods, and even this restriction was entirely removed in the course of Edward III's reign. The restriction as to their place of abode was similarly treated ; and under Edward III they were allowed

Position of
foreign
merchants
in England.

1303.

to prolong their stay for forty days or even more, provided they took their share in ordinary taxation. Indeed, Edward III's whole policy aimed at the encouragement of foreign trade; and while he granted letters of safe conduct to alien merchants who were deterred by the liability to reprisals, his successor relaxed the restriction on the exportation of money to the extent of half the value of the goods imported. But the oligarchical feeling which was as powerful among the English burgesses as it was abroad, proved too strong for the desires of the king. A short spell of absolute freedom was followed 1351-1377. by a similar period of indecision on the part of the executive, and finally the towns procured an Act in 1393 which withdrew from foreign merchants the licence to take part in retail trade.[1]

[1] Cf. Ashley, *Econ. Hist.* vol. i. pt. i. 104-108, pt. ii. 13-17.

The English merchants sought not only to repel the invasion of the foreigners, but to carry the mercantile contest into the enemies' country. For this purpose they gradually organized themselves. The regulation of trade at the English ports began with Edward I, who not only accepted the fixed customs as a parliamentary grant, but, for their better collection, substituted regular customers for the sheriffs and the various officials hitherto employed, and appointed certain ports in England at which the goods for exportation should be collected. Under Edward II the merchants themselves, who already may have been a separate body, were recognized by 1313. charter as a trading association of *Merchants of the Staple*.[2]

[2] Gross, i. 140-147. Cunningham, i. § 99.

In the same reign the staple itself, or place to which the wool should first be taken, was fixed abroad, at Antwerp. But the system of a staple was at first much opposed by the English merchants, for whose convenience it was continually moved about, chiefly between Bruges and Antwerp. For a time it was even abolished; but so obvious was the advantage 1328-1341. of a fixed place for the levy of customs for the king and even for the enjoyment of privileges by the associated merchants, that the staple was again established abroad successively at Bruges and Calais. But in 1353, in pursuance of his policy of encouraging the visits of foreign merchants, Edward III by the *Statute of Staples* removed the staple to several English towns. His successor followed this up by forbidding English merchants to take any part in the trade in wool. But in 1363 Edward himself found it necessary

1390.

to retransfer the staple to the other side of the channel, and it was generally fixed at Calais, which had the double advantage of being an English town abroad. On the loss of Calais in 1556 its rules were considerably relaxed, and it was placed at Bruges, whose waning glory it helped to support against the threatening supremacy of Antwerp. But the staple was an inelastic organization : it did not lend itself to the expansion of trade to new places. As early as 1407 Henry IV gathered together into the Company of Merchant Adventurers all English merchants who were trading to foreign countries and were outside the bounds of the staple.[1] In the course of the next two centuries this new organization had outstripped both its foreign rival—the Teutonic Hanse, and its English rival—the Merchants of the Staple.[2] Indeed, it was itself the first of those *Regulated Companies* which, on the great outburst of English trade under Elizabeth, identified themselves with some definite part of the commercial world. They took one of two forms, trading either as a Regulated Company proper—such as the Russian and Levant Companies—into which any English subject could gain admittance on definite terms, and the members of which traded each with his own capital though in accordance with the regulations of the company ; or they formed Joint Stock Companies such as the East India Company and, in a different sphere, the Bank of England, trading with a common capital distributed into shares and partaking therefore of the nature of a monopoly.[3]

§ 78. The importance of the customs duties from their settlement under Edward III to their resettlement at the Restoration, may be described as political rather than constitutional. We have seen that Parliament actually authorized the Tudors by statute to take measures necessary for the protection of trade ; and so long as this was the evident intention of the royal acts no objection was raised. But it was the obvious employment of this power ' as a source of profit to the Crown and therefore a means of evading parliamentary control '[4] that began the long struggle over the parliamentary right of taxation already described. It does not appear that the actual amount of increase in the customs duties under the first two Stuarts bore hardly on the merchants. At the same time, English commerce was particularly prosperous ; and when by the adhesion

[1] Gross, i. 148-155. Cunningham, i. § 122. Mrs Green, *Town Life in 15th Century*, i. 87-101.

[2] Mrs Green, i. 101-113.

[3] Cunningham, ii. 118-125. Gross, i. 156.

Later history of the Customs.

[4] Prothero, lxxv.

of the navy the parliamentary party obtained command of the coasts and ports, the enhanced customs dues which they exacted added very materially to their revenues. Thus, whereas in 1610 the customs had amounted to £136,000, and at the outbreak of the Civil War to about £720,000; in 1650 they stood at £350,000, and on the eve of the Restoration at no less than £600,000. At the Restoration not only the irregularities of the last half century, but also the changed character of English trade in the last three centuries, must have suggested the propriety of a new settlement of these duties. Accordingly, the old distinctions were abolished and the future liabilities grouped under the heads of (*a*) Tonnage on French wines at £4 10s.; (*b*) Poundage on both imports and exports at an *ad valorem* duty of five per cent.; and (*c*) duties reckoned by the weight on woollen cloth, both the 'old drapery' or broadcloth, and the newer kinds such as serges and crapes which had been introduced by the Flemish refugees in the time of Elizabeth. The articles upon which poundage was taken by the Act of 1660 were known as the Old Subsidy. Subsequent percentages of equal amount were laid on practically the same articles—in 1698, again just after the outbreak of the Spanish Succession War in 1702 and 1703, just after the Austrian Succession War in 1749, and finally during the Seven Years War in 1759—five percentages in all, the last four being known by way of contrast as the New Subsidy, and being laid almost entirely on imported articles. But the whole twenty-five per cent. was not chargeable even on all the articles enumerated in the Book of Rates provided by the Act of 1660. Meanwhile, the export duty on cloth had been repealed in 1700, and Walpole abolished nearly all the remaining export duties on British manufactures. At the same time, a great number of other duties besides the five subsidies were from time to time imposed on articles which had not needed notice in 1660. Some of these were appreciably reduced and even altogether abolished by Walpole. The fact that they were mainly duties on raw material for English manufactures had the additional advantage of effectually checking the smugglers. Walpole even attempted to alter the mode of collection by developing the system of warehousing which, while encouraging trade to come to England, only charged

1642.

1659.

a substantial duty on the goods which were consumed in the
country. This method had been applied to foreign silks in

1733.

1700: Walpole extended it to tea, and would have carried it
further but for the furious party opposition which identified
it with a general scheme of excise.

Mercantile
System.

But Walpole's excellent measures were only a temporary
lightening of the load placed upon English trade in exempli
fication of the mercantile system of commerce. According
to the principles of this system, power—rather than plenty
through mutual benefit—was the aim of trade with foreign
nations. This power was to be obtained by self-sufficiency
at home through prohibitive duties upon foreign imports,
combined with the acquisition of foreign markets for home
manufactures. Thus not only were export duties gradually
withdrawn; but the export of English goods was artificially
encouraged by drawbacks, bounties, commercial treaties and
a monopoly of the colonial trade. *Drawbacks* were customs
or excise which were repaid on the exportation or re-exporta
tion of the articles on which they were levied. The ware
housing scheme of Walpole was intended to do away with
the necessity for such payments; but no general system
of bonding or warehousing came into practice until 1803.
Bounties were extra payments made by the government for
the encouragement of production in certain kinds of goods,
and especially for their exportation to foreign countries. The
chief of these was a bounty of 5s. per quarter upon wheat
so long as the home price did not rise above a certain limit.
This lasted from the Revolution of 1688 to 1814; but so
high did the price of wheat rise during the Napoleonic wars
that not only was it necessary to withdraw the now useless
bounty on exportation, but an attempt was made to attract
sufficient foreign corn into the country by the payment of
bounties upon importation. Other well-known instances of
bounties were those on whale ships at £1 per ton for the
encouragement of the whale fishery, which ceased in 1824;
and on linen and cured herrings which continued till 1830.
The object of *commercial treaties* was to secure a 'sole market'
or the monopoly of each other's trade by the two contracting

1703.

countries. The best-known instance is that of the Methuen
Treaty with Portugal, by which Portuguese wines were to be

admitted into England at two-thirds of the custom imposed on wines from France, while English wool was to be admitted duty free into the markets of Portugal. Finally, the *colonies* were regarded as mere feeders of the mother country, whose business was to grow raw material for the home manufacturers and to afford a market for the surplus goods of English manufacture. As a matter of fact, English statesmen were more generous to the colonies than their French and Spanish rivals ; and Walpole allowed both rice from Carolina and Georgia, and sugar from the West Indies, to find their way direct to Europe provided they were carried in British ships ; while his so-called excise scheme was framed largely in the interests of the colonial trade with countries outside the British Isles.

In the present system of free trade, such customs duties as remain are levied almost solely for purposes of revenue. The acceptance of this system was due, among many others, first and foremost to Adam Smith and later to Richard Cobden, whose principles were carried into action by William Pitt, Sir Robert Peel, and Mr. Gladstone. When Pitt came into office he found the customs duties in a state of great confusion. Not only were there no less than sixty-eight branches of those duties, but each imported article paid several separate customs, some few of them under as many as fourteen different heads. So great was the consequent temptation to smuggling that the estimated loss to the revenue was two millions. The complexity was increased by the prevailing system of appropriating each duty to a particular item of expenditure. In the true principles of the ' Wealth of Nations ' Pitt reduced many of the existing duties—for example, that on tea from 119 to 12½ per cent. With the same object and without any popular demur, he carried out Walpole's scheme of 1733, by transferring the duties on wine from customs to excise. But, perhaps most important of all, he simplified the various heads under which customs had been enumerated, laid a single duty upon each article, and arranged for the accumulation of all the proceeds of the customs into one sum, known henceforth as the *Consolidated Fund*.[1] The great war necessitated an enormous increase of taxation ; and customs duties were imposed on every available article of importation. But the policy of

Walpole in freeing the raw material imported for our manu
factures, and the success of Pitt in the direction of simplifying
the customs duties, gradually found imitators after the strain
of the war was over.   Walpole's mantle fell upon Robinson
(afterwards Lord Goderich) and Huskisson, by whose joint

1824-1825. influence, as Chancellor of the Exchequer and President of the
Board of Trade respectively, the duties on raw silk and wool
and on several metals were considerably reduced.   But it was
Sir Robert Peel who worked a thorough reform in the custom
duties.   He entered on office after a series of deficits in the

1842. annual revenue ; and yet, while reviving the Income Tax to
tide over the immediate loss to the revenue, he so far showed
himself a consistent disciple of Adam Smith and Ricardo
that—of the 1,200 articles bearing customs duties in 1842—he
removed about 750 from the tariff, and in 1845 over 400 more
In 1846 he abolished the duty upon corn.   The few remaining
export duties disappeared, although from 1901 to 1906 there
was a small revival in the shape of a duty of one shilling a
ton upon coal.   The final blow to the old protective system
was dealt by Mr. Gladstone in his budgets of 1853 and of 1860
The immediate losses to the revenue involved in each of these
reductions have been amply compensated by the increased
trade of the country and the consequent yield of other taxes
which chiefly take the shape of Excise and Stamps.

Excise.   § 79. The most permanent methods by which the revenue
was increased after the Restoration, were the Excise and Stamp

[1] Anson, ii. duties.   An *Excise*[1] was originally a duty on articles of con

308-311. sumption produced in England.   Now, there seems to have
been a deep-rooted aversion in the English mind to taxes
on internal trade.   But at the outbreak of the Civil War the
parliamentary party, under the leadership of Pym, braved
the anger of the people, and introduced in succession, though

1643. only 'at the point of the sword,' an excise on ale, beer, cider

1644. and other beverages, followed by one on salt, starch, textile
goods, and victuals of all kinds.   Some of the more common
articles of consumption were removed from the list in 1649
but the exceeding profitableness of the tax induced the statesmen
of the Restoration to incorporate it permanently in the financial
system of the country.   It was necessary to find some com
pensation for the feudal dues which the Crown surrendered

The country had become somewhat reconciled to the excise. Accordingly, in the place of the abandoned feudal dues and the right of purveyance, was made a grant estimated at £100,000 as the proceeds of an excise on beer and liquors, both home-made and imported. This was added to the hereditary revenues of the Crown; while for Charles II's life a temporary excise was given at the same rate. The hereditary excise formed part of the Civil List of the Crown: in 1736 part of it was commuted by Parliament for an annual sum of £70,000; and in 1787 the rest was absorbed, together with all existing excise duties, into the general scheme of the Consolidated Fund.

Throughout the eighteenth century and the early years of the nineteenth the continually increasing expenses entailed by a series of great wars were met, among other ways, by constant *new applications* of the excise. In 1695 began the tax upon malt, in 1711 that upon soap and paper, in 1746 that upon glass; while from time to time such articles of common and necessary use as bricks, candles, calico prints, leather and salt, were added to the list of excisable commodities. The number of these at the end of the eighteenth century has been enumerated at twenty-seven; but the enlightened policy of Robinson and Huskisson reduced them to nearly half that number, and at present they may be counted on the fingers of one hand. Moreover, when the number of excisable articles seemed to have reached its limit, financiers, nothing daunted, proceeded to raise the rate. Thus the charge upon spirits, the earliest of all excisable articles, was only a few pence at its first imposition in 1660, stood at over 3s. just before the outbreak of the French Revolutionary wars and, under the stress of those wars, rose to no less than 12s. 7d. per gallon. 1819.

Meanwhile, the term excise had been *extended beyond its original meaning* of a tax upon articles of home production and Extended consumption. Even under the Commonwealth an excise was to tax on imports, imposed on certain imported articles, which thus paid a duty at the ports as well as an excise in the process of exchanging hands. But the full effect of the misnomer (for such it really was) appeared in the extraordinary agitation produced by Walpole's Excise Bill. This was simply a scheme whereby, 1733. for the prevention of smuggling and the encouragement of foreign trade, the system of warehousing, already introduced in the case of foreign silks, should be applied to wine and tobacco, and—as in the case of tea, coffee, and cocoa—the customs duty on their importation should be turned into an excise duty on their consumption. For this purpose the articles so to be dealt with were brought to English ports and warehoused, and only such of them were rendered dutiable as were taken out for consumption in England; while those re-exported were free from all except a nominal payment. But despite the continuance of the excise after the Commonwealth, the system was anything but popular in England. The feeling about it may be measured by Blackstone's remark that 'from its first original to the present time its very name has been odious to the people of England,' and by the celebrated definition inserted by Dr. Johnson in his dictionary, that an excise was 'a hateful tax levied upon commodities, and adjudged not by the common judges of property, but wretches hired by those to whom excise is paid.' Walpole's proposal was solely concerned with a change in the method of collection; for, the full duty was to be levied by officers of excise. But 'an unscrupulous opposition working upon the general hatred of the name,' turned the name into a description of the character of the tax, and represented it as the first step towards a general scheme of excise necessitating that inquisitorial method of house to house visitation by government officials against which Englishmen have always protested. But the partisan character of the opposition is shown by the ease with which Pitt carried out the very measure which Walpole, despite his parliamentary majority, had felt himself constrained to abandon.

1787.

to licences. An almost equally illegitimate extension of the term 'excise' is that which makes it include various *licences*.[1] These are of two kinds, embracing *authorizations* to carry on certain professions or to trade in certain commodities; and *payments* falling almost entirely on the wealthier classes 'for enjoyment of certain things of convenience or luxury.' Of the first kind the earliest instance may be found in the monopolies of Tudor and Stuart times, and more particularly in the licences on inns and alehouses of the same period, which were the cause of such violent abuses. But the real idea of these levies

[1] Anson, ii. 311.

was no doubt borrowed from the Dutch and was first applied after the Restoration. Under this head, then, would come such payments as the tax upon publicans, upon auctioneers, hawkers, pawnbrokers, foreign-wine dealers, tobacconists, and others; while in the latter list would be included taxes on carriages, horses, men- and (until 1792) women-servants, plate, cards, dice, armorial bearings, dogs. In 1785 all these were grouped together under the head of assessed taxes, and up to 1869 the taxpayer was required to pay for those the liability to which he had incurred in the previous year. But at that date the name of 'assessed taxes' was abolished, and a distinction drawn between excise licences and establishment licences; both of which were now required to be taken out at the moment when the liability was incurred, whether it was at the beginning of the year or at any period in its course.

Alongside of the Excise grew the *Stamp duties*.[1] Indeed, the difference between the two is only a difference of the manner in which the money is conveyed to the Exchequer. We may set aside such exactions as the admission stamp necessary for practising the calling of a barrister or physician; for, it is immaterial whether such tax takes the form of a stamp or, as in the case of a publican, it is paid as a licence. Apart from this these duties fall into two classes, according as they apply, on the one side, to the validity of legal transactions and, on the other, to the devolution of property. Some temporary stamp duties were imposed in 1671; but the first general Act dates from 1694, when stamps varying in value from £2 to one penny were required to such documents, among others, as admission to offices or degrees, marriage certificates, copies and probates of wills. Numerous other documents were from time to time included within the operation of the Act, such as bills of exchange in 1782 and receipts for payments in 1784. At first the amount of the stamp varied in all cases with the length of the documents. But in 1714, in the case of grants to offices, the value of the transaction was taken as the determining point. In 1784 this principle was applied to receipts which were included within the liabilities of the Act, and subsequently to other legal transactions: while in 1853 the stamp upon receipts was made an uniform amount of 1d. for all sums over £2. The most profitable form of stamp duty is the

Stamp Duties.

[1] Anson, ii. 312.

legacy and succession duty which was first imposed by Lord North in 1780; but its careless provisions led to so much evasion that Pitt's measure of 1796 was on entirely new lines. It was not the legatees but the executors who were responsible for the payment.[1] Pitt had intended to include succession to property of every kind; but he was only able to accomplish a measure which provided for the succession to personal property. It was not until 1853 that real property was brought under liability to the same duties, though in a less degree; and Mr. Lowe's attempt in 1871 to assimilate the duties payable on both kinds of property was in the end abandoned. Changes were made by Sir Stafford Northcote in 1880 and by Mr. Gladstone in 1881. Among other things Mr. Gladstone added a new 'account duty,' and in 1889 Mr. Goschen imposed a new 'estate duty.' Finally, in 1894, Sir William Harcourt substituted for all the so-called 'death duties' except those on legacy and succession, a new estate duty consisting of a percentage of the principal value of all property real or personal. This is graduated in amount corresponding to the increasing size of the sum upon which it is paid.

[1] Dowell, iii. 133-134.

Summary. Such were the chief items of national revenue at various times in the history of the country. They may be shortly summarized. The Anglo-Saxon kings were dependent practically on the revenue which came to the Crown from the king's demesne, the profits of justice, and the exercise and enjoyment of various prerogative rights. Not until after the Conquest were these in any way calculable at a money value. Under the Norman kings the feudal dues were added to the revenue; but it was only in Henry II's reign that taxation began to form an important item of the national income. The taxes of a feudal nature—scutage, tallage, and the hidage or carucage, which had taken the place of the earlier danegeld—dragged out their existence until the reign of Edward I, after which they practically disappeared. Besides the royal demesne, which fluctuated almost from year to year according to the checks put upon the lavish generosity of the king, and many pecuniary rights which came from the prerogative, the chief items of income were (1) the tax on moveables begun under Henry II, and under Edward III not only assuming the shape of a levy in the definite proportions of a tenth and a fifteenth, but even becoming a fixed sum of nearly £40,000; (2) the customs, whether as at first in the shape of the ancient customs and subsidy on wool, or the tunnage and poundage of a later period. Up to the Civil Wars the only change was the addition of the Tudor subsidy. Of the old rights of the prerogative some continued in full force throughout the period, while others were revived from time to time as methods of raising money by unscrupulous kings. The experiments of the Commonwealth, borrowed largely from Holland and adopted by the statesmen of the Restoration, began the modern system of taxation. The feudal dues and some of the most vexatious of the old royal rights were entirely abandoned. Even the subsidy gave way to what was intended to be a property tax, but became merely a land tax. The customs were placed on a new basis, and two practically new expedients, the excise and stamp duties, soon proved to be among the most lucrative items of the national revenue. Finally, from the time of the younger Pitt the customs and excise have been gradually decreased, and the deficiencies made good by the Income Tax and Inhabited House duty.

§ 80. But since the Revolution of 1688 the increased facilities for borrowing money have entirely done away with the necessity of making the expenditure of the year tally with its revenue. This has changed the whole method of government finance. But we should gain a very partial view of the financial resources of the country even before the Revolution, if all mention were omitted of the numerous loans contracted from time to time by the government. *Loans.*

The earliest creditors of the king were the *Jews*.[1] There are isolated notices of their presence in England even before the Norman Conquest; but their importance in the financial history of the country dates from their settlement in larger numbers in the Conqueror's reign. From that time until their banishment by Edward I they were the king's financial agents. One of the so-called Laws of Eadward the Confessor describes them as the king's chattels. Indeed, they were absolutely without status in the kingdom, nor was there any foreign government to interfere in their behalf. The king, on the one side, fleeced them most unmercifully. Under Henry II the Commune Concilium, which had agreed upon £70,000 as *The Jews in England.* [1] M'Kechnie, 265-273. Cunningham, i. § 70. 1290.

the sum likely to be yielded by the Saladin Tithe for the Crusade, proceeded to assess the Jewish population for the same purpose at no less than £60,000.   The story of John's treatment of the Jew of Bristol, who was condemned to lose a tooth a day at the cost of 10,000 marks until either his teeth or his treasure were exhausted, and who held out for six days against the king's demand, is perhaps scarcely an exaggerated illustration of the attitude of the king.   In self-protection the Jews gathered together not only into those towns where public chests were maintained for the registration and preservation of their bonds, but even into special quarters of the towns where they could practise, unmolested by any city official, their language and their religion.   At the same time, every effort was made for their conversion.   Converts as being Christians ceased to be chattels of the king ; and in 1233, in what is now known as Chancery Lane, a Domus Conversorum or state-endowed home for Jewish Christians was set up, an example subsequently followed both at Lincoln and at Oxford.   At the same time, Richard I had given the Jews a regular organization. The revenue obtained from them, which came both from extortion and in payment of licences for various purposes, was gathered into a special Exchequer of the Jews presided over by special justices, sometimes themselves of the Jewish persuasion, who also exercised an exclusive civil jurisdiction in cases where a Jew was concerned.   John and Henry III granted further privileges and protection.   But the utmost royal favour could not shield the Jews from the popular hatred. The Scriptures prohibited the taking of interest for loans ; and in the absence of any field for investment of spare capital,

Usury.

a demand for recompense was regarded as an attempt to take advantage of a neighbour's necessities.   Consequently, the exaction of interest was forbidden to Christians under the hateful

[1] Cunning-ham, i. §§ 84-85.

name of usury.[1]   But the Jews were not amenable to Christian law ; and the dangers which they incurred, no less than their proverbial greed, were responsible for the enormous rates which they demanded.   It was out of their loans to extravagant and heavily taxed landowners that the Jews made profits such as were impossible to the thrifty merchant ; while the fact that it was the Crusades which gave them special opportunities for amassing riches out of the necessities of enthusiastic Christians, added further fuel to the fire of popular hatred which ever and anon burst out. It was, however, only by such means that the Jews could keep pace with the royal demands, and thus the king's use of them, which did not diminish their unpopularity, imposed a large indirect taxation upon the industries of the country. It was scarcely likely that their services to learning, as students of physical science and medicine, as teachers of mathematics and Hebrew, and as collectors of valuable libraries, should have received due recognition. From the time of Stephen onwards no story against them was too impossible to be believed; nor are the kings free from the charge of fostering such tales for the purpose of making the Jew pay heavily for protection. At length Edward I, much to his own advantage, yielded to the popular clamours, and in 1290 wound up a series of harsh measures by a sentence of banishment which, despite his best endeavours, was most cruelly carried out.[1] There is abundant evidence that after the decree of banishment Jews remained in England, chiefly in the guise of physicians or foreign merchants; although as a body they were not allowed to return until the Commonwealth. The accusation on which they had fallen had been that of tampering with the coinage; but, whether this were true or false, the real reason is rather to be found in the accumulated hatred of all classes of the people and the formidable rivalry of merchants from Italy, who in many European countries were successfully assuming the position of bankers.

[1] *S. C. H.* § 278.

The success of the Jews had been largely due to the connection, through their co-religionists, with most of the civilized countries of the world. Thus while, on the one side, they were money lenders, on the other they were foreign-money changers. In the latter rôle they were rivalled and forcibly superseded by *Caursines* and other Italian merchants *from Lombardy and Florence,* who had spread themselves all over Europe. From every part of Western Europe large sums of money were annually transmitted as tribute to the Pope. These merchants were employed as papal agents to collect and transmit what was due. Again, the produce of the East found its way to European markets through the ports

Foreign merchants.

of Italy.   For its distribution Italian houses of business formed
a network of connections throughout Europe.   It has been
pointed out that nearly all the early commerce of the country
was in the hands of foreign merchants.   Indeed, the English
tributes to the Pope were paid largely in wool.   Thus the
conduct of the foreign trade both in England and elsewhere
made the merchants also into money changers.   Moreover,
their business could not be carried on without considerable
capital, and, as owners of large sums of ready money, they
became creditors of the king ; while their possession of the
machinery necessary for the prosecution of a valuable trade
caused them to become banks of deposit for the money or
goods of wealthy individuals.   These foreign merchants were
regarded by the English people with scarcely less suspicion
than that which had fallen upon the Jews.   The kings, however, welcomed them and gradually withdrew the disabilities to
which they were subjected.   Yet even with this encouragement
their trade gradually died away.   Edward III not only borrowed
largely from them, but even repudiated his debts ; and the
consequent ruin of the great house of the Bardi is said to have
plunged half Florence into distress.   The merchants not unnaturally became shy of lending to the king, who was forced
to resort elsewhere.[1]   But even their trade gradually declined.
The increased manufacture of English cloth after the reign of
Edward III, and the consequent decrease in the exportation
of English wool, deprived them of their chief article of trade ;
while the obstacles put in the way of their exportation of coin
rendered it hard for them efficiently to conduct the exchanges.
Their chief work came to be merely the negotiation of bills of
exchange.   At the same time, the English towns prevailed
alike over ' the weakness of the Lancastrians and the bourgeois
sympathies of the Yorkists ' ;[2] obstacles were once more placed
in the way of foreigners, and, at the same time, the English
merchants had begun to organize themselves in the associations
and companies already mentioned.

> Meanwhile, the change of opinion on the subject of usury
rendered it possible for the king to have recourse openly to
such of his subjects as were willing or could be compelled
to lend.   With the opening up of fields for investment the
taking of interest gradually came to be no longer regarded as

[1] S. C. H.
§ 278.

[2] Ashley,
Econ. Hist.
vol. i. pt. ii.
15.

Regulation
of Interest.

sinful, but only as needing legal regulation. For, at first there was naturally no real comprehension of the relation between the employment of capital and the rate of interest, and the latter ' was spoken of as a sort of arbitrary compensation to the man who having money was in a manner obliged to do a good turn to a friend.' Thus, although an Act of Henry VII 1488. forbade all lending of money on interest, under Henry VIII 1545. interest was allowed at ten per cent. This permission was withdrawn in 1552, and on scriptural grounds all taking of interest was again forbidden. This, however, had so little effect in checking the practice that in 1571 the Act of Henry VIII was restored, although any rate above ten per cent. was stigmatized as usury and as forbidden by the law of God. The rate was gradually reduced, in 1624 to eight per cent., in 1651 to six per cent., at which figure it remained till a further reduction to five per cent. was made in 1714. It is noteworthy that the laws regulating the taking of interest, commonly called the Usury Laws, remained on the Statute Book until 1855.

As the king's creditors the foreign merchants were followed Origin of by foreign princes, including even the Pope, who was among Banking in the first to set at nought the Christian feeling about usury; England. while at home wealthy communities, such as towns and monasteries, were willing to help the king in his necessities.[2] But [2] *S. C. H.* it was not always so easy to raise money, and then recourse § 278. was had to compulsion, and wealthy individuals were made to lend of their accumulated treasure to the king. The advantage of this method was that it caused no widespread discontent in the country. The difference between a forced loan and a benevolence or free gift is not easy to grasp ; for, a loan taken at the king's pleasure might also be repaid in his own good time, and with a complaisant Parliament to back him the distinction entirely disappeared. But the Great Rebellion deprived the Crown of this method of raising money. Meanwhile, a new source of supply was developing itself. With the increasing facilities for commerce offered by the discovery of the New World, individual wealth was growing ; and until an extensive system of credit was established, this wealth consisted largely in bullion and precious stones. The need of safety caused the owners to entrust their valuables to the care of the *Gold-*

smiths, who would naturally be possessed of places of safety. To the valuables were added sums of money on deposit, and the goldsmiths, borrowing the system from Holland, turned to the profitable trade of banking. They paid six per cent. on the loans of their customers, and made their profit partly by picking the best coin and melting it down for export, partly by short loans to merchants, like the bankers of the present day. After 1640 their business much increased. Hitherto merchants had kept large sums of ready money at the Mint, which was then in the Tower of London. But a few months before the meeting of the Long Parliament Charles I, among other expedients for raising money, seized a sum of £130,000 deposited there, with a promise of repayment six months hence.[1] The matter was compromised ; but henceforth the only secure place of deposit was with the goldsmiths. Under the Commonwealth the government was carried on largely by loans, which were raised chiefly from the goldsmiths on the security of particular branches of the revenue. The system was continued after the Restoration, until in 1672 Charles II closed the Exchequer, that is, suspended repayment to the goldsmiths, the largest creditors of the Treasury, to the amount of £1,300,000. These were unable to answer the demands of their depositors, and were obliged to declare themselves bankrupt. But the consequent distress was so great that, despite the best efforts of the Crown to escape from the necessity of repaying the goldsmiths altogether, it was obliged at last to acknowledge the debt, and to take means, in a manner which will presently be noticed, to satisfy the surviving creditors.[2]

The thorough distrust in the government which these proceedings had engendered, was increased by the political uncertainty which prevailed for some years after the Revolution in 1688. The ministers of William III found it almost impossible to raise money on a sudden emergency, and resorted to all kinds of expedients. For some time the idea of a national bank had been mooted, on the analogy of the Bank of Genoa which had existed for three centuries, and the Bank of Amsterdam which was founded at the beginning of the seventeenth century. The scheme as it was adopted, was submitted by its founder, a Scotsman named William

[1] Gardiner, ix. 170.

1701.
[2] Cunningham, *Eng. Ind. and Com.* ii. 222-223.

The Bank of England.

Paterson, in 1691; but not until **1694** was it put into practice by Montagu. The plan appealed solely to the monied interest, and consequently only just escaped wreck in the House of Lords. But among the merchants of the City it met with immediate success, and the whole capital of £1,200,000 was subscribed in ten days. The interest was eight per cent., secured on a new tax on the tonnage of ships; and the subscribers were allowed to take up the work of the goldsmiths and to act as a bank of deposit and loan.[1] The novelty of this method of raising money lay in the fact that not only was no stipulation made for the repayment of the principal, but it was definitely understood that the interest paid by the government was to be a more or less permanent charge. In other words, this was the beginning of the *National Debt*. The justice or injustice of burdening posterity with the repayment of debts incurred for present purposes, must be left to treatises of economics or practical politics.[2] Here may be noted the historical facts that the monied classes were enlisted on the side of William III, who was enabled to raise loans without provoking any of the disaffection which would have accompanied heavy taxation; that government securities now became a safe and popular investment; and that thus a great inducement was given for the accumulation of capital. But at the very outset of its career the Bank of England was almost wrecked through the hostility of the goldsmiths and the landed gentry. The former, not unnaturally jealous of the new rival, took advantage of the scarcity of metal money which preceded the recoinage of 1697, and, accumulating a large quantity of the bank's notes, presented them for immediate payment. By the patriotic efforts of the proprietors all genuine claims were met, and the satisfaction of the goldsmiths' demands were delayed until the new coinage had been issued.[3] It was exactly a century before the Bank was again placed in a similar predicament, and on the next occasion Parliament came to 1797. the rescue and exonerated the directors from paying their claims in cash. The bank notes thus became legal tender; nor were cash payments resumed until 1819. In the crisis of 1697 the landed gentry took the opportunity of the Bank's inability to negotiate a fresh loan for the king, to revive the project—already mooted by Chamberlayne in 1693—of a Land

[1] Macaulay, iv. 58-60.

[2] Cf. Lecky, i. 337-339.

[3] Macaulay, iv. 152.

Bank, that is, one whose liabilities should be secured on investment in land. In its desire to propitiate the Tories, the government lent a favourable ear. But the crisis of 1697 had already shown the importance of a bank reserve in forms that can easily be realized. Land is of all things the most difficult to dispose of at a moment's notice. Consequently, quite apart from the fact that the proprietors of the Bank enormously overcalculated the value of land, the classes whom it was intended to serve refused to subscribe, the government obtained no benefit in the shape of the expected loan, and the whole scheme fell through.[1]

The National Debt.

1698.

It has been said that the National Debt originated in a loan to government, in return for which the subscribers were allowed to enrol themselves as a corporation with the title of the Bank of England. To this was added a *loan of £2,000,000 from the New East India Company*, in return for its charter. The government indebtedness was further swollen by the ultimate acknowledgement of the *claims of the goldsmiths*, against whom Charles II had closed the Exchequer. In 1706 these were compounded for, and the principal was added to the general debt. A fourth definite item was formed by the *stock of the South Sea Company* which, on the bursting of the South Sea Bubble, was taken over by the government. But this stock or capital had itself represented a floating debt (that is, one payable on demand of the creditor) of some £10,000,000 raised during the early years of the War of the Spanish Succession. In 1711 Harley had induced these creditors to allow the debt to be 'funded,' that is, to leave the capital permanently with the government, and to accept an annual interest secured upon the customs. In return for this they were formed into a company for exercising all the privileges of trade which Spain subsequently granted to England at the Treaty of Utrecht. This operation was repeated in 1720. All the existing government creditors, whose claims amounted to about £32,000,000, were offered the alternative of payment or shares in the South Sea Company. The government thus gained the advantage of having one creditor instead of many. But more than this : so eager was the company to obtain all the credit of the government in order to extend its operations, that it engaged to receive from the government the

1701.

1721.

lower rate of interest of five per cent. on the capital taken over, instead of the seven or eight per cent. at which the loans had originally been contracted. These loans had been and continued to be raised in two ways—redeemable annuities, of which something will be said presently, and *irredeemable or perpetual annuities*, of which the government engaged to pay the interest, but made no stipulation as to the repayment of the principal. The consolidating policy of 1711 and 1720 was repeated in 1751; the floating debts were funded, but the fund so formed was now kept in the hands of the government, bearing the low interest of three per cent., and was the beginning of what we now call 'Consols.' The policy of the government has been severely criticized, for, in order to diminish the interest, it fixed a low rate at which it was willing to borrow, and offered its nominal £100 stock at the price which investors would give for it. Thus, when the credit of the government stood at five or six per cent., it offered three, and in consequence obtained only £50 or £60, while it left posterity to discharge the debt by payment of £100. This system of raising money was begun under George II, and the extent to which it was carried may be illustrated by the fact that between 1793 and 1815, while the average price of three per cent. consols was 65, the addition made to the National Debt under this head was £400,000,000, for which the government actually received £260,000,000. Financial writers have pointed out that not only was the nation thus made liable to pay money which it never received, but it deliberately debarred itself from cutting down the interest in the future. The system has found a defender in Professor Thorold Rogers, who urges that, besides that it was an easy mode of borrowing (which some writers regard as 'a questionable advantage'), had the investor suspected that on the first opportunity the interest would be reduced, he would have demanded eight or ten per cent., whereas he was willing to take what was practically six per cent., since he paid £50 for £100 worth of stock. The government could redeem at par, and it was only fair that the investor should have some advantage for the convenience which he afforded to the government at the time when the loan was raised, as against the inconvenience which might be occasioned by having a heap of money thrown back upon his hands at a

[1] *Econ. Interp. of Hist.* 453.

time when he did not want it.[1] Two other methods have been employed at various times for adding to the permanent debt. In 1694 a system of *lotteries* was introduced, by which a part only of the money subscribed was distributed in prizes among the ticket holders. It was discontinued after 1823. A far more important portion of the present debt is formed by the *terminable annuities* introduced in 1808. The object of this method of raising money is that, while a larger annual interest is paid, the principal lapses to the government either on the death of the investor or in a certain number of years from the time of the investment. At first, owing to careless miscalculations, these annuities resulted in large losses to the government; but this was remedied in 1828, and nearly £80,000,000 of the present debt is held under this head.

All the methods of borrowing hitherto enumerated have formed part of the funded debt or government stock. A far smaller, but an appreciable item of the whole, is composed of the *Unfunded or Floating Debt*, the redeemable annuities lately mentioned. This consists of temporary loans raised upon the security of Exchequer Bills, that is, promissory notes issued by the Treasury under the authority of Parliament, which bear interest from the day of issue until that of payment, and are then either discharged or renewable. They were issued first in 1696 to supplement the scarcity of metal money at the time of the recoinage ; and, being made receivable in payment of taxes and thus guaranteed against risk of depreciation, they form a good investment for capital which may at any moment be required, and are consequently in much commercial demand. The amount so issued varies enormously from year to year, part of it being sometimes funded and thus made into perpetual annuities.

From the very commencement of the National Debt there were frequent prophecies of its fatal and ruinous influence. The names of Davenant, Bolingbroke, Hume, and Chesterfield may be enumerated among the large number of statesmen, economists, and historians who alike shared this view.[2] And the rapidity of its growth seemed almost to justify their predictions. At the end of William III's reign it amounted to over £16,000,000, and absorbed one-third of the entire revenue in payment of interest; at the Treaty of Utrecht it stood at £54,000,000. At the Peace of Aix-la-Chapelle it

[2] Lecky, i. 340-341.

1713.
1748.

had risen to over £78,000,000; at the Peace of Paris to 1763.
£139,000,000, and the interest took £4,800,000 out of an
entire revenue of £8,500,000. At the Peace of Versailles, 1783.
which ended the long War of American Independence, the
debt touched nearly £270,000,000, and cost more than
£9,500,000 out of a total revenue of £13,000,000. It is to
the French Revolutionary and Napoleonic Wars that we must
look for the growth of the debt to its present gigantic dimensions. The twenty-two years of war added no less than 1793-1815.
£620,000,000 to the liabilities of the government, and at the
end of the struggle the debt stood at £885,000,000, and its
interest swallowed up nearly £30,500,000 out of a revenue of
£71,000,000.[1] The long period of comparative peace and the [1] Cunning-
steady efforts of financiers had by the end of the century reduced ham, *Eng.*
the debt to £635,000,000 ; while, owing to the great increase *Com.* ii.
of revenue, the proportion between the interest on the debt 698.
and the revenue had also declined to one-fourth. The South *Whitaker's*
African War added £150,000,000. It would, however, be a *Almanack.*
great mistake to suppose that no efforts at reduction were
made before the nineteenth century, although the constant
recurrence of long periods of war made them unavailing.

It has already been noticed how Harley was led to fund Attempts
the floating debt, and to transfer it to the capital of the South to reduce
Sea Company. One of his motives was the payment of the the
decreased rate of interest which the company were willing to interest.
accept. This system was adopted by Walpole, who thus
strove at least to diminish the annual charges on the country.
As the credit of the government improved, those who had
lent money at a now abnormal rate were offered the alternative
of payment at par or acquiescence in a lower rate of interest ;
and those who chose the former were paid off with money
borrowed at the newer and lower rate. It was by this means
that Walpole turned the greater part of the existing debt
into a 4 per cent. stock, and although his successors generally 1717.
preferred to raise their loans by the wasteful means already
described, and so to preclude all possibility of repayment, they
occasionally betrayed their knowledge of a more enlightened
policy by recourse to his system of lessening the interest on
the whole amount. Thus, in 1751 the 4 per cents. were
reduced by Pelham to 3½, and in 1757 to 3. It was used

more frequently in the second quarter of the nineteenth century, and its latest and greatest effect was produced by Mr. Goschen in the budget of 1887-8, when the 3 per cents., which composed seven-eighths of the Funded Debt, were reduced to 2¾, and ultimately to 2½. This effected an immediate annual saving of nearly £1,500,000, with an ultimate gain of twice that amount.

Attempts to reduce the capital.

The schemes for reducing the principal of the debt have naturally been more varied. The earliest of these was the formation of a *Sinking Fund*, and was also due to the initiative of Walpole. The taxes appropriated to the payment of the interest of the debt yielded more than what was sufficient for the purpose. The surplus was to be set aside annually and to be allowed to accumulate, until it was sufficient to pay off or at least materially to reduce the debt. But the possession of a treasure was too tempting; on the first need a dip was taken into it, and by 1735 the whole had been gradually dissipated.[1] In 1786 the younger Pitt adopted, but without public acknowledgement, a similar scheme which had been propounded by Dr. Price in 1771. According to this, a portion of the surplus, fixed at £1,000,000, was appropriated to the annual purchase and extinction of stock, and was vested in special commissioners in order to guard against its misappropriation by the government of the day. During the time of peace and commercial development which succeeded the American War, this worked extremely well; and by 1793 the debt had been diminished by £10,000,000 at a quicker rate than ever before. But the system was regarded as possessing some inherent virtue; and on the outbreak of the French War, although the surplus revenue diminished until it disappeared, the Sinking Fund was maintained; money was borrowed at high rates of interest, and part of the sum was applied to the extinction of a debt which bore a much lower rate.[2] This ruinous system continued until 1828. A somewhat similar though not equally pedantic scheme is the *application of all surplus revenue* to the extinction of debt. By recent statutes this becomes the duty of every Chancellor of the Exchequer; and at the end of the century the National Debt was being paid off at the rate of £5,000,000 annually. The last method to be noticed, and the one which found especial favour with Mr. Gladstone, is the *conversion of perpetual into terminable annuities*, or, what comes

1716.

[1] Lecky, i. 343.

[2] *Ibid.* v. 49-52.

to the same thing, the raising of money on terminable annuities with which to pay off the principal of the perpetual annuities. This may be regarded as the antithesis to the first-mentioned policy; for, it increases the interest for a time in order that after that time its payment may altogether cease and the capital may be thus extinguished or deducted from the sum total of the debt.

§ 81. Something should be said, in conclusion, of the methods by which at various times the revenue and taxation have been collected and their expenditure has been controlled. *The system of national expenditure.* The first point—the collection—need not detain us long. Since all public moneys were at the disposal of the Crown, it was natural that their collection should be the business of the sheriffs. The uses to which they put the power caused the *Collection.* appointment of special officials. At the present moment the revenue is collected by four great departments of the Treasury—the Commissioners of Customs, who find their origin in the Custumers appointed under Edward I; the Inland Revenue, which began with the taxation of moveables and, under Henry III, was placed in the hands of temporary, but specially appointed officers; the Post Office, which was not organized until the reign of Charles II; and the Commissioners of Woods and Forests, who superintend the now entirely surrendered crown lands.

When the financial system of the country was first organized by the Normans, the Exchequer was divided into two courts —the Upper or Exchequer of Account, and the Lower or Exchequer of Receipt. It was to this latter court, consisting *Issue and Audit.* of the Treasurer and one or two Chamberlains, that the collected revenue was *paid in;* and the money was acknowledged by a system of tallies or notched sticks split in two, of which one half was taken away by the payer and the other half lodged in the Exchequer. The money was *paid out* in accordance with a royal order which, as a slight check upon the king, required the authentication of the Great or the Privy Seal; and the record of the issue was styled the Pells of issue, from the parchment rolls on which it was entered. The *audit* of these moneys lay at first with the Upper or Exchequer of Account, and then with its legitimate successors, the Treasurer and Barons of the Exchequer. But with the accession of the

Tudors the whole system of issue and audit was revised. The *issue* of public money and the duty of keeping the account of it were placed in the hands of four new officers, called Tellers. The Chamberlains became merely honorary officials, though they lasted as long as the system of receipt by tallies, which it was their sole business to prepare and keep. On the other hand, the Treasurer's clerks developed in importance, one becoming the Auditor of Receipts, whose chief duty, however, was connected with the issue of money; and another Clerk of the Pells, who kept the records of both the receipts and the issues of money at the Exchequer. The money continued to be paid out by the king's command, authenticated by letters patent or by writ under the Privy Seal; and as a further security, there grew up 'a complicated system of Treasury warrants, known as "the course of the Exchequer."'[1]   After the appropriation of supplies had become a recognized principle, and especially after the Revolution of 1688, the whole system of issue centred round the Auditor of Receipt, whose authorization of the Treasury warrant was necessary before the Tellers could un-lock the chests at the Exchequer, where the collected revenue was deposited, and hand it over to the credit of the depart-ment for which it was allowed, at the Bank of England. On the accession of George III the Crown surrendered the management of all the royal domains in return for a Civil List of a fixed amount. It thus ceased to take any personal interest in, and therefore to exercise any control over, the Treasury. At the same time, the ministries of the first ten years of George's reign changed rapidly, while large sums of money had to be raised for the American War. The result was disastrous to the financial system of the country. Offices were paid by fees which realized an enormous sum, and the duties were discharged by deputy. The Paymaster of the Forces and the Treasurers of the Navy and the Ordnance kept in their hands the money voted for their respective services, and their delay in accounting for its expenditure rendered an efficient audit impossible. Attempts were made to remedy these evils. In 1783 measures were taken to prevent ministers from keeping money in their hands un-accounted for; while salaries were fixed in amount and secured upon certain branches of the revenue, which in 1787

[1] Anson, ii. 332.

became the Consolidated Fund. Moreover, in 1785 the Auditors of Imprest, who had superseded the Barons of the Exchequer in the reign of Elizabeth, were abolished in favour of a board of five Commissioners of audit. But further changes became necessary. The arrears left by the Auditors of Imprest were so great that it was more than twenty years before the new Commissioners overtook them and got abreast of their work. Meanwhile, in 1806, Lord Grenville's attempt to retain the non-political office of Auditor of Receipt with the post of First Lord of the Treasury, together with his subsequent use of the Auditorship, when in opposition in 1811, to thwart the ministers over the Regency Bill, proved that the system of which that office was the centre, 'was not very valuable as an administrative check, though it might serve the purpose of political obstruction.'[1]

1 Anson, ii. 334.

In 1834 came a complete reorganization. The Exchequer was abolished together with all the sinecure offices which had grown up around it. All payments hitherto made to it and not direct to such officials as the Paymasters and Treasurers mentioned above, were now made to the Exchequer account at the Banks of England and Ireland by a new official, the Paymaster of the Civil Service, who two years later became a Paymaster-General and included in his functions the moneys hitherto set apart to special officials for the army and navy. The place of the Auditor of Receipt and the Clerks of the Pells was taken by the Controller-General, a non-political official, without whose authority no money was to be issued from the Exchequer account at the Bank of England. Until 1866 the audit was in the hands of the five Commissioners; but the final change to the modern system was made when the duties of the Controller-General and the Commissioners of audit were both made over to one official, the Comptroller and Auditor-General, whose functions have been described as not only magisterial, in that he authorizes the issue of money to the proper department; but also judicial, in that he sees that the money issued has been properly expended. Of all this he has to make an annual report to Parliament, which thus learns that the money originally voted has been regularly collected, issued and expended according to the intention of the tax-payers acting through their representatives.

The modern system.

CHAPTER XI

THE CHURCH

The Church as an organized body.

§ 82. THE question of the continuity of the English Church has become the badge of ecclesiastical party politics. It is no part of the business of this book to trace the varying fortunes of ecclesiastical history in England. Our business is with the structure of ecclesiastical organizations and their more permanent relations to the world around. Thus, without pre-judging the question of continuity, it will be convenient to take the Reformation settlement as a dividing line, and to examine (1) the position of the Church itself as organized in England; and (2) the relations of Church and State before and after that momentous period. In this way it will be most clearly apparent what exact changes followed the repudiation of the Roman authority; and thus indirectly materials may be furnished for answering the question of the origin and antiquity of the English Church.

The consideration of the Church as an organized body involves a description of (i) the various classes of churchmen, and (ii) the methods of self-government of the Church. Constitutionally, the orders of which the ecclesiastical organization was composed, were the bishops, the secular and the regular clergy—strictly speaking a cross division, since the bishops were drawn from the secular and regular clergy alike.

Classes of Churchmen.

(1) Bishops. 597-668.

At the time of the Reformation, ecclesiastical England was divided into two archiepiscopal provinces and nineteen episcopal dioceses. This division had been of gradual growth. For the first century after the spread of Christianity among the English there were eight dioceses among the English kingdoms, and Canterbury was regarded as the metropolitan. But, in the year 735, at the advice of Bede, the holder of the See of York obtained from the pope a pallium which secured

his recognition as a metropolitan also ; while for a short period, 787-803.
owing to the influence of Offa of Mercia, Lichfield became
a third archbishopric for Mid-England.   The organizing work
of Theodore of Tarsus included the division and extension of 668-690.
the existing episcopate.   He formed seven new dioceses and
left Wessex to Winchester alone, although shortly after his
death two more bishoprics were added for Wessex.   The only
further additions of Anglo-Saxon times consisted of three more
West-Saxon Sees which owed their foundation to Eadward the
Elder.   But in consequence of the Danish invasions, of the
twenty bishoprics four or five became extinct altogether, while
others disappeared for a time, and in some cases the bishop's
stool or residence was continually transferred from one place
in his diocese to another.   This compulsory migration had no
effect of itself upon the administration of the diocese ; for, the
bishops were rulers of tribes or districts, not (as abroad) of
towns ; and their residences were often mere villages—places
of retirement, not centres of activity.   The Norman Conquest
wrought considerable changes.   The episcopal system was
brought more into harmony with foreign usage by the transference of the Sees to large towns : several new Sees were
created to supply the place of those which had become
extinct : foreigners of learning were appointed to vacant
bishoprics.   But the increase of the intellectual standard
scarcely compensated for the natural alienation of the bishop
from his flock, or for the inevitable tendency of the high
offices in the Church to become more and more the rewards
of political service.   A more remote change effected by the
Conquest was the settlement of the question of precedence
between Canterbury and York in favour of Canterbury.   A
word of explanation is necessary.[1]   The original scheme of [1] Makower,
Pope Gregory gave twelve suffragans apiece to Canterbury and *Const. Hist.*
York, and included Scotland in the province of the northern *of Ch. of Eng.*
archbishopric.   But the Danish invasions for a time swept § 34.
away even York itself, and on its restoration its sole suffragan Hulton,
was Durham.   Meanwhile, the Archbishop of Canterbury had *Primacy of*
superseded the West-Saxon bishop of Winchester as the chief *England.*
adviser of the Crown, and the temporary extinction of York
had set aside all question of precedence.   But, for the last
half century of Anglo-Saxon rule, York, in common with all

Northumbria, enjoyed a position of semi-independence. The maintenance of the uncanonically appointed Stigand at Canterbury by the interest of the House of Godwine, placed Archbishop Ealdred of York at least on an equality. Ealdred's foreign successor, Thomas of Bayeux, appealed to the pope against Lanfranc's claims ; but the matter was referred to the Witan, which decided against York and ordered the holder of the See always to make profession of obedience to Canterbury. The quarrel, however, continued, and was not fairly settled until William of Corbeil, Archbishop of Canterbury, accepted the office of papal legate. But it is to be noted that he then took precedence of York not in the capacity of *Papa alterius orbis* (for so the pope had styled Anselm), but as the servant and local representative of Rome.

1123-1139.

The clergy as a body were divided into two great sections : (*a*) the seculars or parish priests, bound only by their ordination vows ; and (*b*) the regulars, namely monks and friars, bound by some special rule in addition to their ordination vows. For the sake of completeness, mention should be made of two other bodies, which cannot be classed definitely under either head—the capitular clergy, who were seculars living under some rule, and the religious military orders.

(2) Secular clergy.

The division of England into parishes has been attributed to the organizing hand of Theodore. But it was a matter of gradual growth : the chaplain of the local thegn became the parish priest,[1] as the chaplain of the king became the bishop. The patronage was naturally left to the thegn who had endowed the priest with *glebe* land and acknowledged his claim to *tithes* of produce ; while all the parish contributed on occasion to the *fees* which were exacted for the spiritual services of the church. The glebe was taken probably in strips among the common fields of the village. The obligation of tithe seems at first to have been voluntarily acknowledged, then enforced with spiritual penalties by the Church ; and it was paid in the first instance to the bishop, who distributed it among the several parishes of his diocese. The fees included such items as *cyricsceat* or firstfruits paid by every householder, and *sáwlsceat* or mortuary dues. Mediaeval England seems to have contained about 8000 parishes, and the priest was a man of considerable authority within the local area. His Anglo-

[1] Makower. § 44.

Saxon title of mass-thegn [1] indicates the social class with which
he was ranked, and he accompanied the reeve and four men
of the vill as representative of the local interests in the
hundred and shire moots.[2]   In nothing perhaps is the pro-
vinciality which the English Church shared with the English
Nation, so marked as in the fact that nearly every parish
priest was a married man ; and that, notwithstanding the
canon against the ordination of the son of a priest, before
the Norman Conquest there was danger of the formation of
an hereditary clerical caste.   After the Conquest, Lanfranc
became the agent of the reforming party in the Church, and
introduced celibacy : but the previous ill-success of the efforts
of Dunstan's party caused him to move most cautiously.   The
Hildebrandine party would have liked to assert the nullity of
all sacraments performed by a married priest.   Lanfranc contented himself with leaving married secular priests in their
benefices, while for the future he forbade priests to marry or
married men to be ordained.   The feudal ideas of the
Normans wrought a still more important effect on the position
of the parish priest.   Even before the Conquest pious patrons
had bestowed upon monasteries of especial fame the advowson
of, that is, the right of presentation to, a benefice which was
often situated at a distance from the monastery itself.   This
privilege of patronage, with its attendant duty of protection,
passed into a right over the benefice ; and the monastery,
while impropriating to itself the greater tithes of corn and
wool, supplied the spiritual duty by a curate, for whose support
were reserved the lesser tithes and all fees for the offices of the
Church.   The revival of monastic life caused a rapid spread
of this most harmful method of endowment ; and the country
was covered with benefices whose patrons had none except
a pecuniary interest in the parish.   Besides the beneficed
clergy and their curates there was a class of seculars known as
Chantry priests.   They were attached to cathedrals or parish
churches, or ministered in chapels belonging to great houses.
Their sole work was to say masses for the dead ; so that they
were both practically exempt from episcopal supervision and
amenable to no 'rule.'   The greater number of men admitted
to orders must have been ordained to such posts, and consequently they were the most worthless of all the mediaeval clergy.

[1] *S. C.* 66.
§ 5.

[2] *Ibid.* 105,
vii. 7.

(3) Regular clergy. Monks.

In speaking of the regular clergy it must be borne in mind at the outset that MONKS were not necessarily in full orders either as priests, deacons or sub-deacons. They were originally communities of laymen who cut themselves off from the world for religious contemplation. The temptations which naturally beset so idle and unrestrained a life led to the formulation of various rules, that of Benedict of Nursia being the most universally accepted. These communities freed themselves from parochial control by obtaining the ordination of some of their members, and from episcopal supervision by placing themselves directly under the patronage of the pope. They thus practically formed a papal garrison in every European country. In England, as elsewhere, the conversion of the people was accomplished by communities of monks, and for the first two centuries they were the most prominent element in the local Church. The popularity of the monastic life both multiplied monasteries and filled them with inmates of noble birth, whose presence brought insincerity of purpose, relaxation of rules, and a generally luxurious and idle mode of life. Learning, which had been kept up practically only in the larger monasteries, disappeared ; and the Danish invasions destroyed the monasteries and scattered the monks. When Ælfred began a monastic revival with the erection of the monastery of Æthelney, in memory of his deliverance from the Danes, the old English predilection for monks had quite died away, and he was obliged to seek for inmates in foreign lands. Eadred gave a further impetus to the revival by the refounding of Glastonbury and Abingdon ; and under Eadgar the Benedictine rule was first brought from Fleury in Flanders. This revival is generally associated with the name of Dunstan. Whether Dunstan himself or his purely ecclesiastical friends, Æthelwold and Oswald, were the moving spirits, the extent of the movement was limited both by Dunstan's own position as a statesman as well as an ecclesiastic, and by the strong influence of the married secular clergy. Moreover, whatever may have been the immediate success of the reforming movement, it took no real hold of the country. Indeed, the only kind of discipline which at all succeeded in England before the Conquest, was that of Chrodegang of Metz, introduced by the Lotharingian prelates whom Godwine's family supported as

Sixth century.

Before the Norman Conquest.

946-955.

a counterpoise to Eadward the Confessor's French and Norman bishops. This planted round a cathedral a body of canons, that is, secular clergy living in a common dormitory and feeding at a common table. Such, for example, was Harold's great foundation of Waltham.

With the Norman Conquest a great impetus was given to monastic life. Dunstan had already begun the practice of associating a cathedral chapter with a monastery. Lanfranc's monkish instincts prompted him to encourage this peculiarly English system by introducing it into his own monastery of Christ Church, Canterbury ; while he lent his influence to defeat the attempts of Bishop Wakelin of Winchester in behalf of secular canons. At the same time, monasteries which were not connected with a cathedral struggled to free themselves from episcopal jurisdiction. The origin of this evil lay perhaps with the king himself, for William I exerted himself to procure such exemption for his own foundation of Battle Abbey. In this he had not the support of his primate ; for Lanfranc, though a monk, was also a bishop, and meted out heavy punishment to the monks of St. Augustine's, Canterbury, who claimed this very privilege for themselves. But the papacy gave every facility for the growth of these exemptions ; and in the case of England it found assistance in the fact that, for some time after the Conquest, the monasteries were hotbeds of national feeling. The increased connection of England with continental Europe led to the introduction of many of the new monastic orders to which the religious revival of the tenth century had given rise. The only rules known in England before the Conquest were that of St. Benedict of Nursia, and that of Chrodegang of Metz. The orders which were represented in England after the Conquest may be classed as either Augustinians or reformed Benedictines. The *Augustinians*, or canons regular of the Order of St. Augustine, known from their dress as the 'Black Canons,' were a cross between the regulars and seculars ; for, being in origin secular—a protest against monasticism—they leaned constantly towards monastic ways. They spread all over England, and devoted themselves to the work both of the schoolmaster and of the nurse. The Augustinian rule supplied the model to two other orders. The more important of these were the military orders of the religious,

After the Norman Conquest.

of which two were found in England—the *Knights Hospitallers* of St. John of Jerusalem, who were established at Clerkenwell in 1100, and whose Grand Commander in England became in rank the first lay baron of the realm ; and the *Knights Templars*, who were established at the Temple in London at the beginning of Stephen's reign. Both orders grew rapidly in wealth, while their rivalry was sufficiently bitter to array them not infrequently in arms against each other. In 1308 the career of the Templars was brought to an end : the members resident in England were seized and their lands confiscated, and in the following year Pope Clement V abolished the whole order. The Hospitallers enjoyed a longer existence ; for, being driven from Jerusalem, they became knights of Rhodes until the conquest of that island by the Turks forced them to retire to Malta. Until the Reformation their Grand Commander continued a member of the House of Lords. The second offshoot of the Augustinians were the *Premonstratensians*, or 'White Canons,' who came to England in 1140 and occupied thirty-five houses, remaining until 1512 under the direct jurisdiction of the parent house of Premontré or Premonstratum in the diocese of Laon. Of the *Reformed Benedictines* three branches spread themselves into England. The first in order of time were the *Cluniacs*. This was the earliest example of an order within an order ; for, it was a completely separate organization within the Benedictine rule, and it possessed a large number of dependent houses scattered through Western Europe, all under the government of the Arch-abbot of Clugny. The order came to England in 1077. It held about forty houses, most of which were founded before the accession of Henry II, the chief of them being Lewes Priory : they were all governed by foreigners, and for a long time were filled chiefly with foreign monks : they sent contributions to the parent monastery, and were able to be 'visited' only by the foreign heads of their order. Consequently, the French wars often saw them taken into the king's hands as alien priories. The smallest branch of the Reformed Benedictines in England were the *Carthusians*, who came about 1180 ; they possessed only nine houses, the chief of which was the London Charterhouse, founded by Sir Walter Manny in the reign of Edward III. The largest branch, on the other hand, was supplied by the *Cistercians*, who arrived

1309.

1308-1522.

in 1128 and became both numerous and wealthy. They settled in solitary places, where they carried on their great industry of sheep-farming. At the dissolution of the monasteries, of their seventy-five houses no less than thirty-six were among the greater monasteries. They held in addition twenty-six nunneries. The only other order which needs notice is that of the *Gilbertines*, an offshoot of the Cistercians and the one purely English monastic order. It was founded in 1139 by Gilbert of Sempringham as a double order for men and women, and it possessed twenty-six houses, of which at the dissolution four ranked with the greater monasteries.

Early in the thirteenth century, to the monks were added the FRIARS. They consisted originally of the two well-known orders of *Dominicans*, or 'Black Friars,' founded by a Spaniard as a great order of preachers; and *Franciscans*, or 'Grey Friars,' also called Minorites (i.e. less than the least), founded by an Italian for work among the destitute. Both these orders arose within a few years of each other; and under the patronage of Pope Innocent III they spread into almost every country of Europe. At the outset they were devoted to a life of poverty: their friaries were the meanest possible buildings; and all learning and books were forbidden them. They entered England—the Dominicans in 1219, the Franciscans in 1225— and both soon obtained settlements in all the chief towns. Their singular self-devotion speedily made them popular, and their popularity gave birth to other orders. The multiplication was checked by the Council of Lyons in 1274, which among the new orders confirmed only the Augustinians or Austin Friars and the Carmelites. Their popularity also brought immense wealth; but since it was unlawful for the orders to hold possessions, donations of lands and goods were made to corporations of towns to hold to their use. The next innovation was equally subversive of the original intention of the orders; for, their work both in combating heresy and in tending the sick forced them to the acquisition of knowledge. They plunged into the study of philosophy and natural science with such success that their ranks supplied all the great names in the last period of mediaeval thought. Their influence in England was striking and peculiar. For the first half century of their existence they were found in alliance with those classes which were most at variance with Rome, and engaged in the struggle for English liberty. Later on, however, they reverted to their original position of strenuous supporters of the papacy. Again, at the outset of their career their chief work lay among the rising merchant class, whose heretical tendencies they met with their scholastic learning ; and among the destitute, who welcomed the medical knowledge which they brought to the relief of loathsome disease. But with the accumulation of wealth their thirst for knowledge decayed, and they gradually abandoned their work among the poor, rivalling the monks themselves in idleness and luxury. Meanwhile, they undermined the influence of the parish priests ; for, their freedom from episcopal control enabled them to creep in everywhere, and their cunning gave them almost a monopoly of the confessional.

Government of the Church.

§ 83. The *government of the Church as a local organization* involved the power of legislation which was carried out by ecclesiastical councils, and of jurisdiction which was the work of the ecclesiastical courts.

Ecclesiastical Councils.

[1] Makower. § 54.

The *Ecclesiastical Councils* [1] of Anglo-Saxon times were either national synods of the whole Church or provincial assemblies of Canterbury and York respectively, and consisted always of bishops, with an occasional addition of abbots. In his organization of the Church, Theodore provided for the annual meeting of a synod at Clovesho, somewhere in the neighbourhood of London. Councils are frequently mentioned, but they were neither regular nor annual : they were often attended by kings and ealdormen, and in their discussion and legislation the ecclesiastics carefully avoided any interference with secular law or custom.[2] After the Norman Conquest the organization was extended to the gathering of diocesan synods, which were exhaustive assemblies of the local clergy. So long as separate assent was required, these bodies were separately consulted, and at a later stage it was in them that the representatives for the higher assemblies were chosen and the grievances of the local clergy were formulated. Such grievances were submitted to the provincial synods, which continued to be held very much on the Anglo-Saxon model. The second of William's *Consuetudines* forbade any assembly of the bishops 'to enact or prohibit anything but what was agreeable to his will and had

[2] *S.C.H.* i. § 87.

first been ordained by him ';[1] while under Henry I the Archbishop of Canterbury held his provincial assembly at the same
time as the king held his Court. Thus, although in the anarchy
of Stephen's reign the ecclesiastical councils alone deserved the
name of national assemblies, the power of these assemblies
under the Normans and early Plantagenets was considerably
circumscribed. For, in the first place, so entirely did their
power of legislation in matters ecclesiastical depend on the
acquiescence of the king, that in 1127, although the primate
actually held the office of papal legate, the canons needed the
royal ratification. In the second place, it was not until the
power of granting taxes was transferred from the diocesan to
the provincial synod (which did not happen till the reign of
John) that the clergy as a body could be said to have a voice
in the appropriation of their contributions to national purposes.
The acquisition of this privilege brought with it the need for
a representative assembly.[2] Hitherto the only persons entitled
to attend a provincial synod had been bishops, together with
abbots and archdeacons. In **1225** Archbishop Langton for
the first time extended the summons to include not only
(α) bishops, abbots, priors, deans and archdeacons, but also
(β) proctors or representatives for the cathedral, collegiate
and monastic clergy. But there were two grave *defects*. In
the first place, no provision was made for the parochial clergy.
The practical results were seen in the refusal of the bishops in
1254, and, in 1283, of an assembly of bishops, abbots, heads
of religious houses and proctors of cathedral clergy, to assent
to a grant of money on behalf of the unrepresented parochial
clergy. In the second place, neither the number of proctors
nor the mode of their appointment was specified. It was not
till May **1283** that for the first time the bishops were directed
by Archbishop Peckham to assemble the clergy of the diocese,
and to bid them elect proctors—two for the parochial clergy
and one for each cathedral and collegiate chapter. The result
was the formation in each province of a completely representative synod or *Convocation*, which became a permanent assembly.
The constituents of the two Convocations slightly differed.
To the Canterbury assembly there came in person the bishops,
abbots, priors, heads of religious houses, deans of cathedral
and collegiate churches, and archdeacons. To these were

[1] *S. C.* 82,
Eadmer.

[2] *S. C. H.*
ii. § 199.

Convoca-
tion.

added as representatives, two proctors for the parochial clergy of each diocese, and one for each cathedral and collegiate chapter : whereas the unit of representation for the parochial clergy of the northern province was the archdeaconry. These two bodies, so constituted, exercised considerable legislative power.[1] As regards the clergy, it was in these assemblies that the general legislation of Christendom in Lateran and other Councils was accepted as binding on the National Church, and that constitutions affecting the clergy of each province were issued. But the power was by no means unrestrained ; for, William's Consuetudines forbade the introduction of papal bulls without the royal licence,[2] while no ecclesiastical legislation was valid until it had received the royal confirmation. Convocation even included the laity within the scope of its legislative power in all such matters as marriage, wills, tithe, heresy, slander and usury. It is true, however, that these were mostly cases dealt with by the ecclesiastical courts, whose encroachments were met by the issue of prohibitions from the Courts of Common Law. As far as the legislature was concerned, the acceptance of outside legislation was limited by the Common law and the Statute of Praemunire. At the same time, it is to be noted that Convocation did not necessarily, though it did generally, meet at the same time as Parliament. Its proceedings, moreover, were seldom interfered with ; and after the accession of the House of Lancaster, they were not interfered with at all.[3] Now, although in early days the Church organization had set an example of unity to the State, the centralization of the National Church itself stopped short at the two provincial assemblies ; for, the mutual jealousies of the two provinces prevented the convocation of national Church Councils. There were, however, three occasional methods by which this separation was overcome—(a) legatine Councils such as those in which the Constitutions of Otho were published, and the Constitutions of Ottobon were accepted : (b) conference between the two Convocations, which, however, was generally conducted by letter between the two archbishops ; and (c) the meeting of the chief ecclesiastics of both provinces in the National Parliaments. Thus in 1207 John summoned the bishops and abbots of both provinces to grant an aid. Even the lower clergy were sometimes included,

[1] *S. C. H.* iii. § 389.

[2] *S. C.* 82, Eadmer.

[3] *S. C. H.* iii. § 388.

1237.
1268.

as when deans and archdeacons were summoned to the council
in which Henry II arbitrated between the kings of Castile and 1177.
Navarre ; or when Simon de Montfort called deans and priors 1265.
to his Parliament. These formed precedents for Edward I's
summons of the clergy of both provinces to form one estate
in the National Parliament. But three important *differences*
should be noted *between the clergy in Convocation and in
Parliament*—(1) it is obvious that, while Convocation consists
of two provincial assemblies meeting in their respective provinces, the spiritual estate is one element of a general Parliament meeting at the same place : (2) Convocation is summoned
by the writ of the Archbishop addressed through the senior
suffragan to each bishop ; whereas the representatives of the
spiritual estate are summoned by the king's writ directed to
each bishop : (3) before the Reformation, Convocation contained, in the abbots and priors, a class which as a class was
not included in Parliament.

§ 84. The Anglo-Saxon constitution realized the identity of Eccle-
Church and State in a manner which was not possible again siastical
until after the Reformation. Thus, for judicial purposes the Courts.
bishops sat in the local courts and seem to have exercised Before the
there the jurisdiction over cases arising out of the disputes Norman
and offences of the clergy, together with the morals of the Conquest.
laity, with which they appear to have been especially charged.
It is true that, besides this, the bishop had special jurisdiction
in three kinds of cases [1]—(α) in their own franchises, like any [1] Report of
other great thegn, by the ordinary legal methods of compurga- the *Eccle-
tion and ordeal ; (β) a penitential discipline which could be *siastical
put into practice only by the goodwill of the laity ; and (γ) for *Courts
dealing with the spiritual offences of the clergy, such as heresy *Commis-
or disobedience, for which neither the local court nor peni- *sion*, 22, 23.
tential discipline was sufficient. In such cases there must Makower.
have been tribunals answering to the later ecclesiastical courts. § 59.
Here the executive officer was the archdeacon, who could,
however, only exercise his functions by connivance of the
secular power.

William I introduced into England the ideas of ecclesiastical After the
reform prevalent abroad, and with the object of carrying out Norman
the theory of entire separation of the organization of Church Conquest.
and State, he issued an Ordinance by which he both forbade

the bishops and archdeacons to hold ecclesiastical pleas for the future in the local courts, and promised the aid of the secular arm in the enforcement of their sentences.[1] The results of this dualism of Church and State were most important. For the present it is convenient to note the effects upon the jurisdiction exercised by ecclesiastical officers.[2] In the first place is to be remarked the growth of *archidiaconal jurisdiction*. Under the Anglo-Saxons each bishop had as his executive officer an archdeacon, who possibly sat in the hundred courts as representative of the bishop. But after William's Ordinance the archdeacon set up his own court; and in order to meet the increase of ecclesiastical litigation, archdeaconries were multiplied. The holders of the office were carefully trained in Civil as well as Canon law, and they pursued these studies at foreign universities. Thither they were sent at a youthful age, and there they often led such unclerical lives as to provoke the famous mediaeval query, 'whether an archdeacon could be saved.' Moreover, these officials were, as their name implies, kept in deacon's orders, so that priestly hands might not be tainted with the questionable subjects with which the archdeacons often had to deal. Their constantly encroaching jurisdiction was regarded with apprehension by the bishops, and with detestation by the general body of the clergy. The second result—an outcome of the first—was the growth of jurisdiction by *Officials* and *Commissaries*. For, in order to limit and, as far as possible, to supersede the action of the archidiaconal court, about the middle of the twelfth century the bishop began to appoint his chancellor or chief secretary to a newly created office of Official, that is, a judge-ordinary to exercise all the jurisdiction inherent in the person of the bishop himself. No appeal was allowed from the official to the bishop, who, however, generally reserved certain cases for his own personal hearing. The official was at first appointed for the life of the bishop from whom he held his commission; but his position ultimately became permanent. A third result of William I's action was the growth of *Peculiars*. Before the Norman Conquest the bishop and the cathedral chapter held their estates in common, and both the seignorial and the spiritual jurisdictions were exercised by the bishop and his officers. But disputes were

constant; so that after the Conquest, the lands of the
cathedral church, together with the spiritual and secular jurisdiction, were all divided between the bishop, the chapter, and
even individual members of the chapter. There thus came
into existence a number of small ecclesiastical courts known
as Peculiars, with such administrative jurisdiction as was
implied in the right of granting marriage licences, proving
wills, hearing complaints, and inflicting penances. Under this
same head is to be included the jurisdiction exercised by the
greater monasteries and by the king's chapels royal. The
fourth and final result of William's measure was the growth of
a complete hierarchy of ecclesiastical courts.[1] They mounted [1] *E. C. C.*
from (1) the *rural deans*, who only administered custom, not 31.
Canon law; through (2) the *archdeacons*, who possessed a § 60.
double power both of (*a*) ordinary ecclesiastical jurisdiction,
which differed in each diocese and was often regulated by
agreement with the bishop, and of (*β*) visitation to hear complaints when the bishop did not go round. A parallel to the
shire court was found in (3) *the diocesan* or *consistory court* of
the bishop, which heard cases both in the first instance and
on appeal from the archdeacons' courts. This was held by the
chancellor as the official principal in each diocese, and from it
lay appeals to (4) the *provincial court* of the archbishop alone.
Of these provincial courts for the province of Canterbury
there were no less than four—(*a*) the Court of Arches, held at
St. Mary-le-Bow (de Arcubus) Church by the official principal
of the archbishop, which acted as the court of appeal from all
the diocesan courts and as a court of first instance in all
ecclesiastical matters, perhaps by virtue of the archbishop's
authority as papal legate; (*b*) the Court of Audience, held
at St. Paul's in the jurisdiction of the archbishop and of co-
ordinate authority with the Court of Arches; (*c*) the Prerogative
Court, which managed the jurisdiction with regard to wills; and
(*d*) the Court of Peculiars for thirteen London parishes which
were exempt from the Bishop of London's supervision. The
Province of York possessed only two courts—the Chancery, Eccle-
answering to the Court of Arches, and the Prerogative siastical
Court. Law.

An enumeration of the courts carries us naturally to the [2] *E. C. C.*
law administered by those courts.[2] This came from three 24-28.

sources.   The staple part of it consisted, of course, of (1) the

[1] Stubbs,
*Lects. in
Med. and
Mod. Hist.*
xiii. and
xiv.
P. and M.
i. 90 et seq.
Maitland
in *E.H.R.*,
vols. xi.
and xii.

Canon law[1] of Rome.   It was ultimately systematized by Gratian, a monk of Bologna, in his 'Decretum' published between 1139 and 1142.   But this was only an authoritative text-book, although it was practically incorporated into the great collection published by Gregory IX in 1234, which henceforth contained the nucleus of the Canon law.   The procedure and even the maxims of the Canon law were largely drawn from, (2) the *Civil law* of Rome.   The bitter struggle of pope and emperor, round which the whole history of mediaeval Europe centred, encouraged the respective parties to refurbish these two important weapons.   But neither was received as authoritative in the English state.   Stephen drove out Vacarius who attempted to teach Civil law at Oxford; and Henry II fought the claims of the Canon law as personified in Becket.   Consequently, no great school of either law was founded in England.   Yet the effect of both on English law was considerable.   The influence of the Civil law on English Common law has been dealt with.   The Canon law left its mark in no less a degree on national jurisprudence.   Nor are the reasons far to seek.   For, the only training of the ecclesiastical judges was obtained in the foreign schools where Civil and Canon law held complete sway.   Thus, where the Common law neither opposed the principle nor itself provided a remedy, the only appeal was to maxims of the Canon and Civil law.   It is to this fact that we owe our maritime, matrimonial, and equitable law, all of which came from foreign sources.   Nor was it an uninfluential matter that all appeals to Rome were naturally tried by Canon law.   The result is seen in the fact that at the Universities provision began to be made for the study of the two laws.   At nearly every college founded before the Reformation the statutes enjoined the study of the Canon law by a definite number of the fellows, and that of the Civil law as a supplement.   The only native part of Church law was supplied by (3) the *Provincial Law of the Church of England*, which was itself formed of three elements—the *Constitutions* of successive archbishops from the time of Langton ; *Canons* passed in the legatine councils of Otho (1238), and Ottobon (1267), and afterwards accepted by national councils held by Archbishop

Peckham ; and finally, the *Sentences* or authoritative answers
to questions propounded to the popes.

The most important question raised by a description of Extent of
ecclesiastical courts and law concerns the *persons who were* eccle-
                                                            siastical
amenable to ecclesiastical jurisdiction.[1] The claim of the church jurisdic-
courts to exclusive jurisdiction over the clergy led to a struggle tion.
which will best be dealt with in treating of the relations [1] *E . C. C.*
between Church and State. But these courts claimed also an 28-29.
extensive *jurisdiction over the laity.*[2] This would be based on [2] *S. C. H.*
the necessary cognizance by the moral guardian of all matters iii. § 400.
involving breach of faith, and it embraced four important
kinds of cases. In the first place, the jurisdiction over the
laity would include the correction of immorality. Strong
protests were made against this ; but there was no attempt at
its restriction. There was added, secondly, the correction of
breaches of faith. This was the outcome of the penitential
discipline exercised by the Anglo-Saxon Church. The penalties
were of a penitential nature, but they could be commuted for
money. The system could only be carried out by the maintenance of an army of spies and informers : hence its great
unpopularity, and hence also the gradual prohibition to the
ecclesiastical courts to take cognizance of any breaches of
faith which affected contracts between laymen. A third class
of cases was formed by questions arising out of Wills and
Marriages. The former was included in the jurisdiction connected with breaches of faith, and so in the twelfth and
thirteenth centuries was appropriated by the ecclesiastical courts :
the latter was not disputed or even limited. A fourth, and
to modern ideas the most natural work of the spiritual courts,
was the punishment of heresy.[3] Previous to the time of [3] *Ibid.*
Wycliffe the cases of heresy are so rare and isolated as to iii. § 404.
                                                              E. C. C.
demand no notice here. When the question became important 29.
it was complicated with Parliamentary legislation as to the Makower.
assistance of the secular arm. The constitutional history of § 19.
the matter is thus divided into two parts—firstly, the ecclesiastical trial ; secondly, the aid given by the state. With
regard to the trial it may be said that cases of heresy were
seldom, if ever, heard by a court below that of a bishop sitting
in person as *inquisitor natus* in his own diocese ; and there is
no recorded case of appeal in such a matter either to the

archbishop's court or to Rome.   There was, moreover, such a dislike to extreme proceedings in a matter so difficult of proof, that the methods of trial were as various as the cases tried ; until, in 1409, the Constitutions of Archbishop Arundel paralleled it to trials of treason under the Civil law.   But in any case the power of the ecclesiastical judge stopped at a sentence of excommunication.   Here, then, the interposition of the secular arm began.   This was regulated by three statutes.   An Act of 1382, which was passed at Archbishop Courtenay's instigation and in consequence of the Peasant Revolt, ordained that on a certificate from the bishops the Chancellor should issue commissions for the arrest of heretical preachers.   But, in a later Parliament of the same year, the influence of the knights of the shire caused the repeal of this Act on the ground that it had not duly passed the Commons. In **1401**, Archbishop Arundel procured the passing of the celebrated Act *de haeretico comburendo*, by which heretical preachers who had been arrested by the bishop and had refused to recant, should be handed over to the secular arm and the sheriff should burn them.   Finally, by an Act of 1414, passed by the influence of Bishop Beaufort and in opposition to Archbishop Arundel, heresy was made an offence against the Common law : for, not only were secular officers to swear that they would assist the ecclesiastical officers in the suppression of heresy, but Justices of Assize were to have the power of inquiry, to issue an order for arrest, and to hand over the person to the ecclesiastical courts for trial.   The results of these attempts at severity were not encouraging. On the one side, there were several executions.   Already before 1401 a certain Sawtre had been burned : the best known of the later victims were John Badby, a tailor, and Sir John Oldcastle.   But on the other hand, heresy was not stopped, and the Lollards were even encouraged by the attacks made by the knights of the shire in 1404, and again in 1410, on the temporalities of the Church.

§ 85.   The question of the *relations between Church and State* divides naturally into two parts—(1) the influence exercised by the State over the Church, and (2) the attempt of the Church to stand apart from the State.

The influence of the State was exercised over the Church

Margin notes:

5 Ric. II. st. 2, c. 5.

2 Hen. IV. c. 15.

2 Hen. V. c. 7.

1410.
1417.

Church and State in the Middle Ages.

by the maintenance of the *Royal Supremacy*.[1] This may be
said to have always existed in England, and for historical
purposes can be dealt with in two subdivisions. On the one
side is found (*a*) the king's ecclesiastical prerogative, which
was always upheld by English law and, under compulsion,
admitted by the pope. It was asserted by William I in his
Consuetudines ; by Henry I in the compromise which ended
the quarrel over investitures with Anselm ; by Henry II in the
Constitutions of Clarendon, and by the Parliaments of the
Edwards in the successive Statutes Circumspecte Agatis (1285),
Articuli Cleri (1316), Provisors (1351), and Praemunire(1353) ;
while the same motive underlay the practice of issuing prohibitions from the Courts of Common law, and the participation of the lay authority in the legislation on heresy. But, in
addition to this, there was a side of the prerogative which
was (*b*) usurped by the papacy and acquiesced in by the
Crown. This included the papal assumptions of patronage by
provisions, the hearing of appeals at Rome, and the levy of
annates or firstfruits which was begun by Pope Alexander IV
and was made into a general obligation by Pope John XXII.
But the claim of the papacy was at times wider than this.
It put forward not only Gregory VII's general claim of the
inherent superiority of the spiritual to the temporal power,
but a special claim to superiority over England. Gregory VII
demanded homage of William I, but was refused. Henry II
accepted Ireland at the hands of the pope. His alleged submission of England after Becket's murder was only a personal
submission in a spiritual sense, and the offer of the legateship
to him is a fable. It was John's surrender and homage which
first created the idea of a feudal relation between the English
king and the pope. But this was definitely repudiated by
Parliament at Lincoln in 1301, when Boniface VIII interfered
on behalf of Scotland ; and in 1366, when Parliament refused
the further payment of John's tribute and even the satisfaction
of long arrears of payment. Finally, in 1399, in comment on
Richard II's application to the pope to confirm the king's
unconstitutional acts, Parliament roundly declares that the
Crown and the realm of England had been in all time past so
free that neither pope nor any other outside the realm had
a right to meddle therewith.

¹ *S. C. H.*
iii. § 378.

The exercise of this royal supremacy was called forth
chiefly in connection with *the appointment of* bishops.¹ Under
the Anglo-Saxon kings the general rule seems to have been
that bishops were appointed by the king and Witan, of which
they were members, in consultation with the clergy and
people of the diocese.   Like all ecclesiastical business of the
time, it was a matter of arrangement between the parties
concerned.   After the Norman Conquest William I, in the
exercise of the royal supremacy, appointed and deposed
bishops in the same assembly in which he appointed lay
officers; and invested them with ring and pastoral staff, no
less than he received their homage and oath of fealty.   But
the new ultramontane doctrines which insisted on the absolute
separation of Church and State, caused a quarrel between
Henry I and Anselm over the question of the investiture of
a bishop by the temporal authority with the ring and staff—
the emblems of spiritual office.   In 1107 a compromise was
effected by which the king surrendered the claim to invest
with the ring and staff, but kept the oath of homage.   The
twelfth Constitution of Clarendon laid down that an election
should be made by the more important clergy in the
king's chapel, with the consent of the king and his council.
Thus the matter remained until 1214, when John, wishing to
separate the clergy from the barons, granted freedom of election as a bribe to the Church, by allowing the appointment of
bishops to take place in the chapter-house of the cathedral

² M'Kech-
nie, 226.

itself.²   The king, however, still retained a hold on the election
by the issue of his *congé d'élire* or leave to elect, and by the
nomination by letter of the candidate on whom he wished the
choice to fall.

Benefit of
Clergy.

³ *S. C. H.*
iii. § 399.
Makower.
§ 60.

The attempt of the Church to stand apart from the State is
embodied in the struggle for what were comprehensively called
*Clerical Immunities.*³   They included immunity from two things:
(*a*) lay jurisdiction; (*b*) lay taxation.   The claim put forward
by the church courts for *exclusive jurisdiction over the clergy*
was of course the direct result of the separation of the lay and
ecclesiastical courts by William I, and was fostered by the
increased study and formulation of the Canon law.   It included
a claim of jurisdiction over not only breaches of ecclesiastical
law, but even offences committed by the clergy against the

Common law. Further than this, the bishops, as ancient protectors of the clergy, claimed *jurisdiction over laymen* for offences committed by them against the clergy. The Roman Canon which enjoined the separate treatment of laymen and clerk was introduced into England in the reign of Stephen,[1] and the first effect of amenability to merely spiritual penalties seems to have been an increase of violent crime on the part of ecclesiastics. Henry II's attempt to enforce the Common law against criminous clerks led to his quarrel with Becket. The archbishop claimed that for a first offence, however bad, a person in orders was liable only to degradation, so that on a second offence he could incur the full secular penalty; otherwise he would suffer two penalties for one offence. This clearly licensed clerks to commit at least one murder with impunity, and Henry's answer was the Constitutions of Clarendon. By the third clause the king laid down that 'a clerk accused of any matter, when summoned by the king's Justicier, shall come into his court, and there answer for what it shall seem good to the king's court that he should answer for there, and in the church court for what it shall seem good that he should answer for there; so that the king's Justicier shall send into the church court to see how the case is tried there, and if the clerk shall be convict, the Church ought not to defend him further.'[2] In other words, 'Henry did not propose (as the clause is usually interpreted) that a clerk accused of crime should be *tried* in the temporal court, and he did not propose that a *clerk* should be punished by a temporal court. The clerk was to be tried in the bishop's court,' and if convicted and degraded there, he would be brought back into the king's court and would be 'sentenced (probably without any further trial) to the laymen's punishment, death or mutilation.'[3] But whatever the exact point of the king's contention, in 1176 he was obliged at any rate to modify his demands and to agree that no clerk should be tried by a lay court on a criminal charge or charge of trespass, except trespass of the forest, and questions of lay fees for which lay service was due; while he further allowed that murderers of ecclesiastics should forfeit inheritance as well as life, and that the clergy themselves should be exempt from submitting their claims to ordeal by battle. This concession practically recog-

[1] M'Kechnie, 121.

[2] S. C. 138.

[3] Maitland, *E. H. R.* vii. 225-226. Cf. also *P. and M.* i. 430-432, 437-440.

nized the right of what was called 'benefit of clergy,' which was amplified and extended in nearly every subsequent reign up to the Reformation. The resulting evils were enormous; for not only was the procedure of the ecclesiastical courts of the clumsiest kind, but the immunity from the ordinary criminal law was claimed by a host of persons in 'minor orders' living the ordinary layman's life. It has been shown that the 'king's justices, who never loved it, at length reduced it to an illogical absurdity'; for 'they would not be at pains to require any real proof of a prisoner's sacred character. If he could read a line in a book this would do; indeed, it is even said that the same verse of the Psalms was set before the eyes of every prisoner, so that even the illiterate might escape if he could repeat by heart those saving words.' Thus benefit of clergy 'made the law capricious without making it less cruel.'[1]

[1] Maitland, *Social England*, i. 298.

There were, however, two practical limitations; for, in the first place, except in times of political excitement the Church would prefer to save its reputation by disclaiming a clerical criminal; while, secondly, even the most pious kings threatened and sometimes executed bishops and lesser churchmen for political offences. Henry IV's championship of the Church against the Lollardy of his predecessor did not prevent him from hanging a number of friars who were spreading sedition, or stop him even from the execution of Archbishop Scrope. But although benefit of clergy formed the subject of many statutes, they were all practically confirmatory of the privilege until the reign of Henry VII. The first legal limitation was contained in an Act of 1488-89 which enacted that every person accused of murder, rape, robbery or similar crimes, 'which once hath been admitted to the benefit of his clergy (that is in minor orders), eftsoones arraigned of any such offence, be not admitted to have the benefit or privilege of his clergy,' but is to be branded; while a person 'within orders' is to produce proof of his orders on arraignment, or the benefit will be denied to him also. An Act of 1536 seems to be the first which withdrew the privilege from those in higher orders charged with certain grave offences. But it lingered on until comparatively recent times, and even in cases where it was withdrawn from all others who had hitherto claimed it, an Act of Edward VI saved it for 'a Lord or Peer of the Realm

4 Hen. VII. c. 13.

28 Hen. VIII. c. 1.

though he cannot read.' Readers of *Esmond* will remember the escape of Lord Mohun by this means from the penalties of his successful duel with Lord Castlewood.

Exemption from lay taxation involved the claim on the part of the Church to tax itself for secular purposes.[1] Now, clerical property consisted of (*a*) *land* whether held by temporal services or in frankalmoin. The land held by temporal services had the same liabilities as the landed estates of laymen. The objection raised by Archbishop Theobald in 1156 to the payment of scutage by bishops, was perhaps made on the idea that all ecclesiastical payments to the Crown were of the nature of free gifts; but the preliminary demand which Henry II laid upon bishops as well as barons, to send in an account of the knights' fees for which their estates were liable, practically established the king's contention on the point. The second kind of clerical property is comprehended under the term (*b*) *spiritualities*, and consisted of tithes and voluntary offerings. The taxation of the moveables of the laity led by a necessary conclusion to a similar treatment of the spiritualities. All the early cases of this mode of levy can be explained away. Thus, the Saladin Tithe was for an ecclesiastical, not a national purpose; Richard I's ransom was altogether exceptional; and John's demand on the beneficed clergy through the bishops in 1207 was refused. In fact, it was only with the alliance of king and pope under Henry III that the spiritualities came to be placed ordinarily under contribution. Then, by the usual form, the clergy at the pope's request granted a tenth to the king instead of to the pope. The first instance of this grant was in 1226; and after 1252 it became the general method by which the spiritualities of the Church contributed to the needs of the State. The *results* were important. It led, in the first place, to the valuation of ecclesiastical property temporal and spiritual; and the assessment made in 1291 at the instance of Pope Nicholas, remained in force until the Reformation. A second result was the assembly of clergy in distinct bodies for secular business, and the consequent attempt of Edward I to include a representation of the clergy in his Parliament of Estates. But his failure did not prejudice the success of a third result; for, owing to the refusal of the bishops on more than one occasion to grant money in the

Marginal notes:

Clerical self-taxation.

[1] *S. C. H.* iii. § 346.

1188.

1193.

name of the unrepresented clergy, a representative element
was introduced into Convocation.   Thus it was through Convocation that the popes raised the tenths which they directed
the clergy to make over to the king.   The cause of the absten-

P. 151.

tion of the clergy as a body from Parliament has been elsewhere dealt with.   The king ultimately acquiesced in their
absence, but not without a struggle.   He tried first to tax the
clergy otherwise than with the sanction of the pope.   But in
1297 Archbishop Winchelsey, in obedience to the bull *Clericis
laicos* issued by Boniface VIII, refused to make such a grant
to the king.   Edward I outlawed the whole of the clergy, and
the bishops were recommended by the archbishop to make
their submission to the Crown as best they could.   Such
a crisis could not be of frequent occurrence.   Edward II's
councillors tried moral suasion; and from 1311 to 1340 a
special paragraph was inserted into the *praemunientes* clause
of the writ, enjoining the bishop to compel the lesser clergy to
send representatives.   The king ultimately acquiesced in the
absence of the clergy because they voted him, through Convocation, as large a sum as he could expect to get; for, at
the valuation of 1291, the clerical tenth reached £20,000.   But,
like the lay tenth-and-fifteenth, it sank in value until under
Henry VII it was estimated at only half its original sum.

1404.

Under Henry IV the tenth was supplemented by a tax levied
by Archbishop Arundel, probably through the bishops, on the
stipendiary or chantry priests who were unrepresented in Convocation.   It is noteworthy, in conclusion, that, while the
knights of the shire attacked the temporal possessions of the
bishops and monasteries, they never threatened the spiritualities
of the parochial clergy; and, indeed, their only attempt to tax

1449.

the clergy by a repetition of Archbishop Arundel's method of
bringing under contribution the stipendiary priests, was at
once quashed by the king.   Thus the clergy won and maintained their right of self-taxation : but their negative attitude
by which they gained it, prevented them from ever exercising
a direct voice in the bestowal of the money which they had
granted.

Eccle-
siastics in
lay office.

Before passing away from the question of the connection
between State and Church, it is important to note the great
part necessarily played by ecclesiastics in definitely lay offices.

The mediaeval clergy have been divided into three schools or classes : (*a*) the devotional or spiritual, few in numbers and reaching their ideal in Anselm ; (*b*) the ecclesiastical or professional, such as Henry of Winchester, closely connected with Rome and taking a mediatorial attitude in the State to further the interests of the Church ; and (*c*) the secular or statesman, whose preferment in the Church came as a reward for official services. They formed a very important body, and their existence largely influenced the organization of the State. 'The State,' says Dr. Stubbs, 'gained immensely by being administered by statesmen whose first ideas of order were based on conscience and law rather than on brute force,' for 'they laboured hard to reduce the business of government to something like the order which the great ecclesiastical organization of the West impressed on every branch of its administration.'[1] The type of this class is found in Bishop Roger of [1] *S. C. H.* Salisbury and his family, to whom were due the organization § 166. of the Exchequer under Henry I, the peaceable acceptance of King Stephen, and his subsequent rejection. Becket as Chancellor, Hubert Walter as Justiciar, and Stephen Langton, who, however, held no secular office, each in his degree contributed largely to the formation and maintenance of a system of strong and orderly government. On the other hand, the evil of the system was seen both in the refusal of the bishops to support Anselm against William II because, as they said, they were too poor and dependent to have a conscience ; and in their support of Henry II against Becket because they were servants of the State rather than of the Church. Only by slow degrees did the opinion of even the most spiritually minded churchmen turn against the absorption of the abler clergy in secular work. Roger of Salisbury himself, while on the one side he held the justiciarship with the full approval of Anselm and his successors, on the other side refused in the first instance to accept it without the pope's consent. A century later we find, by contrast, Innocent III commanding Archbishop Hubert Walter to resign the same 1198. exalted post. The incompatibility of the simultaneous tenure of the highest offices of Church and State was gaining recognition. But it was some time before the custom was abandoned. Indeed, in the fourteenth and fifteenth centuries

the number of churchmen in lay offices increased ; for, after
the land legislation of Edward I had ensured the safety of
entailed estates, the nobles tried to compensate their younger
sons with ecclesiastical preferment.   The leaders of the Church
became, in consequence, less and less sympathetic with the
lower clergy and increasingly secular in tone and feeling.
How weak was the corporate action of the Church is shown
by the fact that, in the case of both Edward II and Richard II,
only a single bishop was found on the side of the fallen king.
Two results followed from the secularization characteristic of
the fifteenth century.   In the first place, the greater number
of bishops, if they were not altogether foreigners, were at
any rate non-resident.   Their ecclesiastical work was done
by titular prelates, such as the Bishop of Jerusalem, and by
suffragan bishops, of whom there seems to have been one
and sometimes even more, in almost every diocese.   Thus
1428-1454. Kemp, who was Archbishop of York for twenty-six years,
never went near his diocese.   As a second result the bishops
sometimes suffered the extreme fate of unpopular ministers.
1381. Archbishop Sudbury was murdered in Wat Tyler's Rebellion ;
and Bishop de Moleyns of Chichester met a like fate in 1450.
This secular employment of the clergy seemed to reach its
climax on the eve of the Reformation.   Archbishop Warham
as Chancellor was succeeded by Wolsey, while Bishop Fox of
Winchester was Treasurer, the Bishop of Durham Secretary,
and the Bishop of London Master of the Rolls.

The Church and the Pope.
§ 86.   In order to point the full contrast between the position
of the Church in England before and after the Reformation,
it is necessary to conclude this description of the constitution
of the mediaeval English Church with a short account of
its connection with the papacy.   There were five methods by
which the pope endeavoured to obtain a hold over ecclesiastical affairs in England.   Of these the most important

Appointment of bishops.

[1] S. C. H. iii. §§ 381-386.
was his (i) *interference in the appointment of bishops*.[1]   The
gradual growth of this method may be traced through three
stages.   It was begun by the gift of the ' pallium ' or pall to
the archbishop.   This was a kind of woollen collar, a relic of
imperial state, which was at first merely an honorary gift, but
gradually came to be regarded as so necessary that the archbishop would not consecrate bishops until he had received it.

Pope Gregory had in the first instance sent a pall to Augustine ; and until the time of Lanfranc the archbishop usually travelled to Rome to receive it. The claim to refuse the pall placed in the hands of the pope the power of veto on the elections of national churches. A second stage was reached when the pope was able to interfere in the election of prelates as a matter of appeal. At first his power was limited to a decision between the merits and the canonical election of two rival candidates. But in 1204, in the case of the archbishopric itself, Innocent III claimed the right to reject the proffered candidates and to appoint his own nominee irrespective of the royal assent. This principle was asserted in the well-known cases of Stephen Langton, Edmund Rich, Kilwardby, and Peckham. In 1262 it was extended to bishoprics. Finally, to the appellate jurisdiction the pope added a claim to the patronage of vacant sees. On the death of Archbishop Winchelsey he extended to bishoprics 1313. the system of provision and reservation, which since 1226 had been applied to benefices and prebends or canonries. Moreover, he claimed the sole right of translating a bishop from one see to another and of filling the vacant see ; while he regarded as papal perquisites the sees left vacant by bishops who died at the court of Rome. In all these various ways it came about that, by collusion with the king and even after the grant of freedom of election by John, between the reigns of Edward I and Henry V the elective rights of cathedral chapters were practically extinguished. Nor was the recovery of their power under Henry V more than momentary. Indeed, under his successor papal interference was more constant than at any previous time, and Martin V 'provided' to no less than thirteen sees of the province of Canterbury. The Tudors asserted the rights of the king, and from the first the royal nominees were invariably chosen. The constitutional importance of this method of papal interference will be realized when it is remembered that the representatives of the spiritual estate formed the larger half of the members of the House of Lords.

A second and most important method of papal interference in the affairs of the Church, was (ii) *the encouragement of appeals* to Rome.[1] Under the Anglo-Saxons, reference was

Appeals.
[1] *S. C. H.* iii. § 403.
Makower. § 23.

often made to the pope in ecclesiastical matters for which local custom furnished no rules. In the only cases of appeal against a local decision—those of Wilfrid of Northumbria and the Norman Archbishop Robert—the papal interference was either repudiated by the Witan or was simply ignored. The first Norman kings followed the continental custom in allowing appeals to Rome with the royal licence in matters which the local tribunals were incompetent to decide. Under Stephen the divided state of the country caused a great increase in the frequency of appeals. Such appeals fall into *two classes* [1]— (*a*) *extra-judicial*, or appeals *à gravamine*, to stay the action of a superior court in a case which had not yet been heard by the court. This amounted to an invocation of the protection of the pope, and of this kind were by far the largest number of recorded appeals to Rome. (*b*) *Judicial* appeals from a definite sentence were made by a demand of 'apostoli' or letters dimissory from the court against whose sentence the appeal was made. The *subjects* of appeal were of every kind that could be tried in an ecclesiastical court, especially such as concerned disputed elections to bishoprics, cases of marriage and wills, resistance to the authority of bishops and abbots, and the interpretation of ecclesiastical customs. There were two important *exceptions*—(1) questions concerning the title to real property and touching such matters as advowsons, legitimacy and dower, by Henry II's legislation were withdrawn once for all from the church courts; (2) there is no appeal on record against sentences for immorality, heresy or any kind of direct disobedience in ecclesiastical matters; for, no appeal was allowed from a mere corrective judgement. But these exceptions, important though they were, diminished little from the general sum of the appeals to Rome, the great volume of which encouraged the king from time to time to attempt *measures of restraint.* The first of these was the *Constitutions of Clarendon*, by which Henry II provided for appeals up to the court of the archbishop, then to the king by whose command the matter should be reheard and the decision finally given in the court of the archbishop; but no further appeal should be allowed without special leave of the king. [2] This clause, however, Henry was obliged to renounce, and with it disappeared the king's right, maintained

678.
1051.

[1] *E. C. C.*
29-30.

1164.

[2] *S. C.* 139.
§ 8.

by the Normans, of withholding the licence of appeals to Rome.
Henceforth the only restraints which the king could enforce
were the withdrawal of questions of real property from ecclesiastical courts altogether; the limitation of appeals to strictly
ecclesiastical cases; and the maintenance of the common-law
right which forbade a subject to quit the kingdom or to introduce papal letters without royal leave.   This would, however,
be enforced only in times of popular excitement.   A second
attempt to check the action of the papacy was contained by
implication in John's *grant of freedom of election* to cathedral
chapters in 1214.[1]   But the only result has been described as   [1] *S. C.* 288.
'freedom of litigation'; and John's previous surrender to the
papacy [2] was directly responsible for the thirty disputed elec-   [2] *Ibia.* 285.
tions which were carried to Rome between 1216 and 1264.
Indeed, Henry III himself appealed to the pope for a release
from his oath to the barons, and even Edward I dared do no
more than discourage appeals by making it easier to get justice
at home.   The futility of John's grant is proved by frequent
petitions, such as those of the Mad Parliament in 1258 and
the Parliament of Carlisle in 1307, on the subject of freedom
of election.   Indeed, all early legislation on the matter was
defeated by connivance of the pope and the king.   The third
and most deliberate attempt to check appeals to Rome was
made by the *Statutes of Praemunire* [3] (1353 and 1393), which   27 Edw.
decreed sentence of forfeiture and banishment against all who   III. st. 1,
carried their cases beyond the king's court.   But even this did   c. 1.
not entirely stop appeals; for, in the first place, it did not   16 Ric. II.
touch the case of appeals made with the leave of the Crown,   c. 5.
or on subjects with which the local courts were not competent   [3] *S. C. H.*
to deal; while, secondly, no legislation could preclude the   iii. § 393.
collusive dealings of the pope and the Crown.   At the same   Gee and
time the Statute is an index of the feelings of the fifteenth   Hardy,
century.   The diminution in the number of appeals which   103, 122.
characterized the early years of the century, was probably due
to the general discredit which the schism and the general
councils had brought upon the papacy, the increased strength
of the royal courts, and, in some measure, the Statutes
of Praemunire.   The influence of the Statutes was marked
by the use to which Gloucester put them in his contest
with Cardinal Beaufort, and by the fact that they were

Henry VIII's pretext for the overthrow of Cardinal Wolsey. The subjects of appeal were also limited almost entirely to marriages and wills ; and it was over a case arising out of the former set of questions that the Reformation in England began.

Provisions.

Although the papal interference in the appointment of bishops was the most conspicuous mode of papal action on the English Church, it was only the imitation in a higher sphere of (iii) the *system of provisions and reservations*[1] already begun in the case of benefices and canonries, which was a direct attack on the right of private patronage. In 1226 the papal envoy, Otho, began with a demand for the reservation of two prebendal stalls in each cathedral church, which the pope could bestow upon his own nominees. Both this and an attempt in 1239 to apply the same system to benefices in private patronage, were refused. But, nothing daunted, in the following year the pope chose the Bishops of Lincoln and Salisbury from whom to make the unprecedented demand of provision for 300 foreign ecclesiastics. This and subsequent demands led to the strong remonstrances of the devout Bishop Grosseteste himself and of his followers, and to the presentation of petitions from the national council. A royal ordinance of Edward III in 1343 was followed by the *Statutes of Provisors* of 1351 and 1390, the latter of which decreed forfeiture and banishment against all who obtained provisions or reservations.[2] But neither protests nor statutes were of much avail. In 1313 the system was extended to bishoprics, and by collusion with the king the appointment to these high offices and the usurpation of private patronage went on unchecked.

[1] *S. C. H.* iii. §§ 384, 392.

1240.

25 Edw. III. st. 4. 13 Ric. II. st. 2, c. 2.
[2] Gee and Hardy, 112-121.

Legates.
[3] *S. C. H.* iii. § 380. Makower. § 24.

A fourth means of papal influence was (iv) *the appointment of Legates*.[3] Before the Norman Conquest there are only two recorded instances of the visit of papal legates to England. But the early days of the Norman rule were contemporary with the efforts of Gregory VII to make all episcopal authority into a mere delegation from Rome by the employment of legates as the ordinary means of communication. These pretensions of the papacy were met in England both directly and indirectly. To his father's three 'Consuetudines' Henry I boldly added a fourth forbidding the entrance of legates without the king's leave,[4] which Anselm followed up with an assertion that the

[4] *S. C.* 82.

legatine power over England belonged by prescriptive right
to the see of Canterbury. This may have led Archbishop
William of Corbeil to obtain from Rome the legatine authority 1127.
for himself as Archbishop of Canterbury. But the assertion of
Anselm was not really made good until th. time of Stephen
Langton. Henceforth, until the repudiation by Cranmer,
the Archbishop of Canterbury was *legatus natus*, receiving 1221-1534.
the ordinary legatine commission as soon as his election
was confirmed at Rome. The results were important. In
the first place, the supreme jurisdiction of the pope was thus
introduced into the country in a manner which made it almost
impossible for the kings to refuse their recognition; secondly,
it made even the ordinary metropolitan jurisdiction appear
so much a delegated power from Rome that Alexander III
declared this to be the origin of the archbishop's right to exercise jurisdiction in the dioceses of his suffragans. Modern
authorities, however, believe that this power was undoubtedly
exercised from early times. It is to be noticed, as a third result,
that the presence of a perpetual representative of the pope did
not shut out the visits of *legati a latere* or special emissaries,
such as Otho and Ottobon in the reign of Henry III.

Lastly, one method by which the pope made his power felt Exactions.
in the country was through (v) *the papal exactions.*[1] Of these, [1] *S. C. H.*
three kinds were *levied from the whole nation.* The first, and iii. § 395.
best known, was *Peter's Pence*, or Rome-feoh, as the Anglo-
Saxons called it.[2] This probably originated in the tribute paid [2] *Ibid.* i.
by Offa of Mercia for the papal authorization of his new and § 86.
short-lived archbishopric of Lichfield. From the beginning 787.
of the tenth century it became a regular tax of a penny
on every hearth. The institution of a similar tax by Ini of
Wessex for the maintenance of the English School at Rome,
seems unsupported by sufficient evidence. The tax became
commuted for a sum of £201 9s. from the whole kingdom.
It was acknowledged by William I and was paid with fair
regularity. In 1306 Clement V tried unsuccessfully to increase
it by a return to the levy of a penny on every household. In
1366, when John's tribute was repudiated, Peter's Pence was
for a time also withheld. A second papal tax was *John's tribute*
of a thousand marks from England and Ireland, which he
promised on his submission to Innocent III in 1213.[3] The [3] *S. C.* 285.

liability lasted until 1366 when, amid the anti-papal legislation of Edward III's reign, Parliament definitely refused any
further payment of the tribute which had been for many years
in arrears. A third and intermittent tax was formed by *contributions for religious purposes.* These were taken by the
pope's agents in the form of voluntary gifts, the best known of
which was the Saladin Tithe for the Crusade of 1190.[1] The
official collector of the pope was perhaps the best-hated man
in the country. He was petitioned against in 1376, voted
a public enemy in 1390, and imprisoned in 1427. The only
restraint upon him was a stringent oath of fealty to the Crown,
which was exacted from him. But there were two other kinds
of exactions which were *levied from the clergy alone.*[2] They
paid, firstly, *tenths of ecclesiastical revenue.* These were taken
through Convocation, but were practically compulsory. They
were frequently levied under Henry III, and Edward I and II
allowed the exaction because the pope gave them a share in it.
But the king made use of the exiled and divided state of the
papacy in the fourteenth century to continue to take the tenth,
while the papal demands were often refused (1389) or postponed (1427, 1446). Secondly, the clergy were called upon to
pay *Annates* or firstfruits, which amounted to the whole of the
first year's income of a newly appointed bishop or incumbent.
Beginning as a voluntary offering, with the acknowledgement
of the papal right of provision it became compulsory. The
first pope who claimed it in England was Alexander IV, but
it did not become perpetual until John XXII. It reached
a considerable sum, and in 1531 Convocation stated that,
since 1486, £160,000 had been paid under this head.
In conclusion, it should be noted that, besides these payments, there were others, such as fees for Expectatives, or
the right of succession to a benefice at the next vacancy;
for dispensations of all kinds, and for a general traffic in
spiritual things.

§ 87. With the causes of the Reformation we are here not
immediately concerned. Its results on the structure and
position of the Church may be dealt with under the already
familiar heads of (1) the Church as an organized body, and
(2) the Church in connection with the State. To these it will

be necessary to add, as an ultimate effect of the Reformation, (3) the growth of Religious Toleration.

Even before the break with Rome an increase in the number of *bishops* had been contemplated. In 1532 Henry VIII obtained from the pope a bull for the erection of six bishoprics. This bore fruit in 1540 when, after the destruction of the monasteries, some of the proceeds were applied to the foundation of six bishoprics with their chapters. Thus, at Henry VIII's death, the English episcopate was composed of twenty-six archbishops and bishops. Henry had at one time contemplated the creation of as many as eighteen. Not only was there an Act passed, which was repealed in the first year of Philip and Mary (c. 8, § 4), allowing the king to create new sees by letters patent out of the possessions of the monasteries, but as early as 1534 Henry had obtained from Parliament an Act for the erection of twenty-six suffragan bishoprics mentioned by name, which has never been repealed. No new bishoprics were created until 1836, when Ripon was turned from a collegiate church into a cathedral; but this made no increase in the number of the episcopal bench, for Gloucester and Bristol were at the same time united. In 1844 Manchester was made a separate see by Act of Parliament: in 1877 Truro and St. Alban's; in 1878 Liverpool, Newcastle, Wakefield, and Southwell, in 1897 Bristol, in 1901 Birmingham, and in 1905 Southwark, were added to the existing number by a similar method. These, together with the bishopric of Sodor and Man, make up the present number of the episcopal bench to thirty-seven. A limited use has also been made of the Act of Henry VIII to appoint suffragan bishops in some of the larger dioceses; but the chief development of the Anglican episcopate is to be found in the colonies, and in the United States of America.[1] Two hundred and fifty bishops drawn from English-speaking races may be reckoned, a number none too large for the vast populations to which they minister.

The effects of the Reformation on the *lower clergy* were of the utmost importance; for, the regulars were abolished altogether and the seculars were released by degrees from their vow of celibacy.[2] To deal with the last point first:—Under Henry VIII those who had taken advantage of the laxity which followed the breach with Rome, obtained little help.

Bishops.

31 Hen. VIII. c. 9.

26 Hen. VIII. c. 14.

1 Makower. §§ 12, 13.

The lower clergy.

2 *Ibid.* § 22.

In 1535 a royal proclamation forbade those clergy who had taken wives to perform any sacraments or to hold any office within the Church; and in 1539 the Act of Six Articles definitely forbade priests to marry. Under Edward VI came an immediate, though only a temporary, relaxation. In 1547 the first Convocation of the reign affirmed, without a single dissentient, the right of priests to marry; and in 1549, an Act of Parliament, while declaring it better that clerks should remain single, yet legalized their marriage.[1] This was followed by a more ungrudging acknowledgement of the right. But on Mary's accession all this was swept away, and by her Injunctions married priests were to be removed from their benefices and compulsorily divorced. As a result, 1,500 clergy according to one computation, and 3,000 according to a less favourable authority, were thus deprived. Much against her will, Elizabeth was obliged to yield somewhat to the Protestant views. But she put every difficulty in the way. Thus her Injunctions of 1559 allowed no clergyman to marry without the approval of the bishop, two justices of the peace near the woman's residence, and the parents or employers of the intended bride. Again, in 1561, by a royal proclamation, she forbade any member of a college or cathedral church to marry, and was with some difficulty dissuaded by Cecil from extending the prohibition to all persons in Holy Orders.

Two classes of ecclesiastics were entirely abolished as a consequence of the Reformation—the chantry priests and the monastic clergy. The work of the chantry priests had been to say masses for the souls of benefactors. But in 1535 one of the Ten Articles, while allowing prayers, described masses for the dead as superstition and folly. The Act of Six Articles re-established masses for the dead and, consequently, the doctrine of purgatory. But the king's doctrinal preferences were no proof against his greed, and in 1545 an Act for the dissolution of all chantries, hospitals, and free chapels was delayed in execution only by the king's death. An Act of the first year of Edward VI, however, gave over to the new king the chantries and other sacred buildings which had been already doomed.[2] It is only fair to add that the money thus obtained was not entirely diverted to secular purposes; for not only were twenty-two grammar schools founded, but institutions for the

31 Hen. VIII. c. 14.

[1] 2 & 3 Edw. VI. c. 21. Gee and Hardy, 366.

1552.

1554.

1539.

37 Hen. VIII. c. 4.

1 Edw. VI. c. 14.

[2] Gee and Hardy, 328-357.

relief of the poor were largely endowed, such as Christ's Hospital for orphans, St. Thomas' and St. Bartholomew's for the sick, and Bridewell for the ruined.

In his abolition of all the houses of regular clergy, Henry VIII was not acting altogether without precedent.[1] At the outbreak of Henry V's war with France a number of houses affiliated to foreign orders were taken into the king's hands as alien priories. Archbishop Warham, Cranmer's predecessor, had taken an unprecedented course in holding a visitation of the monasteries in his province. Wolsey had gone further; for he had obtained a papal bull for the suppression of forty small monasteries, from the revenues of which he founded his Cardinal College. Henry VIII, too, had supplied himself with a precedent by the suppression of the Order of Observant Friars as opponents of his divorce.[2] The first step towards a general measure was the nomination, in 1535 under the Act of Supremacy, of Thomas Cromwell as the king's vicar-general, with complete power to appoint his own agents and for the time to supersede the jurisdiction of the bishops. The *suppression* itself was carried out by two successive Acts— (*a*) 27 Henry VIII, c. 28, which suppressed all those houses with incomes under £200 a year. These numbered 376 out of 600 houses in all, and their joint incomes reached £32,000. (*b*) The Act 31 Henry VIII, c. 13, both confirmed to the king the abbeys which had been surrendered by their owners who had taken part in the Pilgrimage of Grace, and also provided for the surrender of all the monasteries which yet remained. The *results* of this wholesale destruction were numerous and important. In the first place, constitutionally the balance between spiritual and temporal peers in the House of Lords was altered. In the Reformation Parliament which met in 1529, the Lords comprised forty-four lay peers, twenty bishops, and twenty-eight abbots and priors. These last entirely disappeared—a fate which they thoroughly deserved, for they offered no opposition to the dissolution of the smaller monasteries and were themselves destroyed individually. A second result was the transference of an enormous amount of property.[3] The annual income of the monastic lands has been reckoned at £200,000. The value of their moveables was enormous. Some of the money no doubt was reserved for

Marginal notes:

Suppression of the monasteries.

[1] Gasquet, *Hen. VIII and the Eng. Monasteries*, i. chaps. ii-iii. 1528.

1534.

[2] Gasquet, *op. cit.* i. chap. v.

1536.

1540.

[3] Gasquet, ii. chap. x.

religious purposes. Six bishoprics were founded; some of the monasteries became collegiate churches, such as Ripon and Beverley; many of the abbey churches were left for the parishes. But enough remained in the king's hands to have saved him from the necessity of recourse to Parliament. Fortunately he found himself compelled to buy the acquiescence of the country in the religious changes which had arisen out of his quarrel with Rome; and his lavish grants of monastic property, carrying with them not only lands but the right to tithe, raised up a new class of country gentlemen who took an active part in the literary, religious, and political movements of the time; as justices of the peace, monopolized the local administration; and as members of Parliament, began before long to vindicate its power and privileges against the Crown itself. Other results do not concern us here.

Convocation. § 88. The government of the organized Church may still be dealt with under the twofold division of councils and courts. Among the former, Convocation alone calls for detailed treatment as involving important constitutional questions. It is important to inquire how far Convocation was consulted in the ecclesiastical changes. Two preliminary points must be borne in mind. The first concerns the authority which the sovereigns conceived to have been conferred on them by the title of Supreme Head. Now, none of the three sovereigns who effected the settlement of the Church, had the least intention of subjecting their ecclesiastical authority to the supervision or arbitration of Parliament. Henry VIII used the aid of Parliament to fight a hostile Convocation; but he intended to maintain the old ecclesiastical system as a framework for the exercise of his new ecclesiastical despotism. Edward VI and his ministers were bent on destroying the old framework of Church organization by means of the same despotism; and yet even they submitted many important measures to Convocation. Elizabeth, following in her father's footsteps, was careful first to secure a Convocation which would accept the Prayer Book; but when this was accomplished she would not allow Parliament to interfere with her ecclesiastical prerogative; while at the same time Convocation under her licence passed Canons to which, however, she gave or refused authority at pleasure. A second point to be remembered is

that where the record of Convocation is lost, or when the
journals of Convocation note that silence was imposed on
its members, the presumption is not necessarily against the
co-operation of Convocation in matters which had hitherto
been submitted to it and which were then being transacted in [1] *E. C. C.*
Parliament.[1]   *74.*

    These two points will help to an appreciation of the follow- Its action
ing facts.[2] *Under Henry VIII* the consent of the Church was in the
necessary to two separate kinds of changes—those in the con- Reforma-
stitutional position and organization, and those in doctrine and 26 Hen.
ritual.   As to the first point, the Act of Supremacy was based VIII. c. i.
on the recognition of the royal supremacy by Convocation in [2] *E. C. C.*
1531, and still omitted the words limiting that supremacy which 142-143.
had been omitted both in a form of submission required from
individual clergy in 1534 and in the Act of Appeals in 1533.
The subsequent Acts extending that supremacy, which will
be mentioned presently, do not seem to have been submitted to Convocation.   The second great Act affecting the
constitutional position of the Church, was the Act for the sub- 25 Hen.
mission of the Clergy.   Of this, part was in the Submission of VIII. c. 19.
the Clergy made by Convocation in 1532; and it seems 1534.
probable that the more important part of the Act, which
regulated appeals, was also laid before Convocation.   There
is, however, no direct proof of this.   In the settlement of
doctrine and ritual, the Ten Articles of 1535 were accepted
by Convocation alone; the Six Articles of 1539, reaffirming
some of the prominent Catholic doctrines, had the approval
of both Convocation and Parliament.   Most of the changes
made in these particulars seem to have been authorized by
the king alone, though some were submitted to Convocation.
Thus, in 1537 the king licensed Matthew's Bible; in 1539 he
authorized the possession of Bibles in private houses; in 1546
he forbade the use of Tyndale's and Coverdale's translations.
On the other hand, in 1543 Convocation ordered the curate
in every parish to read the Bible to the people on holydays;
and while the English Litany was authorized by the king,
the Lord's Prayer and other English portions of the breviary
were submitted to Convocation.   Again, the 'Institution of 1537.
a Christian Man' was authorized by the king, though the
'Necessary Erudition' was laid before Convocation.   There are, 1542.

moreover, numerous indications that even when the fully prepared measure was not forthcoming, Convocation was used as a consultative body both in matters authorized by the king and in those legalized by statute. *Under Edward VI*, while, on the one hand, the assent of Convocation may have been given to the first Prayer Book, to the administration of communion in both kinds to the laity, and to the right of clerical marriage, before these were actually legalized ; yet, on the other hand, there is no record that Convocation was consulted with regard to the Ordinal for the consecration of bishops which was published separately in 1550, to the second Prayer Book of 1552, to Cranmer's Catechism and the Forty-two Articles of 1553, and to the 'Reformatio Legum' or Reform of Ecclesiastical Laws. All these were the work of small committees which held such a vague relation to Convocation as might arise from the fact that many of them were appointed in accordance with its petition. The hostility displayed by Convocation at the beginning of *Elizabeth's* reign, caused her to use the sanction of Parliament alone for the restoration of the service-book of Edward VI. But when she had once procured a favourable Convocation, she allowed no interference with its action save such as she conceived to be in accordance with the exercise of the royal supremacy.

Its position towards the Crown.

The whole position of Convocation towards the king was changed by the Reformation. This was the result of the Submission of the Clergy of 1532, followed by the Act for the submission in 1534.[1] By these, Convocation was made to acknowledge (*a*) that no legislation by the clergy was valid without the king's assent and permission for its execution, and that Convocation could be assembled only by the king's command ; (*b*) that a reform of the ecclesiastical laws should be undertaken by a royal commission of laity and clergy, and that meanwhile with the king's approval the ancient laws of the Church should stand good ; (*c*) by the Act of 1534 provision was made for ecclesiastical appeals to be taken to the king in Chancery. The change in the attitude of the king towards Convocation after the Reformation, may be described as the substitution of a positive for the negative attitude. Thus, whereas up to 1532 the king contented himself with prohibiting the ecclesiastical assemblies from enacting

[1] Gee and Hardy, 176, 195.

anything contrary to the law of the land, while Convocation met at the archbishop's summons and not at all necessarily, though for convenience' sake, at the same time as Parliament; *now* Convocation meets only at the sovereign's will; it can do nothing at all without his assent; its legislation is subject to the revision of a royal commission; and appeals against its laws are made to a royal secular court. It was probably this curtailment of its authority even over the clergy, which from 1546 made it necessary that the clerical tenths granted to the Crown should receive confirmation in Parliament, and thus should be raised, if needful, by coercion through the secular power. But it was not until after the Restoration that a verbal agreement between the Chancellor and the Archbishop did away with the clerical right of self-taxation. The result of this surrender was important if not serious. The bulk of the clergy were Tories and even Jacobites: the bishops of William III and of George I were Whigs. The quarrels between the two houses of Convocation caused its abeyance for ten years under William III; and the action of the lower house of Convocation in what is known as the Bangorian controversy, provoked by a sermon of the Whig bishop, Hoadley, determined the Government of George I to silence the whole body. From 1717 until 1840 the Church as an organized body had no constitutional means of expressing its united opinion. Meanwhile, the number of subjects on which Convocation could legislate has been much curtailed: its decrees are not binding on the laity unless accepted by Parliament: it cannot even conduct a trial for heresy, although the condemnation of heretical books is still within its province. Convocation has instituted inquiries and discussions, and has made reports through committees; and a few of its recommendations, chiefly touching matters of services and ritual, have been embodied in Acts of Parliament.

§ 89. The old ecclesiastical courts of archbishop, bishop, archdeacon, and such peculiars as had survived the dissolution of the monasteries, continued to exist after the Reformation, and were held under the authority of the archbishops, bishops, and other ordinaries. The changes made by the Reformation may be conveniently classed under the five heads of Appeals, Judges, Law, Jurisdiction, and Authority. As to *Appeals*,[1] the

(margin notes:) 1664.

Ecclesiastical Courts after the Reformation.
[1] *E. C. C.* 39.
Makower. § 62.

24 Hen. VIII. c. 12.   Act in Restraint of Appeals arranged for appeals from the archdeacon's court to that of the bishop; from that of the bishop to that of the archbishop; and further—but only when the king was concerned—to the upper house of Convocation.   This was

25 Hen. VIII. c. 19.   modified by the Act for the Submission of the Clergy which decided that appeals should go from the archbishop's court to the king in Chancery.   This was the foundation of the Court of Delegates of Appeals which formed the supreme tribunal of appeal in ecclesiastical causes from 1559 to 1832.   Its functions

2 & 3 Will. IV. c. 92.   were transferred, by two statutes of William IV's reign, to the Judicial Committee of the Privy Council.   As to *Judges*, a statute

3 & 4 Will. IV. c. 41.   of 1545 allowed Doctors of Civil Law, though laymen and married, to act in this capacity.[1]   This was most loosely in-

[1] 37 Hen. VIII. c. 17.   terpreted, and even the qualification of Doctor was regarded as unnecessary.   Attempts were made to alter it, and a Canon of 1604, while leaving to the ecclesiastical judge, however qualified, the power of suspension and excommunication, reserved to the bishop the sentence of deprivation or deposition.   The question of the *Law* administered by the courts is rather more complicated.   The Act for the Submission of the Clergy gave to the king the power of appointing a committee of sixteen clergy and as many laymen to revise the existing canons and constitutions.   By subsequent statutes this power was given to

3 & 4 Edw. VI. c. 11.   the king for life.   It was renewed to his successor by an Act of 1549-50, under which three commissions were issued. Meanwhile, in the last year of Edward's reign, Archbishop Cranmer and the foreign reformer, Peter Martyr, completed a 'Reformatio Legum' which, however, was never authorized,

1571.   though it was subsequently published.   The power was again renewed to Elizabeth on her accession; but after some ineffectual attempts in her first Parliament, nothing more was heard of the matter.   The laws, then, which in the absence of

[2] E. C. C. 45.   this revision the ecclesiastical courts had to fall back upon,[2] consisted of (1) the Canon law of the Church so far as it did not run counter to the Common law or the royal prerogative: (2) the king's ecclesiastical laws, such as those relating to the Prayer Book and the Articles, made by virtue of the royal supremacy: (3) the Canons of Convocation licensed by the king: (4) royal proclamations issued by virtue of the Acts of Supremacy and Uniformity.   Of the Canons there were three

sets—those of 1597 and 1604, which, since they have never
received parliamentary sanction, are not regarded as binding on
the laity; and those of 1640, which, owing to the circumstances
under which they were drawn up, are not regarded as having
authority at all. The *Jurisdiction* of the ecclesiastical courts
was of course much diminished. In the first place, the Statute
law quite overrode the Canon law. The authority of the pope
had been annulled by statute, which thus very materially limited
the matter of the Canon law. Prohibitions from the secular
courts to stay trial or sentence in the church courts were no
new thing; but now the judges issued them with greater
freedom, while, even in the ecclesiastical courts themselves,
Common and Canon law were of equal authority, and, in case
of a conflict, the Canon law had to give way. Nor was this all;
for, in the second place, the Courts of Common Law obtained
concurrent jurisdiction with the ecclesiastical courts.

Under these circumstances it is perhaps scarcely astonishing that the church courts decayed. Nor did the fact that
the bishops preferred to gain their ends by use of the
powerful *Court of High Commission* [1] help to strengthen them. [1] *E. C. C.*
Both Edward VI and Mary, at the beginning of her reign, 49-50.
had considered themselves justified by Henry VIII's Act of Prothero,
Supremacy in issuing special commissions for inquiry into xl-xlvii.
heresies. Those of Edward VI, issued in 1549 and 1551, § 30. Makower.
were empowered to exercise full jurisdiction; that of Mary in
1557 was limited to inquiry. Acting upon these precedents
and, moreover, definitely authorized by her Act of Supremacy,
Elizabeth issued an extensive commission to nineteen persons
for the execution of the Acts of Supremacy and Uniformity. 1559.
The inquiry was to be conducted 'as well by the oaths of
twelve good and lawful men as also by witnesses and other
ways and means ye can devise,' and the commissioners were
empowered to hear and determine all cases which could be
included under a wide interpretation of the application of the
two Acts. Thus not only are the punishment of heresy and
absence from church committed to them, but they are even
empowered ' to visit, reform, redress, order, correct and amend
all offences which, by any spiritual or ecclesiastical power,
authority or jurisdiction, can be so dealt with.' Finally, the
commissioners are given the assistance of 'all justices of the

peace, officers and faithful subjects.'[1]   This commission formed a precedent for all those which were subsequently issued, the chief differences being that the execution of other Acts besides the two already mentioned was added to the work of the commissioners; that the powers entrusted to the latter were definitely stated or extended; that the number of commissioners was increased; and that often a commission was issued to take effect only in one of the two provinces or even in a single diocese.   The connection of this court with, and its effect upon, the purely ecclesiastical courts was of immense importance.   For those who came to it, it was a court of first instance and, except for a short period, not subject to appeal. James I's commission of 1620 provided for the appointment by the king's favour of commissions to review its decisions. At the same time, neither did it supersede the ecclesiastical courts of the ordinaries, nor was it, like the Court of Delegates, a court of appeal from them.   Yet a very brief account of its jurisdiction will suffice to prove the blighting effect of its existence on the ordinary Church courts.   'Every offence that could be treated as ecclesiastical was inquired into; every offender, accused or suspected, tried and punished or acquitted; every device for obtaining information was used; every claim for the assistance of secular justice was made and, as far as possible, enforced; every method of instituting a suit was allowed.'[2]   By the grant of writs of Habeas Corpus and by Prohibitions, the Common Law Courts in vain tried to restrict the action of this powerful commission.   It is not difficult to understand that so long as it existed, no important case touching doctrine or ritual could well find its way into the Court of Delegates, whose work was consequently somewhat restricted in range; while, since all important offenders were brought straight before the commissioners, the work of the ordinary courts was confined to such unimportant cases as would not need or would not be allowed an appeal.   It is, however, difficult to understand how the more single-minded bishops of the time permitted themselves to make use of such commissions.   It may be that they 'saw in some such engine the only safeguard against anarchy.'   But in whatever way they justified it to themselves, it seems certainly true that 'the result of the working of the court was morally bad and politically destructive.'

It is no wonder, then, that the Long Parliament abolished the High Commission,[1] and that James II's attempt to revive it in 1686 was met by its condemnation in the Bill of Rights as 'illegal and pernicious.'[2]

[1] Gardiner, *Const. Docts.* 112.

[2] *S. C.* 524.

From the abolition of the High Commission down to 1832, no important change was made in the ecclesiastical courts. The courts were still the old courts of the archbishop, bishop, archdeacon, and such peculiars as had survived the dissolution of the monasteries. The jurisdiction still ranged over an extensive class of cases, including such temporal matters as wills and marriages; matters partly temporal, partly spiritual, such as suits for tithes, Church rates, seats and faculties; and spiritual offences, such as immoral conduct of the clergy, and brawling and defamation of the laity. Both the jurisdiction and the courts have been reduced. As to the former, some offences, such as brawling and defamation, are punished elsewhere; some, such as Church rates and tithes, have been compromised; some, such as testamentary and matrimonial causes, have been handed over to specially constituted courts. As to the courts, the peculiars have practically been extinguished; the court of the archdeacon is rarely used; the powers of the bishop have been regulated and indirectly curtailed in favour of the courts of the province by the Church Discipline Act of 1840, amended by the recent Clergy Discipline Act which provides for the trial of offences against 1892. ecclesiastical law, and by the Public Worship Regulation Act 1874. which deals with the trial of offences against the ceremonial law. Finally, on the formation of the Probate and Divorce Courts in 1857, in both provinces the Prerogative Court of the archbishop lost its jurisdiction over matrimonial and testamentary matters: the Court of Peculiars disappeared with the abolition of the exempt position of the thirteen parishes to which it applied: the Court of Audience, or sphere of the archbishop's personal jurisdiction, has practically fallen into disuse, although, despite the archbishop's declaration to the contrary, it has been thought to have been revived for the hearing of the recent case of *Read* v. *the Bishop of Lincoln* ; 1892. and there remains the Court of Arches alone, presided over originally by the official principal of the archbishop, whose office is now merged in that of the Dean of Arches. But by recent legislation even this official has become little more than a nominee of the Crown ; for, the Public Worship Act of 1874 provided not only that the appointee of the two archbishops as judge to carry out the Act, should be confirmed by the Crown, but that in each province he should succeed as of right to the place of official principal as it became vacant.   The authority of the ecclesiastical court has been further curtailed by the transference of the jurisdiction of the Delegates of Appeals to the Judicial Committee of the Privy Council.

Relations of Church and State after the Reformation.

The royal supremacy.

[1] *E. C. C.* 37. Makower. § 28. Under Henry VIII.

[2] Gee and Hardy, 178. *E. C. C.* 210.

[3] Gee and Hardy, 201. *E. C. C.* 218.

[4] Gee and Hardy, 243. *E. C. C.* 72.

§ 90. All that has been said hitherto concerning the effect of the Reformation upon the organization of the Church, forms a fitting preliminary to the consideration of the changes wrought by that movement in the connection between Church and State.   This may be summed up in an analysis of the interpretation put upon the royal supremacy.   The power claimed by Henry VIII, under the title of Head of the Church, was fourfold.[1]   It included, in the first place, the king's ecclesiastical prerogative which, as we have seen, had always been maintained by English law ; and, secondly, the papal usurpations from the Crown by provisions, appeals, and annates.   These were recovered by two statutes.   The Act in Restraint of Payment of Annates was passed provisionally,[2] then confirmed by the king in letters patent on July 9, 1533, and finally, confirmed and supplemented by parliamentary statute.[3]   The Act of Supremacy or the Style of Supreme Head, defined the king's position as that of 'the only supreme head on earth of the Church of England.'   It gave to the headship two sets of functions—one which has been described as indeterminate, consisting of such powers as were supposed to be inherent in the title of head, namely, the enjoyment of the honours, dignities, privileges, &c., to the said dignity belonging : another determinate set of functions, such as were authorized by the statute, namely, the authority to visit and reform all ecclesiastical mischiefs.[4]   But to these two powers were now added other two which were included under the head of the royal supremacy.   Thus, thirdly, the king claimed the power usurped by the papacy from the Church of England.   This was recovered and added to the Crown by three statutes.   The Acts in Restraint of Payment of Annates provided for the appointment and consecration of bishops within the kingdom.

The Act of Citations,[1] with a view to limiting the power which
the archbishop had exercised in virtue of his legateship, forbade any one to be cited out of his or her diocese.   Finally,
the Act in Restraint of Appeals which was amended by the Act
for the Submission of the Clergy,[2] provided for appeals in
ecclesiastical cases up to the king in Chancery.   A fourth set
of powers included in the royal supremacy, was made up of
claims which the king had never hitherto put forward.   Thus
the Act of Supremacy had given the king authority, through
a vicar-general, to reform all ecclesiastical mischiefs.   The Act
of Six Articles[3] allowed commissions to be given to the archbishops, bishops, and others to hold quarterly sessions for the
trial of those who called in question the definitions arrived
at by the king with Parliament and Convocation; and even
justices of the peace were to make a similar inquiry by the
help of a jury.   The Act concerning Christ's religion stated
that the king had appointed archbishops, bishops, and doctors
of divinity to declare the articles of the Christian faith, and
enacted that all definitions according to God's word and the
Gospel, by the king's advice and letters patent, made by the
archbishops, &c., should have the force of law.   Finally, the
Act that married D.C.L.s should exercise ecclesiastical jurisdiction, stickled not to declare that the king could exercise all
other manner of ecclesiastical jurisdiction; that archbishops,
bishops, and archdeacons have no manner of ecclesiastical
jurisdiction but by, under, and from the king; and that to
him is given by Holy Scripture all authority and power to hear
and determine all causes ecclesiastical, and to correct vice
and sin whatsoever, and to all such persons as the king shall
appoint thereto.   In fact, these Acts claimed for the king
authority to declare articles of faith: but, further, the last two
Acts state this position in the preamble as if merely calling
attention to what was already known and acknowledged.   The
error which underlay the whole point of view was the idea
that the exercise of jurisdiction implied the right of personal
direction.   As the king, although in theory present in all
the courts, has no right to take the place of a secular judge
and administer justice, so in ecclesiastical matters he has
no right to supersede an officer or to issue orders at his own
pleasure.   Under Edward VI the action of the new power

[1] *E. C. C.*
209.

[2] *Ibid.* 213,
216.
Gee and
Hardy,
187, 195.

[3] Gee and
Hardy,
312 et seq.

32 Hen.
VIII. c. 26.

37 Hen.
VIII. c. 17.

Under
Edward VI. acquired by the king as Head of the Church was pushed even
further than it had been under Henry VIII, both Orders of
Council and Acts of Parliament being used for the purpose.
Three illustrations will suffice. (1) With regard to the appointment of bishops, the first Act in Restraint of Payment of
[1] Gee and
Hardy,
181-182. Annates,[1] passed before the final breach with Rome, provided
that, in the case of every one who was presented to the court
of Rome by the king to be bishop of any diocese within
the realm, if the pope delayed or restrained or denied his
appointment by bulls or in any other way, the king's nominee
should be consecrated by the archbishop. It was natural
[2] Ibid.
204-209. that in the second Act[2] this menace should be superseded
by the definite provision that the election to bishoprics should
be made by the deans and chapters of cathedrals under the
king's licence and letters missive naming the person to be
chosen ; and that in default of such election, the king should
1 Edw. VI.
c. 2. present by his letters patent. By one of the earliest Acts
of Edward VI's reign this last method was made the rule,
and it was provided that in every case bishops should be
appointed by letters patent without either the king's *congé
d'élire* or letters missive. (2) With regard to the jurisdiction
of ecclesiastical officers, at the beginning of Edward VI's reign
Cranmer and, possibly, other bishops renewed their commissions for the exercise of their ordinary jurisdiction, as if
its efficacy were dependent on each individual sovereign. In
the same spirit another Act of the same year provided that
all processes in the ecclesiastical courts should run in the
king's name, since their jurisdiction was derived from him and
no courts were held by any authority other than that of the king.
During the same reign two general royal visitations were carried
out—the first in 1547, to press on the reformed doctrines ; the
other in 1549, to enforce the use of the English Prayer Book :
and during each of these visitations the powers of the bishops
were suspended. (3) Doctrinal changes were carried out by
the same means. In 1547 a book of Homilies, and in 1548
a new Communion Office, were published and enforced by
authority of the king alone. So powerful had the title and
authority included in the royal supremacy become, that even
Under
Mary. Mary, with all her desire for the restoration of the papal power,
did not scruple to use it at the very beginning of her reign for

the twofold purpose of repealing the Acts of Edward VI's reign and thus restoring the Church to the position in which it was left on the death of Henry VIII;[1] and of issuing Injunctions[2] after the manner of Cromwell and Cranmer, for the deprivation of the married clergy and other administrative acts. The first statute of Elizabeth's reign was the Act of Supremacy,[3] which, though reviving ten statutes of Henry VIII's reign, did not include among them Henry's Act of Supremacy. It consequently abolished the claim to the title of Supreme Head which Elizabeth's advisers represented to her as unscriptural. The title was changed to Supreme Governor; and as Elizabeth had no intention of parting with the exercise of the ecclesiastical supremacy, all ancient jurisdiction over courts and persons was restored. It has been noticed already that the Act of Supremacy also empowered the Queen to appoint a commission with extensive powers, which armed the Crown with irresponsible authority and was the germ of the High Commission Court. It was by virtue of this same supremacy that another set of Injunctions[4] was published, enforcible by this commission. And yet at the same time, while the power of the Crown was thus extended and strengthened, the method of procedure was altogether more moderate. Thus (i) the Act of Supremacy restored the mode of election of bishops by chapters and in accordance with the *congé d'élire* of the Crown: moreover, (ii) to Convocation was given the duty of reducing the forty-two Articles to thirty-nine, and of authorizing a second book of Homilies; though it will be remembered that Elizabeth used her power to annul, as well as to authorize, canons of Convocation: (iii) Parliament was at the same time carefully restrained from meddling in ecclesiastical laws. Elizabeth and the early Stuarts stoutly maintained the inviolable nature of the royal supremacy. Parliament might have a share in taxation and legislation, but the Church was parallel to and not a department of the State, and, consequently, the dealings of the Crown with the Church were not matters for Parliament to discuss. This attitude could be maintained only so long as the nationality of the Church was insisted on and formed a link between Parliament and the Crown. But after the Restoration, when Charles II used his royal supremacy to publish his two Declarations of Indulgence,

[1] Gee and Hardy, 377.

[2] *Ibid.* 380.

[3] Prothero, 1-13. Gee and Hardy, 442. *E. C. C.* 224. Under Elizabeth.

[4] Gee and Hardy, 418. Prothero, 184.

Under the Stuarts.

Before the Great Rebellion.

1663.

Parliament in each case compelled him to withdraw them. The attempts of James II to use the royal supremacy, as Mary before him, to pave the way for reconciliation with Rome, only hastened on the transference of authority in this respect also from the Crown to Parliament. Outwardly, the Crown still possesses the old powers of Head of the

Church. Convocation is summoned and dismissed by the king, and legislates only with the royal assent ; appeal from the ecclesiastical courts has lain— before 1832, to the Crown in Chancery ; since that date, to the Crown in Council. But the establishment of the Church means more than this. Non-conformity has been recognized at first by toleration of its members, then by their actual inclusion in the ranks of active citizens. But potentially every Englishman is a member of the National Church ; and thus, although there is no guarantee that a single member of the House of Commons should be an actual member of the Church of England, yet Parliament has the right of interfering by legislation in its internal concerns to an extent perhaps difficult to realize ; while the law courts have the duty of considering cases in which, through disputes over property or contracts, the doctrines of the Church themselves may be subject to legal and secular interpretation. The advantages of a religious establishment may be open to debate ; but those who desire all the advantage without any of the necessary compromises, should feel that they must make their choice between a greater and a lesser evil.

§ 91. Now, a chief cause of the Reformation movement had been the growth of the sentiment of nationality in Western Europe as against the universal claims of the papacy. In England old feelings of independence and hatred of foreign interference had been revived, and had found expression in that idea of the Commonwealth which is a familiar thought of Elizabethan writers. For the proper protection of that Commonwealth it was necessary that the ruler should have cognizance of both the religious and the secular sides of the nation's life ; for, whatever else it might be, its religion was a powerful

bond of union in the State. Thus, without pretending in theory to dictate or in any way to notice religious beliefs, except in so far as such beliefs tended to the undoing of the

Commonwealth, the sovereign considered it imperative that he should demand from his subjects an outward uniformity of religious practice, which should at least afford a guarantee that they were not disaffected citizens. But the very feeling which led the Crown to disown any intention of inquisitorial judgement over belief, betrayed a consciousness that such belief was a matter for each individual to settle with himself. This was, in reality, to concede the whole Protestant position. Heresy had so often come to nothing, because the Roman Church, while sparing the heretic, had exterminated his opinions. But the Tudor sovereigns practically made room for the heresy, though they punished the individual. It is little wonder then that the country swarmed with men to whom the judicious but cold compromise of the Elizabethan church was distasteful. On the one side stood the *adherents* (a) Roman *of Roman doctrine and discipline* in its entirety, regarding Catholics; England as a lost inheritance, and obliged to rely upon foreign aid. Treated at first as politically dangerous by reason of their obedience to an alien authority, as the struggle with Parliament proceeded, they began to be courted by the early Stuarts as upholders of the divine right of kings ; while, as the Nonconformists in the Church became more pronouncedly Calvinistic, the assertion of the Catholic position of the English Church disposed the Caroline divines to claim kinship with Rome, and made them seem to be doing everything to bring about a union. Neither James I nor Charles I would ever have betrayed the Church : Charles' sons, on the contrary, did everything to undermine her power, and Romanism once more became the badge of a political party. It was only after all possible danger to the succession to the throne had been for some years removed, that those who had retained the old faith amidst many difficulties and dangers, began once more to be treated as fellow-citizens. On the other side were ranged the *Protestants* in the widest sense, whether Noncon- (b) Protest-formists or Puritans proper, who were willing to remain ant Non-members of the Church provided certain changes in outward conform-ceremonial were made; or Presbyterians opposing to epis-ists. copacy the divine government of a board of presbyters; or Independents, as yet called Brownists or Barrowists, who claimed for each congregation the right of self-control. The

school of Andrewes and Laud showed the incompatibility
between the Calvinistic theology of the Puritans and the
Catholic doctrines which they impressed upon the Church;
the republicanism of the Presbyterians never really obtained a
hold in England; the democratic system of the Independents
caused the Church to identify herself more than ever with the
monarchy.   At the same time Parliament was in the hands of
the Puritans; repressive legislation against Puritanism was
impossible; but, in the disciplinary authority vested in the
royal supremacy, the Crown found a far readier means of
coercing those who professed to remain members of the
National Church, but who desired to effect certain alterations
which should remove it to a safer distance from what they
conceived to be the erroneous Roman model.   But the triumph
over the monarchy worked for the benefit of the extreme
section of their party, who might be described by way of illustration though not of analogy as the religious Jacobins; the discredited Puritans hung their heads before the fervent loyalty and
vindictive churchmanship of the Parliament of the Restoration.
Schemes of comprehension were vain, and the Puritans themselves rejected an indulgence of their worship which must
be enjoyed in company with the Romanists.   At the same
time, the attitude of the Church had turned them from Nonconformists—that is, persons unwilling to conform to certain
outward ceremonials—to Dissenters, or persons who differed
altogether from the doctrines of the Church and stood outside
her pale, repudiating and repudiated.   But although the
Church showed herself more than willing to continue her
services to the Crown, it was the Crown itself which cast
her off and sought to betray her.   The Church became a
powerful emblem of nationality; and while her existence in
nominal supremacy seemed to guarantee the country against
outside interference from Rome and internal anarchy from
a too rampant individualism, the false position in which the
Church had been placed produced a considerable loss of
enthusiasm in her ranks, and rendered her willing, at any
rate, to tolerate the worship of those who had made common
cause with her against the Romanists, and ultimately to
connive at their participation in the government.   From such
toleration to legal recognition was a natural step, but it took

some time to accomplish. Prejudice was strong where argument was weak ; and the utterances of a few persons whose politics were more prominent than their religion, were interpreted as expressing the opinions of the whole religious section to which they nominally belonged.

There were, then, two bodies — the Catholic and the Protestant Dissenters — against whom the Church found it necessary to protect herself, and to whose faith she ultimately extended a legal recognition. The position of the two bodies was so different that it will be well to treat them separately. In each case the process will be similar; for, it will be necessary to notice in order, first, the restraints imposed upon their religious worship and the disabilities in civil life attached to all who were not professing members of the Church, and then the gradual withdrawal of these restraints and disabilities.

The measures of the legislature against Romanists may be marked off into two periods. The first of these was coextensive with the reign of Elizabeth and the early years of James I. Until 1570 religious legislation was occupied with a *definition of the position of the National Church* under the protection of the Crown. This had been begun by Henry VIII's Act of Supremacy, and continued by Edward VI's two Acts of Uniformity, which enforced the use of the two Prayer Books in succession, under penalties which, in the Act of 1549, extended to imprisonment for life for the third offence.[1] The reaction under Mary necessitated the re-enactment, on Elizabeth's accession, of the Acts of Supremacy and Uniformity. The former laid upon all beneficed clergy and all civil officials of the Crown, on penalty of forfeiture, an obligation to take the oath of supremacy renouncing the spiritual jurisdiction of every foreign prince or prelate. The latter[2] forbade the use of any but the Book of Common Prayer and therefore, by implication, the saying of mass ; while, in order to enforce attendance at church, it imposed a fine of one shilling on all absentees on Sundays and holydays. Three years later the abortive conspiracy of the Poles gave the excuse for another Act which rendered all in holy orders, whether beneficed or not, all recipients of University degrees, and all lawyers, liable to be called on to take the oath of supremacy. A refusal protracted beyond three months made the recusant guilty of high

Disabilities of Roman Catholics.

Before the Great Rebellion.

1549.

1552.

[1] Gee and Hardy, 358, 369. *E. C. C.* 220, 223.

[2] Gee and Hardy, 458. *E. C. C.* 229. Prothero, 13.

1562.

treason. The obligation was further imposed on all members of the House of Commons, but Roman Catholic peers were saved for more than a century by Elizabeth's declaration of confidence in the hereditary councillors of the Crown.[1] So far nothing, except by implication, had been enacted in the nature of a proscription of Romanists as such. But in **1571** the bull of deposition issued by Pope Pius V against Elizabeth in the previous year, called forth a measure of direct *defence*. The penalties of high treason were threatened to all who published bulls from Rome or who absolved or reconciled others or were themselves reconciled to the Church of Rome ; in other words, all priests exercising their functions and all converts.[2] The systematic attack of the Jesuits which began in 1580 called forth, for the first time, *offensive* legislation against the adherents of Rome. An Act of **1581**, while repeating the threats of the previous Act, and increasing the penalty imposed by the Act of Uniformity on absentees from church, to £20 a month or imprisonment until they conformed, also subjected to fine and imprisonment the celebrant and the willing attendant at a mass.[3] A later statute authorized the seizure of two-thirds of the delinquent's lands and goods.[4] In 1584 the Jesuits themselves were attacked in a law which not only commanded all kinds of priests, whether Jesuits or others, to leave the country in forty days under penalties of high treason, but even adjudged all who harboured them to be guilty of felony, and threatened with fine and imprisonment any who knew of their presence in the country and did not inform against them.[5] A final Act of this reign aimed against the laity, forbade the persons who, for the first time, were described as 'Popish recusants,' to move more than five miles from their usual place of residence under pain of forfeiture of all their possessions.[6] The general effect of these laws was that they 'compelled every Catholic to attend the Anglican service, suppressed absolutely and under crushing penalties the celebration of the mass, proscribed the whole Catholic priesthood, and made it high treason for any English priest from beyond the sea to come to England, for any Catholic graduate to refuse for the third time the oath of supremacy, for any Protestant to become a Catholic, or for any Catholic to convert a Protestant.'[7] Nor were these laws allowed to

[1] Prothero, 39.

13 Eliz. c. 2.

[2] *Ibid.* 60.

23 Eliz. c. 1.

[3] *Ibid.* 74.
[4] *Ibid.* 88.
27 Eliz. c. 2.

[5] *Ibid.* 83.
Gee and Hardy, 485.

35 Eliz. c. 2.

1592.

[6] Prothero, 92.
Gee and Hardy, 499.

[7] Lecky. *Hist. of Eng.* i. 272.

remain inoperative. About 200 persons suffered the extreme
penalty of death, of whom the majority were priests; and
despite Burleigh's protestation that no one was put to death
solely for his religious opinions, more than half the victims
perished after all danger of foreign interference had been
removed by the destruction of the Armada. Elizabeth's successor began with every intention of leniency, being greeted
on his accession by the pope and helped in the discovery
of plots by the leading Romanists in England. He desired
to leave the laity in peace, and therefore, shortly after his
accession, he remitted the fines incurred under Elizabeth's laws.
But at the same time, he hoped spiritually to starve them into
union with the National Church by banishing the priests. This 1604.
was done by proclamation,[1] and for further security in case of [1] Prothero,
need, all Elizabeth's penal legislation was confirmed.[2] But 420.
such a policy left James the victim of circumstances. A [2] *Ibid.* 253.
rumour of his own intended conversion caused him, in self-
justification, to enforce the recusancy fines; and the Gunpowder Plot, which was the result of this return to severity,
was the occasion of the enactment of the severe law of 1606, 2 Jac. 1.
by which not only was every Roman Catholic debarred from c. 4, 5.
the professions of the law and of medicine, and forbidden
to act as a guardian or trustee, but he was compelled to take
a more stringent oath of allegiance, which contained a denial
of the papal power to depose kings, and his house was liable
to be visited by magistrates in search of arms. But above all,
it was enacted that every recusant should receive 'the blessed
sacrament of the Lord's Supper' at least once a year in his
parish church under penalty of a fine of £60 or the forfeiture
of two-thirds of his lands.[3] This was the beginning of the *use* [3] *Ibid.*
of the sacramental test, which, perhaps more than any other 256-268.
single cause, degraded the ordinances of the Church in the
next century to a mere guarantee of political opinions.

The unwillingness of the kings rendered impossible any After the
further anti-Catholic legislation under the first two Stuarts. Great
James desired to propitiate Spain, and he and his son promised Rebellion.
to humour France by a relaxation of the penal laws. The
only hope of the Romanists lay with the Crown, so that under
the Commonwealth they were proscribed along with all Churchmen, for political as much as for religious opinions. The

triumphant Church of the Restoration attacked primarily the Commonwealth's men in the acts called, somewhat misleadingly, the Clarendon Code.   Incidentally, of course, the Romanists were also hit by the prohibition of all services except those of the Church and the application of the sacramental test to all candidates for municipal office.   Charles II's attempts in the interest of the Romanists, both at indulgence and at comprehension, failed, and Parliament proceeded to close all avenues to them by the *Test Act* of **1673**.   Elizabeth's Act of Supremacy did not make the oath contained in the Act a necessary qualification for any office except membership of the House of Commons ; and both by neglect of the Act and by the use of disingenuous explanations of the oath when taken, Romanists had held offices in the State.   At the moment of the passing of the Act, the Treasurer, Lord Clifford, and the Lord High Admiral, the Duke of York, were both avowed Roman Catholics. It was now enacted that all holders of temporal office must receive the sacrament according to the rites of the Church of England and must make a declaration that they rejected the doctrine of transubstantiation.[1]   The two statesmen resigned their posts, and five years later the Commons, after several unsuccessful attempts, obtained the assent of the Lords to the imposition of a test on members of both Houses, consisting of the oaths of allegiance and supremacy and a declaration that the worship of the Church of Rome is idolatrous.   The requirements of this statute were nothing new to members of the House of Commons ; but for the first time they were made applicable to the House of Lords, and caused the exclusion of about twenty peers, although, much to the chagrin of the country party, the Duke of York was specially exempted from the operation of the statute.   Indeed, it was this exemption which led directly to the introduction of the Exclusion Bill.   The Calvinism of William III did not prevent him from having dealings with the pope against their common enemy, Louis XIV ; and the Tory party, in feigned alarm and with a real desire to annoy the king, passed an Act in 1700 which has been described as 'perhaps the darkest blot upon the history of the Revolution.'   The intention of the Act was to drive the Romanist proprietors of land out of the country.   It required that all adherents of the popish

25 Car. II.
c. 2.

[1] Gee and
Hardy,
632.
30 Car. II.
st. 2, c. I.
1678.

11 & 12
Will. III.
c. 4.

religion should, within six months of reaching the age of eighteen, take the oaths of allegiance and supremacy and subscribe the declarations of 1673 and 1678 against transubstantiation and the worship of saints. The penalties for neglect were an incapacity to purchase land, and the transference of an inheritance to the next of kin who was a Protestant. Nor was this all. Perpetual imprisonment was denounced against all priests exercising their functions and all papists who kept schools or took part in the instruction of youth; nor were children to be sent abroad to be educated as Roman Catholics. The discovery of any who contravened this statute was encouraged by a reward of £100. The English Parliament was merely imitating some of the ferocity of its Irish contemporary; but the statute seems to have taken little effect, even when it was capped by the equally stringent Acts passed in the early years of George I's reign. By these, the oaths of allegiance and supremacy and of abjuration of the Pretender were to be taken by all civil and military officers, members of colleges, teachers, preachers, and lawyers; the two oaths could at any time be tendered by two justices of the peace to any Romanist whom they regarded as disaffected, and his refusal to take them rendered him liable to the penalties of recusancy. Moreover, Catholic landowners who, despite the Act of 1700, had maintained their estates, were required to register them together with all future conveyances and wills. Nor was this all; for, the annual Act which established the land tax imposed it on Catholics at a double rate, and in 1722 an additional tax was levied on their property.

1 Geo. I. st. 2, c. 13, 55. 3 Geo. I. c. 18.

Such were the chief provisions of the penal code which, had it been executed to the letter, would have exterminated the adherents of Rome. These may have been, as a writer of their religion has described them, a half proscribed and socially ostracized section of English society; but they owed their continued existence in comparative security, to the general indifference of the people and the admirable conduct of the judges, who refused to subordinate the law to the petty spite of personal enemies. The Acts of George I's reign are almost justified by the disaffection of the Romanists to the reigning family, and they expressed more nearly than might be supposed, the feeling still cherished by the English people generally

Early relaxations of the penal code in England, 1778-1791.

against the Roman Catholics. For, the first successful attempt at relaxation was followed by the greatest riot recorded in English history. In **1778** Sir George Savile procured the passing of an Act by which the penalties denounced by the Act of 1700 against popish priests and schoolmasters and Roman Catholic heirs or purchasers of land were removed, provided such persons took a special oath abjuring not only the Pretender, but also the temporal jurisdiction and deposing power of the pope, and the doctrine that faith should not be kept with heretics and that heretics may be lawfully put to death. The proposed extension of this Act to Scotland roused an unexpected amount of popular feeling, which culminated in the Gordon riots. For four days London remained entirely in the hands of the mob. But Parliament stuck to its Act. The petitions for repeal of the recent statute were met by a series of resolutions moved by Burke, with the approval of the Government of the day, vindicating the Act and condemning the misrepresentations to which it had been subjected. The only concession, stigmatized by an historian as 'unworthy,' was a bill also introduced by Savile, forbidding Romanists to teach the children of Protestants; but it was thrown out in the House of Lords. But this Act had done nothing to remove the disabilities of Catholic landowners or the disqualifications for nearly all the professions, under which the whole class of Romanists laboured. The removal of some of these was the object of Mr. Mitford's Catholic Relief Act of **1791**. Its introduction was preceded by a statement of opinions obtained from a number of foreign Universities, against the power of the Roman Church to interfere in civil affairs in England or to release English subjects from the oath of allegiance, and against the supposed Romanist belief that faith should not be kept with heretics. This was followed by a protestation of the leading Roman Catholics to Parliament in condemnation of the doctrines commonly attributed to them on the subject of the papal power of deposing or licensing the murder of sovereigns. It was on this protestation and in imitation of an Irish Act of 1774, that an oath was framed which freed its recipients from many penalties and disabilities. Thus the statutes dating from Elizabeth's time against popish recusants were abolished, and the law recognized the exercise

18 Geo. III. c. 60.

1780.

31 Geo. III. c. 32.

of Catholic worship and the existence of Catholic schools.
Moreover, Romanist landowners were freed from the necessity
of enrolling their wills and deeds, and were no longer liable,
on the summons of two justices of the peace, to condemn
themselves by refusing to take the oath of supremacy or to
make a declaration against transubstantiation. Finally, the
restrictions on the exercise by Catholics of all professions
connected with the law were removed, and Catholic peers were
restored to access to the king, though not as yet to their places
in Parliament. But the Act was far from complete. A number
of restrictions were still imposed. Thus, Catholic chapels and
schools, and the names of their priests and schoolmasters had
to be registered, and the services must all be conducted with
open doors. No steeple or bell was allowed to the chapels ;
no endowed college or school must be founded, and no
monastic order introduced ; no priest was to wear his dress or
to perform a service in the open air ; and, as a final security,
no Protestant child was to attend a Catholic school. It should
be noticed in connection with this Act, that from this time the
double land tax was regularly omitted from the annual Land
Tax Act by which it was imposed.

Meanwhile, in Ireland a penal code far more searching
and proscriptive than had obtained in England, was being
subjected to a gradual and steady relaxation. A series of laws
passed under William and Anne banished the Roman Catholic
from civil life. He could neither vote for nor sit in Parliament, he was excluded from the corporations, the magistracy,
the entire legal profession, the army and the navy. He was
denied the care of youth whether as guardian or schoolmaster. If he was not denied the exercise of his religion, the
full means of its continuance was much hampered by the
proscription of all bishops and other ecclesiastics claiming to
exercise jurisdiction ; and while regular clergy were forbidden,
all secular priests had to be registered and were subsequently
compelled to take the oath of abjuration of the Pretender.
The landowner was also worse off than in England. He
could neither purchase nor inherit land, nor bequeath it by
will. He could not intermarry with a Protestant. His estate
descended equally to all his papist sons ; but the eldest,
becoming a Protestant, could turn his father into a life

Disabilities of Roman Catholics in Ireland.

tenant, and so treat the fee simple of the land as his own possession.

Relaxations.

Soon after the middle of the eighteenth century the relaxation of these prohibitions was begun by the action of the Lord-Lieutenant, who in 1759 directed that marines should be raised from the Romanist districts ; and the licence was extended soon afterwards to recruits for the army.

1774.

In 1774, the first Statute which dealt with the matter, merely allowed Catholics to attest their loyalty by taking before a justice of the peace the oath of allegiance and making a form of declaration renouncing the Stuarts and certain doctrines commonly attributed to the Romanists as to the treatment of heretical sovereigns and their followers. Meanwhile, the many attempts which had passed the Irish Commons only to be rejected by the English Privy Council, to allow Catholics to lend money in mortgages upon

1778.

land, ended in the more generous Act of 1778, which not only permitted them, after taking the oaths of the Act of 1774, to hold leases of land and to inherit land, but removed alike the necessity of an equal division among all the sons and the premium hitherto placed by the law upon the apostasy of the

1782.

heir. An Act of 1782 further allowed those who took the oaths of 1774, to purchase and bequeath land so long as it was not in a parliamentary borough. It also abolished the registration of priests and the prohibition on the presence of bishops and regular clergy in the country ; and it opened the teaching profession to Catholics, provided they had no Protestant pupils. Indeed, notwithstanding the wide provisions of the Act, it was limited by a number of restrictions, many of which were after-

1792.

wards copied in the English Act of 1791. In 1792 the legal profession was thrown open by statute, though Catholics were prevented from becoming king's counsel or judges. By the same Act all remaining restrictions on education, whether at home or abroad, and the severe penalties on the intermarriage of Protestants and Catholics were removed. Finally, an Act

1793.

of 1793 did away with the few remaining disabilities under which Catholics laboured as to worship, education, and the disposition of their property. Provided they took the oath of allegiance and a new oath of abjuration of certain pernicious doctrines, they could become elected members of all corporations and receive degrees and hold offices of Dublin University,

Trinity College alone being excepted. They could hold all civil and military posts except the very highest, and they could keep arms with certain restrictions. They could exercise the franchise, but were not eligible for seats in either House of Parliament.

In England, owing to the hostility of the king, after 1791 there was a long pause in the grant of further concessions. Pitt's attempt to fulfil the expectations of those who had helped him in bringing about the Irish Union, wrought his own fall; and when in 1805 Fox took up the cause of the Catholics, Pitt was found in opposition. After Fox's death, Lord Grenville tried to introduce an Army and Navy Service Bill, which proposed to extend to England so much of the Irish Act of 1793 as related to the army and navy, but without the restrictions which closed the highest ranks to Catholics. The king, however, refused to assent to the removal of these restrictions, and the ministry resigned. It was not till 1812 that the movement in favour of Catholic Emancipation became serious. The claims of the Romanists were treated as an open question by the newly formed ministry of Lord Liverpool, and among the advocates of complete concession were Canning, Grattan and Marquis Wellesley. Canning's motion for considering the laws relating to the Roman Catholics was passed in the Commons by a majority of 129, but it went no further: and in the next year (**1813**), although Grattan's proposal for opening Parliament to them was thrown out, an Act was passed enabling Irish Roman Catholics to hold in England all the civil and military offices which the Irish Act of 1793 allowed them to hold at home. This was followed in **1817** by the more general Military and Naval Officers' Oaths Bill, which practically opened all ranks in those services to Roman Catholics and Dissenters alike. But the full measure of enfranchisement did not come for twelve years. Bills were rejected almost annually, until the pressure of the Catholic Association and the disaffected condition of Ireland forced the Tory government of the Duke of Wellington and Sir Robert Peel to concede the demands of the advocates of emancipation at the same time as they suppressed the formidable association. By the Catholic Emancipation Act of

Catholic Emancipation.

10 Geo. IV.
c. 7. § 2.
1829, a new oath was substituted for the oath of supremacy, and Roman Catholics were no longer debarred from either House of Parliament. All corporate and judicial offices except those connected with the ecclesiastical courts, were thrown open to them, as well as all civil and political offices except those of Regent, Lord Chancellor in England and Ireland, and Lord-Lieutenant of Ireland. The restrictions or securities were reduced to a minimum, and the dark prognostications of the continued opponents of the bill were in no sense realized. In 1851 the provision of the pope for the ecclesiastical government of England by bishops with English titles caused the defensive measure of the Ecclesiastical Titles Bill, which prohibited the use of territorial titles by the bishops and made penal the introduction of papal bulls. But no serious effects followed, the titles were retained, the excitement died away, and in 1871 the Act itself was repealed.

Disabilities of Nonconformists.
The Roman Catholics had been proscribed in the first instance as a political party in alliance with a foreign power. The Nonconformists met with similar treatment because they desired some change extending from a modification to the total abolition of the existing system of ecclesiastical rule. The Romanists repudiated the Church of England as heretical and schismatic ; the Church drove out the Nonconformists for disciplinary as well as doctrinal reasons. Before the Great Rebellion the Nonconformists would not accept the position which the Anglican party assigned to them ; indeed, many of the clergy and at least two archbishops after Cranmer, namely Grindal and Abbot, openly sympathized with them. The legislation of a Puritan Parliament restricted itself to the Act of Uniformity, with its penalties for non-attendance at the parish church ; and

[1] Prothero, 89.
Gee and Hardy, 492.
to an Act of 1593 [1]—aimed perhaps against the as yet unpopular Independents—by which any one above the age of sixteen, who should forbear for a month to go to church, should be imprisoned for a month until he made open submission and declaration of conformity. Those who continued obdurate should abjure the realm and not return without licence, on penalty of death. The real coercion of the Nonconformists was carried out by the High Commission Court ; and after the Restoration, since it could not be revived, recourse was had to further legislation, which the predominance of the

cavalier interest in Parliament made it easy to carry. The result was the so-called *Clarendon Code*, a series of four Acts passed for the purpose of securing the triumph of the Anglican party. By the first of these, the *Corporation Act*, the power of the Presbyterians in their strongholds was attacked ; for, the reception of the sacrament according to the rites of the Church of England and of an oath repudiating the Solemn League and Covenant were made the conditions of municipal office.[1] The last *Act of Uniformity*, by re-establishing the Prayer Book and enforcing episcopal ordination, struck at those Presbyterian ministers who had, under the Commonwealth, been lawfully inducted into vacant livings, and had been allowed by the Convention Parliament at the Restoration to retain them.[2] It took effect on no less than two thousand benefice-holders. The *Conventicle Act* broke up all services except those of the Church,[3] and the *Five Mile Act* forbade all clergy who had not taken an oath of non-resistance prescribed in the Act of Uniformity, to reside within five miles of a corporate town.[4] By this means the dissenters, as they had now become, were to be officially proscribed and spiritually starved in the places where they had the greatest influence.

Charles II's attempts at toleration by Acts of Indulgence, and at comprehension by the Savoy Conference and the introduction of a bill in Parliament, came to nothing ; for, the dissenters sacrificed themselves to the interests of Protestantism and accepted the Test Act, which excluded them together with the Roman Catholics from all official posts in the State. Their reward was the *Toleration Act*, by which all persons were exempted from penalties incurred under the statutes enforcing conformity with the Church, who should take the oaths of allegiance and supremacy, and should subscribe a declaration against transubstantiation ; if they were ministers, they must further subscribe all except three and a half of the Thirty-nine Articles, and must register their chapels.[5] Thus the Acts which enforced conformity with the Church were not repealed ; they were only suspended in the case of those who accepted certain tests. Under these conditions meetings of Protestant bodies for worship were legalized, but nothing had been done to remove the civil disabilities which excluded all dissenters from Corporations, offices of State and the Universities.

Side notes:
1661.

[1] Gee and Hardy, 594. 1662.

[2] *Ibid.* 600. 1664.

[3] *Ibid.* 623. 1665.

[4] *Ibid.* 620.

Relaxation by (*a*) Connivance ;

1689.

[5] Gee and Hardy, 654.

But despite this Act no settled policy was pursued towards the dissenters until the accession of the Hanoverians. The Whig influence procured the establishment of the Presbyterian Kirk in Scotland, and the grant by William III of a small endowment under the name of the *regium donum* to the Presbyterian ministers in Ireland; while dissenters of many shades were using the freedom of the Toleration Act to set up schools for the education of their youth. Throughout Anne's reign the Tories made a desperate attempt to go back upon the Toleration Act, and in the end they nearly succeeded. For, in 1711, after many previous attempts had

1711.

failed in the House of Lords, they passed the *Occasional Conformity Act* to prevent the more lax dissenters from qualifying for office by the necessary reception of the sacrament.

1714.

This was followed by the *Schism Act*, aimed against the dissenters' schools. Any one wishing to keep a public or private school or to act as tutor, could not do so without a licence from the bishop; while he must further qualify himself by engaging to conform to the English liturgy and by having taken within the year the sacrament according to the rites of the English Church. The Whigs were strong enough to obtain a few small remissions in this Act; and the accession of the Hanoverians robbed both Acts of their intended effect. The new dynasty and the wealthy dissenters needed each other's support. But for some years the strength of the Tories and the precarious tenure of the Hanoverians forbade the ministers to take any step which might alienate important classes in the country. Consequently, while there could be no more definite legal recognition of their claims, yet the dissenters obtained a considerable relaxation of the laws aimed against them. Thus the Occasional Conformity and Schism Acts were repealed in 1718, although, in view of a late occurrence in the City of London, any mayor or magistrate was forbidden to attend a meeting-house with the insignia of his office. Again, the Test Act compelled an official to receive the sacrament within three months of his admission to office: this limit was now extended to six months. Finally, in the first year of George II's reign it became a custom for Parliament to pass an Act of Indemnity in favour of those who had accepted office, but had not taken the sacrament within the specified time. With a few exceptions, in its early days, probably in order to prevent the dissenters counting upon it, this Act became an annual measure until the Test Act was definitely repealed. 1727-1828. But at the best it was a connivance at the breach of a law which remained upon the statute-book ; and since it professed to meet the case of those who had been prevented from complying with the Act 'through ignorance of the law, absence or unavoidable accident,' it formed no protection for the more conscientious among the dissenters. The extent to which the whole class still lay at the mercy of unscrupulous persons is illustrated by a course of action to which no less a body than the Corporation of the City of London resorted about the middle of the century. A bye-law of 1748 imposed a heavy fine on all who refused to serve in any office of the Corporation to which they were elected ; and, until the severe condemnation of the House of Lords in 1759, it became a regular practice to elect dissenters as sheriffs and then to exact the fine, because by the terms of the Corporation Act of 1661 they could not serve.

The movement in favour of a repeal of the laws which im- (b) Repeal. posed disabilities upon the dissenters was almost coterminous with the similar question as affecting the Romanists. But in the case of the former it was the indirect result of an attempt by the latitudinarian party in the Church to obtain a legislative relaxation from the necessity of signature to the Thirty-nine Articles. This was required not only on ordination, but at Oxford it had been a preliminary to matriculation since 1581, and, at the somewhat more liberal Cambridge, to taking a degree since 1616. This movement ended, as far as the dissenters were concerned, in an Act which, after two failures in the Lords, became law in 1779, and allowed any dissenter to preach and teach on condition that, for the subscription to the Articles hitherto required, he should substitute a declaration that he was a Christian and a Protestant dissenter, and took the Scriptures for his rule of faith and practice. The Irish Parliament in the case of the dissenters also set a worthy example to the English assembly ; for in the same year it admitted them to civil and military offices without enforcing the reception of the sacrament. This was simply to repeal the Test Act in their behalf, and it was soon followed in England by a movement for the repeal of the Test and Corporation Acts. The leaders were Beaufoy, who proposed bills for that purpose in 1787 and 1789, and on the latter occasion was only defeated by twenty votes; and Charles James Fox, whose suggestions, however, were in 1790 thrown out by a large majority. Beaufoy dwelt upon the serious disabilities under which the dissenters laboured and the penalties against which the annual Acts of Indemnity by no means effectually protected them. In answer, Burke instanced the hostility to the Church publicly evinced by such leaders as Drs. Price and Priestley, and the recent overthrow of the apparently strongly established Church in France. The maintenance of a religious test was treated by all speakers as a matter of mere expediency, and the circumstances of the French Revolution lulled the question to slumber for many years. In **1812** a movement in the right direction was made when Lord Sidmouth's attempt to restrict the privileges granted to dissenting ministers by the Act of 1779, called forth an unexpected sympathy with principles of toleration, and an Act was passed relieving dissenters from the oaths and the declaration required by the Toleration Act and the Act of 1779. It was not until 1828 that the question of the repeal of the Test and Corporation Acts was again mooted. Under the championship of Lord John Russell the measure was now effected **(1829)**, and for the sacramental test was substituted a declaration, to which the House of Lords in Committee added the words 'on the true faith of a Christian,' thus rendering it inapplicable to the Jews. Three smaller grievances still remained. Dissenters were obliged to be married at the parish church; they were compelled to pay church rates; and the necessity of signing the Thirty-nine Articles excluded them from the Universities. Lord Hardwicke's Marriage Act had been the first interference with the Canon law which had hitherto prevailed. This had allowed the celebration of a marriage by a priest at any time or place without any restraint of registration or of the necessary consent of parent or guardian. To put an end to the scandals which had arisen from what were known as 'Fleet marriages,' it was ultimately enacted that no marriage should be valid unless performed by a clergyman of the Church of England after the banns had been published thrice in the parish church

52 Geo. III. c. 12.

1753.

and a licence had been procured, which, in the case of a minor, should only be granted with the permission of the parents or guardians. A movement for the amendment of this Act in the interest of Catholic and Protestant dissenters alike had taken place between 1819 and 1827 ; but it was not until 1836 that Lord John Russell ultimately passed two bills — one which provided for the civil registration of births, marriages, and deaths ; and a second, which not only authorized the marriage of dissenters in their own chapels registered for the purpose and after due notice to the official registrar, but even allowed those who required no religious ceremony, to enter into a civil contract before the same official. The compulsory payment of church rates received a blow in the decision of the House of Lords in the case of *Burder* v. *Veley*, in which was established 1857. the power of the majority of a vestry to refuse their levy. But this was not enough. The dissenters required their total abolition, and from 1841 a motion to this effect became almost annual. Not till 1858, however, did it pass the Commons ; and, finally, in 1866 a compromise which made the payment voluntary, passed the Commons and became law in 1868. The abolition of all religious tests for entrance to or participation in the benefits of the Universities, finally received the assent of Parliament in 1871.

It remains to notice shortly three bodies who have received Separate exceptional treatment at the hands of the legislature. From treatment the first recognition of the principle of toleration the *Quakers* (1) The have met with a specially considerate treatment. By the Quakers ; Toleration Act they were required, in the place of all oaths or signatures to declarations, merely to affirm their adherence to the Government, their abjuration of transubstantiation, and their belief in the Trinity and the inspiration of the Bible. In 1695, for the oath required of a witness in a law court, they were enabled to substitute an affirmation 'in the presence of Almighty God.' Even this was withdrawn by a subsequent statute to meet their scruples. They were further exempted from Lord Hardwicke's Marriage Act. In 1833 Mr. Pease, a Quaker, was allowed by the Commons to take his seat on making an affirmation ; and an Act was subsequently passed to enable Quakers, Moravians, and Separatists (extended in

1837 to those who had been such) to substitute an affirmation for an oath on their entrance to Parliament.

There were, on the other hand, two classes—the *Unitarians* and the Jews — to whom Parliament was especially slow in extending religious toleration.   The benefits of the Toleration Act were particularly limited to all believers in the doctrine of the Trinity.   It was not until 1774 that the first Unitarian place of worship was opened by a seceded clergyman ; nor was it until 1792 that Parliament was asked by Fox to extend some toleration to the body.   This was obtained in 1813 and it recognized their religious worship ; while in 1836 they obtained, along with all other dissenters, the benefits of the Marriage Law Amendment Act.

53 Geo. III. c. 160.

(2) The Jews.

The *Jews* had an equally hard struggle.   Together with the Quakers, they had been exempted from Lord Hardwicke's Marriage Act.   But they lay under every civil disability, and the repeal of the Test and Corporation Acts which gave relief to the consciences of other citizens outside the pale of the National Church, was for them only the beginning of trouble. For they could not take the oath of allegiance which was sworn on the Gospels, nor the new oath of abjuration ' on the true faith of a Christian,' and there were now no Indemnity Acts under the shelter of which they could creep into office. Consequently, attempts were made at once to meet their case. In 1830, and again in 1833, four Jewish Relief Bills were introduced, and on the last occasion even passed the Commons. In 1839, by Lord Denman's Act for amending the laws of evidence, they were able to be sworn on the Old Testament and so to take the oath of allegiance ; while in 1845 they were admitted to corporations.   The struggle for admission to Parliament was extended over a long period.   In 1847 Baron Nathan de Rothschild was elected by no less a constituency than the City of London.   After vainly waiting three years for a measure of relief, in 1850 he attempted to take the oaths with the omission of ' the true faith of a Christian ' ; but the House refused him permission.   He continued nevertheless to be elected for the City, and in 1851 Mr. Alderman Solomons not only was elected for Greenwich, but took his seat within the bar of the House and refused to move.   But he found no countenance, as he had hoped, from the law courts, and was obliged to await in patience the action of Parliament, which in a very grudging manner gradually admitted the entrance of Jews. Thus in 1858 the Lords gave way so far as to allow that either House, by resolution in each case, could omit the insurmountable phrase from the oath of abjuration. In 1860 this could be done by a standing order of the Commons ; and finally, in 1866, a new form of oath was introduced which changed the position of a Jewish member of Parliament from good-humoured toleration to definite legal recognition.

The general result of the growth of toleration has been that while the Church of England still maintains a certain connection with the State, although she neither is endowed by the State nor exercises her spiritual functions as a department of the State ; yet all other religious bodies are as efficiently protected by the law in the exercise of their rights, and are far more free from any external interference in the conduct of their affairs.

APPENDIX

SOME IMPORTANT CASES IN CONSTITUTIONAL LAW

ASHBY v. WHITE (1704).

THE House of Commons had recently resolved that the right of election for the borough of Aylesbury was in all inhabitants not in receipt of alms. Ashby, an indigent person recently settled in Aylesbury, had been warned out of the parish by the Overseers of the Poor, unless he would give security; and an application for an order to remove him had been made to the local Justices of the Peace. At this moment a general election took place, and the Constables of the borough refused to receive Ashby's vote, because, not having even contributed to the Church or the poor, he could not be regarded as a settled inhabitant. Ashby brought an action against one of them and obtained a verdict with damages at the County Assizes. A motion was made in the Court of Queen's Bench in arrest of judgement on the ground that the action did not lie; and the Judges (the Chief Justice, Holt, alone dissenting) gave judgement for the defendants. The case was taken by writ of error to the House of Lords, who took the same view as Holt, and reversed the judgement. But the House of Commons claimed by resolution the exclusive right for themselves of determining questions of franchise, and declared Ashby guilty of breach of privilege for taking the case to the Lords. The Lords retaliated by resolutions condemning the whole attitude of the Commons. The quarrel was stopped by the prorogation of Parliament. But when Parliament met, it was resumed; and the Commons committed to Newgate for contempt Ashby and five other burgesses, known as the AYLESBURY MEN, who had brought similar actions. One of these was PATY. Again, with the single dissent of Holt, the judges of the Court of Queen's Bench refused a writ of habeas

Thomas, 30.
Broom, 846-867.
Hallam, iii. 273-276.
Anson, i. 170-171, 176, 178.
Robertson, 268-280.

corpus on the ground that the House of Commons were exclusively judges of their own privileges. The Commons committed all the plaintiffs' counsel for breach of privilege, and petitioned the Queen not to grant a writ of error (which is a writ of right) which should bring the question of the Judges' refusal of the writ of habeas corpus before the House of Lords. The Lords passed some very strong resolutions against the action of the Commons, and petitioned the Queen to grant the writ of error. The Queen, while professing a willingness to grant the writ of error, prorogued Parliament, thus setting all the prisoners at liberty ; and the plaintiffs, resuming their actions, obtained verdicts against the returning officers.

BARNARDISTON *v.* SOAME (1674).

Broom, 800-839.
Thomas, 28-29.

Soame, Sheriff of Suffolk, granted a poll for the election of knights of the shire, and the writ was returned to the Chancery with an indenture bearing the name of Sir Samuel Barnardiston as one of the elected knights. But it seemed doubtful whether some of Barnardiston's supporters had sufficient freehold to qualify them for voting. Consequently, at the advice of several influential persons and in order to prevent an action for a false return, Soame attached a second indenture to the writ bearing the name of a different member. The House of Commons confirmed the election of Barnardiston and committed the sheriff for making a double return. Barnardiston brought an action for malice against the sheriff and obtained a verdict with £800 damages. A motion in arrest of judgement on the ground that the verdict was not sustainable in law, was dismissed by the Court of King's Bench. The case was taken by writ of error into the Exchequer Chamber where this judgement was reversed, and, on a second writ of error, this reversal was upheld by the House of Lords.

It was thus decided that an action did not lie at Common law against an officer for making a double return. In the case of PRIDEAUX *v.* MORRIS, the same was decided in the case of a false return.

By 7 & 8 Will. III. c. 7 (made perpetual by 12 Anne, st. 1, c. 15) provision was made for remedy by the aggrieved party in the case of both a false and a double return by the returning officer.

By 31 & 32 Vict. c. 125, s. 48, remedy was given for neglect or refusal to make a return.

BUSHELL'S CASE (1670).

The Quakers persistently set at defiance the prohibitions placed by the various statutes of the 'Clarendon Code' upon their exercise of public worship. In 1670, two, William Penn and William Mead, were indicted at the Old Bailey Sessions for preaching in a street in London. Despite the hostile tone of the court, the jury, of whom Bushell was one, acquitted them, and were fined forty marks each by the Recorder for their contempt in ignoring the direction of the court, or in default of payment were committed to prison. Bushell obtained a writ of habeas corpus from the Court of Common Pleas, and Chief Justice Vaughan ruled that the return on the writ was insufficient. The prisoners were said to have been committed for finding 'against full and manifest evidence,' but as that evidence was not stated, the court could not decide as to its sufficiency. Moreover, no charge was made against them of knowing the evidence to be full and manifest and yet finding corruptly. As to the further charge, that their verdict was 'against the direction of the court in matter of law,' the court only charged the jury upon the law as arising out of some matter of fact already found by the jury. If the decision of matters of fact were taken away from the jury, it had better be abolished as useless. But as things were, the jury might often act upon evidence of which the judge knew nothing ; for it might be local knowledge. It was absurd, therefore, for a judge to fine a jury for going against their evidence, of which he knew only a part. Thus it was resolved by all the judges that finding against evidence or direction of the court was no sufficient cause to fine a jury : and the prisoners were discharged.

Thomas, 96.
Broom, 115-139.
Thayer, 166-168.
Hallam, iii. 9.

CALVIN'S CASE (1608).

James I wished to promote the union of the two peoples of England and Scotland, as well as of the Crowns. Commissioners were appointed by the two Parliaments to treat of the terms of such union. Their negotiations involved a discussion of the question of naturalization. By royal prerogative, letters of denization could be issued to aliens, allowing them to hold all offices under the Crown, to receive as a gift or to purchase landed property in England, and even to transmit it to their descendants, but not themselves to inherit it. No one proposed that the

Gardiner, i.
chap. viii.
Thomas, 48.
Broom, 4-26.
Stepney Election Petition
Case (17 Q.B.D.
p. 54).

position of Scotchmen born before (*ante-nati*) the king's accession to the English throne, should be altered. But the Commissioners proposed that those born after James' accession (*post-nati*) should be pronounced by a Declaratory Act to possess all the privileges of natives in either kingdom. James desired to save the prerogative power of denization by its definite recognition in the proposed Act. This made the Commons hesitate. The Scotch Parliament agreed to the king's proposals, and James determined to force the hand of the English Parliament by submitting a test case to the English judges, on which their formal declaration of the right of the *post-nati* to naturalization should do away with the necessity of any Act of Parliament. A piece of land was bought in the name of a Scotch child, the grandson of Lord Colvill of Culross, and two actions were brought in his name—one an assize of novel disseisin in the Court of King's Bench, against two persons who were supposed to have deprived him of the freehold ; the other in Chancery against two persons for detaining papers relative to the title of the land. The defendants demurred on the ground that Calvin was an alien, born after the accession of James to the English throne, and therefore could not hold the land. This, the central question, was taken to the Exchequer Chamber to be argued before the Chancellor and the twelve judges. Two alone dissented from the opinion that the *post-nati* were not aliens, and could therefore hold land in England. The argument turns on the meaning of allegiance, which is ruled to be due to the king not in his politic capacity, which is different for his different dominions, but in his natural person. Therefore, all those born under one natural obedience are naturalized subjects.

Goodwin and Fortescue, or *the Buckinghamshire election* (1604).

Hallam, ii. 216-
218.
Gardiner, i.
162-163, 167-170.
Prothero, 325-
333.

The proclamation which James I issued for summoning his first Parliament, among other things, forbade the election of outlaws, and ordered that all returns should be made into Chancery where, if any should be found contrary to the proclamation, they would be rejected, and any one elected contrary to the terms of the proclamation would be fined and imprisoned. The two candidates for Buckinghamshire were Sir Francis Goodwin who had formerly been outlawed, and Sir John Fortescue, a member of the Privy Council. Goodwin was returned as elected ; but his name being rejected by Chancery, a second election resulted in the choice of Fortescue. The matter was brought up in the House of Commons which, after hearing the whole case, declared Goodwin duly elected. At the king's desire the Lords asked for a discussion on the matter, to which the Commons reluctantly assented. At the conference in the presence of the king the Commons maintained that, owing to technical omissions, Goodwin was not an outlaw, but that, even if he were, there were instances of outlaws sitting in the House. The king in answer insisted that the Commons derived all their privileges from him and that they ought not to meddle with the returns. As to the eligibility of outlaws, he directed them to confer with the judges. They drew up a memorial refusing this, which they requested the Lords as mediators to lay before the king. James declaring himself quite distracted in judgement, as an absolute king commanded the conference for his further satisfaction. The Commons again yielded to the king's command; but before the formal conference James acknowledged to the committee of the Commons that the House was a court of record and a proper, though not the exclusive, judge of returns. He suggested as a personal favour that both elections should be set aside and a new writ issued. To satisfy the most punctilious members Goodwin wrote a letter acquiescing in the plan. The House had been so far successful that, unopposed, it investigated two other cases of disputed election (Cardigan and Shrewsbury).

HAMPDEN'S CASE (1637).

In mediaeval times it had been the duty of the maritime ports, especially of the Cinque Ports, to provide ships for defence of the realm. But, like all mediaeval obligations, it could be compounded for. In 1619 a levy was made from a number of port-towns for an expedition against Algiers. In 1634 writs for a similar levy were issued. But since the defence of the country concerned the whole country, in 1628, after Charles' second Parliament, a suggestion was made to extend the levy to the inland counties as well. In 1635 this was done. The opposition roused caused Charles to refer the question of the legality of the levy on inland places to the bench of Judges. Ten out of twelve answered that, although in case of piracy the maritime ports of the country would alone be liable, yet when the whole kingdom was in danger, the country in general should be called upon; and that of the danger the king was the sole judge.

Gardiner, viii. 205-209, 271-280. Const. Docts. of Puritan Rev. 40-54. Thomas, 23-25. Broom, 303-367. State Trials, iii. 825.

In 1636 another similar levy was made and opposition was silenced by another more formal reference to the Judges, all of whom answered to the same effect as on the former occasion. But some of the leaders of the opposition in the country thought that Charles intended to take ship-money as a permanent tax. They, therefore, determined to have the case argued in open court. Some of them refused to pay the small amounts at which their property was assessed. The case of John Hampden was selected as a test. Proceedings were taken against him in the Exchequer and, on his raising a demurrer, the case was transferred to the Exchequer Chamber. There appeared—for Hampden, St. John and Holborne : for the Crown, Solicitor-General Lyttleton and Attorney-General Bankes. The case was argued by counsel for twelve days. In view of the extra-judicial opinion of the judges in favour of the king, *St. John* conceded that the law of England gave the king power, to the extent of compulsion, to provide for the defence of the country and that he was sole judge of the danger. But he contended that such provision must be by means recognized by law. As the king did not apply the law except through the Judges, so he could not raise extraordinary supplies except through Parliament. Otherwise subjects are at the mercy of the sovereign. In cases of extreme danger such as actual invasion, not only the king but any one, in the name of public safety, may do acts which violate the rights of property ; but in this particular case there could have been no such extreme danger, for writs had been issued for the equipment of a fleet seven months hence ; so that there would have been plenty of time to summon Parliament. *Holborne* went further and denied that, except in the extremest cases, the king was the proper judge of danger. On behalf of the Crown, *Lyttleton* laid stress upon the instances in which kings had taken money without consulting Parliament and upon the necessary delays in getting a parliamentary grant. *Bankes* refused to argue the question of the circumstances under which the king could exercise his judgement. He quoted a number of precedents for all kinds of claims on the part of the Crown, and ended by asserting in the strongest form the absolute power of the royal prerogative.

The Judges delivered their opinions two at a time and on only two sittings in each term, so that it was three terms before they were all delivered. Seven pronounced emphatically on the side of the Crown : two as emphatically on the side of Hampden, followed, for technical reasons, by the other three. *Croke* absolutely denied the legality of the writ whether by prerogative, statute or Common law. On the other hand, *Berkeley* pronounced the law to be 'an old and trusty servant of the king's ; it is his instrument or means which he useth to govern his people by : I never read nor heard,' he continued, 'that lex was rex ; but it is common and most true that rex is lex.' *Finch* declared roundly that Acts of Parliament to take away the king's power in the defence of his kingdom were void : no such acts could prevent the king from commanding 'the subjects, their persons and goods, and I say their money too ; for no Acts of Parliament make any difference.'

SEVEN BISHOPS' CASE (1688).

In April, 1687, James II published his first Declaration of Indulgence immediately suspending all penal laws in matters ecclesiastical for non-attendance at Church or non-reception of the sacrament. In April, 1688, a second Declaration of Indulgence was put out followed by an Order in Council that it should be read on two successive Sundays in all the churches and chapels in England. For this purpose the bishops were ordered to distribute copies of it throughout their dioceses. Archbishop Sancroft and six bishops presented to the king in the royal closet a petition stating that, in view of late declarations in Parliament about the king's dispensing power, the Declaration was illegal, and that they could not therefore 'in prudence, honour or conscience' be parties to its distribution or its publication. The Government ultimately determined to indict them before the Court of King's Bench for seditious libel. When called before the Council they refused to enter into their own recognizances to appear for trial, declaring that this could not be required of them as peers in such a case. They were consequently committed to the Tower. A week later, when brought before the King's Bench, the Judges decided this point against them ; but they were allowed to be at large on their own recognizances.

The bishops were defended by some of the ablest advocates of the day ; the Attorney-General and Solicitor-General for the Government were very inferior lawyers. The jury was carefully chosen : the four judges had all shown themselves willing to pronounce in favour of the royal prerogative of dispensation.

Macaulay, ii. 89-109.
Thomas, 16-19.
Broom, 406-492.
Robertson, 249-267.

The trial almost broke down over two preliminary questions. The handwriting of the bishops could only be proved by the testimony of Blathwayt, a Clerk of the Privy Council, who swore that he had heard them acknowledge their signatures to the king. The charge of having published the libel in Middlesex (the petition having been drawn up at Lambeth Palace in Surrey) could only be proved at the last moment by the appearance in the witness-box of the Lord President of the Council, Lord Sunderland, who had admitted the bishops into the royal closet with the petition in their hands.

The chief defence of the counsel for the prisoners lay in the reading of extracts from the Journals of the House of Commons proving the assertion of the petition that the dispensing power claimed by the king had been frequently declared illegal by Parliament. Somers, the junior counsel, referred to the decisions in *Thomas* v. *Sorrel* and *Godden* v. *Hales* as telling against a power of general dispensation amounting to suspension, and pithily declared that the libel could not be, as was alleged, either seditious—because it was presented to the king in private ; or false—because its contentions had been shown to be true ; or malicious—because the bishops had not sought the occasion of publishing it ; or, finally, a libel—because they had only done what the law allows every one to do, namely, to petition the sovereign against a grievance.[1] In reply, the Solicitor-General went so far as to deny that the bishops had any power to petition the king outside Parliament. To this view even the Chief Justice demurred. Three of the Judges avoided a discussion of the dispensing power. Two summed up in favour of the Crown, one—the Chief Justice—merely took exception to the particular wording of this petition. Of the other two who declared in favour of the bishops, Powell utterly denied the king's power 'to dispense with any laws whatsoever. If this be once allowed of,' he concluded, 'there will need no Parliament. All the legislature will be in the king.' After a night's consideration, the jury pronounced the verdict of *Not Guilty*.

[1] Cf. pp. 491-493.

SHIRLEY'S CASE (1604).

Sir Thomas Shirley was elected M.P. for Steyning in James I's first Parliament. Before Parliament met, he was arrested for debt at the suit of a City tradesman, and was imprisoned in the Fleet. On the first day of the session the attention of the House of

E.H.R. viii. 733.
Prothero, 320-325.
Hallam, i. 302-303.

Commons was called to his arrest. The Speaker issued a warrant for a writ of habeas corpus : the warden of the Fleet appeared at the bar of the House with his prisoner and was examined. But he refused to release Shirley because that would make him liable for the amount of the debt to Shirley's creditor. The House committed Shirley's creditor to the Tower, as guilty of breach of privilege, and brought in two Acts—a special bill to exonerate the warden from any liability which he might incur by releasing the prisoner, and a general bill safeguarding creditors against loss through the release of prisoners by parliamentary privilege. The special bill was hurried through the Commons and sent up to the Lords with a request that they would move the king to grant his assent to it at once, otherwise its object would be gone. But the Lords doubted 'whether the king's assent to one bill apart do not conclude the session.' While they delayed, the Commons realized that the appeal made by the wording of the bill to the king and the chancellor, would take out of their own hands the determination of the privilege for which they were fighting. They, therefore, suddenly changed their tactics, and when the warden of the Fleet refused to surrender his prisoner until the king had given his assent to the bill just introduced, they committed him to the custody of their sergeant and, when he persisted in his refusal unless the chancellor issued a writ, they sent him to the Tower. But the warden's wife proved as obstinate to their demands as her husband, and the Speaker with difficulty stopped a proposal that six members with the sergeant should make a forcible entry into the prison. Then a new bill was brought in on the lines of the former special bill, but omitting all reference to the king or the chancellor. This was hurried through both Houses in a couple of days. But the warden still remained obdurate, although the Commons committed him ' to the dungeon known by the expressive name of the Little Ease.' At length, probably owing to the secret intervention of the king himself, the warden gave way and Sir Thomas Shirley was released. The warden, however, was not released till four days later, and then only after a humble apology at the bar of the House of Commons. By this time the general bill had also passed the two Houses, and it seems that both this, which being a public bill found its place among the Statutes of the Realm, and the two special private bills which are not included there, all obtained the assent of the king. It has been suggested that the royal assent to the special bill originally introduced was obtained by the chancellor whose jurisdiction it recognized, in order that he might have a pretext for future interference.

STOCKDALE v. HANSARD (1839).

Thomas, 40-41.
Broom, 875-967.
Erskine May, ii.
78-83.
Anson, i. 171-174.
Robertson, 380-388.
Porritt, i. 584-596.

In 1836 the Inspectors of Prisons for the Home District, in their report to the Government, described as 'indecent and obscene' a certain book which they had found among the prisoners in Newgate. This report was printed by order of the House of Commons. Stockdale, the publisher of the book in question, brought an action for libel against the printers, Messrs. Hansard. The case was tried before Lord Chief Justice Denman, and the verdict was given against Stockdale on the plea of justification. But the Judge had laid it down that the authorization of the House of Commons was no justification to any publisher or seller of a parliamentary report containing libellous matter. The House of Commons answered this by a declaration that the power of such publication at their discretion 'is an essential incident to the constitutional functions of Parliament,' and that the attempt of any person to question or of any Court to decide upon matters of privilege in a sense contrary to the determination of either House, was itself a breach of privilege. Stockdale, thus encouraged, brought another action against Messrs. Hansard, which was tried in the Court of Queen's Bench. The question involved was whether the printers were justified by the privilege and order of the House of Commons. The defendants said that, at the direction of the House of Commons, they appeared and pleaded this action in order to inform the court, but that their appearance did not imply that the House submitted to the decision of an inferior tribunal a privilege which was essential to the discharge of its legislative functions : that court could not enquire into the extent of the privilege : the plaintiff was merely given an opportunity of denying that the act was done under the alleged authority, or of showing that the authority had been exceeded. But the Judges all gave judgement against the defendants. Lord Chief Justice Denman pointed out that neither House of Parliament is supreme by itself, and the opinion of its own privileges by either House may not be correct or its declaration of them binding ; that the courts of law had often discussed questions of parliamentary privilege ; that the publication in question had not been only for the use of the members, nor had it been connected with anything that was under discussion in the House. The only remedy for the Commons was a writ of error which would bring the matter before the House of Lords. From this they were prevented by unwillingness to submit their privileges to the jurisdiction of the other House, and also by the fact that already by their own declaration they had committed themselves to a definite statement. They resolved, therefore, that to future actions Messrs. Hansard should not plead. Consequently, when Stockdale brought another action and gained judgement against Messrs. Hansard by default, the sheriffs levied damages. The House of Commons proceeded vigorously. It committed to the custody of the sergeant-at-arms Stockdale, his solicitor Howard, and the sheriffs (to whom the Court of Queen's Bench refused a habeas corpus because they had been committed by order of the House of Commons for contempt [1]—case of the SHERIFF OF MIDDLESEX 1840).[2] Stockdale brought several other actions, and the House committed several other persons before an Act of Parliament was passed, which provided that such actions should be stayed on the production of a certificate that the paper complained of was printed by order of either House of Parliament.

[1] Cf. p. 280.
[2] Robertson, 388-390.

Two further cases arose out of this contest. Stockdale's solicitor, HOWARD, brought an action of trespass against the officers of the House, who had taken him into custody, and, on the ground that they had exceeded their authority, gained a verdict against them with £100 damages. His second action against Sir W. GOSSETT, the sergeant-at-arms, was, on the ground of the informality of the Speaker's warrant, also given in his favour. But this last case was taken by writ of error to the Court of Exchequer Chamber, which reversed the judgement of the Court of Queen's Bench. The Judges maintained that the House of Commons had the power to institute inquiries and to take into custody for contempt, and that, as to the form of the Speaker's warrant, the mandates of the House of Commons deserved at least as much respect as those of the superior courts, which protect the officers of those courts acting under them.

WILKES' CASES.

John Wilkes, M.P. for Aylesbury, appears as a principal in connection with several important constitutional questions. (1) The question of *General Warrants*. In 1762 Wilkes founded a newspaper called the *North Briton*, in ridicule of the advancement of

Thomas, 67.
Broom, 544-554.
Lecky, iii. 52,
70-81.
Erskine May, ii.
247-250 ; iii. 2-6.
Robertson,
299-314.

Scotchmen to high posts in England under the auspices of the
Earl of Bute. No. 45 of this paper, published on April 23, 1763,
treating the king's speech with which Parliament had just been
closed, as the composition of the Ministry, pronounced it 'the most
abandoned instance of ministerial effrontery ever attempted to be
imposed upon mankind.' But the Court party wished to restore
the personal influence of the Crown, and George Grenville, who
had just succeeded Bute as head of the Ministry, agreed to prosecute
for libel. The Secretary of State, Lord Halifax, issued a general
warrant for the arrest of 'the authors, printers and publishers':
under this forty-nine persons were apprehended, including Wilkes ;
while his drawers were ransacked under a search warrant, and his
papers taken away. Despite his plea of privilege, he was kept in
close confinement in the Tower. The Court of Common Pleas
granted him a writ of habeas corpus and, in pronouncing judgement, Chief Justice Pratt decided not only that Wilkes' arrest was
illegal owing to his privilege, but that the issue of general warrants
by the Secretary of State and of search warrants on a charge of
libel, were equally illegal. Wilkes was released and, in reliance on
this judgement, brought actions against Wood, the Under-Secretary
who had superintended the search for papers, and against Lord
Halifax. The case of WILKES v. WOOD was tried before Lord
Chief Justice Pratt, and a special jury awarded the plaintiff £800
damages. Lord Halifax by legal delays postponed the hearing of
the case against him. The Government retaliated by instructing
the Attorney-General to commence an action for libel against
Wilkes in the Court of King's Bench. Parliament met November
15, 1763, and Wilkes was attacked in both Houses. Although the
case was still before the law courts, the Commons voted that
No. 45 of the *North Briton* was 'a false, scandalous and seditious
libel' which should be burned by the common hangman, and that
privilege of Parliament did not extend to the writing and publishing
of seditious libels. Wilkes had privately printed a parody of Pope's
Essay on Man, called an *Essay on Woman*. Because this contained
notes in imitation of Bishop Warburton's notes to Pope's poem, the
Lords condemned it as a breach of privilege and a scandalous libel.
But, meanwhile, Wilkes had been wounded in a duel with one of the
numerous victims of his attacks in the *North Briton*, and retired to
France. In his absence he was expelled the House of Commons
for having written 'a scandalous and seditious libel,' and in the
Court of King's Bench, being found guilty of reprinting No. 45, and

of printing the *Essay on Woman* and, not appearing to receive sentence, he was outlawed (February, 1764).

Two cases arising out of similar events were—

LEACH *v.* MONEY (1765), in which the printer of the *North Briton* gained a verdict with £400 damages against the king's messenger who had executed the general warrant. The judgement was affirmed by the Court of King's Bench, to which the case was brought by writ of error ; and Lord Mansfield also pronounced against the legality of general warrants. Thomas, 68.
Broom, 522-543.
Robertson,
314-316.

ENTICK *v.* CARRINGTON (1765), in which one of the writers in the *Monitor or British Freeholder* was apprehended on a search warrant which mentioned the plaintiff's name, but authorized the general seizure of papers. A jury found a special verdict [1] for the plaintiff with £300 damages. In the Court of Common Pleas, where the case of the special verdict was twice argued, Lord Camden (Chief Justice Pratt) denied that general search warrants had ever been legal. Thomas, 69.
Broom, 555-607.
Robertson, 316-330.

(2) *The Middlesex Election* (1768). Wilkes returned to England, petitioned the king for his pardon, stood as a parliamentary candidate for the City of London and was defeated, but was elected at the head of the poll for Middlesex. He surrendered at the Court of King's Bench on his outlawry, which, on a technical point, was reversed, and then, for the seditious libel and blasphemy of which he had been found guilty in his absence, he was sentenced to imprisonment for twenty-two months and a fine of £1000. Riots took place in his favour. The Secretary of State, Lord Weymouth, by letter authorized the magistrates to use the military force of a Scotch regiment, and an innocent man was killed. The soldiers were publicly complimented. Wilkes published Lord Weymouth's letter with comments. For the three offences—the *North Briton* (for which he had already been expelled), the *Essay on Woman* (for which he was undergoing punishment), and the comments on Lecky, iii. 128-133, 138-150.
Erskine May, ii.
8-26.
Robertson, 330-336.

---

[1] Blackstone (*Commentaries*, Bk. iii. ch. 23) explains a special verdict to be one in which, some difficult matter of law having arisen, the jury 'state the naked facts, as they find them to be proved, and pray the advice of the court thereon ; concluding conditionally, that if upon the whole matter the court shall be of opinion that the plaintiff had cause of action, they then find for the plaintiff; if otherwise, then for the defendant. This is entered at length on the record, and afterwards argued and determined in the Court at Westminster, from whence the issue came to be tried.'

Lord Weymouth's letter (which was cognizable either by the Lords as a breach of privilege, or by the law courts as a seditious libel)— the Commons expelled him. In February, 1769, he was unanimously re-elected : the House declared him incapable of sitting in that Parliament. In March he was again re-elected : the House again pronounced his election void. Colonel Luttrell vacated his own seat in order to stand against him ; but Wilkes was a third time re-elected by a large majority. The House declared Luttrell duly elected. Wilkes' compensations were that he was elected successively Alderman, Sheriff, and Lord Mayor ; a subscription was raised for him and, his old action against Lord Halifax being resumed, he obtained £4000 damages. At the next general election (1774) Wilkes was elected to Parliament and took his seat unmolested ; and finally, in 1782 the resolutions passed against him were expunged from the journals of the House.

INDEX

633

2 T

2 T*

PRINTED AT THE EDINBURGH PRESS
9 AND 11 YOUNG STREET